Handbook of Research on Engineering, Business, and Healthcare Applications of Data Science and Analytics

Bhushan Patil
Independent Researcher, India

Manisha Vohra
Independent Researcher, India

A volume in the Advances in Data Mining and
Database Management (ADMDM) Book Series

Published in the United States of America by
    IGI Global
    Engineering Science Reference (an imprint of IGI Global)
    701 E. Chocolate Avenue
    Hershey PA, USA 17033
    Tel: 717-533-8845
    Fax: 717-533-8661
    E-mail: cust@igi-global.com
    Web site: http://www.igi-global.com

Library of Congress Cataloging-in-Publication Data

Names: Patil, Bhushan, 1993- editor. | Vohra, Manisha, 1994- editor.
Title: Handbook of research on engineering, business, and healthcare
  applications of data science and analytics / Bhushan Patil and Manisha
  Vohra, editors.
Other titles: Research on engineering, business, and healthcare
  applications of data science and analytics
Description: Hershey, PA : Engineering Science Reference, an imprint of IGI
  Global, [2020] | Includes bibliographical references and index. |
  Summary: "This book explores the application of data science and
  analytics in the engineering, healthcare, and business sectors"--
  Provided by publisher.
Identifiers: LCCN 2019047050 (print) | LCCN 2019047051 (ebook) | ISBN
  9781799830535 (hardcover) | ISBN 9781799830542 (ebook)
Subjects: LCSH: Information resources--Data processing. | Quantitative
  analysis. | Big data. | Engineering--Data processing. | Business--Data
  processing. | Medical care--Data processing.
Classification: LCC ZA3075 .H348 2020 (print) | LCC ZA3075 (ebook) | DDC
  001.4/33--dc23
LC record available at https://lccn.loc.gov/2019047050
LC ebook record available at https://lccn.loc.gov/2019047051

This book is published in the IGI Global book series Advances in Data Mining and Database Management (ADMDM) (ISSN: 2327-1981; eISSN: 2327-199X)

British Cataloguing in Publication Data
A Cataloguing in Publication record for this book is available from the British Library.

For electronic access to this publication, please contact: eresources@igi-global.com.

Advances in Data Mining and Database Management (ADMDM) Book Series

David Taniar
Monash University, Australia

ISSN:2327-1981
EISSN:2327-199X

MISSION

With the large amounts of information available to organizations in today's digital world, there is a need for continual research surrounding emerging methods and tools for collecting, analyzing, and storing data.

The **Advances in Data Mining & Database Management (ADMDM)** series aims to bring together research in information retrieval, data analysis, data warehousing, and related areas in order to become an ideal resource for those working and studying in these fields. IT professionals, software engineers, academicians and upper-level students will find titles within the ADMDM book series particularly useful for staying up-to-date on emerging research, theories, and applications in the fields of data mining and database management.

COVERAGE

- Customer Analytics
- Data Mining
- Data Warehousing
- Profiling Practices
- Enterprise Systems
- Data Analysis
- Predictive Analysis
- Factor Analysis
- Decision Support Systems
- Heterogeneous and Distributed Databases

IGI Global is currently accepting manuscripts for publication within this series. To submit a proposal for a volume in this series, please contact our Acquisition Editors at Acquisitions@igi-global.com or visit: http://www.igi-global.com/publish/.

Titles in this Series

For a list of additional titles in this series, please visit:
https://www.igi-global.com/book-series/advances-data-mining-database-management/37146

Opportunities and Challenges for Blockchain Technology in Autonomous Vehicles
Amit Kumar Tyagi (Vellore Institute of Technolgy, Chennai, India) Gillala Rekha (K. L. University, India) and N. Sreenath (Pondicherry Engineering College, India)
Engineering Science Reference • © 2021 • 316pp • H/C (ISBN: 9781799832959) • US $245.00

Cross-Industry Use of Blockchain Technology and Opportunities for the Future
Idongesit Williams (Aalborg University, Denmark)
Engineering Science Reference • © 2020 • 228pp • H/C (ISBN: 9781799836322) • US $225.00

Applications and Developments in Semantic Process Mining
Kingsley Okoye (University of East London, UK)
Engineering Science Reference • © 2020 • 248pp • H/C (ISBN: 9781799826682) • US $195.00

Challenges and Applications of Data Analytics in Social Perspectives
V. Sathiyamoorthi (Sona College of Technology, India) and Atilla Elci (Aksaray University, Turkey)
Engineering Science Reference • © 2020 • 330pp • H/C (ISBN: 9781799825661) • US $245.00

Handling Priority Inversion in Time-Constrained Distributed Databases
Udai Shanker (Madan Mohan Malaviya University of Technology, India) and Sarvesh Pandey (Madan Mohan Malaviya University of Technology, India)
Engineering Science Reference • © 2020 • 338pp • H/C (ISBN: 9781799824916) • US $225.00

Feature Extraction and Classification Techniques for Text Recognition
Munish Kumar (Maharaja Ranjit Singh Punjab Technical University, India) Manish Kumar Jindal (Panjab University Regional Centre, Muktsar, India) Simpel Rani Jindal (Yadavindera College of Engineering, India) R. K. Sharma (Thapar Institute of Engineering & Technology, India) and Anupam Garg (Bhai Gurdas Institute of Engineering and Technology, India)
Engineering Science Reference • © 2020 • 300pp • H/C (ISBN: 9781799824060) • US $225.00

Neutrosophic Graph Theory and Algorithms
Florentin Smarandache (University of New Mexico, USA) and Said Broumi (Faculty of Science Ben M'Sik, University Hassan II, Morocco)
Engineering Science Reference • © 2020 • 406pp • H/C (ISBN: 9781799813132) • US $245.00

701 East Chocolate Avenue, Hershey, PA 17033, USA
Tel: 717-533-8845 x100 • Fax: 717-533-8661
E-Mail: cust@igi-global.com • www.igi-global.com

List of Contributors

Table of Contents

Detailed Table of Contents

Chapter 1

M. Govindarajan, Annamalai University, India

This chapter focuses on introduction to the field of data science. Data science is the area of study which involves extracting insights from vast amounts of data by the use of various scientific methods, algorithms, and processes. The term data science has emerged because of the evolution of mathematical statistics, data analysis, and big data. Data science helps to discover hidden patterns from the raw data. It enables to translate a business problem into a research project and then translate it back into a practical solution. The purpose of this chapter is to provide emphasis on integration and synthesis of concepts, techniques, applications, and tools to deal with various facets of data science practice, including data collection and integration, exploratory data analysis, predictive modeling, descriptive modeling, data product creation, evaluation, and effective communication.

Chapter 2

Manisha Vohra, Independent Researcher, India
Bhushan Patil, Independent Researcher, India

Data analytics is used to extract necessary information from a given data or data set. It is a concept of technology which can be implemented in various applications and is evolving rapidly. Data analytics analyses the whole data set completely and provides important information from it to the users. In this chapter, a brief description of data analytics is provided. Different types of data analytics are also explained. Along with it, various different aspects of data analytics are described. As the chapter title suggests, this chapter is a brief walk through the world of data analytics i.e., a brief insight of data analytics is provided in this chapter.

Chapter 3

Pankaj Pathak, Symbiosis International University (Deemed), India
Samaya Pillai Iyengar, Symbiosis International University (Deemed), India
Minal Abhyankar, Symbiosis International University (Deemed), India

In the current times, the educational and employment areas are changing at a very fast rate. The change is visible especially in the zone of technology-education. Approximately 4-5 years back, technology education meant coding, using different computer science programming languages. But in the recent times data science and data analytics have become the buzz words. The employment in this area has also undergone a tremendous change effect. Many new employment opportunities have sprung in this area as well with the regular or existing jobs becoming less or extinct. The entire business domain is warming to these buzz words. And the industry preference for these techniques has widened. The chapter discusses both the concepts and the tools being used.

Chapter 4

Ricardo A. Barrera-Cámara, Universidad Autónoma del Carmen, Mexico
Ana Canepa-Saenz, Universidad Autónoma del Carmen, Mexico
Jorge A. Ruiz-Vanoye, Universidad Politécnica de Pachuca, Mexico
Alejandro Fuentes-Penna, Centro Interdisciplinario de Investigación y Docencia en
    Educación Técnica, Mexico
Miguel Ángel Ruiz-Jaimes, Universidad Politécnica de Morelos, Mexico
Maria Beatriz Bernábe-Loranca, Benemérita Universidad Autónoma de Puebla, Mexico

Various devices such as smart phones, computers, tablets, biomedical equipment, sports equipment, and information systems generate a large amount of data and useful information in transactional information systems. However, these generate information that may not be perceptible or analyzed adequately for decision-making. There are technology, tools, algorithms, models that support analysis, visualization, learning, and prediction. Data science involves techniques, methods to abstract knowledge generated through diverse sources. It combines fields such as statistics, machine learning, data mining, visualization, and predictive analysis. This chapter aims to be a guide regarding applicable statistical and computational tools in data science.

Chapter 5

Shatakshi Singh, Mody University of Science and Technology, India
Kanika Gautam, Mody University of Science and Technology, India
Prachi Singhal, Mody University of Science and Technology, India
Sunil Kumar Jangir, Mody University of Science and Technology, India
Manish Kumar, Mody University of Science and Technology, India

The recent development in artificial intelligence is quite astounding in this decade. Especially, machine learning is one of the core subareas of AI. Also, ML field is an incessantly growing along with evolution and becomes a rise in its demand and importance. It transmogrified the way data is extracted, analyzed, and interpreted. Computers are trained to get in a self-training mode so that when new data is fed they can learn, grow, change, and develop themselves without explicit programming. It helps to make useful predictions that can guide better decisions in a real-life situation without human interference. Selection of ML tool is always a challenging task, since choosing an appropriate tool can end up saving time as well as making it faster and easier to provide any solution. This chapter provides a classification of various machine learning tools on the following aspects: for non-programmers, for model deployment, for Computer vision, natural language processing, and audio for reinforcement learning and data mining.

Data analysis is a process of studying, removing non-required data in the view level, and converting to needed patterns for sub decisions to make an aggregated decision. Statistical modeling is the process of applying statistical techniques in data analysis for taking proactive decisions depend requirements. The statistical modeling identifies relationship between variables, and it encompasses inferential statistics for model validation. The focus of the chapter is to analyze statistical modeling techniques in different contexts to understand the mathematical representation of data. The correlation and regression are used for analyzing association between key factors of companies' activities. Especially in business, correlation describes positive and negative correlation variables for analyzing the factors of business for supporting the decision-making process. The key factors are related with independent variables and dependent variables, which create cause and effect models to predict the future outcomes.

#### Chapter 7

Financial ratios are used in a variety of ways today. Empirical research is getting bigger, with a special focus on predicting business failure, the strength of a company, investment decision making, etc. This chapter focuses on two methodologies suitable to deal with many data to evaluate business performance. They are data envelopment analysis and grey relational analysis. The empirical part of the chapter conducts an empirical analysis with the aforementioned two approaches. Firms are ranked based on their performances and detailed interpretations are obtained so that managers within businesses can get useful information on how to utilize such an approach to modelling. This study implicates that using the two mentioned approaches can be useful when making investment decisions based on many data available for the decision maker. This is due to the methodology being suitable to handle big data and correctly quantifying the overall financial performance of a company.

#### Chapter 8

The point of this chapter is to think about the correlation of two well-known European option pricing models – Black Scholes Model and Binomial Option Pricing Model. The above two models not statistically significant at one period. In this examination, it is shown how the above two European models are statistically significant when the time period increases. The independent paired t-test is utilized with the end goal to demonstrate that they are statistically significant to vary from one another at higher time period and the Anderson Darling test being used for the normality test. The Minitab and Excel programming has been utilized for graphical representation and the hypothesis testing.

    Gaurav Nagpal, Birla Institute of Technology and Science, Pilani, India
    Gaurav Kumar Bishnoi, Birla Institute of Technology and Science, Pilani, India
    Harman Singh Dhami, Birla Institute of Technology and Science, Pilani, India
    Akshat Vijayvargia, Birla Institute of Technology and Science, Pilani, India

With the increasing share of digital transactions in the business, the way of operating the businesses has changed drastically, leading to an immense opportunity for achieving the operational excellence in the digital transactions. This chapter focusses on the ways of using data science to improve the operational efficiency of the last mile leg in the delivery shipments for e-commerce. Some of these avenues are predicting the attrition of field executives, identification of fake delivery attempts, reduction of mis-routing, identification of bad addresses, more effective resolution of weight disputes with the clients, reverse geo-coding for locality mapping, etc. The chapter also discusses the caution to be exercised in the use of data science, and the flip side of trying to quantify and dissect the phenomenon that is so complex and subjective in nature.

    Ulkem Basdas, Philip Morris International, Turkey
    M. Fevzi Esen, University of Health Sciences, Turkey

Massively parallel processors and modern data management architectures have led to more efficient operations and a better decision making for companies to process and analyse such complex and large-scale data. Especially, financial services companies leverage big data to transform their business processes and they focus on understanding the concepts of big data and related technologies. In this chapter, the authors focus on the scope of big data in finance and economics. They discuss the need for big data towards the digitalisation of services, utilisation of social media and new channels to reach customers, demand for personalised services and continuous flow of vast amount of data in the sector. They investigate the role of big data in transformation of financial and economic environment by reviewing previous studies on stock market reading and monitoring (real-time algorithmic trading, high-frequency trading), fraud detection, and risk analysis. They conclude that despite the rapid development in the evolution of techniques, both the performance of techniques and area of implementation are still open to improvement. Therefore, this review aims to encourage readers to enlarge their vision on data mining applications.

    James Osabuohien Odia, University of Benin, Nigeria
    Osaheni Thaddeus Akpata, University of Benin, Nigeria

The chapter examines the roles of data science and big data analytics to forensic accountants and fraud detection. It also considers how data science techniques could be applied to the investigative processes in forensic accounting. Basically, the current increase in the volume, velocity, and variety of data offer a rich source of evidence for the forensic accountant who needs to be familiar with the techniques and procedures for extracting, analysing, and visualising such data. This is against backdrop of continuous global increase in economic crime and frauds, and financial criminals are getting more sophisticated, taking advantage of the opportunities provided by the unstructured data constantly being created with every email sent, every Facebook post, every picture on Instagram, or every thought share on Twitter. Consequently, it is important that forensic accountants are constantly abreast with developments in data science and data analytics in order to stay a step ahead of fraudsters as well as address evolving vulnerabilities created by big data.

Chapter 12

Vandana Kalra, Manav Rachna International Institute of Research and Studies, India
Indu Kashyap, Manav Rachna International Institute of Research and Studies, India
Harmeet Kaur, University of Delhi, India

Data science is a fast-growing area that deals with data from its origin to the knowledge exploration. It comprises of two main subdomains, data analytics for preparing data, and machine learning to probe into this data for hidden patterns. Machine learning (ML) endows powerful algorithms for the automatic pattern recognition and producing prediction models for the structured and unstructured data. The available historical data has patterns having high predictive value used for the future success of an industry. These algorithms also help to obtain accurate prediction, classification, and simulation models by eliminating insignificant and faulty patterns. Machine learning provides major advancement in the healthcare industry by assisting doctors to diagnose chronic diseases correctly. Diabetes is one of the most common chronic disease that occurs when the pancreas cells are damaged and do not secrete sufficient amount of insulin required by the human body. Machine learning algorithms can help in early diagnosis of this chronic disease by studying its predictor parameter values.

Chapter 13

Nivethitha V., National Institute of Technology, Puducherry, India
Aghila G., National Institute of Technology, Puducherry, India

Some of the largest global industries that is driving smart city environments are anywhere and anytime health monitoring applications. Smart healthcare systems need to be more preventive and responsive as they deal with sensitive data. Even though cloud computing provides solutions to the smart healthcare applications, the major challenge imposed on cloud computing is how could the centralized traditional cloud computing handle voluminous data. The existing models may encounter problems related to network resource utilization, overheads in network response time, and communication latency. As a solution to these problems, edge-oriented computing has emerged as a new computing paradigm through localized computing. Edge computing expands the compute, storage, and networking capabilities to the edge of the network which will respond to the above-mentioned issues. Based on cloud computing and edge computing, in this chapter an opportunistic edge computing architecture is introduced for smart provisioning of healthcare data.

Chapter 14

Nagaraj V. Dharwadkar, Department of Computer Science and Engineering, Rajarambapu
Institute of Technology, Sakhrale, India
Shivananda R. Poojara, Department of Computer Science and Engineering, University of
Tartu, Estonia
Anil K. Kannur, Department of Computer Science and Engineering, Rajarambapu Institute
of Technology, Sakhrale, India

Diabetes is one of the four non-communicable diseases causing maximum deaths all over the world. The numbers of diabetes patients are increasing day by day. Machine learning techniques can help in early diagnosis of diabetes to overcome the influence of it. In this chapter, the authors proposed the system that imputes missing values present in diabetes dataset and parallel process diabetes data for the pattern discovery using Hadoop-MapReduce-based C4.5 machine learning algorithm. The system uses these patterns to classify the patient into diabetes and non-diabetes class and to predict risk levels associated with the patient. The two datasets, namely Pima Indian Diabetes Dataset (PIDD) and Local Diabetes Dataset (LDD), are used for the experimentation. The experimental results show that C4.5 classifier gives accuracy of 73.91% and 79.33% when applied on (PIDD) (LDD) respectively. The proposed system will provide an effective solution for early diagnosis of diabetes patients and their associated risk level so that the patients can take precaution and treatment at early stages of the disease.

Chapter 15

Valerianus Hashiyana, University of Namibia, Namibia
Jacob Angara Sheehama, University of Namibia, Namibia
Paulus Sheetekela, International University of Management, Namibia
Frans David, International University of Management, Namibia

This chapter showcases a big data platform solution for the Namibian health sector using handheld, portable devices, mobile devices, desktops, and server systems targeted to capture patient information, keep records, monitor and process patient health status. This chapter oversees the architectural design of the system that is more oriented towards specifications of user requirements on usability of mobile devices and their applications for e-health systems. This chapter is looking ahead to the benefits that come along with good investment in the e-health, which require a very philosophical and pragmatic systematic transformation of the hardware, software, and human resources in the health sector. Sustainability of the e-health system in the future is very promising as young professionals embrace these technological advancements from the training time and can take over the system without a big IT support staff as most of them are IT literate.

Chapter 16

Niharika Garg, Optum Global Solutions, India

Healthcare is one of the significant areas of development where the hospitals are turning to innovative models built around advanced medical technologies like electronic health, tele-medicine, and mobile health. Healthcare sector is revolving around big data sets and huge amount of unstructured information produced from these high-tech devices and tools. But the technologies like machine language, big data, and artificial intelligence are turning them to a data-intensive science. The data is used for analysis by medical researchers which in turn is becoming solution for many healthcare challenges like early diagnosis, quality care, portable healthcare, cost- and time-effective treatments, and many more. Therefore, the hospitals are turning to smart hospitals to strengthen their existence in tomorrow's challenging medical service market. This chapter discusses the technology contribution in healthcare, challenges in future, future healthcare and cost model, and challenges for insurance companies.

Human gait analysis plays a significant role in clinical domain for diagnosis of musculoskeletal disorders. It is an extremely challenging task for detecting abnormalities (unsteady gait, stiff gait, etc.) in human walking if the prior information is unknown about the gait pattern. A low-cost Kinect sensor is used to obtain promising results on human skeletal tracking in a convenient manner. A model is created on human skeletal joint positions extracted using Kinect v2 sensor in place using Kinect-based color and depth images. Normal gait and abnormal gait are collected from different persons on treadmill. Each trial of gait is decomposed into cycles. A convolutional neural network (CNN) model was developed on this experimental data for detection of abnormality in walking pattern and compared with state-of-the-art techniques.

COVID-19 is having a huge impact on the society around the world, causing a huge number of deaths, which is increasing day by day. All the countries are fighting against this global pandemic by working on vaccines, implementing complete and partial lockdowns to avoid the spread of virus. On the basis of the various literature surveys done by the authors, it is found that computational intelligence and data analytics can play a vital role in this pandemic and can be really helpful. This chapter explains how data analytics and computational intelligence can serve the world to combat COVID-19.

Knee osteoarthritis (OA) is a degenerative joint disease that occurs due to wear down of cartilage. Early diagnosis has a pivotal role in providing effective treatment and in attenuating further effects. This chapter aims to grade the severity of knee OA into three classes, namely absence of OA, mild OA, and severe OA, from radiographic images. Pre-processing steps include CLAHE and anisotropic diffusion for contrast enhancement and noise reduction, respectively. Niblack thresholding algorithm is used to segment the cartilage region. GLCM features like contrast, correlation, energy, homogeneity, and cartilage features such as area, medial, and lateral thickness are extracted from the segmented region. These features are fed to random forest classifier to assess the severity of OA. Performance of random forest classifier is compared with ANFIS and Naïve Bayes classifier. The classifiers are trained with 120 images and tested with 45 images. Experimental results show that random forest classifier achieves a higher accuracy of 88.8% compared to ANFIS and Naïve Bayes classifier.

Chapter 20
Rohan Jagtap, Sardar Patel Institute of Technology, Mumbai, India
Kshitij Phulare, Sardar Patel Institute of Technology, Mumbai, India
Mrunal Kurhade, Sardar Patel Institute of Technology, Mumbai, India
Kiran Shrikant Gawande, Sardar Patel Institute of Technology, Mumbai, India

Medical services are basic needs for human life. There are times when consulting a doctor can be difficult. The proposed idea is an AI-based chatbot that will provide assistance to the users regarding their health-based issues. The state of the art in the aforementioned field includes extractive bots that extract the keywords (i.e., symptoms from the user's input) and suggest its diagnosis. The proposed idea will be a conversational bot, which unlike the QnA bot will take into consideration the context of the user's whole conversation and reply accordingly. Thus, along with symptom extraction, the user will get a better experience conversing with the bot. The user can also normally chat with the chatbot for issues like if the user is not emotionally sound. For example, the bot will console the user if he/she is feeling stressed by recognizing the emotional health of the user.

Chapter 21
R. Suganya, Thiagarajar College of Engineering, India
Rajaram S., Thiagarajar College of Engineering, India
Kameswari M., Thiagarajar College of Engineering, India

Currently, thyroid disorders are more common and widespread among women worldwide. In India, seven out of ten women are suffering from thyroid problems. Various research literature studies predict that about 35% of Indian women are examined with prevalent goiter. It is very necessary to take preventive measures at its early stages, otherwise it causes infertility problem among women. The recent review discusses various analytics models that are used to handle different types of thyroid problems in women. This chapter is planned to analyze and compare different classification models, both machine learning algorithms and deep leaning algorithms, to classify different thyroid problems. Literature from both machine learning and deep learning algorithms is considered. This literature review on thyroid problems will help to analyze the reason and characteristics of thyroid disorder. The dataset used to build and to validate the algorithms was provided by UCI machine learning repository.

Chapter 22
Boipelo Vinolia Mogale, North-West University, South Africa
Johannes Tshepiso Tsoku, North-West University, South Africa
Elias Munapo, North-West University, South Africa
Olusegun Sunday Ewemooje, Federal University of Technology, Akure, Nigeria

Youth mortality is a challenge in South Africa, where on a daily basis a number of deaths are reported and are related to youth. This study used the 2014 Statistics South Africa data to examine the influence of sociodemographic factors on causes of death among South African youth aged 15-34 years, using a logistic regression model. The results showed that there is a significant relationship between education and causes of death as well as other sociodemographic factors and that the youth mortality will likely reduce if more youth have higher levels of education. The results of this study could be used to improve national prevention campaigns to reduce death among young South Africans, especially adolescents.

Anjali Dixit, Faculty of Juridical Sciences, Rama University, Kanpur, India

Cybercrime is increasing rapidly in this digitized world. Be it business, education, shopping, or banking transactions, everything is on cyberspace. Cybercrime covers a wide range of different attacks such as financial cybercrime, spreading computer viruses or malware, internet fraud, pornography cybercrime, intellectual property rights violation, etc. Due to increased cyber-attacks these days, the online users must be aware of these kinds of attacks and need to be cautious with their data online. Each country has their own laws for dealing with cybercrime. The different measures taken by the government of India to combat cybercrime are explained in this chapter. How the potential use of data analytics can help in reducing cybercrime in India is also explained.

Onur Önay, School of Business, Istanbul University, Turkey

Data science and data analytics are becoming increasingly important. It is widely used in scientific and real-life applications. These methods enable us to analyze, understand, and interpret the data in every field. In this study, k-means and k-medoids clustering methods are applied to cluster the Statistical Regions of Turkey in Level 2. Clustering analyses are done for 2017 and 2018 years. The datasets consist of "Distribution of expenditure groups according to Household Budget Survey" 2017 and 2018 values, "Gini coefficient by equivalised household disposable income" 2017 and 2018 values, and some features of "Regional Purchasing Power Parities for the main groups of consumption expenditures" 2017 values. Elbow method and average silhouette method are applied for the determining the number of the clusters at the beginning. Results are given and interpreted at the conclusion.

Ajinkya Kunjir, Lakehead University, Canada
Jugal Shah, Lakehead University, Canada
Vikas Trikha, Lakehead University, Canada

In the digital era of the 21st century, data analytics (DA) can be highlighted as 'finding conclusions based on observations' or unique knowledge discovery from data (KDD) in form of patterns and visualizations for ease of understanding. The city of Toronto consists of thousands of food chains, restaurants, bars based all over the streets of the city. Dinesafe is an agency-based inspection system monitored by the provincial and municipal regulations and ran by the Ministry of Health, Ontario. This chapter proposes an efficient descriptive data analytics on the Dinesafe data provided by the Health Ministry of Toronto, Ontario using an open-source data programming framework like R. The data is publicly available for all the researchers and motivates the practitioners for conveying the results to the ministry for betterment of the people of Toronto. The chapter will also shed light on the methodology, visualization, types and share the results from the work executed on R.

Preface

Data analytics and data science are two rapidly growing technologies. They can practically be applied in various applications. Data analytics is basically analyzing a large amount of data or data sets with the use of certain protocols and software's which help in understanding the data and gaining information regarding it. Data science is the combination of different algorithms, technologies and systems used to extract information from data and solve complex problems. There lies a great potential in data analytics and data science. They can be very well utilized in various sectors like business, healthcare, etc. where they will prove to be very beneficial. It is very important to encourage data analytics and data science by spreading awareness regarding it as they will change the course of working of different sectors where they will be used and will help them reach new heights for the benefit of the society.

This book titled *Handbook of Research on Engineering, Business, and Healthcare Applications of Data Science and Analytics* provides detailed explanation of what is data science and data analytics, their applications in various sectors like engineering, business, healthcare and it also briefs about application of data science and analytics in other miscellaneous areas. Undergraduate students, graduate students, research scholars, PhD scholars, scientists, faculty members and industry professionals of various sectors, etc. will all benefit and gain knowledge from this book.

Data analytics and data science can benefit various sectors like business sector, industrial sector, engineering, healthcare, etc. They have a great potential and need to be explored but there is a lack of awareness regarding it in our society. The objective of this book is to spread awareness regarding data analytics and data science and help people know its potential and educate them regarding its applications in different sectors and the tremendous benefits possible from it. They can ease the difficulties of various sectors and help them reach new heights and change the way of their working for the better.

This book comprises of total 25 chapters, each written by different author(s) from various countries of the world. The valuable information and details explained in each chapter is as follows:

Chapter 1: This chapter focuses on introduction to the field of data science. Data Science is the area of study which involves extracting insights from vast amounts of data by the use of various scientific methods, algorithms, and processes. The term data science has emerged because of the evolution of mathematical statistics, data analysis, and big data. Data science helps to discover hidden patterns from the raw data. It enables to translate a business problem into a research project and then translate it back into a practical solution. The purpose of this chapter is to provide emphasis on integration and synthesis of concepts, techniques, applications and tools to deal with various facets of data science practice, including data collection and integration, exploratory data analysis, predictive modeling, descriptive modeling, data product creation, evaluation, and effective communication.

Chapter 2: Data analytics is used to extract necessary information from a given data or data set. It is a concept of technology which can be implemented in various applications and is evolving rapidly. Data analytics analyses the whole data set completely and provides important information from it to the users. In this chapter a brief description of data analytics is provided. Different types of data analytics are also explained. Along with it, various different aspects of data analytics are described. As the chapter title suggests, this chapter is a brief walk through the world of data analytics i.e., a brief insight of data analytics is provided in this chapter.

Chapter 3: In the current times, the educational and employment areas are changing at a very fast rate. The change is visible especially in the zone of technology-education. Approximately 4-5 years back, technology education meant coding, using different computer science programming languages. But in the recent times Data Science and Data Analytics have become the buzz words. The employment in this area has also undergone a tremendous change effect. Many new employment opportunities have sprung in this area as well with the regular or existing jobs becoming less or extinct. The entire business domain is warming to these buzz words. And the industry preference for these techniques has widened. The Book chapter discusses both the concepts and the tools being used.

Chapter 4: Various devices such as smart phones, computers, tablets, biomedical equipment, sports equipment, and information systems generate a large amount of data and useful information in transactional information systems. However, these generate information that may not be perceptible or analyzed adequately for decision-making. There are technology, tools, algorithms, models that support analysis, visualization, learning and prediction. Data science involves techniques, methods to abstract knowledge generated through diverse sources. It combines fields such as statistics, machine learning, data mining, visualization, and predictive analysis. This chapter aims to be a guide regarding applicable statistical and computational tools in data science.

Chapter 5: The recent development in Artificial Intelligence is quite astounding in this decade. Especially, Machine Learning is one of the core subareas of A.I. Also, M.L field is an incessantly growing along with evolution and becomes a rise in its demand and importance. It transmogrified the way data is extracted, analyzed and interpreted. Computers are trained to get in a self-training mode so that when new data is fed they can learn, grow, change and develop themselves without explicit programming. It helps to make useful predictions that can guide better decisions in a real-life situation without human interference. Selection of M.L tool is always a challenging task, since choosing an appropriate tool can end up saving time as well as making it faster and easier to provide any solution. This chapter provides a classification of various machine learning tools on the following aspects: for non-programmers, for model deployment, for Computer Vision, Natural Language Processing, and audio for reinforcement learning and data mining.

Chapter 6: Data analysis is a process of studying, removing non-required data in the view level and converting to needed patterns for sub decisions to make an aggregated decision. Statistical modeling is the process of applying statistical techniques in data analysis for taking proactive decisions depend requirements. The statistical modeling identifies relationship between variables and it encompasses inferential statistics for model validation. The focus of the chapter is to analyze statistical modeling techniques in different contexts to understand the mathematical representation of data. The correlation and regression are used for analyzing association between key factors of companies' activities. Especially in business, correlation describes positive and negative correlation variables for analyzing the factors of business for supporting decision making process. The key factors are related with independent variable and dependent variable which creates cause and effect model to predict the future outcome.

Chapter 7: Financial ratios are used in a variety of ways today. Empirical research is getting bigger, with a special focus on predicting business failure, the strength of a company, investment decision making, etc. This chapter focuses on two methodologies suitable to deal with many data to evaluate business performance. They are Data Envelopment Analysis and Grey Relational Analysis. The empirical part of the chapter conducts an empirical analysis with the aforementioned two approaches. Firms are ranked based on their performances and detailed interpretations are obtained so that managers within businesses can get useful information on how to utilize such an approach to modelling. This study implicates that using the two mentioned approaches can be useful when making investment decisions based on many data available for the decision-maker. This is due to the methodology being suitable to handle big data and correctly quantifying the overall financial performance of a company.

Chapter 8: The point of this paper is to think about the correlation of two well known European option pricing models – Black Scholes Model and Binomial option pricing model. The above two models not statistically significant at one period (Dar and Anuradha 2018). In this examination, it is shown how the above two European models are statistically significant when the time period increases The independent paired t-test is utilized with the end goal to demonstrate that they are statistically significant to vary from one another at higher time period and the Anderson Darling test being used for the normality test. The Minitab and Excel programming has been utilized for graphical representation and the hypothesis testing.

Chapter 9: With the increasing share of digital transactions in the business, the way of operating the businesses has changed drastically, leading to an immense opportunity for achieving the operational excellence in the digital transactions. This chapter focusses on the ways of using data science to improve the operational efficiency of the last mile leg in the delivery shipments for Ecommerce. Some of these avenues are predicting the attrition of field executives, identification of fake delivery attempts, reduction of mis-routing, identification of bad addresses, more effective resolution of weight disputes with the clients, reverse geo-coding for locality mapping, etc. The chapter also discusses the caution to be exercised in the use of data science, and the flip side of trying to quantify and dissect the phenomenon that is so complex and subjective in nature.

Chapter 10: Massively parallel processors and modern data management architectures have led to more efficient operations and a better decision making for companies to process and analyse such complex and large-scale data. Especially, financial services companies leverage big data to transform their business processes and they focus on understanding the concepts of big data and related technologies. In this chapter, we focus on the scope of big data in finance and economics. We discuss the need for big data towards the digitalisation of services, utilisation of social media and new channels to reach customers, demand for personalised services and continuous flow of vast amount of data in the sector. We investigate the role of big data in transformation of financial and economic environment by reviewing previous studies on stock market reading and monitoring (real-time algorithmic trading, high-frequency trading), fraud detection and risk analysis. We conclude that there is a huge gap on big data studies in finance and economics in terms of both theoretical and empirical perspectives.

Chapter 11: The chapter examines the roles of data science and big data analytics to forensic accountants and fraud detection. It also considers how data science techniques could be applied to the investigative processes in forensic accounting. Basically, the current increase in the volume, velocity and variety of data offer a rich source of evidence for the forensic accountant who needs to be familiar with the techniques and procedures for extracting, analysing and visualising such data. This is against backdrop of continuous global increase in economic crime and frauds, and financial criminals are getting more sophisticated, taking advantage of the opportunities provided by the unstructured data constantly being created with every email sent, every Facebook post, every picture on Instagram or every thought share on Twitter. Consequently it is important that forensic accountants are constantly abreast with developments in data science and data analytics in order to stay a step ahead of fraudsters as well as address evolving vulnerabilities created by big data.

Chapter 12: Data science is a fast growing area which deals with data from its origin to the knowledge exploration. It comprises of two main subdomains, data analytics for preparing data and machine learning to probe into this data for hidden patterns. Machine Learning (ML) endows powerful algorithms for the automatic pattern recognition and producing prediction models for the structured and unstructured data. The available historical data has patterns having high predictive value is used for the future success of an industry. These algorithms also help to obtain accurate prediction, classification and simulation models by eliminating insignificant and faulty patterns. Machine Learning provides major advancement in health care industry by assisting doctors to diagnose chronic diseases correctly. Diabetes is one of the most common chronic disease which occurs when the pancreas cells are damaged and do not secrete sufficient amount of insulin required by the human body. Machine learning algorithms can help in early diagnosis of this chronic disease by studying its predictor parameters values.

Chapter 13: One of the largest global industry that is driving smart city environments are anywhere and anytime health monitoring applications. Smart health care systems need to be more preventive and responsive as they deal with sensitive data. Even though Cloud computing provides solutions to the smart health care applications, the major challenge imposed on cloud computing is how could the centralized traditional cloud computing handle voluminous data. The existing models may encounter problems related to network resource utilization, overheads in network response time and communication latency. As a solution to these problems edge oriented computing has emerged as a new computing paradigm through localized computing. Edge computing expands the compute, storage, and networking capabilities to the edge of the network which will respond to the above mentioned issues. Based on cloud computing and edge computing, in this chapter an opportunistic edge computing architecture is introduced for smart provisioning of health care data.

Chapter 14: Diabetes is one of the four non-communicable diseases causing maximum deaths in all over the world. The numbers of diabetes patients are increasing day by day. Machine learning techniques can help in early diagnosis of diabetes to overcome the influence of it. In this paper, we proposed the system which imputes missing values present in diabetes dataset and parallel process diabetes data for the pattern discovery using Hadoop-MapReduce based C4.5 machine learning algorithm. The system uses these patterns to classify the patient into diabetes and non-diabetes class and to predict risk levels associated with the patient. The two dataset namely Pima Indian Diabetes Dataset (PIDD) and Local Diabetes Dataset (LDD) are used for the experimentation. The experimental results show that C4.5 classifier gives accuracy of 73.91% and 79.33% when applied on (PIDD) (LDD) respectively. The proposed system will provide an effective solution for early diagnosis of diabetes patients and their associated risk level so that the patients can take precaution and treatment at early stages of the disease.

Chapter 15: This chapter showcases a big data platform solution for the Namibian health sector using hand held - portable devices– mobile devices, desktops and server systems targeted to capture patients information, keep record, monitor and process patient health status. This Chapter oversees the architectural design of the system that is more oriented towards specifications of user requirements on usability of mobile devices and their applications, for e-health systems. The advance of this paper is far looking, to the benefits that come along good investment in the e-health, which require a very philosophical and pragmatic systematic transformation of the hardware, software and human resources in the health sector. Sustainability of the e-health system in the future is very much promising as young professional do embrace these technological advancements, from the training time and the cane latter take over the system without the a big IT support staff, as most of them are IT literate.

Chapter 16: Now a days, Health care is one of the significant areas of the developments where the hospitals are turning to innovative models built around advanced medical technologies like Electronic health, Tele medicine and mobile health. Healthcare sector is revolving around big data sets and huge amount of unstructured information produced from these high tech devices and tools. But the technologies like Machine Language, Big Data and Artificial Intelligence are turning them to a data intensive science. The data is used for analysis by medical researchers which in turn is becoming solution for many healthcare challenges like early diagnosis, quality care, portable healthcare, cost and time effective treatments, and many more. Therefore, the hospitals are turning to Smart hospitals to strengthen their existence in the tomorrow's challenging medical service market. This article discusses about the Technology contribution in healthcare, challenges in future, future healthcare and cost model & challenges for insurance companies.

Chapter 17: Human gait analysis plays a significant role in clinical domain for diagnosis of musculoskeletal disorder. It is extremely challenging task for detecting abnormalities (unsteady gait, stiff gait etc.) in human walking if the prior information is unknown about the gait pattern. A low cost Kinect sensor is used to obtain promising results on human skeletal tracking in a convenient manner. A model is created on human skeletal joint positions extracted using Kinect v2 sensor in place using Kinect-based color and depth images. Normal gait and abnormal gait are collected from different persons on treadmill. Each trial of gait is decomposed into cycles. A convolutional neural network (CNN) model was developed on this experimental data for detection of abnormality in walking pattern and compared with state-of-the-art techniques.

Chapter 18: In the current year 2020, COVID-19 is having a huge impact on the society around the world, causing a huge number of deaths which is increasing day by day. All the countries are fighting against this global pandemic by working on vaccines, implementing complete and partial lockdown to avoid the spread of virus and along with this, various measures are being implemented. On the basis of the various literature survey done by the authors in this chapter, it is found that Computational Intelligence and Data Analytics can play a vital role in this pandemic and can be really helpful. This chapter explains how data analytics and computational intelligence can serve the world to combat COVID-19.

Chapter 19: Knee Osteoarthritis (OA) is a degenerative joint disease that occurs due to wear down of cartilage. Early diagnosis has a pivotal role in providing effective treatment and in attenuating further effects. This chapter aims to grade the severity of knee OA into 3 classes namely, absence of OA, mild OA and severe OA from radiographic images. Pre-processing steps include CLAHE and anisotropic diffusion for contrast enhancement and noise reduction respectively. Niblack thresholding algorithm is used to segment the cartilage region. GLCM features like contrast, correlation, energy, homogeneity and cartilage features such as area, medial and lateral thickness are extracted from the segmented region. These features are fed to Random Forest classifier to assess the severity of OA. Performance of Random Forest classifier is compared with ANFIS and Naïve Bayes classifier. The classifiers are trained with 120 images and tested with 45 images. Experimental results show that Random forest classifier achieves a higher accuracy of 88.8% compared to ANFIS and Naïve Bayes classifier.

Chapter 20: Medical services are basic needs for human life. There are times when consulting a doctor can be difficult. The proposed idea is an AI based chat-bot which will provide assistance to the users regarding their health-based issues. The state of art in the aforementioned field includes extractive bots that extract the keywords i.e symptoms from the user's input and suggest its diagnosis. The proposed idea will be a conversational bot which unlike the QnA bot will take into consideration the context of the user's whole conversation and reply accordingly. Thus, along with symptom extraction, the user will get a better experience conversing with the bot. The user can also normally chat with the chat-bot for issues like if the user is not emotionally sound, for example the bot will console the user if he/she is feeling stressed by recognizing the emotional health of the user.

Chapter 21: Currently, thyroid disorders are more common and widespread among women in worldwide. In India, seven out of 10 women are suffering from thyroid problem every day. Various research literature studies predict that about 35% of Indian women are examined with prevalent goiter. It is very necessary to take preventive measures at its early stages, otherwise it causes infertility problem among women. The recent review discusses various analytics model are used to handle different types of thyroid problems in women. This chapter is planned to analyze and compared different classification models –both machine learning algorithms and deep leaning algorithms to classify different thyroid problems. Literature paper from both machine learning and deep learning algorithm is considered. This literature review on thyroid problem will help to analyze the reason and characteristics of thyroid disorder. The dataset used to build and to validate the algorithms was provided by UCI machine learning repository.

Chapter 22: Youth mortality is a challenge in South Africa, where on a daily basis a number of deaths are reported and are related to youth. This study used the 2014 Statistics South Africa data to examine the influence of sociodemographic factors on causes of death among South African youth aged 15-34 years, using a logistic regression model. The results showed that there is a significant relationship between education and causes of death; as well as other sociodemographic factors and that the youth mortality will likely reduce if more youth have higher levels of education. The results of this study could be used to improve national prevention campaigns to reduce death among young South Africans, especially adolescents.

Chapter 23: Cybercrime is increasing rapidly in this digitized world. Be it business, education, shopping or banking transactions everything is on cyberspace. Cybercrime covers a wide range of different attacks such as financial cybercrime, spreading computer viruses or malware, internet fraud, pornography cybercrime, intellectual property rights violation etc. Due to increased cyber-attacks these days, the online users must be aware of these kind of attacks and need to be cautious with their data online. Each country has their own ways and laws for dealing with cybercrime. The different measures taken by the government of India to combat cybercrime is explained in this chapter. Along with it, how the potential use of data analytics can help in reducing cybercrime in India is explained.

Chapter 24: Data science and data analytics are becoming increasingly important. It is widely used in scientific and real life applications. These methods enable us to analyze, understand and interpret the data in every field. In this study, k-means and k-medoids clustering methods are applied to cluster the Statistical Regions of Turkey in Level 2. Clustering analyses are done for 2017 and 2018 years. The datasets consist of "Distribution of expenditure groups according to Household Budget Survey" 2017 and 2018 values, "Gini coefficient by equivalised household disposable income" 2017 and 2018 values and some features of "Regional Purchasing Power Parities for the main groups of consumption expenditures" 2017 values. Elbow method and average silhouette method are applied for the determining the number of the clusters at the beginning. Results are given and interpreted at the conclusion.

Chapter 25: In the digital era of the 21st Century, Data Analytics (DA) can be highlighted as 'Finding Conclusions based on Observations' or Unique Knowledge Discovery from Data (KDD) in form of patterns and Visualizations for ease of Understanding. The city of Toronto consists of thousands of food-chains, restaurants, bars based all over the streets of the city. 'Dinesafe' is an agency-based inspection system monitored by the provincial and municipal regulations and ran by the Ministry of Health, Ontario. This chapter proposes an efficient Descriptive data Analytics on the Dinesafe data provided by the Health Ministry of Toronto, Ontario using an open-source data programming framework like 'R'. The data is publicly available for all the researchers and motivates the practitioners for conveying the results to the ministry for betterment of the people of Toronto. The chapter will also shed light on the Methodology, Visualization types and share the results from the work executed on 'R'.

This book explains each and everything related to data analytics and data science. It describes in and out about its advantages, possibilities, applications in various sectors and miscellaneous areas, etc. We both editors are really happy put forward this book with the help of the prestigious IGI Global, USA-REG. publication house, their entire team, all the contributing authors and reviewers as this book will be the one go to book when it comes to data analytics and data science.

Thank you.
Regards,

Manisha Vohra & Bhushan Patil

Acknowledgment

We both editors would like to thank IGI Global, USA for providing us with the opportunity to bring out this book, *Handbook of Research on Engineering, Business, and Healthcare Applications of Data Science and Analytics*, in front of the whole world. This is an immensely vital book as data science and analytics are two highly valuable concepts which on implementation in different sectors can bring about really positive and helpful results.

We both editors would also like to thank Jan Travers, Lindsay Wertman, Josephine Dadeboe, Morgan Brajkovich, Kris Byrne, Collen Moore, and the entire team of IGI Global who has in some way or the other helped us on this journey of our book.

We would like to express our gratitude to all the contributing authors and reviewers and thank them for their great dedication, hard work and efforts which helped in making this book successful.

Along with it, I, Mr. Bhushan Patil, would like to thank my mother, Mrs. Jyoti Patil, my father, Mr. Bajirao Patil and my brother, Mr. Jeevan Patil for their love and support. I would also like to thank my co-editor Miss Manisha Vohra without whom this book would not have been possible.

I, Miss Manisha Vohra would like to take this opportunity to thank my mother Mrs. Meena Vohra, my father, Mr. Arun Vohra and my brother Mr. Chirag Vohra for their support, encouragement and love. I would also like to thank my co-editor, Mr. Bhushan Patil for making this book possible.

Chapter 1
Introduction to Data Science

M. Govindarajan
Annamalai University, India

ABSTRACT

This chapter focuses on introduction to the field of data science. Data science is the area of study which involves extracting insights from vast amounts of data by the use of various scientific methods, algorithms, and processes. The term data science has emerged because of the evolution of mathematical statistics, data analysis, and big data. Data science helps to discover hidden patterns from the raw data. It enables to translate a business problem into a research project and then translate it back into a practical solution. The purpose of this chapter is to provide emphasis on integration and synthesis of concepts, techniques, applications, and tools to deal with various facets of data science practice, including data collection and integration, exploratory data analysis, predictive modeling, descriptive modeling, data product creation, evaluation, and effective communication.

INTRODUCTION

Data Science is the science and art of using computational methods to identify and discover influential patterns in data. The goal of data science is to gain insight from data and often to affect decisions to make them more reliable (D.Abbott, 2014).

Data is necessarily a measure of historic information so, by definition, data science examines historic data. Considering this definition data science can be defined as organizing data knowledge that can be used for experiments and prediction. The need for data science has developed due to the immense increase in the amount of raw data such as images, text, video and others.

Every field is contributing to this ever increasing data such as engineering, mining, healthcare, hospitality, energy etc. Data scientists are developing various algorithms and techniques in order to process and analyze this data and make the best use out of it. Previously health industry used hard paper to store data regarding patients and other medical issues. But the new trend has helped doctors to store this data in electronic form (Raghupathi & Raghupathi, 2014).

DOI: 10.4018/978-1-7998-3053-5.ch001

Space exploration has produced a large amount of data considering the recent space missions. Data scientists have also helped to store this data and use it for prediction to carry out further missions. Implementing business logics and strategies need data analysis and predictions which can be now easily done by the use of prediction algorithms.

Energy companies are using data prediction algorithms to manage the energy production based on demands and supply. This prediction has aided to use the available energy efficiently. In coming years machines will have the ability to predict and generate the required resource as per the supply and demand. The current upcoming technology artificial intelligence is also being helped tremendously by the use of data mining and prediction algorithms.

LITERATURE REVIEW

Table 1. Shows various Methods, Tools and Applications used in Data Science

Author	Advantages	Disadvantages
Katerina Lepenioti et al., (2020)	This paper provides clarity on the research field of prescriptiveanalytics, synthesizes the literature review in order to identify the existing research challenges, and outlinesdirections for future research.	The review presented herein is limited to works explicitly scoped as prescriptive analytics. It does not deal with works from different research fields that can potentially contribute to the field of prescriptive analytics.
Ben Kei Daniel (2019)	This paper was inspired partly by insights drawn fromthe literature but mostly informed by experience researching into Big Data in education.	This paper does not discuss privacy, ethics, access and governance issues and identify strategies to support educationalresearchers.
ImanRaeesi Vanani et al., (2019)	This paper discussed the methods of both ML and DL and an ML/DL deployment model for IOT data.	This paper does not discuss the methods of both ML and DL and an ML/DL deployment model for IOT fog and edge computing.
Jeffrey Ray et al., (2018)	This paper provides an overview of the current research efforts in Big Data science, with particular emphasis on its applications, as well as theoretical foundation.	This paper does not consider applications of Natural Language Processing and Network Theory.
Jens Baum et al., (2018)	This paper is based on a broad, systematic literature review consisting of a two-step search approach combined with additional filtering and classification.	This paper considers search strings consisted of the words "big data", "maintenance", "production" and "manufacturing" and did not consider other related terms, such as "factory", "industry 4.0" and so on. This study considered only papers written in English (including the title, abstract and full text); others were excluded.
G. Magesh et al., (2017)	This paper is facilitating future researchers to develop new approaches and algorithms to solve few challenges in big data.	This paper addressed only few challenges in big data and its applications in various fields.
LongbingCao (2017)	This paper provides a comprehensive survey and tutorial of the fundamental aspects of data science.	This paper does not provide algorithms and process of data science.
Yulan Liang et al., (2016)	This paper provides a general survey of recent progress and advances in Big Data science, healthcare, and biomedical research.	This paper does not consider Big Datasets in healthcare, and biomedical research.
SanketMantri (2016)	This paper discussed about data science, current and future development in this field.	This paper does not consider new methods to obtain appropriate values and develop good computational data sets.
PanagiotisBarlas et al., (2015)	This paper provides an overview of open source (OS) data science tools, proposing a classification scheme that can be used to study OS data science software.	The proposed classification scheme provides useful, but limited scope, statistical functionality to the parent tool.

FOCUS OF THE ARTICLE

Data Science is the process of discovering interesting and meaningful patterns in data using computational analytics methods. Analytical methods in the DataScience are drawn from several related disciplines, some of which have been used to discover patterns and trends in data for more than 100 years, including statistics. The purpose of this chapter is to provide emphasis on integration and synthesis of concepts, techniques, applications and tools to deal with various facets of data science practice, including data collection and integration, exploratory data analysis, predictive modeling, descriptive modeling, data product creation, evaluation, and effective communication.

Data Collection and Integration

Data collection is concerned with the accurate acquisition of data; although methods may differ depending on the field, the emphasis on ensuring accuracy remains the same. The primary goal of any data collection endeavor is to capture quality data or evidence that easily translates to rich data analysis that may lead to credible and conclusive answers to questions that have been posed.

Data integration is the process of combining data from different sources into a single, unified view. Integration begins with the ingestion process, and includes steps such as cleansing, extract, transform, loadmapping, and transformation. Data integration ultimately enables analytics tools to produce effective, actionable business intelligence.

Exploratory Data Analysis

Once the data has been cleaned and stored in a way that insights can be retrieved from it, the data exploration phase is mandatory. The objective of this stage is to understand the data, this is normally done with statistical techniques and also plotting the data. This is a good stage to evaluate whether the problem definition makes sense or is feasible.

Predictive Modelling

Predictive modeling is a commonly used statistical technique to predict future behavior. Predictive modeling solutions are a form of data-mining technology that works by analyzing historical and current data and generating a model to help predict future outcomes

Classification

Classification algorithms are used when the desired output is a discrete label. In other words, they're helpful when the answer to your question about your business falls under a finite set of possible outcomes. Much use cases, such as determining whether an email is spam or not, have only two possible outcomes. This is called binary classification.Multi-label classification captures everything else, and is useful for customer segmentation, audio and image visualization, and text analysis for mining customer sentiment.

Naive Bayes

Naive Bayes algorithm based on Bayes' theorem with the assumption of independence between every pair of features. Naive Bayes classifiers work well in many real-world situations such as document classification and spam filtering.

Decision Trees

Given a data of attributes together with its classes, a decision tree produces a sequence of rules that can be used to classify the data.

Neural Networks

Neural Networks are modelled after the neurons in the human brain. It comprises many layers of neurons that are structured to transmit information from the input layer to the output layer. Between the input and the output layer, there are hidden layers present. These hidden layers can be many or just one. A simple neural network comprising of a single hidden layer is known as Perceptron.

KNN

K-Nearest Neighbor deploys to classify objects in the nearest training class of features (Zhang Q et al.2018), and it is known as one of the most widely used algorithms in classification problems in data mining and knowledge extraction. In this method, an object is assigned to its k-nearest neighbors. The efficiency of this method is on the basis of thelevel of features' weighted qualifications.

Support Vectors Machine

Support vector machine (SVM) was proposed in 1995 by Cortes and Vapnikto solve problems related to multidimensional classification and regression issuesas its outstanding learning performance (M. Silva et al., 2017). In this process, SVM constructs ahigh-dimensional hyperplane that divides data into binary categories, and findinggreatest margin in binary categories considering the hyperplane space is the mainobjective of this method (J.Chen et al. 2012). "Statistical learning theory," "Vapnik-Chervonenkis(VC) dimension," and the "kernel method" are underlying factors of developmentof SVM (S.Wamba et al. 2017),which deploys limited number of learning patterns to desirablegeneralization considering a risk minimization structure (A. Gandomiet al., 2015).

Regression

On the other hand, regression is useful for predicting outputs that are continuous. That means the answer to your question is represented by a quantity that can be flexibly determined based on the inputs of the model rather than being confined to a set of possible labels. Regression problems with time-ordered inputs are called time-series forecasting problems, like ARIMA forecasting, which allows data scientists to explain seasonal patterns in sales, evaluate the impact of new marketing campaigns, and more.

Descriptive Modelling

Descriptive modeling is a mathematical process that describes real-world events and the relationships between factors responsible for them. The process is used by consumer-driven organizations to help them target their marketing and advertising efforts.

Clustering

Clustering as a supervised learning method aims to create groups of clusters,which members of it are in common with each other in characteristics and dissimilarwith other cluster members (Shi X et al.2017). The calculated inter point distance of every observation in a cluster is small in comparison with its distance to a point in otherclusters (J. Kozak et al., 2016). "Exploratory pattern-analysis," "grouping," "decision-making," and"machine-learning situations" are some main applications of clustering technique. Five groups of clustering are "hierarchical clustering," "partitioning clustering,""density-based clustering," "grid-based clustering," and "model-based clustering"(Shi X et al.2017).Clustering problems are divided into two categories: generative and discriminativeapproaches. The first one refers to maximizing the probability of samplegeneration, which is used in learning from generated models, and the other isrelated to deploying pairwise similarities, which maximize inter cluster similarities and minimize similarities of clusters in between (R.Sikora et al., 2007).

There are important clustering methods like K-means clustering, kernel K-means, spectral clustering, and density-based clustering algorithms that are at thecenter of research topics for several decades. In K-means clustering, data is assignedto the nearest center, which results from being unable to detect nonspherical clusters. Kernel k-means and spectral clustering create a link between the data andfeature space and after that k-means clustering is deployed. Obtaining feature spaceis done by using kernel function and graph model by kernel k-means and spectralclustering, respectively. Also spectral clustering deploys Eigen-decomposition techniques additionally (X .Gu et al., 2018). K-means clustering works effectively in clustering ofnumerical data, which is multidimensional (L.Zhou et al. 2017).

Density-based clustering is represented by DBSCAN, and clusters tend to beseparate from data set and be as higher density area. This method does not deployone cluster for clusters recognition in the data a priori. It considers user-definedparameter to create clusters, which has a bit deviation from cited parameter in clustering process (X.Shi et al. 2017).

Association Rules

Association Rule Mining, as the name suggests, association rules are simple If/Then statements that help discover relationships between seemingly independent relational databases or other data repositories. Most machine learning algorithms work with numeric datasets and hence tend to be mathematical. However, association rule mining is suitable for non-numeric, categorical data and requires just a little bit more than simple counting. Association rule mining is a procedure which aims to observe frequently occurring patterns, correlations, or associations from datasets found in various kinds of databases such as relational databases, transactional databases, and other forms of repositories. An association rule has two parts:

- An antecedent (if) and
- A consequent (then).

An antecedent is something that's found in data, and a consequent is an item that is found in combination with the antecedent.

Association rules are created by thoroughly analyzing data and looking for frequent if/then patterns. Then, depending on the following two parameters, the important relationships are observed:

- **Support:** Support indicates how frequently the if/then relationship appears in the database.
- **Confidence:** Confidence tells about the number of times these relationships have been found to be true.

So, in a given transaction with multiple items, Association Rule Mining primarily tries to find the rules that govern how or why such products/items are often bought together. For example, peanut butter and jelly are frequently purchased together because a lot of people like to make PB&J sandwiches. Association Rule Mining is sometimes referred to as Market Basket Analysis, as it was the first application area of association mining. The aim is to discover associations of items occurring together more often than you'd expect from randomly sampling all the possibilities. The classic anecdote of Beer and Diaper will help in understanding this better.

Sequential Patterns Mining

The task of sequential pattern mining is a data mining task specialized for analyzing sequential data, to discover sequential patterns. More precisely, it consists of discovering interesting sub sequences in a set of sequences, where the interestingness of a subsequence can be measured in terms of various criteria such as its occurrence frequency, length, and profit. Sequential pattern mining has numerous real-life applications due to the fact that data is naturally encoded as sequences of symbols in many fields such as bioinformatics, e-learning, market basket analysis, texts, and webpage click-stream analysis.

Implementation

In this section, how to use WEKA tool to build the above models for the mushroom dataset will be demonstrated based on execution time.

Interpreting the Results

The performance of classification, clustering and association rule mining and sequential mining algorithms were compared using mushroom dataset based on time complexity. Based on the performance of various classification, clustering and association rule mining and sequential mining algorithms, it has been concluded that K-Nearest Neighbor algorithm outperforms the other algorithms in classification, the Estimation Maximization outperforms the cobweb algorithm in clustering, the CoverRulesOpt outperforms the other algorithms in association rule generation and the SPADE algorithm outperforms the ApriorAll algorithm in sequence mining in time constraint.

Table 2. Evaluation of mushroom dataset

Algorithms	Time (Seconds)				
Classification					
Naive Bayes	0.05				
Decision Trees: C4.5	0.08				
Neural Networks- RBFNN	0.97				
K-Nearest Neighbor	0				
Support Vectors Machine	8.08				
Regression					
Linear Logistic Regression	4.2				
Clustering					
Cobweb	333.7				
Estimation Maximization	002.0				
Association rules – Minimum Support	**0.5**	**0.6**	**0.7**	**0.8**	**0.9**
Apriori	0	16	0	0	16
CoverRules	16	0	0	0	16
CoverRulesOpt	15	16	15	0	0
Sequential Patterns Mining - Minimum Support	**0.5**	**0.6**	**0.7**	**0.8**	**0.9**
AprioriAll	112880	109570	104690	94200	83540
SPADE	60360	60470	57840	57400	57340

Graph and Network Analysis

Graph Algorithms or Graph Analytics are analytic tools used to determine strength and direction of relationships between objects in a graph. The network analysis is a method used to analyze, control and monitoring of business processes and workflows.

Data Product Creation

A data product is the production output from a statistical analysis. Data products automate complex analysis tasks or use technology to expand the utility of a data informed model, algorithm or inference.

Model Evaluation

Model Evaluation is an integral part of the model development process. It helps to find the best model that represents our data and how well the chosen model will work in the future. Evaluating model performance with the data used for training is not acceptable in data science because it can easily generate overoptimistic and overfitted models. There are two methods of evaluating models in data science, Hold-Out and Cross-Validation. To avoid overfitting, both methods use a test set (not seen by the model) to evaluate model performance.

Effective Communication

Making predictions is not enough! Effective data scientists know how to explain and interpret their results, and communicate findings accurately to stakeholders to inform business decisions. Visualization is the field of research in computer science that studies effective communication of quantitative results by linking perception, cognition, and algorithms to exploit the enormous bandwidth of the human visual cortex.

Tools for Data Science

Data Scientists use traditional statistical methodologies that form the core backbone of Machine Learning algorithms. They also use Deep Learning algorithms to generate robust predictions. Data Scientists use the following tools and programming languages:

R: R is a scripting language that is specifically tailored for statistical computing. It is widely used for data analysis, statistical modeling, time-series forecasting, clustering etc. R is mostly used for statistical operations. It also possesses the features of an object-oriented programming language. R is an interpreter based language and is widely popular across multiple industries.

Python: Like R, Python is an interpreter based high-level programming language. Python is a versatile language. It is mostly used for Data Science and Software Development. Python has gained popularity due to its ease of use and code readability. As a result, Python is widely used for Data Analysis, Natural Language Processing, and Computer Vision. Python comes with various graphical and statistical packages like Matplotlib, Numpy, SciPy and more advanced packages for Deep Learning such as TensorFlow, PyTorch, Keras etc. Python is utilized for the purpose of data mining, wrangling, visualizations and developing predictive models. This makes Python a very flexible programming language.

SQL: SQL stands for Structured Query Language. Data Scientists use SQL for managing and querying data stored in databases. Being able to extract information from databases is the first step towards analyzing the data. Relational Databases are a collection of data organized in tables. SQL is used for extracting, managing and manipulating the data. For example A Data Scientist working in the banking industry uses SQL for extracting information of customers. While Relational Databases use SQL, 'NoSQL' is a popular choice for non-relational or distributed databases. Recently NoSQL has been gaining popularity due to its flexible scalability, dynamic design, and open source nature. MongoDB, Redis, and Cassandra are some of the popular NoSQL languages.

Hadoop: Big data is another trending term that deals with management and storage of huge amount of data. Data is either structured or unstructured. A Data Scientist must have a familiarity with complex data and must know tools that regulate the storage of massive datasets. One such tool is Hadoop. While being open-source software, Hadoop utilizes a distributed storage system using a model called 'MapReduce'. There are several packages in Hadoop such as Apache Pig, Hive, HBase etc. Due to its ability to process colossal data quickly, its scalable architecture and low-cost deployment, Hadoop has grown to become the most popular software for Big Data.

Tableau: Tableau is data Visualization software specializing in graphical analysis of data. It allows its users to create interactive visualizations and dashboards. This makes Tableau an ideal choice for showing various trends and insights of the data in the form of interactable charts such as Treemaps, Histograms, Box plots etc. An important feature of Tableau is its ability to connect with spreadsheets, relational databases, and cloud platforms. This allows Tableau to process data directly, making it easier for the users.

Weka: For Data Scientists looking forward to getting familiar with Machine Learning in action, Weka is can be an ideal option. Weka is generally used for Data Mining but also consists of various tools required for Machine Learning operations. It is completely open-source software that uses GUI Interface making it easier for users to interact with, without requiring any line of code.

Applications of Data Science

Data Science has created a strong foothold in several industries such as medicine, banking, manufacturing, transportation etc. It has immense applications and has variety of uses. Some of the following applications of Data Science are:

Data Science in Healthcare

Data Science has been playing a pivotal role in the Healthcare Industry. With the help of classification algorithms, doctors are able to detect cancer and tumors at an early stage using Image Recognition software. Genetic Industries use Data Science for analyzing and classifying patterns of genomic sequences. Various virtual assistants are also helping patients to resolve their physical and mental ailments.

Data Science in E-Commerce

Amazon uses a recommendation system that recommends users various products based on their historical purchase. Data Scientists have developed recommendation systems predict user preferences using Machine Learning.

Data Science in Manufacturing

Industrial robots have made taken over mundane and repetitive roles required in the manufacturing unit. These industrial robots are autonomous in nature and use Data Science technologies such as Reinforcement Learning and Image Recognition.

Data Science as Conversational Agents

Amazon's Alexa and Siri by Apple use Speech Recognition to understand users. Data Scientists develop this speech recognition system that converts human speech into textual data. Also, it uses various Machine Learning algorithms to classify user queries and provide an appropriate response.

Data Science in Transport

Self Driving Cars use autonomous agents that utilize Reinforcement Learning and Detection algorithms. Self-Driving Cars are no longer fiction due to advancements in Data Science.

Data Science in Business

There are many ways by which Data Science is helping businesses to run in a better way:

Business Intelligence for Making Smarter Decisions

Traditional Business Intelligence was more descriptive and static in nature. However, with the addition of data science, it has transformed itself to become a more dynamic field. Data Science has rendered Business Intelligence to incorporate a wide range of business operations. With the massive increase in the volume of data, businesses need data scientists to analyze and derive meaningful insights from the data.The meaningful insights will help the data science companies to analyze information at a large scale and gain necessary decision-making strategies. The process of decision making involves the evaluation and assessment of various factors involved in it. Decision Making is a four-step process:

1. Understanding the context and nature of the problem that are required to be solved.
2. Exploring and quantifying the quality of the data.
3. Implementation of the right algorithm and tools for finding a solution to the problems.
4. Using story-telling to translate our insights for a better understanding of teams.

Through this way, businesses need data science for facilitating the decision-making process.

Making Better Products

Companies should be able to attract their customers towards products. They need to develop products that suit the requirements of customers and provide them with guaranteed satisfaction. Therefore, industries require data to develop their product in the best possible way. The process involves the analysis of customer reviews to find the best fit for the products. This analysis is carried out with the advanced analytical tools of Data Science.

Furthermore, industries utilize the current market trends to devise a product for the masses. These market trends provide businesses with clues about the current need for the product. Businesses evolve with innovation. With the growth in data, industries are able to implement not only newer products but also various innovative strategies. For example - Airbnb uses data science to improve its services. The data generated by the customers, is processed and analyzed. It is then used by Airbnb to address the requirements and offer premier facilities to its customers.

Managing Businesses Efficiently

Businesses today are data rich. They possess a plethora of data that allows them to gain insights through a proper analysis of the data. Data Science platforms unearth the hidden patterns that are presents inside the data and help to make meaningful analysis and prediction of events.

With Data Science, businesses can manage themselves more efficiently. Both large scale businesses and small start-ups can benefit from data science in order to grow further.

Data Scientists help to analyze the health of the businesses. With data science, companies can predict the success rate of their strategies. Data Scientists are responsible for turning raw data into cooked data. This helps in summarizing the performance of the company and the health of the product. Data Science identifies key metrics that are essential for the determination of business performance. Based on this, the business can take important measures to quantify and evaluate its performance and take appropriate management steps. It can also help the managers to analyze and determine the potential candidates for the business.

Using data science, businesses can also foster leadership development by tracking the performance, success rate, and other important metrics. With workforce analytics, industries can evaluate what is best working for the employees.

For example – Data Science can be used to monitor the performance of employees. Using this, managers can analyze the contributions made by the employees and determine when they should be promoted, managing their perks, etc.

Predictive Analytics to Predict Outcomes

Predictive analytics is the most important part of businesses. With the advent of advanced predictive tools and technologies, companies have expanded their capability to deal with diverse forms of data. In formal terms, predictive analytics is the statistical analysis of data that involves several machine learning algorithms for predicting the future outcome using the historical data. There are several predictive analytics tools like SAS, IBM SPSS, SAP HANA, etc.

There are various applications of predictive analytics in businesses such as customer segmentation, risk assessment, sales forecasting, and market analysis. With predictive analytics, businesses have an edge over others as they are able to foresee future events and take appropriate measures in respect to it. Predictive Analytics has its own specific implementation based on the type of industries. However, regardless of that, it shares a common role in predicting future events.

Leveraging Data for Business Decisions

In the previous section, how data science is playing an important role in predicting the future is discussed. These predictions are necessary for businesses to learn about future outcomes. Based on this, businesses take decisions that are data-driven. In the past, many businesses would take poor decisions due to the lack of surveys or sole reliance on 'gut feelings'. It would result in some disastrous decisions leading to losses in millions.

However, with the presence of a plethora of data and necessary data tools, it is now possible for the data industries to make calculated data-driven decisions. Furthermore, business decisions can be made with the help of powerful tools that can not only process data faster but also provide accurate results.

Assessing Business Decisions

After making decisions through the forecast of the future occurrences, it is a requirement for the companies to assess them. This is possible through several hypothesis testing tools. After implementing the decisions, businesses should understand how these decisions affect their performance and growth. If the decision leads to any negative factor, then they should analyze it and eliminate the problem that is slowing down their performance.

There are various procedures through which businesses can evaluate their decisions and plan a suitable action strategy. These decisions revolve around their customer requirements, company goals as well as the needs of the project executives. Furthermore, in order to assess future growth through the present course of actions, businesses can make profits considerably with the help of data science.

Automating Recruitment Processes

Data Science has played a key role in bringing automation to several industries. It has taken away the mundane and repetitive jobs. One such job is that of resume screening. Every day, companies have to deal with hordes of applicant's resumes. Some major businesses can even attract thousands of resumes for a position. In order to make sense of all of these resumes and select the right candidate, businesses make use of data science.

The data science technologies like image recognition are able to convert the visual information from the resume into a digital format. It then processes the data using various analytical algorithms like clustering and classification to churn out the right candidate for the job. Furthermore, businesses study the right trends and analyze potential applicants for the job. This allows them to reach out to candidates and have an in-depth insight into the job-seeker market.

Data Science in Engineering

Data science is revolutionizing the engineering sector. It provides new methods for monitoring, operating, optimizing and maintaining technological assets.The engineering sector is in the middle of a data science revolution. Digitalization is the trend in asset management. Digital twins are the hype of the day. Data science is changing the way of monitoring, operating, optimizing and maintaining assets. Not only in industry, but also in utility companies and in civil engineering.

From Sensor to Information

Sensors are getting cheaper, connectivity is almost ubiquitous and storage is abundant. This makes it relatively easy to collect all sorts of status information from assets. Assets can be industrial installations or engines. But also distribution networks, bridges, roads, canals, pumping stations and lots more.

However, sensor data is notoriously noisy and error prone. Sensors fail or drift from their calibrated settings. Connections may fail. And the systems to collect the data have their own problems once in a while. Also, data may be collected in tremendous volumes (big data) where only a fraction of that volume is actually useful.

Data engineering is used to transform the raw data into a reliable data feed. It cuts down the data to a useful volume and it can detect various sorts of errors. It can correct these errors or remove the incorrect data items. If necessary, estimates can be made for missing data (imputation).

Note that data generated by sensors is not always numerical. In many cases important information is available in log files. Sifting through large volumes of text data and finding exactly the relevant entries is also best done by data science in combination with text mining. The data can also come in the form of images. Then advanced image recognition methods can be used to extract information for further processing.

Extending Sensor Data to a Full 3D or 4D View

Even though sensors may be abundant, there is often still a need to grasp what is going on between the sensors. Or to get insights in parts of the asset that are not open to sensoring. In those cases, a computational model of the asset can be used to interpolate or extrapolate the data to unseen locations or times.

A computational model will generate physically meaningful estimates of the unseen parts of the system. Estimates that are consistent with the data that is actually observed.

Monitoring and Operating Assets

But just collecting data is hardly useful as such. It becomes valuable only in the way it is used.In many cases, the data needs to be presented to the operators in a convenient way. This requires the development of a dashboard that shows the relevant metrics to operators and allows them to dig into the data to understand what is going on. Standard dashboard platforms are available. But proprietary dashboards are also relatively easy to build using modern web technology.

Behind a dashboard is usually a collection of services based on data science. These create derivative information that will help the operator to focus on what is really important. For example, data science can be used to detect abnormal situations and trigger an alert.

Artificial intelligence techniques can be used to assist operators. It can suggest advisable actions, either based on business rules or through machine learning algorithms that have been trained on past information. Also, it can be used to determine the root cause of failure or malfunction, for example through Bayesian networks.

Control and Optimization

Data science plays an important role in the control of installations. Based on what it learned from data in the past, a machine learning algorithm can predict the future development of a system and determine the appropriate actions.

A nice example (based on reinforcement learning) is where a neural network is trained by applying small variations on the settings of a system and then observing the response of the system. This neural network can then automatically control the system to keep it in an optimal state. Such an automatically controlled, smart system can be seen as a form of artificial intelligence.

But this approach will fail if the optimal setting of the system is too far from the actual setting to be reached by small variations or if the system is too critical to allow this kind of experimentation. In that case, a computational model that accurately reflects the underlying processes of the system is often used to find the best setting using various optimization techniques.

But such models are often heavy in terms of computational load. One way to deal with this is by using approximate or reduced models. Here, again, machine learning can be helpful. A neural network can be trained on data that is generated by the computational model so that it becomes a fast approximation of the full model. In an operational setting, the trained neural network can be used to determine the optimal settings of the system.

Maintenance

Predictive maintenance was one of the first applications of data science in engineering and is still one of the best known. Typically, the data scientist will collect a large data set of system failures and, through data science, find early warning signals that predict an impending failure. If a the prediction algorithm is accurate enough, it can be used during operations to predict when the system will fail and plan maintenance accordingly.Usually, this approach will lead to much lower maintenance costs in comparison to predefined maintenance moments that are usually planned too frequently just to be sure that no failures will occur. But it should be stressed that it is not always easy or even possible to collect the right amount of data on failures.

New Inventions in Data Science

Data science covers a vast network of topics under its umbrella including Deep learning, IoT, AI and various others. It is a comprehensive amalgamation of data inference, analysis, algorithm computation and technology to solve multifaceted business problems. With the unabated increasing popularity of data science and new technological and sophisticated developments, the applications and uses of data science are increasing by leaps and bounds over time. The following trends in this field are expected to continue in the coming year as well.

Regulatory Schemes

With the plethora of data being generated every second, and the pace being accelerated by catalysts like IoT, the issue of data security will become more and more important. It can be reasonably expected that more data regulatory schemes will follow in 2019. Data regulatory events like for example GDPR (European General Data Protection Regulation), which was enforced on May, 2018 regulated data science practice by setting certain boundaries and limits on collection and management of personal data. Such regulatory activities will hugely impact future predictive models and different analytic exercises. Moreover, the increasingly sophisticated cyber attacks have mandated the need for a less vulnerable data protection scheme. The high-profile data breaches expose our inadequacy in this aspect. So many more new protocols and procedures to secure data are likely to emerge in 2019.

Artificial Intelligence and Intelligent Apps

The buzz created by AI is unlikely to die down in the coming year. Currently it is in the nascent and initial stage of AI, and the following year will see the more advanced application of AI in all the fields. Harnessing AI will still remain a challenge. More intelligent apps will be developed using AI, Machine Learning and other technologies. Automated machine learning (ML) will become common and it will transform data science with better data management. There will also be the development of specific hardware for training and execution of deep learning. Incorporation of AI will enhance decision-making and improve the overall business experience. Applications and other services will increasingly rely on AI to improve the overall experience. All the new applications will incorporate some form of AI in their program to improve their functioning. So, the number of intelligent apps will be on the rise. Intelligent things that are smarter versions of regular gadgets will continue to flood the market.

Virtual Representations of Real-World Objects and Real-Time Innovations

Digital representations of real-life physical objects powered by AI capabilities will become widespread. These technologies will be used to solve real-life business problems across companies all over the world. The pace of real-time innovations will also accelerate with advanced technologies. ML and neural network design will be extensively used in all the applications. Augmented reality (AR) and virtual reality (VR) applications are already giving way to massive transformations. More breakthroughs in these areas are likely to occur in the coming year and the human-machine interaction is deemed to improve because of this. Human expectations and experiences from digital systems and machines will rise.

Edge Computing

With further growth of IoT, edge computing will increasingly become popular. With thousands of devices and sensors collecting data for analysis, businesses are increasingly doing more analysis and data processing close to the source of origin. Edge computing will be on the rise to maintain proximity to the source of information. Issues related to bandwidth, connectivity and latency will be solved through this. Edge computing along with cloud technology will provide a coordinated structure that simulates a paradigm of the service-oriented model. In fact, IDC predicts, "By 2020, new cloud pricing models will service specific analytics workloads, contributing to 5x higher spending growth on cloud vs. on-premises analytics."

Blockchain

Blockchain is a major technology that underlies crypto currencies like Bitcoin. It is a highly secured ledger and has a variety of applications. It can be used to record a large number of detailed transactions. Blockchain technology can have far-reaching implications in terms of data security. New security measures and processes emulating the blockchain technology can appear in the coming year.

FUTURE RESEARCH DIRECTIONS

Let's have a look at a few factors that point out to data science's future, demonstrating compelling reasons why it is crucial to today's business needs.

Companies' Inability to Handle Data

Data is being regularly collected by businesses and companies for transactions and through website interactions. Many companies face a common challenge – to analyze and categorize the data that is collected and stored. A data scientist becomes the saviour in a situation of mayhem like this. Companies can progress a lot with proper and efficient handling of data, which results in productivity.

Revised Data Privacy Regulations

Countries of the European Union witnessed the passing of the General Data Protection Regulation (GDPR) in May 2018. A similar regulation for data protection will be passed by California in 2020. This will create co-dependency between companies and data scientists for the need of storing data adequately and responsibly. In today's times, people are generally more cautious and alert about sharing data to businesses and giving up a certain amount of control to them, as there is raising awareness about data breaches and their malefic consequences. Companies can no longer afford to be careless and irresponsible about their data. The GDPR will ensure some amount of data privacy in the coming future.

Data Science is constantly evolving

Career areas that do not carry any growth potential in them run the risk of stagnating. This indicates that the respective fields need to constantly evolve and undergo a change for opportunities to arise and flourish in the industry. Data science is a broad career path that is undergoing developments and thus promises abundant opportunities in the future. Data science job roles are likely to get more specific, which in turn will lead to specializations in the field. People inclined towards this stream can exploit their opportunities and pursue what suits them best through these specifications and specializations.

An Astonishing Incline in Data Growth

Data is generated by everyone on a daily basis with and without our notice. The daily interaction with data will only keep increasing as time passes. In addition, the amount of data existing in the world will increase at lightning speed. As data production will be on the rise, the demand for data scientists will be crucial to help enterprises use and manage it well.

Virtual Reality will be Friendlier

Today's world can witness and are in fact witnessing how Artificial Intelligence is spreading across the globe and companies' reliance on it. Big data prospects with its current innovations will flourish more with advanced concepts like Deep Learning and neural networking. Currently, machine learning is being introduced and implemented in almost every application. Virtual Reality (VR) and Augmented Reality (AR) are undergoing monumental modifications too. In addition, human and machine interaction, as well as dependency, is likely to improve and increase drastically.

Blockchain Updating with Data Science

The main popular technology dealing with crypto currencies like Bitcoin is referred to as Blockchain. Data security will live true to its function in this aspect as the detailed transactions will be secured and made note of. If big data flourishes, then IoT will witness growth too and gain popularity. Edge computing will be responsible for dealing with data issues and address them.

CONCLUSION

This chapter gave an overview of concepts, techniques, applications and tools to deal with various facets of data science practice, including data collection and integration, exploratory data analysis, predictive modeling, descriptive modeling, data product creation, evaluation, and effective communication. The new developments in the field of data science will definitely change the world and help humans to predict the data usage. The old methods of statistical analysis will not be completely overpowered but still these new techniques will be more efficient than the old ways. Considering the progress speed there will be accurate and efficient techniques in next few years.

REFERENCES

Abbott, D. (2014). *Applied Predictive Analytics: Principles and Techniques for the Professional Data Analyst*. Wiley.

Barlas, P., Lanning, I., & Heavey, C. (2015). A survey of open sourcedata science tools. *International Journal of Intelligent Computing and Cybernetics*, *8*(3), 232–261. doi:10.1108/IJICC-07-2014-0031

Baum, J., Laroque, C., Oeser, B., Skoogh, A., & Subramaniyan, M. (2018). Applications of Big Data analytics and Related Technologies in Maintenance-Literature-Based Research. *Machines*, *6*(54), 1–12. doi:10.3390/machines6040054

Cao, L. (2017). Data Science: A Comprehensive Overview. *ACM Computing Surveys*, *50*(3), 1–42. doi:10.1145/3076253

Chen, J. (2012). The synergistic effects of IT-enabled resources on organizational capabilities and firm performance. *Information & Management*, *49*(34), 140–152. doi:10.1016/j.im.2012.01.005

Daniel, B. K. (2019). Big Data and data science: A critical review of issues foreducational research. *British Journal of Educational Technology*, *50*(1), 101–113. doi:10.1111/bjet.12595

Gandomi, A., & Haider, M. (2015). Big data concepts, methods,and analytics. *International Journal of Information Management*, *35*(2), 137–144. doi:10.1016/j.ijinfomgt.2014.10.007

Gu, X., & Angelov, P. (2018). Self-organizingfuzzy logic classifier. *Information Sciences*, *447*, 36–51. doi:10.1016/j.ins.2018.03.004

Kozak, J., & Boryczka, U. (2016). Collectivedata mining in the ant colony decisiontree approach. *Information Sciences*, *372*, 126–147. doi:10.1016/j.ins.2016.08.051

Lepenioti, K., Bousdekis, A., Apostoloua, D., & Mentzas, G. (2020). Prescriptive analytics: Literature review and research challenges. *International Journal of Information Management*, *50*, 57–70. doi:10.1016/j.ijinfomgt.2019.04.003

Liang, Y., & Kelemen, A. (2016). Big Data Science and Its Applications in Health and Medical Research:Challenges and Opportunities. *Journal of Biometrics & Biostatistics*, *7*(3), 1–7. doi:10.4172/2155-6180.1000307

Magesh, G., & Swarnalatha, P. (2017). Big Data and Its Applications: A Survey. *Research Journal of Pharmaceutical, Biological and Chemical Sciences*, *8*(2), 2346–2358.

Mantri. (2016). Data Science: Literature Review & State of Art. *Technical Report*, 1-3.

Raghupathi, W., & Raghupathi, V. (2014). Big data analytics in healthcare: Promise and potential. *Health Information Science and Systems*, *2*(3), 1–10. doi:10.1186/2047-2501-2-3 PMID:25825667

Ray, J., Johnny, O., Trovati, M., Sotiriadis, S., & Bessis, N. (2018). The Rise of Big Data Science: A Survey of Techniques, Methods and Approaches in the Field of Natural Language Processing and Network Theory. *Big Data Cogn.Comput*, *2*(22), 1–18. doi:10.3390/bdcc2030022

Shi, X., Chen, G., Heng, P. A., & Yi, Z. (2017). Tracking topology structure adaptively with deep neural networks. *Neural Computing & Applications*, *30*(11), 3317–3326. doi:10.100700521-017-2906-y

Sikora, R., & Piramuthu, S. (2007). Frameworkfor efficient feature selection in geneticalgorithm based data mining. *European Journal of Operational Research*, *180*(2), 723–737. doi:10.1016/j.ejor.2006.02.040

Silva, M., & Cunha, C. (2017). A tabu search heuristic for the incapacitated single allocation p-hub maximal covering problem. *European Journal of Operational Research*, *262*(3), 954–965. doi:10.1016/j.ejor.2017.03.066

Vanani & hMajidian. (2019). Literature Review on Big Data Analytics Methods. *Social Media and Machine Learning*, 1-22.

Wamba, S., Gunasekaran, A., Akter, S., Ren, S. J., Dubey, R., & Childe, S. J. (2017). Big data analyt-icsand firm performance: Effects ofdynamic capabilities. *Journal of Business Research*, *70*, 356–365. doi:10.1016/j.jbusres.2016.08.009

Zhang, Q., Yang, L. T., Chen, Z., & Li, P. (2018). A survey on deeplearning for big data. *Information Fusion*, *42*, 146–157. doi:10.1016/j.inffus.2017.10.006

Zhou, L., Pan, S., Wang, J., & Vasilakos, A. V. (2017). Machine learningon big data: Opportunities and challenges. *Neurocomputing Journal*, *237*, 350–361. doi:10.1016/j.neucom.2017.01.026

KEY TERMS AND DEFINITIONS

Data Science: Data Science is the science and art of using computational methods to identify and discover influential patterns in data.

Descriptive Modeling: Descriptive modeling is a mathematical process that describes real-world events and the relationships between factors responsible for them.

Model Evaluation: Model Evaluation is an integral part of the model development process. It helps to find the best model that represents our data and how well the chosen model will work in the future.

Predictive Modeling: Predictive modeling is a commonly used statistical technique to predict future behavior.

R: R is a scripting language that is specifically tailored for statistical computing. It is widely used for data analysis, statistical modeling, time-series forecasting, clustering, etc.

Support Vectors Machine: Support vector machine (SVM) was proposed in 1995 by Cortes and Vapnikto solve problems related to multidimensional classification and regression issues as its outstanding learning performance.

Tableau: Tableau is data Visualization software specializing in graphical analysis of data. It allows its users to create interactive visualizations and dashboards.

Chapter 2
A Walk Through the World of Data Analytics

Manisha Vohra
https://orcid.org/0000-0001-8010-0076
Independent Researcher, India

Bhushan Patil
https://orcid.org/0000-0003-2407-0022
Independent Researcher, India

ABSTRACT

Data analytics is used to extract necessary information from a given data or data set. It is a concept of technology which can be implemented in various applications and is evolving rapidly. Data analytics analyses the whole data set completely and provides important information from it to the users. In this chapter, a brief description of data analytics is provided. Different types of data analytics are also explained. Along with it, various different aspects of data analytics are described. As the chapter title suggests, this chapter is a brief walk through the world of data analytics i.e., a brief insight of data analytics is provided in this chapter.

WHAT IS DATA ANALYTICS?

Data analytics basically means examining and analyzing data with some specific tools and algorithms. An extremely huge amount of data can be easily examined and analyzed with the help of data analytics. The thing about data analytics which makes it useful is that, it provides a person with crucial information regarding the data. It can put before a person all the important details of the whole data, irrespective of how large the data is.

According to author Acharjya (2017), in digital world, data is generated from various sources and the fast transition from digital technologies has led to growth of big data. Data analytics is doing the task of simplifying an otherwise tedious and time consuming process of analyzing and obtaining information from any given data. The tools used in data analytics are capable enough of analyzing the data thoroughly.

DOI: 10.4018/978-1-7998-3053-5.ch002

HISTORY AND EVOLUTION OF DATA ANALYTICS

Data analytics has gained immense limelight in the recent past. It truly owes this due to the list of benefits it provides. It generates a lot of curiosity regarding its origin, its history. There is no such one particular place of its origin or no particular date that marks its origination day. It is a technological concept that has been around since a very long time. The basic meaning of data analytics is to analyze data and provide information regarding it. So, this work of analyzing data to gain information from it is being carried out since many years. Even before the term data analytics was coined and people came across this term, its concept was being used in the simplest of form. Now whenever anyone wants to apply data analytics and obtain information, they make use of some or the other data analytics tools like R programming, Python, etc. These tools were not always present, despite of that, data analytics would be performed manually. Analyzing data, especially large amount of data manually without any tool obviously means a very time consuming process and it also includes a possibility that some important information which would have been easily obtained through data analytics tools might get missed out while manually performing data analytics. Having said that, matter of fact remains the same that data analytics tools were not existent always. Nevertheless, data analytics was widely used by many people even before coining of the term data analytics and its formal introduction to the world, the only differences were the analysis had separate special term for it and no tools existed. In fact, there were no virtual or online data storage facilities as well, many years back then. Book ledger, diary, etc. form of writing, maintaining and storing data were used. Different industries are present since many years and different businesses are also carried out since many years, it is not something which is started in the recent times. If the first industrial revolution is to be considered, then it took place somewhere in between the year 1760 to 1840. This itself is proof enough of the existence of the different industries and the ongoing of different kinds of business. When there is work been done, there is undoubtedly a lot of data generated and not just in business sector, a lot of data is generated in various sectors which requires analysis. So like explained earlier, a basic manual analysis was always being performed by people which is necessary to handle and manage the work. Only with progress and invention of devices like computer, different programming tools, etc. data analytics concept evolved gained this term and limelight.

WORKING OF DATA ANALYTICS

The working of data analytics is a simple process. It involves six different steps. Collecting the data is the first step, then the data needs to be categorized. After that the data needs to be arranged, filtered, analyzed and only after all these steps the data is provided to the end user which is the final step in the working of data analytics. The six different steps involved in working are as follows:

1. Collecting the data:
    Firstly, the data needs to be collected and put together. Whichever data is to be analyzed, it needs to be collected completely and brought and put together.

2. Categorizing the data:
    All the collected data needs to be set up in properly and be categorized appropriately.

Figure 1. Working process of data analytics

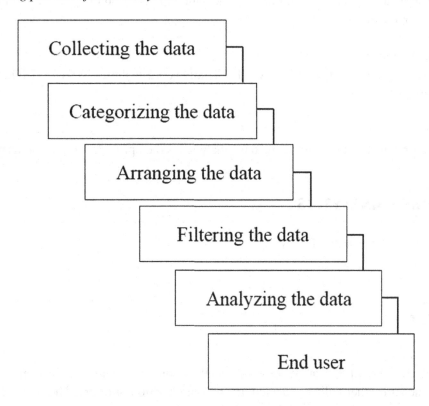

For example, a grocery store owner wants to analyze the sales data of his store. He wants an analysis of all the items sold in the past six months. There is a large variety of items sold in a grocery store, right from breakfast and ready to eat snacks to bathing products, dairy products, etc. All the different types of products needs to be put into a category first like how they are arranged in different categories in the store, likewise for analyzing also, the data needs to be put in a category first. The data of breakfast and ready to eat snacks in one category, dairy products in another category and so on. This is required to make the assessment of the data easier. The sensor has all the data it has received through sensing. The data is in raw form and this data collected from the sensor needs to be sent to the cloud. The sensor makes preparation for sending the data collected to cloud by ensuring all the data remains unaltered and in it exact raw form in which it is collected.

3. Arranging the data:
   The data after being categorized needs to be arranged properly so it can be filtered which is the next step. If the data after being put in different categories is just left like that, possibilities are that the entire data might not be taken for the next step. Some data might be missed out that is why arranging the data is important.

4. Filtering the data:
   There are times when a single data may be entered twice or even thrice in a data set. There can be even a possibility that a certain data entered is incomplete and something is missed out to be

entered and added to the data set. Filtering the data will help find out these kind of errors so that they can be rectified.

5. Analyzing the data:
    Since the data is now ready to be analyzed, a detailed data analytics is performed in this step with the help of tools.

6. End user
    The result obtained by performing the data analytics is then provided to the end user.

TYPES OF DATA ANALYTICS

The types of data analytics are as follows:

1. Descriptive
2. Diagnostic
3. Prescriptive
4. Predictive

All the different types of data analytics are basically helping in finding out answers to certain types of questions which are either telling you about the past information or future. The figure 2 below shows the different types of data analytics and figure 3 below shows which questions are answered by different types of data analytics.

1. Descriptive data analytics:
    This type of analytics is basically answering the question related to the event that has already occurred. To understand descriptive analytics better consider the following example. A company running steel fabrication business wants to understand and know the performance of their company in the past one year. They want to know how much sales took place in the past one year. Their raw data can be taken and descriptive analytics can be performed. This will help them know what happened. Descriptive analytics always deals with the question what happened and gives information about it.

2. Diagnostic data analytics:
    This type of analytics will let one know of the past happening. Using this type of analytics, one gets answers to the question related to why something has happened. So from the given data set, a particular thing that has already occurred will be able to be known that why did it occur. For example to understand diagnostic analytics consider the same example seen above in the descriptive analytics, of the company running steel fabrication business. With descriptive analytics, the company got to know regarding their sales in the past one year and with diagnostic analytics they will come to know how why did it happen, be it an increase or decrease in the sales, diagnostic analytics will let them know why it happened. Diagnostic analytics might require more data to be obtained externally except for the given data set as this will help in finding out the answer to why something happened through correlation of the external obtained data and the given data set.

Figure 2. Types of data analytics

Figure 3. Questions answered by different types of data analytics

Descriptive analytics (for analysis on past happening)

Diagnostic analytics (for analysis on past happening)

Predictive analytics (for analysis on future happening)

Predictive analytics (for analysis on future happening)

3.   Predictive analytics:
This analytics is a future related question answering analytics. Through this analytics, one can find out what will happen. Predictive analytics as the name suggests, will predict and answer this question of what will happen, just like it is giving one an insight into the future. Continuing with the same example of the steel fabrication company, they shall be able to know regarding sales possibilities with predictive analytics.

4.   Prescriptive analytics:
This analytics also answers the question of the future but a different question as compared to the question answered by predictive analytics. This particular analytics will tell one what can be done so that one can decide what step should be taken next. Continuing with the same example of the steel fabrication company, with the help of this analytics, the company would be able to find out what can be done so that the sales can increase.

WHY IS DATA ANALYTICS REQUIRED?

When one has a lot of data to analyze, it is highly possible that one might not be able to manually obtain each and every minute as well as major information from the given data set on which they are working. Data analytics will not only provide a person with all the vital information, it will also, simplify the work, save time, help in planning and taking decisions as it will be bringing forth a very minutely analyzed information. It doesn't have any scope for error. So altogether it is highly benefiting. Thus there is a great need to use as well as encourage and introduce data analytics in different sectors.

TOOLS USED IN DATA ANALYTICS

There are various tools used in data analytics.

1. R
   It is basically a type of programming language. It is used for statistical computing. It provides the users with a software environment and it is highly efficient.

2. Python
   It is a programming language that is very efficient to be used in data analytics. It is useful in integrating various other technology based applications as well.

3. Excel
   It is one of the most common tool used in data analytics. With excel one can easily arrange data into spreadsheets, visualize and analyze it.

4. Tableau
   It is a great tool for data analytics. It allows to quickly connect and access your database.

5. SAS (Statistical Analysis Software)
   Statistical Analysis Software abbreviated as SAS is also yet another amazing tool for data analytics. One can hassle free analyze data using SAS.

The table 1 below shows the comparison of different data analytics tools

ADVANTAGES OF DATA ANALYTICS

1) The need for manual analysis is eliminated
2) All the vital information is obtained
3) There is no scope for error in the information obtained from data analytics (provided the data set is correct)
4) Human work is reduced quite a lot
5) Data gets analyzed very quickly

Table 1. Comparison of different data analytics tools

Data analytics tools	Type	Merits	Demerits
R	Open source	It is very easy to use and is very efficient in data analytics	It cannot be used for web based applications
Python	Open source	It is a beginner friendly tool and provides the user with a lot many libraries that are beneficial in data analytics	The execution speed of Python is slow
Excel	It is available with Microsoft Office. Hence it is not open source	Analyzing the data as well as managing the data becomes quite simplified in excel	Although analyzing and managing data in excel is simple but this stands true only till the time there is not immense amount of data. For large amount of data analyzing and management, excel is not very ideal and effective
Tableau	It is not open source	The overall performance of tableau is highly powerful for analyzing of data	The reports are not refreshed automatically
SAS	It is not open source	It is simple to learn and understand	The graphic representation is not up to the mark as compared to other data analytics tools like R

DATA ANALYTICS IN HEALTHCARE

Healthcare sector is one of the top most priority sector worldwide. Healthcare sector is the one which needs continuous upgradation and improvement. All the possible technologies which can help this sector improve and gain benefits should be integrated in this sector. Different technologies like IoT, robotics, etc. are already being integrated in healthcare sector in some or the other way. Data analytics is also one such technology concept which can be integrated into healthcare sector and help it improve and gain benefits. There are various ways through which data analytics can be integrated in healthcare. Some of them are explained as follows:

1. Analyzing a patient's data
2. Analyzing medicine results
3. Tracking of diseases

1. Analyzing a patient's data:
    Any patient going through any health issue like diabetes, high blood pressure, etc. should always keep a tab on their health and their health records. It is a lot easier for doctors to monitor and track any patient's health history through data analytics. What data analytics does is in this scenario, it helps by putting across the important information of the patient's health record in front of the doctor. The doctor need not minutely go through the entire medical records of the patient for knowing and understanding his/her health issues. The doctor's work will become so convenient and plus the doctor's time will be also saved. Also, the chances of the doctor unknowingly missing out some of the critical information of the patient's health is ruled out as data analytics will ensure no important information is left out and it is put across the doctor.

2.   Analyzing medicine results:

Whenever new types of medicines are being made for any type of disease, their data is stored. If supposing 10 different types of medicines are being made for any particular disease then it is necessary to analyze each medicine's trial result data. At the same time it is also necessary to compare the trial result data of each medicine with the remaining other medicines trial result data and analyze them so that which is best among them all can be known. Data analytics can efficiently and in hassle free manner analyze each medicine's trial result data. Along with it, data analytics can help in comparing and analyzing the trial result data of each medicine with the remaining other medicines result data. Manually comparing and analyzing the data in this case would not be advisable and it would consume a lot of time. Data analytics would be the best resource to be used in this case.

3.   Tracking of diseases

All hospitals maintain records of their patients. Time to time if the data from all hospitals is taken and analyzed then the occurrence of diseases in the recent past can be analyzed using data analytics. It is very important to keep an eye on occurrence of diseases regularly that are taking place in the recent past. Through this if in the recent past any particular disease is found to be on the rise of occurrence or any health epidemic conditions are observed then appropriate measures can be taken on time to prevent health issues. Government bodies or certain health institutes under the government authorities generally collect all this data and keep a tab of this data. Consider the scenario of a city, be it any city in the world, undoubtedly the number of hospitals which include private as well as government one's will be high in count. It is not feasible to manually obtain detailed analyzed information from it quickly. However, data analytics can with great ease do this work and provide a thorough insight of the whole data.

DATA ANALYTICS IN ENGINEERING

Data analytics can be very well be used in various engineering applications. Each engineering area works differently and the work carried out in each engineering area is different. Numerable technologies can be used in different engineering areas. Data analytics is among the numerable technologies that can be implemented and can benefit different engineering areas. For example, industrial engineering is one such area of engineering where data analytics can be used efficiently. In industrial engineering, optimization of available resources is done and along with it new methods are found and tested and implemented to get the best results. To understand how data analytics can be used in industrial engineering, consider the following example. A plastic manufacturing company wants to manufacture plastic containers. There are different techniques or methods using which the plastic containers can be manufactured. The company can try out different methods and manufacture the plastic containers and with the help of data analytics analyze and compare all the data obtained from the different methods. This will give them a clear picture of which method of manufacturing is the most efficient and beneficial. This is one scenario of this example. In another scenario, this company can do a literature survey of the data available of the methods used by other similar companies and then on the basis of their own available resources and with the help of data analytics, get a clear picture of the method they should opt for manufacturing instead of themselves trying all the methods of manufacturing. In both the scenarios, data analytics will play a great role and help in their work. This is just one example of how data analytics can be used in engineering. Likewise data analytics can be used in many more engineering applications. It is extremely useful in engineering applications.

POSSIBILITIES WITH DATA ANALYTICS

Data analytics can be used in almost every sector. It can be used in any work which has generated data and requires analysis to review and make decisions. It not only just puts in front of you the details of events that occurred, it also helps you know what can happen and what can be done. With data analytics, it is possible to always have a plan of action and have to overcome and refrain from the wrong doings and decisions taken in the past for any sector.

CONCLUSION

Data analytics is very beneficial and useful. It has various advantages. It can be easily integrated in healthcare and engineering applications. It eases out the work and provides detailed information of the data which it has analyzed. This chapter thus provided great insights into data analytics.

REFERENCES

Acharjya, D. P. (2017). A Survey on Big Data Analytics: Challenges, Open Research Issues and Tools. *International Journal of Advanced Computer Science and Applications*, 7(2), 511–518.

Jolly, A., & Tripathi, P. (2019). Role of Big Data Analytics in Healthcare. *International Journal of Engineering and Advanced Technology*, 9(1), 4174–4177. doi:10.35940/ijeat.A1421.109119

Raghupati, W., & Raghupati, V. (2014). Big data analytics in healthcare: Promise and potential. *Health Information Science and Systems*, 2(1), 1–10. doi:10.1186/2047-2501-2-3 PMID:25825667

Sonnati, R. (2017). Improving Healthcare Using Big Data Analytics. *International Journal of Scientific & Technology Research*, 6(3), 142–146.

Vijayarani & Sharmila. (2016). Research in Big Data - An Overview. *Informatics Engineering International Journal*, 4(3), 1-20.

KEY TERMS AND DEFINITIONS

Data: Information obtained and put together.
Data Analytics Tools: The computing resources or software used in data analytics.
Dataset: It is a collection of information.

Chapter 3
A Survey on Tools for Data Analytics and Data Science

Pankaj Pathak

ⓘ https://orcid.org/0000-0002-5875-0387

Symbiosis International University (Deemed), India

Samaya Pillai Iyengar

Symbiosis International University (Deemed), India

Minal Abhyankar

Symbiosis International University (Deemed), India

ABSTRACT

In the current times, the educational and employment areas are changing at a very fast rate. The change is visible especially in the zone of technology-education. Approximately 4-5 years back, technology education meant coding, using different computer science programming languages. But in the recent times data science and data analytics have become the buzz words. The employment in this area has also undergone a tremendous change effect. Many new employment opportunities have sprung in this area as well with the regular or existing jobs becoming less or extinct. The entire business domain is warming to these buzz words. And the industry preference for these techniques has widened. The chapter discusses both the concepts and the tools being used.

INTRODUCTION AND BACKGROUND

Database is the container of information i.e. processed data. It is used to store the data. The main objective of a database is storage of data. With the Database comes the database management system, the system to create and manage all operations related to the database. Codd (1990).

The timeline for Database is as follows:

1950s and early 1960s: The Data processing and storage of data mainly done with magnetic tapes. The Magnetic tapes could give a sequential access only. For the input process the "Punched cards" were used.

DOI: 10.4018/978-1-7998-3053-5.ch003

Late 1960s and 1970s: The innovation of Hard disk was done. It allowed direct access to the data. In database handling, the network and hierarchical data models were in reputed and used extensively. Ted Codd put forth the concept of relational data model, which is still relevant in today's world. The relational data model enabled better performance in transactions and helped real time transactions.

1980s: Research in the area of relational DB domain has a great commercial value. During this time, SQL became the industrial de facto standard. Parallel and distributed database systems were launched in the commercial arena for usage. They proved to be most useful for organizations. It was during this time that the Object-oriented databases were also featuring as a new concept in the database domain.

1990s: In this era there was a thrust in decision support systems which were huge. The data-mining applications were also launched and developed during this period. Large multi-terabyte data warehouses were designed. It was the new emergence of a concept called "Web commerce".

2000s: Here the XML and XQuery standards were launched and developed. "Automated database administration" started to feature in the organizations simplifying and easing the lives of database administrators.

Data Science

Data science is both art and science of handling data, mostly big data. Data pre-processing needs to done before using the data for analytics, the data gathered can be of historical data or online real time data, once that is received, various algorithms like the KNN algorithms and Multidimensional scaling algorithms were performed to get the required trends. The people working here are called as "data scientist", Van Der Aalst, W. (2016).

Data scientist understands data from a business point of view and provides accurate predictions and insights that can be used to power critical business decisions. Today R and Python are the major tools used in data analytics.

It can be said that "data science" is connected to computer science, but in principle, it is a distinct and separate field. Computer science as a domain consists of forming programs, algorithms and processing data. Data science covers any type and all types of data analysis. Computers may constitute the process of analysis or can be ignored from the process. Data science is mainly related to the field of 'Statistics'. It includes the steps of data collection, organization of data, analysis of data, and representation of data. The huge amounts of data in the organizations they have resorted to data science for survival and sustenance. Data science has become an integral part of Information Technology. As the technological advancements enable and provide an edge to data science. For example, a company that has huge amount of data can use data science for collecting, storing, managing and also analyzing that data effectively. This data is then run with many tests in a scientific method to extract results. Provost, F. et al. (2013).

Data Science is a bigger picture of data analytics which includes not only simple statistical modeling but also mathematics and calculations. Data science is an umbrella under which all the three parts come up, with subject expertise. Data science mostly tackles big data, data cleansing, preparations and analysis. Data science is used to generate deep insights from the collected data set. It uses the data mining concepts, tools of data mining, predictive analytics and machine learning to generate critical information. Domain knowledge is very important when it comes to data science even more than from data analytics. In the current times Machine learning algorithms also play a pivotal role.

Multidisciplinary data extrapolation, development of algorithm and technology in order to answer complex analytical problems is called data science. Uncovering useful conclusions from data is the basic essence of data science. Data science basically uses hidden insights from data which can help companies in making logical decisions.

Unlike traditional data which was mostly structured, today most of the data lacks proper structuring. This is mainly because the data set generated nowadays is from various kinds of sources such as text files, sensors, images, audio, videos and various other kinds of instruments. Data trends say that more than 80% of the data is unstructured/semi structured.

Simple BI tools are not capable of processing these large volumes of data. This is why more complex and advanced analytical tools and algorithms for processing, analyzing and drawing meaningful insights out of it are required. Here is where Data Science comes into picture. Data Science basically is the use of various tools, algorithms, AI, Machine Learning to discover various patterns in data and based on that pattern get insights and take business oriented decisions.

The Timeline For Data Science Is As Follows

Data Science is fundamentally initiated with statistics and datamining techniques, and now it has evolved to include the current disruptive technologies and concepts. These disruptive technologies are "Artificial Intelligence", "Machine Learning", and the "Internet of Things".

1962: 'John Tukey', marked and discussed about a change in the world of statistics. Tukey here was referring to the merging of two huge concepts of statistics and computers.

1974: 'Data Science' term was discussed in the "Concise Survey of Computer Methods". Peter Naur came up with the new term and concept of data science - "The science of dealing with data". In fields of sciences and business also, once the association of data is established it is easy to implement the concept of data science.

1977: 'IASC', termed as the "International Association for Statistical Computing" was created.

1977: 'Tukey' discussed in his second paper, titled "Exploratory Data Analysis" the further concepts of data science. Here he debated about the significance and importance of hypothesis testing. He also stated further that "confirmatory data analysis and exploratory data analysis should work hand in hand".

1989: the cohort of "Knowledge Discovery in Databases was formed". It transformed into the ACM SIGKDD representing the Association for Computing Machinery's *Special Interest Group on Knowledge Discovery and Data Mining*".

1994: "Database Marketing", which exposed that the organizations were into gathering huge amounts of personal data of customers with a plan to start marketing campaigns. This was a famous revelation by business Week.

1999: 'Jacob Zahavi' came up with the discussion of "the need for new tools to handle the massive amounts of information available to businesses in Mining Data".

2001: Creation and development of "Software-as-a-Service (SaaS)". This was the time cloud had started showing its presence. Many applications were moving to this concept.

2001: The concept of training and educating personnel with the view of future was rooted by 'William S. Cleveland'. He launched the, "Data Science: An Action Plan for Expanding the Technical Areas of the field of Statistics".

2002: "The International Council for Science" was formed. The Committee started publishing on "Data for Science and Technology". This was a Journal. A publication focused on issues of Data Science. It became famous and garnered attention of experts.

2006: "Hadoop 0.1.0", an open-source, non-relational database, was launched.

2008: the title, "Data Scientist" became a catchphrase. It was LinkedIn and Facebook who actually created a buzz for these terms and which lead to acceptability in the minds of other people.

2009: The concept of NoSQL was reintroduced with many modifications.

2011: The job listings for Data Scientists increased by 15,000%.

2011: The organization Pentaho used the concept of Data Lakes. Their strategy was to promote Data lakes rather than Data Warehouses.

2013: More than 92% of the data in the world was created within the span of two years. This was proven by IBM and shared across industries.

2015: This was considered the year of AI. Bloomberg's Jack Clark, declared that it so.AI started to have its presence felt across industries.

2015: The process of Data Science got formulated in a systematic way. The process used techniques like Deep Learning, speech recognition, Google Voice etc. These techniques started being used by vast people. The process constituted the following steps:

Step 1: Frame the problem.

Step 2: Collect the raw data needed for your problem.

Step 3: Process the data for analysis.

Step 4: Explore the data.

Step 5: Perform in-depth analysis.

Step 6: Communicate results of the analysis.

MAIN FOCUS OF THE CHAPTER

Data Analytics

The concept of "Data Analytics" involves the research and discovery of facts. Data analytics is a scope of data science which converts the raw data into some meaningful information for decision making and planning. Data analytics can further process information into knowledge. It also includes data mining in its original form and concept. Since Data mining was all about knowledge discovery. Lee, S. J et. al. (2001).

"Data mining" reflects mining of Data. By mining we mean digging the study or raw data. Data Mining leads to identifying patterns or such arrangements in the data which can impact the business and decision making of the organizations. It has proven its relevance for both business intelligence and data science. There are many data mining techniques organizations can use to turn raw data into actionable insights. These involve all right from making basic data preparation to using algorithms to make the data ready to use for various purposes. Wei, C. P.et. al. (2003)

Following are the various steps constituting Data Mining as a process.

Data cleaning and preparation: This is a vital and most important part of the data mining process. The Raw data i.e. the initial data of study needs to be cleansed and formatted. Only if this is carried out, then one can move on the analysis phase. If this step is ignored or skipped, the data analysis becomes irrelevant and may lead to inaccurate results.

Tracking patterns: This step helps us to track and trace patterns in the study data. This is an essential technique to unearth any visible or hidden patterns. The patterns in data help us to make some quick and intelligent inferences about the outcomes.

Classification: "Classification method in the data mining technique involves analyzing the various attributes associated with different types of data. Once organizations identify the main characteristics of these data types, organizations can categorize or classify related data."

Association: "Association is a data mining technique related to statistics. It indicates that certain data (or events found in data) are linked to other data or data-driven events."

Outlier detection: "Outlier detection determines any anomalies in datasets. Once organizations find aberrations in their data, it becomes easier to understand why these anomalies happen and prepare for any future occurrences to best achieve business objectives."

Clustering: "Clustering is an analytics technique that relies on visual approaches to understanding data."

Regression: "Regression techniques are useful for identifying the nature of the relationship between variables in a dataset."

Prediction: "Prediction is a very powerful aspect of data mining that represents one of four branches of analytics"

Sequential patterns: "This data mining technique focuses on uncovering a series of events that takes place in sequence."

Decision trees: "Decision trees are a specific type of predictive model that lets organizations effectively mine data."

Statistical techniques: "Statistical techniques are at the core of most analytics involved in the data mining process. The different analytics models are based on statistical concepts, which output numerical values that are applicable to specific business objectives."

Visualization: "It grants users insight into data based on sensory perceptions that people can see. Today's data visualizations is dynamic, useful for streaming data in real-time, and characterized by different colors and other visual effects which can reveal different trends and patterns in data."

Big data analytics is where advanced analytic techniques operate on big data sets. Hence, big data analytics is really about two things—big data and analytics—plus how the two have teamed up to create one of the most profound trends in business intelligence (BI) today. Russom (2011). For the computation time, there is no doubt at all that parallel computing is one of the important future trends to make the data analytics work for big data, and consequently the algorithms of datamining and subsequently machine learning and the technologies of cloud computing, distributed systems and machine learning will play the important roles for the big data analytics. Tsai et.al. (2015).

Data analyst produces descriptive statistics and visualizations in order to report information out of the data set provided. Data analytics is a compulsory level for data science. Data wrangling is done before hand in order to make the complex data set ready for analysis. Knowledge of mathematical statistics is very important for data analytics.

Data Analytics can be broadly defined as the process of utilizing different types of available data to draw useful conclusions out of it which is useful in decision making. Data is extracted and categorized to identify and analyze behavioral data and patterns, and techniques vary according to organizational requirements.

Modern forms of Data Analytics have expanded to include:

Predictive Analytics: This means prediction or forecasting. It mainly used techniques like data mining, machine learning, statistical modeling and other data technology.

Big Data Analytics: "big data analytics brings to the table, however, are speed and efficiency. The ability to work faster – and stay agile – gives organizations a competitive edge they didn't have before." Davenport, T. H. et al. (2013).

Cognitive Analytics: "Cognitive Computing is about teaching a computer a way to think like a human would. Coined by IBM, technically the term refers to creation of self-learning systems that use data mining, pattern recognition and natural language processing (NLP) to mirror the way a human brain works."

These systems can:

- Understand human communications.
- Map a sense of their processes on to the real world.
- Continually bolster their learning to anticipate and solve new problems.
- The purpose of cognitive computing is to solve complicated problems without human oversight, much faster than humans ever could. It is turning out that cognitive computing isn't a piece of a puzzle; it is changing the entire playing fields.

Prescriptive Analytics: This method tries to find the best course of action, based on past records, for the future, and for a given scenario.

Descriptive Analytics: This is like describing or summarizing the facts and figures. With the summary it creates a broader, wholesome view of the data. It helps in comprehending and making decisions based on the entire view. The summary must be in an understandable format. It can either inform or prepare data for further analysis. It uses two principal techniques viz: data aggregation and data mining

Enterprise Decision Management: "Enterprise Decision Management (EDM) is an approach that automates, improves and connects decisions across the enterprise"

Retail Analytics: "Retail analytics is the process of providing analytical data on inventory levels, supply chain movement, consumer demand, sales, etc. that are crucial for making marketing, and procurement decisions. The analytics on demand and supply data can be used for maintaining procurement level and also for taking marketing decisions. Retail analytics gives us detailed customer insights along with insights into the business and processes of the organization with scope and need for improvement." "Retail analytics focuses on providing insights related to sales, inventory, customers, and other important aspects crucial for merchants' decision-making process."

Augmented Analytics: "Augmented Analytics Augmented Analytics combines sophisticated Machine Learning (ML) and Natural Language Processing (NLP) to enable users to extract intelligence more quickly and simply."

Web Analytics: "Web analytics is the collection, reporting, and analysis of website data.

Call Analytics: At its core, call analytics on the cloud is the ultimate solution for customer experience. Call center analytics and the cloud are the way forward for today's companies. They allow businesses to identify key pain points for customers, and train agents to respond to those issues accordingly."

Data analytics is the technique to qualitative and quantitative represent the data to enhance productivity and business gain. Data analytics includes various techniques. The techniques are data preprocessing, data warehousing and data cleaning. Tsui, K. L et al. (2019)

The Timeline for Data Analytics is as Follows

Analytics is basically "the study of analysis." Another more acceptable definition for these current times of "Data Analytics" is "An important tool to provide the customers with detailed business insights and from it the personalized responses. Data Analytics is also at times abbreviated as "Analytics.

Earliest examples of Analytics used in business – The famous "time management techniques" propagated by Frederick Winslow Taylor. This was around the 9th century. The other renowned example is that of Henry Ford. He measured the speed of the assembly line in the shop floors of his manufacturing units. Since Data Analytics is based on statistics, it will be ideal to trace this line.

The "tabulating machine" was invented by Herman Hollerith. It was used in the census-survey of the USA. This machine systematically processed data recorded on punch cards and completed the task very fast.

1970-This was the year which saw the rise of relational databases. The RDBMS was being put to its full potential use with SQL being the standard language for all kinds of databases.

1980-The concept of Data Warehouse was introduced and used in the business world.

In 1865, the term "Business Intelligence" (BI) as a keyword was first used. It was used by Howard Dresner in describing as a support tool for better decisions making. The process involved typically collecting, finding and analyzing the accumulated data saved by any organization.

Data Mining began in the 1990s and was used to discover patterns within large data sets.

1990-Internet was the biggest invention which took the world by storm.

2002- NoSql and Big data were introduced.

In 2005, 'Big Data' was identified. It was Roger Magoulas who came up with the initial use of the term big data. He described huge amount of data which could not be managed easily as Big data. Hadoop marked its entry in the markets.

Process involved in Data Analytics -

1. Identify the objective - what needs to be done with raw data -
2. Work on the raw data can be OLTP or OLAP
3. Data preprocessing - Cleaning of data
4. Data Mining - Identifying the trends and patterns in raw data
5. Data analytics - applying different algorithms to create a model
6. Data Visualizations using Tableau / Power BI
7. Decision Making after getting insights

Data Analytics mainly refers to the tools used for analyzing data by cleaning the data set and categorizing into different behavioral patterns. The techniques and the tools used will vary according to the organization/individual. The basic difference between Data Science and Data Analytics is that 'Data Science' focuses mainly on getting insights on what questions are required to be asked while 'Data Analytics' focuses on mainly providing answers to these questions. Both Data Science and Data Analytics are highly interconnected and their end goal is to find patterns from data and generate meaningful insights which in the end will help the business to grow.

Analyzing the data for finding the answers through data analytics captures the broad scope in the field. These techniques widened the scope of data mining and data science. With the use of insights received by data analytics a clear picture of actual position can be ascertained which tells a person where they are and where they should go.

The process of analyzing the data is starts with descriptive analytics. In this process the past trends of data is described. This process fulfills the objective of answering what has happened in the past. The return on investment (ROI) has been measured. The parameters and indicator for different industries are different. Descriptive analytics is only used for meaningful description and it is not used for direct prediction.

Apart from descriptive analytics the next important part is advanced analytics. This advanced analytics part exploits the benefits of tools to extract the patterns from the data. The tools used for data analytics and data science includes statistics, machine learning, neural network, AI and natural language processing and many more techniques within the scope of advanced analytics. Advanced analytics helps in taking the future decisions.

Recently due to availability of AI, machine learning and massive data storage techniques with cheap computing power small industries are also capable of using data analytics and data science techniques. The important component of this process is accurate data, which allows drawing the meaningful conclusions from these massive data sets. These techniques allows for parallel processing and with every kind of the data.

Figure 1. Usage or implementation of data analytics and data science

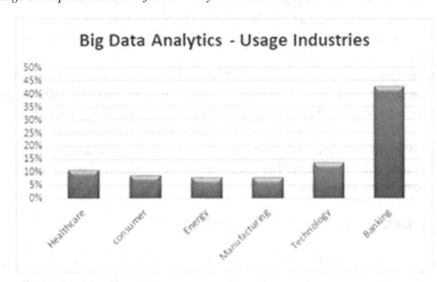

Usage or Implementation of Data Analytics and Data Science

The above diagram depicts the usage of Data Analytics and Data Science in various sectors. As per this diagram, the maximum usage is in banking sector. Followed by technology and rest followed.

1. **Healthcare:** Here variety of decision making happens in identifying diseases which may impact the general public e.g. epidemics. Individual cases to detect, track the status of health status of

people. Government of various countries have started to incorporate data analysis in healthcare. Ekins. S. (2007) describes in detail the integrated data-mining tools applicable to building biological networks.

2. **Consumer Trade**: Here mainly prediction, staffing and inventory requirements are done. Many organizations use the loyalty cards to track the consumers.

3. **Energy**: In this sector, electrical leakages are controlled, load balancing, Analysis of Load patterns, energy consumption based on various parameters.

4. **Manufacturing**: Productivity increase is the base objectivity, along with it supply chain management, optimum resource allocation, optimum resource usage is done considering maximum benefit,

5. **Technology:** Software Development organizations have started making most of their operation based on Analytics in all their tasks.Evans, W. (1996) describes in detail the integrated data-mining tools applicable to building biological networks.

6. **Banking and Securities**: financial markets are managed keeping in view reduction in fraudulent transactions, identifying untrusty consumers, and controlling illegal trade.

The upcoming sectors include:

7. **Communications and Media**: This is the most upcoming area, focussing on real-time events using mobile, web and TV. Music, movies, digital media are the forerunners of this impact.

8. **Sports:** This is one more domain, which has started using analytics big way-with management of sports events, the sports personnel, and inventory in its association.

9. **Education**: Education has also started using for improvement of process improvement, admissions, pedagogy, and student management.

10. **Insurance**: In insurance which is closely related to healthcare industry. Here everything from creation, management of insurance schemes, customers is done. McCabe, (2008) explains the invention in paper provides tools and techniques mainly used in providing technical data protection services.

11. **Transportation**: This domain has a far reaching impact on supply chain and many other related domains along with the consumers. The basic transportation involves better route planning, better traffic monitoring and management, and logistics.

Tools Used In Data Analytics and Data Science

Data Analytics and Data Science has recently came as an emerging field for the business world and considered by them as a key to unlock the door of success. In today's competitive environment most of the companies wish to harvest the crop of advantages gains from Data Analytics. To stay ahead in the race companies are diving deeper into their historical data to increase efficiency, hence they are mastering their use of recent technologies like Data analytics and Data Science. To harness the aim of stay ahead in the race the companies are keen to implement latest technology such as machine learning and Artificial Intelligence. Now business organizations are moving towards more comprehensive analytics strategy to achieve their business goals. Bunney (1997) believes that the credible training is necessary to achieve the success at the very outset in the use of data analytics tools and techniques. Grover (2017) highlighted most of the big data technologies according to their specific services and application. Their study made a clear distinction between the various tools through their analysis platforms, database techniques, warehousing strategy and programming languages.

Leech (2007) discussed about different elements for comprehending multiple techniques for qualitative data analysis and also depicts the advantages and importance of using more than one technique for data analysis. They refer the term analysis triangulation for utilizing multiple data analysis.

Ramsay (1991) discussed on using L-splines for generalizations of principal component analysis (PCA) and linear modelling to analyze the samples which are drawn from random samples. Python still continues to be the most favorite platform for data scientist but at the same time R also retains its popularity. The popularity of R and Python are due to their features like deep learning. While observing past three year trends for the top data analytics tools some interesting facts came to know, and these are, Python stayed at the topmost position, Rapid Miner is another popular tool which shares 51% and proves that it also have a large user base which motivates its users. R has lost its popularity little bit. The reason for that is lack of deep learning features. The other platforms like Tensor flow and Keras has increased their popularity among the Deep Leaning users and it also reflects that Deep Learning has been started using in many applications. Rahaman (2018) highlighted new area in big data analysis for research and development which opens new horizon for the developing the innovative solutions by the researcher.

In 2020 among top 30 big data tools, 15 big data tools are the open source data analysis tools and also utilized for data visualization tools, sentiment tools, data extraction tools and databases. Bonthu (2018) discussed about most popular tools like R, Python, Rapid Miner, Hadoop, Spark, Tableau, and KNIME. MS (2018) also made a comparative assessment of latest tools and framework for big data analytics which are being popular. In their assessment both open source and paid tools were included. Bansal A. (2018) also explained some top tools and draw some important facts of these tools like cost, their data handling capability, graphical capability etc. Rangra (2014) studied the six open source data mining tools and describes the technical specification, characteristics and specialization for each tool with their application areas. Jarvenpaa (1989) investigated the two tools and conducted experiments on Logical Data Structure (LDS) and Relational Data Model (RDM).

Some popular tools for data analytics which are used for deep learning also are described below.

- **TensorFlow** is considered a tool with rich library resources and provides a comprehensible and flexible ecosystem. It is also known for easy model building for machine learning and intuitive high level APIs. The model generated by this tool can be deploy in the cloud, browser or on any device without concerning the language used. It is also popular among the researcher as a powerful research tool.
- **Anaconda Enterprise** is a powerful data science platform with focus on security, scalability, collaboration and readiness for enterprise. With the Anaconda enterprise one can work in ML/AI central development environment.
- **Databricks** provides cross functional environment with focus on security and data science and data engineering tasks. It also provides a collaborative environment for data scientists, data engineers, and data analysts to work together.
- **Keras** is specially focused on fast experimentation with the opportunity to develop neural network API. It is used in the application which needs deep learning library intensively and also facilitates fast prototyping with the support for convolutional networks and recurrent networks, as well as combinations of the simultaneous execution of application from more than one CPU.

Table 1. Tools used for data science and data analytics

Open source	Features	Vendor Based	Features
Google-TensorFlow	Tensor Flow provides open source platform with rich libraries for machine learning capability.	Alteryx	Alteryx is known for data science platform to analyze, develop and deploy the predictive analytics solutions.
Anaconda	Anaconda is a powerful data science platform with focus on security, scalability, collaboration and readiness for enterprise	DataRobot	DataRobot is a global enterprise platform to provide features of AI and collaborative work environment to boost recent Intelligence Revolution.
DataBricks	Open source tool provides Collaboration across the full data and machine learning lifecycle	IBM-SPSS	IBM-SPSS is a great software to perform statistical research which high accuracy and quick decision making. It work with large and complex data sets easily.
Keras	Keras is a tool which specially focused on fast experimentation with the opportunity to develop neural network API.	SAS	SAS is popular for Analytics and Business Intelligence which turns the raw data into knowledge for better decision making.
Apache Spark	Spark is used at a wide range of organizations to process large datasets.	IBM Watson	Watson is Multipurpose suite of IBM to effectively use for Artificial Intelligence and other deep learning services.
R	R provides a wide variety of statistical and graphical techniques, and is highly extensible.	Amazon Lex	Amazon Lex provides interface for effective conversation and utilizes voice and text for deep learning and speech recognition functionalities.
Python	Python provides all features of object-oriented programming language. Python is also known for its clear and easy syntax as well as for its rich libraries	QlikView	QlikView is effective for NLP (Natural Language Processing) and AI based smart visualizations.

- **Spark** is designed to support fault tolerance and applications like MapReduce. MapReduce requires low latency and can share data across multiple parallel operations. It also supports iterative algorithms of machine learning as well as graph algorithms like PageRank.
- **R** is widely used language by statisticians since it provides a wide variety of statistical functions and graphical features. R is also popular for visual analytics since it provides comforts for drawing quality plots and producing mathematical symbol and formulae.
- **Python** is ahead among all data analytics tool and popular among researcher and professional's fraternity. It provides all features of object-oriented programming language. Python is also known for its clear and easy syntax as well as for its rich libraries.

Difference between Data Science and Data Analytics

Just as science is a large term, which includes a number of specialties and emphases, data science is a broad term for a variety of models and methods for information gathering. The scientific method, mathematics, statistics, and other tools used to analyze and manipulate data are under the umbrella of data science. If it is a data-based tool or process to analyze it or obtain some kind of information from it, it is likely to fall under data science. If data science is the house that holds the tools and methods, then data analytics in that house is a particular space. It is related and similar to data science but more oriented and precise. Data analytics is generally more focused than data science because data analysts have a specific goal in mind that they are sorting through data to look for ways to support it rather than just looking for connections between data. In some regions, data analytics are often automated to provide insights.

Data science is a paragliding term that includes data analytics, data mining, machine learning, and a number of related disciplines. While a data scientist is supposed to predict the future based on past events the data analysts derive concrete insights from various sources of data. A data scientist generates questions whilst a data analyst seeks answers to the same problem collection.

Table 2. Nature of functional tasks in data science and data analytics

Professional working as a Data Scientist	Professional working as a Data Analyst
Can do predications on the basis of past data.	Can generate meaningful acumens from existing data.
Deals with unknown data.	Deals with Known Data.
Generates own questions.	Generates solutions for a said set of questions.
Deals with Business problem having highest values	Deals with Business problems.
Deals with many hypothetical scenarios, which may trigger.	Deals with day-to-day analysis.

USE CASE OF DATA ANALYSIS

Use Case 1: Human Smoking Habits and Death Rate

Dataset: smkdth.dat

Source: E.C. Hammond and D. Horn (1954). "The Relationship Between Human Smoking Habits and Death Rates", JAMA, Aug. 7, 1954, pp1316-1328.

Description: Classification of adult males by smoking status, age Classification and occurrence of death during 2 year cohort study.

Variables/Columns

Smoking status 8 /* 0=No, 1=Yes */

Age classification 16 /* 1=50-54, 2=55-59, 3=60-64, 4=65-69 */

Death status 24 /* 0=Survival 1=Death */

Number of cases 28-32

Step 1: Data Formatting

    Converted text data into tabular format using Microsoft Excel

Table 3.

Smoke Status	Age Classification	Death Status	Number of Cases
0	1	0	20132
0	2	0	21671
0	3	0	19790
0	4	0	16499
1	1	0	39990
1	2	0	32894
1	3	0	20739
1	4	0	11197
0	1	1	204
0	2	1	394
0	3	1	488
0	4	1	766
1	1	1	647
1	2	1	857
1	3	1	855
1	4	1	643

Table 4. Data

Age classification	Number of cases
50-54	40637
55-59	33751
60-64	21594
65-69	11840
Sum	**107822**

Distribution of Smokers: Age Wise

- ○ The graph below shows data about people who smoke and is shown in terms of percentage according to age groups.

Figure 2. Number of smokers - age wise

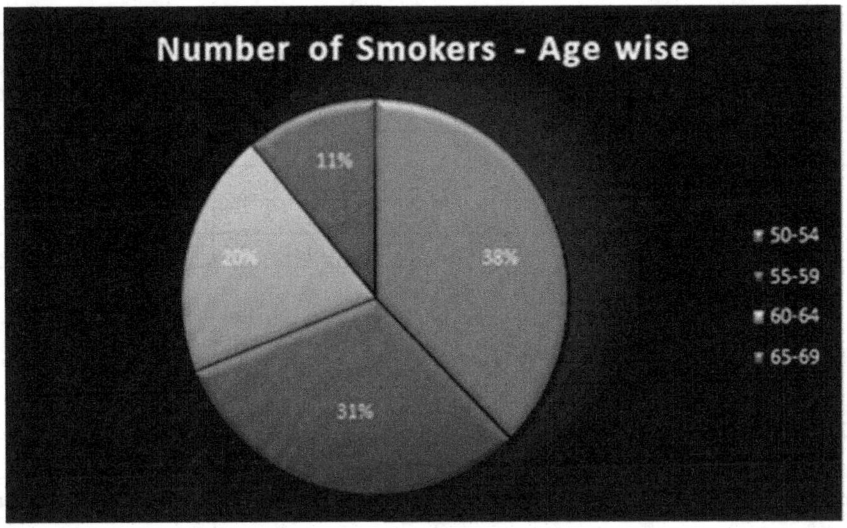

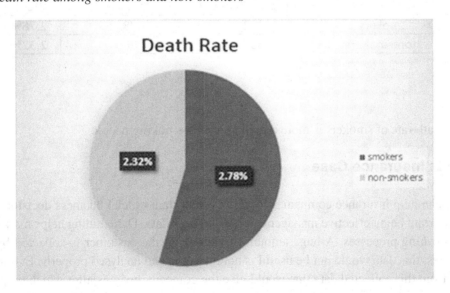

Conclusion

People in the age group 50-54 are maximum in count when it comes to smoking, according to the dataset of 107822 people who smoke between the ages 50-69.

Death Rate

- ◦ The graph below shows data about smokers and non-smokers who have died.
- ◦ Rate is calculated by dividing the number of deaths of people who smoke by total number of smoking people and similarly for non-smokers.

Figure 3. Death rate among smokers and non-smokers

Table 5. Data

Smokers			
Smoking status	**Age classification**	**Death status**	**Number of cases**
1	1	1	647
1	2	1	857
1	3	1	855
1	4	1	643
		Total	3002

Table 6. Data

Non - Smokers			
Smoking status	**Age classification**	**Death status**	**Number of cases**
0	1	1	204
0	2	1	394
0	3	1	488
0	4	1	766
		Total	1852

Table 7. Data

Death			
Smoking status	**Number of cases**	**Out of**	**Rate**
smokers	3002	107822	2.78%
non-smokers	1852	79944	2.32%

Conclusion

Hence death rate of smokers is more than that of non-smoking people

Use Case 2: Insurance Case

Data mining can help insurance companies for taking important crucial business decisions. The main and most important being effective management of Customer data. Data mining helps market specialist for decision-making processes. A huge amount of data about the customer is collected by the insurance companies, this data would not be useful is not managed and analysed properly. Extracting useful information from this collected data that would give the company insights after which proper business decisions can be made.

The steps of the knowledge discovery process would be as follows:

1. Selection
2. Pre-processing
3. Transformation
4. Data mining
5. Interpretation and Evaluation

Areas in which Data mining can be applied:

1. Predicting profits, claims and loss to identify risk factors
2. Customer economical level Analysis
3. Marketing and Sales analysis
4. Introducing and developing new product lines
5. Reinsurance
6. Accounting and Financial analysis
7. Estimating outstanding claims
8. Fraudulent detection

Table 8. Data mining techniques and patterns

Data Mining Techniques	Patterns
Clustering	• Customer with similar behaviour • Analysing customer attrition rate in the insurance sector • Popularity of insurance policies by the customers • Customer Segmentation according to product and other characteristics
Classification & Prediction	• Analysing and predicting behaviour of consumers • Predicting the success rate of insurance policy products • Classification and segmentation of customer base • Retention and drop off rate of insurance policy products • Customer attitude towards any products • Predicting Performance period of specific segment • Prediction of factors to new prospective features of specific product. • Predicting churn rate of customers through the customer base
Association	• Discovery of association rule for promoting business offers
Summarization	• Generation of summarized or aggregated information • Producing multi-dimensional summarized reports • Application of Statistical function to produce summarized information

Use Case 3: Prediction of Churn in Telecom Industry using Python

The telecom market is a churn market because of which telecom companies need to face multiple cases of customer churn. Since there is no variation in the products and services offered by the telecom operators, customers are on the constant look-out for better prices and better service. Using a recommendation engine to figure out the company's most popular and preferred product or service can help the telecom company to find ways to make this product more appealing so as to improve customer satisfaction and also attract new customers. Python and XGboost is used in this case.

The objective of a recommendation engine for telecom companies -

1. Understanding user preferences with respect to popular data/voice packs and data consumption
2. Recognizing various usage patterns
3. Help in building a product portfolio in accordance with user preferences which would result in better customer service and customer retention

The recommendation engine should provide suggestions based on the collected user information on user's preferences and usage patterns.

Methodology

Framework for this case incorporates four significant modules: information shop, field determination, characterization, and suggestion. Fig. 1 is a disentangled design of the framework. In the proposed framework, one can pick up suggestions of plausible client to be addressed. Since here the procedure is application-situated, after advances has been utilized following types can be executed:

-   Exploratory data analysis
-   Feature engineering
-   Logistic Regression
-   Classification model with XGBoost

Figure 4. A simplified architecture of the data analysis system

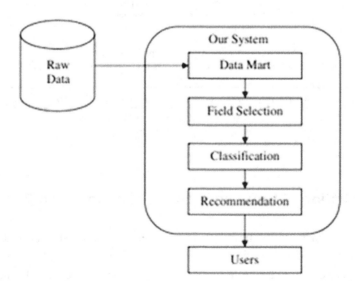

Exploratory Data Analysis

In information mining, explorative data Analysis (EDA) is way to deal with examining datasets to outline their primary attributes, for the most part with visual ways. EDA is utilized for seeing what the data will let us know before the displaying task. It's difficult to look at a column of numbers or a full program and confirm necessary characteristics of the information. It should be tedious, boring, and/or overwhelming to derive insights by staring at plain numbers. EDA is the solution to this problem.

Exploratory data analysis is can be classified in following two ways.

- Non-graphical or graphical
- Univariate or multivariate (usually just bivariate)

The first thing to do is checking how the data is and visualizes how all fields can be related. So to do so initially the authors started with importing few fields of the data and started to analyze its relation with each column. The authors analyzed that broadly the data comes into two main categories:

- Categorical data types: streaming TV, gender, payment method &, many more
- Numerical data types: monthly charges, tenure, total charges and many more

Let's start with the categorical data first. The main task is to know how the data can be utilized to know if the customer will churn or not. In the data set the authors have one column as *Churn* column is string with *Yes and No values.* This is categorical data, so the authors converted it into integer by coding them as 0 and 1 respectively.

Binary Classification Model with XGBoost

XGBoost stands for eXtreme Gradient Boosting. "The name xgboost, though, actually refers to the engineering goal to push the limit of computations resources for boosted tree algorithms. This is the reason why many people use xgboost."— Tianqi Chen, the man behind the method

From XGBoost test it was identified that the churn rate of our data set is 26.5%. This helped the authors to conclude that this model is very good.

Findings

To perform analysis the author's required extensive data, collecting primary data at this scale was not possible. So the authors collected secondary to perform our analysis. The data set used below is customer churn data from Kaggle. Data's description includes each row representing a customer, each column containing customer's attributes described on the column Metadata, the raw data contains 7043 rows (customers) and 21 columns (features) and finally, "Churn", this column was the target.

The data set includes information about:

Customers who left within the last month – the column is called Churn

Services for which each customer has signed up – telephone, multiple lines, email, online security, online backup, computer safety, technology support, and TV and movie streaming

- Customer account details – how long a customer has been, contract, payment method, paperless billing, monthly fees and overall fees
- Customer demographic details-gender, age range, and if they have partners and dependents

Analysis of the Exploratory Analysis

- Male and female, both churn at every 1 in 4 instances.
- Customers with no Device Protection are likely to churn almost twice as compared to those with Device Protection.
- A yearly contracted customer is likely to churn 4 times more than that of a two-year contracted Customer and a monthly contracted is likely to churn 4 times more than that of a yearly contracted.
- Customers streaming TV & Movies are likely to churn at .34, as much as those not streaming at about 31.
- Customers with partners are .57 times less likely to churn than those without.
- Those opted for paperless billings are twice as likely to churn as those who haven't.
- Electronic Check payees are likely to churn .45 times as compared to 0.15-0.20 for other payment methods.
- Online security opted customers churn 2.6 times more than those who haven't opted online security.
- Customers who have opted for online backup churn 2 times more than those who haven't.
- Customers with multiple lines or single are likely to churn between .25-.30.
- Fiber Optic Customers churn at .40 as compared to DSL Customers who churn at less than half of it.
- Customers who do not take Tech Support churn more than twice that of those who do.
- As can be seen, the features Gender, Streaming TV, Streaming Movies and Multiple Lines do not have any major impact on the churn, as the churn is almost same for the various values of these features.
- While there are other features such as the Tenure of Contract and Type of Connection that can give a clear picture of the feature that impacts churn the most.

The next step is called feature engineering. The authors transformed the raw features to extract more information from them. The authors initially made clusters of our continuous variables. So they formed clusters of Total charge v/s Churn, Monthly charge v/s Churn rate and Tenure vs Churn rate.

CONCLUSION

The authors conclude that these new disruptive technologies have a far reaching impact on the way we live our lives. This is a big change in the way even regular, mundane things are carried out. This era of Data Science and Data Analysis will sustain, grow and affect every aspect of decision making in commercial and non-commercial zones.

The data scientist will be required to cultivate multiple skills. The Analysis parts may also become automatic, where it concerns repetitive tasks. Location-based services may dominate the consumer scenes. Forecasting and predictive analysis will dominate across all verticals. Across industries, a real time optimization would be marking a huge presence.

REFERENCES

Bansal, A., & Srivastava, S. (2018). Tools Used in Data Analysis: A Comparative Study. *International Journal of Recent Research Aspects*, *5*(1), 15–18.

Bonthu, S., & Bindu, H. (2018). Review of Leading Data Analytics Tools. *IACSIT International Journal of Engineering and Technology*, *7*. Advance online publication. doi:10.14419/ijet.v7i3.31.18190

Bunney, H. S., & Dale, B. G. (1997). The implementation of quality management tools and techniques: A study. *The TQM Magazine*.

Codd, E. F. (1990). *The relational model for database management: version 2*. Addison-Wesley Longman Publishing Co., Inc.

Davenport, T. H., & Dyché, J. (2013). Big data in big companies. *International Institute for Analytics*, *3*. https://coseer.com/blog/what-is-cognitive-computing/

Domenico, B., Caron, J., Davis, E., Kambic, R., & Nativi, S. (2002). Thematic real-time environmental distributed data services (thredds): Incorporating interactive analysis tools into nsdl. *Journal of Digital Information*, *2*(4), 114.

Ekins, S., Nikolsky, Y., Bugrim, A., Kirillov, E., & Nikolskaya, T. (2007). Pathway mapping tools for analysis of high content data. In High Content Screening (pp. 319-350). Humana Press.

Evans, W. (1996). Computer-supported content analysis: Trends, tools, and techniques. *Social Science Computer Review*, *14*(3), 269–279. doi:10.1177/089443939601400302

Foote. (2016). *A Brief History of Data Science*. Retrieved from https://www.dataversity.net/brief-history-data-science/

Gil Press. (2013). *A Very Short History of Data Science*. Retrieved from https://www.forbes.com/sites/gilpress/2013/05/28/a-very-short-history-of-data-science/#37bd1c1655cf

Grover, P., & Kar, A. K. (2017). Big data analytics: A review on theoretical contributions and tools used in literature. *Global Journal of Flexible Systems Managment*, *18*(3), 203–229. doi:10.100740171-017-0159-3

Jarvenpaa, S. L., & Machesky, J. J. (1989). Data analysis and learning: An experimental study of data modeling tools. *International Journal of Man-Machine Studies*, *31*(4), 367–391. doi:10.1016/0020-7373(89)90001-1

Komal, Ms. (2018). *A Review Paper on Big Data Analytics Tools*. https://www.proschoolonline.com/blog/top-10-data-analytics-tools

La Pelle, N. (2004). Simplifying qualitative data analysis using general purpose software tools. *Field Methods*, *16*(1), 85–108. doi:10.1177/1525822X03259227

Lee, S. J., & Siau, K. (2001). A review of data mining techniques. *Industrial Management & Data Systems*.

Leech, N. L., & Onwuegbuzie, A. J. (2007). An array of qualitative data analysis tools: A call for data analysis triangulation. *School Psychology Quarterly*, *22*(4), 557–584. doi:10.1037/1045-3830.22.4.557

McCabe, R. (2008). *U.S. Patent No. 7,386,463*. Washington, DC: U.S. Patent and Trademark Office.

Provost, F., & Fawcett, T. (2013). Data science and its relationship to big data and data-driven decision-making. *Big Data*, *1*(1), 51–59. doi:10.1089/big.2013.1508 PMID:27447038

Rahaman, A. (2018). *Challenging tools on Research Issues in Big Data Analytics*. https://www.softwaretestinghelp.com/big-data-tools/

Ramsay, J. O., & Dalzell, C. J. (1991). Some tools for functional data analysis. *Journal of the Royal Statistical Society. Series B. Methodological*, *53*(3), 539–561. doi:10.1111/j.2517-6161.1991.tb01844.x

Rangra, K., & Bansal, K. L. (2014). Comparative study of data mining tools. *International Journal of Advanced Research in Computer Science and Software Engineering*, *4*(6). https://towardsdatascience.com/comparison-of-data-analysis-tools-excel-r-python-and-bi-tools-6c4685a8ea6f

Russom, P. (2011). Big data analytics. *TDWI best practices report, fourth quarter*, 19(4), 1-34.

Tsai, C. W., Lai, C. F., Chao, H. C., & Vasilakos, A. V. (2015). Big data analytics: A survey. *Journal of Big Data*, *2*(1), 21. doi:10.118640537-015-0030-3 PMID:26191487

Tsui, K. L., Zhao, Y., & Wang, D. (2019). Big Data Opportunities: *System Health Monitoring and Management. IEEE Access: Practical Innovations, Open Solutions*, *7*, 68853–68867. doi:10.1109/ACCESS.2019.2917891

UW Data Science Team. (2017). *A Modern History of Data Science*. Retrieved from https://datasciencedegree.wisconsin.edu/blog/history-of-data-science/

Van Der Aalst, W. (2016). Data science in action. In *Process mining* (pp. 3–23). Springer. doi:10.1007/978-3-662-49851-4_1

Wei, C. P., Piramuthu, S., & Shaw, M. J. (2003). Knowledge discovery and data mining. In Handbook on Knowledge Management (pp. 157-189). Springer.

KEY TERMS AND DEFINITIONS:

Churn: Customers who left the telco subscription within the last month.

Data Science: Data science is the study of data. It involves developing methods of recording, storing, and analyzing data to effectively extract useful information. The goal of data science is to gain insights and knowledge from any type of data—both structured and unstructured.

Database: A collection of processed data. i.e. storage container of the information.

Structured Data: Data which can be stored in a table structure of two dimensions of row – column.

Tools of Data Science: Business analytics tools are types of application software that retrieve data from one or more business systems to be reviewed and analyzed.

Unstructured Data: Data which cannot be stored in a table structure like an audio file or video and images.

Chapter 4
Tools, Technologies, and Methodologies to Support Data Science:
Support Technologies for Data Science

Ricardo A. Barrera-Cámara
 https://orcid.org/0000-0002-3170-4671
Universidad Autónoma del Carmen, Mexico

Ana Canepa-Saenz
 https://orcid.org/0000-0003-0583-439X
Universidad Autónoma del Carmen, Mexico

Jorge A. Ruiz-Vanoye
 https://orcid.org/0000-0003-4928-5716
Universidad Politécnica de Pachuca, Mexico

Alejandro Fuentes-Penna
 https://orcid.org/0000-0002-4303-3852
Centro Interdisciplinario de Investigación y Docencia en Educación Técnica, Mexico

Miguel Ángel Ruiz-Jaimes
 https://orcid.org/0000-0002-2585-9896
Universidad Politécnica de Morelos, Mexico

Maria Beatriz Bernábe-Loranca
 https://orcid.org/0000-0003-3014-4139
Benemérita Universidad Autónoma de Puebla, Mexico

ABSTRACT

Various devices such as smart phones, computers, tablets, biomedical equipment, sports equipment, and information systems generate a large amount of data and useful information in transactional information systems. However, these generate information that may not be perceptible or analyzed adequately for decision-making. There are technology, tools, algorithms, models that support analysis, visualization, learning, and prediction. Data science involves techniques, methods to abstract knowledge generated through diverse sources. It combines fields such as statistics, machine learning, data mining, visualization, and predictive analysis. This chapter aims to be a guide regarding applicable statistical and computational tools in data science.

DOI: 10.4018/978-1-7998-3053-5.ch004

Data science was initially proposed as a set of areas with a technical point of view made up by operation research, data modelling and data methods, pedagogy, tool evaluation and theory (Cleveland, 2001). Data science encompasses mathematics, automated learning, artificial intelligence, statistics, databases and optimization (Dhar, 2013).

All activities related to data science professionals are classified as follows (Donoho, 2017): 1. Data collection, preparation and exploration, 2. Data representation and transformation, 3. Data calculation, 4. Data modelling, 5. Data visualization and presentation, 6. Science on data science. Furthermore, different roles or professionals with profiles and skills linked to data science have emerged (Government of Spain, 2018) (UC Regents, 2019): 1. Data scientist. A professional with ability to extract, clean and present data through exploration. These professionals aim to find unanswered questions and the data required to answer them. 2. Data analyst. These professionals act as a liaison between a data scientist and a business analyst. They translate the technical analysis into qualitative type data elements and communicate results. 3. Data engineer. These professionals design set up and administer the necessary infrastructure required for the transformation and transfer of data for inquiry.

This chapter is organized in different sections, which are the Related Works section, data analysis, Data Visualization, Dataset, Project Managements in data Science, Data Science Platforms, Machine Learning, Future Research Directions, and finally the Conclusion section.

BACKGROUND

Related Works

This section presents some works related to applicable technology applications in data science. Platforms: Performs an analysis of hardware platforms considering specific features and software framework used in them, as critical elements that must be present for the execution of big data algorithms (Singh & Reddy, 2014); Learning Machine: Some criteria are proposed and analyzed for the selection of opens source tools for learning machine with big data. The experience of processing, libraries and machine learning framework is also considered (Landset et al., 2015); Software: Open source data mining tools are analyzed considering their operational characteristics, license, programming languages, web support, type, domain that are also used in data science (Barlas, 2015); Vizualization: Various tools and techniques of data visualization oriented to large volumes of data are analyzed, presenting their functional and non-functional characteristics (Caldarola & Rinaldi, 2017); Dataset: The availability of data, exchange, access, use recovery, searches make possible the emergence of data stores or data sets available in public access dataset services but from a company with information search services on the internet (Chapman et al., 2019).

In Figure 1, presents a timeline related to the year of launch of the technologies identified in the background of this work.

Data Analysis

Data analysis (Izabella et al., 2019) is the process of inspection, cleaning, transformation and modelling of data with the purpose of finding useful information, reporting conclusions and providing ground for

Figure 1. Timeline of technologies

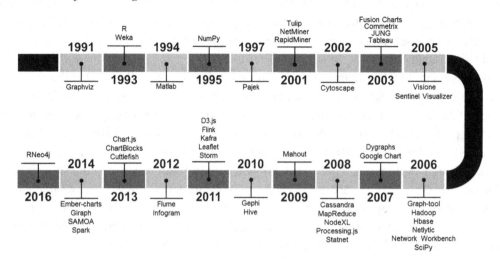

decision-making. Next, a list of examples using data analysis is provided, as well as some of the technologies used for data analysis.

VIDA Project (Sperhac & Gallo, 2019), is developing a Hub which incorporates open source tools for the teaching of data analysis and text mining. In ecology-related professional development courses, the use of statistic tools and data analysis is recommended in order to master skills regarding manipulation, visualization and interpretation decisive to prepare course participants for data science (Farrell & Carey, 2018).

The combination of IT and formal science makes it possible to apply data science in materials thanks to the use of available data sets. Material properties optimization is possible because of data (Rickman et al., 2019). A library is developed in order to obtain raw-materials property data, which is based on a variety data sources ensuring complex materials attributes for a later data analysis (Ward et al., 2018).

The combination of social networks and technical networks creates a socio-cybernetic system implemented with Hadoop and Map Reduce. Map Reduces a framework for parallel computing and GraphX an Apache Spark API for graphics and parallel computing of graphics, considered data sets provided by social networks, health and intelligent transport systems (Ahmad et al., 2019).

In (Comai, 2018), it is conducted an integral analysis of patents, articles and science news based on metadata and text. In the case of structured and unstructured data, Mira Analytics is used for analysis and processing.

In (Akhavan-Hejazi & Mohsenian-Rad, 2018), big data applications are reviewed in energy, as well as the application of big data analytics and algorithms for data mining and statistics.

Pramanik (Pramanik et al., 2017), developed a smart healthcare system framework which enables the engagement of both government and companies. The framework is based on the analysis of projects related to big data technologies, smart systems, and the analysis of advanced healthcare systems. Three technical branches were extracted (3T) which contribute to the promotion of healthcare systems: intelligent agents, machine learning, and text mining. A study related to computational proteomics reviews a diversity of methods and tools for the analysis of protein data (Sinitcyn et al., 2018).

In this study (Nagorny et al., 2017) an analysis is performed on the big data in smart manufacturing systems considering work and technologies used for data storage, analysis and preparation.

Open data is analyzed for the daily forecasting of a bicycle rental service used by tourists in New York. Weather and events are mostly considered (Jiménez Gómez, 2018). With open data, it is possible to predict bicycle rental service demand on a daily basis.

To predict the quality parameters of milk and animal phenotypes to derive mid infrared spectroscopy (MIRS) is used, also converts a compressed domain data (Vimalajeewa et al., 2018).

In Europe, a data processing platform (TEMA) was developed to process driving and mobility pattern data collected through GPS. One of the main purposes is to provide the foundations to support low-carbon road transport policies in the European Union (De Gennaro et al., 2016). Processing of data allows predicting quality as well as pollution in air (Sharma et al., 2018).

A process dashboard located in the operating rooms in a hospital allows to enhance the flow of patients in real time (Martinez-Millana et al., 2019).

In Table 1, examples of work and tools that perform data analysis are listed.

In Table 2 shows the tools used in the work described in the data analysis section.

Dataset

A dataset is a collection of separate sets of information which are treated as a single unit by a computer (Cambridge University Press, 2019). These sets are normally presented as a table made up by a series of instances or registries, and the columns or headings are considered variables. Such sets are made available by the scientific community, academic community and governments. There is a great diversity of datasets which are open-access or fee-based. These contain data from a range of fields, and they can be accessed or downloaded for academic or research purposes. Examples of datasets and a brief description is given in Table 3.

Project Management in Data Science

Projects and data science research use different processes or methodologies which support their development. Knowledge about technological advances and data management are skills which must be present in the formation of environmental scientists (Hernandez et al., 2012), in which knowledge in the management area must be taken into account.

Projects on data science must be taken into account in a greater extent in the way people work. For this reason, methodologies which allow the measurement of their effectiveness and impact must be used (Saltz et al., 2017). Next, we give a general overview on some methodologies and how they relate to some projects. The teams worked on a daily basis by not specifying a methodology, the teams without guidance applied phases and iterations similar to the CRISP methodology. Regarding the quality of the projects developed, they obtained higher average scores with CRISP with 8.4 and Agile Kaban with 7.8. The perception of work obtained a score of 58% with the teams that used Agile Kaban and much lower with 19% and 15% for agile scrum and Baseline. With Baseline he refers to the teams, they were not given suggestions of methodology to follow and the work teams would work as usual.

Data Science methodologies such as KDD Process, SAS SEMMA (Sample, Explore, Modify, Model, Assess), Cross Industry Standard Process for Data Mining (CRISP-DM), Team Data Science Process (TDSP), Foundational Methodology for Data Science (FMDS) are analyzed for cybersecurity application (Foroughi & Luksch, 2018). This type of project requires the execution of four steps: define and formulate the security problem, collect required information, data analysis and prediction, and automatic production.

Table 1. Examples of works and tools with data analysis.

Area	Use	Tool/Technology	Reference
Education	Text Mining training. Data analysis processing training.	RapidMiner PSPP RStudio Jupyter	(Sperhac & Gallo, 2019)
	Data analysis in ecology.	Excel R Phyton	(Farrell & Carey, 2018)
	Educational data mining.	Weka	(Teran et al., 2019)
Construction	Materials properties optimization.	SCI-KIT LEARN TENSOR FLOW	(Rickman et al., 2019)
	Materials characterization in materials mining.	MatMiner	(Ward et al., 2018)
Social media	Social data analysis.	MapReduce and GraphX	(Ahmad et al., 2019)
Text mining	Text mining in documents/Visualization.	Mira Analytic, Open Graph Viz Platform	(Comai, 2018)
Process mining	Processing analysis. Medical processes analysis and monitoring.	ProM PALIA	(Martinez-Millana et al., 2019)
Energy	Energy systems Large volumes of data processing in PMU devices for energy systems in massive database.	Scanda systems and telemetry, BTrDB y DISTIL MapReduce ScaLAPACK.4	(Akhavan-Hejazi & Mohsenian-Rad, 2018)
Tourism	Demand analysis and bicycle traffic.	Weka R by means of RStudio CartoBuilder	(Jiménez Gómez, 2018)
Smart dairy farming	PC calculation with MIRS. Application of the MRA in DWT.	R with R package pls 2.6-0 R package wavelets 0.	(Vimalajeewa et al., 2018)
Health	Data organizer and analytic tool.	Hadoop	(Pramanik et al., 2017)
Manufacturing industry	Data storage tools, generated data analytics, smart manufacturing systems integration.	Hadoop, NoSQL MapReduce, R RapidMiner KNIME Orange Weka Reattle GUI	(Nagorny et al., 2017)
Transportation	Vehicle Mobility patterns analysis.	TEMA	(De Gennaro et al., 2016)
Quality	Descriptive data analysis of air.	RStudio, Tableau	(Sharma et al., 2018)
Biomedicine	Mass spectrometry analysis.	MaxQuant Perseus	(Sinitcyn et al., 2018)

Requirement engineering is applied in healthcare projects by defining a series of steps in order to obtain and establish functional requirements and requirements for the use of data (Liu, 2016). The requirement engineering for data analysis in medical care depends on the available data and is completely different from the software requirements engineering.

Table 2. Tools used in the works described in this section

Tool	Description	Licence
CartoBuilder	Geospatial analysis (Carto, 2019).	Commercial
Excel	Maths calculations in finance using maths functions and various charts (Microsoft, 2019b).	Commercial
GraphX	Apache spark's API and graph-parallel computation (Apache Software Foundation, 2019b).	Apache License
Hadoop	High-volume data processing (Apache Software Foundation, 2019a).	Apache License
Jupyter	A tool which allows cleaning, transformation, simulation, statistical modelling, and visualization of data (Project Jupyter, 2019).	Open source
KNIME	Visual modelling development (KMIME, 2019).	General Public License
MatMiner	Phython library for data mining with application in materials science (Jain, 2015).	BSD-style license
MaxQuant	This tool analyses large mass spectrometry datasets (Max-Planck-Institute of Biochemistry, 2018).	Free
Mira Analytics	This tool allows analysis and visualization of structured and unstructured data based on their contents and relationships (Miniera, 2019).	Commercial
NoSQL	Storage technologies, which do not use SQL as the main query language (nosql-database.org, 2019).	Open Source
Open Graph Viz Platform	Exploration and visualization for graphics and networks (gephi.org, 2019).	Open source
Orange	Data mining and visual predictive analysis (University of Ljubljana, 2019).	General Public License
PALIA suite	Process mining in healthcare services (Commission, 2019).	Commercial
Perseus	Tools for statistical analysis of data in proteomics (Max-Planck-Institute of Biochemistry, 2019).	Freeware
Python	Multi paradigm programming language used for the development of applications and algorithms for use in data science (Python Software Foundation, 2019).	Open Source
ProM	Mining and processing analysis tools (Process Mining Group, 2016).	General Public License
PSPP	Free software for statistical analysis of data (Free Software Foundation, 2018).	General Public License
RapidMiner	Data analysis and mining (RapidMiner, 2019).	Affero General Public License
Rattle GUI	A graphical user interface for data mining using R. It provides statistical and visual information of data (Togaware Pty Lt, 2019).	General Public License
RStudio	Developer's environment using R (RStudio, 2019).	Open source and commercial
SCI-KIT LEARN	Machine learning library using Phyton (Cournapeau, 2019).	Open source, commercially usable - BSD license
Tableau	Data analysis and visualization in maps (Tableau, 2019).	Commercial
TENSOR FLOW	Software for making machine learning applications (Google, 2019c)	Apache License
Weka	Software for data mining and machine learning with a diversity of libraries and algorithms (W. University, 2019).	General Public License

Table 3. Examples of identified datasets

Type	Dataset	Description	Licence
Dataset search engine	UCI Machine Learning Repository	It contains a large variety of datasets generated by the machine learning community (University of California, 2019).	Free access
	Kaggle	It provides access to external datasets related to different areas (Kaggle, 2019a).	Free access
	VisualData	It has datasets related by means of computational vision with searches organized in categories (Visualdata, 2019).	Free access
	Google Dataset Search	This tool searches for datasets in a similar way to Google search (Google, 2019b).	Free access
Public Government	Open data provided by the Mexican government.	Data generated by the Mexican government departments in various aspects such as culture, commerce, health, etc. (Gobierno de México, 2019).	Creative Commons
	U.S. Government open Data	Datasets and information generated by the US government departments under the Open Government Data Act (U.S. General Services Administration, 2019).	Open Government
	INEGI	Data and datasets regarding statistical and geographical information about Mexican territory, resources, population and economy (INEGI, 2019).	Open Government
	UK Data	Economic and social data, both qualitative and quantitative, about the United Kingdom regarding research and education. The information encompasses a diversity of areas and topics (University of Essex & University of Manchester and Jisc, 2019).	Open Government
	Government of Argentina datasets	Datasets from the government of Argentina department (Secretaria de Modernización, 2019).	Open Government
Medicine & Health	HealthData.gov	Government data available for enhancing health (U.S. Department of Health & Human Services, 2019).	Open Government
	The Human Mortality Database	Data on human mortality generated by the national statistics office of an array of countries as well as researchers (Max Planck Institute for Demographic Research, 2019).	Free access
	Life Science Database Archive	Data generated by life scientists in Japan in a stable state as a national public good (Japan Science and Technology Agency, 2019).	Free access
	OASIS	Neuroimaging data sets of the brain available for researchers in basic and clinical (OASIS Brains, 2019).	Open access
	GEO Datasets	Curated gene expression datasets, original series, cluster tools and referential queries (National Center for Biotechnology Information & U.S. National Library of Medicine, 2019).	Open access
	Hospital Compare datasets	Data provided by Medicare & Medicaid Services for comparing the quality of care at over 4,000 certified hospitals (Centers for Medicare & Medicaid Services, 2019).	Open access
	BROAD Institute Cancer Program Datasets	Cancer-related data, categorized by the Institute as cancer, leukemia, etc. (BROAD Institute, 2019).	Open access

continues on following page

Table 3. Continued

Type	Dataset	Description	Licence
Climate, Weather	European Climate Assessment & Dataset project	Data on weather, climate extremes as well as the daily data generated by a group of 31 national meteorological services in Europe (EUMETNET, 2019).	Open access
	Climate data library	Data on weather. The library has tools for visualization, analysis and download of data (Subcretaria del Ministerio de Agricultura, 2019).	Open access
	Climate Change Data by DataHub	Website with an array of data sets on climate change (DataHub, 2018).	Commercial
	NOAA Climate.gov	Data on climate related to the audience (National Oceanic and Atmospheric Administration, 2019).	Free access
Iot/ Smart Home	MERLSense Data	MERL (Mitsubishi Electric Research Labs) motion sensor network data sets from the people working in Mitsubishi's research laboratory (Mitsubishi Electric Research Labs, 2019).	Free access
	Open Data of Ayuntamiento of Malaga	Data sets generated through IoT devices in energy, transportation, sports, manufacturing, weather, smart transportation systems (Ayuntamiento de Málaga, 2019).	Open Government
	WSU CASAS Datasets	Public data on performance of activities of daily living in a two-floor house, an apartment and an office (Washington State University, 2018).	Free access

The combination of science data and operational research allows the development of a methodology for business analysis so that the business objectives of the company are in line with the commercial objectives in company in the food bank sector (Hindle & Vidgen, 2018).

In events (Aalst, 2018) process mining is recommended as an alternative technology which is similar to a spreadsheet for processes initiated on events.

In (Larson & Chang, 2016), an analysis is made on the agile principles approach and the Business Intelligence (BI) delivery, quick analysis and data science in order to propose an agile framework for BI.

The quality of data in discovery tasks allows for the development of a framework based on CRIPSP-DM, SEEMA and data science, regarding the empirical software engineering problem solving (Corrales et al., 2015).

Techniques or methodologies used in the management or development of data science or data mining projects are shown in Table 4.

The different methodologies or frameworks identified in the studies analyzed are explained below:

- Agile Scrum It is a rapid software development methodology in which a series of interactions or "sprints" are developed. The Agile Project is based on five stages: concept, speculation, exploration, review, closure.
- Agile Kanban is a software development methodology, unlike scrum it is not too iterative, it is based on the delivery of functionality and the management of work progress. It consists of five stages: Planning, in progress, development, testing and Completion in which the user requirement acquired is compared to a stage of requirements called backlog.

Table 4. Summary of methodologies of analyzed works

Objective	Methodology	Reference
Methodology evaluation	Agile Scrum Agile Kanban CRISP-DM Baseline	(Saltz et al., 2017)
Cybersecurity problems	KDD Process CRISP-DM FMDS TDSP	(Foroughi & Luksch, 2018)
Requirement engineering for the analysis of health data	DROP	(Liu, 2016)
Combination of data science and operational research	Business Analytics Methodology (BAM)	(Hindle & Vidgen, 2018)
Quality data framework	Sample, Explore, Modify, Model and Assess (SEMMA)	(Corrales et al., 2015)
Spreadsheets with processing mining framework	Spreadsheet as a process	(Aalst, 2018)
Agile framework for BI	Agile Framework BI	(Larson & Chang, 2016)

- Cross Industry Standard Process for Data Mining (CRISP-DM) is based on four levels of abstraction comprising: phases, general tasks, specialized tasks and process instances. The stages followed by the CRIP-DM methodology are Business understanding, data understanding, data preparation, modeling, evaluation, and implementation.
- Knowledge Discovery in Databases process (KDD process), methodology that uses data mining techniques and consists of the following steps: selection, pre-processing, transformation, data mining, Interpretation / evaluation.
- Foundational Methodology for Data Science (FDMS): Methodology similar to KDD process and CRIPS-DM, is oriented to large volumes of data. It consists of ten iterative steps: Business understanding, Analytic approach, Data requirements, Data collection, Data understanding, Data preparation, Modeling, Evaluation, Deployment, and Feedback.
- Team Data Science Process (TDSP). Agile and iterative methodology developed by Microsoft for data science that considers collaboration and team learning through roles; It also uses Microsoft tools and technologies for its use. Its stages are represented as a life cycle that is composed: Business Understanding, Data Acquisition and Understanding, Modeling, Deployment, Customer Acceptance.
- DROP-based requirements elicitation. The steps for determining requirements based on DROP. The steps for determining requirements: D means the acquisition of experience in the domain, R the collection of raw data first, O shared ownership of data and systems and P the perfection of prototype-based products.
- Business Analytics Methodology (BAM). It aims to align business analysis development projects with commercial objectives and strategies. The Stages are: Problem situation structuring, Business model mapping, Business analytics leverage, analytics implementation.
- SEMMA. The SEMMA process developed for SAS Institute in support of SAS Enterprise Miner users. It comprises the following stages: Sample, Explore, Modify, Model, and Assess.

Table 5. Example Platforms used in the reviewed works

Area	Use	Platform used	Reference
Computer vision	Image recognition	Kaggle	(Bogucki et al., 2019)
Social Media	Fake profile identifier	RapidMiner	(Albayati & Altamimi, 2019)
Healthcare	Healthcare data analysis	RapidMiner	(McPadden et al., 2019)
	Disease prediction	RapidMiner	(Naqvi et al., 2018)
	Biomedical texts analysis	CaseOLAP Platform	(Sigdel et al., 2019)
Risks	Risk assesment and early warning	Emerging Risk Knowledge Exchange Platform (RKEP)	(Czyz et al., 2018)
Energy	Demand for energy	IoTEP	(Terroso-Saenz et al., 2019)

- Spreadsheet as a process. Consider spreadsheets as a tool for mining processes that start with events. The events are: Event logs, Exploring event data, Process Discovery, Checking compliance, Analyzing performance, Process animation, Operational support, Tool support.
- Agile Framework BI. This framework is organized by a BI Delivery top layer and a Fast Analytics / Data Science bottom layer linked to each other. In the upper layer five sequential stages are developed: development, implementation and delivery of value, and in the lower layer the sequential stages: scope, data acquisition / discovery, analysis / visualization, validation and implementation.

Data Science Platforms

A platform for data science is an environment in which it is possible to perform activities partial or full processes related to analysis, process visualization, forecast or machine learning with data, in an isolated or collaborative way through a local computer, network or cloud computing services (Table 5, Table 6).

The Baikal Data Science Platform in New Haven was developed using open source technology for the analysis of health care and biomedical research data (McPadden et al., 2019). The prediction of diseases in diabetic patients is possible through the analysis of generated and abstracted data from 130 hospitals in the United States (Naqvi et al., 2018).

Image recognition is an activity that allows the recognition of any individual object. However, it is a time-consuming activity. With the use of the Kaggle platform, recognition of whale images was carried out, applying techniques and tools of greater precision and in an automated way (Bogucki et al., 2019).

The use of tools and platforms such as RapidMiner, which incorporate various algorithms and techniques, analyzes user profile information and network behavior. This makes possible the identification of profiles of fake users on Facebook, the results vary according to the applied algorithm (Albayati & Altamimi, 2019).

CaseOLAP is a cloud computing platform that supports the extraction, analysis and processing of large biomedical textual data published (Sigdel et al., 2019).

In the DEMETER project, a platform called ERKEP was developed for storage, exchange and data analysis for a quick risk assessment (Czyz et al., 2018).

IoT Energy Platform (IoTEP), open source platform that is based on the use of the internet of things to analyze, process and manage data related to the energy demand of buildings (Terroso-Saenz et al., 2019).

Table 6. Example of data science platforms

Platform	Description	License
Anaconda	An enterprise open source data science platform with a variety of tools for professionals and researcher (Anaconda Inc, 2019).	Open Source
Kaggle	A data science platform with tools and data sets where problems can be solved in a collaborative way (Kaggle, 2019b).	Free
Alteryx	The platform allows the preparation, combination, analysis and presentation of data in a predictive fashion for different data science professionals (Alteryx, 2019).	Commercial
RapidMiner	Data preparation, machine learning, modelling development for predictions in a local or distributed network (RapidMiner, 2019).	AGP
Yale New Haven Health Baikal Data Science Platform	The platform allows the storage, processing, and analysis of large volume of healthcare and biomedical data in real time (McPadden et al., 2019).	Private
CaseOLAP Platform	Preprocessing of data, indexation and queries of biomedical text documents analysis (CaseOLAP, 2019).	MIT
KNIME Software	The open source version allows to upload, integrate, transform, analyze, and visualize data. The server version has additional features: collaboration, automation, management and visualization of data (KMIME, 2019).	GPL
H2O	A platform which offers products and services for analysis and machine learning compatible with open source learning (H2O, 2019).	Commercial
Tibco	It provides tools for data analysis, visualization, management, machine learning in big data collaborative environments (TIBCO Software Inc, 2019).	Commercial
Databricks	Platform for analysis using apache spark in the cloud, for data science activities and machine learning with a focus on data engineering. It is capable of communicating with computing services in the cloud (Databricks, 2019).	Commercial
dataiku	This platforms offers functions of explorations, preparation, machine learning, model development, automation, coding, collaboration, security and governance (Dataiku, 2019).	Commercial
Domino Data Science Platform	A data science platform that centralizes all the activities, tools and people across the data science lifecycle (Domino Data Lab, 2019).	Commercial
SiteWhere	Open source platform for implementation of IoT applications (SiteWhere LLC, 2019).	Free software
SAP Cloud Platform Internet of Things	Management of devices and data that can be analyzed later (SAP, 2019).	Commercial
EpiData	IoT open source platform that allows communication with various types of controllers, including industrial ones, and offers automatic learning tools and algorithms (EpiData, 2019).	Commercial
Fairhair.ai	Access to data online through a knowledge graphic with advanced artificial intelligence models (Meltwater, 2019).	Commercial

Data Visualization

Data visualization can be defined as the graphical display in which information and data is presented. In the visualization process, it is possible to use different techniques such as, charts, graphs, maps, and infographics by using different tools which aim to understand tendencies, atypical values and patterns in data. The objectives which can be set for visualization in data science are: order of data and setting a context, exploring data from different perspectives, discovering patterns and outliers (Table 7).

Some examples of visualization methods are (Tableau Software, 2019): area graph, bar graph, bubble chart, bullet graph, cartogram, circular graph, dot distribution map, Gantt chart, heat map, result table, histogram, matrix, networks, polar area charts, radial tree, dispersion graph (2D or 3D), flow graph, text table, time scale chart, tree diagram, stacked pie chart, word cloud, etc.

Table 7. Example of data visualization tools.

Tool	Description	License
Tableu	Drag and drop features, with a wide range of visualization models in an interactive way (Tableau, 2019).	Commercial
QlikView	Visualization software with a wide variety of tools (Qlik, 2019).	Commercial
PowerBI	An interactive data visualization tool for BI (Microsoft, 2019c).	Commercial
Geckoboard Software	A cloud-based computing tool which allows visualizing business metrics in a dashboard. It is possible to import data in real time from different sources such as social networking sites o analytics web services (Geckoboard, 2019).	Commercial
Palladio	It allows the visualization of complex historical data through different displays such as maps, graphs, lists and galleries (Open Palladio projects, 2019).	MIT

Machine Learning

Machine Learning is the scientific study which allows to provide computers with data or observations of a real problem. It is intended that computers learn and improve their learning automatically by means of algorithms (Michalski, 1998). Machine Learning (ML) is directly related to artificial intelligence and their joint purpose is to find non-explicit relationships among data and/or information available. The main objective is to reproduce the process of the generated data allowing analysts to generalize observed data into new scenarios (Giudici, 2003).

Some learning systems are used in self-driving cars, fraud detection, etc. In particular, within data science ML programming languages, the most popular languages are R and Python.

With an automated machine learning model, it is possible to predict the rule and the tendency in materials science, in order to obtain the relationship between atomic and electronic structures of materials in big data (Jie et al., 2019). Tools like MatCALO combine automated learning techniques and semantic knowledge and the combination allows to model the relationships among materials, processes and properties (Picklum & Beetz, 2019).

With the Experience Sampling Method (ESM), data on the daily emotions of people with psychosis spectrum disorder is obtained, and such data is used as a future indicator of mental illnesses and superior patterns, demonstrating that it is possible to apply automated learning and statistical modeling (Stamate et al., 2019).

The combination of the analysis in main components, the non-parametric statistical analysis, support-vector machines, and a machine learning algorithm allows to predict if a team is to win a game (Gu et al., 2019).

The combination of automated learning and big data for crop protection (plant diseases management, weeds and other pests) is explored by means of Markov random fields (MRF) (Ip et al., 2018).

An approach for improving the energy efficiency when gathering and analyzing IoT data implies bit reduction which is periodically transmitted to the edge node before it is sent to the cloud by using a compression method that does not affect the quality of data (Azar et al., 2019).

Computational psychiatry addresses the complexity of mechanical modelling approaches and data-based machine learning approaches to make predictions from data which allows the management of psychiatric disorders (Rutledge et al., 2019).

Extreme learning machine (ELM), Generalized Regression Neural Networks (GRNN), Back Propagation Neural Networks (BPNN) and RF models were used for modeling soil temperature and variables such as air temperature, wind speed, humidity relative, solar radiation and vapor pressure deficit at different depths on the Loess Plateau in China. ELM offers slightly better performance and speed, than the other models with half-hour time scales (Feng et al., 2019).

Through machine learning and statistical analysis, it is possible to predict the demand in restaurants considering location, weather, and events. Bayesian linear regressions, Boosted Decision Tree Regression, and decision Forest Regression are used for machine learning. The Stepwise method is used for the statistical analysis method (Tanizaki et al., 2019).

Driver behavior impacts on traffic density as attested by data collected from the CAN (Controller Area Network) bus. The data is collected from five passenger cars and nineteen trucks driving on the A28 highway in Utrecht region in the Netherlands and restricted to straight roads (Heyns et al., 2019).

It is possible to make a predictive measure of the perceived anxiety through microblogs. The results show inverse correlations among perceived anxiety, expression frequency, degree of popularity and followers' commitment (Gruda & Hasan, 2019).

With predictive analysis, it is possible to improve biogas output in two industrial facilities in China. This can be achieved through the application of machine learning models into the analytical pipeline (De Clercq et al., 2019).

Solar forecasting was performed using 68 machine learning algorithms for 3 sky conditions, 7 locations, and 5 climate zones in the continental United States (Yagli et al., 2019).

Sales forecasting depends on many factors, especially between sales amount and some significant factors which affect demand. For this analysis, an Extreme Learning Machine (ELM) technique was used by using real data from a fashion retailer in Hong Kong (Sun et al., 2008).

Moreover, with the application of a hybrid forecasting model which integrates ensemble empirical model decomposition (EEMD) and Extreme Machine Learning (ELM) represents a good alternative when forecasting computer products sales (Lu & Shao, 2012).

With the application of Extreme Learning Machines (ELMs), it is possible to detect plagiarism in source code from software projects. This was achieved with accurate results by using C programs collected from the Internet obtaining accurate results (Wang et al., 2015).

For example, there are a variety of tools or systems that support data analysis and prediction in Table 8.

FUTURE RESEARCH DIRECTIONS

The deepest study of algorithms and techniques applied to related problems Smart technologies; Comprehensive analysis of services that include platforms and repositories for data science can be addressed

Table 8. Examples of machine learning tools

Tool	Description	License
Bigml	Data training, statistical calculations and operations, validations, preprocessing, various algorithms and adjustments (BigML, 2019).	Commercial/Free access
Deeplearning4j	Distributed, deep learning, open source library, for JVM (Skymind, 2019).	Open source
Google Cloud AutoML	Learning machine products which allow to prepare models according to specific business needs (Google, 2019a).	Commercial
Jupyter Notebook	An application that supports interactive data on science and scientific computing, as well as different programming languages (Project Jupyter, 2019).	Open source
Keras	API for high-level neural networks, developed by Python. It runs in TensorFlow, CNTK or Theano (Chollet, 2019).	MIT
Machine Learning Studio	Clould-based computing tool with a simple interface and learning machine algorithms (Microsoft, 2019a).	Commercial
Natural Language Toolkit NLTK	Libraries and software for the processing of natural language (NLTK Project, 2019).	Free software
Opennn	Neural network libraries with applications in energy, marketing, healthcare using learning machine algorithms for regression, classification, prediction and association (Artificial Intelligence Techniques, 2019).	Free software
PyTorch	A tool for deep neural networks which accelerate and admit GPU (PyTorch, 2019).	BSD
Scikit-learn	A learning library based on Python. It allows the transformation of input data, such as text for learning machine algorithms (Cournapeau, 2019).	BSD
Shogun	Open source library with efficient and unified learning machine methods used by professionals, hackers, scientists and open-source idealists (NumFOCUS, 2019).	GPLv3
TensorFlow	Main framework for all kinds of tasks on machine learning and research, compatible with all devices and operating systems, numerical calculations. Tasks can be complemented with graphs (Google, 2019c).	MIT
NeuroSolutions	Neural network software with artificial intelligence and learning machine algorithms (NeuroSolutions, 2019).	Commercial

with the intention of supporting professionals working in data science. Open access tools and platforms that allow access and use, allow data science researchers to contribute to the best development of data science.

CONCLUSION

The seventy percent of the technologies identified are free software licensing, and the remaining thirty percent are commercial privative (Figure 2). Initiatives such as open government or open data support the solution of problems that affect citizens by making diverse data public, and these are treated by data science professionals. The technologies with marketing or private trends are the computing platforms in the cloud that incorporate many tools for data storage, processing and visualization.

Data management needs have allowed the development of activities; roles and professionals specialized in a wide array of data science areas. These individuals have specific skills and knowledge. Furthermore, technological and scientific advances allow the development of technological tools which allow the storage, cleaning, processing, preprocessing, training, extraction, exportation, visualization and management of data and information. These advances are available under different types of license and accessible to any platform or execution environment, in the cloud, mobile apps, as well as desktop.

Figure 2. Distribution of licenses in analyzed works

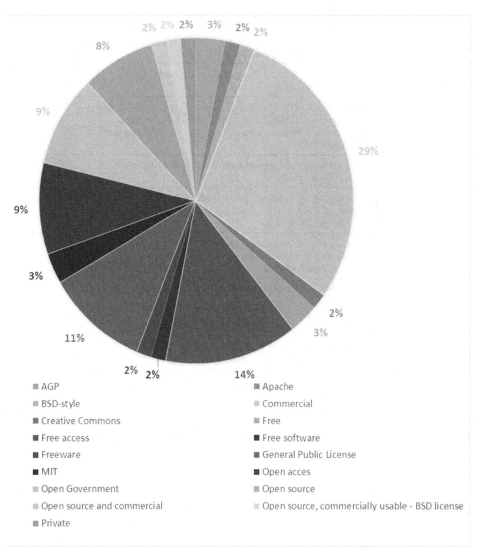

CONFLICTS OF INTEREST

The author(s) declare(s) that there is no conflict of interest regarding the publication of this chapter.

REFERENCES

H2O. (2019). H2O. https://www.h2o.ai/products/h2o/

Aalst, W. (2018). Spreadsheets for business process management: Using process mining to deal with "events" rather than "numbers"? *Business Process Management Journal*, *24*(1), 105–127. doi:10.1108/BPMJ-10-2016-0190

Ahmad, A., Babar, M., Din, S., Khalid, S., Ullah, M. M., Paul, A., Reddy, A. G., & Min-Allah, N. (2019). Socio-cyber network: The potential of cyber-physical system to define human behaviors using big data analytics. *Future Generation Computer Systems*, *92*, 868–878. doi:10.1016/j.future.2017.12.027

Akhavan-Hejazi, H., & Mohsenian-Rad, H. (2018). Power systems big data analytics: An assessment of paradigm shift barriers and prospects. *Energy Reports*, *4*, 91–100.

Albayati, M. B., & Altamimi, A. M. (2019). An Empirical Study for Detecting Fake Facebook Profiles Using Supervised Mining Techniques. Informatica-Journal of Computing and Informatics, 43(1), 77–86. doi:10.31449/inf.v43i1.2319

Alteryx, I. (2019). Alteryx: Self-Service Data Analytics Platform. https://www.alteryx.com/platform

Anaconda Inc. (2019). Anaconda. https://www.anaconda.com/

Apache Software Foundation. (2019a). Apache Hadoop. https://hadoop.apache.org/

Apache Software Foundation. (2019b). GraphX. https://spark.apache.org/graphx/

Artificial Intelligence Techniques, L. (2019). Opennn. https://www.opennn.net/

Ayuntamiento de Málaga. (2019). Data Set del Ayintamiento de Malaga. http://datosabiertos.malaga.eu/dataset

Azar, J., Makhoul, A., Barhamgi, M., & Couturier, R. (2019). An energy efficient IoT data compression approach for edge machine learning. *Future Generation Computer Systems*, *96*, 168–175. doi:10.1016/j.future.2019.02.005

Barlas, P. (2015). A survey of open source data science tools. *International Journal of Intelligent Computing and Cybernetics*, *8*(3), 232–261. doi:10.1108/ijicc-07-2014-0031

BigM. L. (2019). bigml. https://bigml.com/features

Bogucki, R., Cygan, M., Khan, C. B., Klimek, M., Milczek, J. K., & Mucha, M. (2019). Applying deep learning to right whale photo identification. *Conservation Biology*, *33*(3), 676–684. doi:10.1111/cobi.13226 PubMed

BROAD Institute. (2019). BROAD Institute Cancer Program Datasets. http://portals.broadinstitute.org/cgi-bin/cancer/datasets.cgi

Caldarola, E. G., & Rinaldi, A. (2017). *Big Data Visualization Tools: A Survey - The New Paradigms.* Methodologies and Tools for Large Data Sets Visualization., doi:10.5220/0006484102960305

Cambridge University Press. (2019). Dataset. In Cambridge English Dictionary. https://dictionary.cambridge.org/es/diccionario/ingles/dataset

Carto. (2019). Data mapping and visualization tools. https://carto.com/builder/

CaseOLAP. (2019). CaseOLAP. https://caseolap.github.io/

Centers for Medicare & Medicaid Services. (2019). Hospital Compare datasets. https://data.medicare.gov/data/hospital-compare

Chapman, A., Simperl, E., Koesten, L., Konstantinidis, G., Ibáñez, L.-D., Kacprzak, E., & Groth, P. (2019). Dataset search: A survey. *The VLDB Journal*. Advance online publication. doi:10.100700778-019-00564-x

Chollet, F. (2019). Keras: The Python Deep Learning library. https://keras.io/

Cleveland, W. S. (2001). Data Science: An Action Plan for Expanding the Technical Areas of the Field of Statistics. *International Statistical Review*, *69*(1), 21–26. doi:10.1111/j.1751-5823.2001.tb00477.x

Comai, A. (2018). Beyond patent analytics: Insights from a scientific and technological data mashup based on a case example. *World Patent Information*, *55*, 61–77.

Commission, E. (2019). PALIA suite for process mining https://ec.europa.eu/eip/ageing/commitments-tracker/b3/palia-suite-process-mining_en

Corrales, D. C., Ledezma, A., & Corrales, J. C. (2015). A Conceptual Framework for Data Quality in Knowledge Discovery Tasks (FDQ-KDT): A Proposal. *Journal of Computers*, *10*(6), 396–405. doi:10.17706/jcp.10.6.396-405

Cournapeau, D. (2019). scikit-learn. https://scikit-learn.org/stable/

Czyz, M. J., Filter, M., & Buschulte, A. (2018). Application of data science in risk assessment and early warning. *EFSA Journal*, *16*, e16088. Advance online publication. PubMed doi:10.2903/j.efsa.2018.e16088

Databricks. (2019). Databricks Unified Analytics Platform. https://databricks.com/product/unified-analytics-platform

DataHub. (2018). Climate Change Data. https://datahub.io/collections/climate-change

Dataiku. (2019). dataiku. https://www.dataiku.com/

De Clercq, D., Jalota, D., Shang, R., Ni, K., Zhang, Z., Khan, A., Wen, Z., Caicedo, L., & Yuan, K. (2019). Machine learning powered software for accurate prediction of biogas production: A case study on industrial-scale Chinese production data. *Journal of Cleaner Production*, *218*, 390–399. doi:10.1016/j.jclepro.2019.01.031

De Gennaro, M., Paffumi, E., & Martini, G. (2016). Big Data for Supporting Low-Carbon Road Transport Policies in Europe: Applications, Challenges and Opportunities. *Big Data Research*, *6*, 11–25.

Dhar, V. (2013). Data science and prediction. *Communications of the ACM*, *56*(12), 64–73. doi:10.1145/2500499

Domino Data Lab. (2019). Domino Data Science Platform. https://www.dominodatalab.com/platform/

Donoho, D. (2017). 50 Years of Data Science. *Journal of Computational and Graphical Statistics*, *26*(4), 745–766. doi:10.1080/10618600.2017.1384734

EpiData. (2019). EpiData. https://epidata.co/

EUMETNET. (2019). European Climate Assessment & Dataset project. https://www.ecad.eu/

Farrell, K. J., & Carey, C. C. (2018). Power, pitfalls, and potential for integrating computational literacy into undergraduate ecology courses. *Ecology and Evolution*, *8*(16), 7744–7751. doi:10.1002/ece3.4363 PubMed

Feng, Y., Cui, N., Hao, W., Gao, L., & Gong, D. (2019). Estimation of soil temperature from meteorological data using different machine learning models. *Geoderma*, *338*, 67–77. doi:10.1016/j.geoderma.2018.11.044

Foroughi, F., & Luksch, P. (2018). *Data Science Methodology for Cybersecurity Projects*. Academic Press.

Free Software Foundation. (2018). PSPP. https://www.gnu.org/software/pspp/

Geckoboard. (2019). geckoboard. https://www.geckoboard.com/product/

gephi.org. (2019). The Open Graph Viz Platform. https://gephi.org/

Giudici, P. (2003). *Applied Data Mining: Statistical Methods for Business and Industry*. Wiley.

Gobierno de México. (2019). Datos Abiertos de México. https://datos.gob.mx/

Google. (2019a). Cloud AutoML. https://cloud.google.com/automl/

Google. (2019b). Google Dataset Search. https://toolbox.google.com/datasetsearch

Google. (2019c). TensorFlow. https://www.tensorflow.org/

Government of Spain. (2018). The professionals of Data Science teams https://datos.gob.es/en/noticia/professionals-data-science-teams

Gruda, D., & Hasan, S. (2019). Feeling anxious? Perceiving anxiety in tweets using machine learning. *Computers in Human Behavior*, *98*, 245–255. doi:10.1016/j.chb.2019.04.020

Gu, W., Foster, K., Shang, J., & Wei, L. (2019). A game-predicting expert system using big data and machine learning. *Expert Systems with Applications*, *130*, 293–305. doi:10.1016/j.eswa.2019.04.025

Hernandez, R. R., Mayernik, M. S., Murphy-Mariscal, M. L., & Allen, M. F. (2012). Advanced Technologies and Data Management Practices in Environmental Science: Lessons from Academia [Article]. *Bioscience*, *62*(12), 1067–1076. doi:10.1525/bio.2012.62.12.8

Heyns, E., Uniyal, S., Dugundji, E., Tillema, F., & Huijboom, C. (2019). Predicting Traffic Phases from Car Sensor Data using Machine Learning. *Procedia Computer Science*, *151*, 92–99. doi:10.1016/j. procs.2019.04.016

Hindle, G. A., & Vidgen, R. (2018). Developing a business analytics methodology: A case study in the foodbank sector. *European Journal of Operational Research*, *268*(3), 836–851. doi:10.1016/j. ejor.2017.06.031

INEGI. (2019). Datos. https://www.inegi.org.mx/datos/

Ip, R. H. L., Ang, L.-M., Seng, K. P., Broster, J. C., & Pratley, J. E. (2018). Big data and machine learning for crop protection. *Computers and Electronics in Agriculture*, *151*, 376–383. doi:10.1016/j. compag.2018.06.008

Izabella, V. L., Barbara, J. D., & Cees, J. M. L. (2019). Internet of Things and Big Data-Driven Data Analysis Services for Third Parties: Business Models, New Ventures, and Potential Horizons. In M. Natarajan (Ed.), *Strategic Innovations and Interdisciplinary Perspectives in Telecommunications and Networking* (pp. 256–289). IGI Global., doi:10.4018/978-1-5225-8188-8.ch014

Jain, A. (2015). matminer. http://hackingmaterials.lbl.gov/matminer/

Japan Science and Technology Agency. (2019). Life Science Database Archive. https://dbarchive.bio-sciencedbc.jp/index-e.html

Jie, J., Hu, Z., Qian, G., Weng, M., Li, S., Li, S., Hu, M., Chen, D., Xiao, W., Zheng, J., Wang, L.-W., & Pan, F. (2019). Discovering unusual structures from exception using big data and machine learning techniques. Science Bulletin, 64(9), 612–616. doi:10.1016/j.scib.2019.04.015

Jiménez Gómez, C. E. (2018). Análisis predictivo de datos abiertos sobre el uso turístico del servicio de alquiler compartido de bicicletas de Nueva York Universitat Oberta de Catalunya]. http://openaccess. uoc.edu/webapps/o2/bitstream/10609/81516/9/carlosjgTFM0618memoria.pdf

Kaggle. (2019a). https://www.kaggle.com/datasets. https://www.kaggle.com/datasets

Kaggle. (2019b). Kaggle: you home the data science. https://www.kaggle.com/

KMIME. (2019). KMIME. https://www.knime.com/

Landset, S., Khoshgoftaar, T. M., Richter, A. N., & Hasanin, T. (2015). A survey of open source tools for machine learning with big data in the Hadoop ecosystem. *Journal of Big Data*, *2*(1), 24. doi:10.1186/ s40537-015-0032-1

Larson, D., & Chang, V. (2016). A review and future direction of agile, business intelligence, analytics and data science. *International Journal of Information Management*, *36*(5), 700–710. doi:10.1016/j. ijinfomgt.2016.04.013

Liu, L. (2016). Requirements Engineering for Health Data Analytics Challenges and Possible Directions. doi:10.1109/re.2016.48

Lu, C. J., & Shao, Y. J. E. (2012). Forecasting Computer Products Sales by Integrating Ensemble Empirical Mode Decomposition and Extreme Learning Machine [Article]. Mathematical Problems in Engineering. *Article, 831201*. Advance online publication. doi:10.1155/2012/831201

Martinez-Millana, A., Lizondo, A., Gatta, R., Vera, S., Salcedo, V. T., & Fernandez-Llatas, C. (2019). Process Mining Dashboard in Operating Rooms: Analysis of Staff Expectations with Analytic Hierarchy Process. *International Journal of Environmental Research and Public Health, 16*(2), 199. Advance online publication. doi:10.3390/ijerph16020199 PubMed

Max Planck Institute for Demographic Research. (2019). The Human Mortality Database. https://www.lifetable.de/cgi-bin/data.php

Max-Planck-Institute of Biochemistry. (2018). MaxQuant. https://maxquant.org/

Max-Planck-Institute of Biochemistry. (2019). Perseus. https://maxquant.net/perseus/

McPadden, J., Durant, T. J. S., Bunch, D. R., Coppi, A., Price, N., Rodgerson, K., Torre, C. J., Byron, W., Hsiaol, A. L., Krumholz, H. M., & Schulz, W. L. (2019). Health Care and Precision Medicine Research: Analysis of a Scalable Data Science Platform. *Journal of Medical Internet Research, 21*(4), e13043. Advance online publication. doi:10.2196/13043 PubMed

Meltwater. (2019). Fairhair.ai. https://fairhair.ai/about

Michalski, R. S. (1998). *Machine Learning and Data Mining: Methods and Applications*. Wiley.

Microsoft. (2019a). Machine Learning Studio. https://azure.microsoft.com/es-es/services/machine-learning-studio/

Microsoft. (2019b). Microsoft Excel. https://products.office.com/es-mx/excel

Microsoft. (2019c). Power BI Interactive Data Vizualitacion. https://powerbi.microsoft.com/en-us/

Miniera. (2019). MIRA Analytics. http://www.mira-analytics.com/

Mitsubishi Electric Research Labs. (2019). MERL Sense Data. https://sites.google.com/a/drwren.com/wmd/

Nagorny, K., Lima-Monteiro, P., Barata, J., & Colombo, A. W. (2017). Big Data Analysis in Smart Manufacturing: A Review. International Journal of Communications. Network and System Sciences, 10(3), 31–58. doi:10.4236/ijcns.2017.103003

Naqvi, B., Ali, A., Hashmi, M. A., & Atif, M. (2018). Prediction Techniques for Diagnosis of Diabetic Disease: A Comparative Study. *International Journal of Computer Science and Network Security, 18*(8), 118–124.

National Center for Biotechnology Information & U.S. National Library of Medicine. (2019). GEO DataSets. https://www.ncbi.nlm.nih.gov/gds

National Oceanic and Atmospheric Administration. (2019). NOAA Climate.gov. https://www.climate.gov/maps-data/datasets

NeuroSolutions. (2019). Premier Neural Network Software. http://www.neurosolutions.com/neurosolutions/

NLTK Project. (2019). Natural Language Toolkit. https://www.nltk.org/

nosql-database.org. (2019). nosql. https://nosql-database.org/

NumFOCUS. (2019). shogun. https://www.shogun.ml/

Brains, O. A. S. I. S. (2019). OASIS Brains Datasets. http://www.oasis-brains.org/#data

Open Palladio projects. (2019). Open Palladio. http://hdlab.stanford.edu/palladio/about/

Picklum, M., & Beetz, M. (2019). MatCALO: Knowledge-enabled machine learning in materials science. *Computational Materials Science, 163*, 50–62. doi:10.1016/j.commatsci.2019.03.005

Pramanik, M. I., Lau, R. Y. K., Demirkan, H., & Azad, M. A. K. (2017). Smart health: Big data enabled health paradigm within smart cities. *Expert Systems with Applications, 87*, 370–383. doi:10.1016/j.eswa.2017.06.027

Process Mining Group. (2016). ProM. http://www.processmining.org/prom/start

Project Jupyter. (2019). Project Jupyter. https://jupyter.org/

Python Software Foundation. (2019). Python. https://www.python.org/

PyTorch. (2019). pytorch. https://pytorch.org/features

Qlik. (2019). Qlik View https://www.qlik.com/us/products/qlikview

RapidMiner. I. (2019). rapidminer. https://rapidminer.com/

Regents, U. C. (2019). What is Data Science? https://datascience.berkeley.edu/about/what-is-data-science/

Rickman, J. M., Lookman, T., & Kalinin, S. V. (2019). Materials informatics: From the atomic-level to the continuum. *Acta Materialia, 168*, 473–510. doi:10.1016/j.actamat.2019.01.051

RStudio. (2019). Rstudio. https://www.rstudio.com/

Rutledge, R. B., Chekroud, A. M., & Huys, Q. J. M. (2019). Machine learning and big data in psychiatry: Toward clinical applications. *Current Opinion in Neurobiology, 55*, 152–159. doi:10.1016/j.conb.2019.02.006 PubMed

Saltz, J., Shamshurin, I., & Crowston, K. (2017). Comparing Data Science Project Management Methodologies via a Controlled Experiment. doi:10.24251/hicss.2017.120

SAP. (2019). SAP Cloud Platform Internet of Things. https://www.sap.com/sea/products/iot-platform-cloud.html

Secretaria de Modernización. (2019). Datos Argentina-Datasets. https://datos.gob.ar/dataset

Sharma, N., Taneja, S., Sagar, V., & Bhatt, A. (2018). Forecasting air pollution load in Delhi using data analysis tools. *Procedia Computer Science, 132*, 1077–1085. doi:10.1016/j.procs.2018.05.023

Sigdel, D., Kyi, V., Zhang, A. D., Setty, S. P., Liem, D. A., Shi, Y., Wang, X., Shen, J. M., Wang, W., Han, J. W., & Ping, P. P. (2019). Cloud-Based Phrase Mining and Analysis of User-Defined Phrase-Category Association in Biomedical Publications. Jove-Journal of Visualized Experiments, (144), Article e59108. doi:10.3791/59108

Singh, D., & Reddy, C. K. (2014). A survey on platforms for big data analytics. *Journal of Big Data*, *2*(1), 8. doi:10.1186/s40537-014-0008-6 PubMed

Sinitcyn, P., Rudolph, J. D., & Cox, J. (2018). Computational Methods for Understanding Mass Spectrometry–Based Shotgun Proteomics Data. *Annual Review of Biomedical Data Science*, *1*(1), 207–234. doi:10.1146/annurev-biodatasci-080917-013516

SiteWhere LLC. (2019). SiteWhere Open Source Internet of Things Platform. https://sitewhere.io/en/

Skymind. (2019). Deeplearning4j. https://deeplearning4j.org/

Sperhac, J. M., & Gallo, S. M. (2019). VIDIA: A HUBzero gateway for data analytics education. Future Generation Computer Systems-the International Journal of Escience, 94, 833–840. doi:10.1016/j.future.2018.02.004

Stamate, D., Katrinecz, A., Stahl, D., Verhagen, S. J. W., Delespaul, P. A. E. G., van Os, J., & Guloksuz, S. (2019). Identifying psychosis spectrum disorder from experience sampling data using machine learning approaches. *Schizophrenia Research*.

Subcretaria del Ministerio de Agricultura. (2019). Biblioteca de Datos climaticos. https://www.climate-datalibrary.cl/?Set-Language=es

Sun, Z.-L., Choi, T.-M., Au, K.-F., & Yu, Y. (2008). Sales forecasting using extreme learning machine with applications in fashion retailing. *Decision Support Systems*, *46*(1), 411–419. doi:10.1016/j.dss.2008.07.009

Tableau. (2019). tableau. https://public.tableau.com/en-us/s/

Tableau Software. (2019). Data visualization beginner's guide: a definition, examples, and learning resources. https://www.tableau.com/learn/articles/data-visualization

Tanizaki, T., Hoshino, T., Shimmura, T., & Takenaka, T. (2019). Demand forecasting in restaurants using machine learning and statistical analysis. Procedia CIRP, 79, 679–683. doi:10.1016/j.procir.2019.02.042

Teran, H. E. E., Puris, A., & Novoa-Hernandez, P. (2019). Causes affecting the promotion of students of pre-university courses at the state technical university of quevedo: A study applying data mining. Revista. *Universidad y Sociedad*, *11*(2), 61–65.

Terroso-Saenz, F., González-Vidal, A., Ramallo-González, A. P., & Skarmeta, A. F. (2019). An open IoT platform for the management and analysis of energy data. *Future Generation Computer Systems*, *92*, 1066–1079. doi:10.1016/j.future.2017.08.046

TIBCO Software Inc. (2019). TIBCO. https://www.tibco.com/products

Togaware Pty Lt. (2019). Rattle. https://rattle.togaware.com/

University of California. (2019). UC Irvine Machine Learning Repository. http://mlr.cs.umass.edu/ml/

University of Essex, & University of Manchester and Jisc. (2019). UK data Service-Get Data. https://ukdataservice.ac.uk/get-data.aspx

University of Ljubljana. (2019). Orange. https://orange.biolab.si/

U.S. Department of Health & Human Services. (2019). Datasets. https://healthdata.gov/content/about

U.S. General Services Administration. (2019). The home of the U.S. Government's open data. https://www.data.gov/

Vimalajeewa, D., Kulatunga, C., & Berry, D. P. (2018). Learning in the compressed data domain: Application to milk quality prediction. *Information Sciences*, *459*, 149–167. doi:10.1016/j.ins.2018.05.002

Visualdata. (2019). Visualdata. https://www.visualdata.io/

Wang, B., Yang, X. C., & Wang, G. R. (2015). Detecting Copy Directions among Programs Using Extreme Learning Machines [Article]. Mathematical Problems in Engineering. *Article*, *793697*. Advance online publication. doi:10.1155/2015/793697

Ward, L., Dunn, A., Faghaninia, A., Zimmermann, N. E. R., Bajaj, S., Wang, Q., Montoya, J., Chen, J., Bystrom, K., Dylla, M., Chard, K., Asta, M., Persson, K. A., Snyder, G. J., Foster, I., & Jain, A. (2018). Matminer: An open source toolkit for materials data mining. *Computational Materials Science*, *152*, 60–69. doi:10.1016/j.commatsci.2018.05.018

Washington State University. (2018). CASAS datasets for activities of daily living http://casas.wsu.edu/datasets/

Yagli, G. M., Yang, D., & Srinivasan, D. (2019). Automatic hourly solar forecasting using machine learning models. *Renewable & Sustainable Energy Reviews*, *105*, 487–498. doi:10.1016/j.rser.2019.02.006

KEY TERMS AND DEFINITIONS

Dataset: Set of data organized in form tabular where each column usually represents a variable or field.

Framework: Series of conceptual, practical, or normative elements used as a reference to deal with a type of problem used.

Learning Machine: Discipline that uses and develops techniques with the aim of providing intelligence to computers and predicting situations from data.

License: Permission granted by the owner of a product or data to the end user for its use, distribution, modification, or the terms that this or the end user contract specifies.

Methodology: Series of stages that follow a software or data science project, the stages in sets are called the life cycle.

Platform: It is a computer or hardware system on which to run various hardware or software applications or both, with a type of use license.

Repository: Place that has various digital resources such as documents, data, software. These are available under various user licenses and commonly on properly organized websites for access, consultation, or download.

Chapter 5
A Survey on Intelligence Tools for Data Analytics

Shatakshi Singh
Mody University of Science and Technology, India

Kanika Gautam
Mody University of Science and Technology, India

Prachi Singhal
Mody University of Science and Technology, India

Sunil Kumar Jangir
Mody University of Science and Technology, India

Manish Kumar
Mody University of Science and Technology, India

ABSTRACT

The recent development in artificial intelligence is quite astounding in this decade. Especially, machine learning is one of the core subareas of AI. Also, ML field is an incessantly growing along with evolution and becomes a rise in its demand and importance. It transmogrified the way data is extracted, analyzed, and interpreted. Computers are trained to get in a self-training mode so that when new data is fed they can learn, grow, change, and develop themselves without explicit programming. It helps to make useful predictions that can guide better decisions in a real-life situation without human interference. Selection of ML tool is always a challenging task, since choosing an appropriate tool can end up saving time as well as making it faster and easier to provide any solution. This chapter provides a classification of various machine learning tools on the following aspects: for non-programmers, for model deployment, for Computer vision, natural language processing, and audio for reinforcement learning and data mining.

DOI: 10.4018/978-1-7998-3053-5.ch005

INTRODUCTION

In this era of digitalization, data is generated and stored in every field. This data has the potential to be used to predict future possibilities. ML comprises of using this data to train a model for predicting results for new observations without any explicit instructions. It predicts results by analyzing the patterns in the given dataset.

Ranging from a very basic task of separating the spam emails to the revolutionary Cyborg technology ML has a wide range of applications in our life. It not only eases our tasks but has the potential to solve some of the most challenging issues of the society (Anirudhi Thanvi et al., 2019). A lot of research is going on to improve the quality and efficiency of medical care using ML. Digital diagnosis of life-threatening diseases like cancer helps to detect the problem at a very early stage, making it possible to treat it before it turns lethal. ML has great potential across several other domains like Education (Kotsiantis, 2012), Farming (Li et al., 2014; Paul et al., 2016), Environment Conservation (Rahman et al., 2014), Security (Buczak & Guven, 2016), Social Media (Alatabi & Abbas, 2020; ReddyPY.Sushmitha & M.Padma, 2016), Information Verification (Herrera et al., 2010; Sharma et al., 2019) and a lot more(Vyas & Jangir, 2019).

ML tools provide a more convenient way for developers to build, train, and deploy their models. Tools help to speed up the process by automating each step of the process which otherwise needed to be implemented manually from scratch. They help to eliminate the barrier between imagination and implementation of ideas due to a lack of skills. Developers need not be an expert in every step of implementation. They can implement their ideas easily once they are trained to work with a tool (Kumar Jangir et al., 2018, 2019).

The authors reviewed more than 50 papers and more than 100 blogs, articles, and websites that used various data analytics tools for carrying out different processes. The motivation behind carrying out this survey was the unavailability of research work that classified data analytics tools in various categories and gave a brief description of each tool.

This chapter divides data analytics tools into different categories for the simplicity and ease of choosing the right tool. It tells about the needs of tools for data analytics. The rest of the chapter is arranged as follows: Python Libraries used for carrying out various data analytics processes are explained followed by the tools for Big Data Analysis that help to organize and analyze large and complex datasets, which are difficult to be tackled by traditional database and software techniques. Then it states data mining tools that use mathematics, statistics, algorithms, and other scientific ways to provide insights from the given data set. The description is taken further by explaining tools that assist in Natural Language Processing, Voice recognition, face identification, and voice synthesizing which are classified as Tools for Computer Vision, NLP, and Audio. Then tools for Reinforcement learning that helps the agent to learn from its experiences are mentioned. After that tools that help to integrate the ML model with the existing production environment are categorized as tools for Model Deployment. At last, tools that obviate the need for programming skills are categorized under the category of tools for Non-Programmers. Various use cases of tools by different companies are given for each category. The use of some of the tools for research and development is also discussed along with the methodology, dataset description, and results used to carry out that research.

EXIGENCIES OF TOOLS FOR HANDLING DATA

Records of various events are being kept since ancient times. These records generate data that was earlier handled by mathematicians and statisticians in traditional ways. With time, as the volume of this data grew larger there emerged platforms like MS excel for managing this data. It had several features to satisfy the statistical, financial, and engineering needs. It helped to get a better picture of the data and to gain insights from it. Then came python with its libraries like Numpy, Scipy, Pytorch, etc which had several inbuilt functions to obviate the need of applying the algorithms from scratch.

PYTHON LIBRARIES FOR DATA SCIENCE

Data Science (Hunsinger & Waguespaack, 2016) refers to using mathematics, algorithms, statistics, and other scientific methods to get insights from the given data set (Van der Aalst, 2016).

SciPy is a Python-based scientific library for mathematics, science, and engineering. It uses packages including IPython, Pandas, NumPy, etc. to provide libraries for general math computations based programming tasks (S. Developers, 2020; Virtanen et al., 2020). **Dask** provides parallel computing (Rocklin, 2015) for analytics by integrating into other projects like Pandas, NumPy, and Scikit-Learn, etc. It allows parallelizing existing code by making minimal changes in it. Parallel processing saves time in execution and thus giving more time to analyze (D. core Developers, 2019). **Numba** is used to translate Python code to optimized machine code using an industry-standard LLVM compiler library. It easily adapts to CPU capabilities and offers a wide range of options to parallelize the code for CPUs and GPUs (Anaconda, 2018).

Cython is a compiler for Python as well as pyrex based extended Cython language. It provides a simple interface between high level and low-level code thus helps to manage high-level APIs and low-level details in a single codebase (P. S. Foundation, 2020). **High-Performance Analytics Toolkit (HPAT)** is a compiler-based framework for big data. It provides good coverage of Num-py and Pandas operators, basic ASCII string support, and basic integer dictionaries. It helps to speed up the work of ML and analytics on clusters (Totoni et al., 2017).

Since it became easy to handle and process data to gain insights from it, it generated the need for more and more data to get useful insights. Large volumes of data collected from various surveys, sensors, websites, etc made it difficult to handle it and demanded some new ways for data management.

CONTRIVED INTELLECT TOOLS FOR BIG DATA

Big Data refers to a large and diverse set of data. This data is used by ML models to predict future happenings. The larger the data set more is the accuracy of the results predicted by the model. This data may be collected through sensors, through surveys or through some websites or apps. Earlier such data was managed by spreadsheets and other traditional ways. But nowadays these data sets are so voluminous that they can't be managed through the traditional data processing software(Alfred, 2017). Some of the tools which help to organize big data efficiently are as follows:

Hadoop (Bhosale & Gadekar, 2014) is one of the eminent frameworks for working with Big Data (T. A. S. Foundation, 2020a). Facebook's message application is built on Apache Hadoop Platform(Borthakur et al., 2011)(Borthakur et al., 2011). **Talend** (Talend, 2020) is a Hadoop tool for Data Extraction. **Hive** (T. A. S. Foundation, 2020b; Thusoo et al., 2010), **Sqopp** (T. A. S. Foundation, 2018b), and **MongoDB** (MongoDB, 2020) are some tools for Data Storing used by companies like yahoo, Facebook, etc. **HBase** (The Apache Software Foundation, 2020b) and **Pig** (T. A. S. Foundation., 2019) are Data Analyzing tools and **Zookeeper** (T. A. S. Foundation, 2019) and **Pentaho** (Vantara, 2020)are Data Integrating tools in the Hadoop ecosystem.

Apache Spark is a unified analytics engine for Large Scale Data Processing. It is often considered to be a natural successor of Hadoop Big Data. It has 100 times better speed and can run on Hadoop, Kubernetes, standalone, Apache Mesos, or in the cloud. It can access diverse data sources like Alluxio, Apache Cassandra, HDFS, Apache HBase, Apache Hive, etc (T. A. S. Foundation, 2018a). **Neo4j** provides graph databases. With graphs, it becomes easy to analyze and process large data sets (Neo4j, 2020). It has also helped to overcome the challenge of representing and querying the time-varying social network data (Ciro Cattuto, Marco Quaggiotto, André Panisson, 2013).

The large volumes of data collected using these tools contain lots of incorrect, inaccurate, irrelevant, and incomplete entries. Before analyzing this data to get insights and make predictions it is better to process it and clean it to get the highest quality of information out of it. It is a difficult task for humans to clean the vast data sets and would require huge labor to do it. Therefore it raises the demand for tools to prepare data before using it.

The table given below shows the use cases of some of the contrived intellectual tools for big data. A huge amount of data is generated in business firms. Big Data Tools help to store these large data sets in a convenient manner that makes it easy to use for planning strategic business moves. Companies use these tools in various ways, for example, eBay uses Hadoop for search engine optimization and research, Apixio uses it for semantic analysis so that doctors can have better answers to the questions related to patient's health, Skybox Imaging uses it to store and process images to identify patterns in geographic change and many more.

Table 1. Companies using tools for handling Big Data

S.no	Tool Name	Purpose	Company
1.	**Apache Spark**	Apache Spark is used for data analytics and data visualization. It provides a solution for visual analytics processing and analyzing a large amount of data. It also works with the system to distribute data across the cluster and process the data in parallel (Amster, 2016; Education, 2018).	Microsoft
			QA Limited
			Ecolab Inc
			Lottoland
2	**Apache Hadoop**	Hadoop has provided an ultimate solution for handling Big Data. Hadoop is adapted by different companies for different tasks that include identifying customer segments, statistics generation, store and process images, for semantic analysis, etc. (Intellipaat, 2016)	Boston Bruins
			Archrock Inc
			TORI Global Ltd
			Avadyne Health, Inc.
3	**Neo4j**	Neo4j provides a graph database for easy storage, visualization, and analytics of large data sets (Murillo, 2019).	Walmart
			EBay
			Adobe
			Volvo

INTELLIGENCE TOOLS FOR DATA MINING

Nowadays more and more data is being generated in every aspect we can think of. Organizing and Analyzing this data manually is an extremely tedious task. Data mining refers to extracting the information from a large data set. It includes Analyzing, Classifying, and summarizing the huge data into useful information (Chen et al., 2007).

SSDT or SQL Server Data Tools are used to build, debug, maintain, and refactor databases. It provides a visual Table Designer for creating and editing tables in database projects or connected database instances. It allows version control for all the files while working on a group project (Microsoft, 2020b). **Apache Mahout** is a linear algebra framework designed to implement scalable ML algorithms. It includes JAVA libraries to perform mathematical operations (The Apache Software Foundation, 2020a).

Oracle Data Mining is a software that provides powerful data mining algorithms to discover insights, make predictions. It has been used for the predictive analysis of diabetic treatment (Aljumah et al., 2013) and in research on issues like the decline in the number of students in higher education (Zhang et al., 2010). **The rattle** is a Graphic User Interface based software for data mining. All interactions through the GUI are recorded in R-script. This R-script can later be executed in R (Togaware, 2019; Williams, 2009). It can also present the performance of models graphically. **DataMelt** is software for numeric computation, mathematics, statistics, data analysis, and data visualization. It combines the benefits of scripting languages, such as Python, Ruby, Groovy, etc. with the power of hundreds of Java packages (Computation and Visualization environment, 2020).

IBM Cognos is an AI-driven tool for Business Analytics. It provides compelling visualizations and dashboards to work with. Using pattern detection it provides actionable insights for the growth of the organization. It provides an easy way to share insights with people across the organization. With its AI-assisted and automated data preparation, it helps to save time (IBM, 2020a). **IBM SPSS Model** provides an intuitive graphical interface to access data from various data sources and provides a complete range of advanced analytical functions to produce deeper insight and accurate predictions by analyzing the given dataset to improve business outcomes (SPSS Inc., 2015).

SAS Data Mining provides a comprehensive visual and programming interface for all data mining and ML processes. It automatically generates a summary report and useful insights from the given dataset. Its automated feature engineering analyses are given data and assist in selecting the best set of features for modeling our data (SAS Institute Inc., 2020). **Teradata** provides various functions for data profiling and data mining which makes it easy to carry out data mining and analyze trends. Using in-built intelligence it helps to make analytic models efficiently, using inbuilt intelligence (Teradata, 2020). **Tableau** is a tool used by most of the data-driven companies for data visualization. It helps to convert raw data in a processable and understandable format. It also helps to create customized reports and dashboards. It can connect to multiple data sources to find correlations in large volumes of data (SOFTWARE, 2020).

Large sets of data helped to predict a lot about future results. But to use the large amount of data that was captured using cameras there was a need for tools for helping computers to interpret the happenings of the visual world. To resolve the ambiguity in using these applications for speech and text-recognition it was necessary to train computers to understand the patterns of human speech. Computer Vision and Natural Language Processing tools help the computers to interpret information of the real-world and react to it.

The following table shows the names of a few data mining tools used by companies for analyzing the collected data from various perspectives and dimensions. These tools allow users to apply certain data mining algorithms on the collected data to discover the hidden patterns in data and to classify and group the data to summarize the relationship to make it useful in making business decisions.

Table 2. Companies using intelligence tools for data mining

S.no	Tool Name	Purpose	Company
1.	Apache Mahout	Apache Mahout is a Data Mining Framework that helps to analyze large data sets when coupled with Hadoop architecture. It has various libraries containing many useful functions for data mining (HG Insights, 2020).	Allstate
			CBRE
			Proofpoint
			ESRI
2	Oracle Data Mining	Oracle Data Mining software is adopted by companies to solve business problems like to predict customer behavior, to target best customers, to develop customer profiles, to identify cross-selling opportunities, and detect anomalies and potential fraud (Enlyft, 2020).	TriMet
			University of Nevada-Reno
			Inter-American Development Bank
			Contemporary Staffing Solutions
3	IBM Cognos	IBM Cognos is a software used by many companies across the world for Business Intelligence. With Cognos business, users can extract corporate data, analyze and assemble it without having technical knowledge (Thor Olavsrud, 2019).	Deverell Smith
			Enesco, LLC
			Airgas
			J & D RESOURCES, INC
4	Teradata	Teradata provides fast and accurate data mining solutions for enterprises. It delivers real-time, intelligent answers, leveraging 100% of the relevant data, regardless of scale or volume of query (Tehrani, 2019).	Apple
			Capgemini
			BMW
			AWS
5	Tableau	Tableau is a powerful, secure, and flexible end to end analytics platform. It has features that enable businesses to better understand the data with the help of better Data Visualization & Data Analytics (TABLEAU SOFTWARE, LLC, 2020).	Linkedin
			Amazon
			Ferrari
			Skype
6	SAS Data Mining	SAS Data Mining is used by many Business firms for data mining. It searches for patterns, partnerships, specific relations, or trends predictive on large data and provides analysis to make better and more efficient decisions (intellipaat.com, 2016).	Health Quality Ontario
			Fluid Inc.
			Sanofi-Aventis U.S. LLC
			GoAhead Solutions

COMPUTER VISION AND NATURAL LANGUAGE PROCESSING TOOLS FOR VISUAL AND TEXT INTELLIGENCE

Some of the most common application areas of ML include Natural Language Processing, Speech, and computer vision. Natural Language Processing enables humans to communicate with computers in their natural language. NLP uses ML algorithms to find the semantic meaning of a word in a sentence. The neural network finds common patterns among the pronunciation of words and then maps new voice recordings to their corresponding text. With ML, it is also possible to synthesize the human voice. Computer Vision refers to replicating the complex human visual system. It enables computers to identify objects in images and videos.

SimpleCV is a framework for building computer vision applications. It helps to get access to various high-powered computer vision libraries such as OpenCV. It has been used for making motion detection projects like surveillance and monitoring systems (Kurt Demaagd, Anthony Oliver, Nathan Oostendorp, 2012; Sight Machine, 2020). **Detectron** is software open-sourced by Facebook AI Research. It uses state-of-the-art object detection algorithms, including Mask R-CNN to detect the given object. It provides many pre-trained models that support rapid implementation. These models provided by detectron are widely being used to make projects that handle large datasets including images (Jaggi & Templier, 2019; Liu, 2019). **Detectron2** is a ground-up rewrite of Detectron that started with mask can-benchmark. It includes high-quality implementations of state-of-the-art object detection algorithms, including panoptic feature pyramid networks, DensePose, and numerous variants of the pioneering Mask R-CNN model family developed by FAIR (Yuxin Wu, Alexander Kirillov, Francisco Massa, Wan-Yen Lo, 2019). **Stanford Core NLP** provides a set of natural language analysis tools. It makes it easy to apply a bunch of language analysis tools to a piece of text. It is designed to be highly flexible and extensible (Manning et al., 2014; Stanford, 2019). **BERT** is open-source software developed by Google for Natural Language Processing. It stands for Bidirectional Encoder Representation for Transformer. It helps the computers to interpret the message given by humans in their language. It is an expensive yet one-time expense to train a model for each language (Raj, 2019). **Librosa** is a Python package for audio and music signal processing. It provides implementations of a variety of common functions used in the field of Music Information Retrieval (McFee et al., 2015; Raguraman et al., 2019). **Magenta** is an open-source Python library, powered by TensorFlow. It incorporates features for manipulating source data, primarily music and images, to train ML models, and to generate new content using these models (Magenta, 2020). Table 3 shows details about some commonly used tools for Computer Vision, NLP, and Audio.

These software, when exposed to real-world situations face many different scenarios for which they are not trained in prior. It is difficult to train these machines for every situation. Hence there was a need for tools that can train these models by their own experience.

Table 3. ML tools for computer vision, NLP, and audio

Tool Name	Release Year	Developed By	License
SimpleCV	2011	Sight Machine	BSD license
Detectron	2018	Facebook	Apache 2.0
Detectron2	2019	Facebook	Apache 2.0
StandFord Core NLP	2018	StandFord NLP Group	GNU
BERT	2018	Google	MIT License
Librosa	2017	Librosa development team	ISC License
Magenta	2019	Google	Apache 2.0

PLATFORMS THAT AIDS IN TRAINING MODEL USING A REWARD-PENALTY BASED SYSTEM

Reinforcement Learning refers to a learning agent responding to the observation of its environment by choosing actions to maximize a special signal. Here the reward is just another signal that comes from the environment as a result of actions performed by the agent.

Project Malmo is an Artificial Experimentation Platform developed by Microsoft. It is built on the top of the renowned computer game Minecraft to support fundamental research in AI. It exposes the agent to a dynamic 3D environment and helps to expand the capabilities of present AI technology (Johnson et al., 2016; Microsoft, 2020a). **The Unity Machine Learning Agents** is an open-source Unity plugin that enables games and simulations to serve as environments for training intelligent agents. More complex environments give agents more complex and cognitive challenges that provide a flexible, quick, and efficient way to develop and test new AI algorithms (Juliani et al., 2018; Technologies, 2020).

Google Research Football Environment is an environment for Reinforcement Learning where agents are trained to master the football game. It provides a safe and quick platform to test reinforcement algorithms with a complex environment and varying difficulty levels (Karol Kurach, Research Lead and Olivier Bachem, Research Scientist, Google Research, 2020; Kurach et al., 2019). **OpenAI Gym** is an environment for testing reinforcement learning algorithms on different simulated environments to maximize the reward from interacting with that environment. Some papers show how OpenAI Gym is extended to be used in fields like robotics (Zamora et al., 2016) and Network Research (Gym, 2020; Zamora et al., 2016). **TensorFlow** helps to simulate multiple environments in parallel that helps the agents to be well trained for complex real-world problems (Hafner et al., 2017; TensorFlow, 2020a).

Keras is a high-level Neural network API that is capable of running on top of multiple back-ends including TensorFlow, CNTK, or Theano. It is a user-friendly API and is good for research as it enables fast experimentation (Daniel Falbel, JJ Allaire, François Chollet, RStudio, 2020). **DeepMind Lab** is a 3d-game platform designed to support research and development of general AI and ML systems (Beattie et al., 2016). It is used to train the agents to perform real-world complex tasks (Deep Mind, 2020). AlphaGo-a computer program developed by Google's Deep Mind division has set the record of being the first computer program to beat the professional player of the renowned game 'Go'. Doctors have found AlphaGo to be a potential application of ML in clinical medicine (HS Chang, MC Fu, J Hu, 2016; Zhongheng Zhang, 2016).

Once a model is ready to get data and generate insights from it, it is necessary to deploy these trained models in the existing environment to fulfill our needs. This process of deployment can be conveniently carried out using the tools available for model deployment

TOOLS THAT ASSIST IN EXECUTING THE DEPLOYMENT PROCESS

Model deployment is the last stage of ML life-cycle. Once the model is ready and starts generating practical insights from the patterns in the given data set, the next stage is to use these insights for some real-life purposes. This is achieved by integrating the ML model into the existing production environment. This is known as Model Deployment.

ML flow is an open-source platform that integrates ML and AI workflows. It is designed in a way that it can work with any ML library, algorithm, language and deployment tools. It can work with any cloud as well. It is also integrated with several ML frameworks like Apache Spark, Sci-kit-Learn, etc. Moreover, we can also use ML flow with existing code (Databricks, 2020).

TensorFlow.js is the library for performing mathematical computations but it is widely known for building neural networks that power some of the impressive AI Technology that we use today. Users must have a good knowledge of ML to use this software. There is no need for any installation we can use this on the browser itself. It supports Web Graphic Library and is available with GPU acceleration. We can also import pre-trained models that already exist and retrain the entire model using it (TensorFlow, 2020a).

TensorFlow Lite is TensorFlow's lightweight solution designed to make it easy to deploy ML models on mobiles and embedded devices. Its presently supported on Android and iOS (Tang, 2018; TensorFlow, 2020b). **CoreML** was launched by Apple in the annual developer conference WWDC. It is an ML framework used across Apple products. It has the advantage of offline availability as the application runs without an internet connection, privacy because data never leave the device and low cost because there is no data stored on the cloud (Inc, 2020).

With the recent boom in the field of ML many people including those who don't have the slightest idea about programming have shown interest in this domain. People who had good knowledge of mathematics, statistics, and data analytics but can't code needed tools with a graphical user interface for carrying out these processes without writing programs for it.

The following table shows some companies that use ML Flow and TensorFlow.js for the deployment process.

Table 4. Companies using intelligence tools for deployment

S.no	Tool Name	Purpose	Company
1.	**ML Flow**	MLflow is an open-source platform for managing the end-to-end ML lifecycle. It is used to keep track of experiments runs and results across frameworks. It can execute projects remotely on to a Databricks cluster, and quickly, reproduce the experiment runs. Quickly productionize models using Databricks production jobs, Docker containers, Azure ML, or Amazon SageMaker (StackShare, 2020).	Hepsiburada
			DLabs
2	**TensorFlow.js**	TensorFlow.js is a library for ML in JavaScript. for training and using ML models directly in the browser (Ben Gubler, 2019).	ADEXT
			Autea
			Taralite
			Polibase

TOOLS FOR NON-PROGRAMMERS, TO CARRY OUT MACHINE LEARNING PROCESSES

Many companies have launched GUI driven tools that obviate the programming aspects to become a data scientist. A person with minimal knowledge of algorithms can build high-quality ML models using these tools. Along with the intuitive GUI, these tools provide constructive workflow and a fully automated process.

Trifacta Wrangler provides an intuitive and powerful way to view, visualize, and prepare data of various types and formats. Data wrangling and cleaning are the most important features of trifacta. It can connect with various data sources. It monitors the data and performs data normalization by removing inconsistencies (Padmanabhan, 2019; Trifacta, 2020).

Paxata is an easy to use MS Excel-like application for data cleaning and preparation. It provides a user-friendly, powerful, and interactive interface to carry out data preparation. Thus helps to save time for data analysis rather than spending it on data preparation(Paxata, 2020).

Auto-Weka provides a wide range of ML algorithms to perform classification, regression, clustering, anomaly detection, association mining, data mining, etc. It allows developers to test their models on a varied set of possible test cases which helps them to select the model which gives the most precise output (Holmes et al., 1994; Machine Learning Group, 2019).

Datawrapper is an open-source tool that helps to create pie charts, line charts, bar charts, and maps, simply by loading the CSV dataset. It provides several designing options to make good looking charts without the need for actual designing skills. It also supports custom styling and live updating graphics (GmbH, 2020).

MLbase is one of the best open-source platforms to create large scale ML projects. The three main components of this tool are ML Optimizer, MLI, and MLib. It tests data on different models and checks which model provides maximum accuracy (UC Berkeley, 2020).

IBM Watson Studio is an AI-based tool used for extensive data analysis, ML, and data science. It can perform the entire end to end process in a span of a few minutes. It supports various languages like Python, R, etc. It provides drag and drop functionality to build complex ML models with ease (IBM, 2020b).

KNIME provides a drag and drop interface to create an entire data science workflow. It gives a platform to visually implement the entire model workflow, which is very useful while working on complex problem statements. It also provides APIs to integrate with Apache Hadoop. It is compatible with different data sourcing format which includes simple CSV files, PDFs, Excel sheets, etc. It also supports unstructured data formats like images and GIFs. It is further extended for next-generation sequencing data analysis (Jagla et al., 2011; KNIME, 2019). **Visualr** is a tool for data visualization that helps to visualize plain-text data in a pictorial form which helps to gain useful insights from data quickly and easily, simply by uploading the data set. Moreover, it connects with various data providers, including Oracle, MySQL, Excel, CSV, etc. It can also pull data from various online data APIs (S. Solutions, 2020).

MLJar is a browser-based platform with an intuitive interface that is used for fast building and deploying ML models. It comes with a built-in hyper-parameter search and allows training models in parallel. It provides a single interface for many ML Algorithms (MLJAR, 2019).

Amazon Lex helps to create applications that respond using voice and text. It has helped to bring the deep learning technology that powers Amazon Alexa in the reach of every developer (Sam Williams, 2018). With Amazon Lex, anyone can build a chatbot in minutes (Services, 2020).

Orange is a tool for data visualization and data mining (Demšar et al., 2013). It provides interactive data visualization using some amazing visuals like heat-maps, geo-maps, etc. It is widely used in schools and universities because of the hands-on-training it provides for various data science concepts. It supports the feature to add multiple add-ons to complement its feature set (University of Ljubljana, 2020).

Marketswitch Optimization is a mathematical decisioning software solution, focused on optimization, that enables customers to design the best strategies to solve complex business problems and meet organizational objectives. It helps to calculate the impact of every possible decision by evaluating competing business goals, contact protocols, operational constraints, and individual customer needs (E. I. Solutions, 2020).

Logical Glue is a GUI based platform that works from raw data to deployment. It is at the global forefront of Explainable AI (XAI) and helps businesses to unlock the exceptional technological power of AI and ML. It provides explainable, reliable, and interpretable human-centric solutions that deliver actionable insights that can pay dividends for business in the future (Temenos, 2019).

Pure Predictive is a tool that uses AI to create supermodels by combining 1000s of models. It helps a lot to increase the insights that businesses gain from their data by using advanced predictive modeling. It streamlines the process to model and deploys complex predictive models that allow businesses to transform their data warehouses into repositories of revenue (PurePredictive, 2020).

QlikView is one of the most accepted tools used by businesses across the globe. It doesn't provide statistics but has advantages in several other areas. However, its new-gen tool QlikSense is perfect in all areas. It manages to be a super powerful enterprise-scale with its Associative Engine & governed multi-cloud architecture (QlikTech, 2020). **Xpanse Analytics** is the creator of Xpanse AI. It is an automated predictive analytics platform that automates the complete predictive modeling workflow. It helps to reduce the time and cost of an enterprise. It understands the patterns driving customer behavior and provide actionable insights (AI, 2019).

BigML helps to make ML workflows easier. It provides a set of various tools that helps us to access and manage BigML resources even when we are not using our web UI or API (BigML, 2020a).**BigMLer,** an open-source command-line tool to automate ML workflows (BigML, 2020f), **BigML PredictServer** is used to perform millions of predictions in real-time (BigML, 2020d), **BigMLX,** a Mac OS X native app to build models and make predictions by just dragging and dropping on Mac Desktop (BigML, 2020g), **BigML Zapier app** to automate ML workflows (BigML, 2020e), **BigML Bindings** to build models, generate predictions and manage tasks in any preferred programming language (BigML, 2020b) and **BigML-GAS** (BigML, 2020c) are some of the tools provided by BigML.

H2O Driverless AI helps to accomplish ML tasks quickly and more effectively by using automation. It brings in data from various sources, understands it, and builds predictions automatically. Using its model can be deployed across various environments. It generates visualizations and data plots from given data which helps to analyze data before starting the model building process (H2O.ai., 2020).

DataRobot is known to be one of the best tools for data mining and feature extraction. It provides end to end data science solutions for real-world problems. It automatically identifies the most important features and builds a model around these features. It uses test cases to check which model helps to attain maximum accuracy. It is also known for incorporating model evaluation methods like parameter tuning etc (DataRobot, 2020).

Google Cloud AutoML is another tool that supports the entire data mining workflow and helps professionals with limited knowledge of data science to train high-end models that are specific to their business needs. It is integrated with many other google cloud services which help in data mining and data storage. It generates rest APIs while making predictions, which helps to connect with other tools(Google, 2020).

Rapidminer is one of the most widely used ML tools. It takes care of the entire data science workflow from data processing to data modeling and deployment. It provides a very intuitive GUI which can build predictive models to achieve precise outputs using drag and drop methods. It provides a powerful visual environment and comes with an inbuilt RapidMiner Hadoop which helps to integrate with the Hadoop framework for big data analysis. Data cleaning and Data wrangling can be easily done using RapidMiner (RapidMiner, 2014).

Table 5. Companies using Intelligence tools for carrying out various ML processes

S.no	Tool Name	Purpose	Company
1.	**Trifacta Wrangler**	Thousands of companies have switched to Trifacta Wrangler for data cleaning and preparation. It helps in analytics, ML & data onboarding initiatives across any cloud, hybrid and multi-cloud environment (Kelly, 2019).	Google
			Enstar
			CDC
			Pepsico
2	**Paxata**	Paxata is widely used by companies for preparing data collected from various sources, for data analytics software. It checks data quality issues, such as duplicates and outliers. Companies use it for de-duplicating of their marketing data and to improve their customer targeting (Nanduri, 2017).	AdhereHealth
			Cox Automotive
			Nationwide
			OnCourse Learning
3	**Data-Robot**	Data Robot is used by companies to automate their AI development. It enables organizations to leverage the transformational power of AI by delivering the AI platform combined with an AI-native strategic success team to help customers rapidly turn data into value (Magnus Unemyr, 2019).	Accenture
			Lenovo
			Panasonic
			United Airline
4	**Data Wrapper**	Data Wrapper enables business analysts to build predictive analytics without knowing the concepts of ML. Data wrapping uses analytics to make your products more valuable for customers (David Kokkelink, 2019).	Bletchley Park Trust
			intiGrow
			Social Investment Business
			Nesta Impact Investments
5	**KNIME**	KNIME assists companies to visually create data flows or pipelines, and to selectively execute some or all analysis steps, and later inspect the results, models, and interactive views. It is easy to use because of its intuitive and user-friendly GUI (Martyna Pawletta, 2020).	LEGO Group
			Bpost
			Unitedhealth Group
			ASML
7	**Amazon Lex**	Amazon Lex is an AWS service that helps enterprises to create chatbots through voice and text inputs in minutes without any coding knowledge (Vogels, 2017).	Citigroup
			Five9
			Volkswagen AG
			Adobe
8	**BigML**	BigML helps companies more efficiently by enabling multiple users to work on the same project from different accounts at different permission levels. It helps to improve productivity by breaking data silos and organizational barriers (maria jesus, 2019).	ABN AMRO
			Faraday
			Hired
			Mazda

The table given below shows some tools that are used for carrying out various ML processes without having any prior knowledge about algorithms and code. Companies use these tools for better customer targeting, for knowing the customer demand and to turn data into insights and actions for making more profit.

The following table shows the use of some of the intelligence tools for research and development. It contains the description of the approach used by the author and the data set he used along with the conclusion and results of the review or research.

Table 6. Various data analytics tools which are used for research and development along with the description of dataset and results

Tool Name	Author and Year	Methodology	Data Set	Result and Discussion
KNIME	(Syed Muzamil Basha, Dharmendra Singh Rajput, 2019)	Confusion matrix, Decision tree algorithm	Benchmarked and supervised dataset of 1400 records, containing data in the form of text as one of the attributes from UCI ML repository.	It can be concluded that the performance of the decision tree algorithm can be improved by selecting the term frequency as a feature in classifying the sentiment
	(Ranji et al., 2019)	K-means clustering, random forest, linear and polynomial regression	A total of 8241 data were extracted from the ChEMBL database in which 2069 were selected based on the inclusion of IC50 value.	This study indicated that the random forest with auto prediction validation method is the most reliable with the best R2 value of 0.9394. This study paved a way to a simpler process of drug discovery.
	(P. Mazanetz et al., 2013)	Bayes models, fuzzy rules, neural networks, decision tree models, linear and polynomial regression models, support vector machines, and supervised ML.	Datasets of chemical molecules and their activities against biological assays were taken from PubChem.	This review has examined the key features which distinguish KNIME is an open-source data mining platform for drug discovery and it has explored how the vast repository of KNIME nodes provides functionality to cover the diverse needs in a multidiscipline drug discovery environment.
Keras	(Jiang, 2019)	Convolutional Neural Network model, VGG16	Dataset of weeds images containing a total of 12 categories of 3,500 images was taken from Kaggle.	The model performs well with an accuracy of 91.08% in classifying 12 different types of weed images.
	(Kaur & Chhabra, 2014)	J48 Decision Tree	Dataset for this work contains 45 images from the Gold Standard Database.	This paper proves that the J48 Decision Tree Algorithm can achieve accuracy by up to 99.87%.
WEKA	(R.Ramya, Dr.P.Kumar, D.Mugilan, 2018)	Naïve Bayes, Decision tree, simple K-Means, Multilayer Perceptron, SVM, Random forest algorithm	The algorithms were applied on different datasets to compare different algorithms.	The results obtained suggests that among the tested algorithms, Naïve Bayes classifier has the potential to significantly improve the conventional classification methods and SVM performs with an average accuracy.
	(Ramzan, 2017)	J48, naïve-bayes and random-forest	The dataset about the "global burden of diseases "study for the year 1990 and 2010 for analysis taken from the GHDx.	The results show that Random Forest is best classifier for disease categorization of WEKA tool as it runs efficiently on large datasets.
	(Asri et al., 2016)	Support Vector Machine (SVM), Decision Tree (C4.5), Naïve Bayes (NB) and k Nearest Neighbors (k-NN)	Wisconsin Breast Cancer datasets	The results show that highest accuracy i.e. 97.13% was obtained by applying SVM on the given dataset.
Numpy,Scipy,Pandas	(Lemenkova, 2019)	Kernel Density Estimation, stacked area chart, special series of radar charts, stacked bar plots, stacked bar charts, scatterplot matrices	Dataset consists of 25 cross-section profiles having in total 12,590 bathymetric observation points across the Mariana Trench	This paper presented an approach for processing oceanographic data in big data sets on marine geology. The Python language and its libraries adequately perform statistical analysis and represent visualized graphs.
Stanford Core NLP and Hadoop	(ReddyP.Y.Sushmitha & M.Padma, 2016)	Extremely Randomized Trees classification	Raw data is from the Twitter by using Hadoop online streaming tool called Apache Flume	This paper has shown the way for responsibility sentiment analysis using Twitter data.

(Ramzan, 2017) analyzed the dataset about the "global burden of diseases "study for the years 1990 and 2010 using WEKA and found that Random Forest Classifier works best with WEKA. (Nelson et al., 2019) used various techniques on Wisconsin Breast Cancer datasets using R and found that most accurate results i.e. 97.65% were obtained using KNN whereas (Asri et al., 2016) analyzed the same dataset using WEKA and obtained 97.13% accuracy with SVM. (Becari et al., 2016) applied different algorithms on different datasets taken from the UCI ML repository using the same tool WEKA. He concluded that the performance of a classifier depends on the number of attributes in the dataset.(Kesavaraj & Sukumaran, 2013) analyzed the performance of different classification techniques on the Pima Indian Diabetes Data (PIDD) set and found that TANAGRA ML tool works best compared to WEKA and MATLAB for the given dataset. TANAGRA provides accuracy of 100% using Naïve Bayes classifier with training time 0.001 seconds.(R, 2015) conducted experiments on dataset taken from UCI Pima Indian diabetes repository using the frequently used algorithms and found that the J48 algorithm works the best for the dataset.

CONCLUSION

Collecting and Managing data is going on since old-age. The way of doing this work is getting advanced with time, according to the growing demand and new technological advancements. ML has been a widely discussed topic for the last few years.

Python is the widely-used programming language for data analytics because of the libraries it provides for processing the collected data. With the time volume of this data grew larger and emerged a need for big data tools. This large data was cleaned and prepared using various data mining tools that help to prepare this data for training models effectively. There are Computer Vision tools for helping computers to interpret visual data and react to it. NLP tools make it possible for computers to understand human speech patterns.

Reinforcement learning tools put models into a self-leaning mode and make it learn from its own experiences. Tools available for ML have made it easy for developers to build, train, test, and deploy their models. Many tools are being used in industry with millions of funding, some are widely being used by students, and some are at the nascent research stage. A lot of research is going on to discover new ways in which ML can help humanity both at an individual level and for society.

ACKNOWLEDGMENT

The survey for this chapter was carried out with the help of several Blogs, Websites, Research Papers, and other sources available on the web. We are grateful to them for their content about various Intelligence Tools. If we missed out on mentioning some sources here, please consider we are equally obliged to them also.

REFERENCES

H2O.ai. (2020). H2O Driverless AI. Retrieved from https://www.h2o.ai/products/h2o-driverless-ai/

AI. (2019). Retrieved from Xpanse AI. https://xpanse.ai/

Alatabi, H. A., & Abbas, A. R. (2020). Sentiment analysis in social media using machine learning techniques. *Iraqi Journal of Science*, *61*(1), 193–201. doi:10.24996/ijs.2020.61.1.22

Alfred, R. (2017). *The rise of machine learning for big data analytics*. Academic Press.

Aljumah, A. A., Ahamad, M. G., & Siddiqui, M. K. (2013). Application of data mining: Diabetes health care in young and old patients. Journal of King Saud University - Computer and Information Sciences, 25(2), 127–136. doi:10.1016/j.jksuci.2012.10.003

Amster, A. (2016). UC Apache spark. Retrieved from https://www.qubole.com/blog/apache-spark use-cases/

Anaconda. (2018). Numba. Retrieved from http://numba.pydata.org

Asri, H., Mousannif, H., Al Moatassime, H., & Noel, T. (2016). Using Machine Learning Algorithms for Breast Cancer Risk Prediction and Diagnosis. Procedia Computer Science, 83(Fams), 1064–1069. doi:10.1016/j.procs.2016.04.224

Basha & Rajput. (2019). *Classification of Sentiments from Movie Reviews Using KNIME*. Academic Press.

Beattie, C., Leibo, J. Z., Teplyashin, D., Ward, T., Wainwright, M., Küttler, H., Lefrancq, A., Green, S., Valdés, V., Sadik, A., Schrittwieser, J., Anderson, K., York, S., Cant, M., Cain, A., Bolton, A., Gaffney, S., King, H., Hassabis, D., & Petersen, S. (2016). DeepMind Lab. 1–11. Retrieved from https://arxiv.org/abs/1612.03801

Becari, W., Ruiz, L., Evaristo, B. G. P., & Ramirez-Fernandez, F. J. (2016). Comparative analysis of classification algorithms on tactile sensors. Proceedings of the International Symposium on Consumer Electronics, ISCE, 1–2. doi:10.1109/ISCE.2016.7797324

BerkeleyU. C. (2020). ML Base. http://www.mlbase.org/

Bhosale, H. S., & Gadekar, P. D. P. (2014). A review paper on big data and hadoop. *International Journal of Scientific and Research Publications*, *4*(10).

BigM. L. I. (2020a). BigML. Retrieved from https://bigml.com/tools

Big, M. L. I. (2020b). BigML Bindings. Retrieved from https://bigml.com/tools/bindings

Big, M. L. I. (2020c). BigML Gas. Retrieved from https://bigml.com/tools/bigml-gas

Big, M. L. I. (2020d). BigML Predict server. Retrieved from https://bigml.com/tools/predictserver

Big, M. L. I. (2020e). BigML Zapier app. Retrieved from https://bigml.com/tools/bigml-zapier-app

Big, M. L. I. (2020f). BigMLer. Retrieved from https://bigml.com/tools/bigmler

Big, M. L. I. (2020g). BigMLx. Retrieved from https://bigml.com/tools/bigmlx

Borthakur, D., Gray, J., Sen Sarma, J., Muthukkaruppan, K., Spiegelberg, N., Kuang, H., Ranganathan, K., Molkov, D., Menon, A., Rash, S., Schmidt, R., & Aiyer, A. (2011). Apache hadoop goes realtime at Facebook. *Proceedings of the ACM SIGMOD International Conference on Management of Data*, 1071–1080. 10.1145/1989323.1989438

Buczak, A. L., & Guven, E. (2016). A Survey of Data Mining and Machine Learning Methods for Cyber Security Intrusion Detection. IEEE Communications Surveys and Tutorials, 18(2), 1153 1176. doi:10.1109/COMST.2015.2494502

Cattuto, C., Quaggiotto, M., & Panisson, A. A. A. (2013). Time-varying social networks in a graph database: a Neo4j use case. https://dl.acm.org/doi/abs/10.1145/2484425.2484442

Chang, H. S., Fu, M. C., & Hu, J. S. M. (2016). Google DeepMind's AlphaGo.https://www.informs.org/ORMS-Today/Public-Articles/October-Volume-43-Number-5/GoogleDeepMind-s-AlphaGo

Chen, X., Ye, Y., Williams, G., & Xu, X. (2007). A survey of open source data mining systems. Lecture Notes in Computer Science, 4819 LNAI(60603066), 3–14. doi:10.1007/978-3-540-77018-3_2

Computation and Visualization environment. (2020). Data Melt. Retrieved from https://datamelt. org /

Databricks, I. (2020). MLflow. Retrieved from https://mlflow.org/

DataRobot. (2020). Data Robot. Retrieved from https://www.datarobot.com/

David Kokkelink, L. C. R. (2019). UC Data Wrapper. Retrieved from https://blog.datawrapper .de/create-datavisualization-for-free/

Demaagd, Oliver, & Oostendorp. (2012). Practical Computer Vision with SimpleCV: The Simple Way to Make Technology See. Academic Press.

Demšar, J., Curk, T., Erjavec, A., Gorup, Č., Hočevar, T., Milutinovič, M., ... Zupan, B. (2013). Orange: Data mining toolbox in python. *Journal of Machine Learning Research*, *14*, 2349–2353.

Developers, D. core. (2019). Dask. Retrieved from https://dask.org/

DevelopersS. (2020). SciPy. Retrieved from https://www.scipy.org/

Education, L. U. (2018). UC Apache Spark. Retrieved fromhttps://medium.com/@tao_66792/how-are-bigcompanies-using-apache-spark-413743dbbbae

Enlyft. (2020). UC Oracle data mining. Retrieved from https://enlyft.com/tech/products/oracle data-mining

Falbel, Allaire, & Chollet. (2020). Keras. Retrieved from https://keras .rstudio.com/index.html

FoundationP. S. (2020). Cython. Retrieved from https://pypi.org/project/Cython/

Foundation, T. A. S. (2018a). Apache Spark. Retrieved from https://spark.apache.org/

FoundationT. A. S. (2018b). Sqoop. Retrieved from https://sqoop.apache.org/

Foundation, T. A. S. (2019). ZooKeeper. Retrieved from https://zookeeper.apache.org/

FoundationT. A. S. (2020a). Hadoop. Retrieved from https://hadoop.apache.org/

FoundationT. A. S. (2020b). Hive. Retrieved from https://hive.apache.org/

Foundation., T. A. S. (2019). Pig. Retrieved from https://pig.apache.org/

Gmb, H. D. (2020). Data Wrapper. Retrieved from https://www.datawrapper.de/why-datawrapper/

Google. (2020). GoogleAutoML. Retrieved from https://cloud.google.com/automl/

Gubler, B. (2019). UC TensorFlow.js. https://blog.logrocket.com/tensorflow-js-an-intro-and analysis-with-use-cases-8e1f9a973183/

Gym. (2020). OpenAIgym. Retrieved from https://gym.openai.com/

Hafner, D., Davidson, J., & Vanhoucke, V. (2017). TensorFlow Agents: Efficient Batched Reinforcement Learning in TensorFlow. 1–8. https://arxiv.org/abs/1709.02878

Herrera, M., Torgo, L., Izquierdo, J., & Pérez-García, R. (2010). Predictive models for forecasting hourly urban water demand. *Journal of Hydrology (Amsterdam), 387*(1–2), 141–150. doi:10.1016/j.jhydrol.2010.04.005

Holmes, G., Donkin, A., & Witten, I. H. (1994). WEKA: A machine learning workbench. Australian and New Zealand Conference on Intelligent Information Systems - Proceedings, 357-361. 10.1109/anziis.1994.396988

Hunsinger, S., & Waguespaack, L. (2016). A Comparison of Open Source Tools for Data Science. *Journal of Information Systems Applied Research, 9*(2), 33.

IBM. (2020a). IBM Cognos. Retrieved from https://www.ibm.com/products/cognos-analytics

IBM. (2020b). IBM Watson. Retrieved from https://dataplatform.cloud.ibm.com/docs/con tent/wsj/gettingstarted/overview-ws.html

Inc, A. (2020). Core ML. Retrieved from https://developer.apple.com/machine-learning/core-ml/ intellipaat.com. (2016).

Insights, H. G. (2020). UC Apache Mahaout. https://discovery.hgdata.com/product/apache-mahout

Intellipaat. (2016). uc hadoop. IntelliPatt. Retrieved from https://intellipaat.com/blog/how-hadoop helps-companies-manage-big-data/

Jaggi, M., & Templier, T. (2019). *Software Tools for Handling Magnetically Collected Ultra-thin Sections for Microscopy*. Academic Press.

Jagla, B., Wiswedel, B., & Coppée, J. Y. (2011). Extending KNIME for next-generation sequencing data analysis. *Bioinformatics (Oxford, England), 27*(20), 2907–2909. doi:10.1093/bioinformatics/btr478

Jiang, Z. (2019). A Novel Crop Weed Recognition Method Based on Transfer Learning from VGG16 Implemented by Keras. *IOP Conference Series. Materials Science and Engineering, 677*(3), 032073. Advance online publication. doi:10.1088/1757-899X/677/3/032073

Johnson, M., Hofmann, K., Hutton, T., & Bignell, D. (2016). The malmo platform for artificial intelligence experimentation. *IJCAI International Joint Conference on Artificial Intelligence*, 4246–4247.

Juliani, A., Berges, V.-P., Vckay, E., Gao, Y., Henry, H., Mattar, M., & Lange, D. (2018). Unity: A General Platform for Intelligent Agents. https://arxiv.org/abs/1809.02627

Kaur, G., & Chhabra, A. (2014). Improved J48 Classification Algorithm for the Prediction of Diabetes. *International Journal of Computers and Applications*, *98*(22), 13–17. doi:10.520/17314-7433

Kelly, B. (2019). UC Trifacta. https://www.trifacta.com/blog/how-trifacta-is-helping-companies realize-the-massive-value-in-data/

Kesavaraj, G., & Sukumaran, S. (2013). A study on classification techniques in data mining. 2013 4th International Conference on Computing, Communications and Networking Technologies. ICCCNT 2013, 2013(March), 85–97. 10.1109/ICCCNT.2013.6726842

KNIME. (2019). KNIME. Retrieved from https://www.knime.com/software-overview

Kotsiantis, S. B. (2012). Use of machine learning techniques for educational proposes: A decision support system for forecasting students' grades. *Artificial Intelligence Review*, *37*(4), 331–344. doi:10.1007/s10462-011-9234-x

Kumar Jangir, S., Babel, V., & Kumar Singh, B. (2018). Evaluation methods for machine learning. *Journal of Analysis and Computation*, *11*, 1–6.

Kumar Jangir, S., Soni, L., & Goswami, A. (2019). Machine Translation : A Brief Overview. Journal of Analysis and Computation, 1–4.

Kurach, K. (2020). Research Lead and Olivier Bachem, Research Scientist, Google Research, Z. Google Research Football. Retrieved from https://ai.googleblog.com/2019/06/introducing google-research-football.html

Kurach, K., Raichuk, A., Stańczyk, P., Zając, M., Bachem, O., Espeholt, L., Riquelme, C., Vincent, D., Michalski, M., Bousquet, O., & Gelly, S. (2019). Google Research Football: A Novel Reinforcement Learning Environment. Retrieved from https://arxiv.org/abs/1907.11180

Lemenkova, P. (2019). Processing Oceanographic Data By Python Libraries Numpy, Scipy and Pandas. Aquatic Research, 2(2), 73–91. doi:10.3153/AR19009

Li, H., Leng, W., Zhou, Y., Chen, F., Xiu, Z., & Yang, D. (2014). Evaluation models for soil nutrient based on support vector machine and artificial neural networks. TheScientificWorldJournal, 2014, 1–8. doi:10.1155/2014/478569 PubMed

Liu, S. (2019). Detectron. Retrieved from https://github.com/facebookresearch/Detectron

Machine, S. (2020). SimpleCV. Retrieved from http://simplecv.org/

Machine Learning Group. U. of W. (2019). WEKA. Retrieved from https://www.cs.waikato.ac.nz/ml/weka

Magenta. (2020). Magenta. Retrieved from https://magenta.tensorflow.org/

Manning, C. D., Bauer, J., Finkel, J., & Bethard, S. J. (2014). The Stanford CoreNLP Natural Language Processing Toolkit. Aclweb.Org, 55–60. http://macopolo.cn/mkpl/products.asp

maria jesus. (2019). UC BigML. https://blog.bigml.com/2019/03/25/machine-learning-boosts startups-and-industry/

Mazanetz, P., Reisser, C. B. T., Marmon, R. J., & Morao, I. (2013). Drug Discovery Applications for KNIME: An Open Source Data Mining Platform. *Current Topics in Medicinal Chemistry*, *12*(18), 1965–1979. doi:10.2174/1568026611212180004 PubMed

McFee, B., Raffel, C., Liang, D., Ellis, D., McVicar, M., Battenberg, E., & Nieto, O. (2015). librosa: Audio and Music Signal Analysis in Python. Proceedings of the 14th Python in Science Conference, Scipy, 18–24. doi:10.25080/Majora-7b98e3ed-003

Microsoft. (2020a). ProjectMalmo. Retrieved from https://www.microsoft.com/en us/research/project/projectmalmo/

Microsoft. (2020b). SQL Data tools. Retrieved from https://visualstudio.microsoft.com/vs/features/ ssdt/

Mind, D. (2020). DeepMind. https://deepmind.com/blog

MLJAR. (2019). ML Jar. Retrieved from https://mljar.com/blog/

Mongo, D. B. I. (2020). MongoDB. Retrieved from https://www.mongodb.com/hadoop-and mongodb

Murillo, D. J. H. (2019). UC neo4j. Retrieved from https://neo4j.com/news/graph-database-tech elping-improve-businesses-telcos-airbnb/

Nanduri, P. (2017). UC Paxata. Stravium Intelligence LLP. Retrieved from https://www.analytics insight.net/paxatabridging-link-data-business-value/

Neo4j, I. (2020). Neo4j. Retrieved from https://neo4j.com/

Nelson, A., Sunny, B. M., Joseph, J., Shelly, M., & George, S. (2019). Breast cancer prediction techniques : A review. *National Conference in Emerging Computer Applications (NCECA2019)*, 24–26.

Olavsrud, T. (2019). UC IBM Cognos. Retrieved from https://www.cio.com/article/3391920/5 ways-ibmcognos-analytics-is-transforming-business.html

Padmanabhan, A. (2019). Trifacta Wrangler. Devopedia. https://devopedia.org/wrangle-language

Paul, M., Vishwakarma, S. K., & Verma, A. (2016). Analysis of Soil Behaviour and Prediction of Crop Yield Using Data Mining Approach. Proceedings - 2015 International Conference on Computational Intelligence and Communication Networks, CICN 2015, 766–771. 10.1109/CICN.2015.156

Pawletta, M. (2020). UC KNIME. Retrieved from https://www.knime.com/blog?page=1

Paxata. (2020). Paxata. Retrieved from https://www.paxata.com/machine-learning/

PurePredictive. (2020). Pure Predictive. Retrieved from https://www.purepredictive.com/

QlikTech. (2020). QLIK. Retrieved from https://www.qlik.com/us

R, S. (2015). Performance Analysis of Different Classification Methods in Data Mining for Diabetes Dataset Using WEKA Tool. International Journal on Recent and Innovation Trends in Computing and Communication, 3(3), 1168–1173. doi:10.17762/ijritcc23218169.150361

Raguraman, P., Mohan, R., & Vijayan, M. (2019). LibROSA Based Assessment Tool for Music Information Retrieval Systems. Proceedings - 2nd International Conference on Multimedia Information Processing and Retrieval, MIPR 2019, 109–114. doi:10.1109/MIPR.2019.00027. 2019.00027

Rahman, M. M., Haq, N., & Rahman, R. M. (2014). Machine Learning Facilitated Rice Prediction in Bangladesh. Proceedings - 2014 Annual Global Online Conference on Information and Computer Technology, GOCICT 2014, 1–4. doi:10.1109/GOCICT.2014.9

Raj, B. S. (2019). BERT. Retrieved from https://towardsdatascience.com/understanding-bert-is-it a-game-changer-in-nlp-7cca943cf3ad

Ramya, Kumar, & Mugilan. (2018). A Review of Different Classification Techniques in Machine. Academic Press.

Ramzan, M. (2017). Comparing and evaluating the performance of WEKA classifiers on critical diseases. India International Conference on Information Processing, IICIP 2016 - Proceedings. 10.1109/IICIP.2016.7975309

Ranji, R., Thanavanich, C., Sukumaran, S. D., Kittiwachana, S., Zain, S., Sun, L. C., & Lee, V. S. (2019). *Progress in Drug Discovery & Biomedical Science An automated workflow by using KNIME Analytical Platform : a case study for modelling and predicting HIV-1 protease inhibitors*. Academic Press.

RapidMiner. (2014). Rapid Miner. Retrieved from http://edutechwiki.unige.bch/en/RapidMine r _ Studio

Rocklin, M. (2015). Dask: Parallel Computation with Blocked algorithms and Task Scheduling. Proceedings of the 14th Python in Science Conference, Scipy, 126–132. doi:10.25080/Majora-7b98e3ed-013

SAS Institute Inc. (2020). SAS Visual Data Mining. Retrieved from https://www.sas.com/ en_us /software/visualdata-mining-machine-learning.html

Services, A. W. (2020). Amazon Lex. Retrieved from https://aws.amazon.com/lex/

Sharma, R., Thanvi, A., Menghani, B., Kumar, M., & Kumar Jangir, S. (2019). *An Approach towards Information Retrieval through Machine Learning and its Algorithms: A Review*. Academic Press.

Software. T. (2020). Tableau. Retrieved from https://www.tableau.com/

Solutions, E. I. (2020). MarketSwitchOptimisation. Retrieved from http://www.experian. com/ decision analytics/marketswitch-optimization.html

SolutionsS. (2020). VisualAR. Retrieved from https://visualrsoftware.com/index.html

SPSS Inc. (2015). SPSS. Retrieved from http://www.spss.com.hk/software/modeler/

StackShare. (2020). UC ML Flow. Retrieved from https://stackshare.io/mlflow

Stanford. (2019). Stanford NLP. Retrieved from https://stanfordnlp.github.io/CoreNLP/

Sushmitha & Padma. (2016). *Sentiment Analysis on Twitter by using Machine*. Academic Press.

Tableau Software LLC. (2020). UC Tableau. Retrieved from https://www. tableau.com/solutions/high-technology-analytics

Talend. (2020). Retrieved from Talend. https://www.talend.com/

Tang, J. (2018). Intelligent Mobile Projects with TensorFlow. Packt. Retrieved from https://books.google.com/books

Technologies, U. (2020). Unity 3d. Retrieved from https://unity3d.com/machine-learning

Tehrani. (2019). UC Teradata. Retrieved from https://blog.tmcnet.com/blog/rich tehrani/fow/teradata-simplifies advanced-analytics-with-new-solutions-for-future-of-work.html

Temenos. (2019). LogicalGlue. Retrieved from https://www.logicalglue.com/

TensorFlow. (2020a). TensorFlow. Retrieved from https://www.tensorflow.org/

TensorFlow. (2020b). TensorFlowLite. Retrieved from https://www.tensorflow.org/lite

Teradata. (2020). TeraData. Retrieved from https://www.teradata.com/

Thanvi, A., Sharma, R., Menghani, B., Kumar, M., & Kumar Jangir, S. (2019). Bitcoin Exchange Rate Price Prediction Using Machine Learning Techniques. *RE:view*.

The Apache Software Foundation. (2020a). Apache Mahout. Retrieved from http://mah out.apache.org/

The Apache Software Foundation. (2020b). Hbase. Retrieved from https://hbase.apache.org/

Thusoo, A., Sen Sarma, J., Jain, N., Shao, Z., Chakka, P., Zhang, N., Antony, S., Liu, H., & Murthy, R. (2010). Hive - A petabyte scale data warehouse using hadoop. Proceedings - International Conference on Data Engineering, 996–1005. 10.1109/ ICDE.2010.5447738

Togaware. (2019). Rattle. Retrieved from https://rattle.togaware.com/

Totoni, E., Anderson, T. A., & Shpeisman, T. (2017). HPAT: High performance analytics with scripting ease-of-use. Proceedings of the International Conference on Supercomputing, Part F1284. doi:10.1145/3079079.3079099

Trifacta. (2020). Trifacta Wrangler. https://www.tracifacta.com/data-analysis-tools/

UC SAS. (2018). uc sas data mining. https://intellipaat.com/blog/what-is-sas-analytics/

Unemyr, M. (2019). UC Data Robot. Retrieved from https://www.unemyr.com/automl datarobot/

University of Ljubljana. (2020). Orange. https://orange.biolab.si/

Van der Aalst, W. (2016). Process mining: Data science in action. Process Mining: Data Science in Action, April 2014, 1–467. doi:10.1007/978-3-662-49851-4

VantaraH. (2020). Pentaho. Retrieved from https://www.hitachivantara.com/en-us/products/data man-agementanalytics/pentaho-platform.html

Virtanen, P., Gommers, R., Oliphant, T. E., Haberland, M., Reddy, T., Cournapeau, D., Burovski, E., Peterson, P., Weckesser, W., Bright, J., van der Walt, S. J., Brett, M., Wilson, J., Millman, K. J., Mayorov, N., Nelson, A. R. J., Jones, E., Kern, R., Larson, E., & Vázquez-Baeza, Y. (2020). SciPy 1.0: Fundamental algorithms for scientific computing in Python. *Nature Methods*, *17*(March), 261–272. Advance online publication. doi:10.1038/s41592-019-0686-2 PubMed

Vogels, W. (2017). UC Amazon Lex. Retrieved from https://www.allthingsdistributed.com /2017/06/amazonconnect-with-amazon-lex.html

Vyas, A., & Jangir, S. K. (2019). Advances in approach for Object Detection and classification. Na#onal Conference on Informa#on Technology & Security Applications, 978, 1–3.

Williams, G. J. (2009). Rattle: A data mining GUI for R. *The R Journal*, *1*(2), 45–55. doi:10.32614/RJ-2009-016

Williams, S. (2018). Amazon Lex. Packt. Retrieved from https://books.google.com

Wu, K. Massa, & Lo. (2019). Detectron 2. Retrieved from https://ai.facebook.com/blog/-detectron2-a-pytorch-based-modular-object detection-library-/

Zamora, I., Lopez, N. G., Vilches, V. M., & Cordero, A. H. (2016). Extending the OpenAI Gym for robotics: a toolkit for reinforcement learning using ROS and Gazebo. August. https://arxiv.org/abs/1608.05742

Zhang, Y., Oussena, S., Clark, T., & Kim, H. (2010). Use data mining to improve student retention in higher education: A case study. ICEIS 2010 - Proceedings of the 12th International Conference on Enterprise Information Systems, 1, 190–197. 10.5220/0002894101900197

Zhang, Z. (2016). When doctors meet with AlphaGo: potential application of machine learning to clinical medicine. https://www.ncbi.nlm.nih.gov/pmc/articles/PMC4828734/

KEY TERMS AND DEFINITIONS

Artificial Intelligence: Domain of science that deals with the development of computer systems to perform actions like speech-recognition, decision-making, understanding human's natural language, etc., like humans.

Big Data: It refers to a massive volume of structured or unstructured data that is difficult to be processed by traditional data management tools.

Computer Vision: Domain in science that deals with the use of computers in understanding and automating the tasks that a human visual system can do.

Contrived: Something that has not arisen naturally, rather it has been created deliberately or artificially.

Data-Mining: It refers to the process of obtaining useful insights from large datasets by using statistical methods to find patterns followed throughout the dataset.

Data-Science: Field of Science that concerns with the cleansing, preparation and final analysis of data using programming, logical reasoning, mathematics, and statistics.

Deep Learning: Sub-domain in the field of machine learning that deals with the use of algorithms inspired by human brain cells to solve complex real-world problems.

Deployment: The process of putting a resource into action in real-world scenarios.

Machine Learning: It refers to developing the ability in computers to use available data to train themselves automatically, and to learn from its own experiences without being explicitly programmed.

Model: In the context of machine learning, model refers to a transformation engine that helps to express a mathematical problem.e to express the dependent variables as a function of independent variables.

Natural Language Processing: Sub-domain of artificial intelligence that deals with programming of computers to process large amount of natural language data.

Chapter 6
Data Analysis in Context–Based Statistical Modeling in Predictive Analytics

Selvan C.
National Institute of Technology, Tiruchirappalli, India

S. R. Balasundaram
National Institute of Technology, Tiruchirappalli, India

ABSTRACT

Data analysis is a process of studying, removing non-required data in the view level, and converting to needed patterns for sub decisions to make an aggregated decision. Statistical modeling is the process of applying statistical techniques in data analysis for taking proactive decisions depend requirements. The statistical modeling identifies relationship between variables, and it encompasses inferential statistics for model validation. The focus of the chapter is to analyze statistical modeling techniques in different contexts to understand the mathematical representation of data. The correlation and regression are used for analyzing association between key factors of companies' activities. Especially in business, correlation describes positive and negative correlation variables for analyzing the factors of business for supporting the decision-making process. The key factors are related with independent variables and dependent variables, which create cause and effect models to predict the future outcomes.

INTRODUCTION

Data Analysis is defined as finding useful information from existing data and it is used for making concrete decision in critical situations in different areas such as business levels, science, engineering, education etc. In business, decision making process is simplified using business intelligence techniques and company's managers can analyze the performance of company during needs (Scholz et al., 2010). The role of business intelligence is ensured by the impact of performance of business process (Davenport, 2010; Foley & Guillemette 2010). The management point of view, inductive research approach

DOI: 10.4018/978-1-7998-3053-5.ch006

and design with qualitative methods is used for evaluating the business performance to produce cost effective analysis model. For quality management, practical knowledge with theory influenced with business intelligence process (Xia & Gong, 2015). In different levels of business, to challenge the business competitions, managers inclined with scientific solutions as it is used univariate statistics, bivariate associations and multivariate iterations. The univariate and multivariate associations are applied in medical field for analyzing heart decease symptoms and prediction (Baker et al., 2009). The purpose of business analytics is to make immediate analysis of issues for taking instant decision to ensure the business success in critical situation. The business performance aims to meet optimized solution in time. Wide-ranging usage of values or data is utilized by the statistical models to take decisions for supporting management of an organization is called business analytics (Davenport & Harris, 2007; Soltanpoor & Sellis, 2016). In data analysis, various research areas are involved to strengthen the information evaluation like operation research, information retrieval, data science and machine learning (Mortenson, Doherty, & Robinson, 2015). In these circumstances, different models including descriptive analytics has the way for new insights for supporting critical decisions which leads to improve business performance. Finally, the business analytics performances are analyzed in all the ways to face the challenges of competitors (Mikalef et al., 2018; Vidgen & Grant, 2017).

BACKGROUND

Data Analytics is defined as extracting meaningful information continuously with the assistance of specialized system which facilitates modeling the data, information transformation and organization of functions for finding patterns to get feasible solution. It has become an essential process for many companies to take out solution from huge volume of regular storing data in a system for best solution in business context like Google, twitter, Amazon, yahoo etc(Davenport & Jill, 2013). The industries, collected data from different organization might be used for new business income streams and data analytics process involves functions of data collection, sorting and processing to ensure the effectiveness of the data for providing reliable result (Russom, 2013). The data analysis generates an important interest in business intelligence to assist to detect market scenario for making decision in short span of time and higher profit (Chen, Roger, & Veda, 2012). The growth of data analytics has been facing many issues like programming, non-supporting of whole business services. As the datasets volume is so huge, the tools are not able to manage and evaluate the process of operations in time within the cost limit (Jiang & Chai, 2016). The establishment of business processes using business analytics is widely accepted by most of the business industries (Wang & Zhao, 2016). As data analytics is the essential to the business development, each and every operation of business try to accommodate the system facilities in the maximum level for getting feasible solution. The higher facilities are the opportunities of business evaluation in all the ways. The adaptation of new approaches leads to evaluate the available data for best solution based on context (Sosna et al., 2010).

LITERATURE REVIEW

Data Analytics in Business

Data analytics is the analyzing of behavior of a system for finding insights from available information and it is the process of analyzing data to generate patterns for decision making options in business process evaluation (Shirish, Sneha, & Yogesh, 2018). The data analytics methods are classified into three types such as descriptive analytics, predictive analytics and prescriptive analytics where information passed through insights, decision to reach action in business management. In which, the predictive analytics is the process of predicting the future from the existing data using statistical techniques and machine learning algorithms (Vaibhav & Garg, 2018). The umbrella of all type of data analysis is marked as Data science which is the process of extracting knowledge and insights from a multi-disciplinary system (Christophe & Stephane, 2018). As a system acts continuously, a large volume of data generated is called big data. When analyzing a large volume of data, the possibility of output accuracy increases but in other end complexity of system is more concerned (David et al., 2019).

In general, data analytics expect results from the processed data in order to find hindsight, insight, foresight, and finally towards optimized solutions (Chandrima, Siddharth, & Manjusha, 2018). And all the new things find out from data related to time and scientific methods. In day to day life, events occurrences associated with time sequences which can be identified based on incident date and time; fortunately the temporal data accompanied with location information in many applications like predicting location of a culprit, traffic jam, accident zone, rainfall of a region etc (Pal et al., 2019).

Methodology

In data analyzing process, time sequences could be classified into three major divisions such as past, present and future. The past incidents data considered as history of incidents data, which is named as sequence patterns. The present time incident data indicates the current position of an event related with time and location for next immediate move. The future time data can be predicted using sequence pattern and current event information (Sofya et al., 2019).

As shown in figure 1, the temporal based dimensions are segregated into five data analytics for convenience such as diagnostic, descriptive, cognitive, prescriptive and predictive analytics. The source of data for data analyzing and processing starts from human behaviors and system operations which are accumulated for better choices and future references (Zhenhua, Yangsen, & Dangchen, 2018).

Statistics is the scientific methods for figuring out the solution through quantitative data by collecting and analyzing data. The definition of a statistical model is assumptions of sample data from a huge volume of data with mathematical analysis for giving solution which concludes that the value is nearer to expected value. The Statistics is divided into two main branches such as descriptive statistics and inferential statistics. Descriptive statistics refers the finding of mean or standard deviation from sample using indexes. Inferential statistics defines the subject to random variations from process of closely observing errors or sampling variations of population (Gupta & Kapoor, 2013).

Predictive analytics is defined as the finding of new patterns to analyze future performance of a system based on context and historical information. It is segregated into two types, such as predictive modeling and Statistical modeling. Predictive modeling is a process of data mining and probability principles to predict what next using data. In prediction operation, there are n variables influenced to

Figure 1. Classification of data analytics based on temporal dimensions

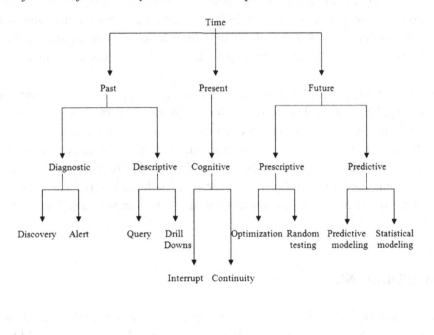

the result or solution. Statistical modeling is used for analyzing data from statistics to infer the relationship among the variables to get useful and new insights. For example in business intelligence, banking relationship parameters are loan default, balance amount, car loan, housing loan, salary etc (Poornima, & Pushpalatha., 2018).

The definition of Descriptive analytics is the process of data visualization with the facilities of generating reports, displaying scorecards, and dashboard is a well defined system. And it is also a statistical method which is used for summarizing historical data to indentify sequence patterns and defined as what happened certain period of time (Faizura et al., 2017). For example, in mobile networks, the movements of the mobile phone users are analyzed to predict the needs of a new base station to provide quality of services for customers.

Cognitive analytics is an iterative learning process of knowledge base for future inferences and it reflects the knowledge of human brain in the process of data analysis. And it is described as applying of various contexts information like text, voice, image, gesture and videos in a system for the purpose of gaining knowledge to decision making process using Artificial Intelligence, Machine Learning, Deep Learning and Semantics methods (Gutierrez-Garcia & Lopez-Neri, 2015). In which, the analytics process finds the solutions from the huge volume of hidden data which is collected from multi-source continuously.

Diagnostic analytics is the process of examining of data for taking deeper look for understanding the causes of behavior in a system and it describes what the reason for happening something in a business. For example, a battery company announced incentives for their dealers the month of June, the end of the year it diagnosis the impact of the incentives in battery sales for particular month. In another context, an ice cream company diagnoses the impact of weather condition in the month of December for analyzing the sales and production ratio. In earlier days, all these process was manually done by experienced analyst to find patterns, anomalies and analyzing relationships between variables. However, there is no guarantee for consistent outcome as it is variety in information, huge volume data and velocity of the data ever increasing continuously (Uskov et al., 2019). Nowadays, machine learning methods are used for diagnostic analytics to avoid the earlier day's contradictions and to reduce the bias in decision making process.

The definition of prescriptive analytics is creating business value, expects best solution for future problem and increasing the ability of data analytics process. In which business improvement is the major focus towards optimized solution for the current and future issues. Prescriptive Analytics is the process of supporting technology to make better decision from an available data. In particular, it analyses all possible situations or scenarios, past history, present performance, suggestions and strategies to take optimized decision (Lepenioti et al., 2020). It represents the both descriptive analytics and predictive analysis. For example, self driving car which works based on two things like environment and moving direction of car.

STATISTICAL MODELING

Statistical modeling plays major role in predictive analytics and it manipulates the data using mathematical representations as per the needs of contexts. In business, general information could be interpreted to fit for computation process, for example sales promotional activities will reflect in the company's expenses prediction. The information interpretation may be varied by domain expert's perception but considering quantitative analysis and mathematical techniques which lead to meet a feasible solution. For example in a company risk analysis, problems could be reviewed in different direction for a simple solution. In statistical model, continuous refinement is done using algorithms and rules related to applications. Nowadays, domain experts believe that statistical models lead their business and predict the business risk in advance. The others business data is accessed through conferences and communications to get outside knowledge about business and issues. For this, enormous techniques are used for continuing the business in the right direction without risk. To analyze all combinations and variances of variables, statistical measures are evidence to record for future use and communicate to others related to needs.

As shown in figure 2, data is collected from different scenarios like historical data, new data and both are coined as patterns, followed that statistical techniques are applied to get predictive models for meeting decision making process. The decision making process includes different criteria like business rules, decision trees, assumptions towards requirements.

Statistics and its Applications

Statistics refers to the scientific methodology which equipped with collecting and analyzing data to figure out valid result using suitable methods in the sense of decision making process. The result is not exactly correct but it is very close to the estimated value which can said to be equal. In hypothesis testing, it cannot be assured the judgment is exactly correct but the chance for wrong judgment is very small. The applications of statistics are nutrition analysis, pollution analysis, designing policies and management in business, analysis of decease prediction, genetic analysis, self driving flight, understanding economic problems etc specifically in business it is viewed for,

Figure 2. Process of predictive analytics

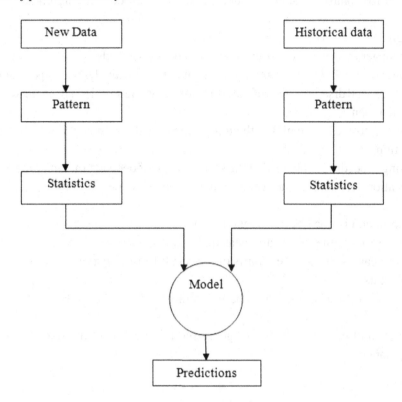

- Deciding new plant location
- Formulating a sales plan
- Expanding established plant
- Introducing new products etc

For instance, deciding for a new plant location, a few points has to be considered like most suitable location, excellent climate and availability of adequate labor, raw materials, markets for selling, transporting facilities for products and employees, cost of living, political climate, tax laws etc.

Decision Making Process in Statistics

The Government and private statisticians typically divide the process into four phases as shown in figure 3, which is study design, data collection, data analysis for solution of a problem.

Figure 3. Phases and steps of the statistical decision making process

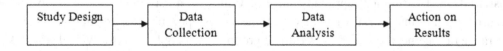

The functions of four phases of statistical decision making process are highlighted as below,

1. Study Design:
    a. The manager frames the questions related to business needs
    b. Alternative procedures for sampling, data collection and analysis are specified by statistician.
    c. Advantages and disadvantages of the alternative feasible solution are evaluated by the manager and statistician.
    d. Strategy of cost and essential of the information for the company is selected by the manager.
2. Data Collection:
    a. Sampling procedure is planned in the second stage of decision making process by Statistician
    b. Observations are chosen and recorded in the second stage
3. Data Analysis:
    a. The estimation is done by statistical methods
    b. Possible errors in the results are measured and computed
    c. Decision makers receive the reports of the result from statistician
4. Action on Results
    a. The management takes the action based on the results of the study

Though the context of the activities is changed, general functions of the statistical decision making process does not change.

DESCRIPTIVE STATISTICS (DS)

Summaries of a sample and measures of data describe the basic features of data is called descriptive statistics. In addition, all the quantitative analysis of data shows in the graphics analysis form for virtually understanding. DS differs with Inferential Statistics (IS) as it shows that what the data is or what the data display. IS derives information from sample data to conclude that what the population would like to convey. The DS is used for displaying quantitative information in a simple and convenient form without deviation in the value, for example large amount of data converted as a single average value which describes large number of discrete numbers.

Univariate Analysis

In Univariate analysis, only one variable is used at a time but single variable viewed as in three perceptions such as distribution, central tendency and dispersion. The univariate is a single variable data sets and it stores a single piece of information for each item. For instance, the income level of people through marketing survey reveals the distribution of incomes, particular income level, variation in the income level and the count of the within the range of the income.

1. **Distribution:** Distribution represents range of values for a variable which tends to summary of occurrences. For instance, the people of income varies upto 'n' numbers, in this case to simplify the range of income, the Indian Government grouped the people into two typical ways like below the poverty line and above the poverty line according to their incomes. In another case, the range

of income slabs grouped into four or five groups for income tax payments and the representation of frequency of occurrences in the each range of values is called frequency distribution.

As shown in figure 4, it is depicted through a table for visual understanding of ages distribution of frequency occurrences and it shows the people's ages versus population of living an area.

Figure 4. Frequency distributions

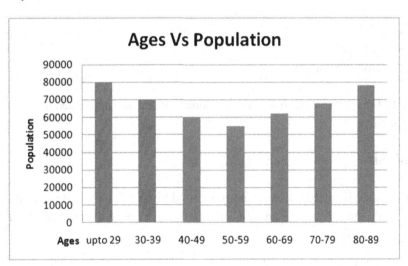

The distribution can be represented as percentages, like various incomes, ages, testing values. In frequency distribution, the main consideration is determining number of classes and deciding the size of the classes.

2. **Central Tendency:** Central Tendency of distribution depicts the estimate of center values which has three types such as mean, median, and mode.

   a. Mean: $\text{Mean}(x) = \dfrac{Sx}{n}$; x is a variable taking different observational values & n = no. of observations, Sx is sum of values of a variable.

In a simple way, $Mean = \dfrac{sum\ of\ testing\ values}{number\ of\ values}$

   b. Median: When observations are arranged in ascending or descending order of magnitude, the middle most value is known as Median.
   c. Mode: In a set of values which occurs most frequently is called mode. For finding the mode of values, the values are ordered.

3. **Dispersion:** Dispersion is a variation in values of same item in different places. The range and standard deviation are the measures of dispersion.

In general, range indicates that Range=highest value – lowest value, Standard Deviation (SD) is the amount of variation of set of values (Bland & Altman, 1996) which represents the square root values of variance for random variable, statistical population, data set, probability distribution etc. SD is often called standard error. The standard deviation is computed as follows, Standard deviation $= \sqrt{\dfrac{\Sigma\left(X - \bar{X}\right)^2}{n-1}}$, where

- X is each score
- $\bar{x}$ is the average
- n is the number of values
- Σ means sum across the values

The square root of the sum of the squared deviations from the mean divided by the number of scores minus one is called SD.

Bivariate Analysis

Two piece of information is stored for every item is called bivariate data. The relationship between two variables is measured using statistical analysis. Predicting the value of one variable is possible when given another value of variable.

Multivariate Analysis

In multivariate data sets, there may be three or more piece of information stored for every item and the interrelationship between all multivariate are analyzed by statistical analysis models. The combining of all variables put together is an estimation analysis to predict the future result (Fangxuan et al., 2019). The multivariate techniques are applied in different contexts like cancer patient response to radiotherapy, developing an index of performance for athletes, developing a rule for separating people who affected by virus, several colleges performances based on common policy implementations etc.

CORRELATION AND REGRESSION

Correlation defined as the degree of relationship between two or more factors or variables. It does not reflect cause and effect relationship between the factors. It is a relative measure and is independent of the units of measurement. The regression denotes the average relationship between two or more factors. It has the cause and effect relationship (David, 2009) between the factors in which cause represents the independent factor (covariates or predictor) and effect is the dependent factor (outcome variable or response).

In statistical modeling, the most commonly known and expected is linear regression which expresses the gradual increase of the both value of x and y axis when plot a graph between independent and dependent factors. For example, let's take the common truth of income, a person salary increases year by

Figure 5. Linear regression

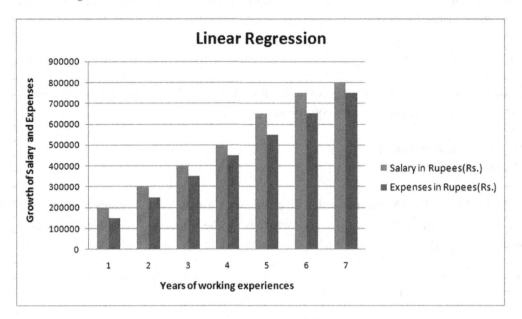

year and his expenses also increases. As shown in figure 5, the x axis is year, salary and his expenses represented in y axis.

Applications of Regression

The regression is applied in different applications for analyzing the various factors of real world environments for decision making process. The applications are,

- Cause and effect in real life
- Rate of change in one variable in term of another variable
- Economic analysis - cost of living increase as consumable and non-consumable prices increase
- Prediction of unknown values in medical field and location analysis
- Determining coefficient of correlation
- Study the nature of relationship between factors

Regression Analysis

Regression analysis is often done by company managers to take decision using key relationship factors and the changes happening between factors are analyzed using regression analysis process. The regression analysis process is used for finding the deficiency and strong bond between factors for taking decision in critical. In general, the statistical processes estimate the relationship between a dependent variable and independent variables; in addition it encompasses unknown parameters and error terms. Predicting the future event, based on existing data sets is possible using regression models and methods. In instance, to improve the marketing process of a company, prediction of marketing demand on the basis of price and advertising expenditure combinations which is used for evaluating the potential changes in a company's marketing strategies and policies.

1. Types of regression lines:

A regression line is a line to best approximate the value of X, for any given value of other variable. There are two types of regression lines considered, namely,

a. Regression line of X on Y
b. Regression line of Y on X

Regression line of X on Y, the line which gives the best estimate for the values of X for an identified value of Y, it is written as $X-\bar{X} = b_{xy}(Y-\bar{Y})$, where b_{xy} is the regression coefficient of X on Y, which is computed using any of the formula under the nature of data.

$$b_{xy} = \frac{\sum xy}{\sum y^2}, \text{ where } x = X-\bar{X} \text{ and } y = Y-\bar{Y}$$

(or)

$$b_{xy} = r\frac{\sigma_x}{\sigma_y},$$

where 'r' is the correlation coefficient, σ_x and σ_y are the standard deviations for X and Y series.

Regression line of Y on X, the line gives the best estimate for the values of Y for an identified value of X. It is written as $Y-\bar{Y} = b_{yx}(X-\bar{X})$, where b_{yx} is the regression line of Y on X, it is computed using any one of the formula depending upon the nature of the data.

$$b_{yx} = \frac{\sum xy}{\sum x^2}, \text{ where } x = X-\bar{X} \text{ and } y = Y-\bar{Y}$$

2. Estimating the sales price based on purchase and sales history

In general, in a business purchasing and selling is a process of business. In which, for meeting profit, fixing the product price with constant percentage of profit is a one of the reasons for failure of business because most of the cases, the business environment is varying based on the seasons in a year. Therefore the purchase and sales history based data analysis is used for predicting or supporting for price fixing for a product using regression methods.

Let's assume the data as shown in table 1, the prices of a product in a year varying based on seasons. The purchasing of a product for business expects to meet the profit only. The purchase and sales are interdependent in a business, purchase depends on sales and sales depend on purchase related to context. The table 2 shows the computational processes for analyzing purchase and sales data.

Table 1. A Product purchase and sales in a year

Sales in Rs.(X)	1	97	108	121	67	124	51	73	111	57
Purchase in Rs.(Y)	71	75	69	97	70	91	99	61	80	47

Table 2. Computational process for prediction

Sales in Rs.(X)	Purchase in Rs.(Y)	$x=\left(X-\bar{X}\right)$	$y=\left(Y-\bar{Y}\right)$	xy	x^2	y^2
91	71	1	-5	-5	1	25
97	75	7	-1	-7	49	1
108	69	18	-7	-126	324	49
121	97	31	21	651	961	441
67	70	-23	-6	138	529	36
124	91	34	15	510	1156	225
51	99	-39	23	-897	1521	529
73	61	-17	-15	255	289	225
111	80	21	4	84	441	16
57	47	-33	-29	957	1089	841
$\Sigma X = 900$	$\Sigma Y = 760$			$\Sigma xy = 1560$	$\Sigma x^2 = 6360$	$\Sigma y^2 = 2388$

n=10, $\Sigma X = 900$, $\Sigma Y = 760$

$$\bar{X} = \frac{\sum X}{n} = \frac{900}{10} = 90$$

$$\bar{Y} = \frac{\sum Y}{n} = \frac{760}{10} = 76$$

By this table, $\Sigma xy = 1560$, $\Sigma x^2 = 6360$, $\Sigma y^2 = 2388$

$$b_{xy} = \frac{\sum xy}{\sum y^2} = \frac{1560}{2388} = 0.6532$$

$$b_{yx} = \frac{\sum xy}{\sum x^2} = \frac{1560}{6360} = 0.2452$$

Regression line of X on Y

$$X - \bar{X} = b_{xy}(Y - \bar{Y})$$

X - 90 = 0.6532(Y – 76)

X – 90 = 0.6532Y– 49.6432

Apply the value of Y =Rs. 90

X=0.6532Y+40.3568

X=0.6532(90)+40.3568

X=Rs. 99.14

The estimated sale is Rs. 99.14 when the product purchase is Rs. 90.00.

Performance-Regression Analysis

The performance of regression analysis objective is to know the difference between actual observed value and predicted value through statistical model for minimizing the error. In the error minimizing process, the actual values observed by nature and predicted values or estimated values to sell the product is computed with 30% profit. As shown in the table 3, the Product sold price(X) is marked in the first row and the actually expected to sell(Y) price is displayed in the third row for analyzing the deviation from the profit.

Table 3. A Product purchased, sold, and estimated to sell with 30% profit

Sold in Rs.(X)	91	97	108	121	67	124	51	73	111	57
Purchased in Rs.	71	75	69	97	70	91	99	61	80	47
Estimated for selling with 30% profit(Y)	92.30	97.50	89.70	126.10	91	118.30	128.70	79.30	104.00	61.10

At the outset, the predicted values are expected to be more close or equal to observed (sold) values for concluding the model is fit or perfect. In general, there is no possibility for concluding the model is fit without knowing the correct value (observed value) which is measured as independent variable and the predicted value is represented as dependent variable.

In general, when analyze a group of data points, a few points may be significantly differ from other observed values which are named as anomaly detection or outlier (Terrades, Berenguel, & Gil, 2020). The outlier may be removed from a dataset or seriously taken for statistical analyses depends the contexts. The error rate of regression model from prediction is analyzed through various models such as,

- Mean Absolute Error (MAE)
- Root Mean Squared Error(RMSE)
- R-Squared method(R2),
- Adjusted R-Squared (R2adj) etc.

In MAE, the average of the error is computed using the following equation,

$$\text{MAE} = \frac{\sum_{i=1}^{n} |y_i - x_i|}{n} = \frac{\sum_{i=1}^{n} |e_i|}{n},$$

where, 'n' is the total number of cases, y_i = predicted or planned value, x_i = sold value, e_i = error or difference..

Table 4. Computation for error analyzing

Sold in Rs.(X)	Estimated to sell in Rs.(Y)	$(y_i - x_i)$	$|y_i - x_i|$	$(y_i - x_i)^2$
91	92.30	1.30	1.30	1.69
97	97.50	0.50	0.50	0.25
108	89.70	-18.30	18.30	334.89
121	126.10	5.10	5.10	26.01
67	91.00	24.00	24.00	576
124	118.30	-5.70	5.70	32.49
51	128.70	77.70	77.70	6037.29
73	79.30	6.30	6.30	39.69
111	104.00	-7.00	7.00	49
57	61.10	4.10	4.10	16.81
$\Sigma X = 900$	$\Sigma Y = 988$		$\Sigma e_i = 150$	$\Sigma(y_i - x_i)$

$$\text{MAE} = \frac{\Sigma e_i}{n} = \frac{150}{10} = 15$$

The MAE error range is more suitable when the range of observed values from 1x to 1xxxxxxx (long range values) and it does not consider the sign of the difference value (Willmott & Matsuura, 2005). As it is not considering the sign of the value, the negative values also summed with positive values so that the error rate is increased unconditionally. When the range of observed value is between 1xxx and 3xxx (short range values) the RMSE performs well using the following equation.

$$RMSE = \sqrt{\frac{\sum_{i=1}^{N} \left(Predicted_i - Observed_i \right)^2}{N}},$$

where N is the total number of observations, from the table 4, $\Sigma(y_i - x_i) = 7114.12$,

$$\text{RMSE} = \sqrt{\frac{7114.12}{10}} = 26.67$$

The RMSE measures square root of average of the squared difference between the predicted values and the observed values. When the outlier or unexpected values occur in a group of data points, it is removed from the group to reduce error. The outlier finding process also called anomaly detection or extrapolation detection which is shown in the table 4, in 7th row, the difference is 77.70. After removing the outlier, the error is computed as,

$$\text{MAE} = \frac{\sum e_i}{n} = \frac{72.30}{9} = 8.03$$

$$\text{RMSE} = \sqrt{\frac{1076.83}{9}} = \sqrt{119.65} = 10.94$$

In a whole, dependent variable values are taken for accounting to analyze the effect of a system. In which, the independent variables play a major role and reason to improve the system. The independent variables can be analyzed with different values using R-Squared model with the following equation,

$$\widehat{R}^2 = 1 - \frac{\sum_{i=1}^{n}\left(Y_i - \widehat{Y}_i\right)^2}{\sum_{i=1}^{n}\left(Y_i - \overline{Y}\right)^2} = 1 - \frac{\frac{1}{n}\sum_{i=1}^{n}\left(Y_i - \widehat{Y}_i\right)^2}{\frac{1}{n}\sum_{i=1}^{n}\left(Y_i - \overline{Y}\right)^2}$$

where $\widehat{R}^2$ is the coefficient of determination, Y is the actual value, $\widehat{Y}$ is the predicted value of Y and $\overline{Y}$ is the means of the Y value.

The R-Squared is also a statistical measure of how close the predicted data to the observed data in regression line (Akossou & Palm, 2017). While R-Squared model adding more independent variables related to significance, the additional variables improve the model but not always. As it is expected best fit model always, the adjusted R-Squared equation is opted to add more variables and 1 is subtracted to meet the requirements and penalty. The Adjusted R-squared equation is

$$R_{adj}^2 = 1 - \left[\frac{\left(1 - R^2\right)\left(n - 1\right)}{n - k - 1}\right]$$

where R_{adj}^2 is the adjusted coefficient of determination, 'n' represents total number of observations (sample size); 'k' represents the total number of independent variables (parameters).

CONCLUSION

The Data analysis methods are related to the mathematical calculations and statistical techniques which are used for predicting the future outcomes in different contexts. All the statistical techniques are analyzed with different error correcting models. In which, the variables values are uncertain in most of the cases so that the outcome of analysis has been changing with time series. Finally, the solution is a feasible one as it is an estimated result but the optimized solution is our needs when considering accuracy and contexts. Therefore, multivariate analysis methods and statistical techniques may be used for converting feasible solution to optimized solution. For getting optimized solution from a complex problem, multivariate analysis will be suitable but effectiveness of the results is strongly related with selection of variables in a data pool and also the selection of variables is varied from domain experts' experiences.

ACKNOWLEDGMENT

This work is supported by the University Grants Commission (UGC), New Delhi, India under the Award of Post-Doctoral Fellowship in National Institute of Technology, Tiruchirappalli, Tamil Nadu, India.

REFERENCES

Akossou, A. Y. J., & Palm, R. (2017). Impact of Data Structure on the Estimators R-Square And Adjusted R-Square in Linear Regression. *International Journal of Mathematics and Computation*, *20*, 84–90.

Baker, A. R., Goodloe, R. J., Larkin, E. K., Baechle, D. J., Song, Y. E., Phillips, L. S., & Gray-McGuire, C. L. (2009). Multivariate association analysis of the components of metabolic syndrome from the Framingham Heart Study. *BMC Proceedings*, *3*(Suppl 7), 1–5. doi:10.1186/1753-6561-3-s7-s42 PMID:20018034

Bland, J. M., & Altman, D. G. (1996). Statistics notes: Measurement error. *BMJ (Clinical Research Ed.)*, *312*(7047), 1654. doi:10.1136/bmj.312.7047.1654 PMID:8664723

Chandrima, R., Siddharth, S. R., & Manjusha, P. (2018). Big Data Optimization Techniques: A Survey. *International Journal of Information Engineering and Electronic Business*, *10*(4), 41–48. doi:10.5815/ijieeb.2018.04.06

Chen, H., Roger, H. C., & Veda, C. S. (2012). Business Intelligence and Analytics: From Big Data to Big Impact. *Management Information Systems Quarterly*, *36*(4), 1165–1188. doi:10.2307/41703503

Davenport, H. T., & Jill, D. (2013). *Big data in big companies*. International Institute for Analytics.

Davenport, T. H. (2010). Business intelligence and organizational decisions. *International Journal of Business Intelligence Research*, *1*(1), 1–12. doi:10.4018/jbir.2010071701

Davenport, T. H., & Harris, J. G. (2007). *Competing on analytics: The new science of winning*. Harvard Business Press.

David, A. F. (2009). *Statistical Models: Theory and Practice*. Cambridge University Press.

David, G., Magnus, J., Higinio, M., & Julian, S. (2019). *Review of the Complexity of Managing Big Data of the Internet of Things.* Advance online publication. doi:10.1155/2019/4592902

Faizura, H., Rosmah, A., Nazri, K., & Sufyan, B. (2017). Descriptive analysis and text analysis in Systematic Literature Review: A review of Master Data Management. *International Conference on Research and Innovation in Information Systems (ICRIIS)*, 1-6.

Fangxuan, L., Jinchao, H., Juntian, L., Wengui, X., & Zhiyong, Y. (2019). Multivariate analysis of clinicopathological and prognostic significance of miRNA 106b~25 cluster in gastric cancer. *Cancer Cell International*, *19*, 1–10. PMID:30622437

Foley, E., & Guillemette, M. G. (2010). What is business intelligence? *International Journal of Business Intelligence Research*, *1*(4), 1–28. doi:10.4018/jbir.2010100101

Gupta, S. C., & Kapoor, V. K. (2013). Fundamentals of mathematical statistics (11th ed.). Sultan Chand & Sons Educational publishers.

Gutierrez-Garcia, J. O., & Lopez-Neri, E. (2015). Cognitive Computing: A Brief Survey and Open Research Challenges. *3rd International Conference on Applied Computing and Information Technology/2nd International Conference on Computational Science and Intelligence, IEEE*, 328-333.

Jeble, S., Kumari, S., & Patil, Y. (2018). Role of Big Data in Decision Making. *Operations and Supply Chain Management*, *11*, 36–44. doi:10.31387/oscm0300198

Jiang, W., & Chai, H. (2016). Research on big data in business model innovation based on GA-BP model. *IEEE International Conference on In Service Operations and Logistics, and Informatics (SOLI)*, 174-177. 10.1109/SOLI.2016.7551682

Kumar & Garg. (2018). Predictive Analytics: A Review of Trends and Techniques. *International Journal of Computer Applications, 182.*

Lepenioti, K., Bousdekis, A., Apostolou, D., & Mentzas, G. (2020). Prescriptive analytics: Literature review and research challenges. *International Journal of Information Management*, *50*, 57–70. doi:10.1016/j.ijinfomgt.2019.04.003

Ley, C., & Bordas, S. P. A. (2018). What makes Data Science different? A discussion involving Statistics 2.0 and Computational Sciences. *International Journal of Data Science and Analytics*, *6*(3), 167–175. doi:10.100741060-017-0090-x

Mikalef, P., Pappas, I., Krogstie, J., & Giannakos, M. (2018). Big data analytics capabilities: A systematic literature review and research agenda. *Information Systems and e-Business Management*, *16*(3), 547–578. doi:10.100710257-017-0362-y

Mortenson, M. J., Doherty, N. F., & Robinson, S. (2015). Operational research from Taylorism to Terabytes: A research agenda for the analytics age. *European Journal of Operational Research*, *241*(3), 583–595. doi:10.1016/j.ejor.2014.08.029

Pal, L., Ojha, C. S. P., Chandniha, S. K., & Kumar, A. (2019). Regional scale analysis of trends in rainfall using nonparametric methods and wavelet transforms over a semi-arid region in India. *International Journal of Climatology*, *39*(5), 2737–2764. doi:10.1002/joc.5985

Poornima, S., & Pushpalatha, M. (2018). A survey of predictive analytics using big data with data mining. *International Journal of Bioinformatics Research and Applications*, *14*(3), 269–282. doi:10.1504/IJBRA.2018.092697

Russom, P. (2013). *Managing big data. The Data Warehousing Institute Best Practices Report.* TDWI Research.

Scholz, P., Schieder, C., Kurze, C., Gluchowski, P., & Boehringer, M. (2010). Benefits and challenges of business intelligence adoption in small and medium-sized enterprises. *18th European Conference on Information Systems, Proceedings*, 1-12.

Sofya, S. T., Valeriy, N. T., Georgios, A., & Jan, P. (2019). Fast implementation of pattern mining algorithms with time stamp uncertainties and temporal constraints. *Journal of Big Data*, *6*, 1–34. doi:10.118640537-019-0200-9

Soltanpoor, R., & Sellis, T. (2016). Prescriptive analytics for big data. *Databases Theory and Applications: 27th Australasian Database Conference, Sydney, NSW, Proceedings*, 245-256. DOI: 10.1007/978-3-319-46922-5_19

Sosna, M., Trevinyo-Rodríguez, R. N., & Velamuri, S. R. (2010). Business model innovation through trial-and-error learning: The Naturhouse case. *Long Range Planning*, *43*(2), 383–407. doi:10.1016/j.lrp.2010.02.003

Terrades, O., Berenguel, A., & Gil, D. (2020). *A flexible outlier detector based on a topology given by graph communities.* Retrieved from https://arxiv.org/pdf/2002.07791

Uskov, V. L., Bakken, J. P., Byerly, A., & Shah, A. (2019). Machine Learning-based Predictive Analytics of Student Academic Performance in STEM Education. *IEEE Global Engineering Education Conference (EDUCON)*, 1370-1376. 10.1109/EDUCON.2019.8725237

Vidgen, R., Shaw, S., & Grant, D. B. (2017). Management challenges in creating value from business analytics. *European Journal of Operational Research*, *261*(2), 626–639. doi:10.1016/j.ejor.2017.02.023

Wang, Z., & Zhao, H. (2016). Empirical Study of Using Big Data for Business Process Improvement at Private Manufacturing Firm in Cloud Computing. *3rd International Conference on In Cyber Security and Cloud Computing (CSCloud)*, 129-135. 10.1109/CSCloud.2016.11

Willmott, C. J., & Matsuura, K. (2005). Advantages of the mean absolute error (MAE) over the root mean square error (RMSE) in assessing average model performance. *Climate Research*, *30*, 79–82. doi:10.3354/cr030079

Xia, B. S., & Gong, P. (2015). Review of business intelligence through data analysis. *Benchmarking*, *21*(2), 300–311. doi:10.1108/BIJ-08-2012-0050

Zhenhua, W., Yangsen, Y., & Dangchen, J. (2018). Analysis and Prediction of Urban Traffic Congestion Based on Big Data. *International Journal on Data Science and Technology*, *4*(3), 100–105. doi:10.11648/j.ijdst.20180403.14

KEY TERMS AND DEFINITIONS

Bivariate Analysis: It is one of the statistical analyses where two variables are involved to figure out the depth of the relationships between variables.

Correlation: The degree of relationship between two or more variables and it does not reflect cause and effect relationship between the factors.

Data Analytics: The science of extracting meaningful information continuously with the assistance of specialized system for finding patterns to get feasible solutions.

Multivariate Analysis: It is a subdivision of statistics for analyzing three or more piece of information for every item to find the interrelationship between variables to predict the future outcomes.

Predictive Analytics: The finding of new patterns is to analyze future performance of a system based on context and historical information and it is used for decision making process.

Regression Analysis: It is a statistical process for denoting the average relationship between two or more factors with the involvement of dependent and independent variables.

Statistical Modeling: It represents a mathematical model which encompasses statistical assumptions to interpret the available data for approximating reality.

Univariate Analysis: It is a simplest form of statistical analysis which involves with single variable for finding solution in predictive analytics.

Chapter 7
Evaluating Business Performance Using Data Envelopment Analysis and Grey Relational Analysis

Tihana Škrinjarić

https://orcid.org/0000-0002-9310-6853

University of Zagreb, Croatia

Boško Šego

University of Zagreb, Croatia

ABSTRACT

Financial ratios are used in a variety of ways today. Empirical research is getting bigger, with a special focus on predicting business failure, the strength of a company, investment decision making, etc. This chapter focuses on two methodologies suitable to deal with many data to evaluate business performance. They are data envelopment analysis and grey relational analysis. The empirical part of the chapter conducts an empirical analysis with the aforementioned two approaches. Firms are ranked based on their performances and detailed interpretations are obtained so that managers within businesses can get useful information on how to utilize such an approach to modelling. This study implicates that using the two mentioned approaches can be useful when making investment decisions based on many data available for the decision maker. This is due to the methodology being suitable to handle big data and correctly quantifying the overall financial performance of a company.

INTRODUCTION

Global business practices place big pressure on companies to achieve the best possible results in terms of profits, sustainability, the social component of the whole business process, etc. The competition is rising almost daily. Thus, companies need to re-evaluate their performances continuously in order to

DOI: 10.4018/978-1-7998-3053-5.ch007

remain competitive as well as increase their competitiveness. On the other hand, investors who seek to employ their resources into companies, expect to achieve excellent returns on investment, based upon excellent results of the business they are investing in.

Both companies and investors need objective information on the performance of the whole business. For a company, this gives insights into where it stands in a similar group, branch or industry regarding the whole process of the business operation. Managers of companies can have a better understanding of the business operation performance when the measurement of such performance is objective and complete. This indicates if a company is performing optimally, with the company's goals brought to completeness or not. If a timely and continuous evaluation is made, this could help achieve business goals more quickly and of better quality, with timely corrections of plans. On the other hand, the information on the company's total performance is important for potential and existing investors to get insights on the quality of the business they are interested in investing in. Based on investor's preferences, goals and limitations, a quality and comprehensive analysis of potential investments can help achieve his goals with fewer costs. Besides managers and investors, business banks could also benefit from such detailed analysis with a strong quantitative base, i.e. mathematical models and methods, due to their valid assumptions and robustness. Financial ratios have been extensively analysed over the last couple of decades. Although it is not difficult to calculate them, the interpretation of their combinations is far more complex. Thus, many different authors have researched such complexity: Hafeez (2002), Lau and Sholihin (2005), Philips and Louvieris (2005), Craig and Moores (2005), Prieto and Revila (2006), Fernandes et al. (2006), Wier et. al. (2007), Chen et. al. (2009), Cardinaels and van Veen-Dirks (2010), etc. To achieve objective comparisons, different models and methods have been developed to rank companies based upon their performances.

The problem observed in this chapter is how to correctly use the financial ratios data when comparing the performance of selected companies, with the basis in finance theory. Namely, big data asks for the correct methodologies to be used. Furthermore, the selection of financial ratios should be based on theory, which is rarely found in existing literature (as it will be seen in the literature review section). That is why the purpose of the paper is to examine previous research on the topic of decision-making based on financial ratios data and to provide insights into the correct analysis based on financial theory. This chapter will primarily focus on two methods which enable objectivity in the decision-making process. The Data Envelopment Analysis (DEA), which was first developed for production companies, is a good stepping stone in evaluating the relative efficiency of companies based upon different criteria. The second methodology, the Grey Relational Analysis (GRA), is a relatively unknown one, belonging to the Grey Systems Theory (GST), a set of models, methods and approaches developed to model uncertain events and concepts.

Both approaches will be observed simultaneously in this chapter in order to evaluate relative business performance among selected companies for which public data is available on a stock market. The complementarities of both approaches will be examined as well, with checking the robustness of results. Thus, the empirical part of the chapter will focus on publicly available data on a sample of companies to evaluate their overall performance, from the individual company's standpoint and the investor's point of view. This is done since a company often does not have full information and disclosure on their competitors. That is because they can only use publicly available information. From the point of view of the investor, he often cannot get some insider information and has to make his investment decisions based upon, again, publicly available data. Data will include a sample of 21 companies which constitute the stock market index as an example to interpret the results on.

Expected contributions are as follows. A critical overview of existing related research will be done with the systematization of the results. This is important for future work to obtain relevant information concisely. Next, the methodology of DEA and GRA will be applied to an empirical sample (a case study) with detailed interpretations and recommendations for investors and businesses of interest. In that way, others interested in such analyses could conduct them in future as well. A gap in the literature is found regarding the use of DEA with missing data, as will be done in this research and a complimentary analysis of the GRA approach. Robustness checking within this chapter will also contribute, as this is also something rarely done in previous research. Managers and investors should base their decisions on robust results which are reliable to use. Finally, the relationship between this chapter and its topics with the data analytics and data science is found in the following. By collecting data on financial ratios of many companies over time, the amount of data a decision-maker is facing with gets huge. Thus, the DEA and GRA methodologies applied to real data in this chapter belong to the area of data science. This means that large amounts of data are being analysed to solve complex problems. The particular data used in this chapter belongs to the area of the business sector, in which the investor or manager needs to make timely decisions on investing or changing the business practices. However, such decisions are based on large amounts of data and information available. Consequently, adequate analysis of such data and information has to be provided.

The main objectives of the study include: giving a comprehensive and critical literature review of financial ratios data analysis; accurate application of the mentioned methodologies for big data analysis on real data; and giving objective advice on how to interpret and use the results from such analysis so that managers and (potential) investors get a basis of good quality for their further research and similar analysis.

ROLE OF FINANCIAL RATIOS IN COMPARING BUSINESSES

Research on utilizing the financial ratios in financial modelling and business comparisons is not new. Different approaches have been taken over the decades, with theoretical and empirical contributions. It seems that the majority of the work is focused on more developed markets where more data is publicly available to test theories and to search for new insights. As time goes by, research spreads to other markets (countries) as well. Probably all financial ratios have been used at least once in the empirical research. Researchers ask different specific questions, and thus a lot of approaches have been taken. In this section, a concise overview is given of some of the most prominent literature regarding the analysis of financial ratios.

Some of the most researched financial ratios in the literature are as follows. The Book to Market ratio (BMR) is observed for several decades now. It is often used in the literature which observes market anomalies related to the Efficient Market Hypothesis and in the asset pricing models it is observed as the value premium (see Fama and French 1992, 1993, 1995). Some of the first empirical research is Stattman (1980), Rosenberg et al. (1985), DeBond and Thaler (1987), and Keim (1988). Maybe the most popular one is from Fama and French (1992, 1993), in which authors have shown that the BMR can explain the differences between stock market returns. Those firms which had bigger BMR were observed as to be overpriced by the stock market, and those firms had greater market leverage. Investors overreact to the market growth of such stocks. Moreover, those firms which had big BMR could have small amounts of non-tangible assets and their stocks could be characterised by small growth opportunities. Some companies are characterized by glamour stocks. This means that the BMR is small but the stock returns are great, which means that the BMR is not a representative ratio which could indicate the business performance and stock returns. Other research which has found significant effects of value premium are Chan et al. (1991) for Japan; Kothari and Shanken (1997) have shown that using the BMR was successful in forecasting the return on DJIA for the period from 1926 to 1991; Fama and French (1998) for UK, Belgium, Germany, Switzerland, France, Singapore, Sweden, Japan, Australia, Hong Kong and Netherlands; Capaul et al. (1993) for USA, UK, Japan, Germany, Switzerland and France; Fraser and Page (2000) for South Africa. This value premium (or value effect) is the most studied cross-sectional anomaly in stock returns today, alongside the size effect. Asness et al. (2015) explain that investors should go long in those stocks which have high fundamental value compared to the market price and short in those stocks which have low fundamental price compared to the market price. This could result in a portfolio which has a low correlation to the market. However, the strategy depends on the investor's preferences.

Dividend yield effects on stock returns and for business comparison purposes have been observed since the 1970s. Some explanations for differences in values of dividend yields between companies (within the same industry as well) include the taxation of capital gains: Brennan (1979), Litzenberger and Ramaswamy (1979). Miller and Scholes (1982), Fama and French (1988), Campbell and Shiller (1988a, b), Capmbell (1991) and Cochrane (1992) agree that the dividend yield is very useful in stock return forecasting, especially for longer periods. When the discount rates and expected returns are big, the stock returns should be small compared to dividends, thus the dividend yield should move alongside expected returns (Fama and French 1988). If the dividend yield is small, the stock is overpriced (Lewellen 2004). Rational pricing theories of asset pricing claim that the dividend yield follows variations of discount rates over time. Research on dividend policies goes as far back as Lintner (1956) who analysed how managers plan dividend policy. Some managers believe that the market has set a premium on those stocks which have stable dividend payouts (first policy, see Leary and Michaely (2011)); residual dividend policy could be a result of it being more profitable for a company to invest the money in other opportunities (Baker and Smith (2006)). Finally, the target payout ratio is based on setting the amount of dividend payouts with respect to some other value, such as earnings. Thus, a ratio is set with the aim of achieving it over the long run (see Leary and Michaely (2011)).

The Price to Earnings ratio (P/E), calculated as the ratio of market value per share and earnings per share ($\frac{\text{market value per share}}{\text{earnings per share}}$), is one of the most researched financial ratios as well. Sometimes, the E/P ratio is examined, as the reciprocal value of P/E. Basu (1977, 1983) has empirically shown that the P/E ratio increases the predicting power of asset pricing models. The research included the relationship between stock returns, company size and a market beta of US companies. Since the results indicated that stocks with higher P/E ratio obtained greater returns compared to others, Ball (1978) concluded that the E/P ratio is the proxy variable which includes all non-named factors that are not explicitly included in asset pricing models. Other examined markets over the years included the Japanese in Aggarwal et al. (1988), Singaporean in Wong and Lye (1990), Taiwanese in Chou and Johnson (1990), etc. La Porta (1996) has found results opposite to previously mentioned ones, due to contrarian strategies resulting with portfolios which had high returns based on investing in low P/E stocks. Chan et al. (1991) have included the ratio of cash flow to price and cash flow yield in their analysis and found that these ratios have significant effects on stock returns. The authors concluded that the significance of fundamental factors in explaining stock price movements are explained as deviances from the market efficiency which is predicted with the Efficient Market Hypothesis.

Bhandari (1988) has shown that stock returns have a positive correlation with the total debt ratio. When mentioning this ratio, the capital structure debate has to be mentioned, since it is present in the literature for several decades. The Modigliani and Miller (1958, 1963) papers are some of the most famous ones within this area of research; which was followed by the pecking order theory in Myers and Majluf (1984) and Myers (1984). Barbee et al. (1996) argue that sales per share ratio could be a better, i.e. more reliable indicator of the relative value of a firm on the market due to different depreciation models which could affect the book values of stock prices. Authors add that their suggested ratio cannot be of negative value, which is often a problem with the P/E and BMR ratios. This leads to problems with estimation of firm value and different models used in asset pricing. Mukherji et al. (1997) have focused on the Korean market and included the following ratios in their analysis: P/E ratio, BMR, the ratio of profit per share and market price of a share, and the ratio of sales and market price. One of the most popular measures of stock evaluation is Tobin's Q (Tobin (1969), the formula: $\frac{\text{total market value of firm}}{\text{total asset value of firm}}$), which is used to measure the market value of a firm in a sense what is the replacement value of physical assets. It is calculated as a ratio, with a value equal to 1 if the value of a firm's assets is equal to its market value. For more details, please see Chung and Pruitt (1994).

Profitability measurement is also important in the analysis. McDonald (1999) showed that profitability measures can predict future profits. Earnings per share ratio (EPS) is a commonly used financial ratio as well. Beaver (1989) has mentioned that investors, when looking at financial statements, look at EPS as some of the first ratios to analyse. Deberg and Murdoch (1994) conducted a 10 year period research on Compustat firms to compare the primary earnings per share (PEPS) and fully diluted earnings per share (FDEPS). Authors found that both EPS ratios contain the same information for investors due to their high correlation. Thus, one or the other ratio can be used in the analysis. Williams (2000) thinks that EPS measures the economic strength of a firm, and it aids in the decision making process about the firm's potential. Wu (2000) has conducted a research on a sample of institutional and individual investors and found that the EPS, receivable turnover ratio (RTR), return on assets (ROA) and liquidity indicators are the most useful and meaningful information about the business when making investment decisions. ROA and return on equity (ROE) have also been proven to be useful in the analysis of the financial statements. ROA gives insights in the effective and efficient usage of the company's assets to generate profits, see Muhammad and Scrimgeour (2014), i.e., it shows how much profit a company generates for every monetary unit invested in assets, Palepu et al. (2010). Muhammad and Scrimgeour (2014) add that investors aim towards greater values of ROA due to it representing a proxy for the firm's performance and the management's efficiency in using the assets to generate profits. It is more useful to compare within the same industries. ROE should also be as big as possible if the management is aiming to maximise the wealth of shareholders. In general, all shareholder return ratios should be aimed to be as big as possible if the goal is to maximise the shareholders' wealth, i.e. obtaining an adequate rate of return, as explained in Hill et al. (2014). Although, the ROE does not state how much the shareholders will obtain when part of the earnings is paid out in terms of dividends. However, it can indicate if the company can generate returns as stated in Berman et al. (2013). Some authors argue that the return on invested capital (ROIC) is a better measure than ROA and ROE, because it is calculated as the amount of return which the company can make above the average cost it pays for its equity capital and debt. Since ROIC focuses on the true operating performance of a company, it should be used the most, which is noted in Copeland et al. (1996) and Jablonski and Barsky (2001).

As can be seen from this overview, many interesting results have been obtained over the years. A great deal of research is focused on predicting stock price returns by including financial ratios in the analysis. This was proven to be useful in most cases. However, it is not an easy task to do such an analysis on a daily or weekly basis, especially with many variables and stocks, i.e. firms which need to be taken into consideration among other important factors of portfolio management. Less research has been found with respect to business comparisons. However, the same variables can be used to compare one company to others (especially within the same industry). Reasoning on why not much work is found within this area of research could be that it requires many data throughout time, it is computationally more difficult compared to some other modelling approaches, often the full data is not available for the researcher (especially the financial ratios data), etc. However, there is some recent research which sheds light on the field, which is shown in the next section.

RELATED RECENT EMPIRICAL LITERATURE FINDINGS

The research on the topic of financial statements ratio is rapidly increasing in size, with many different questions being observed. Thus, the focus of this subchapter is on the most related findings, in which different methodologies have been used. Some authors utilize econometric techniques to see which financial ratios contribute to better stock return predictions; many papers exist on predicting the probability of business failure: Bhargava et al. (1998), Lugovskaja (2009), du Jardin and Severin (2011), Morris (2018), while others try to compare the relative efficiency of one company to another by using DEA approach. The latter approach is also often used in comparisons in the bank industry: Fukuyama (1993), Jemrić and Vujčić (2002), Cielen et al. (2004), Anayiotos et al. (2010), Staub et al. (2010), Adusei (2016), Jiang and He (2018), etc.

Lau et al. (2002) have observed the Malayan stock market for the period from 1988 to 1996. Authors have found that the size of the firm, EPS ratio, BMR and sales growth rate have significant effects on stock returns of the observed firms. This enabled the investors to take advantages of these anomalies in their portfolio strategies. Lewleen (2004) discusses the methodological aspects of the estimation of asset pricing models. Moreover, the author has included a long period in the empirical part of the paper, from 1946 to 2000, to investigate the relationship between the value effects, dividend yields and P/E ratio with respect to stock returns. Again, results have shown significant effects of mentioned variables on stock returns. Australian data was used in the paper Penman et al. (2007), in which authors found a positive relationship between the BMR and stock return. Wang and Ioro (2007) focused on Chinese firms in the period from 1995 to 2002. In this paper, the authors compare the financial ratios to the market variables in forecasting abilities of the firm's value. The financial ratios were found to be more useful in modelling. The American market was observed in Jordan et al. (2007). Here, the authors used a sample of 300 publicly listed firms to estimate the effects of EPS on stock returns. The results indicated that bigger companies had more predictive returns via EPS, compared to smaller ones. Aras and Aylmaz (2008) have analysed 12 developing markets and observed 3 basic financial ratios: BMR, P/E and EPS. The BMR was found to be the best one in predicting returns. Lee and Lee (2008) have investigated the predictive power of BMR, dividend yield and capital gains on the Malaysian market returns and found that the dividend yield had the best predictive power. The Canadian firms were in focus in Deaves et al. (2008), where a longer period was included (1956 – 2003). Authors observed the whole period and shorter sub-periods and concluded that the financial ratios were more useful in longer period predictions and comparisons. Chen and Shen (2009) include macroeconomic variables in the analysis alongside the financial ratios on the US market. Since the authors observed the period from 1961 to 2001, the macroeconomic variable inclusion was explained to capture the bull and bear markets over time. A similar approach was done in Li (2009), where the author was interested in asymmetric effects of financial ratios on stock returns in different economic and financial times, such as the aforementioned bull and bear markets. The effects were found to be greater in bear markets in the observed period (1996 to 2005). Dempsey (2010) focused on Australian data, where the author concluded that this ratio is very useful for the aforementioned market. Gregoriou et al. (2017) have utilized a panel approach in which EPS, net cash from operating activities, B/M ratio, DPS and long-term debt ratio were included as return predictors of mobile companies (from Europe, America, Asia and the Middle East). Majority of the mentioned literature in this paragraph utilizes regression analysis; some apply VAR (vector autoregression) models and cointegration approach. A very small part of research uses more advanced models such as regime-switching methodology or panel model approach.

Research which is methodologically closer to the approach in this chapter is as follows. Powers and McMuller (2002) evaluated 185 stocks on the American and British markets. EPS, market beta (from the CAPM model), standard deviation and other market-related indicators (different return and risk indicators) in a DEA approach. Edirisinghe and Zhang (2007) developed a generalized DEA model. In the empirical part of the paper, the authors have constructed a relative financial strength indicator (RFSI) for 230 American firms based on financial ratios. Here, a simulation was made in which the authors modelled portfolio investing based on the results from RFSI and not including it in the decision-making process. As a result, portfolios based on RFSI were better in terms of risk and return. Chen (2008) considered three years (from 2004 to 2007) for firms listed on the Taiwanese market. The size effect was prominent here as the factor affecting the return series. Lopes et al. (2008) observed Brazilian firms within the DEA model. Firms which were more efficient in terms of the DEA approach based on their financial ratios were those which obtained greater portfolio returns. Pätäri et al. (2010) have included only the market data on firms to compare them in the DEA model. Gardijan and Kojić (2012) have simulated trading on the Croatian stock market based only on market data (risk and return). Strategies based on DEA analysis have beaten the market only 50% of the time. This was due to using static models. Lim et al. (2013) utilized a greater number of market and financial ratio data. Zamani et al. (2014) used a super-efficiency DEA model to form portfolios on the Mumbai stock exchange. Authors found financial ratios to be very useful in differentiating stocks and successfulness of portfolios. Škrinjarić (2014) extended the analysis of Gardijan and Kojić (2012) via dynamic models. In this research, much better portfolio values were obtained. Furthermore, Gardijan and Škrinjarić (2015) have combined both market variables (i.e. characteristics) and obtained better results in terms of portfolio return when incorporating financial ratio data in the analysis. Previously mentioned papers utilize the DEA approach to modelling, with different models which were used as a base to estimate the relative efficiency of a firm's performance based on financial ratio and stock market data. Some authors utilize only financial ratio data, while some just the stock market data (regarding risks and returns and/or return distribution characteristics and moments). The majority is focused on the investor point of view. However, the results obtained in such analysis could be used to compare one firm to another in terms of business success or failure. However, the researcher should be careful, due to different types of industries which are being compared one to another.

Other related groups of studies are those which use similar data as the previous paragraph stated. However, the main methodological approach utilized here is the Grey Systems Theory, i.e. its part regarding the Grey Relational Analysis. This methodology is newer in the literature. Thus, the majority of existing research is from the last decade. Furthermore, there is a great scarcity of papers which utilize such an approach in financial literature and the financial failure prediction, see Huang et al. (2015). Fang-Ming and Wang-Ching (2010) compared the GSD approach (Grey Systems Decision) and the DEA approaches on the electronics sector companies' sample. The GRA approach had a 79% accuracy rate of discriminating good and bad performance companies. There is potential in using the GRA methodology in distinguishing between performances of companies of interest. The Istanbul stock exchange stocks were observed in Hamzacebi and Pekkaya (2011). Authors have compared several scenarios of ranking stocks based on financial ratios. Li et al. (2010) have utilized two approaches: the GRA and the AHP (Analytic Hierarchy Process) to evaluate Chinese companies. In the first stage, authors utilize GRA to rank the financial ratios for the AHP applications in the second stage. Salardini (2013) has used both mentioned approaches as well. 16 companies in the fiscal year 2010 on Teheran Stock Exchange were compared via financial ratios and stock market data. Author ranked the stocks based on the results. Zhao et al. (2014) compared 9 tourist hotels in their business operation performance via 6 financial ratios (Current Ratio, Fixed assets turnover ratio, Debt Ratio, Return on Equity, Growth Rate of Operating Income and Account Receivable Turnover Ratio). The best performing hotel was then a benchmark for others to look upon. Huang et al. (2015) tried to predict financial failure via a two-level DEA model and the GRA combined approaches on the Shenzhen stock exchange (in China). Since the authors utilized many financial ratios, the GRA methodology was used to obtain the best correlations between the company performance and the financial ratios. Then, the second step was the DEA model with the best ranking financial ratios to obtain financial failure prediction. Škrinjarić and Šego (2019) gave insights in comparing 55 stocks on the Croatian market, where the ranking of stocks was made via the GRA approach based on financial ratios and market data. Several simulated portfolios have been compared, which was previously rarely done in the literature. Moreover, this research was based on the investor's utility theory, which was also often ignored in previous research.

From this extensive literature review, some conclusions can be made. Firstly, the interest in utilizing DEA and GRA methodologies is rising over the years. This is especially true for DEA. Moreover, the robustness of checking is not done often, which is important for reliable interpretations. This research fills some of the gaps in the literature by combining the results of the two approaches (DEA and GRA), and by commenting on the results in a simple way so that everyone interested in such research can replicate it for their business.

METHODOLOGY

The two mentioned methodological approaches, DEA and GRA, are described in this subsection. Since the previous literature extensively describes the methodology, a brief description is given here.

DEA Methodology

Data Envelopment Analysis (DEA) is a methodology within the Operations Research, which enables the comparison of the relative efficiency of decision-making units (DMUs). DEA is a set of models and methods which belong to the field of mathematical programming. Each DMU uses a certain number of inputs to produce outputs. These inputs, outputs and the term production have stayed in the terminology of this methodology. This is due to DEA being developed for the production companies. Inputs are usually variables which are observed as inputs of production, i.e. everything which a DMU can reduce or aims to reduce. The opposite is true for outputs. The term relative efficiency is due to comparing the efficiency of one DMU to another, not to some optimal plan or DMU. For a more thorough introduction and basic terminology, please refer to Cooper et al. (2011).

The most famous basic models within DEA are the Charnes-Cooper-Rhodes (CCR) and the Banker-Charnes-Cooper (BCC) models. It is assumed within these models that each DMU j has m inputs $(x_{1j}, x_{2j}, ..., x_{mj})$ and produces s outputs $(y_{1j}, y_{2j}, ..., y_{sj})$; DMU_j, $j=1, 2,..., n$. DMU in this research are the companies which are being compared based on the financial ratios. The data can be compactly written in matrices:

$$X = \begin{pmatrix} x_{11} & x_{12} & \cdots & x_{1n} \\ x_{21} & x_{22} & \cdots & x_{2n} \\ \cdots & \cdots & \cdots & \cdots \\ x_{m1} & x_{m2} & \cdots & x_{mn} \end{pmatrix} \text{ and } Y = \begin{pmatrix} y_{11} & y_{12} & \cdots & y_{1n} \\ y_{21} & y_{22} & \cdots & y_{2n} \\ \cdots & \cdots & \cdots & \cdots \\ y_{s1} & y_{s2} & \cdots & y_{sn} \end{pmatrix}, \tag{1}$$

where X is the matrix of all inputs, Y matrix of all outputs. $x_o = (x_{1o}, x_{2o}, ..., x_{mo})^T$ and $y_o = (y_{1o}, y_{2o}, ..., y_{so})^T$ are respectively the vector of all inputs and vector of all outputs for the DMU j. It is assumed that $x_o \neq 0$, $x_o \geq 0$ and $y_o \neq 0$, $y_o \geq 0$ holds. In terms of this research, the matrix X will consist of those financial ratios which should be as low as possible and matrix Y will include the financial ratios which have to be as big as possible. Each DMU_j is compared to others with respect to their inputs and outputs, i.e. how much a DMU is efficient in using inputs to produce outputs. It is important to define the returns to scale in production. This is what distinguishes the BCC (variable returns to scale, VRS) and the CCR (constant returns to scale, CRS) models. Furthermore, the DMU can be input or output-oriented. If it is input-oriented, the DMU wants to minimize the inputs used in the production with the given amount of outputs. The output-oriented DMU aims to maximize the outputs on a certain level of inputs. The CCR-I (I - input) model in the first phase of the optimization can be written in the envelope form as:

$$\min_{\lambda, \theta} \theta$$
$$\text{s.t.} \quad \theta x_o - X\lambda \geq 0$$
$$Y\lambda \geq y_o \tag{2}$$
$$\lambda \geq 0,$$

where $\lambda = (\lambda_1, \lambda_2, ..., \lambda_n)^T$ is the vector of non-negative constants. The goal is to find the minimal value of θ which radially reduces vector of inputs x_o towards the value θx_o. The optimal value, i.e. the efficiency score θ^* is in the interval $[0,1]$ and is interpreted as the input reduction rate. The second phase of the optimisation is consisted of maximising the sum of input surpluses and output slacks for each DMU, with the inclusion of the optimal value θ^* from the first phase:

$$\max_{\lambda, s^-, s^+} w = es^- + es^+$$

$$s.t. \qquad \theta^* x_o - X\lambda = s^-$$

$$Y\lambda - y_o = s^+ \qquad\qquad (3)$$

$$\lambda \geq 0, \ s^- \geq 0, \ s^+ \geq 0,$$

where $e=(1,1,...,1)$ is the vector of unit values, $s^- = \left(s_1^-, s_2^-, ..., s_m^- \right)^T$ is the vector of input surpluses and $s^+ = \left(s_1^+, s_2^+, ..., s_r^+ \right)^T$ is the vector of output slacks. The optimal solution to the model (3) is $\left(\lambda^*, s^{-*}, s^{+*} \right)$ and is called the max-slack solution. A DMU is CCR efficient if the optimal solution of both phases $\left(\theta^*, \lambda^*, s^{-*}, s^{+*} \right)$ satisfies the conditions $\theta^*=1$, $s^{-*}=0$ and $s^{+*}=0$.

In terms of firms in this study, the firm which will be efficient based on the optimization process, the optimal value of the efficiency score will be equal to 1. This means that its financial ratios will be in such a combination that it will obtain the best business practice and will be the best to invest in from the investor's point of view.

More details on the CCR-O model, the relationship between input and output-oriented models can be found in Cooper et al. (2006). The described model so far was one with the constant returns to scale. If one assumes variable returns to scale, the following constraint should be added to each phase of the model in (2) and (3): $\sum_{j=1}^{n} \lambda_j = 1$. In that way, the linear function of the maximal production possibility set is now being restricted to a convex function.

GRA Methodology

The Grey Systems Theory is being developed since the 1980s in the Far East. The Grey Relational Analysis (GRA) is one part of this theory which is focused on ranking alternatives based on several criteria. The methodology is simpler compared to similar ones in terms of answering the same question of ranking alternatives. Moreover, it includes less subjectivity than some Multiple Criteria Decision Models do. Majority of notations and further details can be found in Liu and Lin (2006, 2010) and Kuo et al. (2008).

The decision maker is comparing data on K behavioural sequences on M alternatives which need to be ranked, $k \in \{1, 2, ..., K\}$ and $m \in \{1, 2, ..., M\}$. The data can be written in a compact matrix form as:

$$X = \begin{bmatrix} x_1(1) & x_1(2) & \cdots & x_1(K) \\ x_2(1) & x_2(2) & & x_2(K) \\ \vdots & \vdots & \ddots & \vdots \\ x_M(1) & x_M(2) & \cdots & x_M(K) \end{bmatrix}, \qquad\qquad (4)$$

where each row denotes the alternative m, and the columns refer to the criterion k. The $(x_m(1), x_m(2), ..., x_m(K))$ represents the behavioural sequence of the alternative m. The normalization of data in (4) has to be done so that comparisons can be made. Huang and Liao (2003) explain the importance of this normalization. It can be done in three ways, depending on the criteria. If the researcher aims to maximize the value of a criterion, the following normalization is done:

$$y_m(k) = \frac{x_m(k) - \min_m x_m(k)}{\max_m x_m(k) - \min_m x_m(k)} , \tag{5}$$

while the smaller the criterion, the normalization is as follows:

$$y_m(k) = \frac{\max_m x_m(k) - x_m(k)}{\max_m x_m(k) - \min_m x_m(k)} . \tag{6}$$

If the researcher is aiming to a reference value of a criterion, $x^*(k)$, due to previous knowledge, industry average or a set value, legislation, etc., the following normalization has to be made:

$$y_m(k) = \frac{\left| x_m(k) - x^*(k) \right|}{\max_m x_m(k) - x^*(k)} . \tag{7}$$

The normalization in (5)-(7) sets the values $y_m(k)$ in the interval [0,1]. The greater the normalized values are, the better is the criterion for some alternative. The next step involves the comparison of each normalized sequence $y_m(k)$ to the desired sequence. Since the values are normalized so that the closer the value is to the unit value the better, the behavioural sequence $y^*(k) = (1, 1, ..., 1)$ is used as a reference one (see Kuo et al. 2008). First, the absolute difference is calculated as follows:

$$\Delta y_m(k) = |\, y_m(k) - y^*(k)\, |, \tag{8}$$

then the Grey Relational Coefficient (GRC) is calculated based on values in (8) as:

$$G_m(k) = \frac{\Delta_{\min} + p\Delta_{\max}}{\Delta y_m(k) + p\Delta_{\min}}, \tag{9}$$

where p denotes the distinguishing coefficient, with $p \in [0,1]$; $\Delta_{\min} = \min\{\Delta y_1(k, ..., \Delta y_M(k)\}\forall k$, $\Delta_{\max} = \max\{\Delta y_1(k, ..., \Delta y_M(k)\}\forall k$. Value of p is usually taken to be 0.5 in the literature (see Liu et al. 2006), but it does not affect the rankings, the values in (9) only get more stretched out or squeezed in a tighter interval. The last step is to calculate the Grey Relational Degree, GRD, as the weighted average of values in (9):

$$GRD_m = \sum_{k=1}^{K} w_k G_m(k) \,\, \forall m \tag{10}$$

where it holds that $\sum_{k=1}^{K} w_k = 1$. Thus, it is a weighted average of GRCs, where the values for weights can be given based on experience, manager's suggestions, etc. This means that some subjectivity can be included in this procedure as well. The greater the value of GRD for the m-th alternative being compared, the better its ranking is.

EMPIRICAL RESULTS

This subsection deals first with describing the data used in the empirical research; namely, the financial ratios which were available at the time of conducting this research. The DEA results are then interpreted and firms are compared based on the results. Next, the GRA results are presented and compared to DEA results for robustness checking.

Variable Description

For the purpose of the empirical analysis, most recent data in the time of writing this chapter has been obtained on 21 stocks which constitute the stock market index CROBEX (Croatian market, Zagreb Stock Exchange) from Investing (2019). The data has been retrieved in August 2019, thus the variables which contain phrases MRQ (most recent quarter) in the title refers to the second quarter of 2019. Financial ratios data which were available to collect are shown in Table 1, with their descriptions. It can be seen that the managers within a company have to deal with a lot of different measures simultaneously, and not only for the particular company which is in centre of focus but for many others as well. Those ratios which should be aimed to be as high as possible are considered as outputs, while the opposite is true for those which should be the smallest possible (inputs).

The output and input classification is based on the DEA terminology, due to the aim of minimizing the values of inputs and maximizing the values of outputs. Table A1 in the Appendix gives the overview of analysed firms, with abbreviations and full names with sector classification. Although the direct comparisons of some financial ratios are meaningful within the same industry, this empirical analysis compares different companies to show the usefulness of the two methodological approaches. Moreover, it is not easy to strictly classify whether a financial ratio is better if it is of greater or smaller value; often it is compared with other ratios or used in combination with several others, due to meaningful interpretations. However, the used methodology asks to classify if a decision maker wants a concrete ratio to be higher or smaller. This is, of course, one of the drawbacks of such analysis, such as every approach has. To partially solve this problem, the selection of inputs/outputs criteria is based on previous empirical findings and conclusions if a value is better if smaller or larger.

DEA Modelling Results

For DEA modelling, variables need to be defined as inputs or outputs, as it was done in Table 1. Since this research deals with 21 companies ($n=21$), the DEA procedure requires that the number of DMUs has to satisfy $n \geq 2(m+s)$ (m and s are the number of inputs and outputs respectively, Golany and Roll 1989); so that the results are more reliable. Thus, the number of inputs and outputs could be at a maximum of 5 for each category. Since the analysis includes 47 different financial ratios, their number has to be reduced. This could be done via the manager's or investor's prior knowledge, experience, legislation, etc. Here, for objective comparison, correlations between all inputs and outputs have been calculated and are shown in Appendix in Table A4 (while Table A3 calculates the correlations between companies, which could give indications on which company performs similarly to others). The basic idea of DEA is that inputs and outputs should be correlated, i.e. with inputs, the DMU should produce outputs. Correlations between inputs should be the smallest possible, as well as between outputs themselves. This is due to containing the same information in data if inputs (outputs) are highly correlated. Findings in Deberg and Murdoch (1994) support this, as is mentioned in the literature review. That is why, based on the greatest correlations between inputs and outputs and lowest coefficients of correlation between inputs (outputs) themselves, the following financial ratios were chosen in the analysis: AT, C/S, OM5Y, OM, PEBS, ROA5Y, ROI5Y and TBV/S, i.e. 3 inputs and 5 outputs. If the decision-maker has data on many more companies, he could use many more inputs and/or outputs for the analysis.

Table 1. Financial ratios used in the study

Full name of financial ratio	Abbreviation	Description	DEA: input vs. output
P/E Ratio TTM	P/E	Ratio of a company's share price to the company's earnings per share. High P/E ratio indicates that the market perceives it as lower risk or higher growth or both when compared to a company with a low P/E ratio.	Output
Price to Sales TTM	P/S	Ratio of a company's market capitalization by revenues. The greater the ratio, the worse the investment is due to paying more for a more than each unit of sales.	Input
Price to Cash Flow MRQ	PCF	Ratio of a company's market capitalization with the company's operating cash flow. The greater the value of this ratio, the lower the value of the stock is (firm is not generating enough cash flows).	Input
Price to Free Cash Flow TTM	PFCF	Ratio of a company's market capitalization to company's free cash flow. Higher value of this ratio indicates that the company could be overvalued; it cannot generate additional revenues.	Input
Price to Book MRQ	P/B	Ratio of company's market capitalization and company's total book value. Empirical research has shown that low P/B stocks outperform high P/B stocks.	Input
Price to Tangible Book MRQ	P/TB	Ratio of company's share price to tangible book value per share. Interpreted as amount of money investor (shareholder) would receive if the company would shut down and liquidate all assets. Lower value of this ratio indicates smaller possible share price losses.	Input
Gross margin TTM	GM	Ratio of difference of company's revenue and cost of goods sold and revenues. The lower the ratio is, the less the company retains on each monetary unit of sales to service costs and debts.	Output
Gross Margin 5YA	GM5Y		

continues on following page

Table 1. Continued

Full name of financial ratio	Abbreviation	Description	DEA: input vs. output
Operating margin TTM	OM	Ratio of company's operating earnings and revenues. Smaller values of this ratio indicate that company is less able to pay non-operating costs.	Output
Operating margin 5YA	OM5Y		
Pre-tax margin TTM	PM	Ratio of company's profits and sales before tax reduction. Greater value indicates better profitability.	Output
Pre-tax margin 5YA	PM5Y		
Net Profit margin TTM	NPM	Ratio of company's net profit and revenues. Greater values indicate that greater percentages of revenues are turned into profits.	Output
Net Profit margin 5YA	NPM5Y		
Revenue/Share TTM	R/S	Ratio of company's total revenues and number of shares outstanding. Higher values indicate greater revenues.	Output
Basic EPS ANN	BEPS	Ratio of company's net income reduced by preferred dividends and the number of shares outstanding.	Output
Diluted EPS ANN	DEPS	Ratio of company's net income reduced by preferred dividends and number of shares outstanding increased with the conversion of dilutive securities. Indicates the worst-case scenario in terms of EPS	Output
Book Value/Share MRQ	BV/S	Ratio of difference between company's total equity value and preferred equity and the number of shares outstanding. If a market share price is smaller compared to the BV/S, the company could be considered undervalued.	Output
Tangible Book Value/Share MRQ	TBV/S	Ratio of company's total tangible assets and number of shares outstanding. Higher values indicate company has a lot in value regarding tangible assets.	Output
Cash/Share MRQ	C/S	Ratio of company's total cash and number of shares outstanding. A great value of this ratio could indicate that a company is performing well, but can also indicate a cost of capital inefficiency.	Input
Cash Flow/Share TTM	CF/S	Ratio of a company's after-tax earnings increased by depreciation and number of shares outstanding. Greater values indicate company's status to generate cash.	Output
Return on Equity TTM	ROE	Ratio of company's net income and equity. Smaller values mean that company is less able to generate income from the equity it uses.	Output
Return on Equity 5YA	ROE5Y		
Return on Assets TTM	ROA	Ratio of company's net income and total assets. Smaller values mean that company is less able to generate income from the assets it uses.	Output
Return on Assets 5YA	ROA5Y		
Return on Investment TTM	ROI	Ratio of company's net income and cost of investment. Smaller values mean that company is less able to generate income from its investments.	Output
Return on Investment 5YA	ROI5Y		
EPS(MRQ) vs. Qtr, 1 Yr, Ago MRQ	EPS_Q	Ratio of company's net profit and number of common shares.	Output
EPS(TTM) vs. TTM 1 Yr, Ago TTM	EPS_TTM		
5 Year EPS Growth 5YA	EPS_G	Growth rate of EPS over the 5-year horizon.	Output

continues on following page

Table 1. Continued

Full name of financial ratio	Abbreviation	Description	DEA: input vs. output
Sales (MRQ) vs. Qtr, 1 Yr, Ago MRQ	S_Q	Growth rate of company's sales, quarter of this year compared to same quarter of last year.	Output
Sales (TTM) vs. TTM 1 Yr, Ago TTM	S_TTM	Growth rate of company's sales, trailing 12 months this year compared to same trailing 12 months of last year.	Output
5 Year Sales Growth 5YA	S_G	Growth rate of company's sales over the 5-year horizon.	Output
5 Year Capital Spending Growth 5YA	CSG	Growth rate of company's investing into capital to maintain and grow business.	Output
Quick Ratio MRQ	QR	Ratio of company's liquid assets and quick liabilities. Best value is if the ratio is around 1:1. (See Tracy 2004).	Unit value; output
Current Ratio MRQ	CR	Ratio of company's current assets and liabilities. Best value is if the ratio is around 1:1. (See Tracy 2004).	Unit value; output
LT Debt to Equity MRQ	LTD/E	Ratio of company's long term debts and the total shareholders' equity. Higher ratio means the company is more risky.	Input
Total Debt to Equity MRQ	D/E	Ratio of company's total liabilities and the total shareholders' equity. Higher ratio means the company is more risky.	Input
Asset Turnover TTM	AT	Ratio of company's net sales revenue and the average total assets value. Higher value of this ratio means that company is generating more revenue per monetary unit of assets.	Output
Inventory Turnover TTM	IT	Ratio of company's net sales and average inventory. Higher value means that company could have inadequate inventory levels (too low); lower value could mean that company is overstocking.	Output
Revenue/Employee TTM	R/E	Ratio of company's total revenue and number of employees.	Output
Net Income/Employee TTM	NI/E	Ratio of company's net income and number of employees.	
Receivable Turnover TTM	RT	Ratio of company's net credit sales and average accounts receivable. If a company is more effective in collecting its receivables, the ratio is bigger.	Output
Dividend Yield ANN	DY	Ratio of company's annual dividend payment and the market capitalization.	Output
Dividend Yield 5 Year Avg, 5YA	DY5Y	Ratio of company's annual dividend payment and the market capitalization; 5 year average.	
Dividend Growth Rate ANN	DGR	Growth rate of the dividend yield.	Output
Payout Ratio TTM	PR	Ratio of company's dividends paid to shareholders and the net income. Greater value indicates that firm is more mature and it does not need to reinvest much more of the net income it earns.	Output

Note: TTM = Trailing Twelve Months, 5YA = 5-Year Average, MRQ = Most Recent Quarter
Source: Investing (2019)

Next, since often not all data is available for the analysis; and the DEA methodology asks for all DMUs to have data in inputs and outputs vectors, this analysis proceeds with the approach of DEA with missing data. Namely, Kousmanenn (2009) advises that penalties should be given to missing data. Otherwise, the DMU has to be dropped in the original models, which could result with few companies to compare. This is not in the interest of the manager or the investor. Kousmanenn (2009) suggests that missing inputs should be set to a large number, which is much greater than all other values which are available for other DMUs. For the missing outputs, it is suggested that a value of 0 is put. Thus, this research follows these suggestions. Four different DEA models have been optimized: with the assumption of the constant (CCR) versus variable (BCC) returns to scale, and input (I) versus output (O) oriented ones. Assumption of returns to scale in production could be determined by previous experience within an industry. This is also true for the input or output orientation. If the industry is such that the inputs or outputs are harder to manipulate within the company (due to legislation or simply due to technology), this can also be resolved via the decision-maker. Here, all possible outcomes have been observed so that as little subjectivity as possible is present in results. Efficiency scores from all four models are shown in Table 2. It is visible that the constant returns to scale produce less efficient companies, which is known in the literature, due to the non-convexity constraint.

The benchmark unit selection within every model and firm's optimization problem is chosen as the firm which has the unit value of the efficiency score as the necessary condition. The sufficient condition is that this unit is the closest on the efficiency frontier to the firm which is under the frontier and currently being evaluated. In other words, the benchmark firm is the one which is efficient within a model and the inefficient firm is closest to that benchmark. Thus, the needed changes which need to be provided regarding the inputs and/or outputs of an inefficient firm are estimated based on the values of inputs and/or outputs of the benchmark firm.

The inefficient companies based on the selected financial ratios were those which did not have an efficiency score of 1. Thus, if a company of interest is inefficient, it has to look at its peers within the industry which were efficient and try to follow good practices. Moreover, the DEA methodology enables calculations on which inputs and/or outputs need to be decreased/increased in order to increase efficiency. Moreover, this analysis can be done every quarter or year, depending on the goals of the management or the investor. Thus, dynamics can be included in the analysis, which would include more useful insights into changes of the (in)efficiencies, how good were the business decisions for increasing business and the whole supply-chain efficiency.

For further detailed analysis, the worst scenario is used from Table 2, where the CCR-I model is chosen, as its results contain the greatest number of inefficient companies. This is to avoid comments on the subjectivity of this research to present the best possible values and efficiencies of companies. On the contrary, by choosing the CCR-I model, companies should aim to see what the worst-case scenarios are for them in which they have to improve their inputs and/or outputs. Best possible scenarios (model BCC-O) could be analysed in the same way as the rest of this subsection does, by obtaining information on the least amount of changes of inputs and/or outputs needed to achieve efficiency. Thus, Table 3 depicts those firms which were referents in calculations of projections to the efficient frontier of the inefficient firms. Such frequency indicates how firm a role model for other companies was. ADPL, LUKA and INGR were the referent firms to calculate projections around for six times each. Thus, if the manager belongs to one of the three mentioned companies, he can be certain with a good probability that the company is operating in a good and desirable way. If the investor is looking at such data, he could

Table 2. Efficiency scores in DEA models

Firm	CCR-I	CCR-O	BCC-I	BCC-O
ADPL	1	1	1	1
ATPL	1	1	1	1
DLKV	1	1	1	1
DDJH	1	1	1	1
INGR	1	1	1	1
LUKA	1	1	1	1
RIVP	1	1	1	1
VART	1	1	1	1
PODR	0.917	0.917	1	1
ZBB	0.585	0.585	1	1
HT	0.347	0.347	1	1
KRAR	0.335	0.335	1	1
ATGR	0.324	0.324	1	1
ERNT	0.309	0.309	1	1
KONL	0.212	0.212	1	1
LKPC	0.091	0.091	1	1
ULPL	0.007	0.007	0.016	1
HIMR	0.325	0.325	0.912	0.966
ADGR	0.185	0.185	0.89	0.947
TPNR	0.537	0.537	0.605	0.673
AREN	0.097	0.097	0.111	0.426

Source: authors' calculation

conclude that the mentioned companies should enter his portfolio. Other efficient companies could also enter the portfolio. Weights of each firm could be determined by the results in Table 3.

The best performing mentioned companies' results is in line with Ghale (2015), Tehrani and Tehrani (2015) and Anwaar (2016), where ROA is found to be a significant factor in determining the successfulness of stock performance; as well as earlier work of Wu (2000) where both EPS and ROA were found to be significant factors when making investment decisions (both institutional and individual investors have been examined). Furthermore, the classification of the inefficient companies based on the operating margins (OM) variable is in line with results of Cengiz and Püskül (2016) and Bayrakdaroglu et al. (2017) where authors found that companies with greater OM-s had worse stock returns compared to others. The TBV/S ratio which should be aimed to be as highest possible was another factor which contributed to distinguish the efficient from inefficient companies. This result is in line with Harc (2015), where the analysis showed that the TBV/S has a positive impact on the long-term debt of companies, as it sends a positive signal to the financial institutions. Moreover, Koksal et al. (2013) found that the tangible assets are easier to collateralize when a company is under stress, and the TBV is positively related to leverage.

Table 3. Frequency of being a referent unit

Firm	ADPL	ATGR	DLKV	DDJH	INGR	LUKA	RIVP	VART
No	12	1	1	1	11	11	0	10

Note: No denotes number of times the firm was a referent unit to others in projection to the efficient frontier.
Source: authors' calculation

Those firms which were found to be inefficient could look at which financial ratios they need to improve in order to become more efficient. Such results are presented in Table 4, where the percentages of each input reduction and/or output increase should be made so that each firm would get to the efficient frontier within the observed model. First three columns refer to ratios which need to be decreased. That is why a minus sign is before the percentages, while last four columns show the needed output increases. The more inefficient the firm is, the greater the values will be in Table 4.

Table 4. Projections of inputs and outputs of inefficient firms

Firm	C/S	OM5Y	OM	AT	BEPS	ROA5Y	ROI5Y	TBV/S
ADGR	-81.53%	-81.53%	-999.90%	999.90%	0.00%	0.00%	327.84%	0.00%
AREN	-90.26%	-90.26%	-248.02%	595.50%	0.00%	0.00%	309.48%	0.00%
ATGR	-67.63%	-67.63%	-67.63%	288.00%	0.00%	0.00%	0.00%	212.88%
ERNT	-69.08%	-69.08%	-999.90%	163.99%	0.00%	36.93%	0.00%	250.02%
HT	-65.30%	-65.30%	-431.37%	168.51%	0.00%	0.00%	51.99%	122.84%
HIMR	-67.49%	-67.49%	-496.33%	966.21%	0.00%	0.00%	177.14%	0.00%
KONL	-78.83%	-78.83%	-999.90%	548.57%	0.00%	0.00%	117.91%	0.00%
KRAR	-66.52%	-66.52%	-565.97%	233.82%	0.00%	0.00%	77.06%	0.00%
LKPC	-90.90%	-90.90%	-999.90%	999.90%	0.00%	0.00%	599.34%	0.00%
PODR	-8.26%	-8.26%	-532.47%	142.64%	0.00%	0.00%	49.45%	0.00%
TPNR	-46.30%	-96.68%	-190.59%	106.99%	0.00%	0.00%	999.90%	0.00%
ULPL	-99.28%	0.00%	0.00%	0.00%	99.35%	80.63%	81.78%	102.83%
ZBB	-41.50%	-41.50%	-423.54%	0.00%	0.00%	486.60%	0.00%	999.90%

Source: authors' calculation

To look at an example, the firm PODR does not need to increase BEPS, TBV/S and ROA5Y, but has to increase ROI5Y and AT regarding outputs. Regarding inputs, it should decrease all of the inputs, but with a smaller rate of C/S and OM5Y (8.26% reduction) and a great reduction of OM (more than 530%). Now, with such information, the manager within this firm should look at the specific values in financial statements and the structure of the business so that he can make further adjustments of the business process. In that way, the company can become more efficient within specific areas. Also, if a manager is satisfied that the projection of an input or output is relatively small (close to zero; e.g. the case of PODR and -8.26%), he can focus on those projections which are sufficiently big (such as the mentioned OM for the PODR). Here, the management could look at operating earnings and revenues to see where the problem lies, due to some potential problems in the core business. Generally speaking, all of the companies (not only those in Table 4) which have, e.g. too high C/S ratio should lower it to some reasonable degree, as this would lead to lower economic uncertainty around the companies themselves. The available cash could be invested in other relevant (to the business itself) parts of the whole business. Similar conclusions can be obtained for other input and output variables when comparing themselves with others in the sample. Overall, inefficient companies should aim to look at the worst performance of their inputs and/or outputs (as in Table 4) and try to, based on the available resources, solve the worst results regarding input reduction and/or output increase. However, another recommendation here is to focus the comparisons within the same industry if possible.

Of course, the analysis would not stop here. Here, only a glance is given in which aspects of the business perform not as desired, expected and/or poorly. In the next steps, a manager would need to carefully consider related aspects of the business of a poor performing financial ratio (indicator). However, it is seen here that such an approach to modelling points at problems immediately.

Table 5. GRA results, with comparisons to DEA

Firm	Scores			Ranks		
	GRD	W_GRD	DEA	GRD	W_GRD	DEA
ADPL	0.583	1.487	1	5	2	1
ADGR	0.559	0.693	0.185	15	19	18
AREN	0.521	0.661	0.097	21	20	19
ATGR	0.569	0.958	0.324	11	15	15
ATPL	0.565	1.67	1	13	1	1
DLKV	0.554	1.418	1	16	7	1
DDJH	0.532	1.372	1	19	8	1
ERNT	0.676	0.877	0.309	1	17	16
HT	0.573	1.023	0.347	9	12	12
HIMR	0.562	0.96	0.325	14	14	14
INGR	0.575	1.486	1	6	3	1
KONL	0.586	0.726	0.212	4	18	17
KRAR	0.572	0.972	0.335	10	13	13
LKPC	0.552	0.423	0.091	17	21	20
LUKA	0.566	1.466	1	12	6	1
PODR	0.592	1.476	0.917	3	5	9
TPNR	0.528	1.246	0.537	20	11	11
ULPL	0.575	0.93	0.007	7	16	21
RIVP	0.574	1.477	1	8	4	1
VART	0.548	1.339	1	18	9	1
ZBB	0.596	1.291	0.585	2	10	10

Source: authors' calculation

GRA Modelling Results

This next methodological approach is suitable both for managers of firms and investors. However, it could be more suitable for investing purposes, due to obtaining ranks of each firm when they are compared one to another, without the analysis of projections as in DEA. Although, it could give very quick and straightforward results for anyone interested in such results and it is faster to do it regularly. Based on the same financial ratios as in the DEA approach, the normalized values of each ratio were calculated, then the GRCs and finally GRDs were estimated by giving equal weights to all financial ratios. Again, as in the DEA approach, the greater the value of a GRD is, the better-ranked the firm is. The scores of the GRA analysis are given in the first column of Table 5. Best ranking firms are now ERNT, ZBB and PODR (see ranks column GRD). The rankings are a bit different due to giving equal weights to all of the ratios. However, if one uses the weights which are obtained in the DEA optimization procedure, and the final GRD scores are re-calculated (column W_GRD), it can be seen that the rankings now follow the original DEA rankings more.

This information can be used in the management process to make a more detailed DEA analysis once in a while; save the weighted results and use them more frequently within the GRA approach of ranking. If the manager or the investor is interested only in the first glance of a company's results, this could be a good and quick approach. Previous literature did not go beyond basic calculations of the GRD coefficients, as it was done here to use the weighted data as it may be more important for the decision-maker. The potential is shown in Figure 1, where the scores of W_GRD and DEA approaches are compared one to another. The coefficient of determination for a linear relationship is around 86% (for a logarithm functional form almost 77% and a second-order polynomial has over 89%); which indicates a great correlation between the two rankings and makes the results very robust. Thus, by utilizing two different approaches, similar rankings of firms can be made with reliability.

Figure 1. Comparisons of W_GRD (x-axis) and DEA (y-axis) rankings
Source: authors' calculations

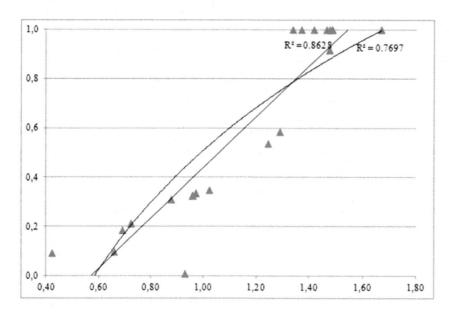

The GRA methodology is useful to calculate the Grey Relational Degree between some objects of interest, i.e. in the case of this study, all of the firms can be compared to the best one, ATPL (see column ranks W_GRD), to see where each firm is mostly correlated in performance to the best one. Now, each financial ratio has been normalized as in the formula (7), and distances have been calculated from the values for ATPL. Values are shown in Table 9 in the Appendix. This can provide the management insights into where do specific companies stand when compared to the best benchmark. This is a similar idea as in DEA projections to the efficient frontier. However, here the decision-maker focuses on one particular firm and compares others to its performance. Such analysis of GRD coefficients can be repeated for comparisons with every firm used as a benchmark in the study. One sample can be used to compare with the best benchmarks and the other for the worst ones. Thus, detailed insights into the good and bad practices can be obtained for future detailed work on sources of those inefficiencies.

DISCUSSION AND CONCLUSION

Based on the results in the previous subsection, some commentary can be given. The existing research on financial ratios analysis is huge and it is not easy to choose only several ratios when making research. A lot of ratios exist which can be useful for examining the efficiency and effectiveness of a business, not only from the managers' point of view but from the investors' as well. However, an objective approach is needed, which would include sufficient enough information on the businesses which are observed and compared. As in any modelling, a parsimonious approach is needed, due to being able to construct and estimate a model and interpret the meaningful results.

Although this research started with a lot of financial ratios, for the analysis to be implemented, the number of those ratios needed to be reduced. The reasoning is found not only in the limitations of the DEA methodology (purely mathematical reasons), but in the economic and business interpretations as well. If several ratios give almost identical information (in mathematical terms, highly correlated), why would the manager or investor use the same information several times in modelling. This research followed the advice within the DEA methodology to focus on those inputs which are highly correlated to outputs. Managers and investors can use that combination of financial ratios which they know from experience and industry common traits. However, further analysis should be consistent in that way. Obtained efficiency scores within the DEA models indicate which company is efficient or not in its conducting of business. The robustness of obtained results can be checked with the GRA approach of ranking. This was done in such a manner that the weights which were used in the optimization process of DEA models have been used to calculate the final GRD values. Combination of both approaches can provide the decision-maker with insights on where are the sources of (in) efficiencies. This reduces time and money needed to improve the business and the whole supply chain process.

Rising globalization, competition, innovations and other many different factors affect businesses today. To remain competitive, a firm needs to continuously re-evaluate its efficiency and total business performance. Managers need to be included in such evaluations due to their knowledge and experience in the total supply-chain process. Moreover, the same analysis which can be done within a company or an industry can be done from the aspect of an investor as well. In that way, such an analysis can provide insights on the performance of companies of interest.

The objectives of this chapter were achieved. Firstly, a comprehensive and exhaustive overview of the theoretical and empirical findings over the decades has been obtained and given in the literature subsection of the chapter. Secondly, the correct usage of financial ratios and the most objective approach of the data analysis have been performed. This is due to the facts that based on the previous literature review; a systematization of the financial ratios and their respective values to be achieved has been performed. This is, to the knowledge of the authors, the first type of such exhaustive systematization found in the literature. To conclude based on things said, the research problems stated at the beginning of this chapter (how to correctly use the financial ratios data when comparing the performance of selected companies, with the basis in finance theory) have been, hopefully, successfully solved. The selected companies and financial ratios have provided the ranking which was obtained in this study. The research included different types of companies (which can be seen in the appendix in the description of each company name and sector classification). Thus, the research is suitable for any type of company (regardless of the type of production). What is important here is that the investor or the manager has to decide which financial ratios are important to them when making their decisions. Thus, a degree of subjectivity is involved in this procedure. But, if the criteria, i.e. the ratios are chosen based on good arguments, there is little doubt that the results of rankings will be non-usable. To check the robustness of the results, the analysis extended to Grey relational analysis approach on the same data to obtain information about how good did the DEA approach rank (in) efficient companies. This is something which is often avoided in empirical research.

Analyses which were examined in this chapter are complementary and are being used together only in the last couple of years. Thus, it is expected that future work will expand upon these initial findings. There is more work to be done. Dynamic analysis should be observed in the future so that decision-makers can obtain information on changes over time. This will be the best indicator if the changes in the business practice have yielded positive results in terms of achieving business goals and wanted values of the financial ratios. Interesting research for future work will be to utilize the GRA methodology to obtain the distances between each financial ratio and the desired value, which the decision-maker can set individually, and then use these distances in the DEA part to estimate efficiencies. This could be helpful within the company itself, but especially for investors who have different preferences and investment goals. Nevertheless, there is still much work to be done within this area of research. Thus, future work related to this chapter will answer some of the remaining questions.

REFERENCES

Adusei, M. (2016). Modelling the efficiency of universal banks in Ghana. *Quantitative Financial Letters*, *4*, 60–70.

Anayiotos, G., Toroyan, H., & Vamvakidis, A. (2010). The efficiency of emerging Europe's banking sector before and after the recent economic crisis. *Financial Theory and Practice*, *34*, 247–267.

Anwaar, M. (2016). Impact of Firms' Performance on Stock Returns (Evidence from Listed Companies of FTSE100 Index London, UK). *Global Journal of Management and Business Research: D Accounting and Auditing*, *16*(1), 1-10.

Aras, G., & Yilmaz, M. K. (2008). Price-earnings ratio, Dividend Yield, and Market to Book ratio to predict Return on stock market: Evidence from the Emerging Markets. *Journal of Global Business and Technology*, *4*(1), 2–20.

Asness, C. S., Ilmanen, A., Israel, R., & Moskowitz, T. J. (2015). Investing with style. *Journal of Investment Management*, *13*(1), 27–63.

Baker, H. K., & Smith, D. M. (2006). In search of a residual dividend policy. *Review of Financial Economics*, *15*(1), 1–18.

Ball, R. (1978). Anomalies in relationships between securities' yields and yield-surrogates. *Journal of Financial Economics*, *6*, 103–126.

Barbee, W. C., Mukherji, S., & Raines, G. A. (1996). Do Sales-Price and Debt-Equity Explain Stock Returns Better Than Book-Market and Firm Size? *Financial Analysts Journal*, *52*(2), 56–60.

Basu, S. (1977). The Investment Performance of Common Stocks in Relation to their Price to Earnings Ratio: A Test of the Efficient Markets Hypothesis. *The Journal of Finance*, *32*, 663–682.

Basu, S. (1983). The relationship between earnings yield, market value, and return for NYSE common stocks: Further evidence. *Journal of Financial Economics*, *12*, 129–156.

Bayrakdaroglu, A., Mirgen, C., & Kuyu, E. (2017). Relationship between profitability ratios and stock prices: An empirical analysis on BIST-100. *PressAcademia Procedia*, *6*, 1–10.

Beaver, W. H. (1989). *Financial accounting: An accounting revolution*. Prentice-Hall, Engle-wood Cliffs.

Berman, K., Knight, J., & Case, J. (2013). *Financial Intelligence. A Manager's Guide to Knowing What the Numbers Really Mean*. Business Literacy Institute, Inc.

Bhandari, L. C. (1988). Debt/Equity Ratio and Expected Common Stock Returns: Empirical Evidence. *The Journal of Finance*, *43*(2), 507–528.

Bhargava, M., Dubelaar, C., & Scott, T. (1998). Predicting bankruptcy in the retail sector: An examination of the validity of key measures of performance. *Journal of Retailing and Consumer Services*, *5*(2), 105–117.

Brennan, M. J. (1970). Taxes, Market Valuation, and Corporate Financial Policy. *National Tax Journal*, *23*, 417–427.

Campbell, J. Y. (1991). A Variance Decomposition for Stock Returns. *Economic Journal (London)*, *101*, 157–179.

Campbell, J. Y., & Shiller, R. J. (1988a). Stock Prices, Earnings and Expected Dividends. *The Journal of Finance*, *43*(3), 661–676.

Campbell, J. Y., & Shiller, R. J. (1988b). The Dividend-Price Ratio and Expectations of Future Dividends and Discount Factors. *Review of Financial Studies*, *1*(3), 195–228.

Capaul, C., Rowley, I., & Sharpe, W. F. (1993). International value and growth stock returns. *Financial Analysts Journal*, *49*(1), 27–36.

Cardinaels, E., & van Veen-Dirks, P. M. G. (2010). Financial versus non-financial information: The impact of information organization and presentation in a Balanced Scorecard. *Accounting, Organizations and Society*, *35*, 565–578.

Cengiz, H., & Püskül, A. Ö. (2016). Hisse Senedi Getirileri ve Karlılık Arasındaki İlişki: Borsa İstanbul Endeksinde İşlem Gören İşletmelerin Analizi. *Yalova Sosyal Bilimler Dergisi, 7*(12), 295–306.

Chan, L. K., Hamao, Y., & Lakonishok, J. (1991). Fundamentals and stock returns in Japan. *The Journal of Finance, 46*(5), 1739–1764.

Chen, H.-H. (2008). Stock selection using data envelopment analysis. *Industrial Management & Data Systems, 108*(9), 1255–1268.

Chen, J.-S., Hung Tai, T., & Huang, Y.-H. (2009). Service Delivery Innovation: Antecedents and Impact on Firm Performance. *Journal of Service Research, 12*(1), 36–55.

Chen, K. H., & Shimerda, T. A. (1981). An empirical analysis of useful financial ratios. *Financial Management, 10*(1), 51–60.

Chen, S. W., & Shen, C. H. (2009). Is the Stock Price Higher than that Implied by the Fundamentals? *International Research Journal of Finance and Economics, 29*, 87–109.

Chung, K. H., & Pruitt, W. (1994). A Simple Approximation of Tobin's q. *Financial Management, 23*(3), 70–74.

Cielen, A., Peeters, L., & Vanhoof, K. (2004). Bankruptcy prediction using a data envelopment analysis. *European Journal of Operational Research, 154*, 526–532.

Cochrane, J. H. (1992). Explaining the Variance of Price-Dividend Ratios. *Review of Financial Studies, 5*, 243–280.

Cooper, W., Seiford, L. M., & Zhu, J. (2011). *Handbook on Data Envelopment Analysis*. Springer.

Cooper, W. W., Seiford, L. M., & Tone, K. (2006). *Introduction to data envelopment analysis and its uses: with DEA-solver software and references*. Springer.

Copeland, T., Koller, T., & Murrin, J. (1996). *Valuation: Measuring and Managing the Value of Companies*. Wiley.

Craig, J., & Moores, K. (2005). Balanced Scorecards to drive the strategic planning of family firms. *Family Business Review, 18*(2), 105–122.

Deaves, R., Miu, P., & White, C. B. (2008). Canadian stock market multiples and their predictive content. *International Review of Economics & Finance, 17*(3), 457–466.

DeBerg, C. L., & Murdoch, B. (1994). An Empirical Investigation of the Usefulness of Earnings Per Share Disclosures. *Journal of Accounting, Auditing & Finance, 9*(2), 249–260.

DeBondt, W., & Thaler, R. (1987). Further Evidence on Investor Overreactions and Stock Market Seasonality. *The Journal of Finance, 42*, 557–581.

Dempsey, M. (2010). The book-to-market equity ratio as a proxy for risk: Evidence from Australian markets. *Australian Journal of Management, 35*(1), 7–21.

du Jardin, P., & Séverin, E. (2011). Predicting corporate bankruptcy using a self-organizing map: An empirical study to improve the forecasting horizon of a financial failure model. *Decision Support Systems*, *51*(3), 701–711.

Edirisinghe, N. C. P., & Zhang, X. (2007). Generalized DEA model of fundamental analysis and its application to portfolio optimization. *Journal of Banking & Finance*, *31*, 3311–3335.

Fama, E., & French, K. (1988). Dividend Yields and Expected Stock Returns. *Journal of Financial Economics*, *22*, 3–26.

Fama, E. F., & French, K. (1992). The cross-section of expected stock returns. *The Journal of Finance*, *47*, 427–465.

Fama, E. F., & French, K. (1993). Common risk factors in the returns on stocks and bonds. *Journal of Financial Economics*, *33*, 3–56.

Fama, E. F., & French, K. R. (1998). Value versus growth: The international evidence. *The Journal of Finance*, *LIII*(6), 1975–1999.

Fang-Ming, L., & Wang-Ching, C. (2010). A precaution diagnosis of financial distress via Grey Situation Decision. *Journal of Grey System*, *22*(4), 395–403.

Fernandes, K. J., Raja, V., & Whalley, A. (2006). Lessons from implementing the balanced scorecard in a small and medium size manufacturing organization. *Technovation*, *26*, 623–634.

Fraser, E., & Page, M. (2000). Value and momentum strategies: Evidence from the Johannesburg Stock Exchange. *The Investment Analysts Journal*, *29*(51), 25–35.

Fukuyama, H. (1993). Technical and scale efficiency of Japanese commerical banks: A non-parametric approach. *Applied Economics*, *25*, 1101–1112.

Gallizo, J. L., & Salvador, M. (2003). Understanding the behavior of financial ratios: The adjustment process. *Journal of Economics and Business*, *55*(3), 267–283.

Gardijan, M., & Kojić, V. (2012). Dea-based investment strategy and its application in the Croatian stock market. *Croatian Operational Research Review*, *3*, 203–212.

Gardijan, M., & Škrinjarić, T. (2015). Equity portfolio optimization: A DEA based methodology applied to the Zagreb Stock Exchange. *Croatian Operational Research Review*, *6*, 405–417.

Ghale, Z. R. (2015). The relation between financial ratio and earnings quality and stock returns. A case study, *GMP Review*, *15*, 6-13.

Golany, B., & Roll, Y. (1989). An application procedure for DEA. *Omega*, *17*(3), 237–250.

Gregoriou, A., Healy, J., & Gupta, J. (2015). Determinants of telecommunication stock prices. *Journal of Economic Studies (Glasgow, Scotland)*, *42*(4), 534–548.

Hafeez, K., Zhang, Y. B., & Malak, N. (2002). Determining key capabilities of a firm using analytic hierarchy process. *International Journal of Production Economics*, *76*, 39–51.

Hamzacebi, C., & Pekkaya, M. (2011). Determining of stock investments with grey relational analysis. *Expert Systems with Applications, 38*, 9186–9195.

Harc, M. (2015). The relationship between tangible assets and capital structure of small and medium-sized companies in Croatia. *Econviews, 28*(1), 213–224.

Hill, C. W. L., Jones, G. R., & Schilling, M. A. (2014). Strategic management theory (11th ed.). Mason: Cengage Learning.

Huang, C., Dai, C., & Guo, M. (2015). A hybrid approach using two-level DEA for financial failure prediction and integrated SE-DEA and GCA for indicators selection. *Applied Mathematics and Computation, 251*, 431–441.

Huang, J. T., & Liao, Y. S. (2003). Optimization of machining parameters of wire-EDM based on grey relational and statistical analyses. *International Journal of Production Research, 41*(8), 1707–1720.

Investing. (2019). https://www.investing.com

Jablonsky, S. F., & Barsky, N. P. (2001). *The Manager's Guide to Financial Statement Analysis*. Wiley.

Jemrić, I., & Vujčić, B. (2002). Efficiency of banks in Croatia: A DEA approach. *Comparative Economic Studies, 44*(2-3), 169–193.

Jiang, H., & He, Y. (2018). Applying Data Envelopment Analysis in Measuring the Efficiency of Chinese Listed Banks in the Context of Macroprudential Framework. *Mathematics, 6*(184), 1–18.

Jordan, C. E., Clark, S. J., & Smith, W. R. (2007). Should Earnings Per Share (EPS) Be Taught as a Means of Comparing Inter Company Performance? *Journal of Education for Business, 82*(6), 343–348.

Keim, D. B. (1988). Stock Market Regularities: A Synthesis of the Evidence and Explanations. In E. Dimson (Ed.), *Stock Market Anomalies* (pp. 16–39). Cambridge University Press.

Koksal, B., Orman, C., & Oduncu, A. (2013). *Determinants of capital structure: evidence from a major emerging market economy*. Available at: https://mpra.ub.uni-muenchen.de/48415/

Kothari, S. P., & Shanken, J. (1997). Book-to-market, dividend yield, and expected market returns: A time-series analysis. *Journal of Financial Economics, 44*, 169–203.

Kuo, Y., Yang, T., & Huang, G.-W. (2008). The use of a grey-based Taguchi method for optimizing multi-response simulation problems. *Engineering Optimization, 40*(6), 517–528.

Kuosmannen, T. (2009). Data envelopment analysis with missing data. *The Journal of the Operational Research Society, 60*(12), 1767–1774.

La Porta, R. (1996). Expectations and the Cross-Section of Stock Returns. *The Journal of Finance, 51*(5), 1715–1742.

Lau, C. H., & Sholihin, M. (2005). Financial and non-financial performance measures: How do they affect job satisfaction? *The British Accounting Review, 37*, 389–413.

Lau, S. T., Lee, T. C., & McInish, T. H. (2002). Stock Returns and Beta, Firms Size, E/P, CF/P, Book-to-market, and Sales Growth: Evidence from Singapore and Malaysia. *Journal of Multinational Financial Management, 12*, 207–222.

Leary, M. T., & Michaely, R. (2011). Determinants of Dividend Smoothing: Empirical Evidence. *Review of Financial Studies, 24*(10), 3197–3249.

Lee, C., & Lee, W. H. (2008). Can financial ratios predict the Malaysian stock return? *Integration & Dissemination, 2*, 7–8.

Lewellen, J. (2004). Predicting Returns with Financial Ratios. *Journal of Financial Economics, 74*, 209–235.

Li, H.-Y., Zhang, C., & Zhao, D. (2010). Stock Investment Value Analysis Model Based on AHP and Grey Relational Degree. *Management Science and Engineering, 4*, 1–6.

Li, M. Y. L. (2009). Value or volume strategy? *Finance Research Letters, 6*(4), 210–218.

Lim, S., Oh, K. W., & Zhu, J. (2013). Use of DEA Cross-Efficiency Evaluation in Portfolio Selection: An application to Korean Stock Market. *European Journal of Operational Research, 236*(1), 361–368.

Lintner, J. (1956). Distribution of Incomes of Corporations among Dividends, Retained Earnings, and Taxes. *The American Economic Review, 46*, 97–113.

Litzenberger, R., & Ramaswamy, K. (1979). The Effects of Personal Taxes and Dividends on Capital Asset Prices: Theory and Empirical Evidence. *Journal of Financial Economics, 7*(2), 163–195.

Liu, S., & Lin, Y. (2006). *Grey Information Theory and Practical Applications*. Springer.

Liu, S., & Lin, Y. (2010). *Grey systems, Theory and Applications*. Springer.

Lopes, A., Lanzer, E., Lima, M., & da Costa, N. Jr. (2008). DEA investment strategy in the Brazilian stock market. *Economic Bulletin, 13*(2), 1–10.

Lugovskaja, L. (2009). Predicting default of Russian SMEs on the basis of financial and non-financial variables. *Journal of Financial Services Marketing, 14*(4), 301–313.

McDonald, J. T. (1999). The Determinants of Firm Profitability in Australian Manufacturing. *The Economic Record, 75*(229), 115–126.

Miller, M., & Scholes, M. (1982). Dividend and taxes: Some empirical evidence. *Journal of Political Economy, 90*, 1118–1141.

Modigliani, F., & Miller, M. (1958). The Cost of Capital, Corporation Finance and the Theory of Investment. *The American Economic Review, 48*(3), 261–297.

Modigliani, F., & Miller, M. (1963). Corporate income taxes and the cost of capital: A correction. *The American Economic Review, 53*(3), 433–443.

Morris, R. (2018). *Early Warning Indicators of Corporate Failure: A Critical Review of Previous Research and Further Empirical Evidence*. Rutledge Revivals.

Muhammad, N., & Scrimgeour, F. (2014). Stock Returns and Fundamentals in the Australian Market. *Asian Journal of Finance & Accounting*, 6(1), 271–290.

Mukherji, S., Dhatt, M. S., & Kim, Y. H. (1997). A Fundamental Analysis of Korean Stock Returns. *Financial Analysts Journal*, 53(3), 75–80.

Myers, S. C. (1984). The Capital Structure Puzzle. *The Journal of Finance*, 39(3), 575–592.

Myers, S. C., & Majluf, N. S. (1984). Corporate Financing and Investment Decisions When Firms Have Information That Investors Do Not Have. *Journal of Financial Economics*, 13(2), 187–221.

Palepu, K. G., Healy, P. M., Bernard, V. L., & Wright, S. (2010). Business Analysis & Valuation: Using Financial Statements (4th ed.). Mason: South-Western Cengage Learning.

Pätäri, E. J., Leivo, T. H., & Honkapuro, J. V. S. (2010). Enhancement of value portfolio performance using data envelopment analysis. *Studies in Economics and Finance*, 27(3), 223–246.

Penman, S. H., Richardson, S. A., & Tuna, I. (2007). The book-to-price effect in stock returns: Accounting for leverage. *Journal of Accounting Research*, 45(2), 427–467.

Philips, P., & Louvieris, P. (2005). Performance measurement systems in tourism, hospitality and leisure small medium-sized enterprises: A balanced scorecard perspective. *Journal of Travel Research*, 44, 201–211.

Powers, J., & McMullen, P. (2002). Using data envelopment analysis to select efficient large cap securities. *Journal of Business and Management*, 7(7), 31–42.

Prieto, I. M., & Revilla, E. (2006). Learning capability and business performance: A non-financial and financial assessment. *The Learning Organization*, 13(2), 166–185.

Salardini, F. (2013). An AHP-GRA method for asset allocation: A case study of investment firms on Tehran Stock Exchange. *Decision Science Letters*, 2(4), 275–280.

Singh, A., & Schmidgall, R. S. (2002). Analysis of financial ratios commonly used by US lodging financial executives. *Journal of Retail & Leisure Property*, 2(3), 201–213.

Škrinjarić, T. (2014). Investment Strategy on the Zagreb Stock Exchange Based on Dynamic DEA. *Croatian Economic Survey*, 16, 129–160.

Škrinjarić, T., & Šego, B. (2019). Using Grey Incidence Analysis Approach in Portfolio Selection. *International Journal of Financial Studies*, 7(1), 1–16.

Stattman D. (1980). Book values and stock returns, *The Chicago MBA: A Journal of Selected Papers*, 4, 25–45.

Staub, R. B., da Silva, S., & Tabak, B. M. (2010). Evolution of bank efficiency in Brazil: A DEA approach. *European Journal of Operational Research*, 202, 204–213.

Tehrani, A. G., & Tehrani, A. (2015). The effect on financial ratios to predict company profits and stock returns. *International Journal of Life Sciences (Kathmandu)*, 5(1), 591–599.

Tobin, J. (1969). A General Equilibrium Approach To Monetary Theory. *Journal of Money, Credit and Banking*, *1*(1), 15–29.

Tracy, J. A. (2004). *How to Read a Financial Report: Wringing Vital Signs Out of the Numbers*. John Wiley and Sons.

Wier, B., Hunton, J., & Hassab Elnaby, H. R. (2007). Enterprise resource planning systems and non-financial performance incentives: The joint impact on corporate performance. *International Journal of Accounting Information Systems*, *8*, 165–190.

Wu, L. S. (2000). A Survey and An Analysis of Investor's Demands for Listed Companies' Accounting Information. *Economic Research Journal*, *4*, 41–48.

Zagreb Stock Exchange. (2019). https://www.zse.hr

Zamani, L., Beegam, R., & Borzoian, S. (2014). Portfolio Selection using Data Envelopment Analysis (DEA): A Case of Select Indian Investment Companies. *International Journal of Current Research and Academic Review*, *2*(4), 50–55.

Zhao, D., Kuo, S.-H., & Wang, T. C. (2014). The Evaluation of the Business Operation Performance by Applying Grey Relational Analysis. In Intelligent Data analysis and its Applications, Volume I. Advances in Intelligent Systems and Computing, (Vol. 297). Cham: Springer.

KEY TERMS AND DEFINITIONS

Business Performance Management: A set of analytics and management measures within the business to achieve business goals.

Data Envelopment Analysis: A set of mathematical models and methods developed to evaluate the relative efficiency of the decision-making units.

Financial Ratios: Relative number indicating the ratio of two financial values from the financial statements to determine the financial health of a company.

Grey Relational Degree: A number indicating the strength of a relationship between the attributes of an observed and the optimal values those attributes could achieve.

Investment Decision: Selecting which type of financial assets will an investor invest his resources, with the selection being based on some kind of analysis.

Mathematical Optimization: The procedure for selecting the best possible values of a variable or alternative between a given set of available variables/alternatives.

Performance Evaluation: The procedure of modeling, optimizing and comparing the results of a given set of alternatives based on defined criteria, in which the results are given in the form of a number with values in a specific interval.

Relative Efficiency: A measure which depicts how much a set of entities/alternatives are efficient in employing their inputs to produce outputs, with the comparison made one to another (and not some ideal values).

APPENDIX

Table 6. Companies used in the study

Firm	Full name	Sector classification
ADPL	AD Plastik, manufacture of parts and accessories for motor vehicles and plastic products	CL 2932, manufacture of other parts and accessories for motor vehicles.
ADGR	ADRIS Grupa, management and investing	MA 7010, management activities
AREN	Arena Hospitality Group, for tourism and hospitality	I 5510, hotels and similar accommodation
ATGR	Atlantic Grupa, for internal and foreign trade	G 4690, non-specialized wholesale trade
ATPL	Atlantska plovidba, international transport of goods and passengers	H 5020, maritime and coastal water transport
DLKV	Dalekovod, for engineering, manufacturing and construction	F 4222, construction of power and telecommunication lines
DDJH	Đuro Đaković group	MA 7010, management activities
ERNT	Ericsson Nikola Tesla, company for the production of telecommunication systems and devices	CI 2630, manufacture of communication equipment
HT	Hrvatski telekom	JB 6110, wired telecommunications activities
HIMR	Imperial Riviera, for tourism	I 5510, hotels and similar accommodation
INGR	Ingra, for construction of investment facilities, import, export and representation	MA 7112, engineering and related technical consultancy
KONL	Končar elektroindustrija	CJ 2711, manufacture of electric motors, generators and transformers
KRAR	Kraš food industry	CA 1082, manufacture of cocoa, chocolate and confectionery
LKPC	Luka ploče, for maritime services, port services, warehousing and freight forwarding	H 5224, cargo handling and transshipment
LUKA	Luka Rijeka, for maritime services, port services, warehousing and freight forwarding	H 5224, cargo handling and transshipment
PODR	Podravka food industry	CA 1039, other processing and preserving of fruit and vegetables
TPNR	Tankerska Next Generation	H 5020, maritime and coastal water transport
ULPL	Uljanik plovidba	H 5020, maritime and coastal water transport
RIVP	Valamar Riviera	I 5510, hotels and similar accommodation
VART	Varteks varaždinska tekstilna industrija, textile industry	CB 1413, manufacture of other outerwear
ZBB	Zagrebačka banka	K 6419, other monetary intermediation

Source: Investing (2019), Zagreb Stock Exchange (2019)

Table 7. Descriptive statistics for financial ratios in the analysis

Financial ratio	Mean	Median	Maximum	Minimum	Std. Dev.	Skewness	Kurtosis	Jarque-Bera	Probability	N
CSG	0.093	0.093	0.532	-0.154	0.169	0.644	3.62	1.62	0.446	19
EPS_G	0.14	0.076	0.656	-0.058	0.216	1.18	3.62	2.99	0.224	12
S_G	0.015	0.013	0.207	-0.163	0.095	-0.056	2.67	0.101	0.951	20
AT	0.57	0.395	1.81	0.09	0.425	1.27	4.47	7.22	0.027	20
BEPS	-3.43	7.55	85.4	-444	104	-3.84	17	224	0.000	21
BV/S	288	204	996	-712	402	-0.11	3.34	0.141	0.932	21
CF/S	18.6	34.6	139	-441	113	-3.27	14.3	148	0.000	21
C/S	75.5	23.1	438	0.27	106	2.07	7.53	33	0.000	21
CR	1.77	1.19	10.9	0.07	2.32	3.19	13.1	119	0.000	20
DEPS	-3.43	7.55	85.4	-444	104	-3.84	17	224	0.000	21
DGR	0.197	0.16	0.783	-0.11	0.25	1.44	4.59	4.06	0.131	9
DY5Y	0.023	0.017	0.0739	0	0.026	0.862	2.33	2.57	0.277	18
DY	0.039	0.026	0.0912	0.022	0.023	1.2	3.07	2.64	0.268	11
EPS_Q	0.293	0.138	6.93	-3.48	2.14	1.69	6.54	21	0.000	21
EPS_TTM	-0.745	0.238	37.5	-44.7	13.2	-0.64	10.1	45.5	0.000	21
GM5Y	0.537	0.493	0.987	0.118	0.211	0.218	2.71	0.217	0.897	19
GM	0.539	0.502	0.854	0.288	0.173	0.241	1.91	1.19	0.551	20
IT	13.4	5.44	70.3	0.65	17.1	2.24	7.55	33.9	0.000	20
LTD/E	0.869	0.337	5.81	0.003	1.42	2.6	8.94	51.9	0.000	20
NI/E	41.2	38.8	190	-52.1	58.9	0.759	4.78	2.97	0.226	13
NPM5Y	-0.0262	0.0499	0.211	-0.848	0.252	-2.32	7.61	35.6	0.000	20
NPM	-0.0418	0.0504	0.36	-1.78	0.414	-3.69	16.2	200	0.000	21
OM5Y	-0.00179	0.0447	0.26	-0.622	0.206	-1.9	6.22	20.6	0.000	20
OM	-0.00377	0.0653	0.422	-1.32	0.328	-3.18	13.7	136	0.000	21
P/E	16.9	14.1	35.2	3.79	8.97	0.549	2.33	0.963	0.618	14
PR	0.384	0.406	0.832	0	0.308	0.023	1.66	1.06	0.590	14
PM5Y	-0.0165	0.0514	0.26	-0.847	0.258	-2.19	7.25	31	0.000	20
PM	-0.0269	0.0614	0.422	-1.78	0.422	-3.55	15.6	182	0.000	21
P/B	1.18	0.935	4.02	0.41	0.847	2.03	7.41	29.9	0.000	20
PCF	77.1	10.9	648	1.1	201	2.65	8.05	22.3	0.000	10
PFCF	172	14.3	1.09E+03	4.25	405	2.04	5.15	6.18	0.045	7
P/S	1.32	0.79	4.25	0.13	1.23	1.21	3.21	5.19	0.074	21
P/TB	1.47	1.08	5.27	0.26	1.28	1.75	5.48	15.3	0.000	20
QR	1.46	0.98	9.95	0.06	2.16	3.27	13.3	125	0.000	20
RT	20.8	5.63	131	2.46	35	2.43	7.5	36.5	0.000	20
ROA5Y	0.008	0.021	0.118	-0.119	0.059	-0.739	3.23	1.86	0.394	20
ROA	0.003	0.021	0.134	-0.302	0.084	-2.32	9.82	59.5	0.000	21
ROE5Y	0.014	0.042	0.569	-0.764	0.253	-1.1	6.85	15.6	0.000	19
ROE	0.014	0.047	0.367	-0.559	0.183	-1.52	6.64	18.7	0.000	20

continues on following page

Table 7. Continued

Financial ratio	Mean	Median	Maximum	Minimum	Std. Dev.	Skewness	Kurtosis	Jarque-Bera	Probability	N
ROI5Y	0.012	0.028	0.265	-0.174	0.1	0.067	4.02	0.83	0.660	19
ROI	0.001	0.028	0.311	-0.504	0.148	-1.69	8.66	36.2	0.000	20
R/E	762	650	1610	249	388	0.983	3.15	2.11	0.349	13
R/S	379	276	1620	5.21	458	1.39	3.97	7.63	0.022	21
S_Q	0.068	0.026	0.735	-0.208	0.197	1.94	7.49	30.9	0.000	21
S_TTM	0.008	0.034	0.18	-0.253	0.128	-0.765	2.48	2.28	0.319	21
TBV/S	251	170	994	-712	377	-0.064	3.81	0.594	0.743	21
D/E	1.15	0.538	7.35	0.003	1.8	2.5	8.53	46.3	0.000	20

Note: Jarque-Bera denotes the test value for the null hypothesis of normal distribution; Probability is the *p*-value for the Jarque-Bera test.
Source: authors' calculation

Table 8. Correlation matrix between inputs and outputs in the analysis

Note: Values below the main diagonal are the correlation coefficients, while values above are the *p*-values in testing the significance of correlations. Notations V1-V47 refer to the financial ratios as depicted in Table 1. Red values in matrix denote statistical significance.
Source: authors' calculation

Table 9. Correlation matrix between companies

Probability	ADGR	ADPL	AREN	ATGR	ATPL	DDJH	DLKV	ERNT	HIMR	HT	INGR	KONL	KRAR	LKPC	LUKA	PODR	RIVP	TPNR	ULPL	VART	ZBB
ADGR	1	0.0006	0.0000	0.0292	0.0000	0.2120	0.2330	0.0765	0.0000	0.0000	0.4640	0.0000	0.0001	0.0000	0.0000	0.0001	0.0000	0.0000	0.0124	0.0000	0.0008
ADPL	0.7600	1	0.0008	0.0000	0.0000	0.0000	0.0001	0.0000	0.0001	0.0000	0.6200	0.0000	0.0000	0.0003	0.0042	0.0000	0.0000	0.0002	0.4750	0.0000	0.0734
AREN	0.9820	0.7520	1	0.0280	0.0000	0.1800	0.1940	0.0538	0.0000	0.0000	0.5450	0.0000	0.0001	0.0000	0.0000	0.0002	0.0000	0.0000	0.0215	0.0000	0.0000
ATGR	0.5440	0.9420	0.5480	1	0.0051	0.0000	0.0000	0.0000	0.0155	0.0027	0.7660	0.0000	0.0000	0.0150	0.0987	0.0000	0.0004	0.0211	0.7920	0.0001	0.2140
ATPL	0.9770	0.8630	0.9500	0.6640	1	0.0569	0.0680	0.0157	0.0000	0.0000	0.4520	0.0000	0.0000	0.0000	0.0000	0.0000	0.0000	0.0000	0.0353	0.0000	0.0064
DDJH	0.3300	0.8460	0.3530	0.9440	0.4850	1	0.0000	0.0000	0.1290	0.0557	0.7980	0.0014	0.0002	0.1110	0.4160	0.0002	0.0106	0.1510	0.2230	0.0014	0.5350
DLKV	0.3160	0.8190	0.3430	0.9210	0.4670	0.9830	1	0.0000	0.1510	0.0695	0.8560	0.0021	0.0004	0.1170	0.4070	0.0004	0.0155	0.1690	0.1490	0.0017	0.5180
ERNT	0.4550	0.9100	0.4900	0.9680	0.5920	0.9770	0.9540	1	0.0383	0.0113	0.8580	0.0001	0.0000	0.0313	0.2070	0.0000	0.0015	0.0528	0.5940	0.0004	0.2350
HIMR	0.9910	0.8120	0.9710	0.5930	0.9920	0.3960	0.3760	0.5210	1	0.0000	0.4790	0.0000	0.0000	0.0000	0.0000	0.0000	0.0000	0.0000	0.0121	0.0000	0.0023
HT	0.9720	0.8640	0.9650	0.6970	0.9760	0.4870	0.4650	0.6150	0.9790	1	0.5470	0.0000	0.0000	0.0000	0.0000	0.0000	0.0000	0.0000	0.0278	0.0000	0.0011
INGR	0.1970	0.1340	0.1640	0.0809	0.2020	0.0696	-0.0494	0.0485	0.1910	0.1630	1	0.5410	0.5750	0.5050	0.6380	0.5640	0.5940	0.4650	0.7810	0.4300	0.8400
KONL	0.8840	0.9690	0.8850	0.8510	0.9480	0.7280	0.7090	0.8140	0.9160	0.9420	0.1650	1	0.0000	0.0000	0.0001	0.0000	0.0000	0.0000	0.2470	0.0000	0.0100
KRAR	0.8220	0.9910	0.8210	0.9020	0.9090	0.8000	0.7770	0.8740	0.8660	0.9020	0.1520	0.9920	1	0.0000	0.0009	0.0000	0.0000	0.0000	0.3720	0.0000	0.0302
LKPC	0.9800	0.7860	0.9960	0.5950	0.9590	0.4140	0.4070	0.5390	0.9710	0.9660	0.1800	0.9120	0.8530	1	0.0000	0.0001	0.0000	0.0000	0.0473	0.0000	0.0001
LUKA	0.9770	0.6740	0.9400	0.4270	0.9500	0.2190	0.2230	0.3330	0.9660	0.9150	0.1280	0.8150	0.7450	0.9350	1	0.0011	0.0000	0.0000	0.0082	0.0001	0.0041
PODR	0.8140	0.9950	0.8030	0.9090	0.9050	0.8040	0.7800	0.8730	0.8590	0.8960	0.1560	0.9870	0.9980	0.8360	0.7390	1	0.0000	0.0000	0.3750	0.0000	0.0468
RIVP	0.9210	0.9350	0.9060	0.7770	0.9730	0.6190	0.5930	0.7250	0.9560	0.9690	0.1440	0.9760	0.9600	0.9180	0.8720	0.9580	1	0.0000	0.0690	0.0000	0.0114
TPNR	0.9910	0.7950	0.9610	0.5700	0.9920	0.3770	0.3610	0.4920	0.9970	0.9650	0.1970	0.9050	0.8520	0.9630	0.9790	0.8470	0.9440	1	0.0147	0.0000	0.0041
ULPL	-0.6080	-0.1920	-0.5690	0.0716	-0.5290	0.3220	0.3780	0.1440	-0.6100	-0.5480	-0.0756	-0.3070	-0.2390	-0.5020	-0.6350	-0.2380	-0.4660	-0.5960	1	-0.2210	0.1180
VART	0.8660	0.9470	0.8450	0.8300	0.9390	0.7270	0.7180	0.7810	0.8930	0.9000	0.2120	0.9810	0.9730	0.8830	0.8180	0.9720	0.9460	0.8960	-0.2210	1	0.5380
ZBB	0.7520	0.4600	0.8510	0.3280	0.6500	0.1680	0.1750	0.3150	0.7050	0.7380	0.0550	0.6220	0.5420	0.8340	0.6760	0.5030	0.6140	0.6760	-0.4070	0.5380	1

Note: Values below the main diagonal are the correlation coefficients, while values above are the p-values in testing the significance of correlations.
Source: authors' calculation

147

Table 10. Distances of financial ratio values from the optimal value of ATPL

	C/S	OM5Y	OM	AT	BEPS	ROA5Y	ROI5Y	TBV/S
ADPL	0.033	0.350	0.338	0.055	0.643	0.474	0.439	0.219
ADGR	0.395	0.334	0.159	0.000	0.564	0.398	0.711	0.190
AREN	0.290	0.391	0.142	0.001	0.514	0.354	0.188	0.168
ATGR	0.223	0.368	0.242	0.069	0.673	0.491	0.336	0.851
ATPL	0.000	0.000	0.000	0.000	0.000	0.000	0.000	0.000
DLKV	0.051	0.305	0.797	0.066	0.409	0.236	0.731	0.103
DDJH	0.053	0.269	0.558	0.036	0.121	0.102	0.730	0.062
ERNT	0.346	0.363	0.245	0.138	1.000	1.000	0.249	1.000
HT	0.039	0.432	0.136	0.020	0.777	0.533	0.521	0.116
HIMR	0.124	0.417	0.059	0.002	0.598	0.405	0.208	0.318
INGR	0.055	0.406	0.523	0.016	0.656	0.507	0.720	0.048
KONL	0.393	0.343	0.384	0.044	0.652	0.476	0.809	0.447
KRAR	0.124	0.348	0.273	0.057	0.582	0.421	0.193	0.424
LKPC	1.000	0.320	0.347	0.013	0.561	0.384	1.000	0.049
LUKA	0.051	0.275	1.410	0.008	0.450	0.314	0.653	0.070
PODR	0.005	0.357	0.265	0.058	0.668	0.476	0.034	0.317
TPNR	0.044	1.000	0.230	0.003	0.482	0.334	0.609	0.035
ULPL	0.014	0.105	5.168	0.009	0.043	0.092	1.981	5.473
RIVP	0.051	0.416	0.094	0.009	0.695	0.474	0.708	0.021
VART	0.055	0.260	0.903	0.009	0.261	0.165	0.660	0.120
ZBB	0.137	0.495	1.000	1.000	0.522	0.334	0.638	0.034

Source: authors' calculation

Chapter 8
Comparison of European Option Pricing Models at Multiple Periods

Amir Ahmad Dar

B. S. Abdur Rahman Crescent Institute of Science and Technology, India

N. Anuradha

B. S. Abdur Rahman Crescent Institute of Science and Technology, India

Ziadi Nihel

High Business School of Manouba, Tunisia

ABSTRACT

The point of this chapter is to think about the correlation of two well-known European option pricing models – Black Scholes Model and Binomial Option Pricing Model. The above two models not statistically significant at one period. In this examination, it is shown how the above two European models are statistically significant when the time period increases. The independent paired t-test is utilized with the end goal to demonstrate that they are statistically significant to vary from one another at higher time period and the Anderson Darling test being used for the normality test. The Minitab and Excel programming has been utilized for graphical representation and the hypothesis testing.

INTRODUCTION

The derivatives are the agreement between the two gatherings in which one gathering consents to purchase and another gathering consents to offer the basic resource at a characterized cost at a future date. The fundamental derivatives are forward, future, swap and options. They are exchanged on both Over-the-Counter (OTC) and exchange market. In this investigation, just European options are utilized. European options will lapse just on the development date. The Black Scholes Model (BSM) and Binomial option pricing model (BOPM) are the celebrated option pricing models. Through the budgetary world, the two

DOI: 10.4018/978-1-7998-3053-5.ch008

option evaluating models are utilizing with the end goal to gauge the estimation of the options (call and put). "An option is an agreement/contact that gives the proprietor the rights, yet not the commitment to purchase (if there should arise an occurrence of call option) or sell (in the event of a put option) at some characterized cost called strike cost at some future date" (Hull 2003). The holder of a call option trusts that the price of an underlying asset value will increment in future date and in the event of the put option, the holder trusts that the estimation of underlying asset price value will fall in future. With the end goal to claim the rights, the holder/purchaser of an option needs to pay some add up to the writer/ seller, that instalment is known as premium.

Options are utilized with the end goal to decrease the future hazard (misfortune) i.e. s hedging or to maximise the profit of an investment. The price of the option relies upon the movement of the price of an underlying stock. Therefore a financial specialist will settle on a option relies upon whether the cost of a underlying asset will climb or down. On the off chance that the underlying asset climbs, at that point the speculator will pick the call option and if the value moves down, at that point he will pick put option. The financial specialists will practice the option if there is a positive result. The result is an arrival at some future date. Fisher and Myron in 1973 separated a hypothetical option value valuation and analysis it with scientifically. That demonstrates the actual price/value varies from the calculated option pricing model. Panduranga (2013a, 2013b) tried whether Black Scholes choice evaluating model is significant to Indian derivatives market. It was distinguished that the actual cost of an option is statistically significant with the calculated price of an option using Black Scholes model. Feng and Kwan (2012) researched that the BOPM which in the end meets to understood BSM as the quantity of Binomial period increment. In the year 2018, Dar and Anuradha distinguished that there is no huge contrast between the BOPM and BSM at one period by utilizing the two measurable techniques – t-test and Tukey strategy.

Initially, we use networks to assess the estimations of the options (call/put) toward the t=0 that gives an incentive to each call and put options at different strike costs at an expiry/develop date subject to the non-benefit paying shares and without premium.

At last, the outcomes we understood that BSM is fundamentally unique in relation to BOPM at the number of time periods increment with the assistance of statistical paired t-test. Minitab and Excel have been utilized as a vital apparatus to compute all the vital outcomes.

Most speculators and dealers new to options markets want to purchase calls and puts as a result of their restricted hazard and boundless benefit potential. Purchasing puts or calls is commonly a path for financial specialists and dealers to hypothesize with just a small amount of their capital. Yet, these straight option purchasers miss a considerable lot of the best highlights of stock and product options, for example, the chance to turn time-esteem rot (the decrease in estimation of an alternatives contract as it arrives at its termination date) into potential benefits. This chapter focused on the option values and its two famous methods for calculating the option values. The traders should know about the methods so that they can easily estimate the premium when people buy options. In this way, this chapter comes under the data science and analytics.

LITERATURE REVIEW

Boyle (1988) has presented five-jump cross section structure for evaluating with two state factors under the suspicion of the bivariate lognormal dispersion of these state factors. Boyle, Evnine and Gibbs (1989) presented a methodology for esteeming multivariate unexpected cases including a few hidden resources under the guess of the lorgarithmic return process, in light of an n-dimensional augmentation of the grid binomial strategy. Kamrad and Ritchken (1991) expands the past model that depends on approximating the logarithmic returns process by a discrete multinomial cross section and consider even bounces, in contrast to the Boyle, Evnine and Gibbs approach. The binomial option model and the Boyle, Evnine and Gibbs models are unique instances of Kamrad and Ritchken model. The model is intended to deal with productively the valuation of unforeseen cases whose qualities rely upon numerous wellsprings of vulnerability. Bollen (1998) presented a "pentanomial" grid that approximates a regim-switching procedure at the cost of the basic; for valuing both European-style and American-style options. System exchanging models are more adaptable than those with SV; permitting the parameters of the stochastic variable conveyance to take on various qualities in various systems. Authors expect two system exchanging model, where the two systems are spoken to by a trinomial that is then joined into one "pentanomial" cross section whose center branch is shared by the two systems. Ritchken and Trevor (1999) proposed a grid approach for evaluating American-style options under the discrete time-varying unpredictability GARCH systems. Lee, Tzeng, Wang (2005) acquainted fluffy set hypothesis with the binomial estimating model to set up the fluffy binomial option valuing model. Their outcomes demonstrate that this kind of model fits the information much better then unique binomial estimating model. Additionally, financial specialists utilizing this model can develop their portfolio system as indicated by their hazard inclinations. The idea of fluffiness is utilized to gauge the riskless loan fee and the unpredictability. The stock value, call value, unpredictability, riskless interest cost and likelihood have as indicated by the triangular fluffy number three qualities, including low, medium and high. In each time interim stock cost have three situations to go up and three situations to descend – can move into six new qualities, where the up, center and low development is described by the high, center and low instability. At that point bond and stock are joined to frame supported portfolio to get the call cost. The estimation of the portfolio can again go up or down with three probabilities (up, center, down) for every development. Option costs are then determined in a similar way is in the binomial technique. This structure takes into account the hazard inclinations of financial specialist.

Option pricing theory aims to find the relations and dependencies between the factors that influence the option price and the option price itself to deduce the option pricing formula or mechanism. Option pricing theory dates back to the very beginning of the 20-th century, when the French mathematician Louis Bachelier deduced an option pricing formula. The formula was based on the assumption that stock prices follow a Brownian motion with zero drift. Option estimating theory plans to discover the relations and conditions between the elements that impact the option value and the option value itself to reason the option evaluating recipe or system. Option evaluating theory goes back to the earliest reference point of the 20-th century, when the French mathematician Louis Bachelier derived an option estimating equation. The recipe depended on the presumption that stock costs pursue a Brownian movement with zero drift. The best improvement (some review to this change as progressive) was activated by crafted by Robert C. Merton (1973) and F. Black and M. Scholes (1973) in 1970's. Black and Scholes exhibited the principal complete balance option estimating model under the suspicion of risk-neutrality. Merton than broadened their model in a few different ways. Black-Scholes model is nowadays most well-known, despite the fact that it abuses the truth in number of ways. The model has for sure framed the reason for some resulting scholarly investigates. The hypothesis of derivatives valuing is helpful in hazard the executives and propelled the hypothetical comprehension of financial markets. Option costs might be too used to give an understanding into the atmosphere the monetary market's assumption regarding the future improvement of costs. Bates (1991) among others tried on the information before the 1987 accident the theory that when out-of-the cash puts are valued higher than out-of-the-money calls the financial specialists expect enormous descending developments in the basic stock costs as for this situation the puts are bound to complete in-the cash than the calls.

DERIVATIVE

It is the financial contract between the two parties in which one party agrees to sell and another party agrees to buy an underlying asset at some future date at some specific price. A derivative is a security or a contract which promise to make a payment at a future date. For example, my two friend's one is a farmer (A) and another is a business man (B), they both make a contract that a business man (B) will buy farmers rice (A) after one year at some price. In other words, it is financial contract whose value depends on the value of the other underlying variables. For example, a stock option whose value is dependent on the price of the stock. The underlying assets are commodities, bonds, market indexes, currencies, the stocks, and interest rate.

Derivative Market

The Derivative market is a financial market where the derivatives like futures contract, forwards contract, options, swap etc. The derivatives market can be classified into two:

Over-the-Counter (OTC)

Over-the-Counter (OTC) derivatives markets are those which are privately traded between two parities and no one is involving between the two parities (no intermediary). The information of those two parties not leaked out. The non-standard derivatives are traded in Over-the-Counter like Swap, forwards contract etc. the Over-the-Counter derivative market consists of the investment banks and include clients like commercial banks, government sponsored enterprises, hedge funds etc. The Over-the-Counter is the largest traded derivative market in the derivative markets.

Exchange-Traded Derivatives (ETD)

Exchange-traded derivatives (ETD) are derivative market where the individual's trade standardized contracts that have been defined by the exchange. An Exchange-traded derivatives (ETD) acts as a middle man (intermediary) to all related transactions and takes initial margin from both sides of the trade to act as a guarantee. The Options and the futures contract are traded in the Exchange-traded derivatives (ETD) market. The Korea Exchange, Eurex and CME group are the largest derivatives exchange market.

TYPES OF DERIVATIVES

There are four main types of derivatives:

1. Futures Contract

It is an agreement between the two parties in which one party agrees to buy and another party agrees to sell an underlying asset at a certain future time for a certain price (that will mention at the beginning of the contract). Unlike a forward contract, the buyer and the seller do not enter into an agreement with one another. Normally the futures contract is traded on an exchange market. The exchanges market act as an intermediate in a futures contract. It is standardised and the two parties are guaranteed that the contract will be honoured. The Chicago Board of Trade (CBOT) and Chicago Mercantile Exchange (CME) are the two largest exchange markets where the futures contract is traded. A non-obligatory contract to buy/sell an asset on or before a future date at a price specified today. It is standardized and traded on exchange. The underlying assets often traded in future contract are cattle, sugar, wool, copper, gold, tin, stock indices, currencies, treasury bonds etc.

Example

Suppose that a person having plan to grow 1 ton kilogram of rice in the next period, he can either grow the rice and then sell it to the market or he can enter into the future contract that obligates him to sell 1 ton kilogram of rice after the harvest for a fixed price (it is price that the two parties fix some price at the beginning of the contract). By entering into a futures contract (or locking the price now), he can eliminate the risk of falling rice prices. But at the end of the period if the price of the rice increases, then he will get only contract entitled him to.

Forward Contracts

It is a simple derivative. It is an agreement between the two parties in which one party agrees to buy and another party agrees to sell an underlying asset at a certain future time for a certain price (that will mention at the beginning of the contract). The benefit of this contract is that the information does not release to the public. An obligatory contract between two parties, where payment takes place at a specific time in the future at today's pre-determined price. It is non-standardized and traded off an exchange. Forward contracts are traded mainly "over the counter" markets between two financial institutions or between a financial institution and one of its clients. The underlying assets often traded in forward contracts are oil, beef, orange juice, gas, wheat, rice etc.

The futures and the forward contract allow peoples to sell or buy an underlying asset at a future date at a specific price. Both are same in explanation but the difference is that the futures contract are standardised that is it can be traded on the exchange market. The exchanges market act as an intermediate and a guarantor.

Options

It is contract between individuals or firms in which one party is ready to buy and another party is ready to sell. Option is a contract that gives owner the rights but not obligation to buy or sell an underlying asset at a fixed price (exercise/strike price) on the future date (maturity/exercise). Options are traded in the over-the-counter and the exchange market.

Option Styles

American Options

An American option is an agreement that can be expiry before the mature date.

European Options

A European option is an agreement that cannot be expiry before the mature date.

Types of Options

There are two main types of options:

Call Option

It gives the holder the right but not obligation to buy an underlying asset at a fixed price/exercise/strike price on the future date

Put Option

It gives the holder the right but not obligation to sell an underlying asset at a fixed price/exercise/strike price on the future date.

Swap

A swap is an agreement between two financial institutes to exchange cash flows in the future date. Swaps are traded in the over-the-counter derivatives market. The agreement defines the dates when the cash flows are to be paid and the way in which they are to be calculated. Usually the calculation of the cash flows involves the future value of an interest rate, an exchange rate, or other market variable. There are two types of swap:

1. **Interest Rate Swap:** An interest rate swap is an agreement between two parties in which the two parties exchange interest payments periodically.
2. **Currency Swap:** A currency swap is an agreement between the two parties in which the two parties deliver one currency against another.

USES OF OPTIONS

Hedge

It reduces the future risk in the underlying by entering into an option contract whose value moves in the opposite direction to the underlying position and cancels part or all of it out. For example, if a person enters into a call option, it means that the buyer of an option is having rights to buy or not the underlying asset at the fixed price/strike price at the mature date. If the price (market price) of the underlying asset at the mature date is higher than the fixed price then he will exercise the option because he will buy it at a lower price and sell it in the market at a higher price. If the price (market price) of the underlying asset at the mature date is lower than the fixed price then he will not exercise the option. In this way, the investor/institute reduces the future loss.

Speculation

It is a sort of winning or losing the amount of money that is gambling, in this, a person even gains a big margin of money or loses a lot of amounts.

Let us suppose that a person believes that the price of underlying asset will increase in next period. Suppose the underlying asset price opened Rs 129.07 on May 15, 2015. Now a person will buy one share of an underlying asset at strike price Rs 130 and the expiration date is July 17, 2015. Suppose he buys a call option.

Therefore, if the stock price increase above 130, the speculator could exercise his rights to buy one share of an underlying asset 1t Rs 130. Let us assume that the underlying asset price increase to RS 140 on July 16, 2015.

The speculator could exercise his rights to buy one share and sell it at Rs 140.

Therefore, the net profit is 140-130= Rs 10

Arbitrage

Arbitrage is a risk-free investment. In simple terms, an arbitrage opportunity is a situation where anyone can make a profit without taking any risk. This is something described as free breakfast. An arbitrage opportunity exists if

1. At some future date T
    a.   The probability of a loss is equal to zero
    b.   The probability that we make a strictly positive profit is greater than zero
2. We can start at time t=0, with a portfolio that has a net value of zero (Zero cost portfolio).

Example: Buy a share from a market and sell the same share in another market with higher price.

FEATURES OF OPTIONS

The following features are common in all types of options.

1. **Contract**: It is an agreement between the two parties to buy /sell an underlying asset
2. **Premium**: Premium is money, in case of options the premium is to be paid by on party (the buyer) to the other party (the seller).
3. **Pay- off**: The profit made by the holder at the expiry date T is called the payoff.
4. **Holder:** The buyer of an option is called the holder

5. **Writer**: The seller of an option is called the holder
6. **Exercise price**: It is the price where the option holder buys (in case of call options) or sells (in case of put options).
7. **Underlying asset**: The underlying assets are: metals, commodities, stock indices, stocks, currencies etc. Simply it is variety of traded instruments.

NOTATION

- t is the current time
- S_t is the current price of an underlying asset (Price of an underlying asset at time t)
- K is the exercise price or strike price
- T is the options expiry time
- c_t is the price of an underlying asset at time t of a European Call option
- p_t is the price of an underlying asset at time t of a European Put option
- r is the risk-free rate of interest

HYPOTHESIS

Based on the objective of this study, the following hypotheses are framed:

H_0 = "There is no mean difference between the BOPM and BSM"
H_1 = "There is mean difference between the BOPM and BSM of options"

METHODOLOGY

First of all, we calculated the price of a European option at multiple period by using the two famous pricing models BOPM and BSM. Later we compare both the models in order to check whether there are any mean differences between the BOPM and BSM at different period with the help of statistical tools t-test.

In order to identify whether the data is following a normal distribution, one of the better way to compare the P-value with the significance level α. There are two cases:

a) If P-value is greater than significance level α (P-value>α), then we don't have enough proof to dismiss the null hypothesis. It implies that the information pursues a normal distribution

b) If P-value is less or equal than significance level α (P-value<= α), then we don't have enough evidence to accept the null hypothesis. It means that the data is not comes from the normal population.

Finally, the authors used Q-Q Plot also to check whether the data follows a normal distribution.

BINOMIAL OPTION PRICING MODEL (BOPM)

The BOPM is a scientific model which assesses the estimations of the option. The BOPM is a basic evaluating model and straightforward. It was first created by J C Cox, S A Ross, and M Rubinstein in 1979. It depends on the no-arbitrage opportunity approach. Arbitrage opportunity implies risk-free trading profit and no-exchange implies that the market is efficient. In this option evaluating model depends on the unique case in which the cost of an underlying asset over some period can either run down with d percent or up with u percent. In the event that S_0 is the current cost of an underlying asset then at the following time frame the cost of an underlying asset will be either

$$S_u = S_0 * (1+u)$$

Or

The payoff of the call option at the maturity date is either

$$C_u = \text{Maximum}(S_u - K, 0)$$

Or

$$C_d = \text{Maximum}(S_d - K, 0)$$

Similarly, for a put option

$$P_u = \text{Maximum}(K - S_u, 0)$$

Or

$$P_d = \text{Maximum}(K - S_d, 0)$$

Assume that the r is the rate of interest and we assume that $d < r < u$
At one period the price of an option is:

$$V_0 = e^{-rt} * (q * C_u + (1-q) * C_d) \text{ for call option}$$

$$V_0 = e^{-rt} * (q * P_u + (1-q) * P_d) \text{ for put option}$$

Where q is not a real world probability, it is known as synthetic probability and it is a number calculated as

$$q = \frac{e^r - d}{u - d}$$

Also, $u = e^{\sigma \sqrt{\delta t}}$ and $d = e^{-\sigma \sqrt{\delta t}}$

Under the BOPM the q are expressed above, and every one of the steps are made autonomous of each other (J. C Hull 2003; Dar and Anuradha 2017a).

The price of an option at time t is:

$$V_t = e^{-r(n-t)} * \sum_{k=0}^{n-t} f\left(S_t * u^k * d^{n-t-k}\right) * \frac{(n-t)!}{k!(n-t-k)!} * q^k * (1-q)^{n-t-k}$$

At time $t = 0$

$$V_0 = e^{-r(n)} * \sum_{k=0}^{n} f\left(S_0 u^k d^{n-k}\right) * \frac{(n)!}{k!(n-k)!} * q^k * (1-q)^{n-k}$$

Where, $f\left(S_0 u^k d^{n-k}\right)$ is payoff

Figure 1. Multiple binomial models

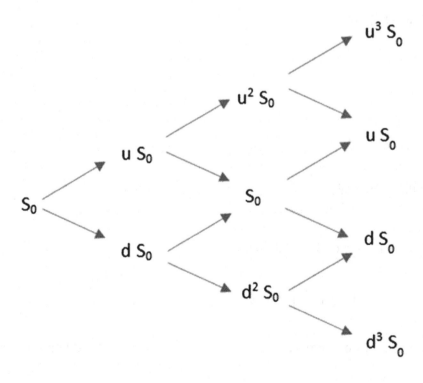

Note: "The binomial pricing model traces the evolution of the option's key underlying variables in discrete-time. This is done by means of a binomial lattice (tree), for a number of time steps between the valuation and expiration dates. Each node in the lattice represents a possible price of the underlying at a given point in time. Valuation is performed iteratively, starting at each of the final nodes (those that may be reached at the time of expiration), and then working backwards through the tree towards the first node (valuation date). The value computed at each stage is the value of the option at that point in time (J. C Hull 2003)"

BLACK SCHOLES MODEL

The Black Scholes option pricing model is the renowned model created by Fisher Black, Myron Scholes and Robert Merton in 1970s. Once in a while it is otherwise called Black-Scholes-Merton demonstrates.

The Back-Scholes formulas for European option at time $t = 0$ on non-dividend paying shares are
For call option

$$c = S_0 * N(d_1) - K * e^{-rT} * N(d_2)$$

For put option

$$p = K * e^{-rT} * N(-d_2) - S_0 * N(-d_1)$$

Where

$$d_1 = \frac{\ln\left(\frac{S_0}{K}\right) + \left(r + \frac{\sigma^2}{2}\right) * T}{\sigma\sqrt{T}}$$

$$d_2 = \frac{\ln\left(\frac{S_0}{K}\right) + \left(r - \frac{\sigma^2}{2}\right) * T}{\sigma\sqrt{T}} = d_1 - \sigma * \sqrt{T}$$

The function "N (*) is a cumulative probability distribution function for a standardised normal distribution".

RESULT AND ANALYSIS

In order to compare the two European option models, we need some values of parameters that are given below:

Give us a chance to consider an European call option with underlying asset cost is Rs 42, the rate of interest is 10% per annum, volatility is 20% per annum, and the strike cost of the European option is Rs 40, and the and the time period is 1, 10, 20, 30,......90 (in years) (J. C Hull page no. 294). this means that $S_0 = Rs42$, $K = Rs40$, $r = 10\%$, $Ã = 20\%$ and $t = 1, 10, 20, \ldots, 90$

In order to compare the BOPM and Black Scholes model for European call option, the above example is enough to calculate the values of the call option at multiple periods.

Table 1. Values of European call option using BOPM and BSM

Time	Call option value (BOPM)	Call option value (Black-Scholes model)
1	7.27	6.84
10	23.26	27.59
20	29.09	36.63
30	31.69	40.02
40	33.20	41.27
50	34.25	41.73
60	35.07	41.90
70	35.75	41.96
80	36.33	41.99
90	36.83	41.99

Paired T-Test

To check whether there is any mean distinction between the samples, the paired statistical T- T-test system is utilized. Statistical T-test is a statistical method for hypothesis testing. The assumption for this method is that the population distribution is at least approximately normal and the variances are equal. The statistical paired T-test strategy thinks about the mean of two factors set for a solitary gathering.

This test used in order to verify whether the average difference between the two datasets is differing from zero.

"Null hypothesis: $H_0 : {}^{1}\!/\!4_{difference} = 0$"

"Alternative hypothesis: $H_1 : {}^{1}\!/\!4_{difference} \neq 0$"

Paired T-Test

The Paired T-test statistics is:

$$T = \frac{\overline{d}}{\frac{S_d}{\sqrt{n}}}$$

Where, d = differences between the pairs of data, $\overline{d}$ = mean of $d_1, d_2, d_3, \ldots \ldots d_n$

n = number of objects

Degrees of freedom = n – 1

If the data is less than 30, then we have to check whether it is following the normal distribution.

It is better to compare the P-value of with $\alpha = 0.05$, if P –value $< \alpha = 0.05$, then we reject the null hypothesis.

Our information is matched yet it isn't sufficiently extensive (under 30) as appeared in table 1, so we have to check whether it pursues a normal distribution at 95% confidence interval. The Anderson Darling measurable test is utilized.

Anderson Darling Test

Test Hypotheses for Anderson Darling test:

H_0: "Data is sampled from a population that is normally distributed (no difference between the data and normal data). We may accept the null hypothesis if $P - value > \alpha = 0.05$.

H_1: "Data is sampled from a population that is not normally distributed".

Note: $\alpha = 0.05$

After calculation we have:

- AD test statistic = 0.6618
- AD* test statistic = 0.726333
- P-value = **0.058244**

From Figure 2, $P - valve > \alpha = 0.05$, we don't have enough proof to dismiss the null hypothesis; it implies that the information originate from the normal distribution. (Dar, A A and Anuradha 2017b).

Normal Q-Q Plot

In order to determine normality graphically, we can use the output of a normal Q-Q Plot as shown in figure 3. If the data are normally distributed, the data points will be close to the diagonal line. If the data points stray from the line in an obvious non-linear fashion, the data are not normally distributed. As we can see from the normal Q-Q plot below, the data is normally distributed. If you are at all unsure of being able to correctly interpret the graph, rely on the numerical methods instead because it can take a fair bit of experience to correctly judge the normality of data based on plots.

Figure 2. Normal probability plot

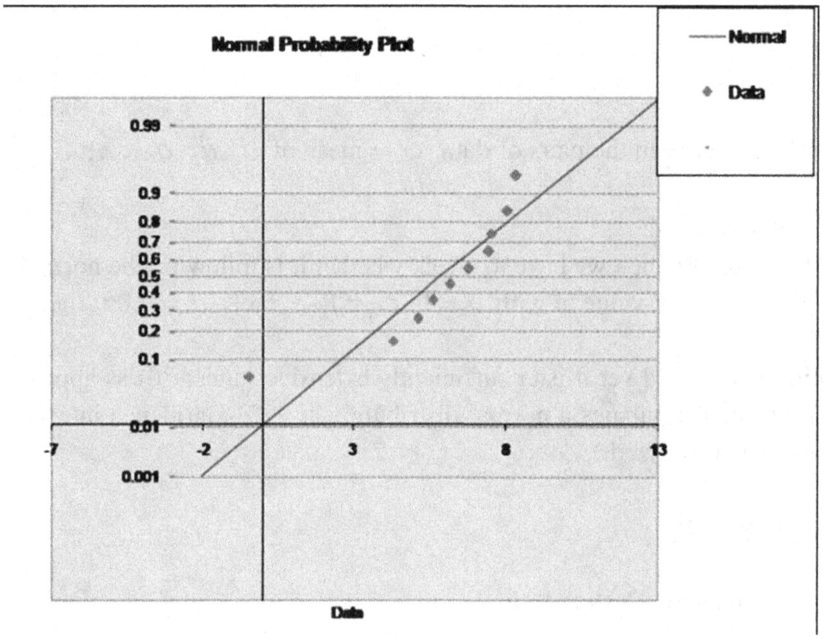

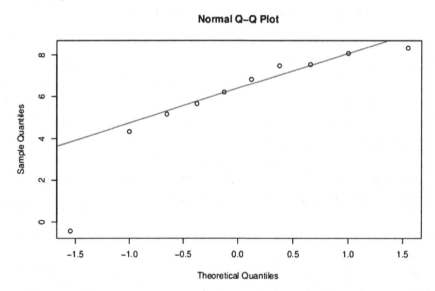

Figure 3. Normal Q-Q plot

Paired T-Test and CI: Call Option (BM), call Option (BSM)

Table 2 displays the basic statistics of BSM and BOPM such as sample size, standard deviation, mean and standard error mean. It is shown in table 2, that the mean of BSM is higher than BOPM while calculating the European call option. The standard deviation reveals that subjects were more variable with respect to BSM than BOPM.

Table 2. Descriptive statistics

Sample	N	Mean	St. Dev	SE. Mean
call option (BOPM)	10	30.27	9.06	2.87
call option (BSM)	10	36.23	11.28	3.57

Table 3. Estimation of paired difference

Mean	St. Dev	SE. Mean	95% CI for μ_difference
-5.961	2.623	0.829	(-7.837, -4.085)

"μ_difference: mean of (call option (BOPM) - call option (BSM)"

- T-Value = -7.19
- P-Value = 0.000

The P-value = 0.000, it may conclude that we don't have enough evidence to accept the null hypothesis because of $P-value < \alpha = 0.05$. The two models are statistical differ from at each other when the time period increases.

Figure 4. values of call option at different time periods

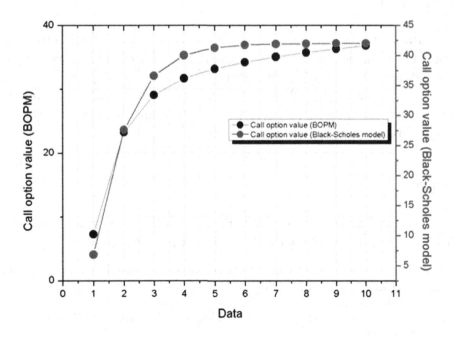

Figure 4, it shows that when the time period increases both the models converges to each other. From the beginning the value of call option using BSM giving the higher value of call option than BM, but when the time period increases both models will merge at some point.

As the number of exercise period between option contacts increases the binomial model converges to the Black Scholes model. It is based on the stochastic principle of random walk and Brownian motion. Though theoretically proven, using excel give more understanding to this poof. The diagram in Figure 4 displays the convergence of the Binomial to the Black-Scholes based on the inputs made in the program.

CONCLUSION

The BSM and BOPM are the two imperative models for assessing the option pricing. The options are utilized with the end goal to lessen the future misfortune that is supporting. The guardian of the call option trusts that at development date the cost of an underlying asset will rise. Our information is combined yet it isn't sufficiently huge (under 30) as appeared in table 1, so we have to check whether it pursues a normal distribution. The Anderson Darling measurable test is utilized. The P-value of (BSM-BOPM) more noteworthy than alpha, which shown that data pursues a normal distribution at 95% confidence level utilizing Darling Anderson measurable test. The BSM gives the higher estimation of consider option than BOPM yet when the day and age increments both the models meets to one another. The measurable combined T-test was utilized with the end goal to explore that whether there is any mean distinction between the two models. It was discovered that P-value $< \alpha=0.05$, that implies they are statistically significant at 95% certainty interim. In future, we will consider put option too.

ACKNOWLEDGMENT

"To my family, particularly my parents and sister, thank you for your love, support, and unwavering belief in me. Without you, I would not be the person I am today. And I would like to thank my wife Samiya Jan for her love and constant support, for all the late nights and early mornings, and for keeping me sane over the past few months. But most of all, thank you for being my best friend. I owe you everything".

"I would like to thank my supervisor for consistent guidance, tutelage, support, unparalleled knowledge, and encouragement".

REFERENCES

Bates, D. S. (1991). The Crash of '87: Was It Expected? The Evidence from Options Markets. *The Journal of Finance*, *46*(3), 1009–1044. doi:10.1111/j.1540-6261.1991.tb03775.x

Black, F., & Scholes, M. (1973). The pricing of options and corporate liabilities. *Journal of Political Economy*, *81*(3), 637–654. doi:10.1086/260062

Bollen, N. P. (1998). Valuing options in regime-switching models. *Journal of Derivatives*, *6*(1), 38–50. doi:10.3905/jod.1998.408011

Boyle, P. P. (1988). A lattice framework for option pricing with two state variables. *Journal of Financial and Quantitative Analysis, 23*(1), 1–12. doi:10.2307/2331019

Boyle, P. P., Evnine, J., & Gibbs, S. (1989). Numerical evaluation of multivariate contingent claims. *Review of Financial Studies, 2*(2), 241–250. doi:10.1093/rfs/2.2.241

Cox, J. C., Ross, S. A., & Rubinstein, M. (1979). Option pricing: A simplified approach. *Journal of Financial Economics, 7*(3), 229–263. doi:10.1016/0304-405X(79)90015-1

Dar, A. A., & Anuradha, N. (2017a). One Period Binomial Model: The risk-neutral probability measure assumption and the state price deflator approach. *International Journal of Mathematics and Trends and Technology, 43*(4), 246–255.

Dar, A. A., & Anuradha, N. (2017b). Value at Risk (VaR) using statistical method. *International Journal of Science. Engineering and Management, 2*(11), 42–49.

Dar, A. A., & Anuradha, N. (2018). Comparison: Binomial model and Black Scholes model. *Quantitative Finance and Economics, 2*(1), 230–245. doi:10.3934/QFE.2018.1.230

Hull, J. C. (2003). *Options futures and other derivatives*. Pearson Education India.

Kamrad, B., & Ritchken, P. (1991). Multinomial approximating models for options with k state variables. *Management Science, 37*(12), 1640–1652. doi:10.1287/mnsc.37.12.1640

Lee, C. F., Tzeng, G. H., & Wang, S. Y. (2005). A fuzzy set approach for generalized CRR model: An empirical analysis of S&P 500 index options. *Review of Quantitative Finance and Accounting, 25*(3), 255–275. doi:10.100711156-005-4767-1

Merton, R. C. (1973). Theory of rational option pricing. Theory of Valuation, 229-288.

Panduranga, V. (2013a). An Empirical Analysis of Black Scholes option pricing model for select banking stocks. *International Journal of Multidisciplinary Research in Social and Management Science, 2*, 23-30.

Panduranga, V. (2013b). Relevance of Black-Scholes option pricing model in Indian derivatives markets– a study of cement stock options. *International Journal of Multidisciplinary Research in Social and Management Sciences, 1*(4), 91–95.

Ritchken, P., & Trevor, R. (1999). Pricing options under generalized GARCH and stochastic volatility processes. *The Journal of Finance, 54*(1), 377–402. doi:10.1111/0022-1082.00109

KEY TERMS AND DEFINITIONS

Call Option: It gives the holder the right but not obligation to buy an underlying asset at a fixed price/exercise/strike price on the future date.

Derivatives: Derivatives are the agreement between the two gatherings in which one gathering consents to purchase and another gathering consents to offer the basic resource at a characterized cost at a future date.

European Options: A European option is an agreement that cannot be expiry before the mature date.

Option Pricing Models: Option pricing models are mathematical models that use certain variables to calculate the theoretical value of an option.

Options: Option is a contract that gives owner the rights but not obligation to buy or sell an underlying asset at a fixed price (exercise/strike price) on the future date (maturity/exercise).

Put Option: It gives the holder the right but not obligation to sell an underlying asset at a fixed price/exercise/strike price on the future date.

Chapter 9
Use of Data Analytics to Increase the Efficiency of Last Mile Logistics for Ecommerce Deliveries

Gaurav Nagpal

(iD) https://orcid.org/0000-0003-1957-7865

Birla Institute of Technology and Science, Pilani, India

Gaurav Kumar Bishnoi

Birla Institute of Technology and Science, Pilani, India

Harman Singh Dhami

Birla Institute of Technology and Science, Pilani, India

Akshat Vijayvargia

Birla Institute of Technology and Science, Pilani, India

ABSTRACT

With the increasing share of digital transactions in the business, the way of operating the businesses has changed drastically, leading to an immense opportunity for achieving the operational excellence in the digital transactions. This chapter focusses on the ways of using data science to improve the operational efficiency of the last mile leg in the delivery shipments for e-commerce. Some of these avenues are predicting the attrition of field executives, identification of fake delivery attempts, reduction of mis-routing, identification of bad addresses, more effective resolution of weight disputes with the clients, reverse geo-coding for locality mapping, etc. The chapter also discusses the caution to be exercised in the use of data science, and the flip side of trying to quantify and dissect the phenomenon that is so complex and subjective in nature.

DOI: 10.4018/978-1-7998-3053-5.ch009

INTRODUCTION

The ecommerce industry has witnessed an exponential growth globally in the past decade. This is the industry of the future, by virtue of the value-add it can provide to the customers. The ecommerce value chain is highly responsive to the customer, and a source of convenient sourcing for him. The ecommerce transactions also result in lesser costs related to inventory carrying, and have a faster inventory turnover. But the last mile logistics cost in such transactions is significantly higher as a percentage of the gross merchandise value of the goods sold. If this cost can be reduced, it can work wonders for this industry.

The logistics sector is not only one of the major contributor to the GDP (Gross Domestic Product) of the nations, but is also a driver for the entire economy since the movement of goods (that ultimately drives the economy) is dependent upon this sector. However, since times, the logistics has been an unorganized industry, which is now being transformed to help the clients achieve their goals. The streamlined logistics can be a major source of competitive advantage for any organization. The organizations, these days, have been outsourcing the logistics function to the specialized logistics services providers so that they can focus more on their core strengths. In order to improve the operational performance of any industry, it becomes paramount to use the data driven approach for structured decision making. Also, the nature of problems is complex and unstructured, which makes the use of structured decision making very important. This scientific decision making can come from the use of data analytics. It is here that data analytics has a big role to play.

Fortunately, the scale of transactions in ecommerce makes sure that we have the plenty of data available from them, which can be used to validate the relevance of the problem statement, generate important insights, arrive at the solutions, implement them, learn from the implementation and improvise the solutions further in a journey of continuous excellence. The data generated by the ecommerce transactions has a significant scale to provide the necessary insights which can be leveraged to achieve the process improvements related to different aspects.

There are multiple ways in which the data can be leveraged. A few of them can be predicting the attrition of the field executives (here-after referred to as FEs), identification of fake delivery attempts by the FEs, reducing the misrouting of the shipments, resolving the weight dispute issues in the shipments, optimizing the delivery route of the field executives, identifying the bad addresses on the shipments, geocoding of the addresses, exploring the economic comparison between fixed staff model and variable staff model, etc.

In this paper, the current Section lays down the motivation for the research. The review of the literature has been performed in the Section 2, and the nine examples of the above mentioned applications of data science have been explained in Section 3, along with the detailed elaboration of the first two applications and the findings of the real-life implementations in firms practicing the last mile deliveries. The Section 4 concludes the paper stating the overall benefits and risks that come with the use of data science in last mile logistics.

LITERATURE REVIEW

The optimization of logistics decisions has become indispensable with the increased movement of goods and services across the geographies in globalized trade (Langevin and Riopel, 2005). Koul and Verma (2011) used advanced analytics to consider the influence of the uncertainties tied to the human cognitive thinking process for vendor selection. Similar studies on the power of analytics in revolutionizing supply chain have been done by LaValle et al. (2011), Chen et al. (2012) and Khan (2013). Waller and Fawcett (2013) said that supply chain will be revolutionized and transformed by predictive analytics to improve the productivity and operational efficiencies. Wu et al. (2016) while doing the review of smart supply chain literature also suggested that there is a tremendous potential on the research for applying analytics in the supply chains. Hanne and Dornberger (2017) also presented how analytics can be used for transportation planning and vehicle routing problems. Deep et al. (2019) presented many of the latest innovations and analytics applications for supply chain, inventory and logistics.

Vehicle routing in case of ecommerce is very peculiar since the demands follow a particular pattern at different times of the day. Considering this interval-varying demand, Erbao et al. (2018) developed a non-linear mixed integer programming model for vehicle routing under interval based demands. Earlier, Sui et al. (2010) had shown how the spatial analysis of GIS data can be used for rioting optimization in last mile.

Although there is significant amount of work on the use of data analytics for logistics and inventory management, but it is hard to find any work in the literature that focusses on the last mile deliveries of the ecommerce. Quante et al. (2019) also suggested that there is definitely the need for more scientific modelling that meets the needs of the industry. That gave the authors a motivation to write this paper.

Also, while the applications of analytics are important, we need to take care on how to apply them. An important consideration in this regard needs to be given to data privacy, ethics, use of right tools, presenting the right findings, etc. Barton and Court (2012) emphasized that the advanced analytics techniques need to be applied in appropriate manner to make them for us. Many other researchers in the field of data science have also conveyed the need for ethics, data privacy in the use of data analytics (Monreale et al, 2014, Buttarelli, 2015 and Fargo et al, 2020).

PERSPECTIVES

In this section, we shall discuss the different ways in which the data science can be used to achieve operational efficiencies in the last mile deliveries. The following approach can be used for solving the problems on the basis of data.

Use of Data Analytics in Forecasting the Attrition of Delivery Executives

In the industries like customer service, construction and hospitality, the unexpected attrition rate is highest. Frequent voluntary attrition has a highly negative impact on employee morale, productivity, and the firm's financials. Recruiting and training a new employee requires numerous resources such as training time and money, and the unplanned nature of the quits disrupts the operations for quite some time. Consequently, the companies need to either pay extra incentive to riders, or outsource the orders. This also leads to poor customer experience. The cost of hiring and training a new staff is typically over a month's salary for the unskilled staff and up to three months for a semi-skilled staff.

Hence determining the probability of field executive leaving the organization becomes very crucial to keep the last mile delivery costs in check and operations running smooth. Having an idea of attrition helps plan accordingly beforehand. Also, predicting the attrition possibilities of the FEs in a given month, using previous year's attrition data offer firms us a greater control over FE attrition administration, and reduces the reduces the risk of inefficiency. For example, if the firm knows that a field executive is likely to quit, it can plan preventive methods for the case where the FE actually quits. Such an exercise of attrition prediction can involve the following steps:

1. Brainstorming the list of variables that influence attrition and can be used in the model.
2. Extracting the data from their respective departments
3. Feature engineering to find the relevant parameters
4. Designing the Machine Learning (ML) model and testing it with the previous data to check the accuracy
5. Using different ML algorithms to find the most appropriate algorithm (the objective is to maximize the recall for 1(Attrition) i.e. the case where models predicts an FE will quit and the data complies, without much change in the other values)
6. Real time monitoring for few weeks until we receive stabile results.

Figure 1. The workable approach for solving the logistics problems using data analytics

Thus, a machine learning model helps predict future attrition if given enough long training data of attrition and factors that affect attrition. Different Algorithms that are effective in predicting attrition are Neural Networks, XGBoost, Random Forest Classifier and Logistic Regression. The parameters affecting attrition in this Industry are broadly classified as: financial (compensation with respect to their peers, Incentives, Deductions, etc.), work-based parameters (distance Covered, shipments delivered, ratio of tougher shipments), demographic parameters (age, Marital Status, City tier, time spent in company, etc.), job market scenario (Similar job availability in the same location), and the recent attendance.

Findings of the Attrition Prediction Model

Mentioned in Figure 2 and Table 1 are the Confusion matrix and the Classification report of a model worked out at one of the Indian ecommerce delivery players that predicted the attritions with an accuracy ranging between 70-85%, and thereby, helping it to take the required action and keep the last mile logistic chain smooth, sturdy and efficient.

Figure 2. Confusion Matrix for attrition prediction model of executives

Actual Values

	Positive (1)	Negative (0)
Positive (1)	TP 3267	FP 718
Negative (0)	FN 208	TN 807

Predicted Values

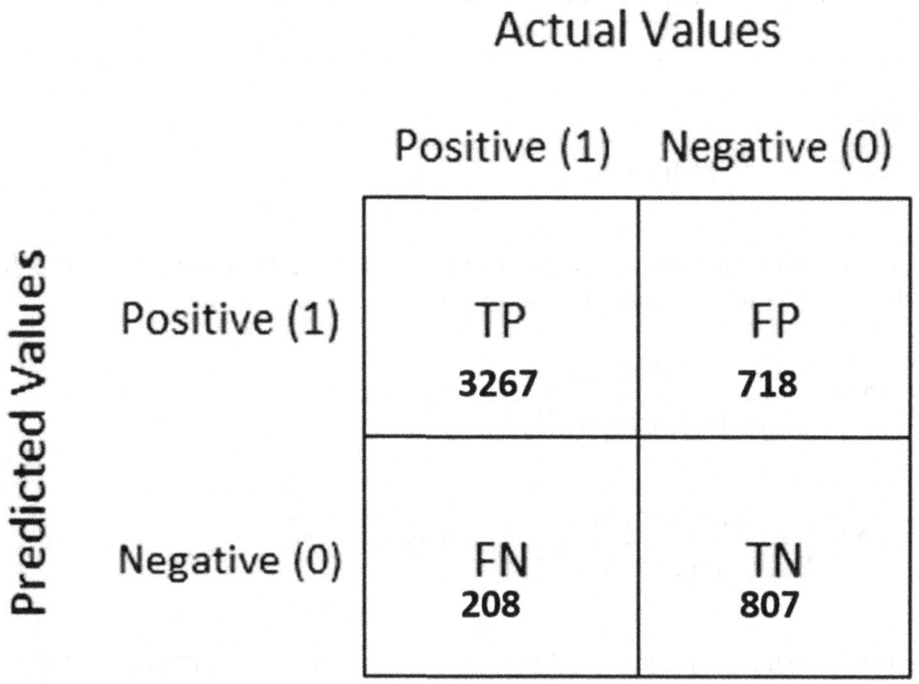

Table 1. Classification report for attrition prediction model of executives

	Precision	Recall	F1 Score
Positive (1)	0.82	0.94	0.88
Negative (0)	0.80	0.53	0.64

The modelling accuracy can be seen with a confusion matrix which mentions:

1. **True Positives (TP):** These are cases in which we predicted yes and the FE actually quits
2. **True Negatives (TN):** We predicted no, and they don't quit.
3. **False Positives (FP):** We predicted yes, but they don't actually quit (Also known as a "Type I error")
4. **False Negatives (FN):** We predicted no, but they do quit. (Also known as a "Type II error.")

The precision is intuitively the ability of the classifier not to label as positive a sample that is negative.

$$Precision(1) = \frac{TP}{TP + FP} = 0.82$$

$$Precision(2) = \frac{TN}{TN + FN} = 0.80$$

The recall is intuitively the ability of the classifier to find all the positive samples.

$$Recall(1) = TP / (TP + FN) = 0.94$$

$$Recall(2) = TN / (TN + FP) = 0.53$$

The F1 score can be interpreted as a weighted harmonic mean of the precision and recall, where an F1 score reaches its best value at 1 and worst score at 0.

$$F1Score(1) = 2 * \frac{Precision(1) * Recall(1)}{\left[Precision(1) + Recall(1) \right]} = 0.88$$

$$F1Score(2) = 2 * \frac{Precision(2) * Recall(2)}{\left[Precision(2) + Recall(2) \right]} = 0.64$$

Our objective is maximize the recall for 1 (the case where mode l s predicts an FE will quit and the data complies) without much loss is other parameters. The model with the highest recall can be comfortably chosen for predicting the attrition.

The utility of such a prediction increases all the more at the time of marketing campaigns so that the increased order rush generated should not be converted into opportunity loss of sales due to insufficient delivery manpower. Similarly, there is also a cost of having excess manpower if the number of expected manpower is over-estimated. Thus, the delivery resources of the last mile can be considered analogous to the inventory assets in an organization, whose under-stocking as well as over-stocking carries some cost, creating a dent on the profitability margins.

Use of Data Analytics for Identification Of Fake Delivery Attempts

The delivery executives, at a time, mark a delivery attempt without having actually attempted, in order to supplement their earnings. This is an unethical practice and hits the profitability of the last mile organizations. There can be data-based rules that can be checked, and the flags can be raised on the instances which may need further investigation. With millions of shipments on daily basis, these flag-raising rules can help bring up such cases at minimum cost. This was actually done at an ecommerce logistics firm. The flags raised are as follows:

1. **No Call Bridge:** The Airway-Bill number was flagged if either both the call talktime and call duration were zero or the call bridge was Null. This essentially implies that the FE never attempted to call the consignee.
2. **Distance Flag:** Any shipment which was marked undelivered within a 20 meters radius of the Distribution Centre (here-after referred to as DC) without a call bridge was flagged.
3. **Odd-Hour Flag:** Any shipment marked undelivered between 9PM and 6AM without a call bridge was flagged.
4. **Time Flag:** Any shipment marked undelivered within 5 minutes of closing time of the Daily Report of Shipments (here-after referred to as DRS) without a call bridge was flagged.
5. **Duplicate Flag:** Multiple shipments in the same DRS marked undelivered on the same latitude-longitude within one minute without a call bridge were flagged.
6. **Same Lat-Long Flag:** Multiple shipments in the same DRS marked undelivered on the same latitude-longitude without a call bridge were flagged.
7. **Ratio Flag:** The DRS was flagged if the percentage of undelivered shipments for a particular DRS was greater than 80% for Pre-Paid Delivery (here-after referred to as PPD) shipments and 70% for Cash-On-Delivery (here-after referred to as COD) shipments.
8. **Aggregate Flag:** If an Airway-Bill fails on any of the above stated parameters, it is flagged here.
9. **Sum of Flags:** It gives the number of parameters on which a particular airway-bill has failed.

All the flagging was used to generate various summaries specific to DCs and FEs. These summaries were generated for different regions as well. The report was then sent to the Operations Team of the organization for further analysis and subsequent action. This made it very easy for the management to track the instances of fake delivery attempts. The check-sheet used for this exercise is shown in the Table 2. The exact percentages cannot be shared for the reasons of confidentiality.

Findings of the Fake Delivery Attempt Model

Based on the analysis above, it was found that approx. 15% of deliveries for first attempt and 30% for second attempt were found to breach the delivery protocol. Also, the DCs and FEs could be categorized into buckets on the basis of their tendency to mark fake delivery attempts. This enabled the management to identify the more notorious DCs and FEs, and put in place selective control measures targeted at these set of resources, so that the 20% of the elements that cause 80% of the problem (as reflected in Table 3) could be controlled. The colours in table 4 signify the percentage of the delivery centres or field executives attempting the fake deliveries within that range. The darkness of a cell is proportional to the percentage of the delivery centers or field executives lying in that range of fake potential. The darker

Table 2. Template for tracking the percentage share of each rule in the flagging for First attempt and further attempts

Rule Description	Flag Count	% share
Shipment marked undelivered within 10 meters of the DC, without Call attempt		
Shipment marked undelivered within 15 minutes of the DRS closure, without any call attempt		
>= 4 shipments marked undelivered at the same time without call attempt		
>= 4 shipments marked undelivered at the same latitude longitude coordinates without call attempt		
Low DRS dlivery conversion, COD- less than 20%, PPD less than 30% (Min 8 shipments). Both without call bridge		
Shipment marked undelivered within b/w 2000 to 0700, without Call attempt		

cells imply that more of the delivery centres or field executives lie in that particular category. So, most of the field executives and delivery centres had the fake deliveries within 10% of the total shipments delivered; and a relatively fewer number of them had fake deliveries exceeding 16% of the total shipments. The exact percentages cannot be shared for the reasons of confidentiality.

Use of Data Analytics for Optimal Scheduling and Assignment of Deliveries

Historical data of Riders, Customers and Time of the day can be analysed and taken into account when deciding routes. The data on the past performance and demographics of field executive can tell us about his skills, preferred time of deliveries and preferred region to work. Similarly. The historical order record of a customer can uncover a lot about his preferred time slots, availability and any special instructions for delivery. Not only this, the insights on the usual traffic conditions in a particular geography, and the opening/ closing time of a building can also be obtained with the past data records. With advanced Machine learning and artificial intelligence, accounting for these is easier today than a few years ago.

Table 3. Template for FE-wise and DC-wise Fake delivery potential

FE Potential Fake	DC Potential Fake					
	> 30%	22-30%	16-22%	10-16%	10% or less	Total
>30%						
22-30%						
16-22%						
10-16%						
10% or less						
Total						

Use of Data Analytics in Route Optimisation

Route Optimization is often thought of the quickest way to reach from X to Y. While this approach would have been satisfactory a few years ago, quest for better margins lead to optimising not only the time but also the cost. There are various aspects of route optimization that can be improved. Instead of manually allocating routes to delivery vehicles, new softwares could be built that manage fleet size, give driving directions and deliver or pick up goods from multiple stops and thereby improving productivity of the vehicle. Route optimization through leveraging technology thus reduces human dependency, saves time and thus labor costs and then saves fuel costs as well. The Figure below shows the visual representation of a typical vehicle routing problem.

A few of the aspects/variables that should be considered when optimising routes are below:

Figure 3. The pictorial representation of the vehicle routing problem in last mile logistics

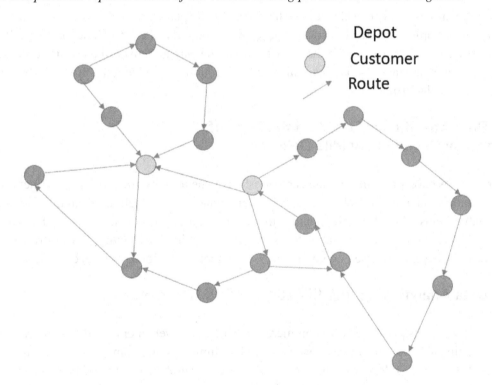

Accounting for Real Time Traffic

Just optimizing distance driven by delivery vehicles would be an incomplete assessment. Even if driving distance is minimized, the vehicle could be delayed in its operations by traffic on the road. Taking the real-time traffic conditions in to consideration will not only lead to lesser cost of logistics but also ensure a quicker and on-time receipt of the consignment by the consignee and thus, enhanced satisfaction to customer. Any robust optimization software can be use for planning the routes and compute expected time of arrival based on dynamic, real-time data.

Geocoding

Optimizing routes would need all of the locations geocoded, so that they can be mapped for the routes. Alphabetical or vernacular addresses need to be correctly understood with appropriate contexts and then mapped to precise latitude and longitudes for route optimisation.

Real Time Shipment Tracking and Performance Monitoring

Even advanced algorithms need human intervention and management. The software for route optimisation should have dashboards showing real time movement of vehicles as well as means to compare performances of various hubs/depots.

Dynamic Route Planning

There are softwares available that can handle the optimal route planning for the scheduled orders as well as the on-demand orders. There also arises a need for re-routing of the shipments occasionally. When the customer changes the order while the rider is out on the way to deliver, the new routes can be created by the route optimization softwares. This needs the routing optimization software to be integrated with the ordering platform.

Use of Data Analytics in Deciding the Type of Vehicle to be Used in Last Mile Delivery

Different vehicles have different carrying capacities. Also, the nature of the vehicle is influenced by the mix of perishable and non-perishable items, light weight and heavy weight items in the shipments. For non-perishable items of light weight, usually motorcycles are used. For non-perishable, heavy items vans/mini-trucks are used. For perishable items like fruits or animal husbandry, freezer-trucks are used. Allocation of these vehicles based on goods mix is an important factor to optimize.

Use of Data Analytics for Identification of Bad Addresses

Whenever an order gets placed on any ecommerce website, the buyer enters an address where that order needs to be delivered. Due to various reasons, including limited written language knowledge and non-awareness of structured address writing rules (writing House number, street number, locality, city etc.), a number of addresses are of inferior quality. Such addresses can't be located for deliveries by a field executive. For a significant chunk of them, even an address parser that converts these addresses into latitude-longitude geocodes doesn't work. Shipping these parcels all the way from the buyer and shipper incurs a significant cost only to not getting fulfilled during the last mile because of inherent properties lead to under-utilisation of resources. Such orders can be not shipped to the last mile operations if they are determined beforehand. Businesses could create a system to check anomalies/best practices. Text Analytics and Natural Language Processing can help significantly in this exercise.

Use of Data Analytics for Locality Mapping

While some of the shipments do not mention the PIN codes, a few of them also carry the wrong PIN codes. Hence, the mapping of the localities with the PIN codes becomes necessary. Locality mapping infers to shifting the base of last mile delivery from pincodes to actual localities in place in the cities. The existing pincode delivery model poses a multitude of problems which leads to increasing misroutes by the day. The problems generally faced are wrong pincodes mentioned against addresses, vague division of areas based on pincode mapping, the indecision in DC allotment for pincode bunches, and huge areas under specific pincodes. These issues lead to a significant increase in the misrouting of delivered goods.

To address this problem, the locality model can be adopted in which the cities are divided into localities. There are four steps involved in such an exercise, as mentioned below:

1. **Locality Extraction:** Localities are extracted online for the various cities under consideration, and an exhaustive list is obtained
2. **Cleaning Junk:** Junk values like house numbers, societies, lane numbers are cleaned off from the list before feeding it into a predesigned program to be run for locality mapping on the mentioned addresses as per the client.
3. **Mapping:** A python code is prepared which takes the clean locality list as input and gives the output from the mentioned address based on a pre-decided algorithm which is a mix of different text matching algorithms for optimised allotment.
4. **DC Mapping:** After getting the localities, they are allotted a DC based on a master file created off historical delivery data, based on allotment of a particular DC to a particular locality which served major deliveries to the locality in the past for a decided period.

The action research done at a leading last mile logistics firm based in India showed that Locality based model reduced misroutes by a whopping 90% in a couple of cities and atleast by 60% in other Tier 1 and 2 cities where the model has been tried and adopted.

Use of Data Analytics in Optimal Mix of Fixed and Flexible Staffing

Logistics companies suffer from a wide seasonal fluctuations and the fluctuations have risen a lot due to increasing number of promotional activities being done by ecommerce companies at regular time intervals. The delivery staff has an upper cap of possible deliveries in a day. The staffing decisions are based on the expected demand generation. If not planned for, it gets difficult for the companies to handle extra orders in the season of sale and a company loses out its share of orders to competition or has to outsource a portion of order delivery and share profit. Hence it becomes important to develop a model which has a flexibility in terms of maximum delivery capacity. Such a model can utilize the existing network of the field executive possessed by the small grocery stores, students, part time workers, and other similar under-utilized workforce, who can supplement their normal earnings as they are paid on per-order-basis when the orders are higher. It is a win-win case scenario for both- the last mile logistics firms as well as the part-time workforce.

Integrating the historical trends the supervised learning and the modelled influence of the promotions can help in better forecasting of the order volumes as well as order densities for the different geographies and delivery localities. This, in turn, when integrated with the cost dynamics of fixed manpower and variable manpower can assist in determination of optimal fixed manpower requirements. While the fixed manpower can result in lesser cost per delivery at the full utilization and can be used for a base demand, the variable manpower can be more economical for the surge in orders beyond the base demand. This, in turn, can help the firms strike the right chord as they juggle between the two conflicting objectives of supply chain responsiveness and supply chain efficiency. While responsiveness increases with the increase in staffing, the efficiency falls down.

Use of Data Analytics in Resolution of Weight Disputes between Service Provider and Client

Data analytics can also be used for automating the already existing plans of resolving weight disputes raised by the clients of these last mile logistics. Whenever the partner company (like Amazon, Flipkart, 1mg etc.) feels that it is being charged somewhat wrong for delivering their shipments either in excess or sometimes even lesser, they raise a dispute about that shipment and then the revenue assurance team of the last mile service providers has to work upon such cases. However, this task being manual and tedious, can be automated to make the work more efficient and accurate. MS Excel and R programming can be used automate such models. The basis of resolution can be provided by the product mix composition of the shipment in terms of the dead weight for the flyer packaging and the volumetric weight for the box packaging.

CONCLUSIONS AND FUTURE DIRECTIONS

This research study that the data analytics, coupled with machine learning algorithms can play an important role in increasing the operational excellence at last mile logistics firms. The paper also shows the deployment of two applications in practice, along with the results obtained. With the increased computing ability of the modern IT infrastructure, the data can be leveraged like never before to enable the logistics managers in making smart business decisions. However, it is worth noting that there is a cost and a risk component also associated with the use of data for making decisions. All this comes at cost of computation tools and resources, computation time and energy, and the need for sophisticated knowledge of data science. Thankfully, the above mentioned risks can be easily covered up if they are managed well with the use of right set of data and applying the right set of tools. Also, training the models at regular intervals to make sure that they evolve with the changing business dynamics, becomes very essential. Using the appropriate sampling procedures in data collection, and ensuring that the over-fitting is not done by the machine learning models, is of prime importance. The managers need to exercise the caution while they try to quantify the behavioral phenomenon in the business situations and convert it into pure science for the purpose of modelling. The data scientists also need to ensure that the benefits of using data science for an activity should far exceed the cost of doing it.

REFERENCES

Barton, D., & Court, D. (2012). Making advanced analytics work for you. *Harvard Business Review*, *90*, 79–83. PMID:23074867

Buttarelli, G. (2015). *Towards a new digital ethics- data, integrity and technology.* Retrieved from https://edps.europa.eu/sites/edp/files/publication/15-09-11_data_ethics_en.pdf

Chen, H., Chiang, R. H. L., & Storey, V. C. (2012). Business intelligence and analytics: From big data to big impact. *Management Information Systems Quarterly, 36*(4), 1165–1188. doi:10.2307/41703503

Deep, K., Jain, M. & Salhi, S. (2019). *Logistics, Supply Chain and Financial Predictive Analytics.* Springer.

Erbao, C., Ruotian, G., & Mingyong, L. (2018). Research on the vehicle routing problem with interval demands. *Applied Mathematical Modelling, 54,* 332–346. doi:10.1016/j.apm.2017.09.050

Forgo, N., Honald, S., & van den Hoven, J. (2020). *An ethico-legal framework for social data science.* International Journal of Data Science and Analytics., doi:10.100741060-020-00211-7

Hanne, T., Dornberger, R. (2017). *Computational Intelligence in Logistics and Supply Chain Management.* Springer.

Khan, K. (2013, May). The transformative power of advanced analytics. *Supply Chain Management Review,* 48-49.

Koul, S., & Verma, R. (2011). Dynamic vendor selection based on fuzzy AHP. *Journal of Manufacturing Technology Management, 22*(8), 963–971. doi:10.1108/17410381111177421

Langevin, A., & Riopel, D. (2005). *Logistics Systems: Design and Optimization.* Springer. doi:10.1007/b106452

LaValle, S., Lesser, E., Shockey, R., Hopkins, M. S., & Kruschwitz, N. (2011). Big data, analytics, and the path from insights to value. *MIT Sloan Management Review, 52*(2), 21–31.

Monreale, A., Rinzivillo, S., Pratesi, F., Giannotti, F., & Pedreschi, D. (2014). Privacy by design in big data abalytics and social mining. *EPJ Data Science, 3*(1), 10. doi:10.1140/epjds13688-014-0010-4

Quante, R., Meyr, H., & Fleischmann, M. (2009). Revenue management and demand management: Matching applications, models, and software. *OR-Spektrum, 31*(1), 31–62. doi:10.100700291-008-0125-8

Sui, M., Shen, F., Wei, H., & Chen, J. (2010). Logistics Route Planning with Geographic Data Considering Multiple Factors. *International Conference of Logistics Engineering and Management (ICLEM) 2010,* 2346-2352. 10.1061/41139(387)327

Waller, M. A., & Fawcett, S. E. (2013). Data science, predictive analytics, and big data: A revolution that will transform supply chain design and management. *The Journal of Business.*

Wu, L., Yue, X., Jin, A., & Yen, D. (2016). Smart supply chain management: A review and implications for future research. *International Journal of Logistics Management, 27*(2), 395–417. doi:10.1108/IJLM-02-2014-0035

KEY TERMS AND DEFINITIONS

Classification Table: A table that captures the predicted number of successes (or failures) to the observed number of successes (or failures).

Confusion Matrix: A table that captures the performance of a classification algorithm on a dataset for which the observed values are known.

Feature Engineering: Application of domain knowhow to pull out features from raw data with the use of data mining.

Predictive Modeling: Application of statistics and data to make prediction of the outcomes using data modelling.

Route Optimization: Finding the least costly or the fastest route for a set of shipments with complicated constraints related to customer time windows, driver availability, vehicle availability, traffic situations, road conditions, etc.

Chapter 10
Review of Big Data Applications in Finance and Economics

Ulkem Basdas
https://orcid.org/0000-0002-7142-149X
Philip Morris International, Turkey

M. Fevzi Esen
https://orcid.org/0000-0001-7823-0883
University of Health Sciences, Turkey

ABSTRACT

Massively parallel processors and modern data management architectures have led to more efficient operations and a better decision making for companies to process and analyse such complex and large-scale data. Especially, financial services companies leverage big data to transform their business processes and they focus on understanding the concepts of big data and related technologies. In this chapter, the authors focus on the scope of big data in finance and economics. They discuss the need for big data towards the digitalisation of services, utilisation of social media and new channels to reach customers, demand for personalised services and continuous flow of vast amount of data in the sector. They investigate the role of big data in transformation of financial and economic environment by reviewing previous studies on stock market reading and monitoring (real-time algorithmic trading, high-frequency trading), fraud detection, and risk analysis. They conclude that despite the rapid development in the evolution of techniques, both the performance of techniques and area of implementation are still open to improvement. Therefore, this review aims to encourage readers to enlarge their vision on data mining applications.

INTRODUCTION

The world has been experiencing the revolution in information and communication technologies (ICTs) in last couple of decades. Big data appeared as a revolutionary phenomenon that influenced decision-making processes. In the 1960s and 1970s, companies' first attempts in data discovery for business purposes proceeded through various stages, shaped by heuristic decision making, simple reporting and

DOI: 10.4018/978-1-7998-3053-5.ch010

statistical analysis (Figure 1). In the 1990s, most companies organized data collections in table based format with rows and columns and they used relational or hierarchical databases to store their data. For cross-functional activities, fast query processing and multiuser environment, they implemented extract, transform and load (ETL) processes that help enterprise data mitigate from day-to-day transactions to data warehouses. The volume of data was measured in gigabytes at the very most.

Figure 1. Evolution of big data

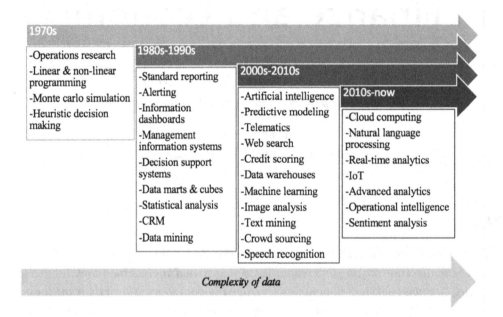

In the early 2000s, companies started to focus on value creation by operational data warehouses that accumulate business transactions. The following decade brought out different kinds of data sources that were actively used as content management repositories and networked storage systems to manage enterprise information, and the size of databases began to increase in volume and scale. Terabyte-scale bases were replaced by petabytes. Traditional form of data types were augmented by unstructured data that either typically have text-heavy format without a data model. To realize business benefits from being able to process high volume of data, companies put emphasis on the speed of new data creation. High velocity data underscored to process large amounts of data at high rates of speed, resulting companies became more analytical and data-driven.

In 2010s, the advent of wireless communication (i.e., WiFi, cellular, GPS, bluetooth, RFID) over a wide area made the connection of devices possible with each other nearly anywhere. This resulted in hundreds of petabytes moving across networks per day. Companies has broadened their data management strategies with considering many kinds of data such as multimedia files, e-mail messages, webpages and other kinds of business documents. As a result of this, data has become a proprietary resource because of its value.

The second half of the 2010s strove to bring a next frontier for innovation in big data. The interconnection of sensing and actuating devices enabled distributed file systems among the connected users, thereby allowing data storage and sharing through a real-time communication network. Such an innovation allowed many companies to allocate their resources for moving, storing and analyzing the huge amount of data by virtual infrastructures. According to NVP (2020), the percentage of companies investing in big data technologies amounted to 39.7% with an average spend of $50 million per company in 2018. The percentage of the companies increased in 2019 and expected to rise sharply to 64.8% in 2020. However, it was also stated that the vast majority of companies are struggling with business adoption of big data and only 37.8% created a data-driven environment (NVP, 2020).

Today, there is a dramatic increase in the amount of generated, mined and stored data, reaching a market size of $50 billion to reach $104.3 billion by 2026 (Fortune, 2019). Companies produce large amounts of raw data in daily basis via IoT, smart devices and cloud platforms. Further developments in the digital transformation enable companies to move with big data solutions using Artifical Intelligence (AI) for organizing and performing business tasks. According to Forrester (2019), big data is considered as a vital dominant driver of competitive advantage that refers the ability to outperform the rivals for businesses. Another big data market survey states that big data has enabled businesses to achieve their goals and that impact is expected to grow immensely over the next years (IDC, 2020).

The use of big data in financial services and economics creates competitive advantage for the businesses. Companies conduct hundreds of millions transactions daily, dealing with a very diverse data types and they implement sophisticated methods by adopting augmented data sources and technologies for better and more informed decisions. They develop big data strategies to identify their businesses' requirements and pay attention to new research methodologies to understand complex networks in financial markets and economics. For example, some companies can deploy big data capabilities to collect data from IoT devices and satellites and they can estimate retail traffic through new and varied ways in financial services. This also enables companies to forecast price movements by using complex interactions between massive integrated data sources. According to DB (2020) report of big data in financial services industry, 80 to 90% of financial institutions' data sources require big data technologies to be analysed and only 55% of the institutions make efforts to achieve big data objectives.

DEFINITION OF BIG DATA

Big data has some different characteristics that seems to be different when compared to the classical definition of datasets. Traditionally, a dataset contains two dimensional tables, in which each column represents a specific type of variable, and each row displays a given record. It also takes considerable time, money and effort to decide the right data collection method and design dataset. However, big data has a broad concept that includes large, comprehensive and always available data, which is nourished by various data sources such as information-sensing mobile devices, software logs, digital images and videos, GPS signals and wireless communication networks etc. in many formats (Pyne et al., 2016).

In general sense, big data is a term used for a large, diverse and complex data collection that is formidable to be stored and processed neither adequately nor efficiently by using traditional technology. Although the discussion on the definition of big data still goes on, there is a general agreement on fivefold definition encompassing the five V's: Volume, Variety, Veracity, Velocity and Value (Nguyen et al., 2018).

First, volume refers the size of data. Data attributes and number of data points are the identifying factors of data volume. In this sense, financial services industry is rife with hundreds of millions transaction daily. Global trading environments are more open and integrated through electronic and automated trading platforms. Such platforms provide real-time data streaming whereby the volume of transactions is being generated and analyzed is much more than yesterday. Moreover, the competition among companies creates large amounts of data at faster intervals. Based on a recent report on global general purpose cards, the total value of the payments made by credit and debit cards was $13.79 trillion from 171.66 billion transactions worldwide in 2018 and the number of transactions generated is expected to increase by about 24% annually (Nilson, 2018). Likewise, the total number of transactions executed on New York Stock Exchange (NYSE) is 2.5-3 million with a total value of $200 billion per day (NYSE, 2020). The global financial data is integrated into financial, company, commodities, trading, investment and advisory work flows across global markets. Data streams through a datasphere that stores a wide range of multi-asset market and pricing data, providing over 7 million price updates per second for over 70 million instruments and 10 billion bytes of real-time pricing data daily over 100 markets (Refinitiv, 2020). Therefore, the volume has been considered as the main feature of big data (Zikopoulos and Eaton, 2011).

Variety is an expanded concept of data types and sources (Philip and Zhang, 2014). It is typically defined as the combinations of different types of structures within the data. This includes both semi-structured (e.g. XML, JSON), and unstructured data (e.g. audio, images, text, click streams). From a business perspective, the utilization of large volumes of unstructured data can increase the revenues and reduce the costs for creating business value. companies can create valuable benefits from the variety in their big data initiatives (Davenport and Dyché, 2013). Social media inputs, audio and video streams are important resources to understand what drives business success and what customers expect from the company. In fact, between 80 to 90% of financial services companies' data are unstructured such as physical and digital channel interactions and geo-location data logs (Oracle, 2015). Moreover, IDC (2019) states that almost 80% of global datasphere will consist of unstructured data by 2025. However, more than 30% of financial services companies seriously lack the skills and solutions for managing unstructured data and this is seen as an obstacle especially across banking, capital markets and insurance companies (Kim and Gardner, 2015).

Banks and insurance companies for years have captured the pictures or scans of large quantities of customer contracts and stored them within a traditional file processing system. In other words, valuable information was hidden in text or pictures and it could mostly be detected by manual inspection. Poor file maintenance, no centralised control of the data, limited data sharing, inadequate file structure, data duplication and lengthy development times were expected conditions when using traditional systems. It was only possible to store and process certain documents in a timely manner, not allowing knowledge discovery from big bunch of datasets.

Financial institutions have adjacent relationship with their customers, regulators and rivals through a variety of channels and they utilize data that is produced in a broad range of activities. Static analysis of financial data is no longer sufficient, and it is not used as often as before. Aside from internal data sources, they started to gain a deeper understanding of customers' preferences and interests by utilizing external data sources such as social networks, web logs, claims data and machine device records as shown in Figure 2. Hence, they adopt data mitigation strategies with real-time processes to store and process huge amounts of both structured and unstructured data. A flexible modeling environment and real-time view can result in better visibility of detailed finance information for longer periods. This not only provides improved corporate performance and accountability to meet compliance targets, but also reduces uncertainty and risks related to data content.

Figure 2. Big data flow in Banking industries

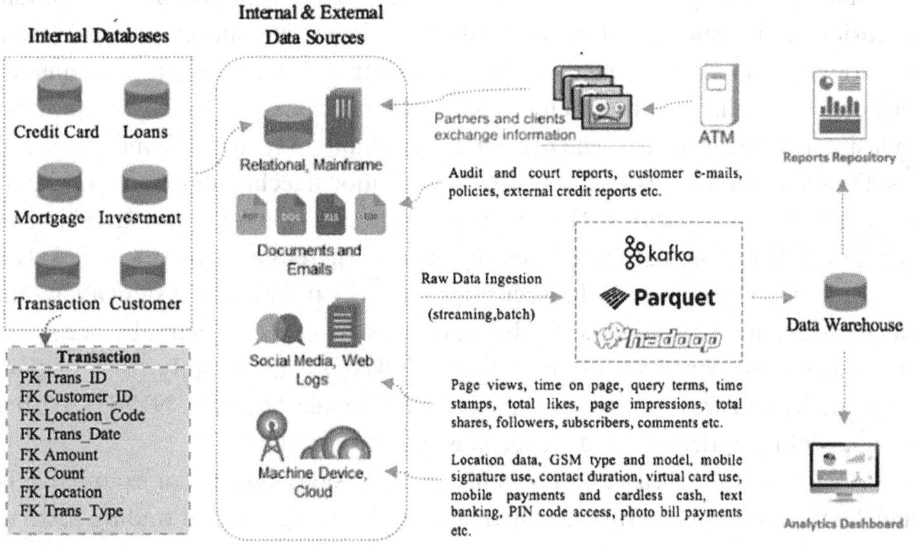

With the increasing complexity of data, erroneous, incomplete or noisy data added too much complexity to data management processes. As the data is obtained from multiple and possibly heterogeneous sources, trustworthiness of data has attracted the attention of data science. Inconsistent and incomplete data can lead to statistical errors and content ambiguities in information (Ohlhorst, 2012). From big data perspective, increasing amount of data can amplify the uncertainty of data especially for unstructered texts and medial files. Therefore, the term "veracity" is added to the definition of big data. To describe how data can be a trusted asset and address the issues related to clean and accurate data, the companies started to invest in the systems that improve data quality. According to Gartner's (2018) research on data quality, poor data quality costs companies $9.7 million, on average, per year.

For financial organizations, veracity is a combination of four dimensions: completeness, consistence, correctness and timeliness. These dimensions apply to both quantitative and qualitative data. The concept of "completeness" refers to an important notion in data quality. It represents a state in which all components of data are available for the full description of considered object. It is basically a measure of the proportion of missing data entries in a dataset. For example, a bank officer requiring eligibility data of credit card applicants from an external source in addition to the personal details and address history provided by the applicant may find the data unfit for the bank's business purposes unless the external data is not available to them. The data will be 100% complete, if it includes all necessary records. The second dimension, consistency, is the taxonomy of data that is practically useful. Data must fulfill all constraints for each observation and it should not violate the semantic rules defined over the given dataset. For example, the amounts of loan payments shown in the document must be the same as those in the operational system. The third dimension is correctness of data. Dejaeger et al. (2010) identifies "correctness" as the degree of accurate representation of real-life values in terms of not only syntactic accuracy but also semantic accuracy. For example; volume of shares traded can not be negative within a transaction record. Lastly, timeliness is the "currency" as immediate update of data. This is a measure of data age that corresponds to the delay between the change in a real world state and when it manifests itself as data (Fleckenstein and Fellows, 2018). For example, the role codes or positions of the insider within the company must be updated on the system, if there is a change in insider's position.

Other dimension of big data, velocity, is defined the frequency of data generation. Big data does not only refer to retrieving and storing data, but also processing it. Data is flowing continuously in huge amounts every single second. Systems in running state generate and transmit large quantities of data in a time-varying fashion at greater speeds, and hence tens of billions of records are moving across networks and machines. Data in motion is difficult to process by traditional technologies and it generally requires high storage and computing capacities. This enabled highly available real-time streaming bulk data architectures for flow, delivery, storage and processing of data. Therefore, many stock market data systems are designed to provide a real-time view for securities and stock trades. The system allows the traders to receive and analyse data in real time. It is also being used as an preventive survelliance system which is able to stop transactions as soon as volume or volatility spiked. In fact, roughly 70% of US equity trades are high velocity trades and are machine driven (Seth and Chaudhary, 2015). NYSE (2020) also reports that median latency of the orders is 26 microseconds in equity markets.

Analysis of streaming data reveals new challenges for decision makers. For example, it is important to detect fraudelent transactions on financial markets by identfying unusual trading patterns that most likely relates to deceptive practices such as stock manipulation, insider trading, short selling abuses and ponzi schemes. It is possible with a wide spectrum of data, which is from transactions, weblogs, financial markets, corporates and historical datasets. In many cases, external sources that rely on call records, e-mails, social networks and claims information are better to conduct in-depth analysis and understand frauds.

In general, data is divided into three categories: static, dynamic and streaming data. Traders and investors use automated systems that require minimum human intervention to execute and monitor huge amounts of trades, bonds, and other financial investments. These systems rely on streaming data and allow traders benefit from the velocity of data processed and analysed. Streaming data can be either structured or unstructured. This also provides an understanding of comprehensive investment strategies for investors within microseconds as the trade execution occurs. In finance, the primary use of streaming data comprises algorithmic trading, surveillance, fraud detection and risk management applications (Esen et al., 2019). Static data resides on repositories and it is unalterable and persistent after being recorded. Financial product information (e.g. name, category, batch number, special identifiers), technical information of the financial trading system (e.g. hardware, modules and special components, system type, storage size) and operation information (e.g. trading entities, currencies, counterparties, prices) can be listed as the examples of static data on financial markets. Static data can be updated regularly and it is not refreshed in real-time, whereas streaming data is in always-flowing nature and it is transferred across real-time systems at a massive scale. In terms of enterprise data management, the definition of dynamic data is slightly different from streaming data. Generally, dynamic data relates to business operations that are likely conducted by a transaction processing system. These are the structured, low-level and detailed records of daily transactions of a company in a wide range of operations such as orders, customers, inventory management, cash & treasury management, financial control and reporting etc. Dynamic data can be updated frequently over different time horizons and it is usually stored in relational databases as shown in Figure 2. For example, the management of the financial accounting and operations is carried out by transaction processing systems. An electronic payment process generated by mobile or computer running applications or PoS terminals often consist of several steps, including buyer's records and requisition, approval of requisiton, purchase order, approval of the order, delivery of order, invoincing and receiving payments from buyer. This process varies depending on electronic payment methods, type of goods or services, trust/security, supply chain and technical specifications of the system such as design, flexibility and ergonomy.

Companies perceive both social and economic value for their business environments by adopting big data technologies, resulting more efficient and effective operations, innovative products and services (Günther et al., 2017). It is estimated that the economic size of big data will reach the size of traditional physical economy by 2030 (Jin et al., 2015). Therefore, big data can be considered as a knowledge productivity tool that constantly creates value for economies.

The fifth dimension of big data is "value". The emergence of technology-driven processes and computational power of devices created new opportunites for networking, storage and analysis of big data. On a company level, it is essential to conglomerate technology and analysis to create business value from new sources and kinds of data. The use of proper data and the ability of gathering meaningful results provide great resources for decision makers. To discover hidden and valuable information from datasets and provide analytical perpectives, big data analytics (BDA) has been implemented to business applications. It is an emerging subdiscipline of business analytics that involves IT architectures, tools, technologies and programming languages. The key principle of BDA is being capable of handling complexity and real-time nature of data and processing very large collections of both structured and unstructured datasets (Shmueli et al., 2019). Descriptive, predictive and prescriptive analytics are the levels of BDA that enable a wide variety of analysis in each level and give foresight for the current and forthcoming conditions in decision making.

Table 1. Valuing data by levels and techniques

Level	Characteristics	Techniques
Descriptive	Retrospective – hand sight view: · Use of historical data, · Usually business reporting and backward-looking	Summary statistics: measures of central tendency and variability, cross-tabulation, correlation and charts, visualization etc.
Predictive	Insight view: · Data modeling, · Detection of trends and patterns, · Forecasting conditions and events	Regression, simulation, neural networks, Naïve bayes etc.
Prescriptive	Foresight view: · Predict, prescribe and adapt, · Decision automation and optimization, · Develop optimized recommendations and foresee the likely implications of each decision option, near-zero break-down approach	Metaheuristics, speech recognition, applied statistics, signal processing, mathematical programming, evolutionary computation combined with rules & algorithms

Descriptive level is the first step of big data analytics. It basically summarizes the raw data regarding day-to-day operations and involves simple techniques as stated in Table 1. The second level is predictive analytics that combine large quantities of data from different sources for the prediction of businesses' future outcomes or events. It provides a forecasting capability and includes a variety of techniques such as regression, classification or clustering algorithms that is generally based on historical and actual data (Olson and Wu, 2020). For example, financial institutions predict credit risk scores or flag suspicious insurance claims of individuals or companies by using predictive analytics. They can detect patterns in customers' spending behaviors by credit cards or forecast profits and order executions in stock markets. In prescriptive analytics, there is an analytical assessment of different possible decisions to assist business executives in their decision-making. According to Gartner (2019) only a small number of companies prioritize prescriptive analytics to improve their decision-making capabilities; however, the market size of prescriptive analytics is expected to reach almost $2 billion by 2022. Prescriptive analytics combines multiple techniques to solve business problems, either using a combination of different methodologies, or switching the techniques during the analysis. It typically involves computer science and mathematical optimization algorithms. For example, financial institutions can develop strategies that improve customer relationships by using social networking data or establish some technical indicators with a set of rules for their automated trading strategies by prescriptive analytics. Exchanges also use natural language processing and behavioral analysis as a real-time surveillance function that monitors order, cancellation, amendment and other market activities. This is critical in investigating and deterring abusive trading practices in line with the regulations as well as increasing transparency and enhancing the integrity in the markets.

APPLICATIONS OF BIG DATA

Today, due to rapid technological advances there is an on-going expansion of the big data implementations. Data mining techniques have been successfully applied in different areas like fraud detection and bankruptcy prediction, strategic decision-making, or financial performance. The number of studies grow with an increasing pace, and it is not anymore possible to squeeze all studies in pages. Unfortunately, due to space limitation this section would review only major categories, where the studies focused on.

Risk Management

Big data application in different areas can be classified from risk management perspective. Big data can be utilized to predict a bankruptcy of a firm (i.e., credit risk), to detect a fraud (i.e., operational risk), or to predict future stock returns (i.e., market risk). In any case, these studies would support to mitigate the risks with accurate and reliable estimations/models. Therefore, different implementation areas would be considered in three major categories: credit risk, operational risk and market risk.

Credit Risk (Financial Distress Modelling)

Financial distress modelling studies focused to detect whether a target company falls into distress in a specific time. Data mining techniques have been implemented to forecast the financial distress (i.e., financial failure) since 1990s. Compared with early empirical methods for financial distress prediction, namely Multivariate Discriminant Analysis and logit as the two mostly commonly used methods, which required some rules on the distribution of variables, big data techniques resulted in better performance.

Among the most popular techniques, kNN was the first one applied to predict financial distress in 1990s. An early study by Jo et al. (1997) implemented case-based reasoning (CBR) with kNN for business failure prediction. Owing to the fact that algorithm of kNN used instance-based reasoning, kNN became popular and followed by several studies (Elhadi, 2000; Li and Sun, 2008; Nanni and Lumini, 2009; Park and Han, 2002; Sun and Hui, 2006; Yip, 2004). Unfortunately, this method was lack of a model in the algorithm, causing the predicting process to be very time-consuming, and the number of nearest neighbors have to be selected empirically. Another line of literature implemented support vector machine (SVM), which showed better predictive performance (Hua et al. 2007; Hui and Sun, 2006; Min and Lee, 2005; Min et al., 2006; Shin et al., 2005; Wu et al., 2007), however predictive results of SVM are not so easy to be interpreted by users.

Sun and Li (2008) claimed that data mining method combining attribute-oriented induction (AOI), information gain (IG), and decision tree could outperform existing financial distress prediction methods, which may not handle dynamic learning or cannot be easily understood. Early statistical techniques like univariate analysis, multiple discriminant or logit analysis were lack of learning from new data dynamically, and neural networks were criticized to have weight values, which are hidden knowledge for classification, making it difficult for investors or practitioners to understand. On the other hand, their decision-tree model involving 35 financial ratios offered an empirical data mining method to forecast the financial distress of companies.

In another paper by Koyuncugil and Ozgulbas (2012), an early warning system (EWS) model was constructed based on data mining for financial risk detection. For their financial EWS, which was used to predict the achievement condition of enterprises and decrease the risk of financial distress, they preferred CHAID (Chi Square Automatic Interaction Detection) as a decision tree implementation technique used for classification of the dataset. They classified 7853 enterprises in 31 different risk profiles via CHAID.

Kim and Upneja (2014) even expanded the implementation of data mining to restaurant industry to investigate the key financial distress factors for publicly traded restaurants by using decision trees. Based on their results, they recommended to use AdaBoosted decision tree as an EWS for restaurants based on the smallest error in overall and type I error rates (i.e., classifying a failing business as successful).

The choice of Kim and Upneja (2014) to implement decision trees was also verified by other studies. Koh (2004) showed that decision tree outperformed ANN and logit analysis by using financial ratios for 165 going concerns and 165 matched non-going concerns. Li et al. (2010) supported classification and regression tree (CART) over MDA, logit, SVM, kNN, and MDA-CART (i.e., stepwise method) for the dataset composed of Shanghai Stock Exchange and Shenzhen Stock Exchange. Indeed, the worst performers were parametric methods. In the analysis of Gepp et al. (2010) CART and Recursive Partitioning Analysis (RPA) decision tree techniques resulted in similar performance over MDA and See5 (a decision-tree building algorithm). On the other hand, Chen and Du (2009) suggested that neural networks perform better than decision trees or alternative approaches.

Not only the financial difficulties at firm level, but also credit default swaps (CDS) and lending decisions for customers and SMEs were an area of interest. To illustrate; based on the assessment of daily CDS at different maturities and rating groups, Son et al. (2016) showed that nonparametric machine learning models with deep learning outperform traditional models in terms of predicting accuracy and proposing hedging measures. In another study, Khandani et al. (2010) suggested a technique based on decision trees and sector vector mechanism, which resulted in cost savings of up to 25% when tested on actual lending data. Figini et al. (2017) proposed a multivariate outlier detection machine learning technique to improve credit risk estimation for SME lending.

Operational Risk (Financial Fraud Modelling)

Operational risk refers the financial losses arising from either internal or external operational breakdowns. Internal factors can be inadequate internal processes, people, or systems whereas external event can be such as fraud, failure in controls, operational error, or natural disaster. Among these topics, the widely studied area has been financial fraud modelling.

Financial fraud modelling can also be considered an implementation of big data in auditing, and it includes fraud detection, prediction, and prevention. Particularly, the studies on this area aimed to correctly classify fraudulent financial statements to be able to forecast future frauds. Even though data mining techniques performed much more than other statistical methods, the best methodology for financial fraud is still inconclusive. Kirkos et al. (2007) discussed that Bayesian network could outperform both the neural network and decision tree by correctly classifying 90.3% of the validation sample. Ravisankar et al. (2011) argued that probabilistic neural networks and genetic programming outperform other methods, such as support vector machines, logistic regression, multilayer feed forward neural network. Perols (2011) logistic regression and support vector machines performed well relative to competing models such as neural networks and decision trees. On the other hand, Bhattacharya et al. (2011) supported the use of genetically optimized artificial neural network based on their tests carried on artificially generated datasets. The comparison of different data mining techniques and judgment of experts in Lin at al. (2015) indicated that neural networks and decision trees reached a correct classification ate of over 90% on a holdout sample, outperforming logistic regression.

Other studies preferred to combine multiple techniques. Abbasi et al. (2012) implemented meta-leaning, which is a machine learning tool that can learn from experience. In another study by Chen (2016) claimed that combination of decision tree models in two staged modelling, specifically Chi-squared automatic interaction classification in stage 1 and classification and regression tree in stage 2 was the most accurate methodology to detect financial statement fraud. Different from previous studies, Chang et al. (2008) suggested an approach to detect suspicious accounts and transactions. They set coordinated visualizations based on identifying specific keywords within the wire transactions. Besides, they introduced a search-by-example technique to detect similar transaction patterns.

A line of the literature also considered the text content for the fraud detection. Among several methods for word classification using supervised machine learning, the most popular has been naïve Bayes method. Despite the difficulty of replicating the results of this method, naïve Bayes method had several advantages over others as (i) being one of the oldest methods to analyze text, (ii) handling large amount of data, (iii) having established rules about analyzing data without the impact of researcher's subjectivity (Loughran and McDonald, 2016). For example; in the two-staged analysis of Purda and Skillicorn (2015), first a decision tree was used to identify a list of words based on the reports of known fraud firms, and then vector order machines was used to forecast the fraud status of financial reports, where their correct classification rate was over 80%. On the other hand, Sadasiyam et al. (2016) employed support vector machine where principal features were extracted through principal component analysis. Basically, they created a score card based on the occurrence of keywords in annual reports and feature set extraction was done based on these score cards. Their experimental results achieved 90% accuracy by using 10 to 25% of the principal features.

Market Risk (Financial Markets)

Market risk includes the risk arising from investing, trading, and exposure to financial markets.

Asset Selection and Investment Allocation

Asset selection refers the selection of most suitable assets among the available investment options to achieve a successful investment strategy. Considering that the screening of assets can necessitate follow-up of several information sources, such as market trends, firm-specific announcements or historical data, automated methods can help handling of big data. To illustrate; artificial neural networks (Quah, 2008), genetic algorithms (Hamzacebi and Pekkaya, 2011), support vector machines (Huang, 2012) for stock selection, genetic programming (Yan and Clack, 2010) and data envelopment analysis, a linear programming tool, (Allevi et al., 2019) for funds selection have been previously used in the literature.

Asset allocation problem covers combining multiple assets into portfolios that would meet the desired risk-return preferences. In that sense, this investment decision problem includes several extensions: cardinally constrained asset allocation to automatically select a pre-defined number of assets among a pool of options (Woodside-Oriakhi, et al., 2011), index tracking portfolio creation to replicate the market index returns (Zhao et al., 2019).

Trading

Trading involves dynamically rebalancing a portfolio of assets to maximize the wealth. In parallel to the development of trading systems, a great range of machine learning methods has been used over time from artificial neural networks, deep learning, support vector machines to genetic algorithms and programming. These approaches helped to study with real-time, dynamic data without making assumptions about statistical properties. Depending on the type of the traded asset, different methodologies were selected. To illustrate; for equity indices artificial neural networks (Chavarnakul and Enke, 2008), for portfolios genetic algorithm (Gorgulho et al., 2011), for index futures boosting method (Creamer, 2012), for forex genetic algorithm (Evans et al., 2013), for stocks genetic programming (Mabu et al., 2013), for ETFs support vector mechanism (Abbaszadeh, et al., 2018), for cryptocurrencies artificial neural networks (Nakano et al., 2018) were implemented. Even though there is no common methodology, for forecasting purposes mostly neural networks were preferred due to their numeric structure (i.e., to better handle financial data), flexibility of not having any data distribution assumptions, incremental mining technique (i.e., new data through trained neural network to update the previous training result), and model-free nature (Lam, 2004).

Research questions of studies also cover different aspects of trading. To illustrate; Chun and Kim (2004) examined the effect of coupling learning techniques with various trading strategies. Specifically, they preferred an implicit learning technique (neural nets) and explicit approach (case-based reasoning) to compare active and passive trading strategies and found out that active trading strategies could outperform the buy-hold policy even net of moderate transaction costs. Lam (2004) also tested whether neural networks can be used to integrate fundamental and technical analysis for rate of return on common shareholders' equity prediction. In another study by Chun and Park (2006) they tried to predict the Korean Stock Price Index (KOSPI) by using past values and volume of the index. Based on their results, regression case-based reasoning significantly performed better than random walk or standard case-based reasoning models. On the other hand, Zhang et al. (2015) implemented a genetic algorithm-based model for stock trading rules that outperformed a decision tree or Bayesian network.

Among other topics, one of the widely known example of how data mining techniques contributed to the evolvement of financial sector is high-frequency trading. Even though there is no formal definition, HFT has some specific features that encourages the implementation of data mining techniques: automation of the trading and high speed of orders. The impact of HFT is still debatable on price discovery, short-term volatility and stock liquidity (Hasbrouck and Saar 2013; Menkveld 2013; Conrad et al. 2015). Specifically, previous studies documented that HFT helped to reduce trading costs (Angel et al. 2015) and improve price efficiency (Brogaard et al. 2014; Chaboud et al. 2014). Considering the implementation of data mining techniques, previous studies suggested different alternatives, such as nonlinear filtering algorithm (Sun and Meinl, 2012) or neural networks (Chu and Chan, 2018).

Some studies also focused on stress testing market models (i.e., model risk management) to validate the trading strategies. Woodall (2017) examined the investment firms to understand how machine learning was used to monitor trading to ensure that the unsuitable assets are not used in trading models. Besides, large trading firms prefer data mining techniques to forecast the impact of their trading on market pricing. Day (2017) showed how large trading firms could avoid the cost of trying to take large positions in illiquid markets. By doing so, firms could identify connections between assets and desired positions through a series of related assets without having a large position in the single asset. Lastly, market trading algorithms have been developed further by adapting future trading by learning from market reactions (Hendricks and Wilcox, 2014). To illustrate; Chandrinos et al. (2018) implemented neural networks and decision tree to give real-time warnings to traders based on trading patterns. In another study by Wu and Olson (2015), support vector mechanism was used to create warning signals to traders.

Next section focuses on text-mining and sentiment analysis in the context of big data. Even though this methodology can be implemented for asset selection, investment selection or trading purposes, a separate section would be provided owing to high number of studies.

Text-Mining and Sentiment Analysis

Text-mining and sentiment analysis refers the study of language or textual properties of any kind of information source. In other words, this line of financial literature investigates whether a sentiment can be derived from a document, such as firm disclosures or newspaper articles, to predict any kind of financial performance. Big data sentiment analysis also gained importance for auditing purposes since negative sentiment would trigger a risk-based audit.

The relationship between the direction of textual content (positive vs. negative) and stock markets had been previously documented by several studies. Tetlock (2007) investigated the impact of pessimist or optimist content of Wall Street Journal news on stock returns and volume and found that pessimist news was associated with price declines and helped to forecast trading volume. Alanyali et al. (2013) also found a relationship between the daily number of mentions of a stock in the Financial Times and daily trading volume. Piskorec et al. (2014) even constructed a news cohesiveness index based on online financial news to show the correlation with volatility. Jensen et al. (2013) also verified an association between firm-specific news sentiment and intraday volatility especially for bad news.

In the earliest use of the naïve Bayes approach in finance by Antweiler and Frank (2004), 1000 out of 1.5 million online stock message postings were used to train the filters of the program. Higher disagreements among the postings were linked with higher trading volume. Das and Chen (2007) also supported that message board postings of 24 high-tech stocks were related with the trading volume and volatility. In another study by Li (2010), average tone of the forward-looking statements, a part of 10-K filings, was positively related with future earnings. Huang et al. (2014) used the naive Bayes machine learning approach to identify the sentiment in analyst reports. The categorization of more than 27 million sentences into positive, negative, and neutral categories helped them to link positive sentences with firm's earning growth rate five years after the publication of the report. Curme et al. (2014) found that increase in Google and Wikipedia searches were related to subsequent stock market falls. Li et al. (2015) captured the investor attention with Google search volume index to analyze trader positions and future crude oil prices. Sun et al. (2014) implemented a trading network to predict individual stock returns, and similarly, Shapira et al. (2014) modeled the stock market in terms of a network with many investors. Lastly, a number of studies tried to create equity portfolios showing better performance than benchmark index portfolios by using Google searches (Kristoufek, 2013) or changes in Google search queries (Preis et al., 2013).

By expanding the implementation area of sentiment analysis, a cryptocurrency price prediction using news and social media sentiment was first introduced in Lamon et al. (2016), followed shortly by Phillips and Gorse (2017), who tried to forecast cryptocurrency price bubbles using social media data. Li et al. (2018) compared price prediction based on historical price values with machine learning with different types of neural networks and proposed a sentiment-based prediction of alternative cryptocurrency price fluctuations using a gradient boosting tree model. Not surprisingly, in the review of Kumar and Ravi (2016) the range of text mining applications in finance over 2000-2016 even varies from FOREX and stock market forecasts to customer relationship management applications including different text mining algorithms (decision trees, neural networks, etc.).

Other Accounting Implementations

Now, it is clear that big data techniques add value to the audit process (Brown-Liburd et al., 2015) and it is recommended to be a complementary to auditing function (Yoon et al., 2015; Moffitt and Vasarhelyi, 2013). The advantages of big data, such as process mining, which analyzes the event logs of business systems (Jans et al., 2014), or process of big data video, audio, and textual information (Crawley and Wahlen, 2014; Warren et al., 2015) were found to improve accounting and auditing process.

The studies on financial accounting, which primarily focus on financial performance and ratio analysis, such as forecasting earnings, textual analysis of disclosures, or identifying risk factors in annual reports, are already covered under market risk management. Apart from aforementioned research questions, managerial accounting topics have been considered as well. These studies cover a wide a range of research topics from forecasting product unit cost (Chang et al., 2012) to developing a project-level cost control system (Petroutsatou et al., 2011) showing the positive impact of these techniques on not on at cost level, but also inventory management. Lastly, in other areas, such as revenue management (Ragothaman and Lavin, 2008) or account reconciliation (Chew and Robinson, 2012) data mining techniques were found to be contributing to the traditional auditing practices.

CONCLUSION

During the last decade, rapid digital transformation has enabled us to utilize the increased amount of generated data in various ways. The implementation area of big data in economics and finance has widened from bankruptcy prediction to modelling profitable trading strategies or forecasting energy prices. Growing literature evidently supports the contribution of big data techniques to every implemented area owing to the fact that these methods can handle vast amounts of data in a more realistic way, without making strict assumptions about distributions, or learning from past trends. Previous studies highlight a couple of points:

There is a rapid development in the evolution of techniques. To illustrate; decision tree models for financial fraud detection evolved from decision trees to combination of multiple techniques at the same time. Over the years text mining benefited from advances in big data techniques, and machine learning strategies became popular in asset pricing. However, different results on the performance of techniques indicate that there is no common big data methodology outperforming the other, and the development of techniques is still underway.

Similar to data mining techniques, the area of implementation is still in-progress. Even though major concepts, such as asset prices or financial distress models, have been reviewed so far, there are more various topics in finance that can be handled with big data techniques. Considering that information accumulated in financial institutions and intermediaries are all examples of big data, the data can be used in different dimensions to improve the market dynamics as well as customer-specific goals.

Last but not least, the benefit of data mining techniques should be more visible and explicit for non-academics. There is not any single paper claiming that data mining technique application did not add value to the implemented area. Nevertheless, it is not still widely known what big data is and how big data techniques can be used even to improve business systems, market structure, or auditing processes. Therefore, communication regarding benefits in various areas would definitely help non-academic society to enlarge their vision on data mining applications in finance.

REFERENCES

Abbasi, A., Albrecht, C., Vance, A., & Hansen, J. (2012). Metafraud: A meta-learning framework for detecting financial fraud. *Management Information Systems Quarterly*, *36*(4), 1293–1327. doi:10.2307/41703508

Abbaszadeh, S., Nguyen, T.-D., & Wu, Y. (2018). Optimal trading under non-negativity constraints using approximate dynamic programming. *The Journal of the Operational Research Society*, *69*(9), 1406–1422. doi:10.1080/01605682.2017.1398201

Alanyali, M., Moat, H. S., & Preis, T. (2013). Quantifying the relationship between financial news and the stock market. *Scientific Reports*, *3*(1), 6. doi:10.1038rep03578 PMID:24356666

Allevi, E., Basso, A., Bonenti, F., Oggioni, G., & Riccardi, R. (2019). Measuring the environmental performance of green SRI funds: A DEA approach. *Energy Economics*, *79*, 32–44. doi:10.1016/j.eneco.2018.07.023

Angel, J. J., Harris, L. E., & Spatt, C. S. (2015). Equity trading in the 21st century: An update. *The Quarterly Journal of Finance*, *5*(1), 1550002. doi:10.1142/S2010139215500020

Antweiler, W., & Frank, M. (2004). Is All That Talk Just Noise? The Information Content of Internet Stock Message Boards. *The Journal of Finance*, *59*(3), 1259–1294. doi:10.1111/j.1540-6261.2004.00662.x

Bhattacharya, S., Xu, D., & Kumar, K. (2011). An ANN-based auditor decision support system using Benford's law. *Decision Support Systems*, *50*(3), 576–584. doi:10.1016/j.dss.2010.08.011

Brogaard, J., Carrion, A., Moyaert, T., Riordan, R., Shkilko, A., & Sokolov, K. (2018). High frequency trading and extreme price movements. *Journal of Financial Economics*, *128*(2), 253–265. doi:10.1016/j.jfineco.2018.02.002

Brown-Liburd, H., Issa, H., & Lombardi, D. (2015). Behavioral implications of big data's impact on audit judgment and decision making and future research directions. *Accounting Horizons*, *29*(2), 451–468. doi:10.2308/acch-51023

Chaboud, A. P., Chiquoine, B., Hjalmarsson, E., & Vega, C. (2014). Rise of the machines: Algorithmic trading in the foreign exchange market. *The Journal of Finance*, *69*(5), 2045–2084. doi:10.1111/jofi.12186

Chandrinos, S. K., Sakkas, G., & Lagaros, N. D. (2018). AIRMS: A risk management tool using machine learning. *Expert Systems with Applications*, *105*, 34–48. doi:10.1016/j.eswa.2018.03.044

Chang, P. C., Lin, J. J., & Dzan, W. Y. (2012). Forecasting of manufacturing cost in mobile phone products by case-based reasoning and artificial neural network models. *Journal of Intelligent Manufacturing*, *23*(3), 517–531. doi:10.100710845-010-0390-7

Chang, R., Lee, A., Ghoniem, M., Kosara, R., Ribarsky, W., Yang, J., Suma, E., Ziemkiewicz, C., Kern, D., & Sudjianto, A. (2008). Scalable and interactive visual analysis of financial wire transactions for fraud detection. *Information Visualization*, *7*(1), 63–76. doi:10.1057/palgrave.ivs.9500172

Chavarnakul, T., & Enke, D. (2008). Intelligent technical analysis based equivolume charting for stock trading using neural networks. *Expert Systems with Applications*, *34*(2), 1004–1017. doi:10.1016/j.eswa.2006.10.028

Chen, S. D. (2016). Detection of fraudulent financial statements using the hybrid data mining approach. *SpringerPlus*, *5*(1), 16. doi:10.118640064-016-1707-6 PMID:26848429

Chew, P. A., & Robinson, D. G. (2012). Automated account reconciliation using probabilistic and statistical techniques. *International Journal of Accounting and Information Management*, *20*(4), 322–334. doi:10.1108/18347641211272722

Chu, C. C. F., & Chan, P. K. (2018). Mining Profitable High Frequency Pairs Trading Forex Signal Using Copula and Deep Neural Network. *2018 19th IEEE/ACIS International Conference on Software Engineering, Artificial Intelligence, Networking and Parallel/Distributed Computing (SNPD)*, 312-316.

Chun, S. H., & Kim, S. H. (2004). Data mining for financial prediction and trading: Application to single and multiple markets. *Expert Systems with Applications*, *26*(2), 131–139. doi:10.1016/S0957-4174(03)00113-1

Chun, S. H., & Park, Y. J. (2006). A new hybrid data mining technique using a regression case-based reasoning: Application to financial forecasting matter. *Expert Systems with Applications*, *31*(2), 329–336. doi:10.1016/j.eswa.2005.09.053

Conrad, J., Wahal, S., & Xiang, J. (2015). High-frequency quoting, trading, and the efficiency of prices. *Journal of Financial Economics*, *116*(2), 271–291. doi:10.1016/j.jfineco.2015.02.008

Crawley, M., & Wahlen, J. (2014). Analytics in empirical/archival financial accounting research. *Business Horizons*, *57*(5), 583–593. doi:10.1016/j.bushor.2014.05.002

Creamer, G. (2015). Can a corporate network and news sentiment improve portfolio optimization using the Black–Litterman model? *Quantitative Finance*, *15*(8), 1405–1416. doi:10.1080/14697688.2015.1039865

Curme, C., Preis, T., Stanley, H. E., & Moat, H. S. (2014). Quantifying the semantics of search behavior before stock market moves. *Proceedings of the National Academy of Sciences of the United States of America*, *111*(32), 11600–11605. doi:10.1073/pnas.1324054111 PMID:25071193

Das, S. R., & Chen, M. Y. (2007). Yahoo! for Amazon: Sentiment Extraction from Small Talk on the Web. *Management Science*, *53*(9), 1375–1388. doi:10.1287/mnsc.1070.0704

Davenport, H. T., & Dyche, J. (2013). *Big Data in Big Companies*. Retrieved from http://www.sas.com/resources /asset/BigData-in-Big-Companies.pdf

Day, S. (2017). *Quants turn to machine learning to model market impact*. Retrieved from https://www.risk.net/asset-management/4644191/quants-turnto-machine-learning-to-model-market-impact

DB. (2020). *Big data: how it can become differentiator*. Deutsche Bank Report. Retrieved from https://cib.db.com/

Dejaeger, K., Hamers, B., Poelmans, J., & Baesens, B. (2010). A novel approach to the evaluation and improvement of data quality in the financial sector. *Proceedings of the 15th International Conference on Information Quality*.

Elhadi, M. T. (2000). Bankruptcy support system: Taking advantage of information retrieval and case-based reasoning. *Expert Systems with Applications*, *18*(3), 215–219. doi:10.1016/S0957-4174(99)00063-9

Esen, M. F., Bilgic, E., & Basdas, U. (2019). How to detect illegal corporate insider trading? A data mining approach for detecting suspicious insider transactions. *Intelligent Systems in Accounting, Finance & Management*, *26*(2), 60–70. doi:10.1002/isaf.1446

Evans, C., Pappas, K., & Xhafa, F. (2013). Utilizing artificial neural networks and genetic algorithms to build an algo-trading model for intra-day foreign exchange speculation. *Mathematical and Computer Modelling*, *58*(5–6), 1249–1266. doi:10.1016/j.mcm.2013.02.002

Figini, S., Bonelli, F., & Giovannini, E. (2017). Solvency prediction for small and medium enterprises in banking. *Decision Support Systems*, *102*, 91–97. doi:10.1016/j.dss.2017.08.001

Fleckenstein, M., & Fellows, L. (2018). *Modern data strategy*. Springer. doi:10.1007/978-3-319-68993-7

Forrester. (2019). Big Data Fabric 2.0 Drives Data Democratization. In *The Insights-Driven Business Playbook*. Forrester Research.

Fortune. (2019). *Big Data Technology Market Size, Share & Industry Analysis*. Fortune Business Insights.

Gartner. (2019). *Forecast Snapshot: Prescriptive Analytics Software, Worldwide*. Gartner Research.

Gepp, A., Kumar, K., & Bhattacharya, S. (2010). Business failure prediction using decision trees. *Journal of Forecasting*, *29*(6), 536–555. doi:10.1002/for.1153

Goloshchapova, I., Poon, S., Pritchard, M., & Reed, P. (2019). Corporate social responsibility reports: Topic analysis and big data approach. *European Journal of Finance*, 25(17), 1637–1654. doi:10.1080/1351847X.2019.1572637

Gorgulho, A., Neves, R., & Horta, N. (2011). Applying a GA kernel on optimizing technical analysis rules for stock picking and portfolio composition. *Expert Systems with Applications*, 38(11), 14072–14085. doi:10.1016/j.eswa.2011.04.216

Günther, W. A., Mehrizi, M. H., Huysman, M., & Feldberg, F. (2017). Debating big data: A literature review on realizing value from big data. *The Journal of Strategic Information Systems*, 26(3), 191–209. doi:10.1016/j.jsis.2017.07.003

Hamzacebi, C., & Pekkaya, M. (2011). Determining of stock investments with grey relational analysis. *Expert Systems with Applications*, 38(8), 9186–9195. doi:10.1016/j.eswa.2011.01.070

Hasbrouck, J., & Saar, G. (2013). Low-latency trading. *Journal of Financial Markets*, 16(4), 646–679. doi:10.1016/j.finmar.2013.05.003

Hendricks, D., & Wilcox, D. (2014). A reinforcement learning extension to the Almgren-Chriss framework for optimal trade execution. In *IEEE Conference on Computational Intelligence for Financial Engineering & Economics (CIFEr)* (pp. 457–464). 10.1109/CIFEr.2014.6924109

Hua, Z., Wang, Y., Xu, X., Zhang, B., & Liang, L. (2007). Predicting corporate financial distress based on integration of support vector machine and logistic regression. *Expert Systems with Applications*, 33(2), 434–440. doi:10.1016/j.eswa.2006.05.006

Huang, A., Zang, A., & Zheng, R. (2014). Evidence on the Information Content of Text in Analyst Reports. *The Accounting Review*, 89(6), 2151–2180. doi:10.2308/accr-50833

Huang, C.-F. (2012). A hybrid stock selection model using genetic algorithms and support vector regression. *Applied Soft Computing*, 12(2), 807–818. doi:10.1016/j.asoc.2011.10.009

Hui, X.-F., & Sun, J. (2006). An application of support vector machine to companies' financial distress prediction. In *Modeling decisions for artificial intelligence* (pp. 274–282). Springer Verlag. doi:10.1007/11681960_27

International Data Corporation. (2019). *Worldwide Global DataSphere IoT Device and Data Forecast, 2019–2023*. IDC Corporate.

International Data Corporation. (2020). *Worldwide Big Data and Analytics Spending Guide*. Available at: https://www.idc.com/getdoc.jsp?containerId=IDC_P33195

Jans, M., Alles, M. G., & Vasarhelyi, M. A. (2014). A field study on the use of process mining of event logs as an analytical procedure in auditing. *The Accounting Review*, 89(5), 1751–1773. doi:10.2308/accr-50807

Jensen, J. B., Ahire, S. L., & Malhotra, M. K. (2013). Trane/Ingersoll Rand combines lean and operations research tools to redesign feeder manufacturing operations. *Interfaces*, 43(4), 325–340. doi:10.1287/inte.2013.0680

Jin, X., Wah, B., Cheng, X., & Wang, Y. (2015). Significance and Challenges of Big Data Research. *Big Data Research*, *2*(2), 59–64. doi:10.1016/j.bdr.2015.01.006

Khandani, A. E., Kim, A. J., & Lo, A. W. (2010). Consumer credit-risk models via machine-learning algorithms. *Journal of Banking & Finance*, *34*(11), 2767–2787. doi:10.1016/j.jbankfin.2010.06.001

Kim, H., & Gardner, E. (2015). The science of winning in financial services — competing on analytics: Opportunities to unlock the power of data. *Journal of Financial Perspectives*, *3*(2), 13–24.

Kim, S. Y., & Upneja, A. (2014). Predicting restaurant financial distress using decision tree and Ada-Boosted decision tree models. *Economic Modelling*, *36*, 354–362. doi:10.1016/j.econmod.2013.10.005

Koh, H. C. (2004). Going concern predictions using data mining techniques. *Managerial Auditing Journal*, *19*(3), 462–476. doi:10.1108/02686900410524436

Koyuncugil, A., & Ozgulbas, N. (2012). Financial early warning system model and data mining application for risk detection. *Expert Systems with Applications*, *39*(6), 6238–6253. doi:10.1016/j.eswa.2011.12.021

Kristoufek, L. (2013). Can Google Trends search queries contribute to risk diversification? *Scientific Reports*, *3*(1), 3. doi:10.1038rep02713 PMID:24048448

Kumar, B. S., & Ravi, V. (2016). A survey of the applications of text mining in financial domain. *Knowledge-Based Systems*, *114*, 128–147. doi:10.1016/j.knosys.2016.10.003

Lam, M. (2004). Neural network techniques for financial performance prediction: Integrating fundamental and technical analysis. *Decision Support Systems*, *37*(4), 567–581. doi:10.1016/S0167-9236(03)00088-5

Lamon, C., Nielsen, E., & Redondo, E. (2016). *Cryptocurrency Price Prediction Using News and Social Media Sentiment*. Retrieved form http://cs229.stanford.edu/proj2017/final-reports/5237280.pdf

Li, F. (2010). The Information Content of Forward-Looking Statements in Corporate Filings: A Naive Bayesian Machine Learning Approach. *Journal of Accounting Research*, *48*(5), 1049–1102. doi:10.1111/j.1475-679X.2010.00382.x

Li, H., & Sun, J. (2008). Ranking-order case-based reasoning for financial distress prediction. *Knowledge-Based Systems*, *21*(8), 868–878. doi:10.1016/j.knosys.2008.03.047

Li, H., Sun, J., & Wu, J. (2010). Predicting business failure using classification and regression tree: An empirical comparison with popular classical statistical methods and top classification mining methods. *Expert Systems with Applications*, *37*(8), 5895–5904. doi:10.1016/j.eswa.2010.02.016

Li, T. R., Chamrajnagar, A. S., Fong, X. R., Rizik, N. R., & Fu, F. (2018). Sentiment-based prediction of alternative cryptocurrency price fluctuations using gradient boosting tree model. *Frontiers in Physics*, *7*, 98. doi:10.3389/fphy.2019.00098

Li, X., Ma, J., Wang, S. Y., & Zhang, X. (2015). How does Google search affect trader positions and crude oil prices? *Economic Modelling*, *49*, 162–171. doi:10.1016/j.econmod.2015.04.005

Lin, C. C., Chiu, A. A., Huang, S. Y., & Yen, D. C. (2015). Detecting the financial statement fraud: The analysis of the differences between data mining techniques and experts' judgments. *Knowledge-Based Systems*, *89*, 459–470. doi:10.1016/j.knosys.2015.08.011

Loughran, T., & McDonald, B. (2016). Textual Analysis in Accounting and Finance: A Survey. *Journal of Accounting Research, 54*(4), 1187–1230. doi:10.1111/1475-679X.12123

Mabu, S., Hirasawa, K., Obayashi, M., & Kuremoto, T. (2013). Enhanced decision-making mechanism of rulebased genetic network programming for creating stock trading signals. *Expert Systems with Applications, 40*(16), 6311–6320. doi:10.1016/j.eswa.2013.05.037

Menkveld, A. J. (2013). High frequency trading and the new market makers. *Journal of Financial Markets, 16*(4), 712–740. doi:10.1016/j.finmar.2013.06.006

Min, J. H., & Lee, Y. C. (2005). Bankruptcy prediction using support vector machine with optimal choice of kernel function parameters. *Expert Systems with Applications, 28*(4), 603–614. doi:10.1016/j.eswa.2004.12.008

Min, S. H., Lee, J., & Han, I. (2006). Hybrid genetic algorithms and support vector machines for bankruptcy prediction. *Expert Systems with Applications, 31*(3), 652–660. doi:10.1016/j.eswa.2005.09.070 PMID:32288331

Moffitt, K. C., & Vasarhelyi, M. A. (2013). AIS in an age of big data. *Journal of Information Systems, 27*(2), 1–19. doi:10.2308/isys-10372

Nakano, M., Takahashi, A., & Takahashi, S. (2018). Bitcoin technical trading with artificial neural network. *Physica A, 510*, 587–609. doi:10.1016/j.physa.2018.07.017

Nanni, L., & Lumini, A. (2009). An experimental comparison of ensemble of classifiers for bankruptcy prediction and credit scoring. *Expert Systems with Applications, 36*(2), 3028–3033. doi:10.1016/j.eswa.2008.01.018

New Vantage Partners. (2020). *Big Data and AI Executive Survey 2020*. Retrieved from https://newvantage.com/

Nguyen, T., Zhou, L., Spiegler, V., Ieromonachou, P., & Lin, Y. (2018). Big data analytics in supply chain management: A state-of-theart literature review. *Computers & Operations Research, 98*, 254–264. doi:10.1016/j.cor.2017.07.004

NYSE. (2020). *Stock market summary*. Retrieved from https://www.nyse.com/market-data/historical

Ohlhorst, F. (2013). *Big data analytics*. Wiley.

Olson, D., & Wu, D. D. (2020). *Enterprise Risk Management Models*. Springer. doi:10.1007/978-3-662-60608-7

Oracle. (2015). *Big data in financial services and banking*. Retrieved from http://www.oracle.com/us//big-data-in-financial-services-wp-2415760.pdf

Park, C. S., & Han, I. (2002). A case-based reasoning with the feature weights derived by analytic hierarchy process for bankruptcy prediction. *Expert Systems with Applications, 23*(3), 255–264. doi:10.1016/S0957-4174(02)00045-3

Perols, J. (2011). Financial statement fraud detection: An analysis of statistical and machine learning algorithms. *Auditing, 30*(2), 19–50. doi:10.2308/ajpt-50009

Petroutsatou, K., Georgopoulos, E., Lambropoulos, S., & Pantouvakis, J. P. (2011). Early cost estimating of road tunnel construction using neural networks. *Journal of Construction Engineering and Management*, *138*(6), 679–6. doi:10.1061/(ASCE)CO.1943-7862.0000479

Philip Chen, C. L., & Zhang, C. Y. (2014). Data-intensive applications, challenges, techniques and technologies: A survey on Big Data. *Information Sciences*, *275*, 314–347. doi:10.1016/j.ins.2014.01.015

Phillips, R. C., & Gorse, D. (2017). Predicting cryptocurrency price bubbles using social media data and epidemic modelling. *2017 IEEE Symposium Series on Computational Intelligence*, 1–7. 10.1109/SSCI.2017.8280809

Piskorec, M., Antulov-Fantulin, N., Novak, P. K., Mozetic, I., Grcar, M., Vodenska, I., & Smuc, T. (2014). Cohesiveness in financial news and its relation to market volatility. *Scientific Reports*, *4*, 8. PMID:24849598

Preis, T., Moat, H. S., & Stanley, H. E. (2013). Quantifying trading behavior in financial markets using Google Trends. *Scientific Reports*, *3*(1), 3. doi:10.1038rep01684 PMID:23619126

Pyne, S., Rao, B. L. S., & Rao, S. B. (2016). Big Data Analytics: Views from Statistical and Computational Perspectives. In *Big Data Analytics: Methods and applications*. Springer.

Quah, T. (2008). DJIA stock selection assisted by neural network. *Expert Systems with Applications*, *35*(1–2), 50–58. doi:10.1016/j.eswa.2007.06.039

Ragothaman, S., Carpenter, J., & Buttars, T. (1995). Using rule induction for knowledge acquisition: An expert systems approach to evaluating material errors and irregularities. *Expert Systems with Applications*, *9*(4), 483–490. doi:10.1016/0957-4174(95)00018-6

Ravisankar, P., Ravi, V., Rao, G. R., & Bose, I. (2011). Detection of financial statement fraud and feature selection using data mining techniques. *Decision Support Systems*, *50*(2), 491–500. doi:10.1016/j.dss.2010.11.006

Refinitiv. (2020). *Big Data & Machine Learning trends in 2020*. Retrieved from https://www.refinitiv.com/perspectives/big-data/big-data-and-machine-learning-trends-to-watch-in-2020/

Sadasivam, G. S., Subrahmanyam, M., Himachalam, D., Pinnamaneni, B. P., & Lakshme, S. M. (2016). Corporate governance fraud detection from annual reports using big data analytics. *International Journal of Big Data Intelligence*, *3*(1), 51–60. doi:10.1504/IJBDI.2016.073895

Seth, T., & Chaudhary, V. (2015). Big data in finance. In book: Big Data: Algorithms. *Analysis and Applications*, 329–356.

Shapira, Y., Berman, Y., & Ben-Jacob, E. (2014). Modelling the short-term herding behavior of stock markets. *New Journal of Physics*, *16*(5), 16. doi:10.1088/1367-2630/16/5/053040

Shin, K.-S., Lee, T.-S., & Kim, H.-J. (2005). An application of support vector machines in bankruptcy prediction model. *Expert Systems with Applications*, *28*(1), 127–135. doi:10.1016/j.eswa.2004.08.009

Shmueli, G., Bruce, P., Gedeck, P., & Patel, N. (2019). *Data Mining for Business Analytics: Concepts, Techniques and Applications in Python*. Wiley.

Son, Y., Byun, H., & Lee, J. (2016). Nonparametric machine learning models for predicting the credit default swaps: An empirical study. *Expert Systems with Applications, 58*, 210–220. doi:10.1016/j.eswa.2016.03.049

Sun, E. W., & Meinl, T. (2012). A new wavelet-based denoising algorithm for high frequency financial data mining. *European Journal of Operational Research, 217*(3), 589–599. doi:10.1016/j.ejor.2011.09.049

Sun, J., & Hui, X. F. (2006). Financial distress prediction based on similarity weighted voting CBR. In X. Li, R. Zaiane, & Z. Li (Eds.), *Advanced data mining and applications* (pp. 947–958). Springer Verlag. doi:10.1007/11811305_103

Sun, J., & Li, H. (2008). Data mining method for listed companies' financial distress prediction. *Knowledge-Based Systems, 21*(1), 1–5. doi:10.1016/j.knosys.2006.11.003

Sun, X. Q., Shen, H. W., & Cheng, X. Q. (2014). Trading network predicts stock price. *Scientific Reports, 4*, 6. PMID:24429767

Tetlock, P. C. (2007). Giving content to investor sentiment: The role of media in the stock market. *The Journal of Finance, 62*(3), 1139–1168. doi:10.1111/j.1540-6261.2007.01232.x

Warren, J. D. Jr, Moffitt, K. C., & Byrnes, P. (2015). How big data will change accounting. *Accounting Horizons, 29*(2), 397–407. doi:10.2308/acch-51069

Woodall, L. (2017). *Model risk managers eye benefits of machine learning*. Retrieved from https://www.risk.net/risk-management/4646956/model-risk-managers-eye-benefits-of-machine-learning

Woodside-Oriakhi, M., Lucas, C., & Beasley, J. (2011). Heuristic algorithms for the cardinality constrained efficient frontier. *European Journal of Operational Research, 213*(3), 538–550. doi:10.1016/j.ejor.2011.03.030

Wu, C. H., Tzeng, G. H., Goo, Y. J., & Fang, W. C. (2007). A real-valued genetic algorithm to optimize the parameters of support vector machine for predicting bankruptcy. *Expert Systems with Applications, 32*(2), 397–408. doi:10.1016/j.eswa.2005.12.008

Wu, D. D., & Olson, D. L. (2015). *Enterprise risk management in finance*. Springer. doi:10.1057/9781137466297

Yan, W., & Clack, C. D. (2010). Evolving robust GP solutions for hedge fund stock selection in emerging markets. *Soft Computing, 15*(1), 37–50. doi:10.100700500-009-0511-4

Yip, A. Y. N. (2004). Predicting business failure with a case-based reasoning approach. In *Knowledge-based intelligent information and engineering systems* (pp. 665–671). Springer Verlag. doi:10.1007/978-3-540-30134-9_89

Yoon, K., Hoogduin, L., & Zhang, L. (2015). Big data as complementary audit evidence. *Accounting Horizons, 29*(2), 431–438. doi:10.2308/acch-51076

Zhao, Z., Xu, F., Wang, M., & Yi Zhang, C. (2019). A sparse enhanced indexation model with norm and its alternating quadratic penalty method. *The Journal of the Operational Research Society, 70*(3), 433–445. doi:10.1080/01605682.2018.1447245

Zikopoulos, P., & Eaton, C. (2011). *Understanding big data: Analytics for enterprise class Hadoop and streaming data*. McGraw-Hill.

KEY TERMS AND DEFINITIONS

Big Data: Big data has a broad concept that includes large, comprehensive and always available data, which is nourished by various data sources such as information-sensing mobile devices, software logs, digital images and videos, GPS signals and wireless communication networks or so on.

Operational Risk: Operational risk refers the financial losses arising from either internal or external operational breakdowns. Internal factors can be inadequate internal processes, people, or systems whereas external event can be such as fraud, failure in controls, operational error, or natural disaster.

Risk Management: It involves prediction of bankruptcy of a firm (i.e., credit risk), detection of fraud (i.e., operational risk), or prediction of future stock returns (i.e., market risk).

Value: Data value refers to creating business value from new sources and kinds of data. The use of proper data and the ability of gathering meaningful results provide great resources for decision makers.

Variety: It is an expanded concept of data types and sources and it is typically defined as the combinations of different types of structures within the data such as semi-structured (e.g., XML, JSON), and unstructured data (e.g., audio, images, text, click streams).

Velocity: It is defined the frequency of data generation.

Veracity: Data veracity is a combination of four dimensions: completeness, consistence, correctness, and timeliness. These dimensions apply to both quantitative and qualitative data.

Volume: It refers the size of data. Data attributes and number of data points are the identifying factors of data volume.

Chapter 11
Role of Data Science and Data Analytics in Forensic Accounting and Fraud Detection

James Osabuohien Odia
University of Benin, Nigeria

Osaheni Thaddeus Akpata
University of Benin, Nigeria

ABSTRACT

The chapter examines the roles of data science and big data analytics to forensic accountants and fraud detection. It also considers how data science techniques could be applied to the investigative processes in forensic accounting. Basically, the current increase in the volume, velocity, and variety of data offer a rich source of evidence for the forensic accountant who needs to be familiar with the techniques and procedures for extracting, analysing, and visualising such data. This is against backdrop of continuous global increase in economic crime and frauds, and financial criminals are getting more sophisticated, taking advantage of the opportunities provided by the unstructured data constantly being created with every email sent, every Facebook post, every picture on Instagram, or every thought share on Twitter. Consequently, it is important that forensic accountants are constantly abreast with developments in data science and data analytics in order to stay a step ahead of fraudsters as well as address evolving vulnerabilities created by big data.

INTRODUCTION

Fraud constitutes a leakage on the resources of businesses and threat to the livelihood for individuals (Deloitte, 2018).It is an intentional and calculated deed that is against the law, precepts or policy, carried with the aim of getting undue economic or personal gains (Sharma & Panigrahi, 2012).The Oxford Dictionary defines fraud as the wrongful or criminal deception intended to result in financial or personal gain. Moreover, the Institute of Internal Auditors' International Professional Practices Framework (IPPF)

DOI: 10.4018/978-1-7998-3053-5.ch011

defines fraud as: "... any illegal act characterized by deceit, concealment, or violation of trust. These acts are not dependent upon the threat of violence or physical force. Frauds are perpetrated by parties and organizations to obtain money, property, or services; to avoid payment or loss of services; or to secure personal or business advantage". Authors Vlasselaer, et al. (2015) provide an all-encompassing by defining fraud as "an uncommon, well considered, imperceptible, concealed, time-evolving and often carefully organized crime which appears in many ways".

The various categories of fraudulent include; confidence tricks, embezzlement, corruption, counterfeit, product warranty fraud, health fraud, bankruptcy fraud, credit card fraud, insurance fraud, telecommunication fraud, money laundering and the use of tax haven countries to carry out illegal activities, click fraud, identity theft and plagiarism (Baesens et al. 2015; Bressler, 2010). Jofre and Gerlach (2018) asserted that committers of financial fraud are driven by personal gains or by explicit or implied contractual commitments such as debt agreements and the strong desire to achieve market projections. Fraud is associated with substantial economic risks that may pose a threat to the profitability and perception of business organisations (Bănărescu, 2015). Fraud is a growing issue for financial institutions, as tech-savvy criminals increasingly target the payments industry in new and inventive ways. Financial frauds are responsible for the sudden failure of many reputable organisations (Sule et al. 2019).

The importance of fraud detection and prevention is due to the colossal consequences. A typical organization is reported to lose 5% of their revenues to fraud annually; the annual insurance fraud in the United States is over $40 billion while fraud is costing the United Kingdom about £73 billion annualy (Baesens et al,2015).According to PwC's Global Economic Crime and Fraud survey of 2018, nearly half (49%) of 7,200 global organisations have experienced economic crime in the past two years, up from 36% in their last survey. Synectics Solutions' latest statistics showed that organised fraud rose to 59.58% during 2017 from 57% in the previous year. Similarly, the Association of Certified Fraud Examiners (ACFE) Report released in 2018 provided a global analysis of the costs and effects of occupational fraud.16% of all the cases in the study resulted in a median loss of USD 118,000 and continued for a median 18 months before they were discovered (ACFE,2018). Ernst & Young Global Fraud survey of 2018 revealed that 11% of companies have encountered a substantial fraud in the last two years while 38% of respondents affirmed that acts of bribery/corruption take place widely in organisations within their countries (Ernst & Young, 2018).The annual online fraud is 12 times larger than offline frauds of companies report, resulting in severe financial losses to the global economy (Zheng et al,2018).It is also reported that 5% of the organination revenues is lost to fraud.

It is evident that financial fraud is a worldwide concern that signifies a major threat to the stability of the economic system because of the consequent weakening of business confidence and trust of regulatory establishments (Jofre & Gerlach, 2018). Financial fraud is a serious concern for businesses and economies around the globe (Gepp et al.,2018). The disastrous outcomes of financial fraud reveal the susceptibility and defencelessness of financial community (Jofre & Gerlach,2018).The inadequacy of statutory audit to curtail the misappropriation of company's financial assets and thwart the increase in economic crime has placed a burden on accountants and legal practitioners to develop better ways of reducing fraud (Oyebisi et al,2018). Forensic accounting has emerged as a veritable means to identify and respond to the rising accounting or financial frauds around the world. Forensic accounting is concerned with the employment of accounting methods, auditing procedures and investigative processes for the purpose of finding solutions to legal issues and providing financial analysis that would be deemed appropriate for litigation, and on which discussions, debates and dispute resolution can be based (Oyebisi et al. 2018). Modugu and Anyaduba (2013) have argued that the increasing intricacies of financial frauds demand the use of forensic accounting methods for effective investigation and prosecution of perpetrators of financial crimes. Again leveraging technology to implement continuous fraud prevention programme could help safeguard organizations from the risk of fraud and reduce the time it takes to uncover fraudulent activity. Technology provides more accurate audit reports and better insight into the internal controls framework, and improves the ability to access and manage business risk.

However, most of the procedures presently applied to inspect journal entries are generally based on familiar fraud scenarios or "red-flag" checks (e.g. postings at odd hours) that are based on guidelines defined by knowledgeable chartered accountants or fraud examiners. Unfortunately, these guidelines often do not make generalisations outside known incidences of fraud, therefore they fail to identify new patterns (Schreyer et al. 2017). In addition, there are fresh concerns regarding big data and the associated processing of extremely large datasets which demand intricate and sometimes difficult techniques to process the data (Iron & Lallie, 2014). Big data is an umbrella term for any group of data sets that are considered difficult to handle when employing traditional data management methods because they are very large or multifarious (Cielen et al. 2016). According to Sivarajah et al. (2016), many organizations are adopting big data analytics (BDA) processes and tools today to help improve operational efficiency, drive new revenue streams, detect frauds and gain competitive advantages over business competitors. The internal control team members were required to consider every transaction that occurred, this is no longer manually possible because of the large volume, hence the use of data analysis tools and data science. Since the companies usually operate with large volumes of data, it is absolutely necessary to implement such processes of continuous monitoring, in order to identify anomalies in the data stream or behavioural patterns, potentially fraudulent (Bănărescu, 2015). However, in the era of big data and internet of things (IoT) where all things are being automated and huge data generated, attacks on data and financial frauds are on the increase. But BDA can help to sift through unstructured data and proactively detect fraud.

Data science is an evolving field that deals with the gathering, preparation, exploration, visualization, organisation, and storage of large groups of data (Proyag et al. 2015). Data science procedures are valuable in the uncovering of anomalies; anomalies could denote deviations from previous actions that are considered uncommon and noteworthy and suggest something and may require a response (Kumar et al. 2017).The procedure for detecting anomalies and fraud involves identifying uncommon patterns in data, probing the data and picking out singular items that may require additional investigation (Dilla & Raschke, 2015). According to Grover and Kar (2017), the importance of data science and BDA is growing very fast as organizations are gearing up to leverage their information assets to gain competitive advantage. Similarly, the flexibility offered through BDA can empower functional and firm's financial performance.

The impact of fraud on organisations could be very significant and staggering. The impacts can be financial, operational and psychological. It can result in the loss of reputation, goodwill and customers relations. While the perpetrators of frauds maybe employees from inside the organization or outsiders, organizations need to have effective fraud management and data analytics system in place to safeguard the organisation's assets and reputation. Therefore, the objective of the chapter is to examine the roles of data and big data analytics in forensic accounting and fraud detection. The rest of the chapter is structured as follows. The immediate section is the background and overview of data science, big data, big data analytics, artificial intelligence and machine learning and fraud detection. Section three considers forensic accounting and fraud detection and why forensic accounting need the new data analytic tools.

Section four dwells on forensic and data analytic tools currently used for fraud detection. Section five is the solutions and recommendations. The section six is the conclusion and suggestions for further study.

BACKGROUND

Data Science and Fraud Detection

According to Wing (2019), data science is the study of obtaining useful insights from data.It is the study of nature of data (Legara,2017). Proyag et al.(2015) viewed data science as an extension of the field of information mining and perceptive investigation, concerned with the extraction of valuable information from large volumes of data that may exist in an unorganised or unstructured form. It covers a range of activities associated with the assortment, linkage and storage of data (Garber, 2019). Data science entails the structures and methods that allow the abstraction of information or insights from data in different forms, which may be structured or unstructured (Berman et al, 2016). Data science implies using techniques to examine great amounts of data and mining the information contained within (Cielen et al,2016). Norrie (2019) sees data science as" a modern and rapidly growing synthesis of large-scale database operations, ML, and statistics. It also includes unstructured data analysis such as text mining, which involves an understanding of both computational linguistics and natural language processing". It is a field that comprises everything related to cleaning, preparing, and analysing unstructured, semi-structured and structured data (Embarak,2018). This field of science uses a combination of statistics, mathematics, programming, problem-solving, and data capture to extract insights and information from data.

Data science has emerged as a means to identify fraudulent behaviour (Banenjee et al,2017). It has evolved from statistics and data administration to include concepts and practices such as AI, ML and deep learning (Accenture, nd; Cielen et al, 2016). Over the years, data science has transformed from being utilised in the somewhat narrow area of statistics and analytics to having a worldwide presence in all aspects of science and business (Proyag et al, 2015). Data science has gradually developed as an interdisciplinary specialisation that incorporates techniques from data analysis related disciplines such as statistics and predictive analytics (Berman et al, 2016).Data science has a substantial overlap with computer science that subsumes artificial intelligence (AI), mathematics, data processing, statistical research, ML and domain expertise (Legara,2017; Norrie, 2019). Data science also includes ML, but not AI as such. Big data is the raw materials that fuel the data science revolution. Data science is both synonymous with data mining, as well as a superset of concepts which includes data mining. Data mining is the process of determining useful patterns and trends from large sets of data and it combines various fields of study such as ML, information science, and statistics. It requires skills in analysis and data manipulation. Machine learning is one of the technical drivers of data science. ML is the engine which allows this process of extraction of insights from data to be automated.

Although data science consists of data analysis as a vital element of the skill set needed for performing many functions, it is far more than just analysing data (Proyag et al, 2015). Wing (2019) argued that data science is more than analysing data using techniques from ML and statistics because obtaining value takes much effort, prior to and subsequent to data analysis. Stanton (2012) also agrees that data science consists of data analysis as an essential constituent of the required skill set but not the only needed skill, concluding that; data science is not the same as other areas, including mathematics and statistics. Therefore, data science appears to be strongly linked with areas which include data base and computer science, there are other diverse skills which may be non-mathematical or statistical that are also required (Proyag et al, 2015).There are also a number of other key terms such as data analysis, data analytics, big data, descriptive analytics, predictive analytics and prescriptive analytics which are very connected to data science (Cao,2017).

Proyag et al (2015) believe that data science as an area of activity is the joint where a number of disciplines meet. They further affirm that a data science specialist has a blend of skills and abilities through a variety of fields, for that reason, it is expected that he has the capacity to mine data and obtain meaning from large quantities of data. Data science is increasingly being accepted as a field of strong influence for driving next-generation transformation, business, and academics (Cao, 2017). A search of "data science" on Google Trends reveals that over the last five years, there has been a sustained increase in the online search interest for data science and other key terms such as machine learning, data analytics, big data and artificial intelligence (Google Trends, 2019). Proyag et al. (2015) identified three parts contained within data science; arranging, bundling and conveying (or ABC of) information. Arranging is concerned with the gathering of data from relevant sources and transforming the data manually from a "raw" state into another form that permits a more appropriate management and manipulation of the data using semi-automated methods. This part is also referred to as data wrangling or munging. Bundling deals with the procedures for evaluating, altering, and representing information with the intention of discovering useful data, making informed recommendations, and facilitating the making of policy and administrative decisions. This is also referred to as the analysis phase. Conveying includes the ways and means of transforming the statistical inferences derived from the data into a form that can be better comprehended and interpreted by users of the information.

The benefits of data science are substantial and as the number accurate predictions made through data science increases, products of data science will become more valuable than ever, thereby increasing interest in the area (Garber,2019). Data science extracts and cleanses data, looks for patterns, provides actionable insights, communicates and helps to make data-driven decisions. Cao (2017) predicts that in the next 50 years, data science will spread further than statistics to identify, examine and define precise foundational scientific issues and tackle significant challenges. Data science has an extremely great potential to become a distinct and comprehensive discipline with extensive interest (Monajemi et al., 2019). Certainly, there is an increasing recognition of the possibility of data science and analytics to facilitate data-driven theory and professional development in core disciplines such as computing, information technology, and statistics in addition to the broad-based areas of business, social and medical sciences.

Big Data, Big Data Analytics and Fraud Detection

Big data is strongly related to the term "data science" and both terms are impossible to separate both (Jofre & Gerlach, 2018). Big data refers to data sets that are so voluminous and complex that traditional data processing application software is inadequate to deal with them. Big data is concerned with data sets characterised by high velocity, high volume and high variety; that due to their nature, cannot be easily organised or analysed with the regular data administration tools, procedures, and infrastructure (Ernst & Young, 2013). Big data concept appeared first in the late 1990s (Cox & Elsworth 1997). It was initially defined in early 2000 in terms of 3Vs- volume, velocity and variety (Garner Inc, 2012), but it has moved to 4Vs (added veracity), 6Vs (added variability and value), 7Vs (added variability, value and visualization) and presently over 10Vs.The convergence of the internet of things (IOTs), cloud and mobile computing and social media have led to exponential increase in the volumes of data being created and collected. In fact, it is estimated that the digital universe will reach 44 zettabytes or 44 trillion gigabytes by 2020.

Irons and Lallie (2014) opined that "for an analytical problem to be a big data problem, it has to pass the 'test' of volume, velocity and/or variety". Connolly (2012) argued that BD is bringing together varied datasets into one data silo to permit the analysis of disparate data to then find new trends, associations and correlations in the data. In defining big data Cukier and Mayer-Schoenberger (2013) warned that "it is misleading to want to solely understand BD in terms of size". They explained that "big data is also characterized by the ability to render into data many aspects of the world that have never been quantified before". For instance "followings", "retweets" and "likes" can now be transformed into data via twitter. BD has a lot of opportunities from helping to improve predictions of economic indicators such as the unemployment level (Vicente, López-Menéndez & Pérez 2015), detect market trends, help policy-makers to monitor faster and more precisely the effects of a wide range of policies and public grants (Blazquez & Domenech,2017).

Ramya and Sumathi (2019) pin-pointed the applications of BD in various field like government or public sector, banking, marketing, healthcare, stock exchange and addresses aadhar card fraud detection by using data-mining techniques like Naive Bayes (NB), C4.5, and Back Propagation (BP) to analyse the customer data and identify patterns that can lead to fraud. Big data provides auditors with internal and external tools to better forecast estimates, concerns, detects fraud and other audit matters (Alles, 2015; Joshi & Marthandan, 2018; Littley 2012).Big data can also help to solve cyber security issues since the mining of precise information from enormous amount of data can give a broader view and real time information of risks and vulnerabilities. Big data has brought with it novel fraud detection and prevention techniques such as behavioral analysis and real-time detection to give fraud fighting techniques a new perspective. The Chinese e-commerce company, Alibaba is using BD to effectively tackle fraud.

The BD tools like Hadoop, MapReduce, Splunk, EC2,Fortscale, IBM Security Intelligence, Action DataRush, Apache Spark, QRadar, Platfora and Apache Metron etc can handle complex and large volume of network data and also used for better analysis of cyber security. BD technologies help to detect application layer distributed denial of service (DDoS) attacks thereby reducing the time taken to analyze the data and process it in real time. They give better insights into the attack data and segregate the attackers from genuine users in real time (Joglekar & Pise,2016; Mahmood & Uzma,2013).The ability of BD tools to handle both structured and unstructured data help to easily identify anomalies.BD tools can quickly process data, build models and do quick analysis, without using complex hardware, analyses of data in present times becomes very easy (Joglekar & Pise,2016).Big data tools are now used for insolvency and forensic professional services, and for teams of dedicated investigators covering financial investigations. The crimes can be traced by analysing structured and unstructured data sources such as bank statements, PDF files, emails, invoices and spread sheets.

Big data analytics (BDA) is an analysis that is based on a large population of data of a variety of types with the aim of uncovering unknown tendencies, correlations and information that will be useful in facilitating the arrival at conclusions based on facts (Ernst & Young, 2013).According to the European Union Agency for Network and Information Security- ENISA (2016), BDA is used to combat fraud by"(i) correlating real-time and historical account activity, "(ii) relying on baselines to spot abnormal user behaviour uncovering trends and patterns in large amounts of data, "(iii) establishing patterns and relationships, and (iv) making non-obvious connections between disparate sources of data". By these means, businesses are able to identify fraud risks at an early stage and thereby prevent crime and help investigations. The technical challenge about fraud analysis involves looking for behavioural patterns and building a profile of normal activities, accessing sparse financial information data and parsing unstructured text, and understanding discrepancies in customer transactions. BDA assists in network security, enterprise analytics, and detect advanced persistent threats (ATP) facing organization today. ATP include stealing intellectual property from targeted organization, gaining access to sensitive customer data, accessing strategic business information that could be used for financial gain, blackmail, embarrassment, data poisoning, illegal insider trading or disrupting an organization's business (Cardena et al,2013)

BDA can be prescriptive, predictive, diagnostic and descriptive analytics. According to Ernst and Young (2013), prescriptive analytics is used to decide WHICH course of action will generate the most effective outcome against a particular set of things to achieve and the associated limitations. Predictive analytics on the other hand, leverages on past data to give meaning to the underlying link between data inputs and outputs for the purpose of forecasting WHAT will occur in the future across several circumstances. Diagnostic analytics enables us to understand WHY a particular thing happened while descriptive analytics extracts historical data to visualize, comprehend and provide information regarding WHAT has happened live, previously or after the fact. Predictive analytics has been tipped as the most powerful technique for detecting financial crime, especially for large populations of clients or transactions (Accenture, nd).

Data analytics (DA) refers to the use of analytics software to identify trends, patterns, anomalies and exceptions within data. The primary reason to use DA techniques to tackle fraud since many internal control systems (ICs) have serious weaknesses.The DA could be simple or advanced, or batch and streaming data analytics. Again DA maybe ad hoc or one-off investigative and exploratory, repetitive and "always on" or continuous approach to fraud detection (ACL,2010; Cardena, Manadhata & Rajan, 2013).The advanced DA (ADA) helps to deal with complex cases and detect sophisticated fraud schemes. ADA can detect deviations from normal behaviour even if normal behaviour has not been defined in terms of rules or thresholds. Some of the DA methods for fraud detection include clustering, support vector machine (for solvency analysis, intrusion detection and verifying financial statement), case base reasoning and k nearest neighbour, artificial neural network and random forest. While batch DA deals with data in high latency application and at rest, processes static files after storage, an attends to periodic jobs with some delay action, streaming DA involves data with low latency application, on-going event stream data in motion which are instantaneously processed before storage. Modern audit paradigm is shifting from traditional cyclical approach to continuous and risk based model owing to the wide range of technology solutions available and the size and sophistication of the audit firm. There is movement of business application from batch DA to streaming DA because of real time data-driven decision making, better efficiency in operation, enhanced customer satisfaction and competitive advantage (Cardena et al, 2013). Technology provides more insights into IC frameworks, more accurate audit reports and enables ability to access and manage business risks. The benefits of DA include: increase efficiency and effectiveness, boost productivity and profitability, reduce sampling errors, assess and improve internal controls, revise or reinforce policies, monitor trends, It also help to identify fraud before it becomes material, focus detection efforts on suspicious transactions, gain insights into how well ICs are operating and compare data from diverse sources to identify instances of fraud or non-compliance and heightened risk of fraud. It is especially useful when fraud is hidden in large data volumes and manual checks are insufficient. Data analytics software is used to reduce the cost, time and complexity associated with fraud and forensic investigations for litigation. It provides more proactive fights against frauds.

The BDA architecture could help to achieve cleaner production processes and optimize product life-cycle management (Zhang, Ren,Liu & Si 2017), forecast economic and social behaviour, trends and changes (Blazquez & Domenech 2018).According to Sivarajah et al (2016), the opportunities of BDA include: value creation, increased organizational output and support in enhancing visibility and flexibility of supply chain and resource allocation. Advanced BDA technologies such as NoSQL Databases, BigQuery, MapReduce, Hadoop, WibiData and Skytree generate greater insights and enable improved business strategies and decision making in some critical sectors like health care, economic productivity, energy futures, and to predict natural catastrophe (Yi, Liu, Liu & Jin 2014) . BDA helps to unlock and analyse all data types. Appelbaum et al (2017a) argued that many engagement clients' systems are now integrating BD with new and complex business analytical approaches to generate intelligence for decision making. The use of BD and DA is helping modern audit engagement of client to remain competitive and relevance. It also results in enhanced audit quality, increased audit effectiveness and improved clients' services. BDA enables auditors to focus on outliers and exceptions and also to identify the riskiest areas of audits .It enables audit by exception (Appelbaum et al, 2017b). Bologa, Bologa and Florea (2010) argued BDA should use the following technologies: business rules, anomaly detection, text mining, database searches and social network analysis (SNA) to prevent insurance fraud. According to them, the applications of these techniques enable rapid detection of abnormal claims, create a new set of tests to automatically narrow the segment potentially fraudulent applications or detect new patterns of fraud not previously known.

Artificial Intelligence

Artificial intelligence(AI) can be viewed as a computer system which simulates some amount of intelligence (Irons & Lallie, 2014). Floridi and Cowls (2019) see AI as a budding resource of interactive, independent and often self-learning agency that can deal with tasks that would otherwise require human intelligence and intervention to be performed successfully. In accordance with history, the phrase "artificial intelligence" was originated in the late 1950's to refer to the strong aspiration of creating an entity, using software and hardware that will have human-level intelligence (Jordan, 2019). AI systems are embodied as intricate volumes of numerical parameters and bespoke mathematical formulae designed or "trained" to suit a specific purpose (Berman et al., 2016). Deloitte (2016) explains AI is progressively becoming a routine aspect of our everyday lives, following the coming to existence of intelligent virtual assistants, music and movie recommendation engines, and cars that can park themselves. Also, smart mobile devices, virtual shopping websites, and music applications learn and adjust on the basis of our preferences. Furthermore, cognitive computing can be employed in teaching computers to spot and diagnose risks.AI is also helping to analyse intricate fraud cases.

Already, AI is having a significant effect on the world, so, the crucial questions now are how, where, when, and by whom the effect of AI will be felt (Floridi & Cowls, 2019). With advancements in ML algorithms, AI has enabled advanced business analytics which are descriptive, diagnostic, predictive, prescriptive and fraud analytics. While predictive analytics uses data, algorithms, and ML techniques to anticipate future outcomes, prescriptive analytics guides predictions into action. AI also facilitates document review in auditing. The BD environment provides opportunity for the external auditors to perform more advanced predictive and prescriptive-oriented analytics. ICAEW (2018a) has predicted that in the decades to come, intelligent structures will to a greater extent, take over decision-making duties from persons, therefore, it is a chance for the accounting profession to thoroughly enhance the value of organisational decisions which is the paramount objective of the profession.

Machine Learning and Fraud Detection

Machine learning is a field that involves more than one branch of knowledge, focused on dealing with pattern recognition issues and developing interdisciplinary prognostic models to make decisions that are based on data (Lo, Siah & Wong, 2019). Machine learning is a type of AI where computer teaches itself the solution to a query discovering patterns in sets of data and matching fresh parts of data the based on probability (Banerjee et al. 2018; ICAEW, 2018b). ML uses statistical analyses to generate predictions or make decisions from the analysis of a large historical dataset. The characteristics of ML procedures reveal its capacity to substantially improve the various areas within the accounting field and can provide accountants with new competencies, in addition to automating several processes (ICAEW, 2018a). Columbus (2019) asserts that computer-based organisations that have a good history of preventing online fraud are those that aggressively employ the use of supervised machine learning to develop models that can identify fraud faster than manually-based methods. Machine learning can aid in enhancing fraud recognition using advanced models of 'normal' events and more effective prediction of fraudulent actions, in addition to easing access to, and analysis of, unstructured information. The various algorithms an establishment employs to manage fraud risks can eventually be joined into a framework that records and categorises various transactions and organisations according to their comparative level of suspiciousness and significance; helping to assign priority to fraud examination and analysis (Deloitte, 2018).

Gepp, Linnenluecke, O'Neill, and Smith (2018) define ML as an all-inclusive term that covers both supervised and unsupervised learning. While supervised learning generates predictive or descriptive models from data with identified outcomes for application to data with unknown outcomes, unsupervised learning uncovers forms in unlabelled data. Supervised learning focuses on finding a relationship between an input value and an output value to predict further output values when more input is provide. The common supervised ML include using logistic regression (LR), artificial or deep neural networks (ANN/DNN),multilayer perception (MLP) random forests (RF) classifier, naïve Bayes (NB),K nearest neighbour (KNN) and support vector machine (SVM), while neural networks, association rules (or market basket analysis) and cluster analysis are associated with unsupervised learning. Unsupervised learning is a technique in which there are inputs but no specific output. While clustering involves grouping of data like market and customer segmentation using confirmatory discriminant analysis, association rules is about co-occurrence of different attributes.

The RF is considered as the state-of-art fraud detection algorithm (Jurgovsky et al, 2018) which can be used to detect credit card fraud. The SVM was also found to be most successful in detecting credit card fraud when tested under more realistic conditions (Banerjee et al,. 2018).On the other hand, Yang and Xu (2019) found that sequential models like Hidden Markov models (HMM) and recurrent neural networks (RNN) were superior to traditional classifiers like SVM, RF, DNN in fraud detection. In fact, SVM performs the worst while DNN outperforms RF. Albashrawi (2015) found that there were 41 ML techniques that were used for fraud detection and LR was the most used based on the review of 65 relevant articles from Emerald, Elsevier, World Scientific, IEEE and Routledge. Given the different outcomes of the various fraud detection models, Shpyrko and Koval (2019) concluded that "the use of one or another model depends on the specific situation, whether clients are ready sometimes get denial of the transaction, but to be sure that their funds will not be obtained by fraud, or they are more interested in ease of use, and security is not that important".

The social network analysis (SNA) extends the ability of the fraud detection system by learning and detecting characteristics of fraudulent behaviour I a network of linked entities.SNA tools combine a hybrid approach of analytical methods which include organisation business rules, statistical methods, pattern/ clustering analysis and network leverage analytics to uncover large amount of data and also show relations via links. SNA identifies fraudulent entities through link and clustering analysis. General Electric (GE) consumer and industrial home services has employed SNA solution-SAS detect suspicious claims from technicians which repair products under warranty.

Python and R are often used in data analysis (Banerjee et al. 2018; Embarak, 2018). Some of Python's built-in libraries like Scikit-learn, Pandas and Matplotlib aid in data analysis and visualization. Numpy allows for large storage of information, Pandas provides for data organization and helps to format data from excels and CSVs into analysable data frames. Scikit-learn has numerous built-in ML algorithms, matplotlib graphs data in various plot types,and Keras, a high-level neural networks API which is run on Python and focuses on fast experimentation. The formatting, analyzing, and visualization techniques help to analyze credit-card transactions and detect fraud. Scikit-learn is one of Python's most notable libraries for ML. Unlike Numpy and Pandas, which are used for data manipulation, Scikit-learn focuses on data modelling like clustering, cross-validation, supervised models, and feature selection.

Machine learning techniques suggest powerful ways to carry out activities relating to data science, especially in areas of prediction and pattern recognition. The Institute of Chartered Accountants of England and Wales (ICAEW, 2018a) is of the opinion that ML techniques draw on our own cognitive strong points which are; pattern recognition and learning, instead of trying to outline complex rules. In addition, the most sophisticated methods in ML such as ANN and deep learning allow important advancements like natural language processing (NLP) and translation, and machine vision. Jordan (2019) revealed the likelihood of ML gaining immense relevance in the business sphere since the early 1990s to the turn of the century. He pointed out that progressive organisations like Amazon were already applying ML in all areas of their business to solve back-end issues in fraud recognition, supply-chain forecasts and develop innovative service like product recommendation systems. Substantial errors, blank fields and other data quality issues are often more prevalent in new datasets, and additional checks and data quality assurance are needed. ML can help improve data quality by automatically identifying anomalies (potential errors) to flag them to the statistician and/or the data-providing source. AI and ML applications in insurance markets could reduce the degree of moral hazard and adverse selection

The Financial Standard Board (FSB, 2017) argued that AI and ML methods are being rapidly adopted for a range of applications in the financial services industry. These range from assess credit quality, to price and market insurance contracts, and to automate client interaction, analyse market impacts of trading large positions, find signals for higher (and uncorrelated) returns and optimise trading execution, regulatory compliance, surveillance, data quality assessment and fraud detection. Applications of AI and ML could result in new and unexpected forms of interconnectedness between financial markets and institutions. ICAEW (2018a) suggested that developments in ML is the main reason for the current publicity around AI. Furthermore, integrating ML with the progress in AI areas like knowledge representation and reasoning enhances the processes of human thinking.

MAIN FOCUS OF THE CHAPTER

Issues, Controversies and Problems

The advent of the internet from the 1980s, digitization and e-commerce have created significant opportunities and challenges for organizations. It has also offered criminals the opportunity to exploit financial systems to do fraudulent transactions (Yang & Xu, 2019). Deloitte (2018) posited that the increase in the number and types of digital devices has increased businesses exposure to risks as fraud schemes driven by technological improvements have continually sprung up, spread and transformed rapidly, creating fresh concerns. Fraudsters have continued to evolve new tactics to explore the technologies. Criminals are constantly finding and innovating new ways and experimenting with new techniques to commit fraud. Therefore, organizations must update their data insights and ability, to detect and prevent fraud fast enough to fight the ever-present threat. They must develop ever-more sophisticated techniques to uncover, stop new threats and be a step ahead of the fraudsters.

Basically the manual handling of frauds is generally very costly. Moreover, the use of sampling techniques, work in silos under the traditional method together with much unstructured data trend in the era of big data and have created opportunity for frauds to be undetected if there is no thorough analysis. Therefore, organizations are looking to leverage advanced analytics detection tools such as ML solutions to protect them against increasingly sophisticated fraud attacks. Again, because the amount of processed data has grown exponentially that the internal control team members and auditors are not able to look at every transaction that takes place. There is need for data science and data analytics tools as well as the ability to uncover actionable insights from large volumes of data which are presently in short supply in many organisations. There is also the challenge of creating a model that could instantly detect and block a given fraudulent transaction in order to provide better security and user experience.

Although BDA are veritable techniques to fraud detection and prevention in organisations, there are also the issues of data provenance, privacy and governance, security, and human-computer interaction that must be addressed to realise its full benefits (Cardena et al. 2013)

According to ACCA (2019), "the next step for auditors and finance analysts is to apply AI and ML algorithms to improve the quality of analysis and forecasting, and to increase the rate of fraud detection". ML 'predictions' can be both backward and forward-looking, with clear applications in risk management, fraud detection and inaccuracy, and risk assessment by comparing historical data sets with current data, which can predict the likely future value of an asset (ACCA, 2019). However, AI and ML present a range of legal issues relating to privacy and data protection, consumer protection, anti-discrimination and liability issues, and cross-border issues. Besides, the lack of interpretability or "auditability" of AI and ML methods could become a macro-level risk and have unintended consequences. (FSB, 2017).

Forensic Accounting and Fraud Detection

Forensic accounting is an area within accounting that is not only interested in performing conventional accounting duties, but also in using acquired experiences and competencies to resolve matters concerning civil disputes and criminal matters (Hamdan, 2018).Forensic accounting is believed to have developed in reaction to some particular fraud linked cases with the general anticipation being that forensic accounting will provide some respite to the apparent weaknesses associated with regular accounting and audit processes to economic fraud (Modugu & Anyaduba, 2013). The Association of Certified Fraud Examiners states that "forensic accountants combine their accounting knowledge with investigative skills, using this unique combination in litigation support and investigative accounting settings" (Association of Certified Fraud Examiners, 2019).With the attention on the accounting profession to provide more effective and efficient solutions to fraud, a new breed of accountants, the forensic accountant has emerged (Charles et al. 2009).The inadequacy of internal auditing system methods in spotting the accounting frauds has made it necessary for the development of specialised procedures, recognised collectively as forensic accounting (Sharma & Panigrahi, 2012).

Forensic accounting encompasses all other areas associated with investigations for the purpose of uncovering economic fraud, having its own models and methodologies that provide advisory services assurance and attestation suitable to be used as legal evidence (Modugu & Anyaduba, 2013). Hamdan (2018) asserts that forensic accounting has been used as a tool to underpin legal involvement in the financial and accounting disciplines, therefore, the forensic accountant uses his experiences in accounting and his knowledge of Law to help detect and report any contravention or lack of compliance. It is important to note that there is no generally acceptable definition of forensic accounting. It is likely that there are as many definitions of forensic accounting as there are authors within the discipline (Oyebisi et al, 2018). However, in order for forensic accountants to be able to accurately recognise fraud indicators, they must be knowledgeable in the areas of investigation in addition to several specialised auditing procedures. In many instances, the financial detective will be a competent auditor and/or accountant (Bressler, 2010).

In the past few decades, incidences of economic fraud have become progressively more regular and consequential (Jofre & Gerlach, 2018). Stone and Miller (2012) suggested that forensic accounting and fraud investigation is a fast developing accounting area in at least three domains; practice, training and certification, research and publication. Accordingly, Oyebisi et al (2018) examined the role of the forensic accountants in the prevention and detection of fraud in the Nigerian banking sector and found that forensic accounting has a significant impact on fraud prevention and detection. Hamdan (2018) linked the practice of forensic accounting to different associated skills sets of forensic accountants and revealed that forensic accounting practice provides an effective system for fraud detection. In addition, Modugu and Anyaduba (2013) findings indicate that there is substantial consensus amongst stakeholders that forensic accounting is effective for fraud management and strengthening internal control. Forensic accounting is the three-way practice of applying accounting, auditing and investigative knowledge to provide support litigation evidence for fraud. Therefore, being an effective accountant does not necessarily translate into being an effective forensic accountant. An effective forensic accountant needs to have a broad range of skills and competencies (Charles et al, 2009).

According to Hamdan (2018), forensic accounting is hinged on a number of pillars which include the personality of accountant, expertise, the necessary tools and familiarity with the law. Similarly, based on an investigation into the perception of professionals in the field and users of forensic accounting services about the essential traits, and relevant skills of forensic accountants, Salleh and Aziz (2014) found that the top five skill traits of a forensic accountant ranked as most important are; analytical, ethical, detail-attentive, self-assured and critical. Furthermore, the top five basic /core skills as investigative capacity, auditing abilities, critical / strategic thinker, recognise vital concerns and understand the purpose of a case while the top five relevant enhanced skills are the ability to evaluate and understand data in financial statements, fraud recognition, audit evidence, asset tracking and internal controls.

Linda (2010) suggested that the forensic accountant must be well trained in the procedures for handling evidence, management of financial data, accounting information systems (AIS) software, effective communication and have the ability to influence a judicial decisions as an expert witness. Hamdan (2018) stressed that the forensic accountants should have adequate investigation skills to enable them build scepticism and gather the necessary evidence to support or refute. The Association of Certified Fraud Examiners outlines some valuable skills, features and knowledge areas of forensic accountants to include analytical skills, research expertise, proficiency in the use of computer applications and knowledge of regression analysis (Association of Certified Fraud Examiners, 2019).

FORENSIC ACCOUNTING AND THE NEW (DATA ANALYTICS) TECHNIQUES

ICAEW (2018) highlights some important reasons why the accounting profession should consider leveraging on the benefits of AI such as; intelligent structures can discover hidden or more intricate patterns in data, they may be better in settings that we consider less predictable and they are not prone to fatigue, tedium and human prejudices. The intricacies and pressures of our present world has made it necessary that organisations are aware of the challenges they are confronted with and take steps towards protecting their assets from fraud, waste, exploitation, and regulatory issues (Deloitte, 2018). PwC's 2018 Global Economic Crime and Fraud Survey reveals that 34% of the C-level and senior management executives said that the current methods to tackling online fraud was generating too many errors in data reporting (PWC, 2018). One of the most popular forms of emerging offensives employs ML and other automation processes to perpetrate fraud that existing methods of fraud management are unable to detect (Columbus, 2019). Deloitte (2018) believes that as fraudsters develop their range of criminality, traditional organisational antifraud procedures are rapidly running out of steam against fraud patterns that are continually growing in both rate of recurrence and inventiveness. Also, following the transformations in financial environments, the growth in the adoption of new technology and the data increase in the velocity and quantity, the challenges associated with identifying anomalies immediately have also increased (Anandakrishnan et al, 2017). Columbus (2019) affirmed most common conventional approaches to tackling online frauds are proving to be no longer effective at combating the more innovative, subtle forms of present-day fraud schemes.

Sathyapriya and Thiagarasu (2017) argued that the "conventional methodologies of performing forensic analysis have changed with the emergence of big data because forensic with big data requires more sophisticated tools along with the deployment of efficient frameworks". Deloitte (2016) is of the opinion that conventional approaches to data analysis are becoming more and more incapable of managing this data quantity, instead, cognitive capabilities such as data mining and machine learning are displacing conventional methods of analytics and being used on these enormous data sets to help find patterns and indicators. Irons and Lallie (2014) posit that the community of digital forensics has to expand its range of skillsets and procedures, and discover more effective means of analysing data and extracting meaning from sources of evidence for the purpose of comprehending the event being examined. Fraud modelling should take advantage of the available additional data by employing big data procedures developed to automatically update whenever fresh information is obtainable (Gepp et al., 2018). ICAEW affirms that "the profession needs to focus on the fundamental business problems it aims to solve, and imagine how new technologies can transform its approach to them" (ICAEW, 2018).Furthermore, to develop an optimistic picture of the future, the accounting profession needs to obtain a deep understanding of the current practical challenges and how accountants can work side by side with artificial systems to provide a solution to organisational problems.

Ernst and Young (2016) affirms that the internet adds new features to data. Accordingly, personnel in many establishments are constantly interacting outside the networks of the organisation using social media platforms, mobile devices or through web pages which exemplifies why conventional investigative analytics procedures used a decade ago may not be effective given the nature and variety of present day data. In addition, there is the fast expanding storage sizes now offered for purchase. For example, typical hard disk sizes have expanded from 10 Gigabytes in the early 1980s to an excess of a Terabyte in the 2010s (Irons & Lallie, 2014).The character, assortment and intricacy of structured and unstructured information is evolving at a rapid rate, demanding that organisations have a rethink on how they keep a track on illegal financial activities (Ernst &Young, 2016).

Big data demands that the statistical techniques employed should be more flexible models because structured conventional regression models will most likely not fit big data well (Gepp et al., 2018). Big data analytics is concerned with the extraction of value from big data which are significant, previously unknown, implicit and potentially useful. Big data analytics enables companies to analyze voluminous amount of data generated during financial transactions, fight cyber attacks, detect fraud and identify theft and facilitate digital forensic analysis (Sathyapriya & Thiagarasu, 2017). Since most of the frauds incidences are high-volume in nature, BDA can help to extract value from huge data, separate what is "normal" from what is "abnormal", separate the patterns generated by authorized users from suspicious or malicious users. By providing means to discover changing patterns of malicious activities hidden deep in large volumes of organizations data, BD tools can indeed empower businesses to better understand if and how they have been attacked (Madmood & Alza,2013)

FORENSIC AND BIG DATA ANALYTICS TOOLS FOR FRAUD DETECTION

Although many companies are seeking to detect frauds using data analytics to search for anomalies and suspicious transactions, very few companies are successfully employing analytics for the detection of frauds. In a recent global survey of KPMG professionals of 750 fraudsters between March 2013 and August 2015, only three (3%) were detected using proactive fraud-focused analysis compared to whistle-blowing (44%) and other methods. The reasons attributed include: the wane in management owing to unsuccessful implementation of analytic anti-fraud programme, lack of understanding of what data analytics can do for them, high cost or expense as well as the lack of trust and confidence underlying the data analytic processes (KPMG,2016). According to Dagiliene et al (2019), Li et al (2018), and Verma and Bhattacharyya (2017), the non-adoption of BDA was due to companies' not realising the strategic value of BDA, and also because they were not ready to make changes owing to technological, organisational and environmental difficulties.

Some of the forensic and data analytic tools currently used in fraud detection include (i) Spreadsheet tools such as Microsoft excel (ii) Database tools such as Microsoft Access or Microsoft SQL Server (iii) Continuous monitoring tools which may include governance risk and compliance (GRC) tools (SAP, SAI Global, Oracle) (iv) Text analytics tools or keyword searching (v) Forensic analytics software (ACL, iDEA) (vi) Social media/web monitoring tools (vii) Visualization and reporting tools (Tableau, Spotfire, QlikView) (viii) Statistical analysis and data-mining packages (SPSS, SAS, R, Stata) (ix) Big data technologies (Hadoop, Map Reduce) (x) Voice searching and analysis (Nexidia, NICE).The wide spectra of specialized tools are capable to support and enhance the antifraud activity in the organization, although there are reports of low use of these tools and other limitations such as high costs, time loss, complexity need of human resource etc (Bănărescu,2015).

According to Maniraj, Sain, Sarka and Ahmed (2019), some of the currently used approaches to fraud detection are artificial neural network (ANN), fuzzy logic, genetic algorithm, logistic regression (LR), decision tree (DT), support vector machines (SVM), Bayesian Networks (BN), hidden Markov Model (HMM) and K-nearest Neighbour. Data mining techniques such as classifications like SVM, Naive Bayes (NB), neural networks (NN), DT, k-mean clustering, association rule mining (ARM) were being used in the banking industry to enhance security and detect unusual behaviour and patterns indicating fraud, phishing, or money laundering, credit card fraud, security trend of mobile/online/traditional banking among others (Hassani, et al. 2018; Jayasree & Balan, 2017; Kharote & Kshirsagar, 2014).

Empirical investigations into the applications of data science and data analytics are on the increase. For instance, Behera and Panigrahi (2015, 2017) demonstrated the hybrid approach for credit card fraud detection by combining Fuzzy Clustering and NN techniques, and achieved over 93% accuracy with the dataset generated. Azimi and Noor Hosseinia (2017) proposed a hybrid approach of genetic algorithm and NN for Greek companies in the banking sector. Devadiga, Kothari, Jain, and Sankh (2017) used e-banking security system of cryptography and steganography to prevent online banking fraud. Oumar and Augustin (2019) examined 284807 transactions of European cardholders with 0.172% fraudulent transactions. They proposed the use of ANN model in credit card fraud detection because its back propagation has high accuracy rate of 99.48% in detecting fraudulent transaction in credit cards. Schreyer et al. (2017) proposed the use of deep auto-encoder NN to identify anomalies in journal entries. They stated that "an auto-encoder or replicator NN defined a special type of feed-forward multilayer neural network that can be trained to reconstruct its input" and established that the trained network's reconstruction error available for a journal entry and normalised by the entry's distinct attribute probabilities can be taken as a very adaptive anomaly evaluation.Their empirical assessment, which uses two real-world accounting data reveals that the reconstruction error of deep auto-encoder networks can be employed as a very adaptive anomaly evaluation of journal records. Ravisankar,Ravi,Rao and Bose (2011) tested techniques which include multilayer feed forward NN,SVM, genetic programming, group method of data handling, LR and probabilistic NN on 202 Chinese companies. They found that probabilistic neural networks and genetic programming outperform other approaches and are similarly accurate. Similarly, Huang (2013) used SVM techniques and LR to generate fraud detection models with a combination of five variables. The results indicate that models with filtered variables is the best suited one to identify financial statement schemes a year before the occurrence of the fraud event. In addition, SVM with complete variables was most appropriate to spot financial statement schemes two years prior to the occurrence of the event. The findings of the study diminished the rising threats faced by investors and other relevant stakeholders.

Anandakrishnan et al (2017) put forward methods for automatic analysis for the general ledgers of organisations to identify anomalies such as fraud or just human errors. The methods were executed within a prototype structure called "Sherlock" which integrates components of outlier detection and classification. The paper presented how to address the following challenges; developing an effective procedure for collecting data from an assortment of sources, teaching classifiers with only affirmative and untagged examples and displaying information in a straightforward and clear fashion. Also, Kotsiantis, Koumanakos, Tzelepis and Tampakas (2006) examined the usefulness of ML procedures such as decision tree, BN, K-Nearest Neighbour and SVM in identifying companies that issued fraudulent financial statements.

SOLUTIONS AND RECOMMENDATIONS

A number of factors may be responsible for the deficiencies in fraud investigation and monitoring such as very large quantities of data, an increasing variety in the sources of data, limited ease of data access and inadequate proficiency to manage and analyse big data (Deloitte, 2018). Industries across the globe are contending with rapid upsurge in the availability of enormous quantities of data, mainly driven by a rise in the composition of both front and back end applications, with a large variety of systems creating constantly evolving data in real time (Anandakrishnan et al., 2017). Consequently, Schreyer et al (2017) argued that detection of anomalies and fraud in wide-ranging financial data is one of the challenges encountered in audits or fraud inquiries that has existed and would continue for a long time. Similarly, structured data alone offers a very restricted assessment of patterns that might reveal fraud schemes, therefore, a combined approach that unites structured with unstructured data from across the organisation, in addition to data from outside sources like social media, will display a more robust representation of events and activities (Deloitte,2018).

Ernst and Young (2016) attested that organisations can obtain enormous benefits by integrating structured and unstructured information in their analysis to obtain a wide-ranging and all-inclusive understanding of their fraud risk situation. A system for analysing social media analysis for example, would be able expose the correct nature of acts that took place on the business trip or connections with third parties that may expose hidden facts regarding a transaction (Deloitte, 2018).

Several fresh and innovative approaches are developing in response to these challenges, including semi-supervised learning procedures, SNA and network/graph founded solutions which are able to function in real time by processing vast amounts of data created in real time (Anandakrishnan et al., 2017). Deloitte (2018) asserts that one action that establishments can take to better identify and investigate incursions and prevent future occurrences is to have a mixture of AI, ML and cognitive analytics, along with experienced forensic detectives. By taking advantage of data derived from various sources, investigators can now carry out analysis on the basis of non-financial data. Using a full complement of tech tools, these experts can drill deep into clients' data (Gale, 2019).

Deloitte (2018)outlines some methods employed to grapple with the challenges created by the availability of massive quantities and assortment of data, including; building an analytics storehouse that brings different data sources together so analytical models can combine signals from the different units of an organisation and network analysis which discovers the nature of a perpetrator's relationships to expose other individuals connected to the scheme or carrying out similar acts. Other methods discussed by Deloitte (2018) are textual and computer vision analytics, which to an increasing extent, are getting to be useful investigative instruments resulting from the rapid increase in unstructured information including emails, audio and text messaging. In a case of economic extortion, for example, where a perpetrator demands payment from a contractor before processing his vouchers, AI can be employed to analyse audio files from the telephone conversations between the perpetrator and the contractor to detect signs of pressurizing. The investigation could include the perpetrators tone of voice and contractor's stress level. Fraud detection requires AI to catch up with the rapidly, ever-increasing intricacy and creativity of present day fraud schemes (Columbus,2019). Therefore, the expectation is that the judgement of computers through AI will start taking preference in the uncovering the digital trails left by fraud perpetrators.

Artificial intelligence creates favourable circumstances for accountants to increase their effectiveness and provide more value to organisations in the short/medium term; while in the long term, AI increases likelihood that a much more radical transformation will occur as computers continue to take over decision-making responsibilities presently done by human beings (ICAEW, 2018a). A combination of supervised and unsupervised machine learning as component of a comprehensive AI driven fraud management strategy will makes it possible for businesses to swiftly and correctly spot automated and ever more complex fraud schemes (Columbus, 2019).Machine learning procedures can be deployed to find patterns of activities and flag anomalies just as neural networks can be taught to model the pattern of behaviour of several computer users so it would flag abnormal use patterns for the user that is logged in (Irons & Lallie,2014).

In computer forensic investigations, intelligent systems can be implemented at the different phases of the investigation life cycle: digital evidence collection, digital evidence preservation, digital evidence analysis and the presentation of the collected evidence (Irons & Lallie, 2014). Deloitte (2018) discussed the concept of forensic accounting analytics, which combines forensic investigative procedures with advanced analytics, facilitated by the progress made in computational strength and data administration. Forensic analytics helps businesses in spotting, stopping, and preventing incursions by adding artificial intelligence centred data analytics to the skill-sets of a competent forensic accountant. Artificial intelligence cognitive technologies employ cutting-edge algorithms to analyse text with the purpose of obtaining sentiment from unstructured information (Deloitte, 2016). Unstructured forensic analytics can be employed to investigate the exchange of information over a period to spot breaches in data sets, execute link analytics to discover who is talking to who, perform emotional tone analysis to estimate stress levels during communication and implement fraud triangle analytics (Ernst & Young, 2013). Similarly, SNA leverages on graph theory and other mathematical procedures to perform an exploration of networks of individuals which can avail an investigator of insights into how a network is structured, helping to pick out conspirators who may not have been part of the earlier stages of the investigation (Irons & Lallie, 2014).

By employing big data analytical tools, real-time evidence generated could be presented using high-tech visualizations and bespoke dashboards in a manner that is more comprehensible than conventional financial information (Gepp et al., 2018). These interactive data visualizations have the potentials to make the process for recognising fraudulent transactions more efficient because the forensic investigator is able to modify the data from script to graphics, sifting out sub-groups of transactions for supplementary investigation (Dilla & Raschke, 2015). Alles and Gray (2015) agreed that big data provides a clearer picture of the client's business, far beyond what can possibly to be captured when using only a sample of the population of data. With big data, investigators can bring together and analyse enormous volumes of data about events; looking for patterns that might help predict future occurrences (Cukier & Mayer-Schoenberger, 2013). Big data sentiment analysis has possible uses in auditing and forensic accounting. For instance a sentiment analysis of emails may aid an investigator to understand an organisation under scrutiny and expose parts with greater risk of fraud (Gepp et al., 2018). Also, financial statement fraud can be identified by analysing indicators concealed in textual information contained in published financial reports by means of text mining which can analyse words or collection of words (Gupta & Gill, 2012).

The contents of big data are materially and conceptually different from conventional accounting data, therefore, fraudsters are less likely to have the capacity to manipulate all relevant big data contents to conceal their actions (Alles & Gray,2015). The long-standing process of identifying fraud was to use computer software to examine several structured information against a set of rules (Deloitte, 2016). However, due to the extensive contents of big data and the notion of making use of the whole population (100% sampling), the possibility of detecting "red flags" and other suspicious anomalies is greater than before (Alles & Gray, 2015). Neural networks can be deployed for massive quantities of text and other information, allowing for the identification of irregularities that would not have possible when using the physical and mental energy of humans alone (Geradts, 2018).Big data analytics is becoming one of the most robust tools employed by organisations and business regulators for performing a number of functions that increase the effectiveness of processes, collect useful information and monitor activities (Hanchett, 2016). Gray and Fata (2017) report the increased use of big data in United States Securities and Exchange Commission (SEC) enforcement, stating that "the impact of the SEC's reliance on big data has allowed the Commission to adopt a much more proactive approach to investigations" They further explain that the use of big data gives the SEC more control over the organisations and actions that it selects for investigation. Analysts at SEC can also identify otherwise unconnected transactions that are similarly timed or yield comparable revenue to detect patterns and relationships among the dealers or to fix attention on a mutual supplier of inside information (Newville & Ansanelli, 2017).

CONCLUSION

The chapter provided an overview of what data science is. Its associated terms including big data analytics, artificial intelligence and machine learning were discussed. Data science was taken as the umbrella term for these terms and others such as social network analysis and neural networks. The relevance of data science and data analytics to forensic accounting and fraud detection were highlighted and the works reviewed revealed several benefits. In embracing data science techniques for fraud investigations, the role of the human factor in the entire process must always be remembered. Again while machines can totally erase the place of humans from the investigative process we see man teaming up with machines to provide proactive and continuous fraud monitoring procedures. We recommend that more researches especially in the development of algorithms and big data analytic tools in fraud detection and fight against corruption in developing countries like Nigeria.

REFERENCES

Accenture. (n.d.). *Financial crime: Data science to the rescue.* Accenture.com.

ACL. (2010). *Fraud detection using analytics in the banking industry.* ACL Services Ltd.

Albashrawi, M. (2016). Detecting financial fraud using data mining techniques: A decade review from 2004 to 2015. *Journal of Data Science : JDS, 14,* 553–570.

Alles, M. G. (2015). Drivers of the use and facilitators and obstacles of the evolution of big data by the audit profession. *Accounting Horizons, 29*(2), 439–449. doi:10.2308/acch-51067

Alles, M. G., & Gray, G. L. (2015). *The pros and cons of using big data in auditing: A synthesis of the literature and a research agenda.* Rutgers Business School.

Anandakrishnan, A., Kumar, S., Statnikov, A., Faruquie, T., & Xu, D. (2017). *Anomaly detection in finance*: Editors' introduction. *Proceedings of Machine Learning Research KDD Workshop on Anomaly Detection in Finance, 71,* 1–7. Retrieved from http://proceedings.mlr.press/v71/anandakrishnan18a/anandakrishnan18a.pdf

Appelbaum, D., Kogan, A., & Vasarhelyi, M. A. (2017a). Big data and analytics in the modern audit engagement: Research needs. *Auditing, 36*(4), 1–27. doi:10.2308/ajpt-51684

Appelbaum, D., Kogan, A., & Vasarhelyi, M. A. (2017b). An introduction to data analytics for auditors and accountants. *The CPA Journal*, 32–37.

Appelbaum, D., Kogan, A., & Vasarhelyi, M. A. (2018). Analytical procedures in external auditing:A comprehensive literature survey and framework for external audit analysis. *Journal of Accounting Literature, 40*, 83–101. doi:10.1016/j.acclit.2018.01.001

Association of Certified Chartered Accountants-ACCA. (2019). *Audit and technology.* Report by Chartered Accountants of Australia and New Zealand.

Association of Certified Fraud Examiners. (2018). *2018 global study on occupational fraud and abuse.* Author.

Association of Certified Fraud Examiners. (2019). *Forensic accountant.* Retrieved from https://www.acfe.com/forensic-accountant.aspx

Azimi, A., & NoorHosseini, M. (2017). The hybrid approach based on genetic algorithm and neural network to predict financial fraud in banks. *International Journal of Information Security and System Management, 6*, 657–667.

Bănărescu, A. (2015). Detecting and preventing fraud with data analytics. *Procedia Economics and Finance, 32*(15), 1827–1836. doi:10.1016/S2212-5671(15)01485-9

Banerjee, Bourla, Chen, Kashyap, Purohit, & Battipaglia. (2018). *Comparative analysis of machine learning algorithms through credit card fraud detection.* New Jersey's Governor's School of Engineering and Technology.

Behera, T. K., & Panigrahi, S. (2015). Credit card fraud detection: A hybrid approach using fuzzy clustering & neural network. *Proceedings of the 2015 Second International Conference on Advances in Computing and Communication Engineering (ICACCE)*, 494–499. 10.1109/ICACCE.2015.33

Behera, T. K., & Panigrahi, S. (2017). Credit card fraud detection using a neuro-fuzzy expert system. In *Computational Intelligence in Data Mining.* Springer. doi:10.1007/978-981-10-3874-7_79

Berman, F., Rutenbar, R., Christensen, H., Davidson, S., Estrin, D., Franklin, M., ... Szalay, A. (2016). *Realising the potential of data science.* National Science Foundation Computer and Information Science and Engineering Advisory Committee Data Science Working Group, doi:10.1126cience.1167742

Blazquez, D., & Domenech, J. (2017). Web data mining for monitoring business export orientation. *Technol. Econ. Dev. Econ. Online (Bergheim)*, 1–23. doi:10.3846/ 20294913.2016.1213193

Blazquez, D., & Domenech, J. (2018). Big data sources and methods for social and economic analyses. *Technological Forecasting and Social Change, 139*, 99–113. doi:10.1016/j.techfore.2017.07.027

Bologa, A.-R., Bologa, R., & Florea, A. (2010). Big data and specific analysis methods for insurance fraud detection. *Database Systems Journal, 1*(1).

Borgman, C. L. (2019). The lives and after lives of data. *Harvard Data Science Review*, (1). Retrieved from https://hdsr.mitpress.mit.edu/

Bressler, L. (2010). The role of forensic accountants in fraud investigations: Importance of attorney and judge's perceptions. *Journal of Finance and Accountancy*, *14*(4).

Cao, L. (2017). Data science : A comprehensive overview. *ACM Computing Surveys*, *50*(3), 1–42. doi:10.1145/3076253

Charles, D., Ramona, F., & Ogilby, S. (2009). *Characteristics and skills of the forensic accountant.* American Institute of Certified Public Accountants.

Cielen, D., Meysman, A. D. B., & Ali, M. (2016). *Introducing data science.* Manning Publications Co.

Columbus, L. (2019). *AI is predicting the future of online fraud detection.* Retrieved from https://www.forbes.com/sites/louiscolumbus/2019/08/01/ai-is-predicting-the-future-of-online-fraud-detection/

Connolly, S. (2012). *7 key drivers for the big data market.* Retrieved from https://hortonworks.com

Cukier, K., & Mayer-Schoenberger, V. (2013). The rise of big data: How it's changing the way we think about the world. *Foreign Affairs*, *92*. https://www.foreignaffairs.com/articles/2013-04-03/rise-big-data

Dagiliene, L., & Kloviene, L. (2019). Motivation to use big data and big data analytics in external auditing. *Managerial Auditing Journal*, *34*(7), 750–782. Advance online publication. doi:10.1108/MAJ-01-2018-1773

Deloitte. (2016). Why artificial intelligence is a game changer for risk management. *Deloitte Advisory.* Retrieved from https://www2.deloitte.com/content/dam/Deloitte/us/Documents/audit/us-ai-risk-powers-performance.pdf

Deloitte. (2018). *The evolution of forensic investigations.* Retrieved July 1, 2019, from https://www2.deloitte.com/us/en/pages/advisory/articles/evolution-forensic-investigations-series.html

Devadiga, N., Kothari, H., Jain, H., & Sankhe, S. (2017). E-banking security using cryptography, steganography and data mining. *International Journal of Computers and Applications*, *7*(164), 26–30. doi:10.5120/ijca2017913746

Dilla, W. N., & Raschke, R. L. (2015). Data visualization for fraud detection: Practice implications and a call for future research. *International Journal of Accounting Information Systems*, *16*, 1–22. doi:10.1016/j.accinf.2015.01.001

Donoho, D. (2015). 50 years of data Science. *Tukey Centennial Workshop*, 1–41.

Embarak, O. (2019). *Data analytics and visualization using Python-analyze data to create visualization for BI system.* APress California.

Ernst & Young. (2013). *Demystifying "big data" analytics.* Retrieved from https://www.ey.com

Ernst & Young. (2016). *Shifting into high gear: mitigating risks and demonstrating returns global forensic data analytics survey 2016.* Author.

Ernst & Young. (2018). *Integrity in the spotlight, the future of compliance; 15th global fraud survey*. Retrieved from https://www.ey.com/Publication/vwLUAssets/ey-global-fids-fraud-survey-2018/$FILE/ey-global-fids-fraud-survey-2018.pdf

European Union Agency for Network and Information Security (ENISA). (2016). *Big data threat landscape and big data practice guide*. ENISA.

Financial Stability Board. (2017). *Artificial intelligence and machine learning in financial services Market developments and financial stability implications*. Financial Stability Board.

Floridi, L., & Cowls, J. (2019). A unified framework of five principles for AI in society. *Harvard Data Science Review*, (1), 1–13. Retrieved from https://hdsr.mitpress.mit.edu/

Gale, C. (2019). Time to tackle technology. *Accounting Today*, *33*(6). www.accountingtoday.com

Garber, A. (2019). Data science: What the educated citizen needs to know. *Harvard Data Science Review*, (1), 1–14. Retrieved from https://hdsr.mitpress.mit.edu/

Gepp, A., Linnenluecke, M. K., O'Neill, T. J., & Smith, T. (2018). Big data techniques in auditing research and practice: Current trends and future opportunities. *Journal of Accounting Literature*, *40*, 102–115. doi:10.1016/j.acclit.2017.05.003

Geradts, Z. (2018). Digital, big data and computational forensics. *Forensic Science Review*, *3*(3), 179–182. doi:10.1080/20961790.2018.1500078 PMID:30483667

Google Trends. (2019). *Google trends*. Retrieved August 1, 2019, from www.trends.google.com

Gray, E., & Fata, C. (2017). Increased use of big data in SEC enforcement. *The Review of Securities & Commodities Regulation*, *50*(12), 145–149.

Grover, P., & Kar, A. K. (2017). Big data analytics: A review on theoretical contributions and tools used in literature. *Global Journal of Flexible Systems Managment*, *18*(3), 203–229. doi:10.100740171-017-0159-3

Gupta, R., & Gill, N. S. (2012). Financial statement fraud detection using text mining. *International Journal of Advanced Computer Science and Applications*, *3*(12), 189–191. www.ijacsa.thesai.org

Hamdan, M. (2018). The role of forensic accounting in discovering financial fraud. *International Journal of Accounting Research*, *6*(2). Advance online publication. doi:10.35248/2472-114X.18.6.176

Hanchett, W. (2016). *SEC uses big data for regulatory compliance*. Retrieved July 1, 2019, from www.kpm-us.com

Hossein Hassani, H., Huang, X., & Silva, E. (2018). Digitalisation and big data mining in banking. *Big Data and Cognitive Computing*, *2*(18), 1–13. doi:10.3390/bdcc2030018

Huang, S. Y. (2013). Fraud detection model by using support vector machine techniques. *International Journal of Digital Content Technology and Its Applications*, *7*(2), 32–42. doi:10.4156/jdcta.vol7.issue2.5

ICAEW. (2018a). *Artificial intelligence and the future of accountancy*. ICAEW Thought Leadership.

ICAEW. (2018b). *Big data and analytics – what's new?* ICAEW Thought Leadership.

Irons, A., & Lallie, H. (2014). Digital forensics to intelligent forensics. *Future Internet*, 6(3), 584–596. doi:10.3390/fi6030584

Jofre, M., & Gerlach, R. H. (2018). *Fighting accounting fraud through forensic data analytics*. SSRN Electronic Journal., doi:10.2139srn.3176288

Joglekar, P. & Pise, N., (2016). Solving cyber security challenges using big data. *International Journal of Computer Applications*.

Jordan, M. I. (2019). Artificial intelligence - the revolution hasn't happened yet. *Harvard Data Science Review*, (1). Retrieved from https://hdsr.mitpress.mit.edu/

Joshi, P. L., & Marthandan, G. (2018). The hype of big data analytics and auditors. *Emerging Market Journal*. Retrieved from http://emaj.pitt.edu

Jurgovsky, J., Granitzer, M., Ziegler, K., Calabretto, S., Portier, P.-E., He-Guelton, L., & Caelen, O. (2018). Sequence classification for credit-card fraud detection. *Expert Systems with Applications*, *100*, 234–245. doi:10.1016/j.eswa.2018.01.037

Kotsiantis, S., Koumanakos, E., Tzelepis, E., & Tampakas, V. (2006). Forecasting fraudulent financial statements using data mining. *International Journal of Computational Intelligence*, *3*(2).

KPMG. (2016). *Using data analytics to successfully detect frauds*. Kpmg.com

Legara, E. F. (2017). *Data science, advanced analytics for modern manufacturing*. Inclusive Innovation Convention.

Leonelli, S. (2019). Data governance is key to interpretation : Reconceptualising data in data science. *Harvard Data Science Review*, (1), 1–7.

Li, H., Dai, J., Gershberg, T., & Vasarhelyi, M. A. (2018). Understanding usage and value of audit analytics for internal auditors: An organizational approach. *International Journal of Accounting Information Systems*, *28*, 59–76. doi:10.1016/j.accinf.2017.12.005

Littley, J. (2012). *Leveraging data analytics and continuous auditing processes for improved audit planning, effectiveness, and efficiency*. Available at http://www.kpmg.com/US/en

Lo, A. W., Siah, K. W., & Wong, C. H. (2019). Machine learning with statistical imputation for predicting drug approvals. *Harvard Data Science Review*, (1). Retrieved from https://hdsr.mitpress.mit.edu/

Mahmood, T., & Uzma, A. (2013). Security analytics: Big data analytics for cybersecurity: A review of trends, techniques and tools. In *Information assurance (ncia), 2nd national conference on*. IEEE.

Maniraj, S. P., Saini, A., Sarka, S. D., & Ahmed, S. (2019). Credit card fraud detection using machine learning and data science. *International Journal of Engineering Research & Technology (Ahmedabad)*, *8*(9), 110–115. doi:10.17577/IJERTV8IS090031

Modugu, K. P., & Anyaduba, J. O. (2013). Forensic accounting and financial fraud in Nigeria: An empirical approach. *Journal. International of Business and Social Science*, *4*(7), 281–289.

Monajemi, H., Murri, R., Jonas, E., Liang, P., Stodden, V., & Donoho, D. (2019). Ambitious data science can be painless. *Harvard Data Science Review*. Retrieved from https://hdsr.mitpress.mit.edu/

Newville, B. J. M., & Ansanelli, J. M. (2017). *SEC continues to use advanced data analytics to investigate insider trading*. Retrieved from https://www.corporatedefensedisputes.com

Norrie, M.A .(2019).An introduction to machine learning. In *Data analytics: Concept, techniques and application*. CRC Press.

Oumar, A. W., & Augustin, P. (2019). Credit card fraud detection using ANN. *International Journal of Innovative Technology and Exploring Engineering*, *8*(7), 313–316.

Oyebisi, O., Wisdom, O., Olusogo, O., & Ifeoluwa, O. (2018). Forensic accounting and fraud prevention and detection in Nigerian banking industry. COJ Reviews & Research, 1–8. doi:10.31031/CO-JRR.2018.01.000504

Proyag, P., Triparna, M., & Asoke, N. (2015). Challenges in data science: A comprehensive study on application and future trends. *International Journal of Advance Research in Computer Science and Management Studies Research*, *3*(8), 1–8.

PwC. (2018). *Global economic crime and fraud survey*. Retrieved from https:// www.pwc.com/fraudsurvey

Ramya, K., & Sumathi, A. (2019). Big data applications in Aadhar card fraud detection. *International Journal on Computer Science and Engineering*, *7*(3), 865–867.

Ravisankar, P., Ravi, V., Rao, G., & Bose, I. (2011). Detection of financial statement fraud and feature selection using data mining techniques. *Decision Support Systems*, *52*(2), 491–500. doi:10.1016/j.dss.2010.11.006

Restrepo, M. (2019). *Explaining data science, AI, ML and deep learning to management-a presentation and a script- part 1 of 3*. Retrieved website: https://towardsdatascience.com/explaining-data-science-ai-ml-and-deep-learning-to-management-a-presentation-and-a-script-4968491eb1e5

Rizkallah, J. (2017). *The big (unstructured) data problem*. Retrieved from Forbes website: https://www.forbes.com/sites/forbestechcouncil/2017/06/05/the-big-unstructured-data-problem/

Salleh, K., & Aziz, R. A. (2014). Traits, skills and ethical values of public sector forensic accountants : An empirical investigation. *Procedia: Social and Behavioral Sciences*, *145*, 361–370. doi:10.1016/j.sbspro.2014.06.045

Sathyapriya, M., & Thiagarasu, V. (2017). Big data analytics techniques for credit card fraud detection: A review. *International Journal of Science and Research*, *6*(5), 206-211.

Schreyer, M., Sattarov, T., Borth, D., Dengel, A., & Reimer, B. (2017). *Detection of anomalies in large scale accounting data using deep autoencoder networks*. Retrieved from https://arxiv.org/abs/1709.05254

Sharma, A., & Panigrahi, P. (2012). A review of financial accounting fraud detection based on data mining techniques. *International Journal of Computers and Applications*, *39*(1), 37–47. doi:10.5120/4787-7016

Shpyrko, V., & Koval, B. (2019). *Models of fraud detection and analysis of payment transactions using machine learning*. Taras Shevchenko National University of Kyiv.

Sivarajah, U., Kamal, M. M., Irani, Z., & Weerakkody, V. (2016). Critical analysis of big data challenges and analytical methods. *Journal of Business Research*, *70*, 263–286. doi:10.1016/j.jbusres.2016.08.001

Stanton, J. (2012). *An introduction to data science in Open Source eBook* (3rd ed.). Retrieved from https://surface.syr.edu/istpub/165/

Sule, S., Ibrahim, S., & Sani, A. (2019). The effect of forensic accounting investigation in detecting financial fraud : A study in Nigeria. *International Journal of Academic Research in Business and Social Sciences*, *9*(2), 545–553. doi:10.6007/IJARBSS/v9-i2/5590

Vasarhelyi, M.A.,& Tuttle, B.M. (2015). Big data in accounting: An overview. *Accounting Horizons,* *29*(2), 381-396.

Verma, S., & Bhattacharyya, S. S. (2017). Perceived strategic value based adoption of big data analytics in emerging economy: A qualitative approach for Indian firms. *Journal of Enterprise Information Management*, *30*(3), 3. doi:10.1108/JEIM-10-2015-0099

Vicente, M. R., López-Menéndez, A. J., & Pérez, R. (2015). Forecasting unemployment with search data: Does it help to improve predictions when job destruction is skyrocketing? *Technological Forecasting and Social Change*, *92*, 132–139. doi:10.1016/j.techfore.2014.12.005

Wing, J. M. (2019). The data life cycle. *Harvard Data Science Review*, (1). Retrieved from https://hdsr.mitpress.mit.edu/

Yang, K., & Xu, W. (2019). FraudMemory: Explainable memory-enhanced sequential neural networks for financial fraud detection. *Proceedings of the 52nd Hawaii International Conference on System Sciences 2019*. 10.24251/HICSS.2019.126

Zhang, Y., Ren, S., Liu, Y., & Si, S. (2017). A big data analytics architecture for clean manufacturing and maintenance processes of complex products. *Journal of Cleaner Production*, *142*(2), 626–641. doi:10.1016/j.jclepro.2016.07.123

Zheng,L., Liu,G., Luan, W., Li, Z., Zhang, Y., Yan, C., & Jiang, C. (2018). A new credit card fraud detecting method based on behavior certificate. In *Networking, Sensing and Control (ICNSC)*. IEEE.

KEY TERMS AND DEFINITIONS

Big Data: Refers to data sets that are so voluminous and complex that traditional data processing application software is inadequate to deal with them.

Big Data Analytics: Big data/analytics is defined as the capability of processing extremely large data sets to identify patterns of relationships (correlation, causality) among data to be used in detecting market trends, consumer behaviour and preferences.

Data Science: This is an evolving field that deals with the gathering, preparation, exploration, visualization, organisation, and storage of large groups of data and the extraction of valuable information from large volumes of data that may exist in an unorganised or unstructured form.

Forensic Accounting: Encompasses all the areas associated with investigations for the purpose of uncovering economic fraud, having its own models and methodologies that provide advisory services, assurance, and attestation suitable to be used as legal evidence.

Fraud: Is a wrongful or criminal deception intended to result in financial or personal gain.

Fraud Detection: Refers to the process of uncovering frauds in an organization.

Machine Learning: Is a type of artificial intelligence where computer teaches itself the solution to a query discovering patterns in sets of data and matching fresh parts of data the based on probability.

Chapter 12
Machine Learning and Its Application in Monitoring Diabetes Mellitus

Vandana Kalra

https://orcid.org/0000-0003-0458-1079

Manav Rachna International Institute of Research and Studies, India

Indu Kashyap

Manav Rachna International Institute of Research and Studies, India

Harmeet Kaur

https://orcid.org/0000-0001-5173-7908

University of Delhi, India

ABSTRACT

Data science is a fast-growing area that deals with data from its origin to the knowledge exploration. It comprises of two main subdomains, data analytics for preparing data, and machine learning to probe into this data for hidden patterns. Machine learning (ML) endows powerful algorithms for the automatic pattern recognition and producing prediction models for the structured and unstructured data. The available historical data has patterns having high predictive value used for the future success of an industry. These algorithms also help to obtain accurate prediction, classification, and simulation models by eliminating insignificant and faulty patterns. Machine learning provides major advancement in the healthcare industry by assisting doctors to diagnose chronic diseases correctly. Diabetes is one of the most common chronic disease that occurs when the pancreas cells are damaged and do not secrete sufficient amount of insulin required by the human body. Machine learning algorithms can help in early diagnosis of this chronic disease by studying its predictor parameter values.

DOI: 10.4018/978-1-7998-3053-5.ch012

INTRODUCTION

The discipline of machine learning is covered under the umbrella of Artificial Intelligence. Analytical and reasoning skills are essential component for building intelligence. Learning from past experience enhances these skills. The current need of all the industries is to inculcate this intelligence into machines. A machine cannot deal directly with the collected data in an intelligent way. It does not have the capability to analyze data on its own. A machine can be made intelligent by training it using past experience. A machine can decide about a disease from its symptoms only when it is trained by the symptoms gathered in the past. Therefore every growing industry needs powerful machine learning algorithms to train machines using past structured or unstructured data.

Machine learning algorithms are the computer programs that make machines learn from old data and enable them to perform predictions, classification, summarization and many more. The learning by machine involves construction of models that takes past data as input and produces the desired output using mathematical functions. Various machine learning techniques are there depending upon the type of data used for learning: supervised, unsupervised and reinforcement. Supervised learning algorithms are using labelled data whereas unsupervised learning algorithms uses unlabelled data. Reinforcement Learning is a machine learning technique in which a learning algorithm is based on a feedback system and no past data is used for training. Supervised learning involves different algorithms for classification task which includes decision tree, regression, support vector machine, k -nearest neighbours etc. The model built from training data is applied on the test data to check its validity (Callahan, A., & Shah, N. H. 2017).

The healthcare sector has always been a quick adapter of technological advances. Nowadays, machine learning plays a major role in many health related realms such as managing patient history and records in hospitals (Bhardwaj, R.et al. 2017), the development of advanced medical methods (Ghassemi, M.et al. 2018), effects of medicine, medical image diagnosis and the treatment of chronic diseases. Computer-aided diagnosis of some chronic diseases uses pattern recognition techniques of machine learning to detect infected structures in the medical image (Panch, T. et al.2018). Here, the labelled data can be in the form of images which are given to the machine learning algorithm as input, such as Bayesian classifier, artificial neural network and support vector machine. The resulting classifier is expected to classify new medical images correctly.

MAIN FOCUS OF THE CHAPTER

This chapter mainly provides detailed description of about data science discipline network, machine learning applications, type of machine learning approaches and machine learning algorithms available in these approaches. The first subsection gives brief about type of machine learning approaches Unsupervised, Supervised, Reinforcement, and deep learning. The next subsection describes the algorithms of unsupervised learning approach and dimensionality reduction technique with the associated python libraries to handle them practically. Further, in the subsection of supervised learning algorithms, all algorithms like Regression, Decision Tree, K-Nearest Neighbours, Support Vector Machine, Artificial Neural Network and Naïve Bayes are discussed in detail with examples and their supportive python libraries and functions are provided for help in practical implementation. Last subsection provides detailed case study of applying simple and weighted K-Nearest Neighbours classification algorithm in Python on diabetes dataset. This subsection also emphasizes on how machine learning KNN algorithm helps in facing the challenge of identifying chronic disease like

diabetes mellitus at early stages with the symptoms given in terms of attribute values in the dataset. Results with analysis are provided to study the behaviour of the classification whether a patient is at high risk of diabetes or not.

ISSUES, CONTROVERSIES, PROBLEMS

Few challenges (Sendak, M.et al.2019) in relation to healthcare are listed below which can be handled using appropriate machine learning algorithms. In the case study provided, one of the challenge of identifying chronic disease of diabetes at early stages is explained in detail using machine learning algorithm K- nearest neighbour.

Challenge 1: Information and Service Integration

Traditionally, hospitals use relational databases to store and retrieve reports of patient data (Gianfrancesco, M. A. et al. 2018). Lots of unstructured information, such as clinical reports and transcripts cannot be efficiently managed by relational databases. As the patient data grows significantly, hospitals are in need of improved data storage structures to handle voluminous data in structured form. Big data advancements (Ngiam, K. Y., & Khor, W. 2019) are greatly adopted by the medical community. However, the implementation algorithms for big data analytics needs lot of computational efforts. Several hospitals and clinics started using non-relational databases that merges patient information from many sources. Machines learning algorithms and predictive modelling algorithms take care of inaccurate and duplication of data very efficiently.

Challenge 2: Effects of Costly Equipment

Big hospitals advise patients to spend lots of money for latest medical equipment to cure diseases (Ghassemi, M.et al. 2018). Earlier, there were no means to study the effectiveness of these equipments, therefore no scope for its improvement. By getting in-depth details of e-records of patients, equipment manufacturers are able to extract stronger insights about the effects of medical products used by patients using machine learning techniques. Additionally, practitioners are now able to discover easy and cost effective solutions for patients.

Challenge 3: Perfect Medical Diagnosis

Sometime practitioners are not able to diagnose the diseases perfectly due to lack of structured records of varying symptoms of diseases (Sendak, M.et al. 2019). Machine learning techniques when applied on an existing patient records will make near perfect diagnoses which improves patient's health with minimum costs. It also helps in recommending best medicines and identify high risk patients.

Challenge 4: Identifying Chronic Diseases

The availability of historical data is of significance only when it provides some inference that can be used for betterment of the patient health. In earlier days, sometimes doctors may not be able to identify chronic diseases at earlier stages. Identifying chronic diseases at early stages is very difficult without analysing the past historical medical data (Zufferey, D.et al.2015). Machine learning techniques are used to extract patterns to identify number of chronic diseases like diabetes, tuberculosis etc. at early stages.

Challenge 5: Incomplete Observations in Data

It is likely that many observations will be missing while identifying important variables in a healthcare dataset. It is often impractical to have truly complete data due to its volume and cost. Building learning models using machine learning algorithms from healthcare dataset having incomplete, or missing, data is of least importance to practitioners (Ghassemi, M.et al. 2018) (Gianfrancesco, M. A.et al. 2018). Healthcare is a dynamic process to measure vital attributes with time, therefore clinical labs are instructed by doctors to record observations over time in response to previous observations to find the dependencies among what attributes are measured earlier and later with their values to avoid getting biased results. Machine learning with pre-processing of data using data analytics techniques is the only powerful mechanism which can handle the missing or incomplete data in efficient manner to provide accurate learning model for any medical practice.

INTRODUCTION TO MACHINE LEARNING

Essence

Data science is an integration of multiple most important disciplines including data analytics, machine learning, statistics, software engineering and many more. Data analytics is the domain that deals with big data. It involves retrieval, cleaning, gathering, assimilation, and transformation of this large volume of data. This polished data is ready for use by various other important procedures of interest. In this era of technological growth, Machine learning is an in-demand branch of trained learning, possessing various algorithms which are applied on this transformed refined data for statistical and predictive analysis, to extract knowledge. Data science is a science that is accountable for shaping big data in such a way that it becomes significant for mining patterns, and guiding decision-makers for bringing effective growth in business. Data analytics and machine learning are two vital tools to complete data science processes as shown in Figure 1.

Learning is the process of understanding and grasping of a subject physically and mentally. Subject can be an entity or any concept of a real world. Learning seems to be complete when one can apply this acquired knowledge about a subject to fit into or relate to the already available concepts of real world. Medically, learning by human involves modification in the nervous system, involving thinning of neural trajectories and stimulation of neurons with strengthening of synapses. These modifications evoke a precise responses to an environmental stimuli. We can say, this learning leads to intelligence, when it enhances the knowledge base and skill of a human being.

Figure 1. Data sciences, data analytics and machine learning

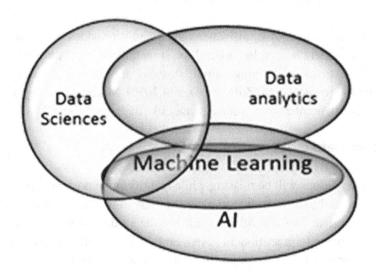

Human intelligence is described as "their intellectual ability". Human possess the cognitive abilities to understand, learn and concepts formulation. Their logical and reasoning ability, capacities to recognize patterns, generate new ideas, solve difficult problems makes human top of all living beings.

The powerful field of Artificial Intelligence emphasize on designing machines in which human intelligence is simulated with the usage of complicated algorithms. AI uses many tools and techniques to get the insights from many areas. The most common are computer science, psychology, cognitive science, linguistics, economics, optimization and logic. AI is considered as cloud having overlaps with areas like robotics, data mining, logistics, speech recognition and facial recognition.

The machine learning is a sub field of artificial intelligence that focuses on system that learn from their environment that is data (Jiang, F.et al. 2017).The overlapping between artificial intelligence and machine learning is depicted in Figure 2. Many powerful computer science algorithms exist which are designed to extract knowledge from the existing data to build learning models and improve them over time when exposed to new data. The final goal is to apply these learning models for new data and obtain some results that can be used for decision making. Data collected over the years in an industry comprises of various useful patterns. Complex algorithms are required to learn these patterns hidden in the legacy data. These algorithms are known as machine learning algorithms. In a real world the knowledge extracted using machine learning algorithms is of great importance for the data driven decision to carry out several tasks in an organization.

There is an edge of machine learning over human intelligence. The working capacity of the machine is far better than human. A doctor may need a break after few hours of working whereas a machine will not stop and can continue work for days and months. Machine learning techniques always provide unbiased outcomes to a problem as compared to humans (Panch, T. et al.2018). Therefore, machine learning can be applied in the following circumstances:

- The result changes or improves with time like optimization, troubleshooting, spam detection, search engines, routing algorithm etc.

Figure 2. Inside artificial intelligence

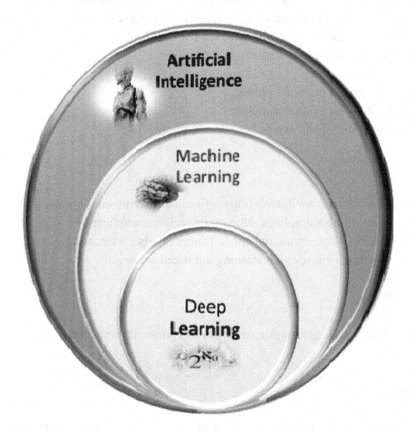

- The human expertise is not available for example it's very difficult to make road map, planting vegetation at moon by human due to inadequate knowledge about moon's area and surface.
- Humans are incapable to describe their expertise for example in handwriting recognition, language Recognition etc.
- Results needs to be reformed to particular cases as sometimes output depends upon user biometrics or user credentials.

History

The quest for artificial intelligence starts from the invention of first general purpose digital computer "ENIAC" (Electronic Numerical Integrator and Computer).

"Give machines the ability to learn without explicitly programming them." said Arthurs Samuel, 1955. Arthur Samuel machine becomes the first learning machine which tended to play checkers as one player and tries to win in this two-player game. His algorithms used heuristic search to learn from experiences which efficiently utilized the limited memory and disk storage space available at that time. At first this algorithm was such that it could easily win over the other player. With time and experience, it learnt all the board position that could ultimately lead it to win or lose and thus finally became a superior player than Samuel himself.

"A computer program is said to learn from experience E with respect to some class of tasks T and performance measure P, if its performance at tasks in T, as measured by P, improves with experience E.". This was a formal mathematical definition given by Tom Mitchell in 1999. When this statement is applied for the board game, the parameters are described as:

E is experience that is number of games played.
T is a task of playing checkers against computer.
P is the performance measure given as win/loss by computer.

Applications

Machine Learning is useful for every automating routine tasks having intelligent insights. Every industry from almost every sector like automobiles, electronics, telecommunications, education, economic and many more (Gopal, M. 2018) are trying to benefit from its tools and techniques.

Few common applications of machine learning are listed below:

Medical Diagnosis

Learning model is trained to recognize diseases from its symptoms collected from various patients over a period of time.

Image Recognition

Machine learning model can be trained for face detection in an image by using image repository which stores voluminous imagery data stored category wise.

Financial Industry and Trading

Various companies and banks use machine learning techniques to reduce risk assessments by credit checks and fraud investigation and prevention.

Speech Recognition

It is the paraphrasing of spoken words into the text. There are many Voice User Interfaces (VUIs) available now a days which allow user to interact with a system through speech commands. Virtual assistants, such as Siri by Apple, Google Assistant, and Alexa from amazon are latest popular examples of VUIs.

Video Surveillance

The video surveillance system is designed to detect abnormal situations with the help of captured movements in video cameras. They track strange behaviour of individuals like standing motionless for a long time and observing, snoozing on benches etc. The system can raise an alarming signal to human attendants, which can finally help to avoid mishaps.

Controlling Wearable Devices

Various machine learning trained devices are also available in the market which have attracted the people most. One of them is wearable fitness tracker Fitbit which monitors all body parameters and analyses the fitness of the body.

Challenges

Main perspective of Machine Learning is how best the past experience is utilized to learn a model. The machine learning algorithms involves complex mathematical computations including functions generating desired output. The accuracy of the output generated by an algorithm is highly dependent on the choice of mathematical functions. Various challenges are faced while applying different machine learning algorithms based on these mathematical functions to the observed data to extract knowledge. As a result, these challenges provide a substantial platform for future research in machine learning domain. (Gopal, M. 2018)Few challenges as observed by researchers in the domain are listed below.

- The identification of algorithms best fit for specific type of observed data.
- Which settings for target function requires any alteration in algorithms to improve the learning model?
- How much volume of training data is sufficient for establishing optimized learning model which provides accurate results if applied on test data?
- How to check the authenticity of the prior knowledge used for building learning model? Whether the past experience is valuable when it is approximately correct and give accurate results with confidence?

MACHINE LEARNING APPROACHES

Broadly, the four main approaches are there for the task of machine learning (Flach, P. 2012).

1. Unsupervised Learning
2. Supervised Learning
3. Reinforcement Learning
4. Deep Learning

Unsupervised Learning

Unsupervised learning is the type of machine learning in which the self-organized learning takes place through machine learning algorithms (Gopal, M. 2018). Algorithms are directly applied on unlabelled data without any guidance. Unknown patterns from the data are extracted as the output which cannot tested for its correctness. Unsupervised learning algorithms perform complex operations on unlabelled data without the use of any trained data(Figure 3). This is the reason that this learning may lead to unpredictable results. It finds out relationships among the input values. The task in unsupervised learning is to find out patterns, similarities and differences in the input data.

Figure 3. Unsupervised learning process

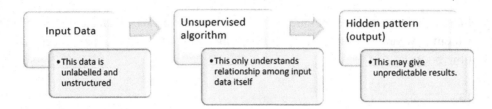

For example, clustering of the healthy and junk food items by observing their characteristics in the given food items input data is an unsupervised learning. Healthy and Junk food items can be clustered separately according to differences in their ingredients, source, calorie value and many more characteristics. Food items with cheese as ingredient, high calorie value and source as processed is identified as junk food and food items with ingredients as nutrients, low calorie value and source as raw as shown in Figure 4.

Figure 4. Unsupervised learning: Clustering

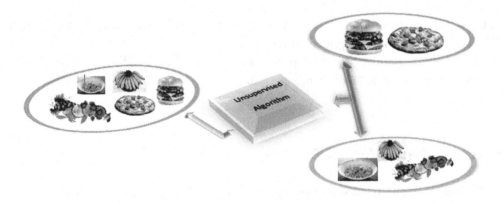

Broadly, there are two types of unsupervised learning algorithms frequently used: association rule mining and clustering.

Unsupervised learning algorithms are useful in various applications:

- Main advantage of using unsupervised learning is easy availability of unlabelled data in real world. These algorithms are mostly used in the area where the analyst wants to understand clearly the behaviour of the real data.
- It helps in pre-processing of the data which is further utilized for supervised learning. The processed data used in supervised learning methods help in the improvement of accuracy results. Also, it leads to less memory utilization and time complexity. Preprocessing of data comprises of various methods for reducing the number of features in a dataset, data transformation and extraction of features.

- Clustering algorithms associates all data objects to their corresponding groups based on their similarity characteristics. It is used for customer relationship management, artificial intelligence, data compression, medicine, statistics and many more.
- Association analysis identifies sets of products which are related to each other in the data. Association rules are designed to help the managers to study the relationships among various products and explore the behaviour of customers.
- The data objects which are not a part of any cluster identified as outliers help in searching uninteresting misleading transactions from the dataset.

In spite of various applications of unsupervised learning, it also has some challenges:

- No precise information regarding the output as data used in unsupervised learning methods is unknown and unlabelled.
- Unlabelled data also leads to less accuracy of the results.
- Interpretation and then allocating label to data is very time consuming

Supervised Learning

We are living in the real world where data objects are identifiable and are already labelled with some name. The categories are already defined for the labelled data. This voluminous available labelled data can be utilized for analysing, classifying and categorize new objects emerged during the execution of real time applications. Identifying characteristics, features and patterns from this available labelled data to build a simulated learned model which is then applied on unseen target data to categorize it, constitutes supervised learning. In comparison to unsupervised learning algorithms where the unlabelled data is used for learning inherent structure, the goal of supervised learning algorithms is to learn the mapping function from the labelled input data to predict the output variables for the test data as shown in Figure 5. These learning algorithms iteratively give improved predictions every time based on training data. This iterative learning process for getting accurate prediction ends when the algorithm level of performance reaches some threshold value.

Figure 5. Supervised learning process

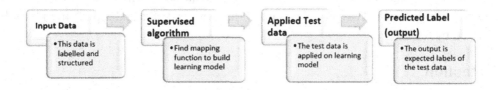

An example of supervised learning algorithm is given in Table 1. It depicts a small sample of heart dataset.

The knowledge about cause of heart disease can easily be extracted using heart disease training data (Table 1). The model can be learned through a mathematical function which maps the features age,

Table 1. Heart dataset

S.No	Smoking Status	Gender	Age	Family History	Heart Disease
1.	yes	Male	50	yes	yes
2.	no	Female	40	no	no
3.	yes	Male	38	yes	Yes
4.	no	Female	55	yes	yes
5.	no	Male	60	yes	yes
6.	yes	Female	44	no	no
7.	yes	Female	59	yes	?

smoking status, gender and family history with the probability of heart disease as category 'yes' and 'no' using this training data. A new set of features values (yes, Female, 59, yes) is supplied as input to the learned model to predict its chances of heart disease. The predicted category for this new feature set after mapping is found to be 'yes'. Therefore, available past knowledge in this world plays a vital role in supervised learning approach. Also, the supervised learning algorithms are computationally simpler and more accurate as compared to unsupervised learning algorithms due to this available labelled data about the specific domain.

Supervised Learning is useful in various real time application domains:

Health Care

Health Industry is one of the fast growing industry adapting new technologies. The effect of various nutrients on human body, identifying cancerous tumours, identifying diseases and diagnosis, drug discovery and manufacturing, medical imaging diagnosis, smart maintenance of patient records and many more (Panch, T. et al.2018).

Speech Recognition

Supervised Learning algorithm learned the samples of speech of individuals and then it is able to recognize the individual from their voice. The well-known virtual assistant available in the market are Google assistant and Apple Siri which learns by the sample questions answer sessions with the owner of the device. After that virtual assistant recognizes the owner's voice and replies immediately to the questions asked by them.

Spam Detection

The weird E-Messages and E-Mails received in mail box need to be blocked. Gmail is preloaded with machine learning algorithm that learns the awkward keywords which could make the email as spam such as "win a BMW car" and "ask for bank details for verification". Some message application algorithm gives right to the user to make the application learn about list of doubtful keywords which need to be blocked. The application then automatically blocks messages containing those keywords.

Recommender System

Machine can learn about human likes and dislikes from the regular activities of the human being like purchase history, time spent on exploring a product, etc. The recommender systems utilize machine learning algorithms to suggest related items, articles, products etc. to users after analysing the past patterns of user preferences and interests. A amazon uses recommender systems to customize online store according to individual customer based on his/her past purchase pattern. Similarly, Netflix uses recommender algorithms to study the interest of the person over a period of time and shows in his account the list of movies and series related to his interests.

Supervised Learning also has several challenges which are encountered while applying its algorithms on the data. Few of them are listed below:

- Overfitting of data occurs by machine learning algorithm many times. Overfitting occurs when a model learns the features along with the noise in the training data to a level which directly impacts the performance of the learned model on fresh data. This means that the outliers or random instabilities in the training data is also included for constructing learning model.
- Accurate and reliable data must be used as a training data.
- Learning algorithms takes more computational time for modelling.
- Applying pre-processing methods on data is the big task.
- Outliers also effect the accuracy of the learning model.

Reinforcement Learning

Reinforcement Learning (Bhatia, P. 2019) is a machine learning approach that is altogether a different in terms of learning procedure than the other two. It does not involve real static dataset for learning. In this approach, the data is generated in the dynamic environment. Reinforcement learning algorithms operate back and forth on data generated in the processing environment to reach a goal of finding optimal solution to a problem. The three main components in the reinforcement learning are agent, environment and actions. Agents are used to explore and accordingly choose the action to be performed which maximize the rewards and finally provide the optimum series of actions. Agents interacts with an environment described by certain set of states at that time. Each time an agent perform some action in some state of environment, the agent receives a reward. The agent final goal is to learn a policy network that maximizes these rewards. This learning process is shown in Figure 6.

Reinforcement learning is mostly used in following application domains:

Computer Games

These machine learning algorithms are used in E-Gaming software where one of the player is the computer system itself like Chess game between human and computer. The machine will be trained by selecting only reward winning game turns by the agent. Agent remembers all reward winning sequences and form control policy network.

Figure 6. Reinforcement Learning process

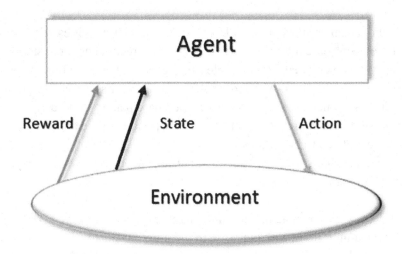

Robotics

Robot, act as agent, has trained sensors to sense the state of the environment and then choose set of actions to alter its state and produce reward. This process is repeated till the sum of rewards collected is maximized and finally reaches its optimal state.

Driverless Cars

Agents in the form of software learns the driving patterns in different real time situation on the road to avoid accidents. Reinforcement algorithms helps the car driving system to learn about the action to be performed after sensing the vicinity of the car and following navigation commands.

There are two important learning models in reinforcement learning: Markov Decision Process and Q learning. Many challenges were faced during Reinforcement learning process implementation.

- It is difficult to decide the design of a reward.
- Complexity is involved in the learning process which may affect the speed of learning.
- Realistic environments can be dynamic and not always be observable for every state.
- Many reinforcement signals may result in surplus states which diminish the final results.

Deep Learning

Deep Learning is a subdivision of machine learning in artificial intelligence (AI) that has artificial neural network based algorithms capable of extracting higher level of features from input data. The data transformation through number of hidden layers in artificial neural network makes it '*deep*' in terms of learning. In deep learning, every hidden layer is responsible for transforming its input data into a little more abstract and cohesive representation. Due to this, it can also be referred as deep neural network(DNN). Learning by deep learning algorithms can be supervised or unsupervised.

Various deep learning architectures are common nowadays such as convolutional neural networks, recurrent neural networks and deep belief networks, which are applied in various application domains including speech and audio recognition, natural language processing, recommendation systems, bioinformatics, image restoration, medical image analysis, drug design and gaming. The results achieved from these deep learning architectures are comparable with human expert analysis of that domain.

DNNs are feedforward networks in which raw data is progressively transformed from the input layer to the output layer without seeing back. The DNN generates a network of virtual neurons and assigns weights to the connections of neurons. The output between 0 and 1 is generated by multiplying weights and inputs. An algorithm will adjust the weights only if the learned network does not recognize a given pattern accurately. These mathematical calculations are performed till the data is fully processed to give the accurate output.

Despite the powerful deep learning algorithms which are able to compete with human intelligence, the algorithms are not looking after the soft relationships among data and abstract knowledge about data objects. The stable quality data is needed to achieve profound and accurate results from deep learning algorithms.

Unsupervised Learning Algorithms

Association Analysis

Many large grocery stores have large amount of data from their routine transaction operations in various sections of food items. For example, an online grocery store like the "big basket" have registered lot of customers who buy variety of products on regular basis from their online store. These stores create separate accounts of their customers with their personal details and keep track of their order history. This complete regular purchase data consist of lot of knowledge in terms of patterns of purchases by the customer. One can easily study the behaviour of the customers from this live data. As the customer buys items from different categories like milk products, fruits, vegetables etc. This data can also be used to infer about the customer's inclination towards type of food intake: healthy or a junk food. The data of products purchased have hidden relationships among them. Such transactions data is known as Market Basket Transactions.

Table 2. Market basket transactions of a grocery store

Transaction -ID	products-purchased
t_1	{Banana, milk, bread, butter}
t_2	{chocolate, milk, burger, sauce}
t_3	{milk, bread, butter, eggs}
t_4	{burger, sauce, onion, tomato}
t_5	{milk, bread, butter, proteinbar}

Consider the transactions in the Table 2 which can be used by retailer to understand that the customer is diet conscious or junk food lover. The retailer can load the store shelves according to behaviour pattern of food habits of the customers. This table shows the Transaction-ID as unique code for each transaction, and a set of products purchased by a given customer. It also shows the purchase behaviour of a given customer. Retailers are mostly concerned in examining the data to learn about the purchasing behaviour of their customers. This valuable information can be utilized to explore business-focused applications for a store such as promotion of related products, inventory management, marketing strategies and customer relationship management. Learning interesting relationships from the huge dataset of purchase transactions of their customers can be done using association analysis methodology. The relationships among products can be represented in the form of sets of products purchased in number of transactions. If set of n products available in a grocery store are represented as $P = \{p_1, p_2, ..., p_n\}$, and set of all transactions of customers are represented as $T = \{t_1, t_2, ..., t_m\}$. For a given Market basket data shown in Table 3. P is given as

$P = \{$milk, bread, butter, eggs, burger, tomato, onion, protein bar, sauce, banana, chocolate$\}$

Number of subsets containing distinct product combinations can be constructed from the set P. These subsets can have one or more than one product combinations. Using the representation for these subsets (candidate sets of P) as $PS_k (k=0,1,2,...,n)$ with respect to number of products a particular subset have. For example, PS_0 denotes the null set having no products, PS_1 denotes all sets having single product. There are 11 PS_1 sets, $^{11}C_2$ PS_2 sets, $^{11}C_3$ PS_3 sets ...... for the market basket data shown in the Table 2.

PS_2: {milk, bread}, {milk, butter}, {milk, eggs}, {milk, burger}, {milk, tomato}, {milk, onion}, {milk, protein bar}, {milk, sauce}, {milk, banana}, {milk, chocolate}...

The PS_3 set, X = {milk, bread, butter} is the subset of transactions t_1, t_3 and t_5. That is,

$$X \subseteq t_1, X \subseteq t_3, X \subseteq t_5$$

To clearly depict the membership of products in all transactions, it is required to transform the Table 2 in binary representation form as shown in Table 3 . The value Zero(0) represents the product is not the member of the transaction set and value one(1) represent the product is the member of the particular transaction set.

Table 3. Customer transactions

Transaction ID	milk	bread	butter	eggs	burger	chocolate	tomato	onion	Proteinbar	sauce	banana
t_1	1	1	1	0	0	0	0	0	0	0	1
t_2	1	0	0	0	1	1	0	0	0	1	0
t_3	1	1	1	1	0	0	0	0	0	0	0
t_4	0	0	0	0	1	0	1	1	0	1	0
t_5	1	1	1	0	0	0	0	0	1	0	0

The characteristic of the product set is described by a measure known as *Support*, symbolized as $Support_X$. It is defined as the number of transactions enclosing particular product set.

Mathematically,

$$Support_X = Count(\{\forall t_k | X \subseteq t_k, t_k \in T\})$$

Therefore,

$$Support_{\{milk\}} = 4$$

$$Support_{\{milk, bread, butter\}} = 3$$

This *Support* measure is always relative to the total number of transactions. So, fractional *support* measure should be taken as

$$\frac{Support_X}{m}, \text{ where } m \text{ is total number of transactions.}$$

Retailers are only interested in frequently occurring product sets to study the pattern of related products in demand by customer for their business growth. The product set which has its *Support* exceeding some user defined threshold value (ϕ) is taken as frequently occurring product set. That is, if $Support_X > \phi$, X is considered as frequently occurring product set. A small $Support_X$ value is improbable to be realistic for a business because it might not be lucrative to promote products that customers seldom buy together.

Algorithmically, generating frequently occurring product sets from support values of its candidate sets is computationally very complex. The Apriori principle is an effective way to reduce this complexity. The Aprori Principle states "if the product set is frequent, then all its subsets are also frequent". Therefore, for generating frequent product set, all its candidate sets are simply removed without counting their support value.

The product sets which mostly appears together in transactions are used to construct association rules. Association rules shows the association strength of two disjoint product sets which generally appears together in transactions. It is represented as following form,

$X \rightarrow Y$ where X and Y are disjoint product sets

Here, X is called antecedent and Y is known as consequent. This association rule is also interpreted as

"if X then Y"

Association rules also use the criteria *Confidence* with *Support* to identify the most important relationships among product sets. *Confidence* indicates how frequently the product set Y appear in the transactions that contain the product set X. Confidence also measures the reliability of the inference made by an association rule. The higher the *confidence* with respect to user defined threshold (ϕ), more likely it is for Y to be present in transactions that contains X.

Mathematically,

$$Confidence_{(X \to Y)} = \frac{Support_{X \cup Y}}{Support_X} \text{ and } Support_{(X \to Y)} = \frac{Support_{X \cup Y}}{m}$$

Another metric, called lift, can be used to compare *confidence* with expected *confidence*. Lift can be found by dividing the $Support_{X \cup Y}$ by the support of product set X times the support of Y, so

$$Lift_{X \to Y} = \frac{Support_{X \cup Y}}{Support_X * Support_Y}$$

A value of lift greater than 1 guarantees high association between *Y* and *X*. High value of lift shows if the customer has already purchased products in set *X*, there are high chances that the customer buys products in set *Y*. Lift is the metric that helps store managers to decide placement of right products on shelves.

Considering association rule analysed from the Table 2:

{milk, bread} → {butter}

These association rules shows the relation between the products milk, bread and butter. Store owners use these association rule relationships to identify new product combinations for cross selling their products to increase the sale. They also observe the choice of food items of the customers, either healthy or unhealthy.

$$Support_{\{milk,bread\} \to \{butter\}} = \frac{Support_{\{milk,bread,butter\}}}{5}$$

$$Support_{\{milk,bread\} \to \{butter\}} = \frac{3}{5} = 0.6$$

$$Confidence_{\{milk,bread\} \to \{butter\}} = \frac{Support_{\{milk,bread,butter\}}}{Support_{\{milk,bread\}}}$$

$$Confidence_{\{milk,bread\} \to \{butter\}} = \frac{3/5}{3/5} = 1$$

$$Lift_{\{milk,bread\} \to \{butter\}} = \frac{Support_{\{milk,bread,butter\}}}{Support_{\{milk,bread\}} * Support_{\{butter\}}}$$

$$Lift_{\{milk,bread\}\rightarrow\{butter\}} = \frac{3/5}{3/5*3/5} = \frac{5}{3} = 1.66$$

Higher values in support and confidence with threshold (ϕ) as 0.5, inferred that milk, bread and butter are frequently occurred products in transactions. These products are associated to each other such that knowledge about inventory of milk and bread can be used to infer about the inventory of butter required in store. The value of lift is greater than 1, signifies that if the customer buys milk and bread there are more chances he will buy butter too. Also, the customer does not belong to junk food lover category. It shows this association rule is reliable to be followed. With this knowledge extracted from this rule, manager always place butter on shelve while loading the shelf with milk and bread.

To check the reliability of another Association rule:

{burger, sauce} → {milk}

$$Support_{\{burger,sauce\}\rightarrow\{milk\}} = \frac{Support_{\{burger,sauce,milk\}}}{5}$$

$$Support_{\{burger,sauce\}\rightarrow\{milk\}} = \frac{1}{5} = 0.2$$

$$Confidence_{\{burger,sauce\}\rightarrow\{milk\}} = \frac{Support_{\{burger,sauce,milk\}}}{Support_{\{burger,sauce\}}}$$

$$Confidence_{\{burger,sauce\}\rightarrow\{milk\}} = \frac{1/5}{2/5} = 0.5$$

$$Lift_{\{burger,sauce\}\rightarrow\{milk\}} = \frac{Support_{\{burger,sauce,milk\}}}{Support_{\{burger,sauce\}}*Support_{\{milk\}}}$$

$$Lift_{\{burger,sauce\}\rightarrow\{milk\}} = \frac{1/5}{2/5*4/5} = \frac{5}{8} = 0.62$$

Lower values in support and confidence with threshold (ϕ) as 0.5, inferred that burger, sauce and milk are not frequently occurred product combination in transactions. These products are not strongly associated to each other. The stock of burger and sauce on shelves cannot be correlated to stock of milk cans in store. Also, for this association rule, the value of lift is less than 1, which clearly states that customer buying burger and sauce not surely buy milk and customer belong to junk food category. It shows this association rule is not reliable to be followed.

Association analysis can also be applied to other data from different domains like medical, web mining, bioinformatics. Association analysis is not so popular for machine learning due to many reasons. One of them is that it is very expensive to mine the patterns from voluminous transaction data as it requires complex algorithms involving high level of computational efforts. Also, few discovered patterns may be unrealistic and even for realistic patterns, some are more remarkable than others. It is required to order the realistic patterns according to their reliability measure.

Python Library

from apyori import apriori

Python Function

```
#Specify the list of datarecords, support threshold(.0059), confidence
threshold(0.3), lift threshold(4),minimum number of items(2)
a_rules = apriori(datarecords, min_support=0.0059, min_confidence=0.3,
          min_lift=4, min_length=2)
results = list(a_rules)
```

Clustering

Clustering is an important unsupervised learning technique which finds patterns in the uncategorized data and group them according to their features and relationship among each other. Algorithms are used to process data for evolution of natural clusters from the collection of data. Data objects in one cluster have similar features and are different from data objects in another cluster. Clusters are more distinct when homogeneity within a group and heterogeneity with the other group is very high. The number of clusters required for meaningful categorization in data varies according to the characteristics of the data. Clustering algorithms helps the user in suggesting the desired cluster parameters.

Various business owners practice these clustering algorithms for the decision making and accordingly create the new business initiatives. The practical application of these techniques is to identify a belongingness of data objects to different groups. For retail businesses, data clustering helps with customer shopping patterns, sales promotions and retention of customer. In banking sector, clustering is used for customer segregation and credit scoring. Clustering is also suitable for fraud detection and identification of risk factor in the insurance industry. Even the Google news make use of clustering algorithm to club the related news of same topic.

Clusters can be defined as subgroups of data objects made by collecting objects based on similarity measure from the given domain of n data objects as shown in Figure 7. Domain knowledge plays important role to interpret clusters build from the data. Clusters do not have fixed shape, size and granularity. It is represented using the measure of central tendency known as centroid of the collection of similar data objects. The objects are allocated to the clusters based on the closeness such that the squared distance from the centroid is curtailed. Data points in the following diagram can be visualized into two clusters.

Types of Clustering

Different type of clustering types are available based on how clusters of data objects are designed:

Figure 7. Data points in two clusters

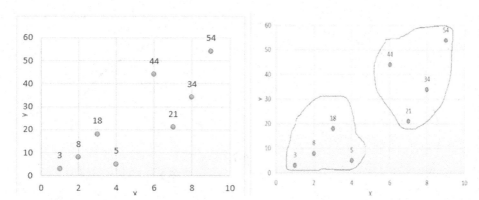

Exclusive (Partitioned)

This technique works upon non-overlapping clusters. Each data object is assigned to a single cluster. For example, employees of marketing department and technical department in an organization. No employee could be a part of both the departments. All data objects are partitioned evidently into groups. A disadvantage of this technique is sometimes a data object which is not a good match for any cluster, could forcibly be placed into a cluster with an approximate match.

Overlapping

This is non-exclusive clustering technique where the data object could be placed in more than one cluster. The data object match the characteristics of more than two clusters. For Example, student opted subject papers from commerce and economics departments. Here, the data object which do not belong to any of the group, may lies in between the two clusters. A disadvantage here is that some data objects may be left floating and clustering do not cover all data objects.

Fuzzy (Probabilistic)

The fuzzy technique treat all clusters like fuzzy sets in which membership weights between 0 and 1 are assigned to every data object. The weight of '0' represent data object does not belong to any group and '1' shows that it definitely belongs to some group. Since it is a must to assign every data object to some cluster, the technique computes the probability with which it can be assigned to clusters. The sum of all probabilities attached with a data object is 1. A drawback of using this technique is that it could not show true allocation of data object which can be surely a part of more than one clusters. Considering the case of a student studying subjects of two departments. On the other hand it has an advantage that data object cannot be allocated to a single cluster based on its approximated match to that cluster. It can be transformed to exclusive clustering when allocation of object to a cluster having highest probability of association.

Agglomerative (Hierarchical)

In this clustering technique, initially every data object is a cluster. This techniques is expensive as compared to other techniques of clustering. This is an iterative methods to repeatedly build union of two

Figure 8. Agglomerative clustering

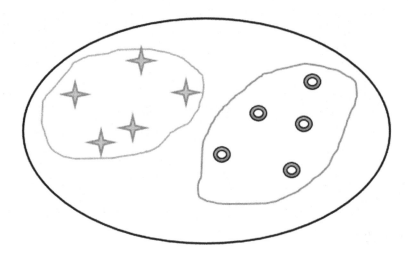

nearest neighbour small clusters as big cluster to reduce the number of clusters. It is a kind of bottom up approach to join the singleton data objects based on distance between them as shown in Figure 8.

The following shows the algorithm for Agglomerative clustering technique:

Step 1: Initially, Every single data object o_i can be taken as a cluster c_i, which forms a collection of clusters C.

$c_i=\{o_i\}$ and $C=\{c_1,c_2,\ldots,c_n\}$

Step 2: Find two nearest neighbour clusters o_i, o_j, join them to build single cluster as $c_k=\{o_i,o_j\}$.

Step 3: Discard singleton clusters for o_i and o_j and replace it with new cluster $c_k=\{o_i,o_j\}$ in the collection C.

Step 4: Repeat this process with every nearby clusters calculated as $\min_{i,j}(distance(c_i,c_j))$

Step 5: Stop the procedure when only one big cluster is left.

Threshold value for the distance metrics calculated between clusters can be set to stop the procedure at certain level to get the distinct number of clusters. Dendrogram can be used to describe the process of cluster formation visually. Figure 9 shows the sample dendrogram with threshold 1150 and two clusters in purple and yellow colour build on dataset.

Python Libraries for Agglomerative Clustering

```
from matplotlib import pyplot as plt
from sklearn.cluster import AgglomerativeClustering
import scipy.cluster.hierarchy as sch
from sklearn.preprocessing import normalize
```

Python Functions for Agglomerative Clustering

```
#Dendogram on Dataframe DFrame from dataset
dendrogram = sch.dendrogram(sch.linkage(DFrame, method='ward'))
plt.axhline(y=1150, color='blue', linestyle='--')
Dframe_scaled = normalize(Dframe)
ACmodel=AgglomerativeClustering(n_clusters=2,affinity='euclidean',
linkage='ward')
ACmodel.fit(Dframe_scaled)
```

Figure 9. Agglomerative clustering with dendrogram

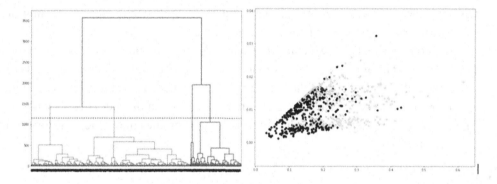

The linkage methods and distance measure used to calculate the distance between data objects will vary the end result of clustering. Some of linkage methods used are single, ward, complete and average. Distance measures used are Euclidean Distance, Manhattan, Mahalanobis etc.

Complete Clustering

In complete clustering, all data objects are to be assigned to a well-defined cluster. All clustering types exclusive, hierarchical and fuzzy are complete clustering.

Partial Clustering

Some of the data objects in the data does not belong to any of the well-defined clusters. These data objects may be represented as noise, outliers. That type of clustering is known as partial clustering.

Clustering Algorithms

There are two categories of clustering algorithms commonly used are centroid based clustering and density based clustering.

Centroid Based Clustering

This is an iterative clustering algorithm in which the proximity of data objects to the centroid of clusters is measured. During the iterations, the cluster centroid is modified in such a way that the distance between all data objects and the centroid is minimum. There is no efficient known solution exists for these algorithms, therefore they are NP-Complete.

- **K-Mean:** This clustering algorithm is most commonly used centroid based method. Here, the whole process involves operations around the centre vector of the cluster (Sohail, M. N. et al. 2019). The procedure is divided into two phases:
  - Any *k* number of centroid points are identified by the user. All data objects in the proximity of every initial centroids are considered as a cluster with that centroid point as centre. Distances between centroid and all data objects of a cluster is measured using any of the distance metrics like Euclidean, Manhattan etc.
  - In the second phase, the new centroids are found such that the distance between the data objects and centroid of every cluster is reduced. This process of updating centroids of clusters is repeated till the centroids of clusters remain unchanged. This algorithm is computationally faster for large values of features, if k is small. It results in distinct clusters without outliers. The main disadvantage of this algorithm is how to predict the value of k for finding well-defined clusters.

Python Library

```
from sklearn.cluster import KMeans
```

Python Function

```
# Specify the number of clusters (3) and fit the data D
    Kmeans_Cl = KMeans(n_clusters=3, random_state=0).fit(D)
```

- **K-Medoids:** In this algorithm the medoids are the data objects itself in the n-dimensional space. The iterative procedure of this algorithm is exactly same as the k-means except in k-means centroid can be any point near to data object or data object itself. Based on the distance calculated between the medoid and the data objects, the updated medoids can be taken as any other data object from the cluster or remain same as the earlier one when no net change in distances is observed.

Python Library

```
from sklearn_extra.cluster import KMedoids
```

Python Function

```
# Specify the number of clusters (3) and fit the data D
        Kmedoids_Cl = KMedoids(n_clusters=3, random_state=0).fit(D)
```

Density-Based Methods

In these methods, the grouping of neighbouring data objects into clusters is based on the density conditions of data objects. Density of data objects in neighbourhood is used to judge the boundary of cluster. High density clusters are separated from other high density clusters with the low density region around them. Data objects in low density portion is taken as noise or outliers. DBSCAN and OPTICS are two examples of density based clustering.

- DBSCAN (Density based spatial clustering of application with noise) - It is a form of clustering in which algorithm automatically determines the number of clusters. The algorithm is able to manage outliers and noise present at region of low density. In this clusters are often incomplete, irregular and intertwined. This algorithm works with two parameters:
  1. ε (The radius of neighbourhood around a data object) and
  2. *MPts* (The minimum number data objects in a neighbourhood to define a cluster)

Using these parameters, data objects are categorized into three major categories: core points, boundary points and outliers.

Python Library for DBSCAN:

```
from sklearn.clusters import DBSCAN
```

Python Function

```
#creating core points of DBSCAN object(dsobj) with a minimum of 20 data objects,
#a radius of 0.7 and fit dataset D
dsobj = DBSCAN(eps = 0.7, min_samples = 20).fit(D)
```

- OPTICS (Ordering points to identify the clustering structure) – It is a density based method used to find clusters in spatial dataset. It is driven from the DBSCAN algorithm and introduces two concepts: core and reachable distance. Core distance is calculated as the lowest value of radius required to categorize a given point as a core point. If the given data object is not a core point, then it's core distance is also not defined. A reachable distance of a data object d1 is measured with respect to some other data object d2. It can be taken as the highest of the core distance of d1 and any distance metric between d1 and d2. If d2 is not a core point, the reachability distance is also not defined.

Python Library for OPTICS:

```
from sklearn.clusters import OPTICS
```

Python Function

```
# creating core points of OPTICS data object(optcobj) with a minimum sample of
2
# data objects, max_eps is default value infinity and fit dataset D
optcobj = OPTICS(min_samples = 2).fit(D)
```

Principal Component Analysis

Various algorithms are used for preprocessing of data involving dimensionality reduction, feature extraction and data transformation.

Principal Component Analysis (PCA)(Deo, R., & Panigrahi, S. 2019) is a statistical procedure used to explain the variance-covariance organisation of variables from a dataset through their linear groupings. It comprises of orthogonal transformations to transform correlated variables into linearly uncorrelated variables which are known as principal components. The principal components holds most of the information from the large set of correlated variables. This technique is used for compressing the data set by reducing data dimensionality. It is commonly applied to find patterns in high dimensional image data for face recognition and image compression. Principal component algorithm involves the following steps on the given dataset having any number of attributes taken as dimensions for number of samples.

Step 1: Get the data without the class attribute.

Step 2: Normalize data by scaling it.

Step 3: Subtract the mean from each dimensional attribute value producing a new adjusted data set whose mean is zero. Mean of each dimensional attribute is calculated as an average of that dimensional attribute values taken from the data set.

$$Mean(x) = \overline{x} = \sum_{i=1}^{n} x_i$$

Find for each dimensional attribute x, $(\overline{x} - x_i)\forall x_i, \ i = 1,\ldots,n$

Step 4: Find the covariance matrix from the given dimensional attributes. Covariance matrix symbolises the covariance measurement of each dimension in the data set with every other dimension attribute. The covariance value computed between the two random variables implies the variables association with one another. Positive covariance value indicates the two attributes increase and decrease together and the negative covariance value specifies the attributes are inversely proportional. As the covariance is always measured between two dimensions therefore for more than two dimensions the values of covariance can be placed as a matrix. If the non-diagonal elements in the covariance matrix are positive, then both the attributes increase and decrease together.

$$Covariance(x, y) = cov(x, y) = \frac{1}{n-1} \sum_{i=1}^{n} (x_i - \overline{x})(y_i - \overline{y})$$

Covariance matrix for n dimensional attributes can be shown as

$$C = \begin{bmatrix} cov_{1,1} & \cdots & cov_{1,n} \\ \vdots & \ddots & \vdots \\ cov_{n,1} & \cdots & cov_{n,n} \end{bmatrix}$$

Step 5: Calculate the eigenvectors and eigenvalues of the covariance matrix. These eigenvectors are best fit lines that describe the given dataset. Every dimensional attribute data point should be projected on these eigenvectors. Following equation is used for calculating eigenvalue λ, with the covariance matrix C and Identity Matrix I,

$$|\lambda I - C| = 0,$$

Further to compute an eigenvector V_k associated with each eigenvalue λ_k, the equation is given as

$$(\lambda_k I - C) * V_k = 0$$

Step 6: Choose principal components. The eigenvectors V_k are computed from eigenvalues λ_k, for the covariance matrix C. The eigenvectors are computed from high eigenvalues are called principal components showing more significant relationships among the dimensional attributes. Eigenvectors with small eigenvalues are less significant and can be ignored. Dropping least significant components leads to dimension reduction in the final dataset.

Step 7: Form a feature vector *FV*, which is a matrix of eigenvectors having only significant eigenvectors in column and transposed.

$$FV = [V_1, V_2, \ldots, V_k]^T$$

Step 8: To compute the final adjusted data set with the reduced dimensions,

Final adjusted dataset= $FV*$ (mean adjusted values of the dimension attribute)^T

where FV is the matrix with the eigenvectors in the columns transposed so that the eigenvectors are in rows, with the most significant eigenvector at the top and the mean-adjusted dimension attribute values transposed so that the attribute values are in each column and each row holding a separate dimension.

Python Libraries

```
from sklearn import decomposition
from decomposition import PCA
```

Python Functions

```
#Assigning the number of component(4), fit the data D and apply dimensionality
reduction to data D.
pca = PCA(n_components=4)
pca.fit(D)
D = pca.transform(D)
```

SUPERVISED LEARNING ALGORITHM

Regression

Regression (Gopal, M. 2018) is the well-accepted statistical supervised learning tool to study the predictive relationship between a dependent variable and various independent variables. In this simple model, the mapping function is learned that maps input independent variables to continuous target dependent variable with minimum error. Each independent variable is taken as separate dimension in multidimensional space to find the best fit curve for a dependent variable. Simple linear regression is beneficial when dependencies among number of covariates is to be retrieved. (Valsamis, E. M.et al. 2019) To study the temporal effect of patient mortality, simple regression model can be applied on dataset of patients. The curve in regression model will be a straight line if the variables have strong linear relationship among them whereas the nonlinear curve shows either weak or no relationship among variables.

The strength of relationship between each independent variable with dependent variable can also be measured using correlation. The coefficient of correlation is a measure illustrating strength of relationship between variables. Its value varies from -1 to 1. The coefficient of correlation of value 1 indicates perfect positive relationship between variables whereas a value of 0 signifies no relationship and value of -1 indicates perfect negative relationship.

The Multivariate regression model to fit the independent attributes x, $(x_0, x_1, x_2, x_3, ..., x_n)$ to get dependent predicted variable y' using linear relationship function $f(x,w)$, where w represents weights, η represent error variable.

$$y' = f(x, w) = w_0 + w_1 x_1 + w_2 x_2 + ... + w_n x_n + \eta$$

The goal is to find the adjusted values of w_0, w_1, w_3, ..., w_4 such that the mean square error is minimized. This gives the best fit regression learning model based on training data.

$$MSE = minimize \left(\frac{1}{2n} \sum_{i=1}^{n} (y_i' - y_i)^2 \right)$$

For example, to predict the target value of nurse salary for the given number of experience 2.5 and 5 years from the given salary training dataset of nurses in a hospital in Table 4. In this simple regression model, experience of nurse is the only independent attribute (x) and Salary of nurse is the dependent variable (y). To predict the value of salary for the given experience in years, the relationship between these two attributes is to be depicted using mapping function f. Simple Linear regression model is used to find this mapping function.

$$y' = f(x, w) = w_0 + w_1 x_1 + \eta \tag{1}$$

Where w_0 is the intercept, w_1 is the slope and x_1 is the experience.

Consider Nurses Salary Training dataset shown in Table 4

Calculating values of w_0 and w_1, given n(no. of observations in trained data) = 16,

$$w_0 = \frac{\sum y \left(\sum x^2\right) - \left(\sum x\right)\left(\sum xy\right)}{n\left(\sum x^2\right) - \left(\sum x\right)^2},$$

(2)

$$w_1 = \frac{n\sum xy - \left(\sum x\right)\left(\sum y\right)}{n\left(\sum x^2\right) - \left(\sum x\right)^2},$$

(3)

The coefficient of correlation r^2 to show the strength of relationship among two attributes is given as

$$r^2 = \frac{\left(n\sum xy - \left(\sum x\right)\left(\sum y\right)\right)^2}{\left(n\left(\sum x^2\right) - \left(\sum x\right)^2\right) * \left(n\left(\sum y^2\right) - \left(\sum y\right)^2\right)}$$

Using equations (2) & (3),

$$w_0 = \frac{854 * 173.85 - 49.5 * 2787.1}{16 * 173.85 - 49.5 * 49.5} = 31.7080$$

$$w_1 = \frac{16 * 2787.1 - 49.5 * 854}{16 * 173.85 - 49.5 * 49.5} = 7.0034$$

The learning model generated using linear regression using (1) is given by equation

$$y' = f(x, w) = 31.7080 + 7.0034 x_1$$

Finding r^2,

$$r^2 = \frac{\left(16 * 2787.1 - 49.5 * 854\right)^2}{\left(16 * 173.85 - 49.5 * 49.5\right) * \left(16 * 46962 - 854 * 854\right)} = 0.7362$$

The value of $r^2 = 0.7362$ shows the two attributes are strongly related to each other.
Finding predicted values of salary for experience 2.5 years and 5 years:

$$y'_{2.5} = f(2.5, w) = 31.7080 + 7.0034 * 2.5 = 49.2165$$

$$y'_5 = f(5, w) = 31.7080 + 7.0034 * 5 = 66.725$$

The predicted values of nurse salary using learning model equation for experience 2.5 years is approximately rupees 49000 and for experience 5 years is approximately rupees 67000 per month. Graphically the linear model is depicted in Figure 10.

Table 4. Nurses salary training dataset

S.No	Experience (in years)(x)	Salary(in Thousand) (y)	x^2	y^2	x*y
1	1.1	39	1.21	1521	42.9
2	1.3	46	1.69	2116	59.8
3	1.5	37	2.25	1369	55.5
4	2	43	4	1849	86
5	2.2	39	4.84	1521	85.8
6	2.9	56	8.41	3136	162.4
7	3	60	9	3600	180
8	3.2	54	10.24	2916	172.8
9	3.2	64	10.24	4096	204.8
10	3.7	57	13.69	3249	210.9
11	3.9	63	15.21	3969	245.7
12	4	55	16	3025	220
13	4	56	16	3136	224
14	4.1	57	16.81	3249	233.7
15	4.5	61	20.25	3721	274.5
16	4.9	67	24.01	4489	328.3
å	**49.5**	**854**	**173.85**	**46962**	**2787.1**

Figure 10. Regression Model Fitting-Salary Data

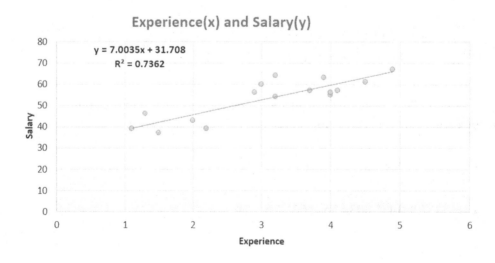

Python Libraries

```
from sklearn.linear_model import LinearRegression
from sklearn import datasets, linear_model
from sklearn.metrics import mean_squared_error, r2_score
from sklearn.metrics import classification_report, confusion_matrix, accuracy_
score
```

Python Function for Multiple Regression Classifier

```
Mregression = linear_model.LinearRegression()
# Train the model using the training sets
Mregression.fit(Xtrain, ytrain)
# Make predictions using the testing set
ypred = Mregression.predict(Xtest)
```

Logistic Regression

Logistic Regression is the augmentation of multivariate regression model which is used to fit the data having binary dependent variable. The independent variables can be a categorical or continuous value. It is an appropriate regression model to measure the relationship between dichotomous dependent variable and one or more continuous independent variables by calculating probabilities using logistic mapping function. The algorithm accurately predicts the class of outcomes for distinct cases after learning coefficients of the regression model.

The training data is used to estimate coefficients of logistic function in logistic regression model. This logistic regression function is a non-linear sigmoid function which include exponentiation of linear combination of independent variables (x) with weights (w) to predict a binary dependent variable (y'). Here, the model is predicting the probability that independent variables (x_0, x_1, ..., x_n) belongs to some default class. This probability output lies between 0 and 1. The equation is given as

$$p\left(x_0, x_1, \ldots, x_n\right) = \frac{e^{w_0 + w_1 x_1 + \ldots + w_n x_n}}{\left(1 + e^{w_0 + w_1 x_1 + \ldots + w_n x_n}\right)}$$

It is mainly used for image segmentation and categorization, geographic image processing, handwriting recognition, text analytics and healthcare systems. Logistic regression is an efficient technique and require computationally simple resources as compared to other classification and predictive techniques.

Regression models are easy to understand and compute because they are based on simple algebraic equations. These models can include all independent variables for prediction. Various statistical measures are easily available to find the strength of regression models.

Python Libraries

```
from sklearn.linear_model import LogisticRegression
```

Python Function for Logistic Regression Classifier

```
MLogistic = LogisticRegression(random_state = 0)
MLogistic.fit(xtrain, ytrain)
ypred = MLogistic.predict(xtest)
```

Decision Tree

Decision Tree (Bhatia, P. 2019) is a tree based hierarchical supervised learning model of machine learning. This predictive model is applied on learning set of instances and on a category allotted to those instances. The decision tree algorithm splits the learning patterns from the dataset on the basis of the target class variable (Induja, S. N., & Raji, C. G. 2019). These splits will be perceptible as a subtree leading to a path depicting some rule to reach the final class target. The construction of decision tree is following a top-down approach when applied on the learning patterns available in the dataset.

This tree classifier algorithm analyse the target class value from the rules built while traversing a particular path towards leaves of a tree. This makes the decision tree learning model accurate and useful in medical science, customer relations, market research etc. The common decision tree algorithms used are C5, CART, CHAID. These algorithms vary due to three different key criterion: Choosing split variable, Stopping criteria and Pruning. Different measures like Information gain and Gini's Index are calculated to choose the best split variable. Dataset having large features set can have many split variables which generates huge complex tree and may lead to overfitting. Pruning is to reduce the size of tree by removing the subtrees having features with little importance. This makes the tree balanced and precise.

For example, the hypothetical drug A and B is prescribed by the doctor based on patient characteristics as shown in the following patient training dataset Table 5: The decision tree based learning model is built based on this training dataset for finding future patients prescription Figure 11:

Table 5. Patients training dataset

S.No	Patient ID	Age(in years)	Sex	BP	Drug
1	A1	10	Male	Normal	A
2	B1	40	Female	Normal	B
3	A2	55	Female	Low	B
4	B2	15	Female	Low	A
5	B3	77	Female	Normal	B
6	A3	80	Female	High	B
7	A4	68	Male	Low	A
8	B4	63	Female	Low	A
9	A5	38	Male	High	A
10	B5	42	Male	Normal	A

Figure 11. Decision tree patient dataset

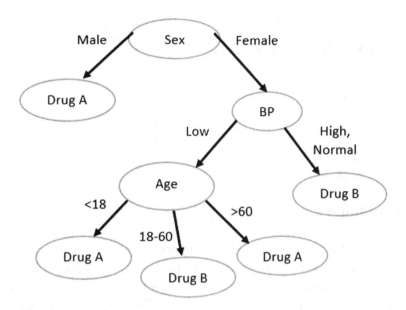

General Rules can be derived from this decision tree which can be treated as learned model from the given training dataset. The following general rules can be formulated which can be further used to predict the decision of drug for the new instance arrived later.

Rule 1: If Patient is male, prescribe Drug A
Rule 2: If Patient is Female, BP is Normal, prescribe Drug B
Rule 3: If Patient is Female, BP is High, prescribe Drug B
Rule 4: If Patient is Female, BP is Low and Age < 18, prescribe Drug A
Rule 5: If Patient is Female, BP is Low and Age is between 18 to 60 years, prescribe Drug B
Rule 6: If Patient is Female, BP is Low and Age > 60, prescribe Drug A

Using these set of rules, inferring which Drug is to be prescribed to new patients with characteristics:

a.   (A6, 90, Male, Normal) - Rule 1, Drug A
b.   (A7,85, Female, Low) - Rule 6, Drug A
c.   (B7,73, Female, High) - Rule 3, Drug B
d.   (B6,50, Female, Low) - Rule 5, Drug B

Python Library

```
from sklearn.tree import DecisionTreeClassifier
from sklearn import tree
from sklearn.tree import DecisionTreeClassifier, plot_tree
```

```
from sklearn.metrics import classification_report, confusion_matrix, accuracy_
score
```

Python Function for Decision Tree Classifier

```
MDTgini=DecisionTreeClassifier(criterion="gini",random_state=100,
        max_depth =3,min_samples_leaf=5)
# Performing training
MDTgini.fit(Xtrain,ytrain)
#Train the model using the training set and get predicted values
ypred = MDTgini.predict(Xtest)
```

K-Nearest Neighbours

K-Nearest Neighbours(KNN) is the most common supervised machine learning algorithmic approach for categorization. It is also called a lazy learning algorithm because it doesn't learn any unique mathematical function from the training data but identify points from the memorized training dataset. The category of the test object is predicted based on categories of its k-closest pre classified training objects found in the feature space. Various Proximity distance metrics (Table 6) are used to find the distance between the training and test objects.

Euclidian distance is commonly used where squares of the distance between the test object and training objects are calculated and find the first k objects having minimum distances from test objects. (Induja, S. N., & Raji, C. G. 2019).The category of test object is the category of majority of the k closest objects. The results vary according the different values of K and the proximity distance formula used.

k-nearest neighbours(KNN) classifier have two issues while classifying the data objects. First, the performance of KNN varies with the different values of parameter K. If value of K is taken as small, outliers affects the accuracy of the classification. If k has larger value, many points from other class may be included which leads to wrong classification of the test object. Second, some techniques is needed to combine the class labels. Majority voting technique is not working properly if the nearest training objects vary widely in their distance Due to these issues, a modified version of KNN is used which is known as weighted KNN.

A kernel function is needed to give weights to the neighbours. In weighted KNN, high weight is given to those training objects which are close to the test object and low weight to those which are farther. Any kernel function can be used for the weighted KNN classifier whose value decreases as the distance from the test object increases. Inverse distance function is the commonly used kernel function.

For example, a dataset of students is given as shown in Table 7 having their height, weight and their category as *Underweight* and *Normal*. This classification can be used by dietician to guide the student for the routine diet intake to remain healthy.

Euclidean Distance:

$$Dist(d) = \sqrt{\left((57-51)^2 + (170-167)^2\right)} = \sqrt{(36+9)} = \sqrt{(45)} = 6.7$$

$$Dist(d) = \sqrt{\left((57-62)^2 + (170-182)^2\right)} = \sqrt{(25+144)} = \sqrt{(169)} = 13$$

$$Dist(d) = \sqrt{\left((57-69)^2 + (170-176)^2\right)} = \sqrt{(144+36)} = \sqrt{(180)} = 13.4$$

$$Dist(d) = \sqrt{\left((57-64)^2 + (170-173)^2\right)} = \sqrt{(49+9)} = \sqrt{(58)} = 7.6$$

...

Let k= 3

Three least distances are 1.4,3,2

Majority of categories in these three records are Normal

Therefore Class of Test object is Normal.

Table 6. Proximity distance metrics

S.No	Proximity Metrics	Definition Function
1.	Euclidean Distance	$D(x,y) = \sqrt{\sum_{i=1}^{m}(x_i - y_i)^2}$
2.	Manhattan	$D(x,y) = \sum_{i=1}^{m}|x_i - y_i|$
3.	Minkowsky	$D(x,y) = \left(\sum_{i=1}^{m}(|x_i - y_i|)^r\right)^{1/r}$
4.	Chebychev	$D(x,y) = \max_{1\le x\le m}|x_i - y_i|$

Table 7. Students dataset used by dietician

S.No	Weight(kg)	Height(cm)	Class	Euclidean distance
1.	51	167	Underweight	6.7
2.	62	182	Normal	13
3.	69	176	Normal	13.4
4.	64	173	Normal	7.6
5.	65	172	Normal	8.2
6.	56	174	Underweight	4.1
7.	58	169	Normal	1.4
8.	57	173	Normal	3
9.	55	170	Normal	2
10.	57	170	?(Normal)	

Python Libraries

```
from sklearn.neighbors import KNeighborsClassifier
from sklearn.metrics import classification_report, confusion_matrix,
    accuracy_score
```

Python Function KNN Classification

```
MKNN = KNeighborsClassifier(n_neighbors=K,p=2,metric='euclidean',
    leaf_size=30,weights='uniform')
MKNN.fit(Xtrain, ytrain)
ypred = MKNN.predict(Xtest)
```

Naïve Bayes

The Naïve Bayes classifier (Bhatia, P. 2019) is a supervised machine language algorithm which is based on Bayes theorem stated by Thomas Bayes(1701-1761). It is a simple and effective probabilistic feature model with robust independent assumptions between the features. It is most popular algorithm for the categorization applications (Kotsiantis, S. B et.al 2007) involving high dimensional training datasets. Several healthcare applications like study the pattern of the symptoms of diseases, chronic disease predictions(Induja, S. N., & Raji, C. G. 2019), suggesting effective activities to patients suffering from depression and many more involving high dimensional data can be effectively done by this classifier. Some of the other applications involving high dimensional data are spam filtration, news articles classification, sentiment analysis etc. It learns the probability of an object with its independent features speedily and then quickly predicts the class of the test data.

This learning probabilistic model is called naïve because it works with assumption that the occurrence of particular feature in a class is unrelated to the existence of other features present in the class. For example, to identify the fruits with three of its features colour, taste and shape. Apple is identified with its red colour, spherical shape and sweet taste. Although all these features are required to find that there is a probability of identifying the fruit as apple but their contribution is independent of each other.

Bayes theorem describes the conditional probability of occurrence of any event based on previous knowledge of already existed events. Mathematically, It states as following equation:

$$P(A|B) = \frac{P(B|A)P(A)}{P(B)}$$

Where,

$P(A|B)$ = conditional probability of occurrence of event A given that the event B is already existed.

$P(B|A)$ = conditional probability of occurrence of event B given that the event A is already existed.

$P(A)$ and $P(B)$ = Probability of occurrence of event A and B respectively.

Methodology

By Definition of conditional probability

$$P(A|B) = \frac{P(A \cap B)}{P(B)} \tag{4}$$

$$P(B|A) = \frac{P(B \cap A)}{P(A)} \tag{5}$$

Combining equations (4) and (5),

$$P(A|B)\ P(B) = P(B|A)\ P(A)$$

$$P(A|B) = \frac{P(B|A)P(A)}{P(B)}$$

Algorithm

Let multiple features be $x_1, x_2, x_3, \ldots, x_n$ and classes be $C_1, C_2, C_3, \ldots, C_k$.

Conditional probability of an object with feature vector $x_1, x_2, x_3, \ldots, x_n$ belongs to a particular class C_i is given as equation (6).

$$P(C_i \mid x_1, x_2, x_3, \ldots, x_n) = \frac{P(x_1, x_2, x_3, \ldots, x_n \mid C_i)P(C_i)}{P(x_1, x_2, x_3, \ldots, x_n)} \quad \text{for } 1 \leq i \leq k \tag{6}$$

Rearranging (6)

$$P(x_1, x_2, x_3, \ldots, x_n | C_i)P(C_i) = P(x_1, x_2, x_3, \ldots, x_n, C_i)$$

By definition,

$$P(x_1, x_2, x_3, \ldots, x_n, C_i) = P(x_1 \mid x_2, \ldots, x_n, C_i)P(x_2, x_3, \ldots, x_n, C_i)$$

and,

$$P\left(x_1, x_2, x_3, \ldots, x_n, C_i\right) = P(x_1 \mid x_2, \ldots, x_n, C_i)P(x_2 \mid x_3, \ldots, x_n, C_i)P\left(x_3, x_4, \ldots, x_n, C_i\right)$$

Therefore, $P\left(x_1, x_2, x_3, \ldots, x_n, C_i\right)$ can be written as

$$P\left(x_1, x_2, x_3, \ldots, x_n, C_i\right) = P\left(x_1 | x_2, \ldots, x_n, C_i\right)P\left(x_2 | x_3, \ldots, x_n, C_i\right)\ldots P\left(x_{n-1} \mid x_n, C_i\right).P\left(x_n \mid C_i\right)P\left(C_i\right)$$

(7)

Since assumption is that the features are independent

$$P\left(x_j | x_{j+1}, \ldots, x_n, C_i\right) \approx P\left(x_j | C_i\right) \quad \text{for all } j$$

(8)

Substituting value of $P\left(x_j | x_{j+1}, \ldots, x_n, C_i\right)$ from (8) in (7)

$$P\left(x_1, x_2, x_3, \ldots, x_n, C_i\right) = \prod_{j=1}^{n} P(x_j \mid C_i)P\left(C_i\right)$$

(9)

Substituting value of $P(x_1, x_2, x_3, \ldots, x_n, C_i)$ from (9) to (6)

$$P\left(C_i \mid x_1, x_2, x_3, \ldots, x_n\right) = \prod_{j=1}^{n} P(x_j \mid C_i) \frac{P\left(C_i\right)}{P\left(x_1, x_2, x_3, \ldots, x_n\right)} \quad \text{for } 1 \le i \le k$$

As $P(x_1, x_2, x_3, \ldots, x_n)$ is constant for all classes,

$$P\left(C_i \mid x_1, x_2, x_3, \ldots, x_n\right) \propto (\prod_{j=1}^{n} P(x_j \mid C_i))P\left(C_i\right) \quad \text{for } 1 \le i \le k$$

A Go For Walk Dataset is given as Table 8, to find probability whether to go for a walk or not on

1. **15th Day** with {Season=summer, Day Time=noon, Holiday=true, Wind=strong} and
2. **16th Day** with {Season=spring, Day Time=evening, Holiday=true, Wind=strong}

The conditional probabilities for attributes with domain of Go for Walk class attribute is calculated as shown in Table 9. Using these conditional probabilities, class attribute of 15th and 16th Day can be calculated:

Table 8. Go for walk dataset

Day	Season	Day Time	Holiday	Wind	Go For Walk?
1	summer	evening	true	weak	yes
2	summer	evening	true	strong	no
3	spring	evening	true	weak	yes
4	winter	morning	true	weak	yes
5	winter	noon	false	weak	yes
6	winter	noon	false	strong	no
7	spring	noon	false	strong	no
8	summer	morning	true	weak	yes
9	summer	noon	false	weak	no
10	winter	morning	false	weak	yes
11	summer	morning	false	strong	no
12	spring	morning	true	strong	yes
13	spring	evening	false	weak	yes
14	winter	morning	true	strong	no
15	**summer**	**noon**	**true**	**strong**	**??**
16	**spring**	**evening**	**true**	**strong**	**??**

Table 9. Processing of naïve bayes method on season dataset

S.No	Attribute	Conditional Probability Statistics		
Total Rows(14)		**yes(8) no(6) p(yes)=8/14 p(no)=6/14**		
1.	**Season**(14)	**summer**(5)	**spring**(4)	**winter** (5)
		yes(2) no(3) p(summer|yes)=2/8 p(summer|no)=3/6	yes(3) no(1) p(spring|yes)=3/8 p(spring|no)=1/6	yes(3) no(2) p(winter|yes)=3/8 p(winter|no)=2/6
2.	**Day Time**(14)	**evening** (4)	**morning**(6)	**noon**(4)
		Yes(3) no(1) p(evening|yes)=3/8 p(evening |no)=1/6	yes(4) no(2) p(morning|yes)=4/8 p(morning|no)=2/6	yes(1) no(3) p(noon|yes)=1/8 p(noon|no)=3/6
3.	**Holiday**(14)	**true**(7)	**false**(7)	
		yes(5) no(2) p(true|yes)=5/8 P(true|no)=2/6	yes(3) no(4) p(false|yes)=3/8 p(false|no)=4/6	
4.	**Wind**(14)	**Weak**(8)	**Strong**(6)	
		yes(7) no(1) p(weak|yes)=7/8 p(weak|no)=1/6	yes(1) no(5) P(strong|yes)=1/8 P(strong|yes)=5/6	

* The value within the bracket shows number of records having that value. yes(8) means 8 records have value 'yes'

15th Day?

Feature vector for 15th day(x) = {summer, noon, true, strong}

$p(x|yes) = p(yes) * p(summer|yes) * p(noon|yes) * p(true|yes) * p(strong|yes)$

$p(x|yes) = 8/14 * 2/8 * 1/8 * 5/8 * 1/8 = 0.0014$

$p(x|no) = p(no) * p(summer|no) * p(noon|no) * p(true|no) * p(strong|no)$

$p(x|no) = 6/14 * 3/6 * 3/6 * 2/6 * 5/6 = 0.029$

Comparing,

$p(x|yes) < p(x|no)$

$0.0014 < 0.029$

So, NO has more impact on decision. It is not feasible to go for a walk on that day with given features.

16th Day?

Feature vector for 15th day(x) = {spring, evening, true, strong}

$p(x|yes) = p(yes) * p(spring|yes) * p(evening|yes) * p(true|yes) * p(strong|yes)$

$p(x|yes) = 8/14 * 3/8 * 3/8 * 5/8 * 1/8 = 0.0063$

$p(x|no) = p(no) * p(spring|no) * p(evening|no) * p(true|no) * p(strong|no)$

$p(x|no) = 6/14 * 1/6 * 1/6 * 2/6 * 5/6 = 0.0033$

Comparing,

$p(x|yes) > p(x|no)$

$0.0063 > 0.0033$

So, 'yes' has more impact on decision. It is feasible to go for a walk on that day with given features.

Python Libraries

```
from sklearn import neighbors
from sklearn.metrics import mean_squared_error
from sklearn import model_selection, naive_bayes
```

Python Function Naïve Bayes Classifier

```
MNaive = naive_bayes.MultinomialNB()
MNaive.fit(Xtrain,ytrain)
# predict the labels on validation dataset
ypred = MNaive.predict(Xtest)
```

Support Vector Machine

"Support Vector Machine" (SVM) (Gopal, M. 2018) is a supervised machine learning algorithm which can be used for text categorization, image classification, character recognition etc. This algorithm is applied on linearly separable binary sets. In this algorithm, training vectors with their associated classes are used to build a learning machine. We plot each training vector as a point in n-dimensional space (where n is number of features) having coordinate values as features. The goal is to design a hyper plane that classifies all training vectors into two classes. The optimal hyper plane which leaves the maximum margin between classes is used to give best classification results. The classification whether the person is diabetic with number of independent attributes with admissible level accuracy can be done (Kumari, V. A., & Chitra, R. 2013). Another common application for finding number of patients suffered from acute and chronic diseases by categorization using the past e-records of patients.

A SVM (Akbani, R et.al 2004) is a classifier that selects the hyper plane with largest margin between two classes. Let us consider a binary set with N Training vectors, each vector is represented as tuple (x_i, y_i) (i = 0,1,2,3...,N) where $x_i = \left(x_{i1}, x_{i2}, x_{i3}, ..., x_{id}\right)^T$ the feature values for ith training vector and $y_i \in$ {class1, class2} denotes its class label. The hyper plane of SVM classifier is given by function $g(x)$

$$g(x_i) = w^T x_i + b$$

Where w and b are parameters of the model. Also, the training phase of SVM involves estimating the parameters w and w_o in such a way that the following inequalities are met.

$$g\left(x_i\right) \geq 1, \quad \forall x_i \in class1$$

$$g\left(x_i\right) \leq -1 \quad \forall x_i \in class2$$

To compute the total margin between hyper plane and support vectors is given by z

$$z = 2 / \|w\|$$

To maximize the margin, minimize the term $\|w\|$.

A patient is categorized as suffering from acute or chronic disease using number of times patient admitted to hospital and for how many number of days in total. Patient disease category training dataset with 3 data points is given as shown in the Table 10 and Figure 12. Applying support vector method classifier gives categorisation into two disease classes Chronic and Acute.

Table 10. Patient disease category dataset

Patient ID	Times Admitted	Number of Days	Disease Category
p1	1	1	Acute
p2	2	3	Chronic
p3	2	0	?

Figure 12. Patient disease category training dataset

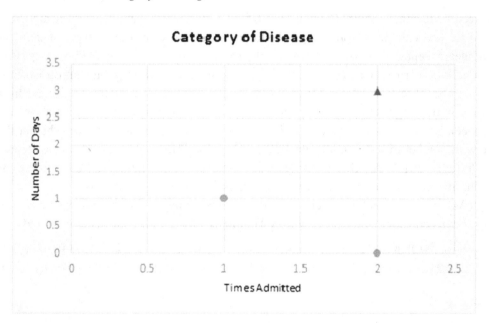

The maximum margin weight vector will be parallel to the shortest line connecting points of the two categories 'Acute' and 'Chronic', that is, the line between p1(1,1) and p2(2,3), giving a weight vector of (1,2). The optimal decision surface is orthogonal to that line and intersects it at the halfway point.

Weight Vector $w = (2,3) - (1,1) = (a,2a)$ for some a

For patient p1(1,1) $g(1,1)= -1$

$$w_0 x_0 + w_1 x_1 + b = -1$$

$$a + 2a + b = -1 \tag{10}$$

For patient p2(2,3) $g(2,3)=1$

$$w_0 x_0 + w_1 x_1 + b = 1$$

$$2a + 6a + b = 1$$

$$b = 1 - 8a$$

Substituting in value of b in (10)

$$3a + 1 - 8a = -1$$

$$a = 2/5$$

$$b = 1 - \frac{16}{5} = -\frac{11}{5}$$

$$w = \left(\frac{2}{5}, \frac{4}{5}\right) \tag{11}$$

The equation of hyperplane using weights w from (11) is given as

$$g(x) = \frac{2}{5}x_1 + \frac{4}{5}x_2 - \frac{11}{5}$$

$$g(x) = x_1 + 2x_2 - 5.5$$

For finding the category of patient p3(2,0):

$$g(x) = 2 + 0 - 5.5 = -3.5 < -1$$

Therefore, the patient p3(2,0) and p1(1,1) lies in same category 'Acute'.

Python Libraries:

```
from sklearn import neighbors
from sklearn.metrics import mean_squared_error
from math import sqrt
import matplotlib.pyplot as plt
```

SVM Classification Function

```
MSVM = svm.SVC(C=1.0, kernel='linear', degree=3, gamma='auto')
MSVM.fit(Xtrain, ytrain)
ypred = MSVM.predict(Xtest)
```

Artificial Neural Network

The neural network (Gopal, M. 2018) (Tan, P. N. et al.2016) is a tool of machine learning which is mainly used for solving complex problems. Earlier the computers follow the set of instructions given by programmer who knows how to solve a problem. This restricts the problem solving capability of conventional computer system. If a programmer do not know the specific steps to solve a problem, the computer cannot solve the problem. With the fast growing world of technology number of the complex problems need to be solved within seconds. The traditional approach is a failure in such scenarios where a complex problem is not understood by the programmer. Neural network gives solution to this problem of solving complex problem. The neural networks are inspired by human brain cells "neuron" which are the building blocks of brain. The biological neuron receives the information from the other neurons through the dendrites which then send it to the cell body of the neuron. Here the information is processed and output generated is sent to other neuron through axons. Artificial neural networks simulate the process of recognition of object by biological neurons. A neural network learns by example or by its own experience. With the advent of GUI and availability of voluminous data from social media help neural networks to solve complex problems.

An artificial neural network is a computing system that is designed to analyse and process the complex problems. It is the interconnected assembly of artificial neurons with directed links. It has self-learning capabilities to enable it to produce better results. Training a network with more data always give accurate results of classification. We can configure artificial neural network for specific task for example health care(Shahid, N. et al. 2019) pattern recognition, text classification etc. Both feedforward and backpropagation are very effective in various hospital management activities and in classification for diagnosis of diseases. The study provided by (Nwiabu, N. D., & John, A. O. 2019) explained neural network as an efficient model for evaluating hospital management performance.

Perceptron

The simplest single artificial neuron is known as perceptron. It comes under the category of supervised learning algorithms for binary classifiers. It provides a class to the certain set of inputs at steady state. A perceptron consists of input layer, hidden layer and output layer. Number of nodes in Input layer depends upon number of features used to train the network. Number of nodes in output layer is the number of classes of the output attribute. Weights allotted to the input features and non-linear activation function with threshold value constitute the hidden layer required to generate the output function as shown in Figure 13.

Perceptron takes in a linear combination of inputs representing features as vector of numbers (x_0, x_1, x_2, ..., x_n) which belongs to particular class. Each input is multiplied with a feasible weight (w_0, w_1, ..., w_n) and summation of these linear combination with a **bias** value is taken as input to activation function. The **bias** value allows the activation function to be shifted to the left or right, to better fit the data. A bias unit is incorporated as an "extra" neuron (w_0) added to each hidden layer that stores the value of 1 and is not affected by the values for previous layers. Activation function with some threshold value is used to generate the binary class output as [1, -1].

$$Weighted \ Sum = \sum_{i=1}^{n} w_i x_i, \quad w_0 = 1 \left(bias \right)$$

$$output = \begin{cases} 1 & if \ \sum_{i=0}^{n} w_i x_i > 0 \\ -1 & otherwise \end{cases}$$

Figure 13. Unit of perceptron

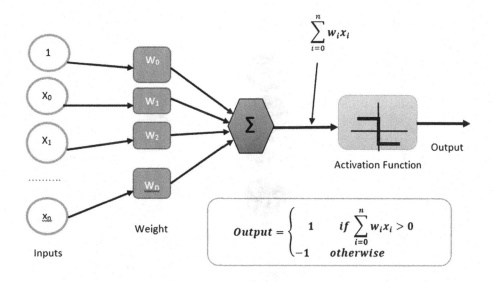

Feedforward Neural Network

Single artificial neuron with single layer architecture is not sufficient to solve the complex problems. According to Universal Approximation theorem single artificial neuron can't deal with non-linear data. Connecting multiple neurons in an effective way can solve any complex relationship between input and the output, required to deal with non-linear data. Several such artificial neurons have their own activation functions to solve such complex problems. A multilayer perceptron has many hidden layers where output of one hidden layer is taken as input to the subsequent hidden layer in series leading to give the output on output nodes. A MLP can be seen as a classifier where the features with varying importance taken as input are first transformed using a learnt non-linear transformation function. This transformation projects the input features into a space where it becomes linearly separable. This is also classified as feedforward neural network or static neural network. This does not involve any feedback loops and time delays for mapping of input feature vector to output response variables.

Backpropagation Neural network

The problem of feedforward neural network is to minimize the error at the output node which is the incorrect classification for certain sets of input features. As this error function is highly non-linear, the only solution to minimize error is to adjust learning parameter which are the weights of the inputs in the training perceptron. Using gradient descent optimization algorithm the adjustment in the weights can be done iteratively by means of error backpropagation. The basic idea of backpropagation algorithm is to propagate errors from the output layer back to the input layer by a chain rule and adjust weights till the model is adequately trained. Training perceptron requires complex computations to adjust the weights at hidden layer (Figure 14) to fit the relationship between input and output attributes.

Figure 14. Backpropagation neural network

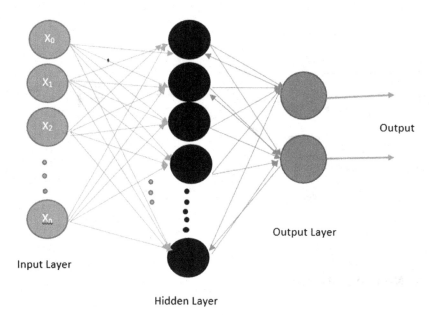

The process begin with the random weight then iteratively apply the perceptron to each training example, modify the perceptron weight till it gives the precise output. Huge number of iterations are required to obtain a precise output for a complex problem. Revised weights w_i associated with input x_i are modified using the perceptron learning rule:

$$w_i = w_i + \Delta w_i$$

Where $\Delta w_i = \eta(d - o)x_i$

Here, d is the desired output for current training example, o is the output generated by perceptron, and η is the positive constant called the learning rate. The learning rate is normally a small value, say 0.1. It is needed to control the degree of change in the weights in each iteration.

Table 11. Activation functions

S.No	Activation function	Description	
1.	Linear	Equation: $y=ax$ It is used at output layer. It is linear function of input values at first layer. It allows muti value outputs. Value range: -inf to inf	
2.	Step(signum)	Equation: $f(x) = \begin{cases} 1, & x \geq 0 \\ 0, & x < 0 \end{cases}$ Simplest activation function Value of input say x is greater than the threshold value then the neuron is activated. It does not allow multi-value outputs. Value range:[-inf,inf]	
3.	Sigmoid	Equation: $y = \dfrac{1}{\left(1 + e^{-x}\right)}$ It is non- linear smooth function having 'S' shaped graph. It is used in output layer of binary classification. Value range: 0 to 1	
4.	Tanh	Tangent hyperbolic function Equation: $f(x) = \tanh(x) = \dfrac{2}{1 + e - 2x} - 1$ OR Tan$h(x)$=2*sigmoid(2x) – 1 It is the non-linear function which is generally used in hidden layers of neural network. It mostly brings the data at centre because mean of data is close to 0. This also makes learning of next layer easy. Value range: -1 to +1	
5.	Relu	Rectified linear unit Equation: $f(x)$=max(0,x) $output = \begin{cases} x, & x > 0 \\ 0, & x \leq 0 \end{cases}$ It is non-linear function involving simple computations with activation of few neurons so less costlier than tanh and sigmoid function. It uses multiple layer perceptrons. Due to simple computations errors are easily propagated to get the desired output. Value Range: [0, inf]	

Activation Function

It is the non-linear complex function used to do complex mapping of input features attributes and output class variable. Non-linear activation functions permit neural networks to compute nontrivial problems using small number of nodes. Therefore, the purpose of the activation function is to maintain non-linearity into the output of a neuron. Many variants of activation functions, as shown in Table 11, are available which does complex mapping between input and output.

Methodology

Parameters:

Inputs vector x(m): $[+1, x_0(m), x_1(m), \ldots, x_n(m)]^T$

Weight vector w(m): $[b(n), w_0(m), w_1(m), \ldots, w_n(m)]^T$

b(m): bias
y(m): actual output
d(m): desired output
η: learning rate (constant value <1)

Let w(0)=0 for time step m = 1,2....
At time step m, input vector x(m) is activated and desired output d(m) received.

$$Y(m) = sgn[w^T(m)x(m)]$$

where *sgn* is *signum* function

$$sgn(x) = \begin{cases} +1, & x \geq 0 \\ -1, & x < 0 \end{cases}$$

Threshold function $\varnothing(v)$

$$\varnothing(v) = \begin{cases} 1, & v \geq 0 \\ 0, & v < 0 \end{cases}$$

Changing weight vector of the perceptron,

$$w(m+1) = w(m) + \eta[d(m) - y(m)]\, x(m)$$

where

$$d(m) = \begin{cases} +1, & \text{if } x(m) \text{ belongs to class } C_1 \\ -1, & \text{if } x(m) \text{ belongs to class } C_2 \end{cases}$$

Increment time step m by one and activate next input vector to repeat the process.

The hyperplane $\sum_{i=1}^{n} w_i x_i + b = 0$ is the decision boundary.

For two class problem, the decision boundary is $w_1 x_1 + w_2 x_2 + b = 0$

Table 12. Patient Cure Dataset

		weight (pounds)	cure period(years)
Patient class C$_1$		121	16.8
		114	15.2
Patient class C$_2$		210	9.4
		195	8.1

Patient Cure dataset is given in Table 12, with attributes as weight and cure period of patient category C_1 and C_2. Following steps are required for classification using neural network classifier.

Step 1: Train the single layer neural network model using features weight and cure period to classify patient into two categories.

Step 2: Use the above model to find the category of patient having feature weight = 140 pounds and cure period = 17.9 years.

Let feature weights and bias be assigned values randomly,

$w_0(0) = -30$ $w_1(0) = 300$ $b(0) = -1230$ $\eta = 0.01$

Decision boundary equation using initial given values:

$-30x_1 + 300x_2 - 1230 = 0$

Train the network with known features values

$x(m) = x(0) = [+1, 121, 16.8]^T$ and $d(0) = +1$

$w(m) = w(0) = [-1230, -30, 300]^T$

$y(m) = y(0) = sgn(w^T(0)x(0))$

$= sgn(-30 * 121 + 300 * 16.8 - 1230 * 1)$

$= sgn(180) = +1 = d(0)$

Hence weights are correct, no need to recalculate

$w(m+1) = w(1) = [-1230, -30, 3000]^T$

$x(1) = [+1, 114, 15.2]^T$ and $d(0)=+1$

$w(1) = [-1230, -30, 300]^T$

$y(1) = sgn(w^T(1)x(1))$

$= sgn(-30 * 114 + 300 * 15.2 - 1230 * 1)$

$= sgn(-90) = -1 \neq d$ (1)

Hence weights are not correct so now need to recalculate
To recalculate weights,

$w(m+1) = w(m) + \eta[d(m) - y(m)] \, x(m)$

$w(2) = w + \eta[d(1) - y(1)] \, x(1)$ (1)

$y(1) = -1$

$w(1) = [-1230, -30, 300]^T$

$w(2) = [-1230, -30, 300]^T + 0.01[+1 - (-1)] \, [+1, 114, 15.2]^T$

$w(2) = [-1230, -30, 300]^T + [0.02, 2.28, 0.304]^T$

$w[2] = [-1229.08, -27.72, 300.304]^T$

$x(2) = [+1, 210, 9.4]^T$ and $d(2) = -1$

$= sgn(w^T(2) \, x(2))$

$= sgn(-27.72 * 210 + 300.304 * 9.4 - 1229.08 * 1)$

$= sgn(-4227.4224) = -1 = d$ (2)

Hence weights are correct so now no need to recalculate

$w(3) = [-1229.08, -27.72, 300.304]^T$

$x(3) = [+1, 195, 8.1]^T$ and $d(3) = -1$

$y(3) = sgn(w^T(3) \, x(3))$

$= sgn([-1229.08, -27.72, 300.304]^T[+1, 195, 8.1]^T)$

$= sgn(-27.72 * 195 + 300.304 * 8.1 - 1229.08 * 1)$

$= sgn(-4202.0176) = -1 = d$ \hfill (3)

No need to recalculate weights

$w(4) = [-1229.08, -27.72, 300.304]^T$

$x(4) = [+1, 121, 16.8]^T$ and $d(4) = +1$

$y(4) = sgn(w^T(4) \, x(4))$

$= sgn([-1229.08, -27.72, 300.304]^T[+1, 121, 16.8]^T)$

$= sgn(-27.72 * 121 + 300.304 * 16.8 - 1229.08 * 1)$

$= sgn(461.91) = +1 = d$ \hfill (4)

Now correctly classified …

$w(5) = [-1229.08, -27.72, 300.304]^T$

$x(5) = [+1, 114, 15.2]^T$ and $d(5) = +1$

$y(5) = sgn(w^T(5) \, x(5))$

$= sgn([-1229.08, -27.72, 300.304]^T[+1, 114, 15.2]^T)$

$= sgn(-27.72 * 114 + 300.304 * 15.2 - 1229.08 * 1)$

$= sgn(175.46) = +1 = d$ \hfill (5)

No need to recalculate

$w(6) = [-1229.08, -27.72, 300.304]^T$

$x(\text{unknown}) = [+1, 150, 17.9]^T$ and $d(5) = +1$

$y(6) = sgn(w^T(6) \, x(\text{unknown}))$

$$= sgn([-1229.08, -27.72, 300.304]^T[+1, 150, 17.9]^T)$$

$$= sgn(-27.72 * 140 + 300.304 * 17.9, 1229.08 * 1)$$

$$= sgn(265.56) = +1 = d \tag{5}$$

So unknown patient belongs to class C_1

Python Libraries

```
import matplotlib.pyplot as plt
from sklearn.metrics import confusion_matrix
from sklearn.neural_network import MLPClassifier
```

Artificial Neural Network Classification Function

```
MMLP= MLPClassifier(solver='sgd', activation='tanh',alpha=1e-5,
      hidden_layer_sizes=(1,n), random_state=0)
MMLP.fit(Xtrain,ytrain)
    ypred=MMLP.predict(Xtest)
```

HEALTH CASE STUDY USING PYTHON

Diabetes mellitus is a disorder, common in India, in which the sugar level in the blood is raised. Also, the body is not able to produce the required insulin. This disease adversely effects the nervous system by damaging the nerves and causing difficulty in sensation. It also harms blood vessels escalating the possibility of cardiac arrest, stroke, kidney malfunctioning, and loss of vision. Doctors detect diabetes by gaging blood sugar levels. People with diabetes must follow a healthy routine diet with low saturated fat, sugar and processed foods. There is no direct cure exists for this disease. With the advent of machine learning algorithms, one can study the predictors and symptoms of disease to make the learning model and discover the population that is at high risk of inception of diabetes (Kavakiotis, I et.al 2017). Therefore, appropriate drugs intake at proper time with regular physical exercise lowers the blood sugar level and control the disease at early stages.

There are two types of diabetes mellitus: Type 1 and Type 2 diabetes (Alberti, K. G. M. M., & Zimmet, P. Z. 1998). Type 1 diabetes is most common in children. It is also called insulin-dependent diabetes. In this diabetes, the pancreas cells are damaged which are responsible for producing insulin. This happens when pancreas is attacked by antibodies. In recent decades, the occurrence of type 2 diabetes has intensified to an epidemic extents. This chronic disease shows significant increase in morbidity and mortality rate from the past. The two major effects of Type 2 diabetes are increased insulin resistance in liver and impaired β-cell function.

The diabetes dataset used in this case study is based on a population of women from Pima Indian heritage living near Phoenix, Arizona in 1990 and with minimum age of 21 years. This population has been under constant observation by the National Institute of Diabetes and Digestive and Kidney Diseases since 1965 due to high prevalence of diabetes. The dataset is used to predict whether a patient has diabetes or not, based on their diagnostic measurements. The instance in the dataset represents each female patient medical parameters along with their diabetes classification. The dataset comprises of 768 instances with 8 independent attributes: Pregnancies, PG Concentration, Diastolic BP, Tri Fold Thick, Serum Ins, BMI, DP Function and Age. Description of diabetes attributes are given in Table 13. Some attributes have a zero value which can be interpreted as noise in the data. The attributes PG Concentration, Diastolic BP, Tri Fold Thick, Serum Ins and BMI cannot have zero value. Data analytics with machine learning classification algorithms are the best suitable techniques in health care industry to analyse hidden knowledge from huge medical data (Sisodia, D., & Sisodia, D. S. 2018). It makes the diagnosis of disease convenient and fast. Applying machine learning techniques for classification in a diabetic dataset (Maniruzzaman, M. et.al 2017) helps in describing a population which have high probability of suffering from diabetes(Ali, A. et.al 2020).

Description of the attributes belongs to diabetes dataset are given in Table 13

Table 13. Description of attributes in diabetes dataset

Attribute	Description	Type	Mean	Range
Pregnancies	Number of times pregnant	Integer	3.845	0-17
PG Concentration	Plasma glucose concentration a 2 hours in an oral glucose tolerance test	Integer	120.895	0-199
Diastolic BP	Diastolic blood pressure (mm Hg)	Integer	69.105	0-122
Tri Fold Thick	Triceps skin fold thickness (mm)	Integer	20.536	0-99
Serum Ins	2-Hour serum insulin (mu U/ml)	Integer	79.799	0-846
BMI	Body mass index (weight in kg/(height in m)^2)	Decimal	31.993	0-67.1
DP Function	Diabetes pedigree function	Decimal	0.472	0.078-2.42
Age	Age (years)	Integer	33.241	21-81
Diabetes	Class variable (0 or 1)	Boolean	-	False500 (65.1%) True 268 (34.9%)

Implementation of K-Nearest Neighbour on *Diabetes* dataset

The following packages and libraries of python were used for applying KNN classifier, training test split, reading dataset, plotting graph and calculating classification report, confusion matrix and accuracy:

```
import pandas as pd
import matplotlib.pyplot as plt
from sklearn.neighbors import KNeighborsClassifier
from sklearn.metrics import classification_report, confusion_matrix,
    accuracy_score
from sklearn.model_selection import train_test_split
```
Commands used to read the dataset into dataframe **df** and applying training-test split of **80-20**

```
df = pd.read_csv('diabetes.csv')
X=df.iloc[:,0:7]
y=df.iloc[:,8]
Xtrain, Xtest, ytrain, ytest = train_test_split(X, y, test_size=0.20,
                                 random_state=0)
```

To generate the KNN classifier with **K** neighbours, distance measure '**Manhattan**', weight as '**uniform**' or '**distance**' to neighbouring points as explained in section 4.3 and predicting classification (**ypredmanh**) for test set data(**Xtest**) as after fitting the learning model on training data (**Xtrain, Ytrain**) was done using python commands:

```
classifier_manh = KNeighborsClassifier(n_neighbors = K, metric=
                  'manhattan', weights ='uniform')
classifier_manh.fit(Xtrain, ytrain)
ypredmanh = classifier_manh.predict(Xtest)
```

To check the accuracy of KNN classifier with this diabetes training test split dataset, python support various performance measure functions accuracy_score, confusion_ matrix and classification_report giving precision, recall and F1-score.

```
accuracy_manh=accuracy_score(ypredmanh, ytest)*100
confusion_matrix(ytest,ypredmanh)
classification_report(ytest,ypredmanh)
```

Graphically, plotting the line graph of accuracy scores against K values for weight as uniform as well as distance using python library panda and pyplot, can be done by building dataframe **curve_manh** with list **acc_val_manh** of accuracy scores stored as column **acc_manhatta_nuniform** and index as **K.**

```
curve_manh=pd.DataFrame(acc_val_manh,columns=
           ['acc_manhattan_uniform'])
curve_manh.index.name='k'
a=curvemanh.plot(title='Accuracy with Manhattan weight=
  uniform',color='red')
a.set_ylabel("Accuracy score weight=uniform")
```

To plot the both graphs on one plane, python gca() function is used to get current axis on which all the graphs have to be shown together.

```
a=curve_manh.plot(kind='line',color='red',linewidth=3,title='Accuracy
                  Manhattan with weight=uniform and distance')
a.set_ylabel("Accuracy score")
ax = plt.gca()
```

RESULT AND DISCUSSIONS

The k-nearest neighbour classifier is applied to diabetes dataset with distance metric 'Manhattan'. There are two possible predicted classes of diabetes: "Healthy" and "Sick". If we were predicting the presence of a disease, "Healthy" indicates patient don't have the disease and "Sick" indicates patient is under a high risk of having disease. The dataset is applied with 80%-20% training-test split function.

Table 14. Performance Measure for KNN Classifiers on diabetes dataset

K	Weight = 'Uniform'				Weight = 'Distance'			
	Accuracy	Confusion Matrix	Precision	Recall	Accuracy	Confusion Matrix	Precision	Recall
1	64.94	[80 27] [27 20]	0.75	0.75	64.94	[80 27] [27 20]	0.75	0.75
3	75.97	[92 15] [22 25]	0.81	0.86	75.97	[92 15] [22 25]	0.81	0.86
10	80.52	[100 7] [23 24]	0.81	0.93	75.97	[93 14] [23 24]	0.80	0.87
16	79.22	[97 10] [22 25]	0.82	0.91	80.52	[98 9] [21 26]	0.82	0.92
30	77.27	[96 11] [24 23]	0.80	0.90	77.92	[96 11] [24 23]	0.81	0.90

Figure 15. Graph showing Accuracy Score with different value of k

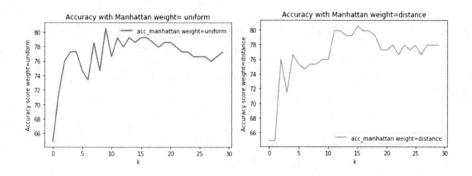

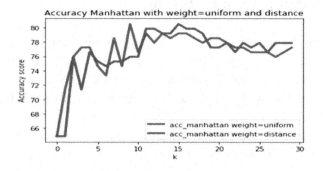

Table 14 and graphs (Figure 15) clearly shows how accurately the KNN classification algorithm classify the healthy and sick patients with different values of k (number of neighbouring points). The different number of neighbouring points (k) considered for classification effects the accuracy of the learning model. The value of k is taken from 1 to 30 and classification accuracy with healthy patient precision and recall is observed. Precision parameter tells that about the ratio of how many instances are relevant among the retrieved instances, whereas recall denote the ratio of the total amount of relevant instances that were actually selected. The minimum classification accuracy observed is around 65% at k = 1, which also signify theoretically that taking only one neighbouring point may mislead by allotting wrong category to the test data point. This diabetes dataset shows classification accuracy of more than 80% in both cases:

1. When distance is measured from 16 neighbouring points with weights as the inverse of their distance.
2. When distance is measured from 10 neighbouring points with uniform weight irrespective of their distance.

KNN Classifier with Uniform Weights (k=10):

The classifier made a total of 154 predictions that is 154 patients were being tested for the presence of diabetes. The classifier predicted 123 "Healthy" and 31 "Sick" patients out of 154. In reality, 107 patients in the test data do not have the disease, and 47 patients have disease. The values of confusion matrix at k =10, distance metric 'Manhattan' and weights as 'uniform' to neighbouring points are interpreted as shown in table 15.

Table 15. Confusion matrix interpretation

True positives (TP)	100	100 instances out of 154 test instance are correctly classified as 'Healthy'.
False positives (FP)	23	23 instances are actually belong to Sick category but wrongly categorized as 'Healthy'
False negatives (FN)	7	7 instances are actually belong to 'Healthy' but wrongly categorized as 'Sick'
True negatives (TN)	24	24 instances are correctly classified as 'Sick'

Using these Confusion matrix values, the performance of KNN Classifier on diabetes dataset with weights as 'uniform' is calculated as shown in Table 16.

KNN Classifier with Distance Weights (k=16):

The classifier made a total of 154 predictions that is 154 patients were being tested for the presence of diabetes. The classifier predicted 119 "Healthy" and 35 "Sick" patients out of 154. In reality, 107 patients in the test data do not have the disease, and 47 patients have disease. The values of confusion matrix at k =16, distance metric 'Manhattan' with weights as 'distance' to neighbouring points are interpreted as shown in Table 17:

Using these Confusion matrix values, the performance of KNN Classifier on diabetes dataset with weights as 'distance' is calculated as shown in Table 18.

Table 16. Performance of KNN classifier on diabetes dataset

Measure	Formula	Value
Accuracy	$\dfrac{(TP+TN)}{(P+N)}=\dfrac{(100+24)}{154}$	0.8051
Misclassification/Error Rate	$\dfrac{(FP+FN)}{P+N}=\dfrac{(7+23)}{154}$	0.19
Recall (True Positive Rate)	$\dfrac{TP}{(TP+FN)}=\dfrac{100}{107}$	0.93
Fall-out (False Positive Rate)	$\dfrac{FP}{FP+TN}=\dfrac{23}{47}$	0.49
Specificity(True Negative Rate)	$\dfrac{TN}{(TN+FP)}=\dfrac{24}{47}$	0.51
Precision	$\dfrac{TP}{(TP+FP)}=\dfrac{100}{123}$	0.81
Prevalence	$\dfrac{(TP+FN)}{(P+N)}=\dfrac{107}{154}$	0.69
F1-Score	$2*\dfrac{((precision*recall))}{(precision+recall))}=2*\dfrac{(0.93*0.81)}{(0.93+0.81)}$	0.87

Table 17. Confusion matrix interpretation

True positives (TP)	98	98 instances out of 154 test instance are correctly classified as 'Healthy'.
False positives (FP)	21	21 instances are actually belong to Sick category but wrongly categorized as 'Healthy'
False negatives (FN)	9	9 instances are actually belong to 'Healthy' but wrongly categorized as 'Sick'
True negatives (TN)	26	26 instances are correctly classified as 'Sick'

CONCLUSION

Now-a-days, challenges faced by health care sector can be efficiently tackled with the advanced machines learning and predictive modelling algorithms. These algorithms with data analytics techniques take care of inaccurate, missing and duplication of patient e-records and then extract interesting patterns from the patients data recorded in hospitals. Several diseases can be identified perfectly before it causes severe damage to body and proper medication can be suggested by the doctor. Many machine learning algorithms make use of collected e-patient records with images to mine hidden knowledge from it accurately. Doctors may use these mined rules for research on varying symptoms of chronic diseases. Doctors and medical equipment manufacturing companies are able to discern cost effective improved equipment solutions for current patients.

Table 18. Performance of KNN classifier on diabetes dataset

Measure	Formula	Value
Accuracy	$\dfrac{(TP+TN)}{(P+N)} = \dfrac{(98+26)}{154}$	0.8051
Misclassification/Error Rate	$\dfrac{(FP+FN)}{P+N} = \dfrac{(9+21)}{154}$	0.19
Recall (True Positive Rate)	$\dfrac{TP}{(TP+FN)} = \dfrac{98}{107}$	0.92
Fall-out (False Positive Rate)	$\dfrac{FP}{FP+TN} = \dfrac{21}{47}$	0.45
Specificity(True Negative Rate)	$\dfrac{TN}{(TN+FP)} = \dfrac{26}{47}$	0.55
Precision	$\dfrac{TP}{(TP+FP)} = \dfrac{98}{119}$	0.82
Prevalence	$\dfrac{(TP+FN)}{(P+N)} = \dfrac{107}{154}$	0.69
F1-Score	$2 * \dfrac{((precision * recall))}{(precision + recall))} = 2 * \dfrac{(0.92 * 0.82)}{(0.92 + 0.82)}$	0.87

Detection of diabetes mellitus at its early stages is one of the most challenging real-world medical problem. In this chapter, various machine learning algorithms of unsupervised and supervised approach were discussed with the appropriate python libraries. Out of these many algorithms may give accurate results in the prediction of disease like diabetes. In depth study of various machine learning classification algorithms shows that each requires certain specific and important parameters to implement on dataset. Also, each algorithms classification strength can be assessed using various accuracy measures. Supervised learning classification algorithm K-Nearest Neighbour is applied on Pima Indians Diabetes Database. Experimental results conclude that simple KNN algorithm achieve an accuracy of 80.51% at *k* equal to 10 whereas the weighted KNN achieves the same accuracy at *k* equal to 16. In future, these machine learning classification algorithms can be used to predict or diagnose other diseases. This chapter can be enhanced further by applying other machine learning prediction algorithms for the automation of diabetes analysis.

REFERENCES

Akbani, R., Kwek, S., & Japkowicz, N. (2004, September). Applying support vector machines to imbalanced datasets. In *European conference on machine learning* (pp. 39-50). Springer. 10.1007/978-3-540-30115-8_7

Alberti, K. G. M. M., & Zimmet, P. Z. (1998). Definition, diagnosis and classification of diabetes mellitus and its complications. Part 1: Diagnosis and classification of diabetes mellitus. Provisional report of a WHO consultation. *Diabetic Medicine*, *15*(7), 539–553. doi:10.1002/(SICI)1096-9136(199807)15:7<539::AID-DIA668>3.0.CO;2-S PMID:9686693

Ali, A., Alrubei, M. A., Hassan, L. F. M., Al-Ja'afari, M. A., & Abdulwahed, S. H. (2020). DIABETES DIAGNOSIS BASED ON KNN. *IIUM Engineering Journal*, *21*(1), 175–181. doi:10.31436/iiumej.v21i1.1206

Bhardwaj, R., Nambiar, A. R., & Dutta, D. (2017, July). A study of machine learning in healthcare. In *2017 IEEE 41st Annual Computer Software and Applications Conference (COMPSAC)* (Vol. 2, pp. 236-241). IEEE. 10.1109/COMPSAC.2017.164

Bhatia, P. (2019). *Data Mining and Data Warehousing: Principles and Practical Techniques*. Cambridge University Press. doi:10.1017/9781108635592

Callahan, A., & Shah, N. H. (2017). Machine learning in healthcare. In *Key Advances in Clinical Informatics* (pp. 279–291). Academic Press. doi:10.1016/B978-0-12-809523-2.00019-4

Deo, R., & Panigrahi, S. (2019, November). Performance Assessment of Machine Learning Based Models for Diabetes Prediction. In *2019 IEEE Healthcare Innovations and Point of Care Technologies (HI-POCT)* (pp. 147-150). IEEE.

Flach, P. (2012). *Machine learning: the art and science of algorithms that make sense of data*. Cambridge University Press. doi:10.1017/CBO9780511973000

Ghassemi, M., Naumann, T., Schulam, P., Beam, A. L., & Ranganath, R. (2018). *Opportunities in machine learning for healthcare*. arXiv preprint arXiv:1806.00388

Gianfrancesco, M. A., Tamang, S., Yazdany, J., & Schmajuk, G. (2018). Potential biases in machine learning algorithms using electronic health record data. *JAMA Internal Medicine*, *178*(11), 1544–1547. doi:10.1001/jamainternmed.2018.3763 PMID:30128552

Gopal, M. (2018). *Applied Machine Learning*. McGraw-Hill Education.

Grus, J. (2019). *Data science from scratch: first principles with python*. O'Reilly Media.

Induja, S. N., & Raji, C. G. (2019, March). Computational Methods for Predicting Chronic Disease in Healthcare Communities. In *2019 International Conference on Data Science and Communication (IconDSC)* (pp. 1-6). IEEE. 10.1109/IconDSC.2019.8817044

Jayalakshmi, T., & Santhakumaran, A. (2010, February). A novel classification method for diagnosis of diabetes mellitus using artificial neural networks. In *2010 International Conference on Data Storage and Data Engineering* (pp. 159-163). IEEE. 10.1109/DSDE.2010.58

Jiang, F., Jiang, Y., Zhi, H., Dong, Y., Li, H., Ma, S., Wang, Y., Dong, Q., Shen, H., & Wang, Y. (2017). Artificial intelligence in healthcare: past, present and future. *Stroke and Vascular Neurology, 2*(4), 230-243.

Kaur, H., & Kumari, V. (2018). *Predictive modelling and analytics for diabetes using a machine learning approach.* Applied Computing and Informatics. doi:10.1016/j.aci.2018.12.004

Kavakiotis, I., Tsave, O., Salifoglou, A., Maglaveras, N., Vlahavas, I., & Chouvarda, I. (2017). Machine learning and data mining methods in diabetes research. *Computational and Structural Biotechnology Journal, 15*, 104–116. doi:10.1016/j.csbj.2016.12.005 PMID:28138367

Kotsiantis, S. B., Zaharakis, I., & Pintelas, P. (2007). Supervised machine learning: A review of classification techniques. *Emerging Artificial Intelligence Applications in Computer Engineering, 160*, 3-24.

Kourou, K., Exarchos, T. P., Exarchos, K. P., Karamouzis, M. V., & Fotiadis, D. I. (2015). Machine learning applications in cancer prognosis and prediction. *Computational and Structural Biotechnology Journal, 13*, 8–17. doi:10.1016/j.csbj.2014.11.005 PMID:25750696

Kumari, V. A., & Chitra, R. (2013). Classification of diabetes disease using support vector machine. *International Journal of Engineering Research and Applications, 3*(2), 1797–1801.

Maniruzzaman, M., Kumar, N., Abedin, M. M., Islam, M. S., Suri, H. S., El-Baz, A. S., & Suri, J. S. (2017). Comparative approaches for classification of diabetes mellitus data: Machine learning paradigm. *Computer Methods and Programs in Biomedicine, 152*, 23–34. doi:10.1016/j.cmpb.2017.09.004 PMID:29054258

Manning, C. D., Raghavan, P., & Schütze, H. (2008). *Introduction to information retrieval.* Cambridge university press. doi:10.1017/CBO9780511809071

Ngiam, K. Y., & Khor, W. (2019). Big data and machine learning algorithms for health-care delivery. *The Lancet Oncology, 20*(5), e262–e273. doi:10.1016/S1470-2045(19)30149-4 PMID:31044724

Nwiabu, N. D., & John, A. O. (2019). Model for Evaluating Hospital Management Performance using Artificial Neural Network. *International Journal of Computer Science and Mathematical Theory, 5*(1), 30–43.

Panch, T., Szolovits, P., & Atun, R. (2018). Artificial intelligence, machine learning and health systems. *Journal of Global Health, 8*(2), 020303. doi:10.7189/jogh.08.020303 PMID:30405904

Saru, S., & Subashree, S. (2019). Analysis and Prediction of Diabetes Using Machine Learning. *International Journal of Emerging Technology and Innovative Engineering, 5*(4).

Sendak, M., Gao, M., Nichols, M., Lin, A., & Balu, S. (2019). Machine Learning in Health Care: A Critical Appraisal of Challenges and Opportunities. *EGEMS (Washington, DC), 7*(1), 1. doi:10.5334/egems.287 PMID:30705919

Shahid, N., Rappon, T., & Berta, W. (2019). Applications of artificial neural networks in health care organizational decision-making: A scoping review. *PLoS One, 14*(2). doi:10.1371/journal.pone.0212356 PMID:30779785

Sisodia, D., & Sisodia, D. S. (2018). Prediction of diabetes using classification algorithms. *Procedia Computer Science*, *132*, 1578–1585. doi:10.1016/j.procs.2018.05.122

Sohail, M. N., Ren, J., & Uba Muhammad, M. (2019). A Euclidean Group Assessment on Semi-Supervised Clustering for Healthcare Clinical Implications Based on Real-Life Data. *International Journal of Environmental Research and Public Health*, *16*(9), 1581. doi:10.3390/ijerph16091581 PMID:31064121

Tan, P. N., Steinbach, M., & Kumar, V. (2016). *Introduction to data mining*. Pearson Education India.

Valsamis, E. M., Ricketts, D., Husband, H., & Rogers, B. A. (2019). Segmented linear regression models for assessing change in retrospective studies in healthcare. *Computational and Mathematical Methods in Medicine*. PMID:30805023

Wu, H., Lu, Z., Pan, L., Xu, R., & Jiang, W. (2009, August). An improved apriori-based algorithm for association rules mining. In *2009 sixth international conference on fuzzy systems and knowledge discovery* (Vol. 2, pp. 51-55). IEEE. 10.1109/FSKD.2009.193

Zhu, C., Idemudia, C. U., & Feng, W. (2019). Improved logistic regression model for diabetes prediction by integrating PCA and K-means techniques. *Informatics in Medicine Unlocked*, *17*, 100179. doi:10.1016/j.imu.2019.100179

Zou, Q., Qu, K., Luo, Y., Yin, D., Ju, Y., & Tang, H. (2018). Predicting diabetes mellitus with machine learning techniques. *Frontiers in Genetics*, *9*, 515. doi:10.3389/fgene.2018.00515 PMID:30459809

Zufferey, D., Hofer, T., Hennebert, J., Schumacher, M., Ingold, R., & Bromuri, S. (2015). Performance comparison of multi-label learning algorithms on clinical data for chronic diseases. *Computers in Biology and Medicine*, *65*, 34–43. doi:10.1016/j.compbiomed.2015.07.017 PMID:26275389

KEY TERMS AND DEFINITIONS

Accuracy: It is the ratio of number of accurate predictions produced by classification algorithm to the total number of input data samples.

Artificial Neural Network: Artificial neural network is a collection of connected input/output units called neurons. Each connection has a weight associated with it to develop and test computational analysis of neurons. This neural network learns by adjusting these weights iteratively till it is able to predict the correct class label of the input data.

Classification: Classification is the scientific procedure for predicting the class label or category of given test data objects. Classification is also a task of predictive modelling in which a mapping function is approximated using inputted feature variables to produce output target variable.

Clustering: Clustering is a type of unsupervised learning technique where data objects are placed into different collections called clusters, based on their degree of dissimilarity. All like data objects are a part of the same cluster.

Confusion Matrix: A confusion matrix is a two-dimensional table depicting summary of classification or prediction outcomes produced by applying classification algorithm on the given dataset. The accurate and inaccurate predictions produced with respect to each class are summarized with their count values. It gives the insight of the errors being made during classification process by a classifier.

Data Science: It is a science of multiple disciplines used for exploring knowledge from data using complex scientific algorithms and methods.

Diabetes Miletus: It is a chronic disease in which the body's capability to produce or react to the insulin hormone is reduced. This effects absorption of carbohydrates and also raised the glucose level in the blood.

F-Score: F-score is a statistical measure which expresses the balance between the precision and the recall. It considers both the precision p and the recall r of the test to compute accuracy. It is the harmonic mean of the precision and recall with its best value at 1 and worst at 0.

Machine Learning: Machine learning is a scientific approach to analyse available data using algorithms and statistical models to accomplish a specific task by utilizing the patterns evolved.

Naive Bayes: It is a classification method based on Bayes' Theorem using an assumption that predictor variables are independent to each other. Naive Bayes classifier believes that the existence of one feature in a class is not surely tells about the existence of any other feature.

Precision: It is an accuracy measure calculated as the ratio of number of true positives predictions to the total of number of true positives and the number of false positives predictions. True positive cases are those cases which the classifier correctly labelled a data point as positive whereas false positive predictions are cases in which a data point is incorrectly labelled as positive by the classifier that are actually negative.

Recall: It is an accuracy measure calculated as ratio of the number of true positives predictions to the total of number of true positives and the number of false negatives. True positives cases are those cases where data point is classified as positive by the classifier that actually are positive and false negatives are cases with such data points that are identified as negative by classifier but actually are positive.

Chapter 13
Opportunistic Edge Computing Architecture for Smart Healthcare Systems

Nivethitha V.
National Institute of Technology, Puducherry, India

Aghila G.
National Institute of Technology, Puducherry, India

ABSTRACT

Some of the largest global industries that is driving smart city environments are anywhere and anytime health monitoring applications. Smart healthcare systems need to be more preventive and responsive as they deal with sensitive data. Even though cloud computing provides solutions to the smart healthcare applications, the major challenge imposed on cloud computing is how could the centralized traditional cloud computing handle voluminous data. The existing models may encounter problems related to network resource utilization, overheads in network response time, and communication latency. As a solution to these problems, edge-oriented computing has emerged as a new computing paradigm through localized computing. Edge computing expands the compute, storage, and networking capabilities to the edge of the network which will respond to the above-mentioned issues. Based on cloud computing and edge computing, in this chapter an opportunistic edge computing architecture is introduced for smart provisioning of healthcare data.

1. INTRODUCTION

The evolution of the Internet of Things and technology has led to the unbelievable growth in the deployment of smart sensors, actuators, and low power consuming hardware chips, smart devices in various fields like telecommunication, manufacturing, aerospace, smart homes, smart city etc .Smart health care systems are one of the important fields that are witnessing this change (Sodhro, Pirbhulal, & Sangaiah, 2018). This development of smart environment creates a great burden on the network due to the enor-

DOI: 10.4018/978-1-7998-3053-5.ch013

mous data transmission. This creates a challenge for the existing cloud infrastructure to provide timely service to the end users(Zhang et al., 2015). The burden that is put on the data processing and analytics on the cloud computing paved the way for the development of new computing paradigm that brings the compute, storage, and processing to the edge of the network that are closer to the user premises. The method of computing at the edge of the network is called "Edge Computing" (Yu et al., 2017).

According to the predictions that are made by (Koop et al., 2008), the present hospital-based health care systems will take a drift to hospital and home balanced by the year of 2020 and will eventually lead to home-based by the year 2030. To make this happen new architectures, technologies and new computing paradigms should be developed specifically to health care domain. Sending the data for computation to the cloud involves latency delay and health care applications are not tolerant of this delay. Hence Edge computing will provide solutions to this data intensive health monitoring system by reducing the network communication for data transfer, storage issues and latency. This chapter demonstrates the use of Edge computing wherein, the real-time data can be monitored, stored and later can be sent to other storages or clouds if required

Contribution of Edge Computing To Data Science and Analytics

Data science and analytics uses various methods, algorithms, and machine learning models to gain knowledge about the data that are analysed. Edge Computing has evolved to overcome many challenges and issues of cloud computing. They provide a way to make analysis and computation at the IOT domain level and at a level that are one step next to the IOT plane. Edge computing enables different stake holders and systems to perform analytics near to the users with the available resources. Developing various analytics and machine learning models at the edge level may reduce the computation time, response time, latency, bandwidth consumption and improve the quality of service.

Role of Edge Computing in Health Care Domain

The technology advancement in today world has created a need for anywhere and anytime responsive service to the end users. The health care monitoring systems are in no way less and be the most needed of the hour. Now a days the health care monitoring systems enable the humans to wear smart watches and trackers that are in charge of continuously monitoring the human health in terms of heart beat, blood pressure, diabetic, body temperature, footsteps covered, calories of food consumed etc. These data are continuously streamed to the cloud storage where data analytics and processing are done to make inferences and predict the health conditions of the individuals. These health care data are data intensive and they are sensitive in nature.

(i) The health care monitoring systems should be quick, responsive as they deal with intensive data. Any delayed response to the end users of these services might lead to fatal situations. For example, a delayed alert generated for a patient whose heart beats are abnormal might give a delayed assistance to the patient and increase the complexity.

(ii) Data gathered and analysed from e-health records, sensor equipment's, medical sensors, devices, and smartphones are analysed over the edge computing. This analysis enhances the decision-making power of healthcare professionals, and helps patients have an active role in managing their personal health. The health care monitoring systems should be reliable and trustworthy to handle the data

(iii) The health care monitoring systems should provide a secure means of analysis, processing and storage. They should preserve the user's privacy and integrity of the data by providing secure mechanisms. Edge computing provides a secure localized computing and preserves the user data

(iv) The health care monitoring systems should be cost effective and be affordable by the end users who can use them for wellbeing of one's life. The edge computing can reduce the cost of transmission of data, bandwidth consumption and network resources. Thus providing a cost effective provisioning of data.

Bringing the Computation and Analytics to the Edge

The edge computing is a new concept in the evolution of computing paradigm. It brings the service and utilities of cloud computing closer to the end user and enables fast processing and less response time (Khan, Ahmed, Hakak, Yaqoob, & Ahmed, 2019). The developing Health care industry that are connected to internet requires a delay resistant and quick response time. Edge computing gives promising solutions as they support mobility of the users, location aware, low latency and close proximity to the users.

The terminology that are used in Edge computing are:

Table 1. Terminology used in edge computing

Terms	Definition
Edge (Khan et al., 2019)	Any device or entity closer to the user, sensors having a computing capacity.
Edge device (Shi, Cao, Zhang, Li, & Xu, 2016)	Any device that produce /consume data
Edge gateway(Yousefpour et al., 2019)	It is the window that separates the edge computing processing and the large network environment
Edge Server (Yousefpour et al., 2019)	Edge server is a computer that exists at the logical extreme or "edge" of a network. Edge servers will connect with multiple different networks.

Edge Computing Architecture

Edge computing moves the data processing and analytics, applications, and services from the far end cloud servers to the edge of a network. The service providers and application developers, end users can use the Edge computing systems for better quality of service and optimal usage of resources. Edge computing is characterized in terms of less energy consumption, less communication latency, high bandwidth, and real-time access to the network data that can be used by several applications.

Edge computing architecture can be devised into three planes

(i) **IOT Device Plane**: This plane has all the smart IOT devices like the mobile phones, smart sensors and actuators, smart wearables, embedded systems, vehicles and any Edge device that produce data and consume data. These edge devices stream data continuously to the cloud for analysis and storage.

(ii) **Edge Server Plane**: This part of the edge computing architecture comprises the gateways, switches edge servers and small data centres that has some constrained memory and processing capability.

(iii) **Cloud Plane:** The cloud plane possess the cloud computing data centres and servers that are able to perform large big analytics, processing and storage.

The Edge computing allows the application developers and service providers to make the computing possible at the edge server plane and thus reducing the burden imposed on the existing cloud architectures.

Characteristics of Edge Computing

Bandwidth Utilization

Bandwidth describes the maximum data transfer rate of a network or Internet connection. Bringing the computational and storage to the edge of the network can reduce the bandwidth consumption and thus reduce the data transfer rates(Hassan, Gillani, Ahmed, Yaqoob, & Imran, 2018). Optimal use of the bandwidth resources led to the cost effective provisioning of the data.

Latency

Latency refers to delays that is incurred during transmitting or processing data, which can be caused by varied reasons. Edge computing addresses this issue for many data intensive applications and provide a quicker service delivery to the end users.

Response Time

As the computation, analytics, data mining, data pre-processing and some decision making are done at the edge level of the network that are in close proximity to the user, the response time of any service or data access is very less(Hassan et al., 2018) . When compared to the centralized cloud computing, the quality of service in terms of response time is much better.

Energy Consumption

The transmission of the data from the user devices to the far end cloud servers incurs a lot of bandwidth energy(Zhang et al., 2015), thus edge computing develops new architectural models and solutions that reduces the usage and consumption of network resources like bandwidth and thus reduce the server overheads by reducing the load of the central cloud servers.

Storage

Storage at the edge is the methods capture and keep information at the edge of the network, as close to the originating source as possible(Jalali, Hinton, Ayre, Alpcan, & Tucker, 2016). The storage capacity of the edge is minimal when compared to storage capacity of the central data centres. Thus all data cannot be stored near to the sources. Storage at the end aims to provide intermittent and fast connectivity access to data that are needed for computing. Thus data that are needed indefinitely are archived at the edge of the network.

Server Overhead

In Edge computing, the server overhead is relatively low when compared with the overhead that is caused to the servers of the central cloud(Jalali et al., 2016). In edge computing the load is distributed among the servers and they have parallel processing of data unlike cloud servers where all the client request are addressed. Communication overhead is also reduced as the data originating from the source can be processed at the edge instead of communicating them to the central cloud.

2. LITERATURE REVIEW

In this research(Ray, Dash, & De, 2019), the authors presents a taxonomical classification of edge computing and the industrial use cases of edge computing paradigm. A novel edge-IoT based architecture for e-healthcare named as EH-IoT and developed a demo test-bed. EH-IoT architecture encompasses three key modules such as, (i) Apache Edgent engine, (ii) embedded hardware-based sensing unit and (iii) IoT-based cloud repository. The experimental results showed results towards reducing the dependency over IoT cloud for processing, analytics and storage facility.

Md. Golam Rabiul Alam et al., proposed an Edge-of-Things (EoT)-based healthcare services(Dubey et al., 2015). In this paper an optimized selection of virtual machines (VMs) of edge and cloud computing that are offered by service providers is proposed. A dynamic pricing model for an EoT health service is considered by the EoT broker for optimal usage of VM in an EoT environment.

Considering the emergency situations of patients,(Chen, Li, Hao, Qian, & Humar, 2018)an Edge-Cognitive-Computing-based (ECC-based) smart-healthcare system is proposed. This system monitors the physical health of the end users by the use of cognitive computing. Based on the health risk grade of each user, the system uses an optimal resource allocation in the edge computing network. The experimental results show cased that ECC-based healthcare system enhances the user experience and optimizes the computing resources.

To enable awareness and prevention of Chikungunya disease a new paradigm in Smart Health is devised in (Rani, Ahmed, & Shah, 2019). Information about causes of growth of mosquitoes is collected and transmitted to the cloud. This approach is validated at the bottom layer of the network and data is transmitted to the cloud with the help of edge nodes. In this framework, edge servers are deployed at the predefined locations in the city. They are responsible for collecting the data from the users and pre-processing it before communicating to the cloud. They trace the location and will send it for further analysis at cloud.

A wearable sensor-based activity prediction system (Uddin, 2019)was developed to facilitate edge computing in smart healthcare system. In this work, the activity prediction is enabled by Recurrent Neural Network (RNN) on an edge device (personal computer or laptop). GPU of the edge device has been utilized to accelerate the computational speed. Healthcare services are enhanced by using the RNN for real-time analysing and predicting human activities combined with newest technologies IOT, Edge of Things, and Cloud of Things.

The research (Subahi, 2019)work presents a conceptual architectural design, for the IoT Edge based healthcare management system. The nodes located closer to the user are called edges. In this architecture these edge nodes are responsible for getting data from smart sensors and IoT devices. This data is been processed and analysed at local premises, to infer an make decisions on unusual health patterns and also reports to the health service providers in the network to respond.

Prabal Verma et al., (Verma & Sood, 2018) proposed the remote patient health monitoring in smart homes by using the concept of fog computing at the smart gateway . The proposed model uses advanced techniques and services, such as embedded data mining, distributed storage, and notification services at the edge of the network. Event triggering-based data transmission methodology is adopted to process the patient's real-time data at fog layer.

In this Paper(Rahmani et al., 2018), the authors determine the feasible positions of the gateways at the edge of the network and these gateways offer high –level services for the data that are transferred to the cloud. Thus Smart e-Health Gateway is proposed which offers a local data processing, local storage and real- time data processing. The Smart Health Gateway called UT-GATE is implemented in an IoT-based Early Warning health monitoring to show the competence and significance of the system in addressing medical situations.

The authors (Lin, Pankaj, & Wang, 2018)proposed an edge computing framework for health care systems. They developed an efficient task offloading and resource allocation schemes for edge of thing. A fruit fly optimization algorithm is proposed to leverage the data analytics at the edge level for further processing and analysis. The novel FOTO algorithm that is proposed reduces the energy consumption, minimizes the task completion time and optimal cost for the data centre when unloading the jobs from smart devices to the cloudlet. This algorithm has been applied in smart health care systems using Edge-of-things computing.

In (Greco, Ritrovato, & Xhafa, 2019) an architectural solution, based on big data technologies to perform real-time analysis of streaming data that are obtained from the wearable sensors. The proposed architecture is defined by four abstract layers: a sensing layer, a pre-processing layer (Raspberry Pi), a cluster processing layer and a persistence layer. The proposed architecture taking into account of Medical Things situation, the data collected from sensing devices make it possible for the system to rise alarms or initiate automatic reactions whenever an emergency medical situation arises.

Thus the recent related works of edge computing in the health care domain depicts the advantages of localized computing in latency intensive applications. Even though edge computing provides solution to many problems faced by cloud. Scalability, energy consumption of edge servers, dynamic adaptation as per the needs of the health care services is challenging and still there is a need for resource aware and cost effective computing model.

3. NEED FOR OPPORTUNISTIC EDGE COMPUTING

Unlike edge computing, opportunistic are centrally managed networks which provide better quality of services to the applications. OEC architectures allows the dynamic creation of resource pools at the user end as per the need and requirement of the application(Casadei et al., 2019). The need of opportunistic edge computing in smart health care domain are as follows

1. The health monitoring systems are smart systems that deal with sensitive data and the applications should be delay resistant and be responsive. Processing and analysing the data at distributed environment may be a tedious method as the data has to collected and send to the distributed data

centres. This acquires a lot of network resources like bandwidth that may lead to communication latency, delayed responses and the end user may not be benefitted with the available resources.

2. To overcome the challenges of analysing data at the remote cloud, edge computing a hyper distributed computing paradigm came into existence. But there are many challenges that edge computing paradigm faces with respect to the health care domain. As the health care applications require continuous monitoring of patients, the static placement of edge servers and resources at the user end may not support the dynamically changing nature of the health care applications and addition to this the system has to be scalable also.

3. Due to the increasing demands of quick response and optimal use of resources, the analysis and processing of health care monitoring systems data will be deployed at edge level. Without a proper framework for amalgamating, orchestrating and allocation of the distributed resources a lot of available compute and storage resources may go in vain.

4. The health care applications need 24*7 services for which the data servers at the edge layer should be fully dedicated and available. The energy and the resource consumption in terms power backup, battery for the edge servers is a challenging problem. Thus scaling of the edge servers to meet the emergency needs of the health monitoring systems can be difficult. Alternate solutions like peering the neighbour resources and using opportunistic resources can be used.

4. OPPORTUNISTIC EDGE COMPUTING(OEC) IN SMART HEALTH CARE DOMAIN

The opportunistic edge computing tries to push the computing capability to the edge of the network unlike edge computing which locates the available resource pools at static pre-determined edge locations(Casadei et al., 2019). It tries to provide an instant access to the resources which are on demand by using the available resources and infrastructures. The main participants of the OEC models in figure 2 are (i) Resource owners (ii) Broker (iii) Service Providers (iv)End-users. The OEC broker is responsible for creating resource pools at the edge of the network using the resources contributed by the end user's. The resources pooled are not permanent. The broker module is responsible for managing the resources in the pool by leasing the resources for certain duration based on the demand and correspondingly incentives will be computed. If resources are withdrawn by resource owners before the completion of the leased duration then they are considered as less trust worthy and faulty resources. OEC based architectures benefits the health care applications in a major way as they can be deployed very close to the end users. The latency and communication, response time are reduced. They are auto scalable where the resources that are pooled is proportionally equivalent to the participating end users.

OEC Model

The OEC Model has 4 major participants

(i) *Resource Owners*: They are the ones who own the physical computing and storage resources for example the desktops, laptops, LAN's Mobiles. The broker leases the resources from the owners.

(ii) *Broker*: Brokers are responsible for managing the resource pools. They are responsible for making contracts with the resource owners and offers them to the service providers.

(iii) *Service Providers*: The Service providers lease the resources from the brokers and runs their application or services. The clients may also run their applications on the opportunistic edge clouds.

(iv) *End Users*: End users are those who the consumers of the services offered by the service providers.

Figure 1 gives a diagrammatic representation of the participants involved in OEC Model

Figure 1. Opportunistic edge computing Model

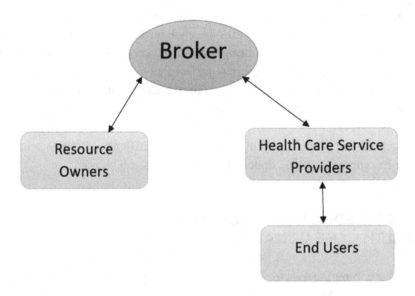

The development of health care monitoring systems and provisioning of the health care data is a challenging area. Many approaches have been proposed to efficiently process and provision the data. In this proposal, an Opportunistic Edge Computing is introduced for health care domain that gives a better response and efficient use of network resources. Considering the dynamic demands of the health care domain a new opportunistic edge architectural model for the smart provisioning of health care application data is proposed that overcomes the challenges of the traditional computing and edge computing models. The proposed architecture model provides an opportunity for processing and analysing data at the edge level by dynamically pooling the available resources thus overcoming the drawbacks of the traditional computing methods.

OEC Architectural Model for Health Care Monitoring

The main architectural elements of the OEC framework are the resource management module of the broker that is responsible for creating the pool of resources at the user end using the resources contributed by the participants. The service providers make use of the broker to run their health care applications that aims to provide fast and quick response to the requests made by the clients for health care services.

Figure 2 show cases the arrangement of OEC framework for health care monitoring of the systems into three layers

Figure 2. OEC Architecture for smart Health care Domain

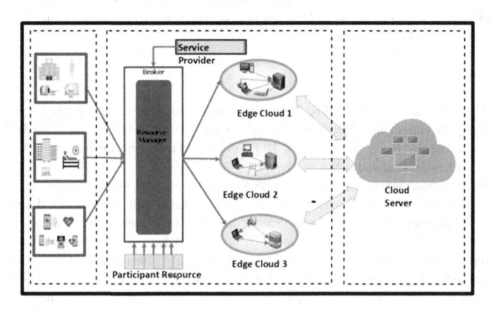

The opportunistic edge computing frame work proposed in this chapter gives to the broker the effort of building and managing the opportunistic edge cloud. In this architecture, the resources are contributed to the broker for computation by the participants and registered with the resource managers.

The OEC framework determines the characteristics of the resources and correspondingly create the virtualized resource units that can be allocated to the service providers to deploy the application. In OEC based health care systems a novel trust management scheme guarantees the broker-to-participant trust and determine how far the broker can rely on resources and infrastructures that are offered by the participants .This scheme allows the participants to take more informed and proper decisions taking into account expectations in terms of reliability, performance and availability

The three layered architecture can be detailed as follows

Medical Sensors Unit

This module is responsible for sensing and recording the health data like temperature, blood pressure, heart rate, sleep pattern from the end users. This data is communicated to the next level through the gateways by WIFI, ZigBee or Bluetooth for further analysis.

Edge Cloud Layer

The broker and its resource manager in the edge layer is responsible for handling the client requests. Based on the demand the resources are pooled and processing of the data is done. Edge clouds are constructed based on the availability of the resources. In this, each contributed and available resource OEC broker module is responsible for analysis of the type, availability, cost of usage, location and reliability The OEC broker also determines the demand for the resources and determine their incentives and pricing models for the resource owners and the service providers respectively. The service providers lend the resources from the brokers and run the application that provide inference on the sensed data. This layer provides higher level services like Data filtering, aggregation, Data pre-processing, Data mining, Decision making, local notifications.

Cloud Layer

The cloud layer is responsible for holding the details of the patients/ individual records that are updated periodically by the edge clouds. They possess the cloud data centres and takes care of the data storage, data analytics, data warehouse. The collected data is stored and represents the big data that are further involved in epidemiological and statics analysis

The OEC framework is in charge for resource monitoring which continuously observe the contributed resources and provide relevant information to the other modules. Lastly, the resource database keeps track of all the statistics, along with relevant information about the stake holders involved in this computing like the participants, the service providers /clients, request description and the allotted resources.

The proposed OEC architecture for health care monitoring solves the problem of static placement of edge servers and make it scalable as per the needs of the application. The resource that are available and contributed by the participants are also considered for the creation of resource pools. The architecture is cost efficient by reducing the needs for providing a continuous power backup and infrastructure needs. Though the opportunistic computing model is efficient in various aspects there are many challenges that has to be explored.

5. RESEARCH SCOPE

The opportunistic edge computing model enables to bring the cloud computing to the edge of the network. The dynamic nature of the edge cloud enables to scale as per the demands of the application but there are many challenges that has to be addressed. The research challenges that are associated with OEC framework are

Resource Management in Opportunistic Edge Computing

OEC resource management is a very challenging area as the resources that are involved in computation are not stable resources. They are dynamic in nature and are not permanent. They are not homogeneous and differ with processing capacity, duration of availability, speed and memory. So the major resource management challenges in this area are

- **Resource Orchestration and Monitoring**
  The health care domain application requires continuous monitoring and availability of resources for computation thus presenting reliable resources is the burden of the OEC resource management. The OEC architecture delegates the process of managing the resources and analysing the characteristics of the resources to the broker. The broker creates the virtualized resource units for processing of health care data based on the needs of the end user and service provider. The dynamic creation of resource pool and organizing the pools is very difficult as the resource availability vary with time.

Thus new orchestration techniques that could share the work of the broker making it a distributed approach should be developed.

- **Data Placement**

  Data placement is the technique of placing the needed or frequently accessed data near to the edge of the network for better response time and fast access of data. In health care applications, the main requirement is a delay resistant system as they deal with emergency situations. The resource pools are not stagnant and they are opportunistically created based on the needs of the service. The data placement approaches that are designed for the edge computing scenario (Li, Tang, Tang, & Luo, 2019) may not be efficient for the OEC framework. Thus data-placement algorithms with respect OEC framework has to be developed to enhance the users experience.

- **Resource Allocation and Scheduling**

  There are number of smart devices that are involved in monitoring the individual's health and they continuously stream data to the cloud for processing. With OEC framework, the data can be filtered and processed at the edge of the network. Scheduling the resources on unchanging topology is relatively easy when compared to resource allocation in a dynamic environment. The scheduling should consider more parameters like the device lifetime, availability, reliability, speed and time duration along with network parameters. Thus new scheduling and allocation schemes should be proposed that ensure the accessibility of the resources by the service providers.

Service Management

The research challenges that are associated with OEC architecture are

- **Building opportunistic edge clouds**

  As per changing needs of the health care application the OEC framework should be scalable to process the requests of the end users and improve the quality of service. To create resource pools resource and the characteristics of the resource should be analysed. The designing schemes should be able to discover the appropriate and available resources to involve in edge computing. As the health care application deal with sensitive data the resource should be carefully selected. New resource discovery schemes should be proposed for dynamically selecting the resources and devices for participation

- **Incentives**

  The participants who contribute the resources for service should be incentivized. Incentives can be either be budgetary or simple services to be offered to the participants who offer their resources. The incentives should be based on the demands for the particular services. A resource in high demand should be incentivized with higher prices and that with low demand with low pricing. More attractive incentive mechanism should be designed by the broker components of the OEC architecture to make more participants contribute resources.

- **Pricing Model**

   Pricing models determine the prices that are to be charged by the brokers for lending their resources to the service providers. The widely used pricing model 'Pay as you go' in cloud computing infrastructure may not be supportive for edge scenarios as the resources are limited and in high demand. Thus novel model for pricing has to be devised taking into consideration the OEC parameters of resource. They should consider the type of resource, reliability and availability over time.

Security and Privacy

Security concerns are the ones that have direct impact on the system performance. OEC resources has many challenging security issues as they deal with shared resources contributed by the participants. OEC framework should earn the trust of all the stake holders including the end user, resource owners and the service providers. The failure or withdrawal of any resource should not hamper the privacy of the user data. New security mechanisms has to be carefully designed to overcome the drawbacks of the issues that arise with OEC model.

Machine Learning in Edge Computing

Machine learning is currently widely used in a variety of applications. With the growing advancements in technology and Internet of things large amount of data are generated at the network edge. Machine Learning models are developed on this gathered data for classification, analysis, and forecast the future events. In OEC, machine learning models can be built on the edge cloud layer where some machine learning algorithms can be run on resource constrained environments to perform data filtering and data processing.

Federated Learning in Resource Constrained Edge Computing Systems

To analyse large amounts of data and gain useful facts for classification, and prediction, machine learning techniques are often applied. The machine learning model has the ability to learn or train the machine using the large set of data. The training is usually done on centralized environment. New machine learning models have been proposed that gathers data from different systems and train based on distributed approach. The main challenging part is to perform machine learning on resource constrained edge computing systems. To enable the distributed learning, the concept of federated learning came into existence.

Federated learning makes it possible to train the machine learning models while not transferring probably sensitive user data from devices or native deployments to a central server. The trained model can further be used to predict and discover new inference. This federated machine learning approach can be used or deployed on the OEC models for creating the resource pools by making appropriate classification based on the type of resources.

In addition they can be used to determine the user's preference or the content popularity for placing the needed content (data) at the edge of the network and improve the data access in OEC models.

This Machine learning approaches can further be improved to run on resource constrained edge devices for various application.

6. APPLICATION OF OEC MODEL IN REAL WORLD SCENARIOS

The various scenario of health care domain are as follows

Scenario A: Smart Health Care System Considering the Emergency Situation in Hospitals / Home

In hospitals/homes consider a scenario where patients/ individuals are monitored continuously. Various parameters such as heartbeat, blood pressure, heart rate etc. are sensed by different sensors and the sensed data are streamed. Any difference or unusual patterns observed in the readings of the patients/ individuals has to be immediately responded and taken action to save the patients/ individuals from critical situations.

i)   Using the cloud computing models

The data are sensed and streamed to the far end cloud servers through different layers of the network. In cloud data centres, decision making and unusual patterns are identified by running different algorithms. Consider an emergency situation where a patients readings of heart rate are unusual. The heart rate sensed are sent to the cloud, the intelligent algorithms determine the unusual patterns and notify to the health care service providers/ Emergency units/ local care takers to give immediate first aids to the patients/ individuals.

Figure 3. Smart health care system using cloud computing models

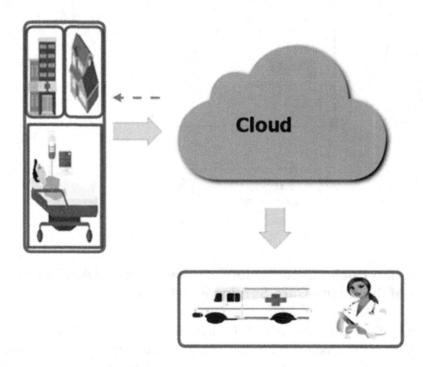

During this process, in cloud computing as depicted in figure 4, the data are routed to multiple layers and then the unusual patterns of the readings are identified. The notification to the care takers/ medical practitioners may be delayed due to the existence of communication latency. Apart from this, the streaming of the data also incurs cost because of bandwidth consumption and network resources. This delay might lead the individuals/ patients to a critical condition.

ii)   Using opportunistic edge computing models

While using opportunistic edge computing model in considered emergency situations instead of cloud computing, any difference in health patterns are determined near to the edge of the network, and they can quickly respond to the patients/ individuals who suffer from disorders.

In this model, the data is processed near to the user premises as shown in figure 5, computation time will be relatively low than the cloud computing model which has to stream the data to far end data centres. The cost of the computation and service are low as the computation and analysis is done using the resources that are available and contributed by the users. The servers need not be dedicated to this application and can be scalable to various needs of the application.

Figure 4. Smart health care system using opportunistic edge computing models

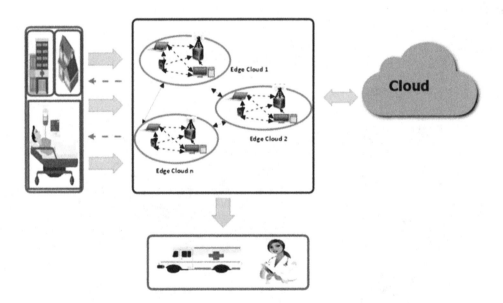

Scenario B: Smart Health Care System, Considering the Availability and Location of the Health Care Service Providers

Consider a scenario where the availability of the doctors/ health care units are scarce. The available services has to be optimally allocated to intensive care units where the patients need immediate attention. In this situation, hence a location aware scheduling to the individuals who need service is required

i)   Using the cloud computing models

The cloud computing provides a location aware service but still there are many challenges that has to be addressed. Consider a situation where a patient who is located in a place where there is no hospitals/ emergency care units and the patient is in a critical condition. Determining the location of medical professionals / emergency care units and then intimating them is long process. This involves tracking and location detection which is difficult and time consuming for the cloud environment.

ii)   Using Opportunistic Edge Computing Model

When a patient is in critical condition, in place where there are no care takers in nearby premises, it would be easy for the opportunistic models to scale as per the needs, process and determine the location of the nearby emergency units and respond quickly. As the OEC models supports the mobility feature, this location aware service delivery will be consuming less time and leading to a cost effective system too.

Scenario C: Edge Computing as a First aid

i)   Using cloud computing Models

Consider a critical condition of a patient/ individual who is under monitoring at home and needs a first aids immediately, For example a need for oxygen immediately. For the considered scenario the data is streamed and decision making will be done at the cloud and the first aid will be given to the patients by opening the oxygen mask. This response may be delayed if there is traffic and congestion at the network. There is a possibility of a failure where the cloud fails to communicate to the devices that are responsible for providing the first aid which will eventually lead the patient to more critical conditions.

ii)   Using opportunistic edge computing Models

For the considered case, the intelligence of decision making will be given to the equipment's sensing and the home computers, laptops that are not in use at present can be contributed. So there will be quick determination of the critical condition and first aid will be given to the patients with no delay which could save them from fatal conditions.

CONCLUSION

In this work, an OEC architecture for healthcare service provisioning which enables personalized and smart-healthcare systems by leveraging healthcare data processing at the edge of the networks is proposed. It clearly shows that OEC architecture succeeds to lower the latency and consumption of the bandwidth. The chapter gives an insight about the emerging edge computing paradigm in health care services and their characteristics. The OEC architecture proposed overcomes the main challenges that are imposed by the cloud computing in health care domain. The proposed architecture aims to reduce request time for the health care services that are requested by the users. They give more appropriate and quick decisions to the stake holders involved in the smart health care systems. This work also explores the possible research challenges that has to be developed to improve the Opportunistic model of edge computing (Amir Ahmad Dara,2017). Various application scenario are also discussed which gives an understanding about the advantages of the opportunistic edge computing than traditional cloud computing models. The cost-effective health-care system is the demand in need which has to be further developed. The chapter can be explored to improve and the model could be implemented.

REFERENCES

Casadei, R., Fortino, G., Pianini, D., Russo, W., Savaglio, C., & Viroli, M. (2019). A development approach for collective opportunistic Edge-of-Things services. *Information Sciences*, *498*, 154–169. doi:10.1016/j.ins.2019.05.058

Chen, M., Li, W., Hao, Y., Qian, Y., & Humar, I. (2018). Edge cognitive computing based smart healthcare system. *Future Generation Computer Systems*, *86*, 403–411. doi:10.1016/j.future.2018.03.054

Dara & Anuradhab. (2017). *Use of orthogonal arrays and design of experiment via Taguchi L9 method in probability of default*. Growing Science Ltd., doi:10.5267/j.ac.2017.11.001

Dubey, H., Yang, J., Constant, N., Amiri, A. M., Yang, Q., & Makodiya, K. (2015). Fog Data: Enhancing Telehealth Big Data Through Fog Computing (#4). Proceedings of the ASE BigData & SocialInformatics 2015, 14:1-14:6. 10.1145/2818869.2818889

Greco, L., Ritrovato, P., & Xhafa, F. (2019). An edge-stream computing infrastructure for real-time analysis of wearable sensors data. *Future Generation Computer Systems*, *93*, 515–528. doi:10.1016/j.future.2018.10.058

Hassan, N., Gillani, S., Ahmed, E., Yaqoob, I., & Imran, M. (2018). The Role of Edge Computing in Internet of Things. *IEEE Communications Magazine*, *56*(11), 110–115. doi:10.1109/MCOM.2018.1700906

Jalali, F., Hinton, K., Ayre, R., Alpcan, T., & Tucker, R. S. (2016). Fog computing may help to save energy in cloud computing. *IEEE Journal on Selected Areas in Communications*, *34*(5), 1728–1739. doi:10.1109/JSAC.2016.2545559

Khan, W. Z., Ahmed, E., Hakak, S., Yaqoob, I., & Ahmed, A. (2019). Edge computing: A survey. *Future Generation Computer Systems*, *97*, 219–235. doi:10.1016/j.future.2019.02.050

Koop, C., Mosher, R., Kun, L., Geiling, J., Grigg, E., Long, S., Macedonia, C., Merrell, R., Satava, R., & Rosen, J. (2008). Future delivery of health care: Cybercare. *IEEE Engineering in Medicine and Biology Magazine*, *27*(6), 29–38. doi:10.1109/MEMB.2008.929888 PubMed

Li, C., Tang, J., Tang, H., & Luo, Y. (2019). Collaborative cache allocation and task scheduling for data-intensive applications in edge computing environment. *Future Generation Computer Systems*, *95*, 249–264. doi:10.1016/j.future.2019.01.007

Lin, K., Pankaj, S., & Wang, D. (2018). Task offloading and resource allocation for edge-of-things computing on smart healthcare systems. *Computers & Electrical Engineering*, *72*, 348–360. doi:10.1016/j.compeleceng.2018.10.003

Rahmani, A. M., Gia, T. N., Negash, B., Anzanpour, A., Azimi, I., Jiang, M., & Liljeberg, P. (2018). Exploiting smart e-Health gateways at the edge of healthcare Internet-of-Things: A fog computing approach. *Future Generation Computer Systems, 78*, 641–658. doi:10.1016/j.future.2017.02.014

Rani, S., Ahmed, S. H., & Shah, S. C. (2019). Smart health: A novel paradigm to control the chickungunya virus. IEEE Internet of Things Journal, 6(2), 1306–1311. doi:10.1109/JIOT.2018.2802898

Ray, P. P., Dash, D., & De, D. (2019). Edge computing for Internet of Things: A survey, e-healthcare case study and future direction. *Journal of Network and Computer Applications, 140*(December), 1–22. doi:10.1016/j.jnca.2019.05.005

Shi, W., Cao, J., Zhang, Q., Li, Y., & Xu, L. (2016). Edge Computing: Vision and Challenges. IEEE Internet of Things Journal, 3(5), 637–646. doi:10.1109/JIOT.2016.2579198

Sodhro, A. H., Pirbhulal, S., & Sangaiah, A. K. (2018). Convergence of IoT and product lifecycle management in medical health care. *Future Generation Computer Systems, 86*, 380–391. doi:10.1016/j.future.2018.03.052

Subahi, A. F. (2019). Edge-Based IoT Medical Record System: Requirements, Recommendations and Conceptual Design. *IEEE Access : Practical Innovations, Open Solutions, 7*, 94150–94159. doi:10.1109/ACCESS.2019.2927958

Uddin, M. Z. (2019). A wearable sensor-based activity prediction system to facilitate edge computing in smart healthcare system. *Journal of Parallel and Distributed Computing, 123*, 46–53. doi:10.1016/j.jpdc.2018.08.010

Verma, P., & Sood, S. K. (2018). Fog assisted-IoT enabled patient health monitoring in smart homes. IEEE Internet of Things Journal, 5(3), 1789–1796. doi:10.1109/JIOT.2018.2803201

Yousefpour, A., Fung, C., Nguyen, T., Kadiyala, K., Jalali, F., Niakanlahiji, A., Kong, J., & Jue, J. P. (2019). All one needs to know about fog computing and related edge computing paradigms: A complete survey. *Journal of Systems Architecture, 98*(February), 289–330. doi:10.1016/j.sysarc.2019.02.009

Yu, W., Liang, F., He, X., Hatcher, W. G., Lu, C., Lin, J., & Yang, X. (2017). A Survey on the Edge Computing for the Internet of Things. *IEEE Access : Practical Innovations, Open Solutions, 3536*(c), 1–1. doi:10.1109/ACCESS.2017.2674687

Zhang, B., Mor, N., Kolb, J., Chan, D. S., Lutz, K., Allman, E., Wawrzyne, J., Lee, E., & Kubiatowicz, J. (2015). The Cloud is Not Enough: Saving IoT from the Cloud. 7th USENIX Workshop on Hot Topics in Cloud Computing, HotCloud'15. Retrieved from https://dl.acm.org/citation.cfm?id=2827740%0Ahttps://www.usenix.org/conference/hotcloud15/workshop-program/presentation/zhang

KEY TERMS AND DEFINITIONS

Bandwidth: Bandwidth describes the maximum data transfer rate of a network or Internet connection.
Broker: The intermediate layer that are responsible for managing the resource pools.

Communication Latency: Latency refers to delays that is incurred during transmitting or processing data, which can be caused by varied reasons.

Edge Computing: It is a distributed computing paradigm which brings computation and data storage closer to the needed location and near to the users, in order to improve response times, bandwidth consumptions.

Machine Learning: Machine Learning models are scientific and statistical model that are developed on gathered data for classification, analysis, and forecast the future events.

Opportunistic Computing: Opportunistic computing use the resources, services, applications, and computing resources, contributed by the devices connected in an opportunistic network, for performing the execution of distributed computing tasks.

Service Providers: A service provider is a vendor that provides IT solutions and/or services to end users and organizations.

Chapter 14
Risk Analysis of Diabetic Patient Using Map–Reduce and Machine Learning Algorithm

Nagaraj V. Dharwadkar

 https://orcid.org/0000-0003-3017-0011

Department of Computer Science and Engineering, Rajarambapu Institute of Technology, Sakhrale, India

Shivananda R. Poojara

Department of Computer Science and Engineering, University of Tartu, Estonia

Anil K. Kannur

Department of Computer Science and Engineering, Rajarambapu Institute of Technology, Sakhrale, India

ABSTRACT

Diabetes is one of the four non-communicable diseases causing maximum deaths all over the world. The numbers of diabetes patients are increasing day by day. Machine learning techniques can help in early diagnosis of diabetes to overcome the influence of it. In this chapter, the authors proposed the system that imputes missing values present in diabetes dataset and parallel process diabetes data for the pattern discovery using Hadoop-MapReduce-based C4.5 machine learning algorithm. The system uses these patterns to classify the patient into diabetes and non-diabetes class and to predict risk levels associated with the patient. The two datasets, namely Pima Indian Diabetes Dataset (PIDD) and Local Diabetes Dataset (LDD), are used for the experimentation. The experimental results show that C4.5 classifier gives accuracy of 73.91% and 79.33% when applied on (PIDD) (LDD) respectively. The proposed system will provide an effective solution for early diagnosis of diabetes patients and their associated risk level so that the patients can take precaution and treatment at early stages of the disease.

DOI: 10.4018/978-1-7998-3053-5.ch014

INTRODUCTION

In last one decade, the health care systems in all over the world have grown and in the same phase, the large volume of data has proportionally increased in the form of patients' records. These patients' records include the x-rays, images, clinical information reports, diagnosis, prescriptions, etc. Nowadays the health care systems are generating and maintaining the data in digital form. This data has particular type such as structured, unstructured, semi-structured or combination of these types. The data generated at health care systems will be helpful not only for the treatment of the patients but also to track what possible may happen to patients' health in future. Health care systems are concerned with all the diseases and with possible diagnosis and treatment of the patient. The Health care system faces many challenging health hazards in day-today, and one of such challenging health hazards is diabetes. Diabetes is one among the four major non-transmissible diseases that is under attention of healthcare sector. Diabetes is caused when a human body does not generate enough insulin. Diabetes has become the most dangerous health issue in this very world. The numbers of diabetes patients are increasing day by day since past few years. On the basis of WHO (World Health Organization) worldwide survey report on diabetes says that, in the year 1980,108 million people were Diabetic and in 2014, the count of people increased up 422 million suffering from diabetes. From 1980 to 2014, the average percentage in increase of diabetic patients randomly changed and as on today more than 600 million suffering from diabetes. There are three types of diabetes that can be characterized into: type-1, type-2 and gestational diabetes. The type-1 diabetes is an insulin-dependent diabetes that occurs due to the inability of patient's pancreas to generate insulin. In this case, the patient needs to inject insulin externally for the survival. The type-2 diabetes is non-insulin dependent diabetes, caused due to unsuccessful utilization of insulin produced by human body cells. The gestational diabetes is third type which is occurs during pregnancy, this is a temporary condition from which pregnant woman may suffer. This condition can lead patient towards the development of type-2 diabetes. It may cause complications in pregnancy (World Health Organization, 2016). Diabetes of each category can make complications in the human body. It leaves long term bad impact on human body. Due to diabetes patient may suffer from different diseases such as heart stroke, attack, eye blindness, leg amputations, kidney failure etc. For pregnant women, diabetes may lead to the possibility of fatal death or other complications in pregnancy. As diabetes has long-term complications associated with it, the patient may suffer from economic loss through regular medical checkups cost, prescription cost (World Health Organization, 2016). Hence it is necessary to control this rising serious disease. There is no permanent and complete solution for diabetes as on date. Hence to make an easy living with diabetes better solution is an early diagnosis of diabetes or diseases that can be caused due to diabetes. To reduce the influence of diabetes contribution of everyone is required. The government, health care industries, technology specialist, the scientists must provide solutions to overcome this issue (World Health Organization, 2016). With the help of technologies such as machine learning, data mining it is possible to analyze diabetes data and accordingly provide early diagnosis, precautions and pre-treatment to the patient (Eswari, T, 2015). The digital data generated in health care systems will be helpful in analyzing the risks in patients. Not only the health care systems researching on the diabetics but also the engineering and biotechnology disciplines are working in the same sector of diabetes to provide the solutions in preventing the risks in patients. One of the engineering disciplines is computer science, there are many techniques available for analyzing the digital data of patients and predict what may possibly happen. The problem statement for the work is to analyze the risk of the diabetic patient, and we propose the methodology for the same using Map-reduce and decision tree-based algorithms. In the proposed work, we are focusing on the analysis of diabetes data. The system first imputes the missing values in diabetes dataset and then parallel process the data by using machine learning algorithms integrated with Hadoop Map-Reduce environment to discover patterns from it. The system uses these patterns for the diabetes patients' diagnosis and prediction of associated risk levels. Many researchers from the different disciplines contributed through their research on the same problem statement. The next section gives the overview of the prior work carried out by other researchers.

Literature Review

The survey on earlier work gives numerous outcomes on health care analysis of information which was carried out by various techniques, methods. Numerous researchers or authors have developed and actualized different analysis and predictive models utilizing various data mining, information management and Hadoop systems or mixture of these methods. Eswari et al. (2015) proposed Hadoop and Map-Reduce based methodology for the analysis of diabetic information. Through this analysis the created framework can be foresee diabetic sort's pervasive and intricacies related with it. Based on such analysis, the framework can help in curing the patient by appropriate treatment as on right time as could reasonably be expected. The framework depends on Hadoop henceforth it is moderate to any medicinal services association. V. H. Bhat et al. (2009) proposed a methodology of combination of relapse, characterization, hereditary and neural system which manages the missing qualities just as exception esteems in the diabetic informational index and supplanted the missing qualities by the comparing property area. For expectation they utilized old style neural system and tested it on the available preprocessed informational index. Aiswarya Iyer et al. (2015), utilized order strategy to discover designs from the diabetes informational indexes. They utilized Credulous Byse and Choice Tree calculations by utilizing Weka instrument. Creators likewise thought about execution of the two calculations against Pima Diabetes dataset. Exploratory outcomes indicated adequacy of each proposed grouping model. Sabibullah M. et al. (2013) built up the forecast model dependent on delicate registering to locate the amassed dangers of diabetic patients. They have utilized hereditary calculation for the experimentation on ongoing restorative informational collection. From the consequences of the analyses the hazard level of patient and as needs be the danger of heart stroke can be anticipated. The created framework will assist the specialist with diagnosing the patient accurately. K. Rajesh et.al. (2012) utilized grouping strategy to discover valuable data from diabetic informational collection. They utilized C4.5 calculation to discover designs from the informational index additionally for effective characterization. They utilized Pima Indian Diabetes Informational index (PIDD) for experimentation. While playing out the order creators didn't consider missing qualities in informational index. They treated PIDD as a total informational index. Vaishnav, et.al. (2015) looked into the changed techniques for dealing with missing information. They evaluated various strategies, for example, K-Means, KNN, order and so forth utilized for the missing qualities ascription and furthermore contrasted and their points of interest and weaknesses. Dai W. et.al. (2014) actualized a Guide Decrease based c4.5 choice tree calculation. They put the first calculation into the instrument of Guide and Diminish process. Creators directed various analysiss on gigantic manufactured informational indexes and looked at execution and exactness on single v/s multi hub Hadoop bunch. From the aftereffects of this work creators recommend that actualized calculation can give time proficiency just as versatility. Loads of research work utilizing various procedures like information mining, Weka, Hadoop and its biological systems and so forth effectively is accomplished for investigating the medicinal services information and growing great analysis models.

For the diabetic analysis, information numerous developers favored decision tree-based algorithm for classification, pattern recognition, rules generation etc. as explained by Sungyoung Lee et.al. (2015). Akkarapol et.al (2012), proposed method for forestalling the diabetes ailment is a continuous region important to the human services network. Albeit numerous analyses utilize a few data mining methods to evaluate the main sources of diabetes, just little arrangements of clinical hazard components are considered. Thusly, not just numerous possibly significant factors, for example, pre-diabetes wellbeing conditions are dismissed in their analysis; however, the outcomes delivered by such strategies may not speak to important hazard factors and example acknowledgment of diabetes suitably. In this analysis, the three diverse spotlights dependent on the patients' social insurance costs. Authors point inspect whether progressively complex expository models sing a few data mining methods in SAS® Undertaking Miner™ 7.1 can all the more likely foresee and clarify the reasons for expanding diabetes in grown-up patients in each cost class. The starter analysis demonstrates that hypertension, age, cholesterol, grown-up BMI, complete pay, sex, respiratory failure, conjugal-status, asthma and dental checkup conclusion are among the key hazard factors.

There is another procedure created by Md. Maniruzzaman et.al. (2018) to streamline and powerful AI (ML) framework under the presumption that missing qualities or anomalies whenever supplanted by a middle design will yield higher hazard stratification exactness. This ML-based hazard stratification is structured, upgraded and assessed, where: (I) the highlights are removed and streamlined from the six element choice methods (irregular woods, calculated relapse, shared data, head part analysis, analysis of change, and Fisher discriminant proportion) and joined with ten distinct kinds of classifiers (straight and quadratic discriminant analysis, innocent Bayes, Gaussian procedure grouping, bolster vector machine, fake neural system, Adaboost, strategic relapse, choice tree, and arbitrary woodland) under the speculation that both missing qualities and anomalies when supplanted by figured medians will be able to improve the hazard precision. "Pima Indian Diabetic Dataset" (A total record of 768 patients: out of which 268 diabetic patient record and 500 controls) were considered in this work. Our outcomes exhibit that on supplanting the missing qualities and anomalies by gathering middle and middle qualities, separately and further utilizing the mix of irregular timberland highlight determination and arbitrary backwoods arrangement method yields an exactness, affectability, explicitness, positive prescient worth, negative prescient worth and territory under the bend as: 92.26%, 95.96%, 79.72%, 91.14%, 91.20%, and 0.93, individually. N.Sneha et.al. (2019), the developers likewise chipped away at the analysis is to utilize huge highlights, structure an expectation calculation utilizing AI and locate the ideal classifier to give the nearest result contrasting with clinical results. The proposed strategy means to concentrate on choosing the characteristics that trouble in early recognition of Diabetes Miletus utilizing prescient analysis. The outcome demonstrates the choice tree calculation and the Arbitrary woods has the most elevated particularity of 98.20% and 98.00%, individually holds best for diabetic analysis information. Gullible Bayesian result expresses the best precision of 82.30%. The analysis additionally sums up the determination of ideal highlights from dataset to improve the characterization precision. Ioannis Kavakiotis et.al. (2017), the exceptional advancement in area of biotechnology and medical sciences has provoked a critical collection of data, for example, high-throughput hereditary data and diagnosis based clinical data, has generated vast data from "Electronic Healthcare Records" (EHRs). For the analysis of these data, AI and data mining models used in biosciences is by and by, like never before previously, essential and imperative in endeavors to change brilliantly all accessible data into important learning. Diabetes Mellitus (DM) is characterized as metabolic accumulation issue in patients' body with huge weight on human health. Broad research in all parts of diabetes has prompted the age as one of the measures of vast data. The point of the present analysis is to lead an efficient survey of the utilizations of AI, information mining methods and apparatuses in the field of diabetes inquire about as for a) Expectation and Finding, b) Diabetic Difficulties, c) Hereditary foundation and condition d) Social insurance and The executives with the main classification having all the earmarks of being the most mainstream. A wide scope of AI calculations was utilized. As a rule, 85% of those utilized were described by administered learning draws near and 15% by solo ones, and all the more explicitly, affiliation rules. Support vector machines (SVM) emerge as the best and widely utilized calculation. Concerning the kind of information, clinical datasets were basically utilized. The title applications in the chose articles venture the value of separating important information prompting new theories focusing on more profound understanding and further analysis in DM.

Based on the survey of prior work carried by many other researchers, still there is lot of scope of improvement in proposed problem statement. Therefore, in the proposed system we have used c4.5 decision tree-based algorithm for the recognition of the diabetes pattern of the data set to determine the risk level of patients.

PROPOSED SYSTEM

The Big-data analytics is a method of examining the huge dataset volume that includes various data types. The big-data analytics identifies the undiscovered hidden patterns to generate the knowledge from the huge dataset volume. The big-data analytics process can be executed by using any one of the software tools and applications types. The basic objectives of analysis is to forecast or predictive the behavior of data pattern using data analytics, optimization and mining. There are various domains in which the big data analytics is used for forecasting or predictive decisions. The domains such as travel, hospitality, healthcare, retails, Government, finance and banking were big-data analytics domain area that gained more popularity in recent years. The advantages of the big-data analytics in healthcare systems are many. By digitizing, storing, combining and effectively utilizing the large volume data, health care providers from individual doctors' hospital and large hospital networks are providing noticeable care early and more health solutions.

Figure 1. System Architecture

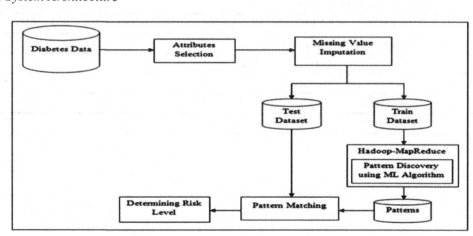

311

Big data analytics in healthcare benefit comprises identification of diseases at very early stages so that patients can get medical care early and more easily. Analytics in health care is also used to find fraud in drugs more quickly and efficiently. In addition, big-data analytics can be utilized effectively in subdomain of healthcare such as: Evidence-based medicine, Genomic analytics, Remote or Device monitoring, risk management and the patients' profile analytics. In this work, we are classifying diabetic and non-diabetic patient and accordingly predicting the risk levels of the patient. The Figure 1 shows overall system architecture which includes different phases such as a) data collection, b) missing-values imputation, c) pattern recognition, d) pattern matching and e) the results. Each phase is briefly described in following sub-sections.

Diabetes Data

The first and foremost important is data related to diabetes patients. The diabetes dataset has been collected by considering various cases of diabetes and every level of the patients' health. In this work, we used two diabetes patients' datasets for the experimentation. One of the standard datasets available is "Pima Indians Diabetes Dataset (PIDD)" and another one is "Local Diabetes Dataset (LDD)".

Pima Indians Diabetes Dataset (PIDD)

The PIDD is used in this work for the experimentation. The dataset is collected from the "UCI Machine Learning Repository": Pima Indians Diabetes Dataset (PIDD) consists of eight attributes and one class variable. Table 1 shows the names of attributes present in (PIDD). This dataset contains records of both diabetic and non-diabetic patients with age above 21 years, and a total of 768 patients' records in the dataset. The dataset included all the numerical attributes. The data set contains some missing values in it.

Table 1. Names of Attributes

Sl. No.	Name of Attributes
1.	Number of times the patient is pregnant
2.	Plasma glucose concentration taken at every 2 hours for testing oral glucose tolerance
3.	Diastolic blood-pressure (mmHg)
4.	Skin fold thickness of Triceps (mm)
5.	Serum insulin at every 2-Hour (mu U/ml)
6.	Bodymass index (weight: in kg and height: in m)
7.	Pedigree function of Diabetes
8.	Age (in years)
9.	Class-variable (0 or 1)

Local Diabetes Dataset (LDD)

The LDD is prepared by collecting patient's records from local hospitals and labs. Some of the data is generated under the guidance of doctor. The dataset contains total 1000 diabetic and non-diabetic patients' records between the ages 21 to 70. The dataset contains 4 attributes and one class variable. The names of attributes in LDD are plasma glucose, diastolic blood-pressure, pedigree function of diabetes and the age in years.

Attributes Selection

Attributes selection is based on the risk factors associated with the diabetes patient. Diabetes patient may suffer from other health related problems and diseases such as kidney failure, heart attack, eye blindness etc., World Health Organization (2016). Hence to overcome this problem it is necessary to diagnose the risk of developing such diseases from current health conditions at early stages. The future risk of developing such diseases can be predicted using different risk factors such as tolerance test of plasma glucose, blood pressure, stress, BMI, diabetes pedigree patient, age etc. Plasma glucose tolerance test is used to diagnose type-2 diabetes, pre-diabetes, and gestational diabetes during pregnancy, insulin resistance World Health Organization (2016). Pre-diabetes also called as borderline diabetes and it is raising problem in all over the world. Pre-diabetes is a condition in which patient has a high level of blood sugar as compared to the normal, but still not that much higher that patient can be labeled with diabetes disease. If pre-diabetes is not diagnosed or treated early, it can turn into type 2 diabetes. Patients who have blood pressure, type-2 diabetes in family history and age above 40, have a high risk of getting the type-2 diabetes. Type-1 of diabetes typically occurs in children and adults. Patients of any age may suffer from this type-1 diabetes. The risk factors of type-1 diabetes are environmental conditions, geography, and type-1 diabetes in family history, etc. Type-2 of diabetes mostly occurs in patients whose ages are above 40 to 45. The risk factors of type-1 diabetes are high blood pressure, stress, age, type-2 diabetes in family history, gestational diabetes etc. About 25% of type-1 diabetes patients and 85% of type-2 diabetes patients usually have high blood pressure.

Diabetes patient with high blood pressure may develop the risk of heart attack, stroke, kidney disease etc. Gestational diabetes occurs in pregnant women whose body is unable to effectively respond to insulin. If gestational diabetes is not treated at early stages, it can be converted to type-2 diabetes. Pre-diabetes, type-2 diabetes in family history and gestational diabetes, high blood pressure, age above 25 are the risk factors of getting gestational diabetes. Testing of plasma glucose tolerance, patients' age in years, blood pressure and pedigree function of diabetes are major factors for the diabetes diagnosis and diabetes related issues. Hence these 4 attributes are selected for the analysis of diabetes data in order to classify patients into diabetes and non-diabetes class and to predict their associated risk level with the minimum complexity of results. To get maximum accuracy of results, missing value imputation is done on (PIDD).

Missing Value Imputation

Analysis of data which contains missing values can end with wrong results. Data analysis techniques are facing a big problem in the form of missing data. Missing data may hide important information that can be used for the accurate analysis of data. Missing data can be occurred due to improper collection of data, or irrelevant data, or due to confidentiality issues of accessing the data. This incomplete data causes difficulties to classifier while extracting significant information from it and hence causes loss of accuracy in results Rahman, G. and Islam, Z. (2011). Because of this, it is necessary to impute missing data before the analysis of it to improve the results.

PIDD consists a number of missing-values in various attributes in the form of '0'. In the dataset, many patients have 0 value for plasma glucose concentration, blood pressure. Hence it is impossible that any patient who has 0 plasma glucose level or has 0 blood pressure in his body. Hence to improve the efficiency of results we designed and implemented classification based Missing Value Imputation Algorithm for the missing-values imputation in PIDD Kalyankar, G.D. et al. (2017). PIDD contains two types of patients, diabetic and non-diabetic. The input PIDD is divided into two subsets of which one subset contains diabetic patients 'records and another contains non-diabetic patients 'records. Each subset is treated separately for the missing value imputation. For each subset, missing values present in each attribute are identified and then replaced them with their respective attribute mean Kalyankar, G.D. et al. (2017). Algorithm 1 gives detail description of steps followed to impute missing values in PIDD. PIDD does not contain any missing value. Hence, we used this algorithm only for PIDD.

Algorithm 1 Missing Value Imputation Algorithm
Input: *PIDD(X)* having missing values
Output: *PIDD(X)* at the end of "missing values imputation"

1. Retrieve attribute 'A' of binary class variable from the attribute A_i, $i = 1,......, N$ (where N is total number of attributes) in dataset X.
2. Divide the dataset X in to X_d and X_{nd} based on the class variable
    I. X_d = Sub-dataset consists of all diabetic records
    II. X_{nd} = Sub-dataset consists of all non-diabetic records
3. Identify the missing values from all the attributes $A \in A_i = \{A_1, A_2, A_3,....., A_N\}$, in each dataset X_d and X_{nd} (by considering 0 as missing value)
4. For each attribute $A \in A_i = \{A_1, A_2, A_3,....., A_N\}$, in dataset X_d, calculate attribute mean M_i, i = 1,..,N.
5. For each attribute $A \in A_i = \{A_1, A_2, A_3,....., A_N\}$, in dataset X_{nd}, calculate attribute mean $M n_i$, i = 1,.....,N.
6. Impute "missing values" in dataset X_d with attribute mean M_i.
7. Impute "missing values" in dataset X_{nd} with attribute mean $M n_i$.
8. Combine dataset X_d and X_{nd} .
9. Return (X)

Table 2. Threshold Values of Attributes Used To Define Risk Level of Diabetes Patient

Name of Attribute.	Low	Medium	High
Plasma glucose concentration at every 2-hour for testing oral glucose tolerance	<95	95-141	141+
Diastolic blood-pressure (mmHg)	<80	80-90	90+
Pedigree function of Diabetes	<0.42	0.42-0.82	0.82+
Age (in years)	<41 (R1)	41-60 (R2)	60+ (R3)

After the imputation of missing value in dataset, all the numerical data is converted into categorical data by using appropriate threshold values of attributes Han, J. et al. (2008) used to define risk level of diabetes patient as shown in Table 2. LDD is also converted to the categorical dataset using threshold values of attributes as shown in Table 2.

After the imputation of missing value in dataset, all the numerical data is converted into categorical data by using appropriate threshold values of attributes Han, J. et al. (2008) used to define risk level of diabetes patient as shown in Table 2. LDD is also converted to the categorical dataset using threshold values of attributes as shown in Table 2. The both categorical input dataset are divided into train dataset and test dataset for the further processing. This train dataset is provided as input for the machine learning algorithm for the pattern discovery from it.

Machine Learning

Machine learning is a sub-domain of artificial intelligence Bell, J. (2014) which contains different techniques used for computing. By using machine learning techniques, system can be designed in such a way that it can learn from data, recognize patterns from the data and then based on learned knowledge it can predict results for decision making. Hence, to improvise the quality and effectiveness of predicted results and decisions, machine learning techniques are widely used in the analysis of diabetes data Kavakiotis, I. et al. (2017). There are various types of algorithms those can be implemented using machine learning. Machine learning are categorized into two types, one is supervised learning and another is unsupervised learning Talwar, A. and Kumar, Y. (2013); Bell, J. (2014). Both of these methods are described below:

(a)   Supervised Learning: In this type of learning, the system can be learned from the historic dataset in which input and output values are already exist. According to the learnt knowledge, system is able to predict results for new dataset. Various diverse classification techniques such as Decision Tree, Rule learning, Naive Bayes etc follow supervised learning technique Talwar, A. et.al. (2013); Bell, J. (2014).
(b)   Unsupervised Learning: in this learning type, system can be learned from a dataset which contains only input values. There are no corresponding output values exist in the dataset. By applying different clustering techniques system can learn from data. Hence this type of learning also referred as cluster analysis. Different clustering techniques such as K-Means Clustering, KNN etc follow unsupervised learning technique Talwar, A. et.al. (2013); Bell, J. (2014).

In this work, both the diabetes dataset used for the experimentation contain input and their associated output values. Hence supervised learning technique is used for the analysis of diabetes data. For this C4.5 decision tree algorithm is implemented to discover patterns from the data. This c4.5 decision tree-based algorithm is implemented using Map-Reduce for the parallel processing of diabetes data.

Hadoop Map-Reduce

Hadoop is the open source Java based solution which provides parallel processing of large volume data in a disseminated way Apache Hadoop Tutorial. Hadoop comes with Map Reduce programming framework which comprises two phases, Map and Reduce. Mapper takes input data and transforms it into key-value a pair which is referred as intermediate data. Reducer takes this intermediate data as input

Figure 2. Map-Reduce Architecture

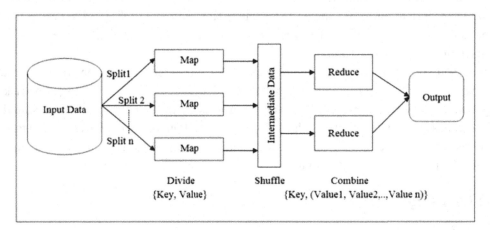

with the addition of all the values related to the key, generates the final output. This framework helps in processing huge dataset volume in parallel and in a reliable manner Hadoop Map-Reduce. Figure 2 describes general architecture of Map-Reduce framework.

In this work, c4.5 decision tree-based algorithm using Map-Reduce framework implementation of c4.5 algorithm using Hadoop Map-Reduce Paradigm for the pattern discovery. The steps used for the implementation of Map-Reduce based C4.5 algorithm are as follows:

(a) Load the diabetes dataset in "Hadoop Distributed File System (HDFS)" and give it as an input to the Missing-Value Imputation algorithm to impute the missing-values present in diabetes dataset.

(b) Convert the numerical data into categorical data.

(c) Divide the diabetes dataset to train dataset and test dataset.

(d) Give train dataset as an input to C4.5 Decision Tree Algorithm.

(e) Call the functions of C4.5 algorithm.

(f) Start with the current attribute in dataset.

(g) Call the Map function from Map-Reduce framework to verify, whether the instances are belonging to the current attribute or not. For all the remaining attributes Map function gives the output in the form of attribute index with its instance and class label of related instance.

(h) Call Reduce function to calculate the total occurrences of the combination of attribute index and its instance and class of that instance.

(i) Use the output of Reduce function to calculate entropy, Information gain and information gain ratio of the attributes using C4.5 decision tree algorithm.

(j) Discover patterns from the data and apply them on test dataset to classify diabetic and non-diabetic persons and to predict their associated risk level.

Pattern Discovery

From the available set of strings with various sequences, various patterns can be recognized. This pattern can be used to analyze the data and accordingly to take important decisions. The numbers of techniques are used for pattern discovery. Classification technique is one of most appropriate techniques used for the discovery of the patterns. A decision tree is most effective classification technique whose aim is to build a model which will be able to predict the output value based on the input value Daghistani, T. et.al. (2016). The working of decision tree algorithm is based on the supervised learning. A decision tree is easy to build and understand and also it performs well with the commensurable power of computing Bell, J. (2014). In this work c4.5 decision tree is implemented for pattern discovery. C4.5 is improved from the ID3 algorithm and is developed by Ross Quinlan. The c4.5 algorithm can deal with both continuous and discrete attributes. The C4.5 algorithm calculates information gain ratio using entropy. Based on the highest valued information gain ratio, the testing attribute is chosen at each node of the tree for the split Rajesh, K. et al. (2009); Dai, W. et.al. (2014). Algorithm 2 gives the pseudo code of c4.5 decision tree-based algorithm.

Algorithm 2 C4.5 Decision Tree
Input: The Training dataset (T); the attributes(S)
Output: The Decision Tree (T)

1. **if** T is NULL, **then**
2. **return** failure
3. end if
4. set Tree = { }
5. **for** a ∈ S **do**
6. set *SplitInfo* (a,T)=0,*Entropy* (a) = 0
7. Compute *Entropy*(a),*SplitInfo*(a, T), *Gain*(a, T),*GainRatio*(a, T))
8. **end for**
9. a$_{best}$ = *argmax{GainRatio*(a, T)}
10. attach a$_{best}$ to *Tree*
11. **for** U ∈ Values(a$_{best,}$ T) **do**
12. call *C* 4. 5 (T$_{a,U}$)
13. **end for**
14. **return** *Tree*

Let c be the total number of classes and the instances proportion that are assigned to j[th] class is denoted by p(S, j). Therefore, entropy of the attribute S is computed using equation (1) as defined by Dai W. et.al. (2014):

$$Entropy\left(S\right) = -\sum_{j=0}^{c} p\left(S,j\right) \times \log p\left(S,j\right) \tag{1}$$

The information gain is computed by using training dataset T is defined by Dai W. et.al. (2014):

$$Gain\left(S,T\right) = Entropy\left(S\right) - \sum_{v \in Values} \frac{\left|Ts,v\right|}{\left|Ts\right|} \times Entropy\left(Sv\right) \tag{2}$$

Where T_s is the values set of S in T, T_s is subset of T induced by S, and $T_{s;v}$, is subset of T that has attribute S has 'v' value in it. Thus, information gain-ratio of the attribute S is defined by Dai W. et.al. (2014):

$$Gain\_Ratio(S,T) = \frac{Gain(S,T)}{SplitInfo(S,T)}$$
(3)

Where *SplitInfo(S; T)* is splitting information computed as defined by Dai W. et.al. (2014):

$$SplitInfo(S,T) = \sum_{v \in Values} \frac{|Ts,v|}{|Ts|} \times \log \frac{|Ts,v|}{|Ts|}$$
(4)

The entropy, gain, gain-ratio and the splitting information *SplitInfo* are computed recursively at each level of the tree using equations (1), (2), (3) and (4) respectively Dai, W. et.al. (2014).

Figure 3 shows the classification of diabetes class and level of risks in patient. An internal node in tree represents various attribute tests as listed in Table 2. The outcome of the tests is represented as a branch in the tree. The class label is represented by leaf node in tree also known as class label distribution. At each node in the tree, one of the attributes is selected for the splitting training dataset into separate classes with maximum possibilities and a new case is assigned to the class by matching path towards specific leaf node. Top-down approach is adopted for determining risks in diabetic patients. At beginning all the training dataset are fed at root and partition of the dataset is carried out recursively by selecting one of the attributes each time. At every node, attributes are evaluated based on separating classes of the training dataset. A Goodness function is considered for this purpose: Entropy, gain and gain-ratio of the attributes.

Figure 3. Decision tree for classification

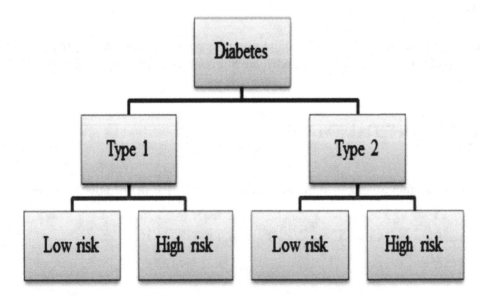

Example, for the random selected sample in training set, the attributes selected are used in computing the entropy, gain and gain-ratio considering the information (equation 1, 2, and 3 respectively) as given below:

To illustrate with an example, suppose S is a randomly selected samples containing 5 examples that has 2 positive and 3 negative samples. Then, entropy of attribute 'S' relative to classification is given as:

$$\text{Entropy}(2/5, 3/5) = -2/5\log(2/5) - 3/5\log(3/5) = 0.971$$

Entropy is 0 if all members of the attribute 'S' that belong to same class. That is, if all the members are positive, then entropy produces 0 value. And entropy produces 1 value if the example consists of equal number of positive and negative samples. If the sample contains an unequal number of positive and negative samples, entropy is between 0 and 1. Now the information gain as an effectiveness measure of an attribute in classification of the training dataset for the same sample set S is given as:

$$\text{Gain} = \text{info}([2,3]) - \text{info}([0,1],[1,1],[1,1]) = 0.940 - 0.693 = 0.247$$

An alternative measuring parameter to gain is gain-ratio as defined by Quinlan et.al. (1986). Gain-ratio adjusts the gain's bias to make it near to attributes at most possibility values by considering the denominator to gain and resulting is known as split information.

$$\text{Split\_info}(1,1,\ldots,1) = 5 \times (-1/5 \times \log 1/5) = 3.807$$

$$\text{Gain\_ratio} = \frac{0.940}{3.807} = 0.246$$

Pattern Matching

The discovered patterns from train dataset of *PIDD* and *LDD* are applied on test dataset of *PIDD* and *LDD* respectively to categorize diabetic and non-diabetic persons and for the prediction of their associated risk levels. Following algorithm 3 shows the steps followed to perform pattern matching task.

Algorithm 3 Pattern Matching
Input: i. Local (Testing) Dataset (Ts) having diabetes patients' records (Ds)
      ii. Discovered Patterns from training dataset (Tr) with associated risk level (Pr)
Output: Predicted class label and corresponding risk level of diabetic patients

1. Match diabetic patterns (Pr) discovered by C4.5 algorithm from training dataset (Tr) with diabetic records in testing dataset (Ts)
2. **if** discovered pattern (Pr) is matched with diabetes patient record (Ds) **then**
3. Assign class label with appropriate risk level to diabetes patient record (Ds)
4. **else** mark diabetes patient record (Ds) as not tested record

5.   **Return** Dataset (Ts') having diabetes patients' records (Ds') with predicted risk level
6.   End

In pattern matching process, discovered patterns are matched with each record from test dataset. The patient who exactly matches the any of the discovered patterns is classified according to the pattern and risk level of the patient is predicted accordingly. To implement risk analysis system for diabetes data, we implemented missing value imputation algorithm for the pre-processing of diabetes data to get more accurate results. To discover patterns, we implemented C4.5 decision tree algorithm integrated into Map-Reduce environment. Discovered patterns are used to predict class and corresponding risk level of the patient.

RESULTS AND DISCUSSION

In this work, the experimentation is done on single node Hadoop cluster. Two datasets, *PIDD*, and *LDD* are used for the experimentation. Both the datasets are divided into train dataset and test dataset in the ratio of 7:3. 70% of data is utilized for training and the rest 30% data is used for the testing. In *PIDD* out of 768, 538 records are used for training and 230 are used for the testing. In *LDD* out of 1000, 700 records are used for training and 300 are used for the testing.

Pattern Discovered by C4.5 Algorithm

The c4.5 algorithm is discovered total 45 patterns from *PIDD* and 67 patterns from *LDD*. According to the highest information gain ratio, for both the dataset, attribute plasma glucose test(0) is selected as a root node. As the tree graphs are easy to understand and interpret, the discovered patterns are represented as decision tree graphs. According to the possible decision values of root node, patterns are categorized into three types such as diabetes case of low plasma, diabetes case of medium plasma and diabetes case of high plasma and accordingly the decision tree graphs are drawn for these three cases separately for the easy understanding. The tree graphs contain nodes and edges. Each node in tree represented as one of the input attributes. The total possible decision values are described by edges. The leaf node represents the output based on values which are given as an input to the root node till it reaches to the desired leaf Bell, J. (2014). For representation of attribute, we used index associated with each attribute. Following Table 3 shows the name of attribute and its associated index.

Table 3. Name of Attribute and its Index

Name of Attribute	Index
Plasma glucose concentration at every 2-hour for testing oral glucose tolerance	0
Diastolic blood-pressure (mmHg)	1
Pedigree function of Diabetes	2
Age (in years)	3

Decision Tree Graphs

Following Figure 4, Figure 5, and Figure 6 represents tree graphs of diabetes case of low plasma, diabetes case of medium plasma and diabetes case of high plasma for PIDD respectively. With the help of these graphs it's become easy to decide whether patient is of diabetes class or not. These patterns also help in predicting the risk level of diabetic patient. According to the pattern, the patient is assigned with low, medium or high-risk level. For example, in diabetes case of low plasma as shown in fig 3, if the patient has the low pedigree, normal blood pressure and age below 41 (low) then patient falls into non-diabetic class and according to the risk factors described in section 2.2, the pattern of patient indicates that patient has fewer chances of developing health problems. Similarly, classification of patients and prediction of associated risk level is done for all cases.

Figure 4. Diabetes Case of Low Plasma (PIDD)

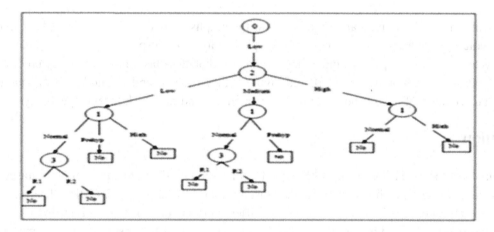

Figure 5. Diabetes Case of Medium Plasma (PIDD)

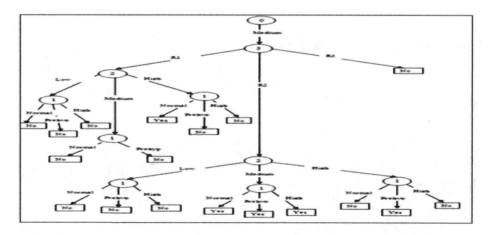

Figure 6. Diabetes Case of High Plasma (PIDD)

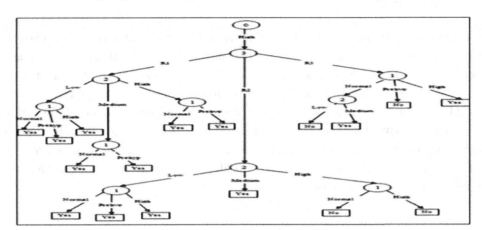

Following Figure 7, Figure 8 and Figure 9 show the graphs of diabetes case of low plasma, diabetes case of medium plasma and diabetes case of high plasma for *LDD* respectively

The system categorized patients into diabetes and non-diabetes class and accordingly predicted their risk levels. From the following Figure 10 and Figure 11, it is easy to understand how many patients are present in test dataset of PIDD and LDD with low, medium and high-risk level respectively.

Evaluation

The accuracy of the classification algorithm can be calculated by the percentage of test dataset records that are accurately classified by the classifier Daghistani, T. and Alshammari, R. (2016). There are various performance measures available to check the classifiers performance in terms of accuracy and others. Some of those are explained below. The confusion matrix is one of the best performance measurement tools for the analysis of classifier accuracy. The confusion matrix can be defined as follows Kedia, A. et.al (2017).

Figure 7. Diabetes Case of Low Plasma (LDD)

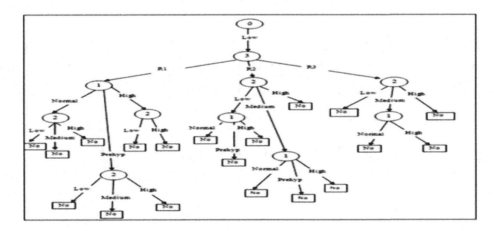

Figure 8. Diabetes Case of Medium Plasma (LDD)

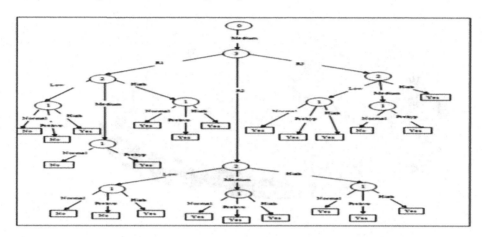

Figure 9. Diabetes Case of High Plasma (LDD)

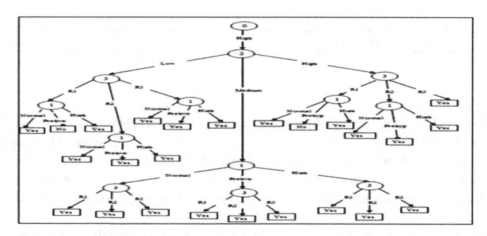

Figure 10. Predicted Risk Levels of Patients (PIDD)

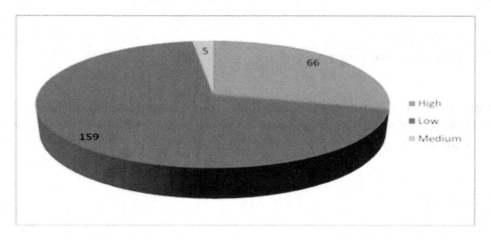

Figure 11. Predicted Risk Levels of Patients (LDD)

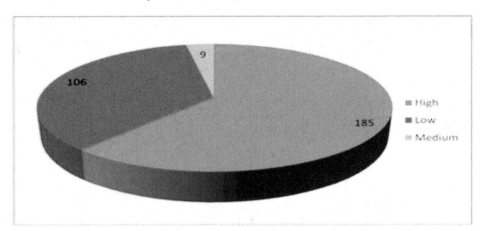

Table 4. Confusion Matrix

	Class 1	**Class 2**
Class 1	True Positives	False negatives
Class 1	False positives	True Negatives

True positives (*TP*) are those positive records which are accurately categorized by classifier. The True negatives (*TN*) are those negative records that are accurately categorized by classifier. The False positives (*FP*) are positive records which are incorrectly categorized by classifier. The False negatives (*FN*) are those negative records that are incorrectly categorized by the classifier. Following are some performance measures of the classifier are used for evaluation. Daghistani, T. et.al. (2016); Kedia, A. et.al. (2017).

1. **Accuracy** can be calculated by the percentage of records that are exactly classified by classifier. Following is the formulae for calculating accuracy Daghistani, T. et.al. (2016); Kedia, A. et.al (2017).

$$Accuracy = \frac{(Tp + TN)}{(TP + TN + FP + FN)} \tag{5}$$

2. **Recall** also called as sensitivity is defined as the ratio of exactly categorized positive records to the total number of records which are under the positive class label. Recall can be calculated by using following formulae Daghistani, T. et.al. (2016); Kedia, A. et.al (2017).

$$Recall = \frac{(TP)}{(TP + FN)} \tag{6}$$

3. **Precision** is defined as the ratio of accurately labeled positive records to the total number of predicted positive records. Precision can be calculated by using following formulae defined by Daghistani, T. et.al (2016); Kedia, A. et.al (2017).

$$Recall = \frac{(TP)}{(TP + FP)} \tag{7}$$

4. **F1 Score** calculates the harmonic mean of the recall and the precision. This performance measurement considers both the FP and the FN. F1 score are more functional for calculating accuracy if there is uneven class distribution. F1 score are computed using following formulae Kedia, A. et.al (2017).

$$F1Score = \frac{2 \times (Recall \times Precision)}{(Recall + Precision)} \tag{8}$$

The results obtained by implementing C4.5 decision tree algorithm are considered for the performance evaluation of the algorithm. Following Table 5 shows the performance measures values (accuracy, recall, precision and the F1 score) of C4.5 classifier when applied on PIDD and LDD respectively. The C4.5 classifier gives 73.91% accuracy for PIDD and 79.33% accuracy for LDD.

Table 5. Performance Evaluation of C4.5Classifier

Dataset	Accuracy	Recall	Precision	F1 Score
PIDD	0.7391	0.6619	0.5662	0.6103
LDD	0.7933	0.8195	0.8548	0.8367

CONCLUSION

Diabetes has become a big health hazard as the numbers of diabetes patients are increased since last decade. Early diagnosis of diabetes and its associated risk is the best solution for preventing from diabetes. In our work, the system has been implemented utilizing the C4.5 machine learning algorithm integrated into Hadoop Map-Reduce environment, which is able to do effective classification and prediction of risk levels associated with diabetes patients. We used PIDD and LDD for the experimentation. The experimental results show that C4.5 classifier gives better accuracy when applied on LDD. The developed system provides an effective solution for the early diagnosis of diabetes patients and their associated risk level so that patients can take precaution and treatment at early stages. Improvement in accuracy of the C4.5 classifier will be the future research topic.

REFERENCES

Adil, A., Kar, H. A., Jangir, R., & Sofi, S. A. (2015), Analysis of multi-diseases using big data for improvement in healthcare. *IEEE UP Section Conference on Electrical Computer and Electronics (UPCON)*. 10.1109/UPCON.2015.7456696

Apache Hadoop Tutorial. (n.d.). Available: https://www.tutorialspoint. com/ hadoop/

Bell, J. (2014). *Machine learning: hands-on for developers and technical professionals*. John Wiley & Sons publications. doi:10.1002/9781119183464

Bhat, Rao, Shenoy, Venugopal, & Patnaik. (2009). An Efficient Prediction Model for Diabetic Database Using Soft Computing Techniques. In *International Workshop on Rough Sets, Fuzzy Sets, Data Mining, and Granular-Soft Computing*. Springer. 10.1007/978-3-642-10646-0_40

Brejová, B., Vinar, T., & Li, M. (2003), Pattern Discovery. In Introduction to bioinformatics. Humana Press.

Choubey, D. K., & Paul, S. (2016). Classification techniques for diagnosis of diabetes: A review. *International Journal of Biomedical Engineering and Technology*, *21*(1), 15–39. doi:10.1504/IJBET.2016.076730

Daghistani, T., & Alshammari, R. (2016). Diagnosis of Diabetes by Applying Data Mining Classification Techniques. *International Journal of Advanced Computer Science & Applications*, *1*(7), 329–332. doi:10.14569/IJACSA.2016.070747

Dai, W., & Ji, W. (2014). A mapreduce implementation of C4. 5 decision tree algorithm. *International Journal of Database Theory and Application*, *7*(1), 49–60. doi:10.14257/ijdta.2014.7.1.05

Delen, D., Fuller, C., McCann, C., & Ray, D. (2009). Analysis of healthcare coverage: A data mining approach. *Expert Systems with Applications*, *36*(2), 995–1003. doi:10.1016/j.eswa.2007.10.041

Diabetes and high blood pressure. (n.d.). Available: http://www. bloodpressureuk. org/Blood Pressure-andyou Yourbody/

Diabetes.co.uk. (n.d.a.). *Pre-diabetes*. Available: https://www.diabetes.co.uk/pre-diabetes.html

Diabetes.co.uk. (n.d.b). *Type1diabetes*. Available: http://www.diabetes.co.uk/ type1 -diabetes.html

Diabetes.co.uk. (n.d.c). *Type2Diabetes*. Available: http://www.diabetes.co.uk /type2-diabetes.html

Eswari, T., Sampath, P., & Lavanya, S. (2015). Predictive methodology for diabetic data analysis in big data. *Procedia Computer Science*, *50*, 203–208. doi:10.1016/j.procs.2015.04.069

Gestational Diabetes. (n.d.). Available: https://www.diabetesaustralia.com.au /gestational-diabetes

Hadoop Map-Reduce. (n.d.). Available: https://www.tutorialspoint.com/ hadoop/ hadoop_mapreduce.htm

Han, J., Rodriguez, J. C., & Beheshti, M. (2008), Diabetes data analysis and prediction model discovery using rapidminer. In *Future Generation Communication and Networking, 2008. FGCN'08. Second International Conference on* (Vol. 3). IEEE.

Hussain, S., & Lee, S. (2015), Semantic transformation model for clinical documents in big data to support healthcare analytics. *Tenth International Conference on Digital Information Management (ICDIM)*. 10.1109/ICDIM.2015.7381876

Implementation of C4. (n.d.). *5 Algorithm using Hadoop Map Reduce Paradigm*. Available: http://btechfreakz.blogspot.in/2013/04/_implementation-of-c45- algorithm-using.html

Iyer, Jeyalatha, & Sumbaly. (2015). *Diagnosis of diabetes using classification mining techniques.* arXiv preprint arXiv:1502.03774

Iyer, Jeyalatha, & Sumbaly. (2015). *Diagnosis of diabetes using classification mining techniques.* arXiv preprint arXiv:1502.03774

Kalyankar, G. D., Poojara, S. R., & Dharwadkar, N. V. (2017), Predictive Analysis of Diabetic Patient Data Using Machine Learning and Hadoop. *International Conference on IoT in Social, Mobile, Analytics and Cloud*, 619-624. 10.1109/I-SMAC.2017.8058253

Kamath, S. (2014). Closed-loop control strategy for type I diabetic patients. *International Journal of Medical Engineering and Informatics*, 6(4), 345–354. doi:10.1504/IJMEI.2014.065438

Kavakiotis, I., Tsave, O., Salifoglou, A., Maglaveras, N., Vlahavas, I., & Chouvarda, I. (2017). Machine Learning and Data Mining Methods in Diabetes Research. *Computational and Structural Biotechnology Journal*, 15, 104–116. doi:10.1016/j.csbj.2016.12.005 PMID:28138367

Kavakiotis, I., Tsave, O., Salifoglou, A., Maglaveras, N., Vlahavas, I., & Chouvarda, I. (2017). Machine Learning and Data Mining Methods in Diabetes Research. *Computational and Structural Biotechnology Journal*, 15, 104–116. doi:10.1016/j.csbj.2016.12.005 PMID:28138367

Kedia, A., Narsaria, M., Goswami, S., & Taparia, J. (2017). Empirical Study to Evaluate the Performance of Classification Algorithms on Healthcare Datasets. *World Journal of Computer Application and Technology*, 5(1), 1–11.

Machine Learning Repository, U. C. I. (n.d.). *Pima Indians Diabetes Data Set*. Available: https://archive.ics.uci.edu/ml/datasets/pima+indians+diabetes

Maniruzzaman, M., & Jahanur Rahman, M. (2018). Accurate Diabetes Risk Stratification Using Machine Learning: Role of Missing Value and Outliers. *Journal of Medical Systems*, 42(5), 92. doi:10.100710916-018-0940-7 PMID:29637403

Mian, M., Teredesai, A., Hazel, D., Pokuri, S., & Uppala, K. (2014). Work in Progress - In-Memory Analysis for Healthcare Big Data. *International Congress on Big Data (BigData Congress)*, 778-779. 10.1109/BigData.Congress.2014.119

Muni Kumar, N., & Manjula, R. (2014). Role of Big data analytics in rural health care-A step towards svasth bharath. *International Journal of Computer Science and Information Technologies*, 5(6), 7172–7178.

Patel, J. A., & Sharma, P. (2014), Big data for better health planning. *International Conference on Advances in Engineering and Technology Research (ICAETR)*.

Praharsi, Y., Miaou, S.-G., & Wee, H.-M. (2013). Supervised learning approaches and feature selection–a case study in diabetes. *International Journal of Data Analysis Techniques and Strategies, 5*(3), 323–337. doi:10.1504/IJDATS.2013.055346

Raghupathi, W., & Raghupathi, V. (2014). Big data analytics in healthcare: Promise and potential. *Health Information Science and Systems, 2*(1), 3. doi:10.1186/2047-2501-2-3 PMID:25825667

Rahman, G., & Islam, Z. (2011), A decision tree-based missing value imputation technique for data pre-processing. *Proceedings of the Ninth Australasian Data Mining Conference-Volume 121.* Australian Computer Society, Inc.

Rajesh, K., & Sangeetha, V. (2012). Application of data mining methods and techniques for diabetes diagnosis. *International Journal of Engineering and Innovative Technology, 2*(3).

Rallapalli, S., Gondkar, R. R., & Ketavarapu, U. P. K. (2016). Impact of processing and analyzing health-care big data on cloud computing environment by implementing Hadoop cluster. *Procedia Computer Science, 85,* 16–22. doi:10.1016/j.procs.2016.05.171

Rao, R., Chhabra, A., Das, R., & Ruhil, V. (2015). A framework for analyzing publicly available health-care data. *17th International Conference on E-health Networking, Application & Services (HealthCom),* 653-656. 10.1109/HealthCom.2015.7454585

Sa-ngasoongsong, A., & Chongwatpol, J. (2012). An Analysis of Diabetes Risk Factors Using Data Mining Approach. Paper PH10-2012, Oklahoma State University.

Sabibullah, M., Shanmuga Sundaram, V., & Priya, R. (2013). Diabetes patient's risk through soft computing model. *International Journal of Emerging Trends & Technology in Computer Science, 2*(6), 60–65.

Sadhana, S., & Shetty, S. (2014). Analysis of diabetic data set using hive and R. *International Journal of Emerging Technology and Advanced Engineering, 4*(7), 626–629.

Shao, H. C., Chiu, Y. S., & Dai, S. Y. (2014). Duplicate drug discovery using Hadoop. In *International Conference on Big Data (Big Data),* IEEE.

Sneha, N., & Gangil, T. (2019). Analysis of diabetes mellitus for early prediction using optimal features selection. *Journal of Big Data, 6*(13), 13. doi:10.118640537-019-0175-6

Talwar, A., & Kumar, Y. (2013). Machine Learning: An artificial intelligence methodology. *International Journal of Engineering and Computer Science, 2,* 3400–3404.

Vaishnav & Patel. (2015). Analysis of Various Techniques to Handling Missing Value in Dataset. *International Journal of Innovative and Emerging Research in Engineering, 2*(2).

World Health Organization. (2016). *Global report on diabetes.* World Health Organization.

Wu, J.-H., Chen, Y.-C., & Greenes, R. A. (2009). Healthcare technology management competency and its impacts on IT–healthcare partnerships development. *International Journal of Medical Informatics, 78*(2), 71–82. doi:10.1016/j.ijmedinf.2008.05.007 PMID:18603470

Yaramala, D. (2016). *Health care data analytics using Hadoop* (Diss.). San Diego State University.

KEY TERMS AND DEFINITIONS

Hadoop: It is distributed processing framework used for data processing and storing for big-data applications which runs on clustered systems.

Machine-Learning: It is a system with ability to learn and improve by experience automatically without being programmed explicitly.

Map-Reduce: It is framework that allows processing the data with distributed and parallel algorithms.

Pattern-Discovery: It is process of recognizing the patterns using machine learning algorithms.

Pattern-Matching: It is process of checking the given sequence of strings for the presence of the elements in the pattern.

Plasma-Glucose: It is blood sugar level at particular time period.

Testing: It is process of making a machine learning model to test the unknown sample from testing datasets for the predictions.

Tolerance: The capacity to sustain continued weakness to glucose level conditions without adverse effect.

Training: It is process of making a machine learning model to learn from the training datasets.

Chapter 15
Integrated Big Data E-Healthcare Solutions to a Fragmented Health Information System in Namibia

Valerianus Hashiyana
University of Namibia, Namibia

Jacob Angara Sheehama
University of Namibia, Namibia

Paulus Sheetekela
International University of Management, Namibia

Frans David
International University of Management, Namibia

ABSTRACT

This chapter showcases a big data platform solution for the Namibian health sector using handheld, portable devices, mobile devices, desktops, and server systems targeted to capture patient information, keep records, monitor and process patient health status. This chapter oversees the architectural design of the system that is more oriented towards specifications of user requirements on usability of mobile devices and their applications for e-health systems. This chapter is looking ahead to the benefits that come along with good investment in the e-health, which require a very philosophical and pragmatic systematic transformation of the hardware, software, and human resources in the health sector. Sustainability of the e-health system in the future is very promising as young professionals embrace these technological advancements from the training time and can take over the system without a big IT support staff as most of them are IT literate.

DOI: 10.4018/978-1-7998-3053-5.ch015

INTRODUCTION

The ministry of Health and Social Services is the entity responsible for facilitating the well-being of the Namibian citizens by making sure the nation has put in place awareness programs on how to prevent diseases, adequate hospitals, health care centers and pharmacies in the country. This should be facilities with qualified professional and state of the art medical equipment for use to diagnose and treat diseases. The ministry is also responsible for the provision of medicine, hence the need for an integrated pharmaceutical service centers with treatment centers (Schultz, 2013).

The health system has more than 340 hospitals and clinics, as well as more than 1150 small service points across the country including emergency centers (Services, 1990). Although this seems to be a lot of facilities in the country looking at the population of only above 2 million people, the county is vast populated and many people still live in remote and rural areas where there are less or not health care center at all. Most people still work distances to reach certain health care center.

In remote rural areas inadequate housing, information and communication technology infrastructures, and lack of social services in the country contributes lack of professional residing to such health care centers. Thus, most health care centers in remote rural areas have limited medical services due to unqualified or lack of specialists in the country (Dr B. Haufiku, 2018).

Since independence in 1990 the Namibian Healthcare sector uses a manual system to keep patients records. The information about the patient is written down on a manual Passport (fig 1). All the illness and the prescription of medication are written in the manual health record Passport pages. This makes it difficult for doctors and nurses to keep track of the patient's treatment, medication prescription and record if the patient's health record Passport is not available.

Historically, traditional frameworks and solutions generally placed policies and regulations that mostly entails ethical control measures of data use at the initial data generation and gathering stages by getting consents from patients and family members.

Even though people make use of the existing health care centers, there is still many gaps within the health care service provision system of the country to make it interoperability functionalities for proper health services delivery in the country.

Figure 1. Namibian Healthcare patients Passport.

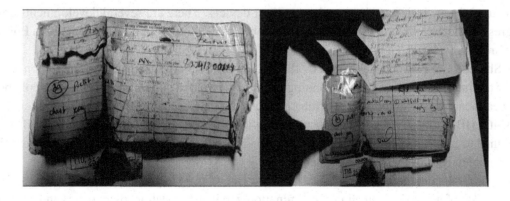

The healthcare patient record passport is hand written in an unorderly manner by the nurses, doctors and specialists. Making it cumbersome for the follow-ups and medical diagnosis of the record of a patient's health status and illness communication not properly done. It makes it difficult for the health professionals to evaluate promptly the patient's history.

The Namibian patients based healthcare Passport (record) has many disadvantages:

- It can be easily get lost;
- It can be easily damaged by fire, water or teared off;
- It can be easily stolen or get confused among others;
- It is not 100% linked to hospital records, and national health database.

The Namibian healthcare patient record passport has the following advantage:

- Secure record keeping between the patients, nurses and doctors.

The Namibia health system established to promote, improve and maintain the well-being of its citizen's good health by preventing, curing diseases and rehabilitate those that fell victims of different illnesses (Seen Environmental Learning Information, 2012).

Namibia faces numerous challenges to provide adequate health care to its citizens (Titus, et al., 2015). The country has a dual system of public health service providers, consists of public and private service providers. The public health service serve most of the population compared to the private health service serve (Services, 1990).

The majority of the population is poor and cannot always afford the country health care facilities that are readily available to them. Certain services like dialyses and organ transplantation are only available from private service providers, putting aside the majority of Namibian citizens out of reach of these services and treatments.

BACKGROUND

Technology evolved over the past years, and enormous development in the health care sector emerged with the use of new devices and secured network of devices. There are several developments done and in progress in the use of big data to solve health problems in various countries especially in Europe and Asia (Miroslav, Fedor, & Gabriel, 2012).

The Shared Care Platform developed by the Region of Southern Denmark in cooperation with IBM is one of the internet's Information Technology (IT) platform that supports a cross sector collaboration within healthcare by facilitating the coordination between the general practitioner, the municipality and the hospital (IBM, 2013). The system focus to provide solutions to patients with chronic illnesses but it is planned to broaden its application (IBM, 2013). This system does not support the pharmacological services and analysis of medication availability.

In Russia (Lokshin) the Mobile Telemedicine Treatment-and-Diagnostic Unit MTTDU «Baikal» is a project intended for carrying out clinical examination, medical inspection, diagnostics and cure of basic nosology of population in remote and hard-to-access districts and the transmission of medical information to stationary medical institutions via satellite communication.

Similar to (IBM, 2013), the emphasis of this project is to provide real time medical information to stationary medical center with high professionals across the country for analysis. This could be a system needed to serve the Namibian population living in remote and rural areas that could not reach specialized health service centers in towns as it provide interoperability between health centers with specialists to provide real time treatment to patients in said communities.

This System is aimed to provide comprehensive insight to improve the quality and comprehensiveness of care for patients with chronic illness. The goal of the program is to facilitate real-time communication among patients, physicians, pharmacists, mental health professionals and specialists so all parties have insight into patient care plans to provide adequate solutions for treatment.

FOCUS

The Big data Integrated e-Healthcare Systems of Namibia will seek to be used for standardized procedures and analyze data efficiently across the sequential rules of care and social services. This will help in developing a complete assessment of each patient to improve the level of care rendered by health professionals both in the public and private hospital, after released from health facilities on treatment and as they continue in everyday life.

The system will not only focus on the illness treatment, prescriptions and follow-ups by health professional but also to analyze the treatment methods for specific illnesses and diseases, medicine prescriptions effectiveness. The system will enable the health specialists to share knowledge and skills across the country including remotely rural areas health care facilities.

Requirements

The systems will be comprised of a central processing system with decentralized processing capabilities. The system is composed of a Data Center, diagnostic machines, End User devices, computers, laptops, tablets, or handheld or PDAs to feed, access information from the central processing system.

There can be two methods of feeding and accessing the data from the central processing infrastructure.

Online Communication

This is required for use and queries to feed and access the data live to and or from the central systems such as of recording the symptoms and queries on specific illness, possible symptoms, and prescriptions of medication and diagnosis of patient's on possible illness. The systems will be required to give live access information on methods of treatment to specific illness, with analysis of such possible symptoms, and prescriptions of medication diagnosis of patient's.

This will be required also by user who are using the accessing their profiles from new devices for the first time. The methods of authentication can be done using biometric data of fingerprints to ensure security of information access and patients medical records by themselves only.

Figure 2. Integrated Systems Big Data Solutions stakeholders

Figure 3. Integrated Data Processing Systems for Big Data solutions

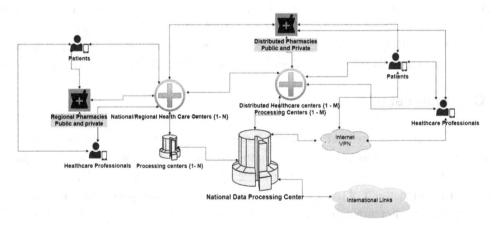

Offline Communication

This method will be require in remote areas and in specific hospital processing center to offload queries to the central processing systems. This will help also with the authentication process mechanism that will allow user authentication on their device and synchronizing mechanism with the central server for profiles update.

System Architecture

The system architecture of the big data solutions for the Integrated E-Healthcare Systems for Namibia will be comprised of the following components.

Input Component

This component will be capturing data and keeping record in the database. The input mechanisms should be synchronizing with the platform database in real-time and provide offline record keeping and synchronize when the remote systems/device connect with the central server systems.

Figure 4. Patient Profile Access Authentication Architecture

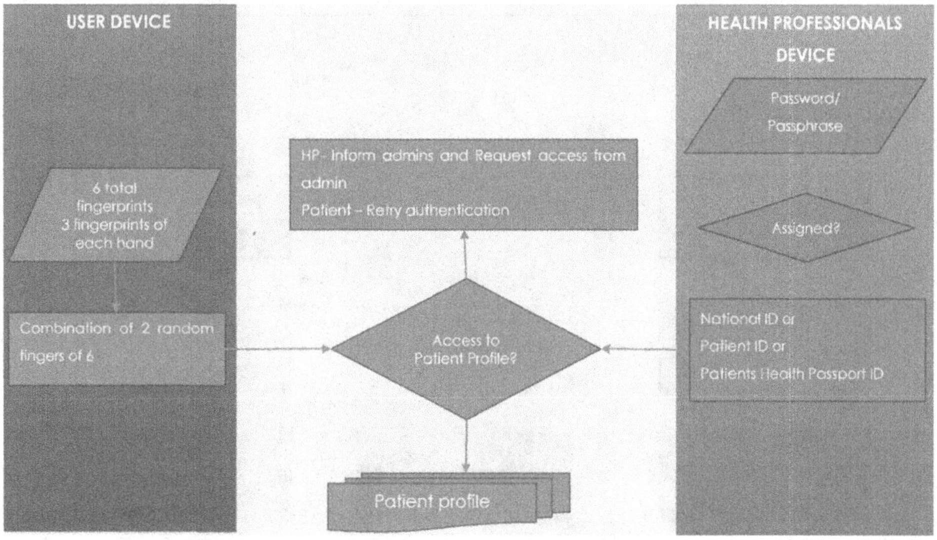

Output Component

The output component is responsible for the output of data from the system on possible solutions to the patient's disease symptoms, prescription of medication and further consultations required.

This mechanism should be able to give thorough information analysis using knowledge base information in the systems and expertise of the specialists through fast processing mechanism of the processing component. If there are no human specialist involved in the decision making of the patients treatment case the systems provides experts knowledge to the health professional determined by patterns of diagnosis by the processing component. In the case of output information where human specialists are involved, the systems should have communication mechanisms with at least three specialists in the specific medicinal field.

Figure 5. Input component

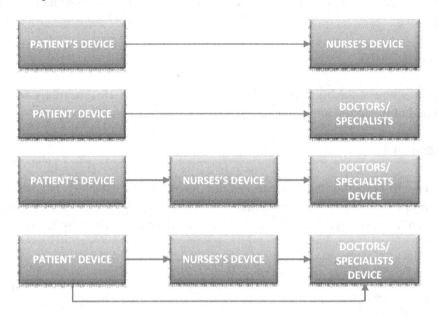

Figure 6. Output component

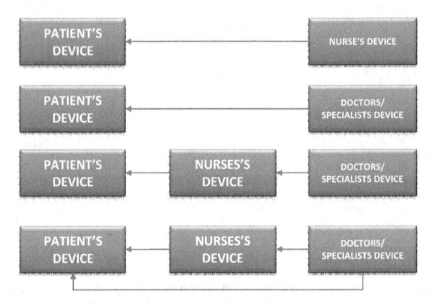

Processing Component

Expert Knowledge

The expert knowledge base, which is a collection of information on symptoms, treatments, diagnosis, treatment, medication and feedback should be stored in the central server system and distributed to remote health care center systems.

The knowledge base information should be distributed intelligently to healthcare's centers systems and to health professional's devices with records of patients on specific cases. Patient's devices will have a mobile application that can do remote processing on providing feedback of expected outcomes of the treatment, diagnosis and medication. This will help in offloading the central processing component on queries transactions to minimal and provide faster feedback and information required by other systems components.

Methods and Analysis

Wearable devices like biochips, biosensors that can be implanted in human bodies and pedometers and heart rate monitors could be used to detect anomaly in patient's treatment methods by sending out information to the systems, both patient's devices and central processing systems, health professionals simultaneously. The patient is been informed of possible abnormalities; warned and can be given early treatment and help prevent cases of a severe disease and illnesses. By getting information from wearable devices, the patient can exercise treatment methods subscribed by the application on his device with feedback from specialists. This method will simplify patients inconvenience and reduce cost of treatment. Additionally to healthy citizens this wearable devices will be used as preventable measures for precautions and abnormalities and prevent healthcare flooding of sick patients. This will enhance the health governing agencies to plan and budget accordingly on treatment, diagnosis and medication.

The big data solutions requires a Mobile Application that will do treatment analysis depending on symptoms in patients. These mobile applications should be embedded with the knowledge base, synchronized with the central knowledge base and remote health care centers knowledge bases intuitively. This mechanism will enhance the processing of information to the patients' needs and requirements regarding the input information both from wearable devices and from analysis with knowledge base information in a distributed manner and provide personalized patient care.

Techniques

Medical data is sensitive and can cause severe problems if manipulated. Data science in healthcare can protect this data and extract many important features to bring revolutionary changes. Every year, many patients die due to the unavailability of the doctor in the most critical time. This underdeveloped technology of data science in healthcare uses the power of wearable health-tracking devices to predict the diseases that a patient can be suffering from in the future. It connects the results generated from health devices with other trackable data to eliminate the risk of being potential patients. Besides, it also helps the doctor to identify the symptoms of certain diseases for providing better service. Big Data application enables health system manage accurately and predict the doctors required to serve the patients efficiently and a specific time and facility according to data's availability.

- Helps to find and predict solution to the problem of identifying a required doctor at a specific time.
- Patients' medical archives of more than 10 years of records from the hospitals and apply Time Analysis techniques to measure the rate of admission into the health care organizations.
- Focuses on reducing the waiting time for patients and extending the quality of health care services.

- • Provides an easy to use platform for all type of users, including doctors, shift managers, nurses, and soon.

The Big Data application is can serve the individuals as well as the society to reduce the untimely loss of lives. It aims to help the treatment to the people even before they start suffering. Many people have died already as an outcome of arriving at the hospital very late. So, this Big Data application in health services tracks any patient at real-time and share the necessary data with doctors so that they can take action before the situation gets critical.

Figure 7. Data processing component device at hand levels for online mechanism

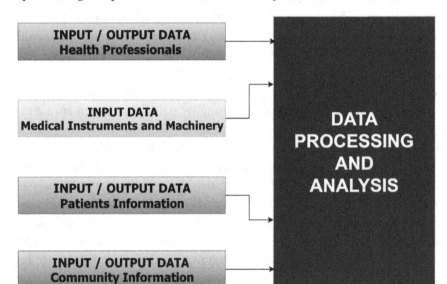

Feedback Mechanisms

This provides output feedbacks and much of big data analytics will be performed in this component. The patient's cases recorded by the systems is gathered in manner that will enhance the knowledge base on both devices and systems. This component will do the visualization of information analysis, diagnosis, and treatment offered in categories of patients, illnesses and classifications of several methods used for treatment and medication prescriptions. This method will require complex algorithms on genomic analysis and cases comparison that would require high performance computing capabilities.

The analysis and provision of information in real-time and the complexity of communication methods of gathering patterns from the knowledge base and information from health professional specialists across the country will entail the development of specialized devices and computing power in health care industries.

Figure 8. Feedback component.

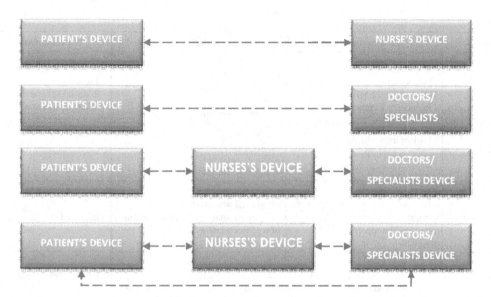

System Description

The proposed system will record all information and medication about the patient in a database using a hand-held device that doctors and nurses would carry. The patients' treatment record and prescribed medication will be available to him/her through the mobile/web application that he/she only has access and the doctors in charge now. In terms of not having a mobile application the prescribed information can be insured to the patients in the printed format Passport and the system will keep record of patient's illness and treatment thereof for future references and monitoring by doctors in charge. This system will enable a platform of information sharing (between private and public sector) and provide the health care sector with information to analyze best treatments and solutions to health in the country.

The system's record should be shared and accessed in a secured network between health care centers and pharmacies. It will provide an integrated platform with easy access to patient's record, profiling, treatment. This will enable interoperability with pharmacies to indicate the availability of medication required and thereof improve the quality of service.

The health systems information will also provide statistics to assess the best solution providers to the private and public sector at an affordable rate, for managing an Electronic Patient Health Passport.

SOLUTIONS

The development and implementation of the concept system will provide the indicated flow benefits to the patients in fig 9.

Table 1. Summary of barriers, benefits and patient outcomes of Electronic Patient Health Passport use in ED

Domain	Barriers	Benefits	Patient Outcomes
Patient safety	· Poor training and awareness · Poor system interface between HIS, EHR and EMR · Poor ethics of practice	· Access to critical information in an emergency situation · Reduced duplication of diagnostic imaging · Reduced duplication of pathology	· Reduced inappropriate admissions · Reduced adverse drug reactions · Reduced radiation exposure
Quality of care	· Lack of trust with content · Poor accessibility · Missing clinical information	· Improved and timely access to information for complex patients with multiple comorbidities · Improved decision-making	· More appropriate care
Efficiency	· Poor integration with workflows · Poor useability and navigation of content, · Lack of IT support services in hospitals	· Improved workflow · Improved sourcing and documenting of a patient's history	· Improved communication
Effectiveness	· Lack of content · Lack user-friendly technology tools (tabs/ipads)	· Improved treatment plans, · Reduced medical costs, · Ease identification and verifications	· Reduced readmissions

Figure 9. Benefits for patients and citizens

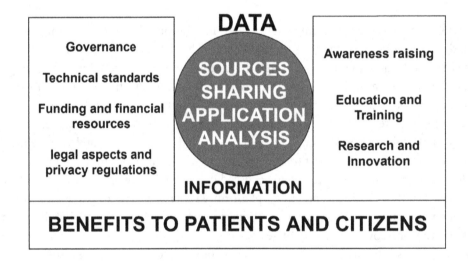

Source, Sharing, Application and Analysis of Data

Data collection in health care systems allows creating holistic views of patients, personalizing treatments, advancing treatment methods, enhancing health outcomes and improving communication between health care professionals and patients.

The approach of managing data allows institutions to balance the needs of gathering data and securing processed data. In addition balancing the privacy and security to provide access to valuable information. This valuable information contains financial data besides patients' personal and health information.

Institutions needs to manage and utilize this information appropriately as this could be most important prized asset they can possess.

Our approach is providing a big data solution that could aid health institutions in managing health information throughout its lifespan, starting from the initial stage of a population information from birth, continuously assess and monitor population health status. This lifecycle includes things like treatment, prescriptions, payment, education, research, results improvement, and institution reporting to inform decision-making bodies.

This solution will help institution widely to make accurate policies, regulations and practices can achieve the following aims:

- enhance quality service experience and satisfaction for patients;
- uplift and maintain populations health status;
- make the health accessible and affordable to the populations;
- decrease budget cost of the institutions.

The comprehensive valuable utilization of health information depends on the information being available and accessible for the overall population benefit by the right users.

Big data solution in a developing country like Namibia will provide comprehensive framework for data governance that defines the balanced conditions of data access and security, the tasks and responsibilities of users and the principles of benefit sharing to the population.

This big data solution will eliminate cumbersome traditional methods of ethical control at initial treatment stages in the future, as data have been collected and information is available whenever they are required.

The effective balanced conditions, fair privacy and security mechanism can simplify data access to various institutions and allow institutional systems easily integrate and become flexible.

The big data solution framework will accelerate legal transformations on data protection and privacy in Namibia. This will inform the electronic transaction and cybersecurity bill currently under draft in the country in balancing the data subjects' privacy, further fairly controls access and openness on data sharing and usage.

Nevertheless, the control of access to data require covering ethics in transfer of any benefits of the manipulation of personal data and the populations' appropriateness of such utilization.

Results Big Data Solutions

The big data health care solution will lead to the development and advancement of health information systems (HIS), digital health records (EHRs) which are different to the electronic medical record (EMR). The EMR is mostly an internal system of healthcare organisations such as, hospitals, clinics and primary healthcare centers. Currently the EMR is only accessible by healthcare professionals and providers in that domain. The big data healthcare solution and integrated e-health services will move the whole Namibian heath care services toward the following qualities:

- Better patient identification if not precise,
- Better patients health records availability,
- Better diagnostic outcomes,

- Better treatment outcomes,
- Better prescriptions of medications,
- Better preventive interventions,
- Cost-effective medical services.
  - Reduce turnaround time medical investigation/diagnostic
  - Reduced diagnostic costs
  - Reduced pharmaceutical costs,
  - Reduced overall budget to health care;
- Improved population health conditions and status.

In the 21 century there is substantive innovative technology that offer multi biometric patient identification solution, supporting fingerprint, palm vein, iris and face recognition. Existing biometric patient identity solution will allows hospitals to retrieve quickly patient's medical records with a fast biometric identification. Using biometrics as the patient identifier enables healthcare organizations to prevent duplicate medical records and control fraud while improving patient safety.

DISCUSSIONS AND RECOMMENDATION

With the increase of information technology usage and theological advancement for health services, electronic health passport will be a reality, for easy identification of patients. This will lead to improved patient's treatment outcomes while reducing readmissions, costs and time.

Figure 10. Big data Legal framework interoperability in Healthcare.

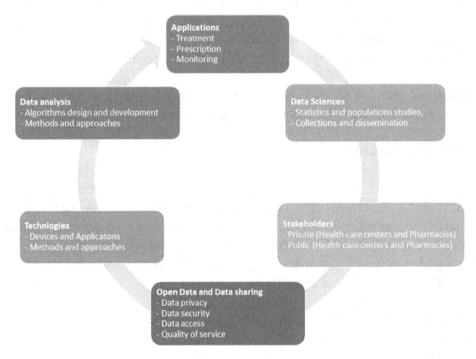

It will reduce a number of diagnostic test as health workers can relate clinical diagnosis with recent laboratory results. Adoption of mobile technology at the point of care will enable easy patient's identification and registration on the health database. Electronic patients' health passport will for sure reduce fraudulent activities toward medical services.

CONCLUSION

It will help to reduce clinical diagnostic turnaround time, as the treating doctor will have sufficient information on the patient (previous and current) medical issues

It will reduce laboratory cost burden on the patient and state, as the treating will be able to request almost correct laboratory test only.

Help monitor and manage pharmaceutical stock and on time supply
Help determine the system wastage and lack of capacity timely

FUTURE RESEARCH DIRECTIONS

This big data platform solutions needs collaboration with the health ministry, public and private healthcare centers and pharmaceutical services in the country. It will also require legal and policy frameworks on data privacy and protection mechanisms to be embedded in the e-healthcare systems for data sharing and distribution across systems components.

REFERENCES

Dr, B., & Haufiku, M. (2018, May 6). Namibia considers PPP to boost public health care. *Namibia considers PPP to boost public health care.* Retrieved from https://southerntimesafrica.com/site/news/namibia-considers-ppp-to-boost-public-health-care

IBM. (2013, May 15). *Southern Denmark to use IBM's Shared Care Platform to improve care for patients with chronic illness.* Copenhagen, Denmark: IBM. Retrieved from https://www.news-medical.net/news/20130515/Southern-Denmark-to-use-IBMs-Shared-Care-Platform-to-improve-care-for-patients-with-chronic-illness.aspx

Lokshin, D. (n.d.). Mobile Telemedicine Treatment-and-Diagnostic Unit (MTTDU) «Baikal» for carrying out of clinical examination, medical inspection, diagnostics and cure of basic nosologies of population in remote and hard-to-access districts project by. Moscow: National Telemedicine Agency Research-and-Production Union.

Miroslav, K., Fedor, L., & Gabriel, V. (2012). *Multi-Platform Telemedicine System for Patient Health Monitoring.* doi:10.1109/BHI.2012.6211525

Schultz, T. (2013). Turning Healthcare intoBig Data Opportunities: A Use-Case Review Across thePharmaceutical Development Lifecycle. *Bulletin of the Association for Information Science and Technology*, *39*(5), 34–40. doi:10.1002/bult.2013.1720390508

Seen Environmental Learning Information. (2012, November 19). Health and the Environment. *Health Services in Namibia*, 4. Retrieved 2017, from http://www.mcanamibia.org/files/files/bd5_Health%20 Services%20in%20Namibia%20-%20Seen%20Environmental%20Learning%20Information%20Sheet%20 No.%206.pdf

Services, M. o. (1990, March 21). *Ministry of Health and Social Services*. Government of the Republic of Namibia. Hosted by the Office of the Prime Minister. Retrieved June 20, 2017, from http://www. mhss.gov.na/

Titus, M., Hendricks, R., Ndemueda, J., McQuide, P., Ohadi, E., Kolehmainen-Aitken, R.-L., & Katjivena, B. (2015). *Namibia National WISN Report*. Ministry of Health & Social Services.

KEY TERMS AND THEIR DEFINITIONS

Artificial Intelligence: Is the theory, development, and practical use of computer systems able to perform tasks normally requiring human intelligence, such as medicine prescription, perception, speech recognition, decision-making, and translation between languages.

Big Data: Is an extremely large amount and varied data sets that may be analyzed computationally to reveal valuable information like patterns, trends, relations, and associations, especially relating to human treatments and behaviour and interactions that can help institutions make informed decisions.

Big Data Analytic: Is a complex process of examining extremely large amount and varied data sets, or big data, to uncover or reveal valuable information – such as patterns, unknown correlations, trends and preferences that can help patient caring institutions make informed decisions.

Cross-Platform: Refers to a software or a multi-platform software or hardware platform-independent software) is computer software that is implemented on multiple computing platforms like specific equipment, laptops, smartphones and tablets.

Data Privacy: Is the aspect of information and communication technology that deals with the ability an organization or individual to determine what data and information in computer system can be shared with third parties.

Data Protection: Is the process in information and communication technology that deals with the ability an organization or individual to safeguard data and information from corruption, theft, compromise, or loss.

Diagnosis: Is the process of identifying the nature of an illness or other patient's problem by examination of the symptoms and possible treatment.

Healthcare: Is the organized provision of medical or patient care to individuals or a community.

Integrated E-Healthcare System: Is a combination information system and platforms embedded to work together to provide information about patient's contacts with primary health care facilities and professionals as well as subsets of information about treatment, prescriptions, and hospitalizations.

Medication: A drug or other form of medicine that is used to treat or prevent a disease.

Medicine: The science or practice of the diagnosis, treatment, and prevention of disease using drugs and or therapy methods.

Patient: A person receiving or registered in health care providing institution to receive medical treatment.

Patient Care: The process in which a person is receiving or registered to receive medical treatment.

Pharmacy: An institution dispensary where medicinal drugs are prepared to be given for free or sold to patient.

Telemedicine: Is the practice of providing medical treatment and caring for patients remotely when the provider and patient are not physically present with each other.

Chapter 16
Technology in Healthcare:
Vision of Smart Hospitals

Niharika Garg
Optum Global Solutions, India

ABSTRACT

Healthcare is one of the significant areas of development where the hospitals are turning to innovative models built around advanced medical technologies like electronic health, tele-medicine, and mobile health. Healthcare sector is revolving around big data sets and huge amount of unstructured information produced from these high-tech devices and tools. But the technologies like machine language, big data, and artificial intelligence are turning them to a data-intensive science. The data is used for analysis by medical researchers which in turn is becoming solution for many healthcare challenges like early diagnosis, quality care, portable healthcare, cost- and time-effective treatments, and many more. Therefore, the hospitals are turning to smart hospitals to strengthen their existence in tomorrow's challenging medical service market. This chapter discusses the technology contribution in healthcare, challenges in future, future healthcare and cost model, and challenges for insurance companies.

INTRODUCTION

The Health care is one of the most important development areas in a country which requires efforts and attention in transition to an innovative technological model based on the high-tech medicine methods and advanced digital technologies. Over the past years, hospitals are extending their sizes and services to meet the needs of the rising demands of the community. The change in the patient expectations and advances in the technology has led to a new direction towards the hospital structures. They are on a new road of consumer- oriented healthcare services.

Technology has already pervaded the healthcare with technologies like electronic health records (EHR); Tele medicine; Mobile Health applications (m-health) and 3D printing (Y. Yin et al. 2016). These technologies where on one side provide the services which attract the consumers/patients but on the other side produces a huge amount of complex data sets and unstructured information. Further, it

DOI: 10.4018/978-1-7998-3053-5.ch016

is adding challenges for the hospitals like development challenges, cost and re-imbursement models, connectivity, scalability and resistance by providers in adopting the new models. These challenges are imposing questions on the best usage of the technology by developing a cost-effective care for everyone. These challenges are not only for providers and consumers but for the hospital designers also. With the rising use of technologies like m- Health, Tele medicine and virtual physicians, is there really a need of physical buildings? Or should the hospitals be virtual hospitals? If there is a capability of remote sensing and presence of medical data in cloud, patients are not required to come to hospitals for monitoring. The consultations will take place over the internet. The diagnosis can be done through virtual doctors. Prescriptions can be done through tele medicine. We will have robot doctors in the hospitals with space age machines where even the surgeries will be carried out at home. This disruptive shift will affect the complete nature and meaning of hospitals. How the care will be delivered to the patient? What will be the look of hospitals in future? The transition to the Smart or Virtual Hospital will be the need of medical services market.

With small and fewer infrastructures of hospitals, the overall cost will be reduced which will affect not only the consumers and doctors but also the insurance companies. There will be a drastic shift in the premiums of insurance and the healthcare companies will be more focused on Care and preventive healthcare services. Like with EHR, prediction of chronic diseases will be much easier and better health plans will be recommended to the members. Need for the preferred provider network and fee-for-service model will be eliminated.

This article discusses about the two sides of the advancing digital tech in the healthcare. It also highlights on the changing requirements, changes in the healthcare cost and insurance models and the various challenges for the healthcare and insurance companies. How the future hospitals will look like and what will be the changes to the providers and members with the new cost and insurance models, will also be discussed in this article.

HEALTH CARE TRANSFORMATION FACTORS: A SURVEY

There are various transformations factors in Health care sector which are changing the shape of the whole industry and re-shaping per the demands and needs of the patients and customers. As per the market trends and Transparent Market Research, the forecast is that telehealth global market will reach US$19.5 billion by 2025 (Market Research 2018). That is an estimated CAGR (compound annual growth rate) of 13% from US$6 billion in 2016 (Market Research 2018).

Among the top priorities of health care systems are reducing the length of stay and re-admission rates. Continuous efforts towards these goals are important with the rise in value- based re-imbursement schemes. Future health care systems will highlight telehealth and outpatient care which would be the key enablers of the systems. A telehealth program launched at Frederick Memorial Hospital in 2016 for patients with high risk chronic conditions, such as chronic heart failure, has already shown encouraging results (Wicklund E. 2019). Emergency room visits have so far been cut by half, hospitalizations have been reduced by almost 90%, and the cost of care for these patients has been cut by more than 50% (Wicklund E. 2019).

Per the study of Definitive Health in 2017, as estimated 70% of patients already use a telemedicine service (Inpatient Telemedicine Study 2017). Now a days, the patients are equipped with modern tools and self-help oriented that they don't find any value in personally visiting the doctor just to share minor details and for the renew of their existing prescriptions. Many patients completely skip visiting their primary care physicians and just use their on-demand healthcare services during any sickness or physical injury (Glauser W. 2018).

Another major transformation factor in the healthcare sector is the AI (Artificial Intelligence). AI is not only used for the radiology tests like X-rays, CT Scans and MRI's, but the methods are used to diagnose any disease by analyzing the physical appearance of patients (H A Haenssle et al. 2018),(Jonah Comstock 2018), (Gurovich, Y. et al. 2019). For example, the mobile app, Skin Vision is used to for skin cancer patients. This app allows users to perform self-checks regularly by capturing their pictures and analyzing them (Gurovich, Y. et al. 2019).

3D Printing which is another powerful tool in the medical field is also forecasted to be worth US\$3.5 billion by 2025. Comparing to US\$713.3 million which was in year 2016, this steep rise represents a CAGR of 17.7% between the years 2017 to 2025 (Nawrat A. 2018).

The patients are more involved in the management of their own health with the availability of wearables in the market now a days which provide an effective opportunity to health care business. Research shows that more engaged patients have better health outcomes and care experiences than patients who are less engaged (Hibbard JH et al. 2013). With the presence of these technology enabled solutions for patients, the physicians are also expected to use the large size data collected from the devices and using that for the better treatment and care of their patients (Simone Edelmann 2019). Also, these wearables are changing the prototype for many clinical trials by making the monitoring of these trials more accessible remotely (Munos B et al. 2016).

TECHNOLOGY IN HEALTHCARE: KEY DRIVERS IN PAST

Technology in Healthcare is pervaded with many innovations which have impacted the health sector. But out of all, projecting developments are in Electronic Health Records (EHR), Telemedicine, Mobile Health applications and 3D Printing.

Electronic Health Records (EHR)

Electronic health Records (EHRs) started to evolve in the year 1960. It became mandate for industries and healthcare professionals to adapt electronic health records models by 2014. Penalties were also charged for those failed to incorporate this into their systems.

EHR systems was a big invention which changed the whole meaning of the healthcare. They enabled the healthcare professionals like physicians, nurses and technicians to record the patient's data electronically instead of manual maintenance of the paper records. Patient's health data like their different allergies, lab test results, vital signs, weight, diagnosis codes, immunizations and many more are all recorded electronically through EHR. Also, it is used in various administrative tasks like scheduling of the appointments, admission process of patients, medical claims submission and updating the diagnostics code for patient records thus reducing the overall cost.

Need of EHR Systems

EHR systems make it convenient for the physicians and medical professionals to view and assess a patient's medical history at one location. This helps to analyze and quick diagnosis of the problems with less probability of errors. Also, medical researchers use the data to analyze and gain important insights on the health of people like viral detections and major bacterial outbreaks (Roxanne Nelson 2016).

Patients and providers are benefitted from EHR in following areas:

- *Drug endorsement:* Based on patient's health records and allergies, better medicines/drugs can be recommended.
- *Planning and Scheduling:* EHR tracks the pending tests pf the patients. For example, if a patient calls the hospital for scheduling an appointment with a doctor and EHR shows the pending tests. In this case, hospital recommends patient to get the lab test done first and then appointment will be scheduled. This enables both the hospitals and patients plan the appointments in a better and efficient way.
- *Cost estimation:* Better cost estimations can be done based on patient's previous conditions and medical history.
- *Claims Processing:* Availability of patient's medical records and past expenses help the insurance companies and payers to easily authorize their claims.

EHR Challenges

The biggest challenge is errors found in the patient medical records due to software glitches. Some of the errors like, patient reports inconsistencies in their own records like blood sugar, blood pressure, interchange values in the records of different patients. Incorrect start and stop dates of the prescribed medicines, wrong prescriptions uploaded. Along with the physical errors, there are other challenges with EHR also like transmitting and maintaining the huge data on a single central database servers. It's a biggest challenge for physicians and doctors to spend almost half of their day in clicking and navigating through various menu options in the software rather than interacting with their patients.

But do we have any standardized model which is acceptable by all? There are so many vendors and software in the markets which are available and it is again a challenge to make an agreement and bring them all on a single platform.

However, we have technologies emerging that can answer these challenges as shown Figure 1.

Figure 1. Emerging technologies

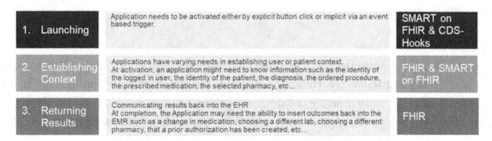

EHR Future

- FHIR and SMART on FHIR standards recognizes these challenges and are proposing solutions for solving some or all of them.
- Requires adoption of FHIR and SMART on FHIR by key EHR vendors.
- EHR customers must be on current release.
- Unpredictable timeline and adoption rate.

Telemedicine

Smartphones have become the lifeline of everyone now-a-days. Everything is so easily accessible through just a single touch on mobile phones. Healthcare care providers are also entering the mainstream where patients can do the virtual consultations with their physicians without leaving the comfort of their home and unnecessary hassle of traffic. A mobile or a tablet or a computer, any of the smart device can be used to virtual chat with doctors or a two-way communication between them.

MD Live or Practo are some of the applications which enables the virtual chat sessions with doctors, dermatologists or counselors. The physicians can diagnose the illness through online consultation where patients share their symptoms. Even medical professionals can monitor their vital signs and medicines can be prescribed from the pharmacy. This not only improves the time efficiency but also helps to ease the risks and inconsistencies while travelling to the hospital or doctor's clinic and waiting in long queue of other sick patients. Also, it is steering to a lot of savings for both patients and providers by improving the access of healthcare to patients in the rural areas too.

Need of Telemedicine

a. Ease of access to Healthcare:
When it was a big challenge for healthcare sector to reach the rural areas, telemedicine is targeting to offer the series to remote patients and hospitals. Through the telemedicine technology, it is easy for patients to access provider and any kind of clinical services. With the assistance of specialized healthcare professionals in urban areas, many hospitals in rural areas are now enabled to provide the emergency services to their patients.

b. Better Health outcomes:
With the availability of medical records on a central database and quick connection of doctors with their patients and the symptoms, early diagnosis and treatments is possible. This provides the improved health outcomes and thus lesser complications as there is an immediate transmission of health data and records.

c. Shrinking Healthcare costs:
As telemedicine is a cost effective substitute for hospital admissions, the healthcare costs for patients will reduce subsequently. Health monitoring programs on smart phones are becoming an edge over the high consultation fees of doctor visits and admission in hospitals. Even, during the emergencies, the delays and high costs of ambulances can also be reduced through telemedicine.

d. Recovering Healthcare shortages:

In rural areas of India, there is a big shortage of health services because of unbalanced distribution of healthcare providers. But Telemedicine is a showing new directions and assisting the hospitals and providers in addressing the issues of shortages by providing access to healthcare services irrespective of location and time when required (Haenssgen et al. 2016) .

e. Remote access of patient medical data:

Telemedicine is a two way communication between patients and their physicians. It creates a passage and communication channel for doctors to monitor the patient health remotely. This model of telemedicine is very beneficial to the critical patients who are homebound and immediate assistance is required.

The Future

The top 3 challenges in the Telehealth and Telemedicine sector are the cost/re-imbursements, engagement with patients and network connections.

Telemedicine has been great revolution with advance technology in devices and communication for medicines. More advanced devices means, more data collected at patient end to collect key vital for patient and this makes patients visits limited to doctor office. Although telemedicine has expanded access and improved care for patients, we have to ensure that we don't forget that face-to-face, personal patient care is still the best way for us to care for patients when possible, especially when difficult news must be delivered. One of the scenario might be a patient in an ICU is being seen by a doctor remotely and doctor tells his relatives that his heart condition is not good and there is nothing that can be done. It can be very hard for doctor to communicate this. We need to ensure that telemedicine gives our patients feel of family physicians, not just convenience. Also patients might take prescribed medicines by just talking to some random doctor through the telemedicine apps.

Figure 2. Development Challenges for Telehealth

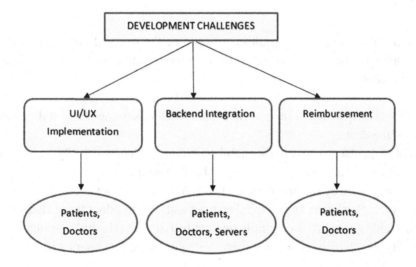

As shown in Figure 2 above, along with patient doctor relationship challenges, there are development challenges involved too. When the patients interact with their doctors/physicians, there is communication channel through various UI (User Interfaces) and backend integrations also. The data stored on the servers should be secure from unauthorized access of patient health records. In turn, the reimbursement cost increases for patients when a more secure channel is provided.

Mhealth (Mobile health)

Smartphones are the most popular among the doctors after their stethoscope. Many of the physicians are using the tablets for the point-of-care. According to the digital health consulting firm research2guidance, as of 2017, there were around 325,000 mHealth apps available for download from different app stores. The days are gone when we used to call and visit the lab to collect the paper reports. Everything is available on a single click. Through mobile health operating systems and cloud computing, patient's data is available on the touch of a screen. The physicians can seamlessly access the patient's data available on the cloud. Services to patients on demand is the need of the hour for the organizations and the hospitals also. Mobile health or mHealth is a framework built around the cloud computing technology and various devices like mobile phones, tablets and the PDAs (personal digital assistants).

The various mobile apps which are designed for healthcare purposes are as follows:

- Tools for Healthcare providers
- Point-of-care diagnostics with wearable sensors.
- Maintenance of the records of various diseases.
- Educating the patients
- Decision making
- Management of Healthcare

These different apps are not only supporting the patients but also providing them with the needs of healthcare.

The Challenges

With the mobile health and various e-health applications, the medical data is available anytime and anywhere. But along with the ease to access, it must be secure and portable. The various road blockers for mHealth are as follows:

- The security and the privacy of the patient's data which raises concerns on the confidentiality and anonymity of the data.
- Management of the data storage in the mobile devices and the availability and maintenance of this data in the network which can be shared by in healthcare network.
- The financial expenses by the organization to build the mobile networks.
- Resistance by the physicians and hospitals nurses and staff to adopt these changes.
- Not all mHealth apps are in compliance with HIPAA (Health Insurance Portability and Accountability Act) which means that there is no guarantee that users will be notified in case of any data breach situation.

- Accuracy of the data like inaccurate results in the blood pressure measurements.
- Availability of data at a single point makes it easy for the healthcare providers to pursue this information and use in the advances in the medical field.

The new World of mHealth

mHealth is becoming the future of Healthcare in the new era. With the presence of thousands of mobile apps and wearables, they have become the part of millions of people's lives. But where this technology is taking the healthcare industry? Who actually can rely on it?

It will offer not only better access to healthcare especially in developing countries but will target in decreasing the overall cost of healthcare in the developed countries by transforming the high cost systems to the patient focused systems. The highlight and key of the model will be to provide low-cost and high-quality healthcare by a direct relationship between physician and patient. The patient's needs will be addressed quickly by medical professionals

3- D Printing

Tiny Eye wash cup was the first discovery using 3D printer by Chuck Hall, in 1983. That was just a small and ordinary looking cup, but it changed the healthcare industry drastically. 3D printing technology has played a major role in the growth of health care so far. Many medical imaging techniques like X-Rays, MRI (magnetic resonance imaging) scans, ultrasounds, CT (computed tomography) scans are used to make the original digital model and then it is fed to the 3D printer. The biggest and main inventions in the medical field using 3D Printing are surgical tools, custom-made prosthetics, tissues and organoids creations, complex blood vessels, hearing aid, designed pills by combination of several drugs to treat problems like diabetes and hypertension.

There are copious benefits of 3D printing to surgeons, patients and hospitals. They are as follows:

- It helps and allows the surgeons to experiment the approach in a risk-free environment.
- It provides the surgeon a kind of simulation model where they can practice before performing the actual surgery.
- The best approach can be figured out by minimizing any waiting time for patients.
- It helps in reducing the overall surgery cost involved in the longer duration and complex surgeries.
- Early identification of risks and complications in surgery.

Challenges

- High cost of manufacturing is the major barrier for hospitals
- Absence of reimbursement costs for the setting up of 3D printing lab.
- Environmental issues with the use of metals and plastics used in different parts and wires.
- Lack of awareness as currently there are no medicine programs on 3D printing in colleges and universities. It is totally based on self-learning model as of now.
- Lack and high cost of raw materials used for printing.
- Lack of experience in this area which results in trial and errors.

CHALLENGES WITH CHANGING CONSUMER DEMANDS

Technology has revolutionize healthcare and the medical methods of past will not be able to meet the consumer demands in the future. Over the past around 10 years, much has been accomplished to meet those challenges but still there are gaps which needs to be filled in order like increasing demands of consumers for quality and cost effective healthcare medical services. Following are some of the challenges:

- Increasing aging population
- More demand for healthcare services with new technology and innovative treatments
- Higher levels of chronic diseases due to lifestyle and work life unbalances.
- Disproportions and discriminations in outcomes for specific population groups.
- Consumers and patient's high expectations and requirements.
- Financial constraints of consumers due to high cost.

These challenges are a concern in the growth of healthcare sector and it requires a rigorous and integrated effort to address them. We must act now so that we are ready for the future of the health system and make sure the solution is sustainable in the long run. It not only requires skills and innovations but a clear vision of the system which would be able to meet the desired needs.

HEALTHCARE FUTURE: HOW EMERGING TECHNOLOGIES CAN CHANGE IT?

The future of Healthcare will be very diverse than today. It will change radically. With changing customer needs and emerging technologies, the global economy will change the traditional methods of health care and relationships of patients and physicians. Technologies like Artificial Intelligence, Machine Learning and Block Chain, the health system will be transformed to totally a digitalize affordable system for all. These technologies are the playing a key role in the redefining of healthcare with better management of demand of inpatient and outpatients, patients demands and their relationships with care providers (Olaronke, O. Oluwaseun 2016) .

Figure 3. Future vision of Healthcare

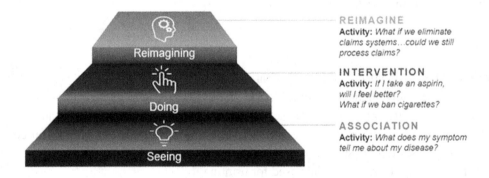

IT and healthcare leaders have this future vision and adopting the path as shown in Figure 3 above. Today, in healthcare we have huge data that can give all vital information to a Machine Learning algorithm to make predictions for future.

- Government plans like Medicare and Medicaid can analyze past claims data and predict claims percentage of different illness and category of members. Even it can be location based.
- Similarly Health Insurance companies and predict costs and launch plans with right cost and services balance.
- Member will be well aware about their health and will be able to take preventive measures.
- Wil help member to choose medical services, labs and provides.

This will have big impact on preventive health services and will help to boost care quality and bring down medical cost.

Similarly Block Chain will also play major role. Block chain technology basically changes how data is managed. It also changes how Business processes are developed. So companies can move from a process where each organization maintains their own copy of dataset to the one with shared dataset having controlled access. Block chain is the answer for that. Its new way of managing data in a distributed system/ledger with secure and confidential information sharing.

Block chain can

- Improve access to Electronic Health Records
- Improve claim adjudication process
- Improve provider networks and payment process.
- Help stopping Fake/Banned Drugs.
- Track medical credentials of providers.
- Improve Medical record Keeping

Overall better data sharing in secured manner will streamline process and make things easy and transparent.

FUTURE HEALTHCARE: A VISION

The future of Healthcare is evolving around the migration of hospitals to Smart Hospitals and challenges to the physicians and other healthcare providers. They are on vanguard of almost of every healthcare intercession including day-to-day lingering conditions of patients to the life threatening illnesses. But with the innovative existing and new emerging technologies, the growth of healthcare sector would take a big jump and would enter into a new era of rapid change. This would change the meaning of how diseases would be prevented, diagnosed and cured. Following are the areas and segments in the healthcare which will be reshaped:

Convenient Portable Personal Care

More personalized and portable patients care will be possible with an array of advancements in the healthcare technologies which includes EHR, robotics, 3D- printing, mHealth and tele medicine. The various healthcare diagnostics equipment and the monitoring devices are getting more portable and smaller in size which in turn will make the treatments more targeted and diagnosis would be more precise and mobile. The clinics and the hospitals may be able to perform the various medical tests at near patient's bedside only. There would be no need of transporting them to different sections of the hospitals. This will not only improve the patient's outcomes but also improve the efficiency of whole process. The hospitals and clinics will be able to find the best and quick treatments for patients rather than trying multiple intercessions. Not only the diagnosis but the medications to the patients will be more personal based on their medical and genetic history. Even, the medicines will be delivered to them by robots. The rooms in hospitals would be equipped with smart devices like touch screens for continuous monitoring of patient's health and test results. This will result in their faster recoveries in absence of medical interventions (Landers, S. et al. 2016).

Automation of Healthcare Logistics

Hospitals are a kind of small logistics companies which transport a large volume of data and materials through pharmacies, admin units, laboratories and pantries. The various medicines through the pharmacies in the hospitals, the test reports from the labs, the linens of the rooms travel so many miles in a day in a daily life of a hospital (David Maguire 2016). This logistics function involves a lot of cost, safety, security and quality. This is not even the core activity of the hospitals which has the mission of providing efficient care to their patients. For example, nurses spend a lot of time out of their work shift in just doing the paper work including supplying the medicines to patients, coordinating their lab results and even timely delivery of meals to their patients in their rooms (Rhonda Collins 2017). But with the presence of robots, with just a single touch of the screen, robots can assist the nurses in their administrative work like delivering medicines, collecting the blood samples, lab reports, food deliveries to the patients, scheduling of linens in the rooms . Also, they can assist in the accounts sections for running the financial reports and even the processing of claims. Using robots in the automation of the logistics, the cost and time efficiencies will be enhanced and also improves the reliability.

Simplification of Admission and Discharge Process

Most of the times, hospitals are stumbling during their admission and discharge process for patients. It is always a concern in terms of patient's satisfaction. They have always complaints about the complex and long procedure of admission where they fill out multiple forms and provide the redundant data. Also, during the discharge, follow-up instructions from the nurses or physicians are hard to understand and memorize. But with the presence of technologies like AI (Artificial Intelligence) and ML (Machine Learning), these processes can go digital which in turn will improve the overall efficiency of the process. In the near future, there will be no registration process during the admission. Patients can just walk- in to the hospitals and will be provided with a welcome package and RFID wrist bands. These bands will then direct them to their rooms. Their medical history will be pre-populated in the smart device with them. This information will be available on cloud and hence it will be easily accessible to the physicians, medical staff, nurses and other key stakeholders. AI will support in selecting the desired room type by the patient per their diagnosis. During the discharge workflow, instead of nurses delivering the instructions, robots will be providing the after discharge instructions like explaining the prescribed medicines, food diets through their recovery.

Secure Contracting Using Block Chain

Over the last few years, hospitals tend to invest ominously in the various data and management systems for EHR, mHealth, supply chain and revenue functions. However, inefficiencies in the process for the data security and interoperability is a challenge for many. Currently, their manual processes for supply chain management leads to inflated costs and integrity issues of data. But Block Chain has the potential to transform many of these processes. It is an absolute distributed system where data is written once and read only available, thus reducing the data theft. The record of digital transactions is shared among many stakeholders or users in the network without the fear of hack. Without any central intercessor, a hacker must target multiple users to amend the data available on network. Few of the scenarios where Block Chain can impact the processes in hospitals:

a.   **Interoperability of data:** The security can be alleviated for Health information Exchanges (HIEs) by Block Chain. Each time a patient is provided with a service by their physicians, they update their patient's health data like diagnostics code, procedure codes, or any referral provider on a block chain enabled HIE. The member of this block chain are provided with a private key and a public key for the visible identifiers. Because of these permissions network, patients can restrict the usage and access of their medical data to the labs, clinics and physicians (John Toussaint et al. 2014).

b.   **Tracking in Supply chain network:** Hospitals has a big inventory of their medical supplies and drugs. Their management includes planning, purchasing and tracking across the supply chain network. But Block chain can make the whole process secure, safe and efficient in deliveries. Normally, in supply chain networks, many wholesalers, distributors, retailers and manufacturers are included which are located all over the world. With such a long distance networks and complex chain, more delays and damages are expected, hence increasing the cost to hospitals. But a block chain enabled supply chain network, not only facilitates the transferring of materials but takes its ownership also. The materials can be easily traced through block chain over a peer-to-peer network (Edwin Lopez 2017).

c.   **Claims processing system:** The revenue system of a hospital is the most prone area for billing errors. Patients and customers often feel downcast when their bills are coded incorrectly leading to the rejections by the insurance companies and bad debt. But Block chain if implemented in the revenue cycle of the hospitals, it can improve the validity and an efficient payment processing system. Claims adjudication using Block chain eliminates the need between patients, customers and various 3rd party insurance companies. This not only reduces the administrative costs but also automated the claims processing which is manually in many hospitals now a days.

d.   **Group health management:** With the availability of large health data sets of the patients on one place, the health outcomes of a specific group of patients can also be managed in a cost effective manner with the data driven approaches.

e. **Data Analysis:** With so many apps, tools and mobile technologies, there would be new long data streams available for physicians and the hospitals. These data sets would be an asset and will be the source of analytics for them. Doctors would be able to diagnose early and provide exact care based on studying the common symptoms data of the group of people. Not only doctors, but the Smart Hospitals would be able to build their services based on the data collected from their patients.

SMART HOSPITALS

With the emerging technologies in the healthcare, the expectations of the consumers have led to new expectations of the customers from the hospitals of the future. With the changing needs, hospitals have to redefine the size, shape, look and services to meet the desired need.

Imagine a Smart Hospital which is automating the tasks like admission and discharge process, own choice of rooms and even medications with robots as shown in Figure 4 below. The patients are connected through smartphones with their physicians where they can do the consultation and medications can be prescribed. Below is given a case study on how a Smart Hospital will look 10 years from now (Aethon Inc. 2017),(Karen Taylo 2017).

Smart Hospital After 10 Years From now: A Case Study

John is accompanying his father to visit a hospital in his hometown. He is totally surprised to see the facility to see the changes. They are welcomed by a robot at the reception. The various elements of the Smart Hospital will be as follows:

*   During admission process, EHR can automatically records information of the patients like medical history, allergies and current medications. There was no manual filling of the papers during admission process by patients.
*   Robot then directs us to our room which was prepared per our preferences, demographics, as well as our physician's inputs.
*   There was a console near the bed side which was not just for entertainment but for ordering the lab and diagnostic tests and then retrieving the medical information like lab reports, prescribed medicines, physician's information.
*   My father was provided with a wristband which was used to monitor and analyze his vital signs.
*   There were no nurses in the hospital instead robots were providing the prescribed medications. Even the discharge and post-discharge process was planned in advance per the predictive analytics based on my father's medical history and how he is responding to the treatment.

TECHNOLOGY IS COST OR INVESTMENT

A million dollar question in front of leading healthcare groups is, "**Whether they should bear cost of new technology**?" Answer is yes. Actually its cost today, but it's like investing for future. With rising healthcare cost, it's required to adopt low cost alternatives for infrastructure and technology that enable to integrate with emerging technology solutions. The challenge for hospital designers is huge. They don't

Figure 4. Future Vision of Tomorrow Hospital

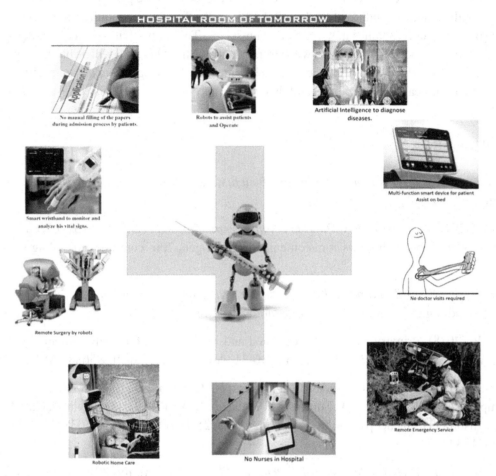

start from zero. With increasing demand, they will have to accommodate existing infrastructure as well as the political, economic and technology change.

Patients are more demanding as they are more aware about the health issues and expect better services. Healthcare is becoming more of a business to their patients where their goal is to provide them with a highest quality, affordable, portable, flexible and convenient care for everyone (Angel Gurría 2017), (Sebastian, M. P. 2017), (Siegel, C et al. 2017). But with continuous increase in healthcare cost in last 2 decades, its big challenge in front of healthcare leaders to keep cost low for health insurance premiums and care cost.

It's high time to optimize process and technology to control this cost. So we should really look forward for future and invest for betterment.

CONCLUSION

Health care should be in top priority development areas with special attention in the transition to the innovative management models based on the use of advanced medical concepts and digital technologies. Healthcare can drive the economy and become a national strategic priority. This disruptive shift in technology will change the nature of the hospital profoundly. The system requires allegiance and brand much as social media companies now promote themselves. This future will still require physical infrastructure but more dispersed, smaller but with strong identity. Smart hospital will be baseline of the future healthcare, therefore, the transition to the Smart Hospital and the design of smart architectural solution become critical for health organizations and this is the right time to disrupt and invest in future vision.

REFERENCES

Aethon Inc. (2017). *TUG Robots—Healthcare Benefits*. Accessed from https://www.aethon.com/tug/tughealthcare/

Comstock. (2018). *Skin Vision gets $7.6M to continue expanding skin cancer app Skin Vision*. Retrieved from https://www.mobihealthnews.com/content/skinvision-gets-76m-continue-expanding-skin-cancer-app

David Maguire. (2016). *Interoperability and the NHS: are they incompatible?* Accessed from https://www.kingsfund.org.uk/blog/2016/08/interoperability-and-nhs

Glauser, W. (2018). Primary care system outdated and inconvenient for many millennials. *Canadian Medical Association Journal*, *190*(48), E1430–E1431. doi:10.1503/cmaj.109-5688 PMID:30510054

Gurovich, Y., Hanani, Y., Bar, O., Nadav, G., Fleischer, N., Gelbman, D., Basel-Salmon, L., Krawitz, P. M., Kamphausen, S. B., Zenker, M., Bird, L. M., & Gripp, K. W. (2019). Identifying facial phenotypes of genetic disorders using deep learning. *Nature Medicine*, *25*(1), 60–64. doi:10.103841591-018-0279-0 PMID:30617323

Gurría. (2017). *OECD Health Ministerial Statement - The next generation of health reforms*. The Next Generation of Health Reforms.

Haenssgen, M. J., & Ariana, P. (2016). The Social Implications of Technology Diffusion: Uncovering the Unintended Consequences of People's Health-Related Mobile Phone Use in Rural India and China. *World Development*. Advance online publication. doi:10.1016/j.worlddev.2017.01.014

Haenssle, H. A., Fink, C., Schneiderbauer, R., Toberer, F., Buhl, T., Blum, A., Kalloo, A., Ben Hadj Hassen, A., Thomas, L., Enk, A., & Uhlmann, L. (2018). Man against machine: Diagnostic performance of a deep learning convolutional neural network for dermoscopic melanoma recognition in comparison to 58 dermatologists. *Annals of Oncology: Official Journal of the European Society for Medical Oncology*, *29*(8), 1836–1842. doi:10.1093/annonc/mdy166 PMID:29846502

Hibbard, J. H., & Greene, J. (2013). What the Evidence Shows About Patient Activation: Better Health Outcomes and Care Experiences; Fewer Data on Costs. Health Affairs: New Era of Patient Engagement, *32*(2).

Inpatient Telemedicine Study: HIMSS Analytics. (2017). Retrieved from https://www.himssanalytics.org

Landers, S., Madigan, E., Leff, B., Rosati, R. J., McCann, B. A., Hornbake, R., MacMillan, R., Jones, K., Bowles, K., Dowding, D., Lee, T., Moorhead, T., Rodriguez, S., & Breese, E. (2016). The Future of Home Health Care: A Strategic Framework for Optimizing Value. *Home Health Care Management & Practice*, *28*(4), 262–278. doi:10.1177/1084822316666368 PMID:27746670

Lopez. (2017). *Survey: Hospital supply chain practices are outdated.* Supply Chain Dive. Accessed from https://www.supplychaindive.com/news/hospital-supply-chain-survey-cardinal-inventory/436505/

Market Research. (2018). Retrieved from https://www.transparencymarketresearch.com/pressrelease/telehealth-market.htm

Munos, B., Baker, P. C., Bot, B. M., Crouthamel, M., de Vries, G., Ferguson, I., Hixson, J. D., Malek, L. A., Mastrototaro, J. J., Misra, V., Ozcan, A., Sacks, L., & Wang, P. (2016). Mobile health: The power of wearables, sensors, and apps to transform clinical trials. *Annals of the New York Academy of Sciences*, *1375*(1), 3–18. doi:10.1111/nyas.13117 PMID:27384501

Nawrat, A. (2018). *3D printing in the medical field: four major applications revolutionising the industry.* Retrieved from https://www.medicaldevice-network.com/features/3d-printing-in-the-medical-field-applications

Rhonda Collins. (2017). *Bringing Nurses Back to the Bedside.* https://www.fortherecordmag.com/archives/0915p10.shtml

Roxanne Nelson. (2016). *Personalized Medicine Delivers Better Outcomes: More Proof.* Retrieved from https://www.medscape.com/viewarticle/863499

Sebastian, M. P. (2017). High-Value Health System for All: Technologies for Promoting Health Education and Awareness. *International Journal of Educational and Pedagogical Sciences*, *11*(8), 2060–2065.

Siegel, C., & Dorner, T. E. (2017). Information technologies for active and assisted living—Influences to the quality of life of an ageing society. *International Journal of Medical Informatics*, *100*, 32–45. doi:10.1016/j.ijmedinf.2017.01.012 PMID:28241936

Simone Edelmann. (2019). *6 technologies that will transform healthcare.* Retrieved from https://healthcaretransformers.com/healthcare-business/technologies-transform-healthcare

Taylo. (2017). *By 2020 the Smart Hospital will be a reality.* Accessed from https://www.philips.com/a-w/about/news/archive/future-health-index/articles/20170613-by-2020-the-smart-hospital-will-be-a-reality.html

Toussaint & Mannon. (2014). Hospitals Are Finally Starting to Put Real-Time Data to Use. *Harvard Business Review*. Accessed from https://hbr.org/2014/11/hospitals-are-finally-starting-to-put-real-time-data-to-use

Wicklund, E. (2019). *Hospital's Telehealth Program Reduces ER Visits, Treatment Costs.* Retrieved from https://mhealthintelligence.com/news/hospitals-telehealth-program-reduces-er-visits-treatment-costs.htm

Yin, Y., Zeng, Y., Chen, X., & Fan, Y. (2016). The Internet of Things in healthcare: An overview. *Journal of Industrial Information Integration*, *1*, 3–13. doi:10.1016/j.jii.2016.03.004

KEY TERMS AND DEFINITIONS

3D Printing: It is a process of making three dimensional objects from a digital model by laying down many thin layers.

Artificial Intelligence: It is an ability of a machine or computer or program to think and learn and thus making machines smart.

Block Chain: It is distributed database of the transactions in bitcoin or cryptocurrency and maintained in multiple computers which are linked in a network.

Electronic Health Records (EHR): It is an electronic r digital version of the patient's medical data including the diagnosis, medications, medical history, immunizations, and lab results.

Health Information Exchanges: It allows the doctors, nurses, pharmacists, and patients to securely share and access the patient's data across organizations or hospitals in a region.

HIPAA (Health Insurance Portability and Accountability Act): It is an US Law defined for privacy standards to protect patient's medical data and other health information to doctors, hospitals, or healthcare providers.

Machine Learning: It is an application of artificial intelligence which makes the computer programs learn by themselves using the existing data and experiences.

Medicaid: It is United States' healthcare insurance program for low-income individuals and those with disabilities.

Medicare: It is a program run by US federal government which provided health care insurance to Americans who are 65 years of age or older.

Mobile Health Applications (M-Health): It refers to the use of mobiles phones or tablets in medical care.

Physicians: It is referred to a qualified doctor of medicine.

Tele-Medicine: It allows healthcare professionals to exchange medical information to diagnose and treat the patients in remote locations.

Chapter 17
Gait Abnormality Detection Using Deep Convolution Network

Saikat Chakraborty
National Institute of Technology, Rourkela, India

Tomoya Suzuki
Tokyo University of Agriculture and Technology, Japan

Abhipsha Das
International Institute of Information Technology, Bhubaneswar, India

Anup Nandy
National Institute of Technology, Rourkela, India

Gentiane Venture
Tokyo University of Agriculture and Technology, Japan

ABSTRACT

Human gait analysis plays a significant role in clinical domain for diagnosis of musculoskeletal disorders. It is an extremely challenging task for detecting abnormalities (unsteady gait, stiff gait, etc.) in human walking if the prior information is unknown about the gait pattern. A low-cost Kinect sensor is used to obtain promising results on human skeletal tracking in a convenient manner. A model is created on human skeletal joint positions extracted using Kinect v2 sensor in place using Kinect-based color and depth images. Normal gait and abnormal gait are collected from different persons on treadmill. Each trial of gait is decomposed into cycles. A convolutional neural network (CNN) model was developed on this experimental data for detection of abnormality in walking pattern and compared with state-of-the-art techniques.

DOI: 10.4018/978-1-7998-3053-5.ch017

INTRODUCTION

Automatic diagnostic systems for pathological gait based on machine learning (ML) techniques have become a popular approach in rehabilitation centers and clinics (Khokhlova et al., 2019; Rueangsirarak et al., 2018). ML-based automatic gait assessment techniques have surpassed all other classical approaches with its quantitative assessment, preciseness in prediction, and effectiveness to deal with high dimensional data (Figueiredo et al., 2018). Examination of the progress of gait treatment using such automated systems is vital for certain neuromusculoskeletal diseases (Papageorgiou et al., 2019).

Periodic assessment of gait pattern using these systems helps the clinicians to prescribe patient-specific intervention and plan future treatment (Figueiredo et al., 2018). Qualitative analysis of gait pattern is highly laborious and prone to the experience level of the doctors for precise assessment (Rueangsirarak et al., 2018). Quantitative analysis based on statistical methods or mathematical transform often fails to model complex nonlinear relationship of gait data (Figueiredo et al., 2018). Automatic diagnostic systems based on ML algorithms detect gait abnormality by classifying normal and pathological gait using some salient features. In literature, different supervised classification models have been used for gait diagnosis (De Laet et al., 2017; Zhang et al., 2009), out of which support vector machine (SVM) was reported to be the best (Figueiredo et al., 2018). Recently, Convolutional Neural Network (CNN) model has gained popularity due to its effectiveness to deal with high dimensional data (Castro et al., 2017; S. S. Lee et al., 2019). But, the investigation of the usability of this model to diagnose human gait is still in its infant state.

Most of the existing gait diagnosis systems contain highly expensive sensors which make them non-affordable for most of the clinics, especially in the developing countries. An affordable gait diagnosis system is an urgent need for the modern society. Low-cost Microsoft Kinect sensor, demonstrated to be worthy for gait diagnosis (Bei et al., 2018; Khokhlova et al., 2019) due to its portability, affordability, and unobtrusive sensing property, seems to be promising gait diagnosis.

The rest of this chapter is organized as follows. In section 2, relevant state-of-the-art literature is provided. In section 3, data processing, experimental setup and proposed CNN model for the classification of human gait as Normal and Abnormal is provided. In section 4, the results and comparison with other existing models are presented. Finally, this chapter concluded with future research directions in section 5.

Related Work

Considerable amount of works has been done to construct automatic diagnostic system. Vaughan et al. (2005) constructed a diagnostic system based on fuzzy clustering technique. Using spatio-temporal feature they have identified five different clusters which represent different walking pattern of Cerebral Palsy (CP) patients. Schmidt et al. (2006) established a fuzzy rule-based expert system using surface EMG signal and investigated its clinical applicability. Carriero et al. (2009) used principal component analysis (PCA) and fuzzy C-mean clustering to diagnose CP gait pattern. They found some overlapping clusters representing variable gait type of CP patients. Laet et al. (2017) combined expert knowledge with ML-based gait diagnosis techniques and reported a better performance than fully quantitative method. But, all of these diagnostic systems for CP patients associates high cost. Dolatabadi et al. (2017) proposed an automated gait diagnosis system for acquired brain injury (ABI) and stroke patients using two Kinect (v2) sensors. Two Kinect v2 sensors were placed at the opposite ends of walking track. The authors examined the ability of k-nearest neighbor (k-NN) and Gaussian Process Latent Variable Model

(GPLVM) to distinguish between pathological and normal gait pattern using upper and lower body joint kinematic features. The performance of those models were reported as satisfactory in detecting gait disorder. However, they have used high dimensional feature vector which may produce an over-fitted result. Instead-of applying feature selection before the classification, feature importance was ranked separately. In addition, Kinect sensors were not used simultaneously to capture single directional walking data, instead one Kinect sensor was used at a time to capture data from the subject walking towards it. Hence, the proposed system was not multi-sensor based in true sense. Bei et al. (2018) reported SVM and Bayesian as the best classifiers while performing gait abnormality detection on a large data set using a single Kinect. They have proposed an algorithm to compute step length and gait cycle. However, their system suffered from limited range of depth sensing problem of Kinect. Also, the authors did not provide any clear information on the types of the abnormal gait. Nguyen et al. (2016) constructed a hidden Markov model (HMM) which was trained using sequence of gait cycles. Instantaneous pose captured from a Kinect sensor was converted to codewords which were used as feature vector. Sequence codewords were used to construct a normal gait sequence model. Gait cycles were classified using a normality likelihood threshold. Experiment was performed on data acquired from gold standard system as well as from Kinect sensor. Substantial accuracy (90.12%) was obtained in classifying normal and abnormal gait. Li et al. (2018) analyzed gait abnormality by segmenting Kinect skeletal data into some fixed size motion windows. They have provided a walking cycle invariant gait representation. They also demonstrated the efficiency of their algorithm in presence high amount of noise. The authors diagnosed abnormal gait using k-nearest neighbor (KNN) classifier where a covariance-based gait descriptor was given as input feature. Urcuqui et al. (2018) proposed a Kinect-based automated gait detection system for patients with Parkinsons disease (PD). After testing different classifiers, the authors reported Random Forest as the best one with accuracy of 82%, false negative rate of 23%, and false positive rate of 12%. However, the authors have used a graphical method to reduce feature dimension which possibly resulted in suboptimal output. Khokhlova et al. (2019) have used an ensemble model based on Long-Short Term Memory (LSTM) and obtained 82% accuracy while detecting gait pathology. They have provided a multi-modal gait database where abnormality was simulated. In addition, they have proposed a new feature based on 3D flexion angles of lower limb joints. They reported that joint orientation data acquired from Microsoft Kinect v2 sensor can be used efficiently to construct a low-cost gait assessment system. Their results were competing with respect to state-of-the-art for gait pathology detection problem. Prochazka et al. (2015) detected Parkinsonian gait using normalized stride length and obtained overall 91.7% classification accuracy. Recently, CNN has been successfully in gait analysis (Castro et al., 2017; S. S. Lee et al., 2019) as well as in other research fields (Ajao et al., 2018; Conneau et al., 2017). Castro et al. (2017) have used low-level motion features (i.e. optical flow components) as input to CNN. Using four different architectures, they have provided a competing result for person identification using gait. Lee et al. (2019) used CNN to classify gait data collected from a smart insole with different sensors. Lee et al. (2017) used 1D CNN to classify walking pattern into 3 groups (i.e. standing, walking, and running). This study uses CNN to detect gait abnormality using low-cost Kinect sensor.

DATASET PREPARATION FOR DEEP CONVOLUTION NETWORK

Data Collection

A lost cost Kinect device is used in clinical gait analysis for gait abnormality detection using skeletal data. It supports skeletal tracking in a convenient manner. A model was generated based on human skeletal joint positions by using kinect v2 sensor. The data of normal and abnormal gait were collected for different persons. The developed model is able to classify the normal and abnormal walking patterns efficiently and accurately.

Figure 1. experimental setup

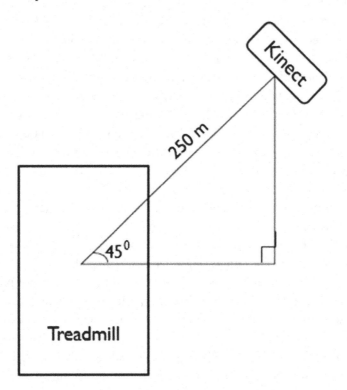

Kinect was placed at 45° from the treadmill at a distance of 250 cm. (see figure.1). Experiment was performed with 6 normal persons (4 male subjects and 2 female subjects) and 4 abnormal persons who simulated hemiplegic gait walking pattern. Data was collected while the subjects walking on treadmill at a speed of 3 kmph. Ten trials were taken for each of the subject. A brief training was given to the participants before performing the experiment. The Kinect SDK was used to obtain the data during the experimental protocol as shown in figure 2. Kinect v2 sensor was able to track joint positions in human skeleton using time-of-flight principle in real time (see figure.2). Kinect was placed at a height of 3 ft. 5 inch. from the floor with a tilt angle of 1°. Horizontal and vertical field-of-view of Kinect (v2) are 70° and 60° respectively. Theoretically allowable distance of subject from the Kinect (v2) sensor is on the range of 0.5 to 4.0 meter. The experimental setup was established empirically to visualize full body

Figure 2. Skeleton of human body can be captured from Kinect v2

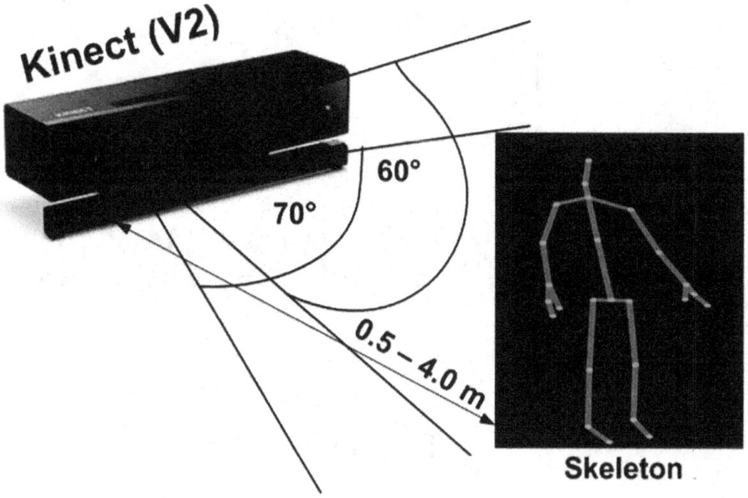

of the subjects. The subjects were agreed to participate in the experiments according to the ethics board of the local institution.

A training session was given on simulation of Hemiplegic gait to the normal persons. For each normal person the data was collected as 5 trails of normal gait and 5 trails of abnormal gait. Each trail is around one-minute time span.

GAIT Cycle Extraction

Three dimensional body-point data were analyzed and processed using deep learning architecture to detect gait abnormality. To do deep learning analysis, matrix data were fed into learning model. Since the authors considered static convolutional neural network (CNN) model, it is needed to prepare fixed size matrix data. Generally, gait analysis define one gait cycle starts from heel-strike to toe-off. Time series was manually labelled by an expert to identify gait events. The obtained data include multiple gait cycle during one minute. Each gait cycle was manually extracted and interpolated at 30 Hz using linear spline interpolation. The positions of x-axis value of left ankle joint were taken as reference to identify each gait cycle clearly (see figure.4).

The walking pattern from the raw-data was extracted manually by removing the noise part as shown in figure 3. Then the segments points from the walking pattern were chosen manually.

Dataset Formation

The dataset was composed of total number of d =1650 gait cycles. 75 (25 joints x 3 coordinates) features were obtained from Kinect v2. Each gait cycle extracted was a feature matrix (f) (rows=30, columns=75). The feature matrices were saved for all the cycles. In a feature matrix, each feature value is normalized using mean μ and standard deviation σ of their respective group as defined below:

Figure 3. Raw data from Kinect for x-axis value of left-ankle joint

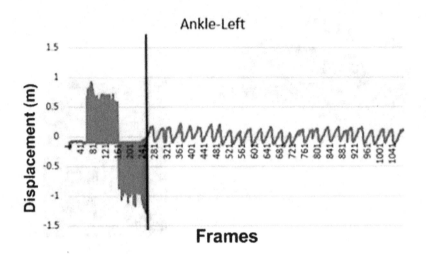

$$f_{i,j} = \frac{f_{i,j-u}}{\sigma} \tag{1}$$

Then, each data (feature matrix and label) in the dataset was represented as $D_i = \{f_i, Y_i\}$ for i=1 to n, with n the number of feature matrices and Y_i is the corresponding output label(normal/abnormal) of feature matrix f_i.

Proposed CNN Model

In the figure 4, N1, N2, N3, N4 represent the number of channels (also called feature map) created after each convolutional layer and their values are respectively 16, 16, 32, 32. RelU represents the activation function. The output of ConvNet was feed into 2 dense layer of neural network. In the neural network, 12000 neurons were used in the input layer, 4096 neurons in hidden layer-1, 1024 neurons in hidden layer-2 and 2 neurons in the output layer.

Figure 4. CNN architecture

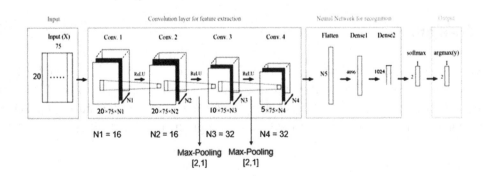

RESULTS AND DISCUSSION

80 percent of data used for training and the remaining 20 percent was used for the testing purpose. When the number of epochs in neural network of CNN model was increasing, the authors obtained better results with improving accuracy. This may be due to better learning. By fixing number of epochs as 10, the authors got the following results as shown in Table 1.

Table. 1 Normalized confusion matrix of CNN model

	Normal	Abnormal
Normal	0.992	0.008
Abnormal	0	1

Using the dataset prepared as described above, k-nearest neighbors (KNN) and support vector machine (SVM) models was implemented. These KNN and SVM models were trained on 80 percent data samples and tested on remaining 20 percent data. Results of the predictions were presented in confusion matrices as shown in Table 2 and Table 3 for SVM and KNN respectively.

Table. 2 Normalized confusion matrix of SVM model

	Normal	Abnormal
Normal	0.982	0.018
Abnormal	0.012	0.988

Table. 3 Normalized confusion matrix of KNN model

	Normal	Abnormal
Normal	0.965	0.035
Abnormal	0.006	0.994

It was found that CNN was giving high accuracy among all the three models.

FUTURE RESEARCH DIRECTIONS

As future work, the proposed model can be improved to classify multiple variations of human motion to perform human cognitive state estimation. Also, the CNN model can be implemented for a multiple Kinect setup data instead of using a single Kinect setup. The CNN model can be implemented for the classification of people based on their gait using Kinect and it will provide the identification of a person from a great distance.

CONCLUSION

The aim of this study was to classify normal and abnormal gait using low cost Kinect V2 sensor through deep learning model i.e. CNN. The proposed CNN model provides relevant features to classify these two different gait motions. By comparing the accuracy of three different models CNN, KNN and SVM, CNN outperformed SVM and KNN.

ACKNOWLEDGMENT

The authors would like to be extremely thankful to Department of Science and Technology (DST), Govt. of India and Japan Society for the Promotion of Science (JSPS) to support this research work (Grant No. DST/INT/JSPS/P-246/2017).

REFERENCES:

Ahmed, F., Paul, P. P., & Gavrilova, M. L. (2015). Kinect-based gait recognition using sequences of the most relevant joint relative angles. Journal of WSCG.

Ajao, O., Bhowmik, D., & Zargari, S. (2018). Fake news identification on Twitter with hybrid CNN and RNN models. In ACM International Conference Proceeding Series (pp. 226-230) doi:10.1145/3217804.3217917

Bei, S., Zhen, Z., Xing, Z., Taocheng, L., & Qin, L. (2018). Movement Disorder Detection via Adaptively Fused Gait Analysis Based on Kinect Sensors. *IEEE Sensors Journal*, *18*(17), 7305–7314. doi:10.1109/JSEN.2018.2839732

Carriero, A., Zavatsky, A., Stebbins, J., Theologis, T., & Shefelbine, S. J. (2009). Determination of gait patterns in children with spastic diplegic cerebral palsy using principal components. *Gait & Posture*, *29*(1), 71–75. doi:10.1016/j.gaitpost.2008.06.011 PubMed

Castro, F. M., Marin-Jimenez, M. J., Guil, N., Lopez-Tapia, S., & Perez De La Blanca, N. (2017). Evaluation of Cnn Architectures for Gait Recognition Based on Optical Flow Maps. In Lecture Notes in Informatics (LNI), Proceedings - Series of the Gesellschaft Fur Informatik (GI) (pp. 1-5). doi:10.23919/BIOSIG.2017.8053503

Conneau, A., Schwenk, H., Le Cun, Y., & Barrault, L. (2017). Very deep convolutional networks for text classification. 15th Conference of the European Chapter of the Association for Computational Linguistics, EACL 2017 - Proceedings of Conference. doi:10.18653/v1/E17-1104

De Laet, T., Papageorgiou, E., Nieuwenhuys, A., & Desloovere, K. (2017). Does expert knowledge improve automatic probabilistic classification of gait joint motion patterns in children with cerebral palsy? *PLoS One*, *12*(6), 1–18. doi:10.1371/journal.pone.0178378 PubMed

Dolatabadi, E., Taati, B., & Mihailidis, A. (2017). An automated classification of pathological gait using unobtrusive sensing technology. *IEEE Transactions on Neural Systems and Rehabilitation Engineering*, *25*(12), 2336–2346. doi:10.1109/TNSRE.2017.2736939 PubMed

Figueiredo, J., Santos, C. P., & Moreno, J. C. (2018). Automatic recognition of gait patterns in human motor disorders using machine learning: A review. *Medical Engineering & Physics, 53,* 1–12. doi:10.1016/j.medengphy.2017.12.006 PubMed

Khokhlova, M., Migniot, C., Morozov, A., Sushkova, O., & Dipanda, A. (2019). Normal and pathological gait classification LSTM model. *Artificial Intelligence in Medicine, 94*(November), 54–66. doi:10.1016/j.artmed.2018.12.007

Lee, S. M., Yoon, S. M., & Cho, H. (2017). Human activity recognition from accelerometer data using Convolutional Neural Network. In *IEEE International Conference on Big Data and Smart Computing, BigComp 2017,* (pp.131-134). 10.1109/BIGCOMP.2017.7881728

Lee, S. S., Choi, S. T., & Choi, S. (2019). Classification of gait type based on deep learning using various sensors with smart insole. Sensors (Switzerland), 19(8), 1–15. doi:10.3390/s19081757 PubMed

Li, Q., Wang, Y., Sharf, A., Cao, Y., Tu, C., Chen, B., & Yu, S. (2018). Classification of gait anomalies from kinect. *The Visual Computer, 34*(2), 229–241. doi:10.1007/s00371-016-1330-0

Nguyen, T. N., Huynh, H. H., & Meunier, J. (2016). Skeleton-Based Abnormal Gait Detection. *Sensors (Basel), 16*(11), 1–13. doi:10.3390/s16111792 PubMed

Papageorgiou, E., Nieuwenhuys, A., Vandekerckhove, I., Van Campenhout, A., Ortibus, E., & Desloovere, K. (2019). Systematic review on gait classifications in children with cerebral palsy: An update. *Gait & Posture, 69,* 209–223. doi:10.1016/j.gaitpost.2019.01.038 PubMed

Procházka, A., Vyšata, O., Vališ, M., Ťupa, O., Schätz, M., & Mařík, V. (2015). Use of the image and depth sensors of the Microsoft Kinect for the detection of gait disorders. *Neural Computing & Applications, 26*(7), 1621–1629. doi:10.1007/s00521-015-1827-x

Rueangsirarak, W., Zhang, J., Aslam, N., Ho, E. S. L., & Shum, H. P. H. (2018). Automatic Musculoskeletal and Neurological Disorder Diagnosis with Relative Joint Displacement from Human Gait. *IEEE Transactions on Neural Systems and Rehabilitation Engineering, 26*(12), 2387–2396. doi:10.1109/TNSRE.2018.2880871 PubMed

Schmidt-Rohlfing, B., Bergamo, F., Williams, S., Erli, H. J., Rau, G., Niethard, F. U., & Disselhorst-Klug, C. (2006). Interpretation of surface EMGs in children with cerebral palsy: An initial study using a fuzzy expert system. *Journal of Orthopaedic Research, 24*(3), 438–447. doi:10.1002/jor.20043 PubMed

Urcuqui, C., Castano, Y., Delgado, J., Navarro, A., Diaz, J., Munoz, B., & Orozco, J. (2018). Exploring Machine Learning to Analyze Parkinson's Disease Patients. In Proceedings - 2018 14th International Conference on Semantics, Knowledge and Grids, SKG 2018, (pp.160–166). doi:10.1109/SKG.2018.00029

Vaughan, C. L., & O'Malley, M. J. (2005). A gait nomogram used with fuzzy clustering to monitor functional status of children and young adults with cerebral palsy. *Developmental Medicine and Child Neurology, 47*(6), 377–383. doi:10.1017/S0012162205000745 PubMed

Zhang, B., Zhang, Y., & Begg, R. K. (2009). Gait classification in children with cerebral palsy by Bayesian approach. *Pattern Recognition, 42*(4), 581–586. doi:10.1016/j.patcog.2008.09.025

KEY TERMS AND DEFINITIONS

Codewords: A word used for secrecy or convenience instead of the usual name for something.

Intervention: In clinical experiment, intervention is a standard procedure to investigate suitability of a drug or any therapy.

Neuromusculoskeletal Diseases: Diseases which affect neural system or/and muscular system or/and bone structure of human body.

Pathological Gait: It is an altered gait pattern due to deformities, weakness, or other impairments.

Rehabilitation: The action of restoring someone to health or normal life through training and therapy after imprisonment, addiction, or illness.

Supervised Classification: This is a learning technique where labelled dataset is used to train the underlying model. The model then estimates the label of unseen data based on its learning.

Unobtrusive Sensor: The sensors which can acquire data without direct interaction of the subjects.

Chapter 18
Exploration of Computational Intelligence Insights and Data Analytics to Combat COVID-19

Prakash J.
PSG College of Technology, India

Vinoth Kumar B.
PSG College of Technology, India

ABSTRACT

COVID-19 is having a huge impact on the society around the world, causing a huge number of deaths, which is increasing day by day. All the countries are fighting against this global pandemic by working on vaccines, implementing complete and partial lockdowns to avoid the spread of virus. On the basis of the various literature surveys done by the authors, it is found that computational intelligence and data analytics can play a vital role in this pandemic and can be really helpful. This chapter explains how data analytics and computational intelligence can serve the world to combat COVID-19.

INTRODUCTION

There are around 7.8 billion people around the world. However, there is one major threat to the lives of all this population which is the disease that can be easily transmitted from one person to the other. Such diseases lead to pandemic. In the current year 2020, the world is experiencing a pandemic.

Corona virus Disease 2019 (COVID-19) is the disease currently causing the pandemic. This virus is caused by SARS-CoV-2, which affects the respiratory system of the human body and can also lead to death (Chan et al., 2020). This virus can easily spread from one person to the other making rapid increase in the infected rate. It is reported that COVID-19 has affected over 200 countries and millions of people got affected by it. Many people recovered from this disease but however there are many people who lost their lives due to COVID-19. The World Health Organization (WHO) has declared this COVID-19 outbreak as Public Health Emergency of International Concern (PHEIC).

DOI: 10.4018/978-1-7998-3053-5.ch018

Data analytics and Computational intelligence can be used in the pandemic situation for determining the patients with high risk, tracking the virus spread in the early stages and predicting the risk of mortality using the historical data of the patients. Artificial intelligence can be used for applications like medical help, awareness notification, screening, etc., Also it is found that these computational intelligence techniques has been applied in many countries and improvements are made as they are implemented (Vaishya, 2020).

The role of big data analytics comes into play when there is a need for huge data processing like prediction (Sivanandhini, 2020) (Rajesh, 2017) (Sandhya et al., 2020). In this pandemic like COVID-19 data analytics can be applied in the Analysis of Health records, tracking of travelling information about an individual, Government notices, report of affected cases all over the globe and predicting the cause and source of illness.

The main objective of this book chapter is to provide an overview of how computational intelligence applications are used in in different stages of COVID-19 treatment. This chapter also provide how the data analytics used in combating COVID-19.

BACKGROUND

Various pandemic like Plague of Galen, Black Death, Spanish flu, etc., have occurred before. All these pandemics were very severe. Plague of Galen which is also referred as Antonine plague erupted in 165 A.D. was very severe and caused millions of deaths. Black Death pandemic outbreak in 1346 also caused millions of deaths, so did Spanish flu pandemic outbreak in 1918 took the lives of millions of people (Srivastava et al., 2020). Currently Coronavirus Disease also known as COVID-19 which occurred in 2019 is declared a global pandemic. This pandemic is hugely impacting almost all the countries. Many people till now across various countries have lost their lives due to this COVID-19 pandemic.

Computational intelligence has been emerged as a significant technology in the field of healthcare and is applied in many medical applications in clinical diagnosis and clinical assessment. In this COVID-19 pandemic the technology of computational intelligence has many contributions in terms of products in combating the corona virus (Shi et al., 2020). The accessibility of data analytic tools in the healthcare has a significant transformation in personal medicine, epidemiology and medical operations (Allam et al., 2019).

WHAT IS COMPUTATIONAL INTELLIGENCE?

Computational intelligence is a part of artificial intelligence, which is used to understand the versatile approaches of human being like learning, understanding, thinking, recognition, etc., and empower them in real world. Computational Intelligence includes many computational paradigms that are differing from various intelligent systems. These computational intelligence methods play a vital in part in increasing learning ability and agility. Some of the major applications of computational intelligence include fuzzy systems, neural networks, evolutionary algorithms, etc.

Applications of Computational Intelligence in Covid-19 Prevention

There are various ways through which computational intelligence can help in COVID-19 prevention. Some of the computational intelligence in prevention are as follows:

Computational Intelligence in Face Mask Detection

The WHO has suggested some guidelines for prevention of the corona virus. One among it is wearing of face mask which shall reduce the spread of the virus from person to person. All the countries have instructed the people to wear face mask in public to avoid the spread of the corona virus. It is found that many people are not wearing a face mask which may increase the spread of the virus. Manual detection of people wearing face mask or not could need huge manpower which is difficult at this current situation. To overcome this computational intelligence can be used in automatic detection of face mask or not. Some of the work on face mask detection are discussed below.

Jiang (2020) proposed a face mask detection system which is used to determine whether a person is wearing a face mask or not. In this proposed system methodology, a dataset is taken and multiple feature maps are used in mask detection and complex semantic information are fused with feature pyramid networks. Algorithms like cross-class object removal and along with-it context attention detection head are used in the effective detection of face mask. Since the availability of face mask datasets is difficult, transfer learning is applied for face mask detection on wide datasets. The flow of the proposed methodology is shown in the Figure 1. The model was tested on the dataset having different kind of images like images with only faces, images with both face and face mask, images without face mask, etc. The experiments were conducted by comparing the proposed method with state-of-the-art results and the proposed method achieved results with 2.3% higher precision in face detection and 1.5% higher precision in mask detection and higher recall of 11% and 5.9% for face and face mask detection respectively.

Computational intelligence in Determining Social Distancing

Social distancing is a major solution in preventing the spread of COVID-19. In order to ensure that there is a social distancing followed among the people, the government of various countries has closed the places, where public gathering will be more like Tourism, shopping malls, playgrounds, parks, theme parks, worship places, etc., Some countries have lockdown the entire countries except for the essential utilities. Computational intelligence could be applied in determining the social distances in the public places, which may ensure the spread the COVID-19. Some of the application in determining the social distancing are detailed below.

Punn (2020) proposed a deep learning model YOLO v3 to determine the social distancing with person detection. In this YOLO v3 model and deep sort method is used to monitor the social distancing in video surveillance. Initially the object detection YOLO V3 model is applied to separate the people and the background. Once the portion of people is isolated then, deep sort approach is applied to determine the people and represent them with boundary box and assigning then with IDs. Finally, closeness among people is determined using pairwise vectored approach. This approach was compared with Faster RCNN model and Single shot detector (SSD).

Figure 1. Flowchart of method proposed to determine Retina Face Mask

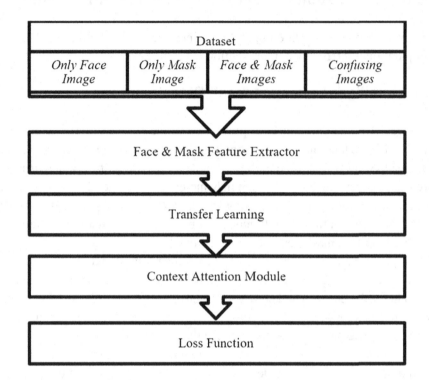

Faster RCNN is a method resulting from RCNN and fast RCNN models. It is on the approach of selective search, which was found to be 10 times faster than fast RCNN. Single shot detector is also a model to identify object. These models are used in the real time video surveillance to identify the people, which is based on feed-forward convolution network.

The results suggested that fast RCNN model has a lowest frames per second, which is difficult for applications used in real time. In comparison of YOLO v3 and SSD, it was determined that YOLO v3 model has better mean average precision, frames per second and training. Suggesting that YOLO v3 model can be applied for monitoring the social distancing on the surveillance video.

Usage of Computational Intelligence in Drone

The drone is an autonomous flying device in performing a vital role in this COVID pandemic situation, where it is used for many applications like surveillance, disinfectant spraying, medicine and grocery deliveries, etc.,

Applications of Computational Intelligence in Covid-19 Detection

The detection of COVID-19 patients is necessary to isolate them and make treatment to avoid spread of the virus. Testing of a sample for corona and getting its result takes one day. There are also rapid test kits for corona detection that give results within a few minutes but it was found in some places that the accuracy of it is not great as some cases positive cases were tested to be negative and vice versa.

Computational intelligence can be used in detection of corona using the X-Ray, CT Imaging, chatbots, etc., which are discussed below.

COVID-19 Classification Using X- Rays

Abbas (2020) proposed a deep learning model to classify COVID-19 using Decompose, Transfer, and Compose (DeTraC). The convolutional neural networks (CNNs) model is used for classification of images and image recognition. Transfer learning is used, as the availability of medical images is very less. By using the X ray image of the chest, the COVID-19 are classified using the deep CNN model called DeTraC, which uses the mechanism of class decomposition in investigating the class boundaries to determine the irregularities. The process flow of the model is shown in Figure 2. X-Ray images of Chest are obtained from various institutions and hospitals for evaluating the model. The evaluation results showed that the DeTraC model has achieved an accuracy of 95.12%, with sensitivity and specificity of 97.91% and 91.87% respectively in COVID-19 detection from the cases of acute respiratory syndrome and normal cases.

Figure 2. Flowchart of method proposed to classify COVID-19 from chest X-Ray

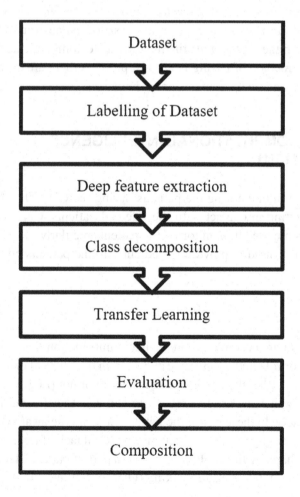

COVID-19 Classification Using CT Imaging

Dai (2020) made a study on Computed Tomography image of lung by comparing the other lung diseases and COVID-19. The study suggested that the testing of COVID-19 using Nucleic Acid Amplification Test (NAAT) of SARS-CoV-2 has some limitations like low detection rate when the viral load is low resulting false negative, Testing of samples takes a day, Progression of the virus cannot be determined as these test can say only positive or negative. To overcome these limitations diagnosis of COVID-19 based on CT Imaging was recommended, which may improve the detection rate of SARS-CoV-2.

By examining 50 patient's information, it was inferred that in early stages of COVID-19 the CT images reveals pure GGOs (Ground Glass Opacities). The progressive stage of COVID-19 is confirmed, if the CT images shows multiple GGOs, crazy-paving pattern and consolidations in lesions. Lung whiteout and diffuse exudative lesions in CT images suggests the advanced stage of COVID-19. In some cases, if the test results are found to be contradictory in NAAT and CT Imaging, then the patient should be kept isolated and start the treatment to ensure the non-spread of COVID-19.

COVID-19 Discovery Using Chatbot

Rudini (2020) implemented a Chatbot to determine whether a person is affected by COVID-19. The chatbots are based on computational intelligence technology like AI, etc. Generally the chatbot ask virus symptoms related questions to individuals and on the basis of the answers if the individual is having virus related symptoms then the chatbot tells the individuals to communicate with hospital and isolate themselves. Although this method of testing is not full proof as there are even asymptomatic cases of this virus but still it will be helpful till some extent at least.

APPLICATIONS OF COMPUTATIONAL INTELLIGENCE IN COVID-19 TREATMENT

Computational Intelligence in monitoring the patients during the COVID -19 care is essential, as this may reduce the people getting in contact with the infected patients. Currently, many computational intelligence-based devices are used in monitoring the patients regularly.

An AI based robot can be used in providing medicines to the patients who are isolated and taking treatment.

Data Privacy

Nowadays, the medical data are becoming more valuable information than the financial data, because the hackers can play a major role in the insurance claims with the medical data of an individual. It takes long time for determining whether the medical data is hacked or not (Legato et al., 2020). The medical robots are being installed with cameras, data recording and data transfer facility which enable them to monitor the patients remotely. In these cases, the patients may not be aware of where the data is being transferred and who are accessing the data, which may result in lack of trust and confidence by the patients as this data may be shared with people who are not a part of patient's family and healthcare team. However, these are essential in the decision making (Olaronke et al., 2017). So, Data privacy is most likely the major challenge in the Healthcare field of Computational intelligence. This issue needs to be addressed by protecting the medical data of the patients by deploying some strategies. Dolice (2019) suggested that Datahub could be one of the solutions to protect patient's data. Data hub are distributed and centralized service that is used to manage the connections data flow among the network and sharing. These are typically used in an enterprise application, where many point to point connections could be established within them.

WHAT ARE DATA ANALYTICS?

Data analytics is a process of investigating the data to determine the trends of data and to extract inference from it. These data analytic plays a major role in commercial industries in enable them to make expert decisions. It is also used by various researchers to prove their scientific models and hypothesis. There are many techniques and process of data analytics which is used in serving different goals.

The process of data analytics includes some of the primary steps like data management, statistical analysis, data mining and data presentation. Data mining is the initial stage of data analytic process, which comprises of data extraction from several data sources. The data may of text, image, sensor data or databases. This phase transforms the raw data into meaningful information which can be easily handled. This stage is usually a time intensive. In the data management stage, the databases required for data mining are designed and implemented. The purpose of the databases is to make the mining task easier in accessing the data. One of the essential stage of data analytics is the Statistical analysis. In this stage the various perceptions of the data are been created to analyze the data. These are also used in decision making and prediction from the new data. In data presentation, the overall vision is shared with the stakeholders by data visualization. These will be very much helpful in understanding the importance and perceptions of the data. These practices can be useful in complex systems, with many researchers are using it for various application in healthcare, agriculture, wildlife, etc.

TYPES OF DATA ANALYTICS

The primary categories of data analytics include: Descriptive Analytics, Diagnostic Analytics, Predictive Analytics and Prescriptive Analytics. The detailed description about the types of data analytics are as follows:

Descriptive Analytics

Descriptive analytics is a statistical method, which is used to infer and determine the meaning or the patterns of the historical data by analyzing.

Consider an example of a health organization during COVID-19 pandemic, where many number of people are admitted and many people are treated in emergency units. Using descriptive analytics, one can infer the information of number of people admitted, details of the patients, date of the happenings, etc. The descriptive analytics can also be used to show how a health organization has handled their work and help them understand it.

Diagnostic Analytics

Diagnostic analytics looks into the problems source and try to determine the cause. It examines about the source of the problem and helps in understanding the data faster. This type of analysis is also stated as root cause analysis.

Consider the same above example of a health organization during COVID-19 pandemic. If supposing any problem occurs in this health organization then diagnostic analytics can help in determining why it was caused.

Predictive Analytics

Predictive analytics uses the data from the past and predict the possibility of the future. It uses many models and techniques to determine the details of the data and predicts its behavior in the future. It will take the current as well as the past data and make predictions about the future.

Consider the same example of a health organization during COVID-19 pandemic discussed in the above section. In this case the predictive analysis can be used to predict the total number of new cases that could come up in the upcoming week and the severity that may be caused, by analyzing the past and current details of the patients.

Prescriptive Analytics

Prescriptive analytics uses the historical data from descriptive analytics and predicted data from predictive analytics and comes out with the finest solution. It aims to determine the accurate activities need to be done. It is also used to make decisions and recommendations based on computational outcomes.

Consider the same example of a health organization during COVID-19 pandemic discussed in the above section. The prescriptive analytics with the information of the patients details and the predicted information form predictive analytics, if more patients are found to be admitted, it may suggest to increase the infrastructure and medical facilities in the hospitals like increase number of beds, equipments, more people staff to attend the patients, etc.,

In summarizing the four types of data analytics, diagnostic analytics and descriptive analytics uses the past historical data to describe what and why it is happened. While prescriptive analytics and predictive analytics uses the past historical data and predict what may occur in the future and what are the suggestive actions need to be taken to overcome. Using the diverse analytics together a smart decision could be made.

DATA ANALYTICS IN COMBATING COVID-19

These data analytics plays a vital role in the current prevailing global pandemic, which is used in many applications. Some of the application of data analytics in combating COVID-19 are as follows:

- Data analytics is very much helpful in determining the people with high risk of getting infected with COVID-19. Despite of strict government and health organizations' advisory and rules of being in quarantine after travel, many people are found of not following it and freely going from one place to another, putting their lives as well as the lives of other people whom they come in contact with them in danger. People with immediate recent travel history during the outbreak of covid19 are more prone to getting infected with it. In order to determine those people, the data of people in any particular area can be taken, using data analytics the people with immediate recent travel history can be found and keep them isolated. Along with this data, information about the recently travelled people can be collected from travel agencies, toll booths etc. and using data analytics all this data can be analysed quickly and efficiently and such people who have travelled recently can be quarantined under strict supervision. This can help in preventing spread of COVID-19.

- The data of the infected people can be taken and by analysed the data using data analytics, the infected people with profession that requires meeting many people on a daily basis such as food home delivery people, grocery store vendors, etc. can be identified and people who have come in their contact can be found and quarantined after testing.

- The real time information of the infected peoples is obtained from various sources and updated in the COVID-19 dashboard. Some of the information in the dashboard could include the total positive cases, total new cases, total deaths, number of people kept in isolation, number of test samples tested, etc., using the data analytics these data can be processed and the impact of COVID-19 and their severity in various countries can be projected among the people publicly to create awareness about the virus.

- With many people are under COVID-19 treatment and some are kept under isolation, it is necessary to monitoring their health regularly to prevent them from the virus. The data about the treatment and test taken by the infected and isolated people can be obtained regularly and using data analytics the data can be handled rapidly in identifying the progress of the health during the treatment in suggesting the further treatment to be made.

- Location data of COVID-19 patients can be obtained and analysed using data analytics to find out which regions and which areas are having large number of active COVID-19 cases.

Use of Data Analytics in Computational Intelligence Applications

Data analytics can be used to analyze the result of computational intelligence applications in COVID-19 detection, prevention and treatment. Data analytics can also help in comparing the results obtained from computational intelligence and this will help in finding out how these applications are performing and the scope for improvement in these applications will be known.

CONCLUSION

This chapter discussed about the various computational intelligence and data analytics applications that are useful to combat COVID-19. Some of the applications that were considered includes; Determining social distancing and face mask, usage of drone, identification of the virus using Chatbots, etc. Various privacy issues that may occur under the usage of computational intelligence in healthcare were also discussed. This chapter also discussed about data analytics and the different types of analytics that are currently evolving. Along with it, how data analytics can help in combating COVID-19 and how it can help the computational intelligence applications is also discussed. Data analytics can be used in effective prediction of corona virus spread in advance, which will be helpful for many countries in combating COVID-19.

REFERENCES

Abbas, A., Abdelsamea, M., & Gaber, M. (2020). Classification of COVID-19 in chest X-ray images using DeTraC deep convolutional neural network. doi:10.1101/ 2020.03.30.20047456

Allam, Z., Tegally, H., & Thondoo, M. (2019). Redefining the use of big data in urban health for increased liveability in smart cities. Smart Cities, 2(2), 259–268. doi:10.3390/smartcities2020017

Chan, J. F., Yuan, S., Kok, K., To, K. K., Chu, H., Yang, J., Xing, F., Liu, J., Yip, C. C., Poon, R. W., Tsoi, H., Lo, S. K., Chan, K., Poon, V. K., Chan, W., Ip, J. D., Cai, J., Cheng, V. C., Chen, H., & Yuen, K. (2020). A familial cluster of pneumonia associated with the 2019 novel coronavirus indicating person-to-person transmission: A study of a family cluster. *Lancet*, *395*(10223), 514–523. doi:10.1016/ S0140-6736(20)30154-9 PubMed

Dai, W., Zhang, H., Yu, J., Xu, H., Chen, H., Luo, S., Zhang, H., Liang, L., Wu, X., Lei, Y., & Lin, F. (2020). CT imaging and differential diagnosis of COVID-19. *Canadian Association of Radiologists Journal*, *71*(2), 195–200. doi:10.1177/0846537120913033 PubMed

Dolice, Z., Castro, R., & Moarcas, A. (n.d.). Robots in healthcare: a solution or a problem? Workshop proceedings. https://www.europarl.europa.eu/committees/en/ supporting-analyses/sa-highlights

Jiang, M., Fan, X., & Yan, H. (2020). Retina Face Mask: A Face Mask Detector. arXiv: 2005.03950v2

Legato, M. J., Simon, F., Young, J. E., Nomura, T., & Sánchez-Serrano, I. (2020). Roundtable discussion III: The development and uses of artificial intelligence in medicine: A work in progress. Gender and the Genome, 4, 247028971989870. doi:10.1177/2470289719898701

Olaronke, I., Oluwaseun, O., & Rhoda, I. (2017). State of the art: A study of human-robot interaction in healthcare. *International Journal of Information Engineering and Electronic Business*, *9*(3), 43–55. doi:10.5815/ijieeb.2017.03.06

Punn, N. S., Sonbhadra, S. K., & Agarwal, S. (2020). Monitoring COVID-19 social distancing with person detection and tracking via fine-tuned YOLOv3 and Deepsort techniques. arXiv:2005.01385v2 [cs.CV]

Rajesh, R., & Mathivanan, B. (2017). Predicting Flight Delay using ANN with Multi-core Map Reduce Framework. In *Communication and power engineering* (p. 280). Walter de Gruyter GmbH & Co KG.

Rudini, A. A. (2020). *Implementation of chatbot in the health industry to detect COVID-19 plague.* SSRN Electronic Journal., doi:10.2139srn.3590815

Sandhya, R., Prakash, J., & Vinoth Kumar, B. (2020). Comparative Analysis of Clustering Techniques in Anomaly Detection Wind Turbine Data. *Journal of Xi'an University of Architecture & Technology*, *12*(3), 5684–5694.

Shi, F., Wang, J., Shi, J., Wu, Z., Wang, Q., Tang, Z., He, K., Shi, Y., & Shen, D. (2020). Review of artificial intelligence techniques in imaging data acquisition, segmentation and diagnosis for COVID-19. IEEE Reviews in Biomedical Engineering, 1–1. doi:10.1109/RBME.2020.2987975 PubMed

Sivanandhini, P., & Prakash, J. (2020). Crop Yield Prediction Analysis using Feed Forward and Recurrent Neural Network. *International Journal of Innovative Science and Research Technology*, *5*(5), 1092–1096. doi:10.38124/volume5issue5

Srivastava, N., Baxi, P., Ratho, R. K., & Saxena, S. K. (2020). Global trends in epidemiology of coronavirus disease 2019 (COVID-19). *Medical Virology: From Pathogenesis to Disease Control*, 9-21. doi:10.1007/978-981-15-4814-72

Tay, M., Low, Y., Zhao, X., Cook, A., & Lee, V. (2015). Comparison of infrared thermal detection systems for mass fever screening in a tropical healthcare setting. *Public Health*, *129*(11), 1471–1478. doi:10.1016/j.puhe.2015.07.023 PubMed

Vaishya, R., Javaid, M., Khan, I. H., & Haleem, A. (2020). Artificial intelligence (AI) applications for COVID-19 pandemic. *Diabetes & Metabolic Syndrome*, *14*(4), 337–339. doi:10.1016/j.dsx.2020.04.012 PubMed

KEY TERMS AND DEFINITIONS

Chatbot: It is an application which act as a live agent.

Combating: Fighting against the virus through some protective measures.

Computational Intelligence: It is the ability to make computer learn to perform specific task through training.

COVID-19: Corona Virus Disease 2019 is a virus that cause illness to the people by affecting their respiratory system.

Data Analytics: It is a process of investigating the dataset and deriving meaningful information from it.

Isolation: Keeping them separate from others contact.

Pandemic: It is an epidemic that may spread all over the world.

Chapter 19
Computer–Aided Diagnosis of Knee Osteoarthritis From Radiographic Images Using Random Forest Classifier

Pavithra D.

Avinashilingam Institute for Home Science and Higher Education for Women, India

Vanithamani R.

Avinashilingam Institute for Home Science and Higher Education for Women, India

Judith Justin

Avinashilingam Institute for Home Science and Higher Education for Women, India

ABSTRACT

Knee osteoarthritis (OA) is a degenerative joint disease that occurs due to wear down of cartilage. Early diagnosis has a pivotal role in providing effective treatment and in attenuating further effects. This chapter aims to grade the severity of knee OA into three classes, namely absence of OA, mild OA, and severe OA, from radiographic images. Pre-processing steps include CLAHE and anisotropic diffusion for contrast enhancement and noise reduction, respectively. Niblack thresholding algorithm is used to segment the cartilage region. GLCM features like contrast, correlation, energy, homogeneity, and cartilage features such as area, medial, and lateral thickness are extracted from the segmented region. These features are fed to random forest classifier to assess the severity of OA. Performance of random forest classifier is compared with ANFIS and Naïve Bayes classifier. The classifiers are trained with 120 images and tested with 45 images. Experimental results show that random forest classifier achieves a higher accuracy of 88.8% compared to ANFIS and Naïve Bayes classifier.

DOI: 10.4018/978-1-7998-3053-5.ch019

INTRODUCTION

Knee Osteoarthritis (OA) is a chronic disease caused by the degeneration of cartilage, which leads to sclerosis and osteophytes. Cartilage helps the easy glide of bones and prevents them from rubbing against each other. In addition to the knee, osteoarthritis can occur in various parts of the body like toes, fingers, pelvis and even in the spine. The significant risk factors of osteoarthritis are ageing, obesity, decreased physical activity and injury. In primary stages, treating osteoarthritis includes non-surgical treatments such as medications, physiotherapy and lifestyle modification. If the disease is left untreated, it leads to the formation of bone spurs, deterioration of connective tissue that attaches muscle to bone and inflammation of joint lining. This adversely affects the individual's ability to move. Complete loss of cartilage characterized by bone-on-bone contact is an indication for end-stage OA. In such conditions, surgical treatments such as joint replacement surgeries, arthroscopy, osteotomy and arthroplasty are suggested. Several imaging methods include Magnetic Resonance Imaging (MRI), Computed Tomography (CT), and Ultrasound are used for diagnosis of augmented OA, however, X-rays are considered the gold standard.

According to National Health Interview Survey, arthritis which includes the knee OA, is expected to increase in the forthcoming years. By the year 2030, an estimated 67 million adults would have arthritis. Globally, OA ranks eighth in all diseases and has impact over 50% of population. In India, OA has a prevalence of 22% to 39% which is comparatively higher than in several countries. Data analytics and technology integration in healthcare improve population health and individual care outcomes. Data science application in medical imaging has caused tremendous impact and most significant potential for future development in healthcare. Hence, the development of expert systems for the diagnosis of knee osteoarthritis from medical images is in demand.

RELATED WORK

Machine intelligence models have received impressive results in various healthcare problems. This is attributed to the availability of data and advancements in algorithms. Several studies have been carried out on the diagnosis of knee osteoarthritis employing the computer-aided methods. Each study applied various segmentation techniques, feature extraction methods and classifiers to diagnose the knee OA. This section describes various researcher's works and studies of related research problems.

Brahim et al. (2019) applied circular Fourier filtering to retain necessary information related to tibial trabecular bone structure. Independent Component Analysis (ICA) was adopted for feature extraction and the first ten discriminant components were used for classification using Naive Bayes and Random Forest classifier. This method classified radiographic images with an accuracy of 82.98%, a sensitivity of 87.15%, and a specificity of 80.65%.

Thomson et al. (2015) developed an automated grading method by identifying the outlines of bones to standardise the measurement of OA features of the knee. The features derived from both bone shape and image texture in the tibia were given to Random Forest classifiers. The weighted sum of the outputs of two Random Forest classifiers improved the performance. Alternatively, the experimental results proved that Random Forest classifiers trained on simple pixel ratio features are as effective as the texture and shape features.

Anifah et al. (2013) employed Gabor kernel, template matching, row sum graph and gray level center of mass method for segmentation. A classic Self Organizing Map algorithm was trained with Gray Level Co-occurrence Matrix (GLCM) features. The experimental results proved excellent classification accuracy for grade 0, 1 and 4, whereas the grade 2 and 3 were failures.

Wahyuningrum et al. (2016) applied Structural 2-Dimensional Principal Component Analysis (S2D-PCA) for feature extraction and Support Vector Machine (SVM) for classification. The maximum average classification accuracy was compared with Gaussian kernel and Polynomial Kernel. The experimental results proved that the hybrid of S2DPCA and SVM could differentiate KL grade 0 from the other grades with accuracy up to 94.33%.

Subramoniam et al. (2013) proposed a novel classification system based on Local Binary Pattern (LBP) features. The extracted LBP features are fed to K-Nearest Neighbor (KNN) classifier with various distance measures such as Euclidian, Manhattan, cosine and correlation distance measure. The experimental results proved that the correlation distance performed better than other distance measures.

Oka et al. (2008) proposed an automated system that measures major parameters for OA diagnosis such as Joint Space Area (JSA) and the minimum JSW at medial and lateral sides, osteophyte area, and Tibiofemoral Angle (TFA) on plain anteroposterior radiographs. Robert's filter is applied to extract the rough outlines of the tibia and femur. Canny's filter is applied to remove the noise of the line. A horizontal neighbourhood difference filter is applied to measure the osteophyte area and TFA. The limitation of this system was that the pre-articular disorders are not included which might possibly lead to failures.

Shamir et al. (2009) proposed an automatic classification of the knee OA into four classes using the nearest neighbour rule. Features such as Zernike features, Tamura texture features, Haralick features, Chebyshev statistics, Multiscale histograms and first four moments of mean, standard deviation, skewness and kurtosis were extracted after localizing the knee joints. Each descriptor is assigned with a Fisher score to select the most informative descriptor while neglecting noisy features. Experimental results show that doubtful OA was classified with a much lower accuracy when compared with other classes.

Kluzek et al. (2019) studied various machine learning algorithms in OA research and demonstrated that employing big data analysis, improved algorithms including the recent emergence of quantum tools will possibly open the door to exciting new avenues for OA research community.

The usage of machine learning algorithms in OA research enables more clinically relevant subgrouping of OA affected patients. As an alternative to a classification problem, some researchers employed machine learning algorithms to identify relatedness or differences in features of OA and non-OA cases. Kinds et al. (2013) evaluated the relationship of various features extracted from knee radiographs with their clinical characteristics during a 5-year follow-up. The extracted features were joint space width, varus angle, osteophyte area, eminence height, and bone density. The relationships were commonly found for osteophyte area and joint space width, whereas clinical outcomes varied over time.

Hirvasniemi et al. (2014) proposed image analysis methods to quantify differences in bone texture in the healthy and osteoarthritic knee. Density-related and structure-related parameters like homogeneity index, entropy based on Laplacian and local binary pattern were extracted. The results interpreted that structural analysis of bone was more reproducible and better suited for quantitative analysis of radiographic images.

Neogi et al. (2009) established a strong relationship between the severity of radiographic knee osteoarthritis and knee pain. The pain measures taken into consideration are frequency, consistency and severity of pain experienced by participants in MOST and Framingham Osteoarthritis studies. The radiographic features accurately reflected the presence of painful pathology.

Vijayakumari et al. (2019) presented the use of Particle Swarm Optimization (PSO) algorithm along with inertia weights to segment the cartilage. Applying PSO gives a low contrast gray image and thresholding is performed to extract cartilage from the background. The standard value of cartilage thickness was set to 1.65 mm and below standard value is notified as to the presence of OA.

Mu et al. (2011) presented an algorithm to extract knee bone contours from X-rays based on bone sweep using decomposition and a graph search. Horizontal sweep lines and rotary sweep rays are used to segment tibia and femur. Circles are used for segmenting the patella instead of sweep lines as the patella contains many irregular curves. The final segmentation is performed using a graph search to refine the results. This approach proved to extract the contours of overlapped bones in a better way.

In recent years, the medical imaging research community is focusing on deep learning. The potential for deep learning in OA disease detection has created a greater impact. Tiulpin et al. (2018) proposed a more robust model of the deep Siamese neural network using random seeds. It consisted of two branches, each with convolution layers followed by batch normalization, ReLU layer and a max-pooling layer. The outputs from two branches were concatenated using a softmax layer. Instead of comparing image pairs, it used the symmetry in the image to learn identical weights. This method yielded a quadratic kappa coefficient of 0.83 and an average multiclass accuracy of 66.71%.

Hegadi et al. (2019) proposed a simple Artificial Neural Network (ANN) based classification system to diagnose the knee OA from X-ray images. The boundaries of the synovial cavity are extracted using a global threshold-based segmentation. False contours are removed using open morphological operation. Image features such as mean, standard deviation, range, skewness and edge curvature are given to a two-layer feed-forward network to classify into the normal or affected knee.

Bhat et al. (2019) applied Otsu's segmentation method to acquire the region of interest. Feature extraction techniques include Discrete Wavelet Transform (DWT) followed by Histogram of Gradients (HoG). These features were provided as input to the SVM classifier for normal and abnormal cases. The experimental results of the SVM classifier were compared with ANN and proved to be superior in time effectiveness and iterative learning with an accuracy rate of 85.33%.

Wahyuningrum et al. (2019) proposed a Convolutional Neural Network that combines pre-processing and feature extraction process, followed by Long Short-Term Memory (LSTM) as a classification process. LSTM is an upgraded model of the Recurrent Neural Network. The experimental results have shown that CNN architectures have performed well in extracting high-level features, therefore enabling the LSTM to effectively discriminate between Kellgren-Lawrence (KL) grades 0 to 4 with a mean accuracy of 75.28%.

Yoo et al. (2016) presented a convenient scoring system and ANN to identify the risk for the knee OA. The predictors of the scoring system were selected as inputs of ANN. The neural network was trained to provide output variables with a five graded scale of radiographic severity. It was established that the performance of the scoring system was improved significantly by ANN.

Recent findings by Moustakidis et al. (2019) revealed that deep learning offers the most efficient solution in the task of OA diagnosis with classification accuracies up to 86.95%, however, it was unfortunately accompanied by computational complexity. It was based on patients' self-reported data about joint symptoms, disability, function and general health from the baseline visit. The advent of quantum computing offers the potential to alleviate such complexities. It was also established that the highest specificity was achieved by Random Forest and the results of Deep Neural Network (DNN), SVM, Adaboost and Random Forest were significantly superior.

With the growth of big data, various researchers conducted disease prediction tasks employing statistical data. Lim et al. (2019) adopted medical utilization and health behavior information of subjects aged 50 years and older as statistical data. To avoid overfitting issues, dropout and batch normalization techniques were adopted. DNN was experimented with four various combinations of Principle Component Analysis (PCA) techniques. Comparatively, DNN and PCA with quantile transformer revealed satisfactory results.

Blessia et al. (2011) proposed the application of a fuzzy logic interference system to automate the diagnosis of osteoarthritis from medical data of patients such as pain, morning stiffness, warmth on joints, bony tenderness, and C - Reactive Protein test and so on. A rule base consisting of 33 rules was constructed, and the fuzzy outputs were aggregated to one fuzzy set. The centroid defuzzification method was addressed to obtain crisp detection with an accuracy of 91%.

Suvarna et al. (2014) presented three models of OA disease using Mamdani, Sugeno and Adaptive Neuro-Fuzzy Inference System (ANFIS) techniques. Statistical data such as age, morning stiffness, warmth in joints, crepitus and bony tenderness were used. The experimental result proved that the ANFIS model offers promising results with an average error 0.3638 in comparison with Mamdani, Sugeno models.

The dataset used by various researchers in the survey is tabulated in the Table.1.

Table 1. Dataset used in previous researches

Authors	Dataset
Brahim et al. (2019)	OsteoArthritis Initiative (OAI)
Anifah et al, (2013)	OAI
Wahyuningrum et al. (2016), (2019)	OAI
Tiulpin et al. (2018)	Multicenter Osteoarthritis Study (MOST) and OAI
Neogi et al. (2009)	MOST and Framingham Osteoarthritis studies
Yoo et al. (2016)	Korean National Health and Nutrition Examination Survey (KNHANES) and OAI
Thomson et al. (2015)	OAI
Kinds et al. (2013)	Cohort Hip & Cohort Knee (CHECK) study
Oka et al. (2008)	ROAD study
Lim et al. (2019)	KNHANES

In previous researches, there were certain drawbacks such as overfitting issues, accuracy, misclassification, time efficiency, performance and so on.

Extracting useful information from unstructured data such as medical images invariably remain in data science community. Such frameworks would benefit medical experts to test enormous volume of unstructured data for better decision making. Data scientists in the field of radiology informatics engineer ways to handle data from images. The present study aims to develop a computer-aided diagnosis method for assessing the severity of the knee OA from radiographic images.

METHODOLOGY

The proposed method is illustrated in Fig.1. This method grades knee OA into three categories namely normal, mild OA and severe OA using X-ray images.

Figure 1. Block diagram of proposed method

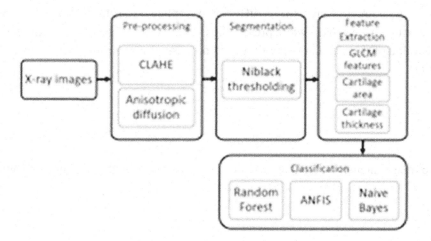

X-ray Images

The dataset for this work is taken from Mendeley Data (Chen & Pingjun, 2018), that is publicly available for research. This dataset is originated from the Osteoarthritis Initiative (OAI), a multi-center longitudinal study for men and women sponsored by the National Institutes of Health (NIH). This dataset includes data from 4976 subjects, aged between 45-79 years. The images in this cohort are independently graded with KL grades 0 to 4 indicating different severity levels as shown in Table.2. For this study, the database has been split into three classes as follows: the absence of OA class contains grade 0 images, mild OA class contains grade 2 images and severe OA class contains grade 4 images. Knee anteroposterior (AP) view represents a standard projection to access knee joints. In this work, a subset of the dataset, i.e. 165 knee AP images with a spatial resolution of 224 X 224 pixels are used which includes 55 images in each of the three classes.

Table 2. KL grading system

KL Grade	Description
Grade 0	Definite absence of OA
Grade 1	Doubtful OA
Grade 2	Minimal or early OA
Grade 3	Moderate OA
Grade 4	End-stage OA

(Data Source: Kellgren, J. & Lawrence, J., 1957)

Preprocessing

In the field of medical imaging, the quality of images is extremely significant for accurate diagnosis and treatment planning. In general, a raw X-ray image may contain a poor quality of the image due to overexposure or underexposure which is not suited for diagnosis. The purpose of pre-processing is to provide better visibility of features of interest. Contrast Limited Adaptive Histogram Equalization (CLAHE) is implemented for enhancing minute details, textures while limiting the overall contrast. After the enhancement process, anisotropic diffusion is applied. Anisotropic diffusion is a technique of smoothing the textures in an image while preserving the edges. The level of smoothing can be adjusted by varying the value of the standard deviation. The process of anisotropic diffusion can be expressed as in equation (1).

$$\frac{\partial I}{\partial s} = div\left(F.\nabla I\right) \tag{1}$$

where I denote image intensity, F denote diffusion function and ∇ is the gradient operator.

$$F = e^{-\left[\frac{\nabla I}{C}\right]} \tag{2}$$

where C is the diffusion constant that triggers the smoothing process. The resultant images of CLAHE and anisotropic diffusion are shown in Fig.2.

Figure 2. Pre-processing results

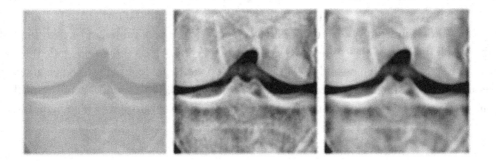

Segmentation

After the image enhancement and noise removal steps, the resultant image is suitable for segmenting the cartilage region using an appropriate segmentation method. In the proposed work, Niblack threshold-based segmentation method (Jan Motl, 2020) is adopted to extract the cartilage region. The threshold value is calculated employing the formula provided in equation (3).

$$Niblack\ threshold = Mean + 0.2 * Standard\ Deviation \tag{3}$$

Mean and Standard Deviation are computed using the equation (4) and (5).

$$Mean = \frac{1}{n}\sum rp(r) \tag{4}$$

$$Standard\ Deviation = \sqrt{\sum p(r)(r - Mean)} \tag{5}$$

where p(r) is the probability of occurrence of gray value r and n is the total gray values.

The segmented images are shown in Fig.3. It could be interpreted that the smoothing attained by the application of anisotropic diffusion, improved the segmentation accuracy.

Figure 3. Segmentation results

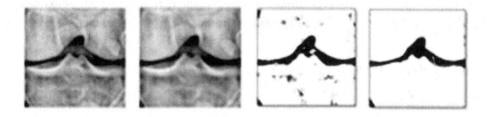

Feature Extraction

GLCM refers to the occurrence of a pair of gray levels in the image at a certain distance and at a particular angle. In simplest form, it exploits the higher order distribution of grey values based on neighborhood criterion. It is a statistical measure of examining the texture and it considers the spatial relationship of pixels. Four textural features such as contrast, correlation, energy and homogeneity are derived from the GLCM matrix.

- Contrast - It measures the extent of variation in pixel intensity.
- Correlation – It measures the joint probability occurrence of the specified pixel pairs.
- Homogeneity – It measures the closeness of the distribution of elements in the GLCM.
- Energy – It is a measure of uniformity and returns the sum of squared elements.

GLCM features are calculated using equations (6), (7), (8) and (9).

$$Contrast = \sum_{i}\sum_{j}(i - j)^2 p \tag{6}$$

$$Correlation = \frac{\sum_i \sum_j p - \mu x \, \mu y}{\sigma x \, \sigma y} \tag{7}$$

$$Homogeneity = -\sum_i \sum_j p / \left(1 + |i - j|\right) \tag{8}$$

$$Energy = \sum_i \sum_j p^2 \tag{9}$$

where p is the matrix element, i, j are spatial coordinates, μx, μy and σx, σy are mean and standard deviation of p along rows and columns respectively.

The major clinical feature of knee osteoarthritis is the reduction in cartilage thickness which leads to joint space narrowing. The cartilage thickness is calculated at seven equally distanced regions as shown in Fig.4 which provides the medial and lateral thickness of cartilage. Since the reduction in cartilage thickness indicates the degradation of cartilage, the area of cartilage is also calculated. The cartilage area is computed by calculating the total number of pixels in the region. The features extracted from 165 X-ray images were divided into training (73%) and testing data (27%). There is no overlapping of data.

Figure 4. Regions of cartilage thickness measure in 3 classes of OA

Classifcation

The proposed method grades the images into 3 classes, namely the absence of OA, mild OA and severe OA. For the classification process, supervised classifiers such as Random forest, ANFIS and Naive Bayes classifiers are adopted. These three classifiers were selected in particular because of the following features:

- Overfitting issues and time efficiency are considered as limitations discussed in some previous researches. Random Forest and Naive Bayes classifiers have a low propensity to overfit.
- Random forest, ANFIS and Naive Bayes classifiers have rapid learning capacity.
- Though the Random Forest and Naive Bayes classifier were adopted in previous researches, alternate segmentation and feature extraction techniques are applied.

- ANFIS classifier was not adopted for OA disease detection from X-rays, though it was adopted using statistical data in previous researches.

A detailed description of these classifiers is delineated in the rest of this section.

Random Forest Classifier

Random Forest is an ensemble learning method for the classification task. It is also known as random decision forest since it is a collection of fully grown decision trees as shown in Fig.5. Every tree in the ensemble is grown on an independent bootstrap replica of input data. The most important feature of this classifier is that it returns feature importance. The Random Forest classifier calculates and selects the most relevant and influential features. The output of each tree is considered as a vote for that particular class. The final output of the Random Forest classifier is assigned using the majority class votes.

Figure 5. Architecture of Random Forest classifier

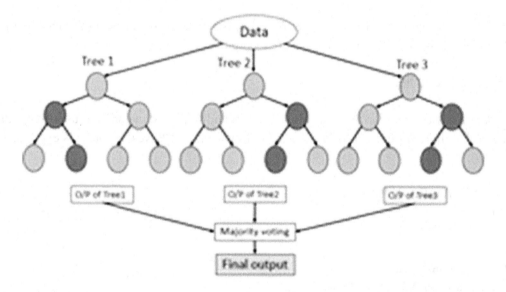

ANFIS Classifier

Adaptive Neuro-Fuzzy Inference System is a combination of Artificial Neural Network and Fuzzy Inference System. ANFIS uses a hybrid learning algorithm that works only with Sugeno-type fuzzy inference systems. It is trained with least-squares method in combination with backpropagation gradient descent method to emulate the training dataset. The training process ceases whenever the specified epoch number is reached.

The architecture of ANFIS consists of six layers as shown in Fig.6. The extracted features are applied to layer 1 where fuzzification operation (F) occurs. In layer 2, the membership grades are assigned for inputs that are denoted by S_f. Layer 3 and 4 perform product operation denoted by Π, whose output is a product of all inputs. The output of layer 3 undergoes the normalization process (N) based on firing

Figure 6. Architecture of ANFIS classifier

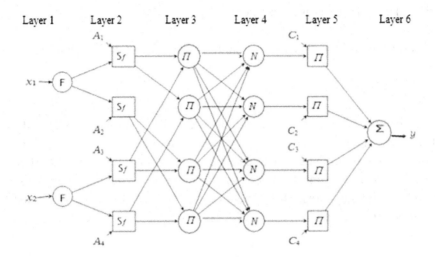

strengths in layer 4 and fed to layer 5. Layer 6 performs summation operation (Σ). The fuzzification output from layer 6 is rounded off to obtain a crisp output.

Naive Bayes Classifier

Naive Bayes classifier works on the basis of probability and statistical methods. It uses Bayes theorem to predict probabilities for each class in a supervised manner. The Bayes Theorem is expressed as the equation (10).

$$P(A|X) = \{P(X/A). P(A)\}/P(X) \tag{10}$$

where

X - Data with unknown class
A - The hypothesis of X is a specific class
$P(A)$ - Probability of the hypothesis A (also known as a prior probability)
$P(X)$ - Probability of data with an unknown class (also known as predictor prior probability)
$P(A|X)$ - Probability of the hypothesis A that refers to X (also known as a posterior probability)
$P(X|A)$ - Probability of X in the hypothesis A (also known as likelihood)

Since the classification process requires various clues to determine the class for the data being analysed, the Bayes theorem can be rewritten as in equation (11).

$$P(A|X1 \ldots Xn) = \{P(A) \, P(X1 \ldots Xn|A)\}/ \, P(X1 \ldots Xn) \tag{11}$$

This equation is used in Naive Bayes classification model.

RESULT AND DISCUSSION

The proposed method precisely extracts the cartilage region. The result of the Random Forest classifier is compared with ANFIS and Naive Bayes classifier with the help of the confusion matrix as shown in the Tables 3, 4 and 5. The confusion matrix contains information about the predicted and true label. The percentage of correctly classified samples is calculated using accuracy provided in the equation (12).

$$Accuracy = \frac{Correctly\ classified\ samples}{Total\ samples} \qquad (12)$$

From the experiment, the best results are obtained for the Random Forest classifier with an accuracy of 88.8%. Comparatively, ANFIS and Naive Bayes classifier underperformed with an accuracy of 86.6% and 77.8%.

Table 3. Confusion matrix of Random Forest classifier

Predicted label				
	Category	Absence of OA	Mild OA	Severe OA
True label	Absence of OA	14	1	0
	Mild OA	1	13	1
	Severe OA	0	2	13

Table 4. Confusion matrix of ANFIS classifier

Predicted label				
	Category	Absence of OA	Mild OA	Severe OA
True label	Absence of OA	13	2	0
	Mild OA	1	13	1
	Severe OA	0	2	13

Table5. Confusion matrix of Naive Bayes classifier

Predicted label				
	Category	Absence of OA	Mild OA	Severe OA
True label	Absence of OA	12	3	0
	Mild OA	2	11	2
	Severe OA	0	3	12

To fully assess the performance of the classifiers, precision and recall metrics are calculated using equation (13) and (14).

$$Precision = \frac{Correctly\ classified\ samples\ as\ class\ X}{Total\ samples\ classified\ as\ class\ X} \qquad (13)$$

$$Recall = \frac{Correctly\ classified\ samples\ as\ class\ X}{Total\ samples\ actually\ present\ in\ class\ X} \qquad (14)$$

From Table.6, it can be interpreted that the absence of OA and the severe OA cases were successfully classified with better precision and recall values, but the presence of mild OA was classified with low accuracy by all three classifiers.

Table.6. Evaluation metrics of different classifiers

Class	Precision	Recall
Random forest		
Absence of OA	0.93	0.93
Mild OA	0.81	0.86
Severe OA	0.93	0.86
ANFIS		
Absence of OA	0.93	0.86
Mild OA	0.76	0.86
Severe OA	0.93	0.86
Naive Bayes		
Absence of OA	0.86	0.80
Mild OA	0.64	0.73
Severe OA	0.86	0.92

CONCLUSION AND FUTUREWORK

Early and accurate diagnosis of the knee OA from radiographic images is a challenging task. Medical diagnostics are fundamentally a data problem that requires tools and techniques to convert medical images into clinically relevant insights. This paper focused on the tri-class classification of the knee OA employing Random Forest classifier. The outcomes of the proposed method are cross-checked with clinical inferences. In most of the cases, the outcomes are appropriate with clinical inferences. Nevertheless, some limitations of this research need to be addressed. The proposed method is primarily based on medial and lateral cartilage thickness and area. Previous researches stated that joint space narrowing was highly associated with cartilage volume. In contrast, presence of osteophytes which is a key feature in severe stages of OA does not have a significant impact on cartilage volume. In this chapter no bone texture descriptors indicating the presence of osteophyte was used which is considered as a drawback. Despite this limitation, it is still evident that the proposed method could highly benefit the clinicians to diagnose the knee OA from X-ray images in a more effective way. Future work will focus on multiclass classification of the knee OA based on KL grades which include both cartilage and bone texture descriptors.

REFERENCES

Anifah, L., Purnama, I. K. E., Hariadi, M., & Purnomo, M. H. (2013). Osteoarthritis Classification Using Self Organizing Map Based on Gabor Kernel and Contrast-Limited Adaptive Histogram Equalization. *The Open Biomedical Engineering Journal*, 7(1), 18–28. doi:10.2174/1874120701307010018 PMID:23525188

Bhat, A. Y. (2019). Normal and Abnormal Detection for Knee Osteoarthritis using Machine Learning Techniques. *International Journal of Recent Technology and Engineering*, 8(2), 6026–6033. doi:10.35940/ijrte.B3733.078219

Blessia, T. F., Kumar, A., Singh, S., & Vennila, J. J. (2011). Application of Knowledge Based System for Diagnosis of Osteoarthritis. *Journal of Artificial Intelligence*, 4(4), 269–278. doi:10.3923/jai.2011.269.278

Brahim, A., Jennane, R., Riad, R., Janvier, T., Khedher, L., Toumi, H., & Lespessailles, E. (2019). A decision support tool for early detection of knee OsteoArthritis using X-ray imaging and machine learning: Data from the OsteoArthritis Initiative. *Computerized Medical Imaging and Graphics*, 73, 11–18. doi:10.1016/j.compmedimag.2019.01.007 PMID:30784984

Chen & Pingjun. (2018). *Knee Osteoarthritis Severity Grading Dataset*. Mendeley Data. doi:10.17632/56rmx5bjcr.1

Hegadi, R. S., Navale, D. I., Pawar, T. D., & Ruikar, D. D. (2019). Osteoarthritis Detection and Classification from Knee X-Ray Images Based on Artificial Neural Network. *Communications in Computer and Information Science*, 1036, 97–105. doi:10.1007/978-981-13-9184-2_8

Hirvasniemi, J., Thevenot, J., Immonen, V., Liikavainio, T., Pulkkinen, P., Jämsä, T., & Saarakkala, S. (2014). Quantification of differences in bone texture from plain radiographs in knees with and without osteoarthritis. *Osteoarthritis and Cartilage*, 22(10), 1724–1731. doi:10.1016/j.joca.2014.06.021 PMID:25278081

Jones, G., Ding, C., Scott, F., Glisson, M., & Cicuttini, F. (2004). Early radiographic osteoarthritis is associated with substantial changes in cartilage volume and tibial bone surface area in both males and females11Sources of support: National Health and Medical Research Council of Australia, Masonic Centenary Medical Research Foundation. *Osteoarthritis and Cartilage*, 12(2), 169–174. doi:10.1016/j.joca.2003.08.010 PMID:14723876

Kellgren, J., & Lawrence, J. (1957). Radiological assessment of osteo-arthrosis. *Annals of the Rheumatic Diseases*, 16(4), 494–502. doi:10.1136/ard.16.4.494 PMID:13498604

Kinds, M. B., Marijnissen, A. C. A., Bijlsma, J. W. J., Boers, M., Lafeber, F. P. J. G., & Welsing, P. M. J. (2013). Quantitative Radiographic Features of Early Knee Osteoarthritis: Development Over 5 Years and Relationship with Symptoms in the CHECK Cohort. *The Journal of Rheumatology*, *40*(1), 58–65. doi:10.3899/jrheum.120320 PMID:23118113

Kluzek, S., & Mattei, T. A. (2019). Machine-learning for osteoarthritis research. *Osteoarthritis and Cartilage*, *27*(7), 977–978. doi:10.1016/j.joca.2019.04.005 PMID:31002937

Lim, J., Kim, J., & Cheon, S. (2019). A Deep Neural Network-Based Method for Early Detection of Osteoarthritis Using Statistical Data. *International Journal of Environmental Research and Public Health*, *16*(7), 1281. doi:10.3390/ijerph16071281 PMID:30974803

Motl. (2020). *Niblack local thresholding*. Error! Hyperlink reference not valid. 40849-niblack-local-thresholding

Moustakidis, S., Christodoulou, E., Papageorgiou, E., Kokkotis, C., Papandrianos, N., & Tsaopoulos, D. (2019). Application of machine intelligence for osteoarthritis classification: A classical implementation and a quantum perspective. *Quantum Machine Intelligence*, *1*(3–4), 73–86. doi:10.100742484-019-00008-3

Mu, J., Liu, X., Luan, S., Heintz, P. H., Mlady, G. W., & Chen, D. Z. (2011). Segmentation of knee joints in x-ray images using decomposition-based sweeping and graph search. *Medical Imaging* 2011. *Image Processing*, *7962*, 159–166.

National Statistics | Data and Statistics | Arthritis | CDC. (2003). Retrieved from https://www.cdc.gov/arthritis/data_statistics/national-statistics.html

Neogi, T., Felson, D., Niu, J., Nevitt, M., Lewis, C. E., Aliabadi, P., & Zhang, Y. (2009). Association between radiographic features of knee osteoarthritis and pain: Results from two cohort studies. *BMJ (Clinical Research Ed.)*, *339*(7719), 498–501. doi:10.1136/bmj.b2844 PMID:19700505

Oka, H., Muraki, S., Akune, T., Mabuchi, A., Suzuki, T., Yoshida, H., Yamamoto, S., Nakamura, K., Yoshimura, N., & Kawaguchi, H. (2008). Fully automatic quantification of knee osteoarthritis severity on plain radiographs. *Osteoarthritis and Cartilage*, *16*(11), 1300–1306. doi:10.1016/j.joca.2008.03.011 PMID:18424107

Shamir, L., Ling, S. M., Scott, W. W., Bos, A., Orlov, N., Macura, T. J., & Goldberg, I. G. (2009). Knee X-Ray Image Analysis Method for Automated Detection of Osteoarthritis. *IEEE Transactions on Biomedical Engineering*, *56*(2), 407–415. doi:10.1109/TBME.2008.2006025 PMID:19342330

Subramonia, M., & Rajini, V. (2013). Local Binary Pattern Approach to the Classification of Osteoarthritis in Knee X-ray Images. *Asian Journal of Scientific Research*, *6*(4), 805–811. doi:10.3923/ajsr.2013.805.811

Suvarna, M, & Patil, A., & Mudholkar, R. (2014). Exploring ANFIS Model for Osteoarthritis Disease Classification. *International Journal of Current Engineering and Technology*, *4*(3), 2124–2130.

Thomson, J., O'Neill, T., Felson, D., & Cootes, T. (2015). Automated Shape and Texture Analysis for Detection of Osteoarthritis from Radiographs of the Knee. *Lecture Notes in Computer Science*, *9350*, 127–134. doi:10.1007/978-3-319-24571-3_16

Tiulpin, A., Thevenot, J., Rahtu, E., Lehenkari, P., & Saarakkala, S. (2018). Automatic Knee Osteoarthritis Diagnosis from Plain Radiographs: A Deep Learning-Based Approach. *Scientific Reports*, *8*(1), 1–15. doi:10.103841598-018-20132-7 PMID:29379060

Vijayakumari & Holi. (2019) Assessment of Joint Space in Knee Osteoarthritis using Particle Swarm Optimization Technique. *International Journal of Innovative Technology and Exploring Engineering*, *9*(1), 502–507.

Wahyuningrum, R. T., Anifah, L., Eddy Purnama, I. K., & Hery Purnomo, M. (2019). A New Approach to Classify Knee Osteoarthritis Severity from Radiographic Images based on CNN-LSTM Method. *2019 IEEE 10th International Conference on Awareness Science and Technology (ICAST)*, 1-6.

Wahyuningrum, R. T., Anifah, L., Purnama, I. K. E., & Purnomo, M. H. (2016). A novel hybrid of S2D-PCA and SVM for knee osteoarthritis classification. *2016 IEEE International Conference on Computational Intelligence and Virtual Environments for Measurement Systems and Applications (CIVEMSA)*, 1-5. 10.1109/CIVEMSA.2016.7524317

Yoo, T. K., Kim, D. W., Choi, S. B., Oh, E., & Park, J. S. (2016). Simple Scoring System and Artificial Neural Network for Knee Osteoarthritis Risk Prediction: A Cross-Sectional Study. *PLoS One*, *11*(2), e0148724. doi:10.1371/journal.pone.0148724 PMID:26859664

ADDITIONAL READING

Arden, N. (2018). *Atlas of osteoarthritis* (2nd ed.). Springer.

Dhawan, A. P. (2011). *Medical image analysis*. Wiley-Interscience. doi:10.1002/9780470918548

Kalaiselvi, K., & Deepika, M. (2020). Machine Learning for Healthcare Diagnostics. *Learning and Analytics in Intelligent Systems Machine Learning with Health Care Perspective*, 91-105.

Latif, J., Xiao, C., Imran, A., & Tu, S. (2019). Medical Imaging using Machine Learning and Deep Learning Algorithms: A Review. *2019 2nd International Conference on Computing, Mathematics and Engineering Technologies (iCoMET)*.

Verma, O. P., Roy, S., Pandey, S. C., & Mittal, M. (2020). *Advancement of machine intelligence in interactive medical image analysis*. Springer. doi:10.1007/978-981-15-1100-4

KEY TERMS AND DEFINITIONS

Arthritis: A disease causing painful inflammation and stiffening of bones.

Computer-Aided Diagnosis: Systems that assist medical professionals in analysis and interpretation of medical data.

Osteophytes: Abnormal bony outgrowth or projection that form along the joint margins.

Radiology Informatics: A field of imaging informatics that is concerned to apply information science to radiology.

Sclerosis: Hardening or stiffening of tissues caused by diseases such as osteoarthritis, diabetes, scleroderma.

Chapter 20
Healthcare Conversational Chatbot for Medical Diagnosis

Rohan Jagtap

(iD) https://orcid.org/0000-0003-0861-5053

Sardar Patel Institute of Technology, Mumbai, India

Kshitij Phulare

Sardar Patel Institute of Technology, Mumbai, India

Mrunal Kurhade

Sardar Patel Institute of Technology, Mumbai, India

Kiran Shrikant Gawande

Sardar Patel Institute of Technology, Mumbai, India

ABSTRACT

Medical services are basic needs for human life. There are times when consulting a doctor can be difficult. The proposed idea is an AI-based chatbot that will provide assistance to the users regarding their health-based issues. The state of the art in the aforementioned field includes extractive bots that extract the keywords (i.e., symptoms from the user's input) and suggest its diagnosis. The proposed idea will be a conversational bot, which unlike the QnA bot will take into consideration the context of the user's whole conversation and reply accordingly. Thus, along with symptom extraction, the user will get a better experience conversing with the bot. The user can also normally chat with the chatbot for issues like if the user is not emotionally sound. For example, the bot will console the user if he/she is feeling stressed by recognizing the emotional health of the user.

INTRODUCTION

Chatbots are one of the most popular applications of Artificial Intelligence (AI). A chatbot is an AI software that can chat or converse with users in a way another human being would. Chatbots are basically used to simplify user interactions with computers via text or speech. There are many ways through

DOI: 10.4018/978-1-7998-3053-5.ch020

which users can chat or converse with chatbots. Some of them are messaging apps, mobile phone apps or websites. Chatbots are one of the most advanced and promising technologies of human to computer interactions. Now how does a chatbot actually work? The answer is - Chatbot must have the ability to understand the intent of the user, extract the data accordingly and provide correct answers to the users. If it does not understand the user's request, it won't be able to give correct answers. AI technologies like Natural Language Processing (NLP) and Machine Learning (ML) are used for teaching the chatbots to read, analyze and interpret human language. These technologies help chatbots in understanding the language and its meaning. Deep Learning (DL) is used to improve chatbot's response to user requests.

There are many applications of chatbots present in the real world. Personal Assistants like Google Assistant, Siri, Alexa are some complex chatbots designed to answer a wide range of user queries like news updates, current weather, personal calendars, random questions. There are chatbots used for customer services as well with a limited scope of queries and responses. Nowadays chatbot applications are rapidly growing in the medical field. Some of the most popular uses of chatbots in the medical field are day-to-day assistance in patient care and wellness, tracking user's physical health, providing food and diet recommendations and for the mental health of patients.

There are many times when consulting a doctor can be difficult. Even Google searching for symptoms can be a headache due to thousands of search results, many contradicting suggestions or misleading sites. At such times, a trained and tested chatbot dealing mainly with such cases is like heaven. There are many chatbots integrated with mobile apps that help patients in scheduling appointments, managing test reports, issuing reminders, providing diet and personalized recommendations. These chatbots are trained based on customized requests of users and their responses are handled by physicians. Thus a chatbot can very well play the role of a health coach. Some of the examples of chatbots in this field are Florence, Your.MD, Safedrugbot, Babylon Health. Thus Chatbots replacing humans in some functions makes the process more efficient, more effective and also cost-saving for patients and healthcare providers.

LITERATURE SURVEY

The medical domain is vast and hence there exist numerous contributions. The concept of healthcare assistants took off with the advancements in chatbots in general. Chatbots possess the potential to deliver medical assistance effectively and efficiently. The concept of chatbots has been broadly classified into 2 major types - Unintelligent Chatbots, that are built to respond to only predefined inputs; and Intelligent Chatbots, which are built on machine learning (Madhu, Jain, Sebastain, Shaji, Ajayakumar, 2017). The rule-based unintelligent chatbots have been in charge for a few years and many leading chatbots were rule-based with smart answering algorithms. (Madhu et al., 2017) defines a system for medical assistance involving a chatbot which is based on an API and the medical assistance based on another API. The chatbot works by extracting the symptoms from the user input and then the medical API generates the diagnosis based on the given input. Here, the symptoms are in JSON format wherein the symptoms and the corresponding diseases are predefined and matching those criteria, the bot suggests the medication to the user. Revisiting the mention of a 'system' for medical assistance, the system also includes user authentication. The main aim is to eliminate the descriptive nature of medical websites. (Rosruen, Samanchuen, 2018) describes the nature of chatbots and how AI-based chatbots help in generating better responses. (Rosruen, Samanchuen, 2018) attempts to create an AI-based chatbot that is trained on Google's

DialogFlow chatbot engine. The system is capable of replying to the user based on their medical queries to a limited number of intents. Here, at a base level, the chatbot first extracts the intent of the user from their inputs, then the symptoms to medication mapping are done by additional code and then the system responds with a solution to the users' problems. The 'MedBot' (Rosruen et al., 2018) has 34 intents with 16 intents of symptoms. The chatbot is mainly concerned with only the simple types of diseases which come under the sixteen symptoms. The solution is designed taking into consideration factors such as feasibility in responding (for example time taken to respond), compatibility, usability, ease of installation of the software. With healthcare assistant bots, these chatbots can also assist the pharmaceutical businesses. (Ahmad et al., 2018) presents a similar system for Sharifah Nur Pharmacy which includes a bot that is able to give all the details regarding medication for a given illness. The system has basic registration modules for the maintenance of customer databases. Additionally, the system, for an illness, suggests a list of medicines, gives the description of the suggested medication, explains the dosage of the given medication. The only user input provided is the description of the illness; basically symptoms and effects. The bot is a rule-based bot that extracts the illness from the inputs and fetches the corresponding data in the databases and in case if data is not present in the database, replies with a suitable prompt.

Along with the development in symptom-disease based chatbots, the psychological health of a human can also be assisted by pseudo-doctors like chatbots. The main aspect of these systems is to consider the emotional state of the user by judging their input (which is assumed to be in natural language) and recognizing the correct way of responding to them. Lee et al. (2017) proposes a chatbot that recognizes the emotional state of the user based on their inputs. It does this with the concept of emotion recognition. The data is classified based on the intent of the user and for the response finally, it consults a database and replies to the user. The system uses the concepts of neural networks for classification i.e extraction of the user's intent. The chatbot initially needs to perform NLP based emotional recognition, for this GRU-based sentence analysis is used (Lee et al., 2017). According to authors Vaswani et al. (2017) the mechanism also uses attention to focus on specific parts of the given input for extraction of the important portions of the text which define or help to depict the emotion of the user. These features are learned and weights are assigned to such parts of the sentences. Similar to this, Oh et al. (2017) designed a chatbot that provides text-to-speech support for a smart chatbot that is capable of analyzing the emotional state and responds with a decent amount of scrutiny on the user input. The system provides psychiatric counseling to the user by means of NLU and emotion recognition based on a multi-model approach (Oh et al., 2017). The architecture of the system flow is given as, first, the dialogue is analyzed by the RNN encoder network, where the features i.e. emotion is extracted from the input. The simultaneous use of emotion recognition mechanisms and psychiatry based dictionary enhances the process of extraction. Further, the model recognizes the emotional changes and then the response is generated accordingly. A Response inference engine is used to generate the response based on additional questionnaires (based on psychiatric counseling) and rule base knowledge as well. This is decoded by the RNN decoder i.e is the NLG followed by the text-to-speech module finally to complete the response generation process. The biggest challenge in the model is the generation of a response. The system uses Point Network Model for this. Here, the important keywords in the sentences are learned from the datasets. The attention on sentences is learned from the feature maps generated from the corpus of language. Since the psychiatric assistant can affect the quality of life of the user, the chatbot also ensures ethical behavior from the chatbot. If the technology is advanced, it will apply unethical situations based on the human ethics code model as per (Oh et al., 2017).

Rai et al. (2018) aims at building a chatbot by taking advantage of developments in the fields of Artificial Intelligence. The Architecture of the system proposed here has 10 modules working. The system here uses The Facebook Messenger API which services user queries at a rapid pace. The data is stored at a remote server called Heroku. The query is sent to the Darwin bot on Facebook. Webhook handler is then used to receive the message. Then there is a trained model which is used by the system to understand the intent of the message (using Tensorflow) (Rai et al., 2018) followed by appropriate generation of replies based on the user and his previous history and then the reply is sent back to the user. (Leong, Goh, Kumar, 2017) targets building a medical kiosk using an International Conversational Agent. It aims at improving the current kiosk to get instant, relevant and intelligent responses to customer queries. Innovations in DL, ML, AI, NLP assists the kiosk in achieving its task. It can serve as a replacement for the customer service response desk and thereby overcome its shortcomings like the unavailability of a human during some emergency situation. The system developed here is heavily reliant on the concepts of Deep Learning, Machine Learning, Artificial Intelligence to find correlations and patterns to improve the chatbot (Leong et al., 2017). This is an improvement over the previous chatbots which used the supervised Learning approach for training (Leong et al., 2017). The system developed in (Leong et al., 2017) takes input via text as well as speech and does the appropriate preprocessing. After the conversation is over it's also stored for further analysis to try and improve the responses in the future. Ambekar & Phalnikar, (2018) state that in spite of the advancement in technology related to chatbots, there are certain issues that are still faced due to limitations with the amount of training they receive as well as the programming. Thus the aim here is to involve a Human in the loop and thus build a Human aided chatbot. The concept used here is that of crowd computing. Data Analysis plays a crucial role in handling large amounts of data in healthcare. Due to a large amount of data growth in the healthcare field, accurate analysis becomes favorable for the prediction of disease. However, accuracy decreases if some medical data goes missing. Thus data cleaning needs to be performed to transform incomplete data to complete data. Most of the data contain hidden information and thus makes decision making a difficult task. Machine learning plays a very important role in finding hidden information and performing data analysis. In the medical field, machine learning has been used in disease prediction and diagnosis. The convolution neural network extracts the features automatically from large datasets to get accurate results. CNN-UDRP has been used for structured data, for extracting features from datasets and prediction of disease is carried out based on that dataset (Ambekar & Phalnikar, 2018).

Shankar et al. (2015) build a system to find out the similarity between two diseases or how likely a person is to contract a particular disease given he had some different disease in the past. This is done by studying the medical history of that particular person as well as the history of other patients with similar medical records. An unweighted graph is constructed with nodes representing the diseases and links between them representing their coexistence. A suitable link prediction method is then used for completing the structure. Aalipour et al. (2018) proposes a conceptual framework with five components that covers the enterprise chatbot capabilities which are not covered by the general framework.

To get the best results from the chatbot conversations, there are several aspects to be focused on. The main focus of a conversation should be on keeping the contexts of a conversation which will ensure the best responses from the bot since it is able to memorize everything the user has talked about. The state of the art technologies in this field includes the attention mechanisms (Vaswani et al., 2017). The main concern of the RNN networks is the element 'memory', there is not enough of it. LSTM networks outperform vanilla RNNs in terms of this in keeping a better sense of context. However, for applications like chatbots, which require a lot of contextual information in a given conversation, even the LSTMs and its variants don't prove to be enough. One approach to overcome this can be focusing on what to remember rather than how much to remember. This can highly enhance the quality of these networks; basically the literal meaning of giving something more importance over others; giving attention. Here along with training on the inputs and calculation and optimizing the losses, the model also learns which inputs provide a higher context in a given text i.e. the occurrence of what objects in a sentence improves the predictability of the model. The model learns these features simultaneously. Weights are assigned to various parts of the sentences and the higher weights have greater attention and more contribution (involvement) in the context of the sentence. These features are made sure to be kept. This concept is proposed by authors Vaswani et al. (2017).

One flavor of attention is widely-known as bahdanau attention (Bahdanau et al., 2014). The implementation of these mechanisms cannot be done directly in a single sequential neural network with multiple layers and mechanisms to learn the attention weights. The main challenge in dealing with the natural language data is the length. The length of the text and its reply (in case of chatbot) will not be the same. The sequential model demands this. Thus to overcome such kinds of restrictions several model designs have been proposed. The simplest is the encoder-decoder architecture in the Sequence-to-Sequence model (Sutskever et al., 2014). Here the basis is on RNN networks. There are 2 major elements viz encoder and decoder. The encoder processes the input data, extracts and keeps quality information from it; the context information. This context is passed on to the decoder and it generates the output sequences using this context. In training phases, the expected output is provided with one offset to the decoder so that it predicts the next element of the output sequence. This prediction can be carried forward in the next timesteps. Here the issue of the same input and output lengths in sequential models can thus be overcome since two separate RNN networks are used at encoder and decoders hence supports variable lengths. An extension to the sequence-to-sequence architecture is the Hierarchical Recurrent Encoder-Decoder (HRED) architecture (Sordoni et al., 2015). Here a common context vector is used between separate sequence-to-sequence pairs.

With state of the art models and architectures to get efficient results from the NLP tasks, it also demands great preprocessing of data. Since textual data cannot be directly processed in neural networks, some representations for text in terms of numbers are required. For this, there can either be a character-level representation or word-level representation. However, word-level representations have proven better since it stores more information. One method of doing this can be one-hot encoded vectors for words occurring in a given corpus. However, this representation doesn't give any notion of the relationship between the words. So Google's research team came up with word2vec for the embedding of words in vectors giving some notion of context for words occurring in a given text (Mikolo et al., 2013; Pennington et al., 2014). This uses the skip-gram and the continuous bag of words model to predict the probability of a word to occur in a given context. However, this training process has proven expensive when it comes to huge dimensions since comparing each word with every other word in a given window multiple times. Thus came the concept of a co-occurrence matrix to initially count the number of times a given word to occur in the context of others thus reducing repetition while training (Pennington et al., 2014). So the glove model uses both these concepts of windows and co-occurrences to train vectors on web-scraped data. It has given outstanding results when relationships among words are concerned (Pennington et al., 2014).

Several notable state of the art research in fields of Neural Machine Translations include Google's well known Transformers model, Bidirectional Encoder Representations from Transformers (BERT) which is based on the transformers model (Vaswani et al., 2017; Devlin et al., 2019). Facebook's Dynamic Memory Networks too, tackles a similar kind of problem. The idea behind these models is to use the highest available data on the web to train on this corpora and to respond to natural language queries by humans. All these in one way or another, implement a way to remember significant data from large corpora, for example, dynamic memory networks maintain a separate external data structure to store the contextual information (Kumar et al., 2015).

HEALTHCARE CONVERSATIONAL CHATBOT

The authors in this chapter propose a methodology that aims to develop a chatbot that can predict diseases based on symptoms and provide a diagnosis. The proposed chatbot is using the Generative NLP technique which will actually generate the responses after reading the user queries. Along with the diagnosis of diseases, the chatbot will also be prescribing medicines for certain common diseases which will be added to the database of the chatbot after thorough consultation with the doctors. Along with the symptom recognition and disease prediction, the chatbot will also focus on the mental health or mental aspect of the human body. That is the chatbot will be able to converse with the patient just like a human would. The aim here is to cheer up or console the person if he/she is feeling emotionally depressed or feeling down. The most important part of this proposed work is context. The context needs to be remembered so that appropriate replies can be expected from the chatbot. Recurrent Neural Network or RNN is a class of Artificial Neural Network that serves as a basic model that remembers the previous input and thus helps in remembering the context. It basically uses the previous output along with the current input as a combined input to the neurons. The issue with RNN is that the amount of data it can remember is not too much. Long short term memory (LSTM) and Gated Recurrent Units (GRU) are improvements over RNN. However, using a Sequential model for a Neural Machine Translation problem like this will lead to 'word-to-word' message-response. Hence, the proposed work uses the sequence to sequence model with the Attention Mechanism for training the bot. The sequence to sequence model consists of an encoder and decoder. The encoder consists of a number of LSTM layers that are used to take the input. The 'message' sequence is read by the encoder, encoded in an intermediate context vector representation and then passed on to the decoder. For better training of the model, the proposed work uses 'Teacher Forcing' wherein the expected outputs are provided as the decoder inputs because cascading the obtained outputs while training will create cascaded inaccuracies and hence, poor model performance. The proposed chatbot models the inference model separately which implements the cascade. But again, focusing on the major contribution; context, LSTM networks still fall short of memory. The issue mostly arises when there are multiple numbers of sentences and the word to be predicted is at the end of the last sentence. So now the focus is on 'what to remember' over 'how much to remember'. Hence, the proposed work uses the attention mechanism, where an additional layer of the network is trained to 'learn' what to remember. When talking about the standard seq2seq model, as stated above, they have an issue with long input sequences. This mainly arises because only the last hidden state of RNN is used as the context Vector. A Mapping is created between each time step of the decoder and all the encoder hidden states. This results in the Decoder having access to the entire input sequence and thus can accurately pick out the words it needs to make the accurate predictions. There are 2 major types of Attention - Bahdanau Attention and Luong Attention. In the proposed work, the Bahdanau model has been implemented.

Now after paying 'attention' to the most significant part of a sentence, let's also take into consideration the inter-sequence context. For this, the Hierarchical Recurrent Encoder-Decoder (HRED) Architecture (Sordoni et al., 2015) is used. Here, there is a 'bus-type' common context vector wherein it keeps on updating after each response to the message, hence passing the context of each sequence. Along with this, the training data is also modeled in such a way that after responding to a message, the response becomes the message.

The proposed work also implemented Google's state of the art model Bidirectional Encoder Representations from Transformers (BERT) (Devlin et al., 2019). The model could have performed better, however, these models are meant to train on large corpora and then to respond to natural language queries on the learned information. Hence, it failed in this case as the proposed work considers message-response type chatbot which learns from past experiences of spontaneous conversations.

DESIGN OF THE CHATBOT

The proposed methodology aims to develop a chatbot that can predict diseases based on symptoms and provide a diagnosis. This bot will also deal with the mental health of patients. The flow of the system as shown in Figure 1 is described below:

1. User Input
   Users will make a request or a message (input) in the form of text to the chatbot. This should be a simplified input that the bot can understand.
2. Generate Response Message
   The input is converted into a processable form for a Machine Learning model
   a. First, the input is taken into its raw form and it is cleansed; i.e. all the punctuational intricacies are removed so as to only have words that contribute to the meaning of the request/message (request and message to be used interchangeably henceforth).
   b. The cleansed input is then tokenized and sanitized i.e breaking of a sentence into tokens, i.e. separating the sentence into a list of words and then substituting an integer equivalent for each word. This representation is unique for the entire corpus.
   c. If the input has any symptom names present in it, then it is given to a classifier model for prediction of disease and it's diagnosis. Here, the algorithm tends to extract more insight into the user's sickness by adding facets to the user inputs, i.e. by asking questions regarding the illness. Once the bot procures enough information about the symptoms, the classifier predicts the sickness and generates a user-friendly response for the same.
   d. If the input does not contain any symptoms, the proposed chatbot uses the generative model to predict a response. In this methodology,
      i. First, the tokenized input sequence is padded with '0' to a fixed 'maxlen' so that all the sequences have the same length. The words are then substituted with the equivalent word embeddings which is a representation for the words as vectors that elicits a notion of context among the other words. For this, 'glove' embeddings are used. These inputs are ready to be processed in the encoder-decoder architecture.
      ii. After embedding, the completely preprocessed inputs first pass through an attention LSTM layer in the encoder and an encoded hidden state is obtained. This encoded state is used as an initial state for the decoder LSTM. The outputs from all the units of the LSTM are then processed in 2 fully connected neural network layers and finally, the

output words are predicted in a one-hot encoded format. This sequence is reversed pre-processed to obtain the textual sequence.

3.   Display response

The final response of the system is then displayed to the user.

Figure 1. Healthcare Conversational Chatbot

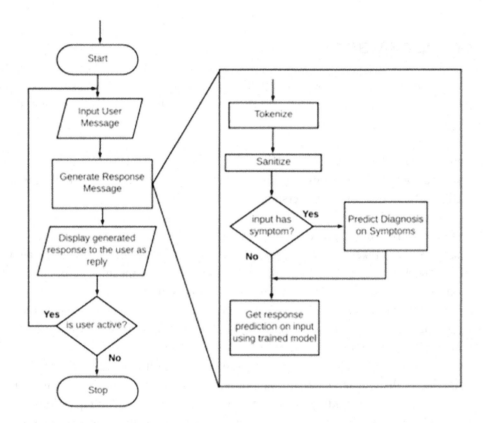

DATASET

Several different datasets have been combined while training the proposed conversational model. The main dataset used is the Cornell Movie--Dialogs Corpus. This dataset contains 220,579 conversational exchanges between 10,292 pairs of movie characters. The idiosyncrasy of this dataset is marked by a grouping of conversations. This enabled the training to implement one of its most impacting mechanisms. However, this dataset is purely meant to train a language model for regular chatbot conversation. To introduce medical domain-specific conversations, various medical question-answering datasets have been used. The GitHub repository for these datasets is https://github.com/LasseRegin/medical-question-answer-data.

MODEL SPECIFICATION

The aforementioned data is trained on a sequence to sequence architecture with attention. The major manipulation in data that induces the context element in the model is essentially the ordering of the responses in the conversation. For a given conversation (set of messages and corresponding responses), the data is modeled as follows:

1. The message is paired with a given response.
2. The response is then taken as a message in the next input.
3. The response obtained for this modeled message is the second message of the conversation. This is repeated.
4. For example, considering ['I need help', 'What do you want?', 'I need information about my appointments', ...] as the conversation, then the chat will be:
    a. Message: I need help; Response: What do you want?
    b. Message: What do you want?; Response: I need information about my appointments
    c. Message: I need information about my appointments; Response: ... (and so on)

This ensures that the model will maintain a notion of context in the conversation which is a major overcoming of the proposed model over others.

The model is trained on the TensorFlow library on the Google Colab platform on Nvidia K80 GPU. The model includes an LSTM layer in the input and output each. The encoder layer is an attention layer. At the decoder, the next word prediction is a classification task to predict the probability distribution of the one-hot encoded word matrix. This is done by 2 Fully Connected Feed Forward Neural Net Layers with a Softmax activation at the end. As in any other sequence to sequence architecture, the proposed model has separate models for training and inference. The architectures for training and inference are summarized below in Figure 2, Figure 3 and Figure 4 respectively:

RESULTS

The chatbot was trained on various models. The training verbose of three such models have been displayed in three parts in Figure 5. The first part is a vanilla sequence to sequence architecture. Second, is a refined sequence to sequence architecture with GRU and bidirectional layer in the encoder. The third verbose is of the proposed architecture with attention which had the best results after the complete training. The objective function is to minimize categorical cross-entropy loss. With stochastic weights, it started off with loss close to 10 and reduced to 4.6 after 17 hours of training on the Nvidia Tesla K80 GPU on the Google Colab platform. The most relevant metric to evaluate a chatbot would be human evaluation. However, the losses show the closeness of the predicted words with the expected output response. The best model was human evaluated as well.

Figure 6 shows symptom extraction by the chatbot and the corresponding diagnosis. As discussed previously, the chatbot tries to dig in with the analysis of the symptoms to a point where it has a sufficient insight into the symptoms to predict the disease.

Figure 2. Training Model

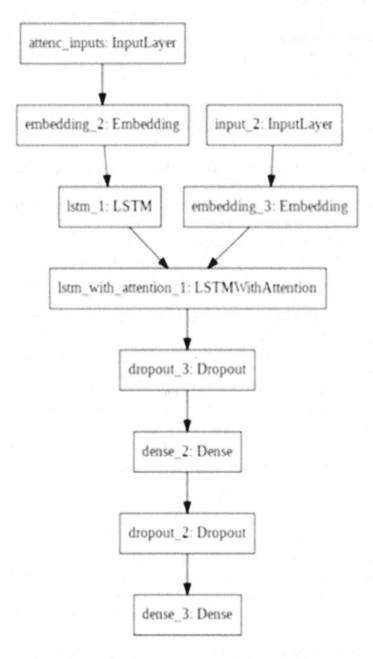

Figure 7 shows the casual behavior of the chatbot wherein the chatbot tries to console the user who seems to be emotionally drained. It demonstrates the chatbot's behavior when the user tries to talk to it without mentioning any symptom of any disease. In this case, the chatbot, unlike the others, tries to converse with the user considering it a regular conversation. Whilst doing so, it is observed that the chatbot preserves the context of the conversation for more than 3-4 messages (here, it remembers what the user is talking about, first the 'gift' then, the fact that the user isn't feeling well).

Figure 3. Encoder Inference Model

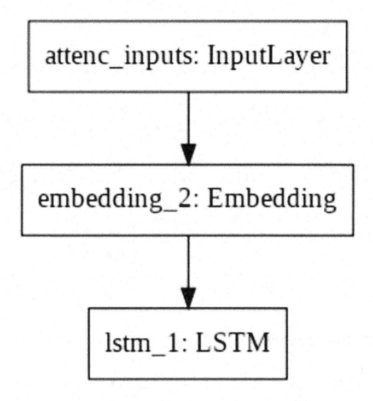

Figure 4. Decoder Inference Model

Figure 5. Losses While Training the Chatbot

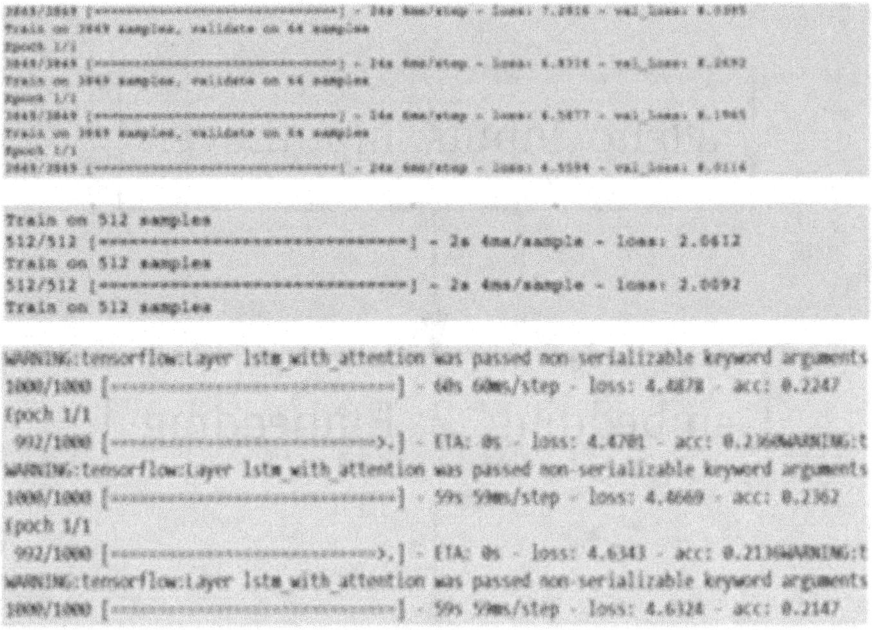
Train on 512 samples
512/512 [==============================] - 2s 4ms/sample - loss: 2.0612
Train on 512 samples
512/512 [==============================] - 2s 4ms/sample - loss: 2.0092
Train on 512 samples
WARNING:tensorflow:Layer lstm_with_attention was passed non-serializable keyword arguments
1000/1000 [==============================] - 60s 60ms/step - loss: 4.4878 - acc: 0.2247
Epoch 1/1
992/1000 [============================>.] - ETA: 0s - loss: 4.4701 - acc: 0.2360WARNING:t
WARNING:tensorflow:Layer lstm_with_attention was passed non-serializable keyword arguments
1000/1000 [==============================] - 59s 59ms/step - loss: 4.4669 - acc: 0.2362
Epoch 1/1
992/1000 [============================>.] - ETA: 0s - loss: 4.6343 - acc: 0.2130WARNING:t
WARNING:tensorflow:Layer lstm_with_attention was passed non-serializable keyword arguments
1000/1000 [==============================] - 59s 59ms/step - loss: 4.6324 - acc: 0.2147

Figure 6. Chatbot Working - Fever Input

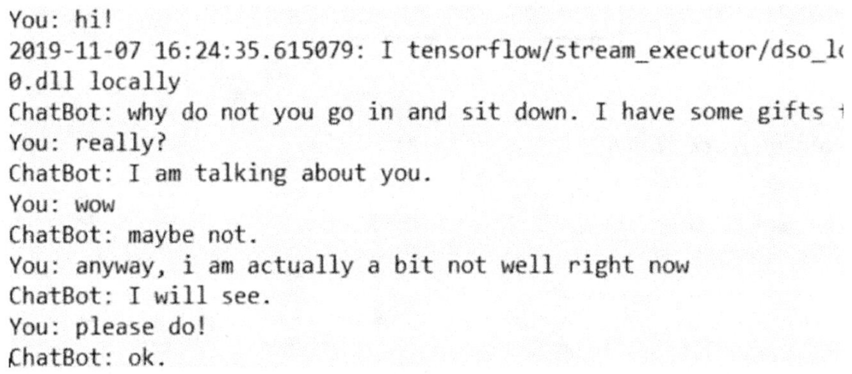
You: hi!
2019-11-07 16:24:35.615079: I tensorflow/stream_executor/dso_l
0.dll locally
ChatBot: why do not you go in and sit down. I have some gifts
You: really?
ChatBot: I am talking about you.
You: wow
ChatBot: maybe not.
You: anyway, i am actually a bit not well right now
ChatBot: I will see.
You: please do!
ChatBot: ok.

Figure 7. Chatbot Working - Emotional Input

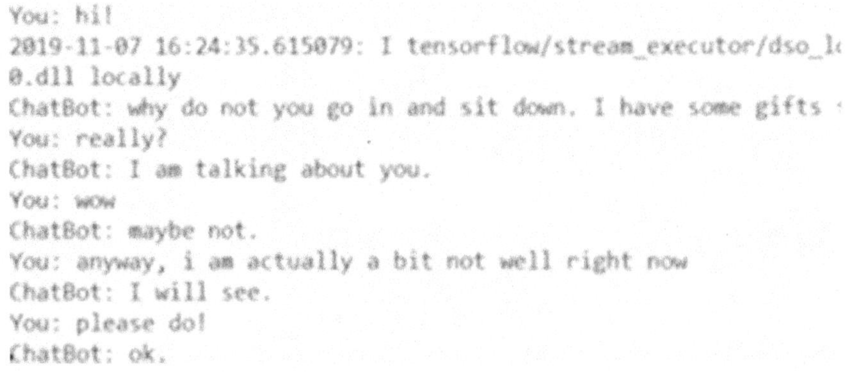
You: hi!
2019-11-07 16:24:35.615079: I tensorflow/stream_executor/dso_l
0.dll locally
ChatBot: why do not you go in and sit down. I have some gifts
You: really?
ChatBot: I am talking about you.
You: wow
ChatBot: maybe not.
You: anyway, i am actually a bit not well right now
ChatBot: I will see.
You: please do!
ChatBot: ok.

CONCLUSION

The sole purpose of chatbots is to improve user experience. The problem addressed is the inefficiency of the existing chatbot systems to diagnose and converse efficiently at the same time. The proposed chatbot obtained a decent evaluation when tested with humans. Also, the diagnosis when compared to germane online resources showed pretty accurate results. The chatbot preserves the context of a given conversation for at least 3-4 chats and also relevance in the responses is observed. This can be a stronghold replacement for the rule-based conversation systems with room for improvement. With improvements in language modeling architectures, high dimensional data with deep Neural Nets on fine-tuning with such state of the art language models can produce even better results. With access to enhanced resources, the proposed architecture with even deeper Neural Networks and complex functions can definitely produce better results. Hence, the proposed system is capable of diagnosing the patient based on the symptoms (if any) provided and/or conversing with the user if they are in distress to improve his/her emotional health.

REFERENCES

Madhu, D., Jain, C. J., Sebastain, E., Shaji, S., & Ajayakumar, A. (2017). A novel approach for medical assistance using trained chatbot. *International Conference on Inventive Communication and Computational Technologies (ICICCT)*, 243-246. 10.1109/ICICCT.2017.7975195

Rosruen, N., & Samanchuen, T. (2018). Chatbot Utilization for Medical Consultant System. *3rd Technology Innovation Management and Engineering Science International Conference (TIMES-iCON)*, 1-5.

Ahmad, N. S., Sanusi, M., Wahab, M. H., Mustapha, A., Sayadi, Z. A., & Saringat, M. Z. (2018). Conversational Bot for Pharmacy: A Natural Language Approach. *IEEE Conference on Open Systems (ICOS)*, 76-79.

Lee, D., Oh, K., & Choi, H. (2017). The chatbot feels you - a counseling service using emotional response generation. *IEEE International Conference on Big Data and Smart Computing (BigComp)*, 437-440.

Oh, K., Lee, D., Ko, B., & Choi, H. (2017). A Chatbot for Psychiatric Counseling in Mental Healthcare Service Based on Emotional Dialogue Analysis and Sentence Generation. *18th IEEE International Conference on Mobile Data Management (MDM)*, 371-375. 10.1109/MDM.2017.64

Rai, S., Raut, A., Savaliya, A. A., & Shankarmani, R. (2018). Darwin: Convolutional Neural Network based Intelligent Health Assistant. Second International Conference on Electronics, Communication and Aerospace Technology (ICECA), 1367-1371.

Leong, P. H., Goh, O. S., & Kumar, Y. J. (2017). MedKiosk: An embodied conversational intelligence via deep learning. *13th International Conference on Natural Computation, Fuzzy Systems and Knowledge Discovery (ICNC-FSKD)*, 394-399.

Ambekar, S., & Phalnikar, R. (2018). Disease Risk Prediction by Using Convolutional Neural Network. *Fourth International Conference on Computing Communication Control and Automation (ICCUBEA)*, 1-5.

Shankar, M., Pahadia, M., Srivastava, D., Ashwin, T. S., & Reddy, G. R. (2015). A Novel Method for Disease Recognition and Cure Time Prediction Based on Symptoms. *Second International Conference on Advances in Computing and Communication Engineering*, 679-682.

Aalipour, G., Kumar, P., Aditham, S., Nguyen, T., & Sood, A. (2018). Applications of Sequence to Sequence Models for Technical Support Automation. IEEE International Conference on Big Data (Big Data), 4861-4869.

Bozzon, A. (2018). Enterprise Crowd Computing for Human Aided Chatbots. *IEEE/ACM 1st International Workshop on Software Engineering for Cognitive Services (SE4COG)*, 29-30.

Gul, S., Kaya, M., & Kaya, B. (2016). Predicting links in weighted disease networks. *3rd International Conference on Computer and Information Sciences (ICCOINS)*, 77-81.

Telang, P. R., Kalia, A. K., Vukovic, M., Pandita, R., & Singh, M. P. (2018). A Conceptual Framework for Engineering Chatbots. *IEEE Internet Computing*, 22(6), 54–59. doi:10.1109/MIC.2018.2877827

Huang, C., Yang, M., Huang, C., Chen, Y., Wu, M., & Chen, K. (2018). A Chatbot- supported Smart Wireless Interactive Healthcare System for Weight Control and Health Promotion. *IEEE International Conference on Industrial Engineering and Engineering Management (IEEM)*, 1791-1795. 10.1109/IEEM.2018.8607399

Kanchan, B. D., & Kishor, M. M. (2016). Study of machine learning algorithms for special disease prediction using principle of component analysis. *International Conference on Global Trends in Signal Processing, Information Computing and Communication (ICGT- SPICC)*, 5-10.

Bahdanau, D., Cho, K., & Bengio, Y. (2014). *Neural Machine Translation by Jointly Learning to Align and Translate*. CoRR, abs/1409.0473

Vaswani, A., Shazeer, N., Parmar, N., Uszkoreit, J., Jones, L., Gomez, A. N., Kaiser, L., & Polosukhin, I. (2017). *Attention is All you Need*. NIPS.

Sutskever, I., Vinyals, O., & Le, Q. V. (2014). *Sequence to Sequence Learning with Neural Networks*. NIPS.

Mikolov, T., Sutskever, I., Chen, K., Corrado, G. S., & Dean, J. (2013). *Distributed Representations of Words and Phrases and their Compositionality*. NIPS.

Pennington, J., Socher, R., & Manning, C. D. (2014). *Glove: Global Vectors for Word Representation*. EMNLP.

Sordoni, A., Bengio, Y., Vahabi, H., Lioma, C., Simonsen, J.G., & Nie, J. (2015). *A Hierarchical Recurrent Encoder-Decoder for Generative Context-Aware Query Suggestion*. ArXiv, abs/1507.02221

Devlin, J., Chang, M., Lee, K., & Toutanova, K. (2019). *BERT: Pre-training of Deep Bidirectional Transformers for Language Understanding*. NAACL-HLT.

Kumar, A., Irsoy, O., Ondruska, P., Iyyer, M., Bradbury, J.H., Gulrajani, I., Zhong, V., Paulus, R., Socher, R. (2015). *Ask Me Anything: Dynamic Memory Networks for Natural Language Processing*. ArXiv, abs/1506.07285

KEY TERMS AND DEFINITIONS

Categorical Cross-Entropy: Also regarded as log loss, this function takes the negative log-likelihood of a normalized logit to be equivalent to the desired output and penalizes unlikeliness accordingly.

Conversation Context: The ongoing topic of the conversation; the object on which the conversations tend to emphasize or the object that gives meaning to a conversation.

Diagnosis: The process of perceiving the patient's medical issues and hence analyzing it on the basis of prior medical knowledge followed by inferring the cause, effect and medication to it (if applies).

DL: Deep learning, a subset of machine learning that deals with 'Deep' Neural Networks; the name 'Deep' comes from the fact that a neural net can be many layers deep.

Feed-Forward Neural Network: The vanilla Neural Network architecture where an output neuron is the weighted sum of the inputs.

GRU: Gated Recurrent Unit, a variant of Long Short-Term Memory wherein the 'input' and 'forget' gates are combined to form one 'update' gate.

Inference Mode: The mode of processing input in a Neural Network wherein the output obtained won't be contributing to the gradients and weight updation of the Network.

Model: The mathematical function of a machine learning algorithm that consists of all the weights and which when fed with a structured input as modeled, produces the output trained by the algorithm.

Softmax: A mathematical function that exponentiates the input and divides it by the sum of the exponentiation of all the inputs in a given set of inputs, hence defining a probability distribution of that input for a given set of inputs.

Teacher Forcing: An approach in training the sequence to sequence architecture wherein one provides the expected output as the input to the decoder, so as to minimize the cascading error resulting from the incorrect output been fed to the next decoder timesteps.

Tensorflow: Google's Deep Learning library that helps to build Neural Networks with or without utilizing the system's GPU with enhancement in performance for GPU based systems.

Word-Embedding: A way of representing words in the form of vectors wherein each element of the vector contains some notion of the value of the word with respect to other words in a given corpus.

Chapter 21
A Literature Review on Thyroid Hormonal Problems in Women Using Data Science and Analytics:
Healthcare Applications

R. Suganya
iD https://orcid.org/0000-0003-1874-6479
Thiagarajar College of Engineering, India

Rajaram S.
Thiagarajar College of Engineering, India

Kameswari M.
Thiagarajar College of Engineering, India

ABSTRACT

Currently, thyroid disorders are more common and widespread among women worldwide. In India, seven out of ten women are suffering from thyroid problems. Various research literature studies predict that about 35% of Indian women are examined with prevalent goiter. It is very necessary to take preventive measures at its early stages, otherwise it causes infertility problem among women. The recent review discusses various analytics models that are used to handle different types of thyroid problems in women. This chapter is planned to analyze and compare different classification models, both machine learning algorithms and deep leaning algorithms, to classify different thyroid problems. Literature from both machine learning and deep learning algorithms is considered. This literature review on thyroid problems will help to analyze the reason and characteristics of thyroid disorder. The dataset used to build and to validate the algorithms was provided by UCI machine learning repository.

DOI: 10.4018/978-1-7998-3053-5.ch021

INTRODUCTION

According to statistics and analytics, thyroid problems are on the rise in Indian women. Data science algorithms provide simple way to solve problem in medical data analysis. The life style of every person is changes due to various factors such as food, culture, environment and social media. It is very difficult to maintain their health. There is no conscious of regular exercise and diet. The hormonal changes of every person are changing drastically. The serious problem should need to take care in hormonal changes is thyroid stimulating hormones. The symptoms of thyroid are hair growth in face, rough skin, stress, depression and obese. The neural network models which explain the complexities of thyroid gland and different types of diseases have been explored. The complications results in thyroid disease are growing rapidly and provides data scientist to find new insights into thyroid hormonal problems by using deep leaning algorithms.

Data sciences afford most important aid in thyroid dataset with different algorithms for classification, clustering, association etc. The authors have used different types of machine learning and deep learning frameworks for thyroid dataset classification. Several startup companies like BUDDI.AI have come forward to carry out research in Thyroid problems.

Machine Learning (ML) is a subset of Artificial Intelligence (AI) is dominating in analytics era can provide prediction for most of the medical analytics problems. It is able to produce more accurate models based on the dataset. It permits the models to train on dataset before being installed. There are two types of models: online and continuous. Based upon the size and complexity of data, the patterns and relations could easily be perceived by common layman. Machine learning algorithms are essential to progress the correctness of predictive models. Deep learning is a subset of ML that includes the architecture of artificial neural networks in consecutive layers to study from data in an iterative nature. DL is particularly applied for huge unstructured data (otherwise called big data). The advantage of both data science and analytics algorithms models are used to predict outcomes.

This chapter is focused on thyroid hormonal problems, factors affecting thyroid hormones, types of thyroid diseases followed by machine learning algorithms, deep learning algorithms and literature survey for both with UCI machine learning repository dataset. Finally discussion and conclusion for complete literature review on thyroid problems in women using data science and analytics is presented.

BACKGROUND

Thyroid diseases are the most common endocrine disorder problem among Indian women. Banu (2016) explained that the thyroid is a butterfly formed organ situated in the human neck and ace organ of digestion. Chen et al. (2012) discussed that thyroid gland secreted two thyroid hormones namely triiodothyronine (T3) and thyroxin (T4). T3 and T4 are composed 50% of iodine. These hormones are in charge for regulation of metabolism. The shortage of iodine decreased T3 and T4 level and enlarges the thyroid tissue called simple goiter. The effects of triiodothyronine (T3) results increase cardiac arrest in man and infertility problems in women. When the level of thyroid hormones T3 and T4 go down too low, the pituitary gland segregates' Thyroid Simulating Hormone (TSH) which stimulates the thyroid gland to produces more hormones. Around 42 million people in India have thyroid disorders. Approximately one in 10 Indian women suffer from hypothyroidism, which means the thyroid gland does not segregate sufficient thyroid hormones to meet up the needs of the women body. Most of the girl from the age 18 is suffering from thyroid problems.

A 2016 literature study carried out in nine states in India and inferred that 13.3% of pregnant women suffered by hypothyroid due to Thyroid stimulating hormone (TSH) during first trimester, because of over stress. Abnormal levels of thyroid hormones during pregnancy are connected with a high risk of complication / hurdle such as miscarriages, anemia, postpartum bleeding and placental abruption. If affects both mother and new born baby's weight and sometimes fetal death. Therefore, treating thyroid problems is important for both maternal and child health.

Vivian et al. (2019) stated that the Indian Thyroid Society has launched an operation, MITA – Making India Thyroid Aware in partnership with Abbott India, to force consciousness amongst doctors and patients for early detection and treatment of thyroid disorders amongst women in the age group of 25 to 45 years. Thyroid syndromes are diverse from other diseases in terms of their ease of diagnosis, user-friendliness of medical treatment, and the visibility of small inflammation of the thyroid glands. Early diagnosis and treatment remains the cornerstone of management. The thyroid hormones and its normal levels for women are given below in the table 1.

Table 1. Thyroid Hormonal Levels

Hormones	Normal levels
FSH	3-9 mIU/ ml
LH	2-10 mIU/ ml
TSH	0.4 – 4.0 mIU/ ml
Total T3	80 -220 ng/ dL
Free T3	260- 480 pg /dL
Total T4	5.4 – 11.5 mcg / dL
Free T4	0.7 -1.8 ng/ dL
Estradiol	27 – 161 pg/ml
Progesterone	5-20 ng/ ml (on day 21)
Prolactin	0-20 ng / ml
AMH	0.7 -3.5 ng /ml

There are several factors that reduce proper production of thyroid hormones. They are Stress, Infection, trauma, and radiation medications, Fluoride, Toxins such as pesticides, mercury, cadmium and lead. Ecological factors are witness for the appearance of autoimmune thyroid diseases (AITD). Increased iodine intake and vitamin D deficiency are environmental factors for increasing AITD. Due to social media and peer pressure, women students at the age of 15 to 17, are acquired thyroid problems. According to recent statistical report, Hypothyroidism reports for 15% of pediatric thyroid problem called Graves' disease more common among girls between the ages 10 to 15 years.

Sometimes, Cold exposure may increases in serum TSH levels in infants and young children. Thyroid hormones play a central role in the regulation of total body metabolism. Balanced diet can helpful to prevent thyroid in an early stages. There are some factors that play a major role in the proper production of thyroid hormones: - Nutrients like iron, iodine, tyrosine, zinc, selenium and Vitamin E, B2, B3, B6, C and Vitamin D. Thyroid disorder can be avoided by doing regular exercise. Sometimes thyroid disorder leads to liver and kidney dysfunction.

Imaging technology is very important for the diagnosis of thyroid diseases. Several modalities like x-ray, ultrasound, CT scan, MRI scan and SPECT are commonly used for medical imaging. Out of these modalities, ultrasound imaging has the several advantages like low cost and less harm to human body compare to other modalities. It is widely used to capture thyroid diseases.

THYROID DISCORDER

Issues

Thyroid disorder is conditions that influence the thyroid gland, a butterfly shaped gland in the front of the neck. Ma et al. (2017) explained, this gland is very essential for regulating several metabolic developments throughout the whole body. Different types of thyroid disorders are there, namely hypothyroid, hyperthyroid, goiter, thyroid nodules and thyroid cancer. Thyroid problem can sometimes enlargers the thyroid gland in the neck.

Hypothyroidism

Hypothyroidism is due to the deficiency of hormones T2 and T4. It results from the thyroid gland manufacturing an inadequate amount of thyroid hormone. It can enlarge as thyroid gland in the neck among most of the women. Ozyilmaz (2002) stated the symptoms of hypothyroidism are fatigue, dry skin, constipation, fluid retention and muscle and joint aches. A current study found that nearly one third of patients with hypothyroidism were over treated. Over treatment was associated with an increased risk for cardiac arrest and sudden stroke. Lower thyroid functionality has an unfavorable control on reproductive phase in the women.

Hyperthyroidism

Hyperthyroidism explains too much production of thyroid hormone called thyroxine, a less common condition than hypothyroidism. It can accelerate whole body's metabolism causing inadvertent weight reduction and irregular heartbeat. The following symptoms are associated with hyperthyroidism:

- Excessive sweating
- Increased bowel movements
- Weight loss
- Fatigue and
- Weakness

Graves' disease is the most widespread reason of hyperthyroidism, can normally be a connected with eye diseases. Treatments for hyperthyroidism include antithyroid medications, radioactive ablation and surgery. Hyperthyroidism defines to an amplified production of thyroid hormone by the thyroid gland, while hypothyroidism refers to a stipulation in which a person has too little thyroid hormone or under-production of thyroid hormones.

Goiter/ Iodine Deficiency Disorders

Iodine deficiency is the main cause of goiters. A goiter describes enlargement of the thyroid gland, may be due to hypothyroidism, hyperthyroidism or normal thyroid function. The main reasons of a goiter are autoimmune disorder. Thyroid goiters are benign (non-cancerous) and if not treated properly leads to cancer. The primary symptom of a goiter is visible inflammation /enlargement in the neck. The following are the symptoms of goiter.

- Difficulty swallowing or breathing
- Coughing
- Dizziness
- Hoarseness in voice

There are two types of goiter: Colloid goiter (endemic) and nontoxic goiter (sporadic).

Hashimoto's Thyroiditis

Hashimoto's thyroditis also called as chronic lymphocytic thyroiditis is an autoimmune disease in which the thyroid gland is gradually destroyed. Initially no symptoms are recognized, but later it forms painless goiter. Women are 10-15 times more likely than men to develop hashimoto's thyroiditis. The common symptoms are

- Brittle nails
- Fatigue and sluggishness
- Constipation
- Hair loss
- Enlargement of the tongue

Thyroid Cancer

Thyroid cancer is far more common among adult women than men or youth. About 2/3 of cases occur in people under age 55. There are different kinds of thyroid cancer: Papillary thyroid cancer (85%), medullary thyroid cancer (3%), follicular thyroid cancer (10%) and anaplastic thyroid cancer (1%). Females are most likely to have thyroid cancer at the ratio of 3:1. It occurs in any age group after age 30. Although as many as 75% of the population will have thyroid nodules called benign.

All the above thyroid disorder is examined by Blood test, imaging test, thyroid scans and biopsy. Blood tests are typically done to measure levels of thyroid hormones and TSH. Imaging tests are commonly used when thyroid nodules or enlargement are found. Ultrasound modality can visualize the consistency of the tissue within the gland and reveal cysts or calcifications. Thyroid scans using radioactive iodine are used to perform the function of thyroid nodules. Biopsy is techniques that remove a sample of cells or tissue from the thyroid gland for examinations.

MACHINE LEARNING ALGORITHMS

Machine learning algorithms comprise supervised learning, unsupervised learning, reinforcement learning and deep learning. ML uses the above variety of algorithms that iteratively learn from data to improve, describe data and predict outcomes. It creates output when you train your ML algorithm with given dataset. Dogantekin (2011) stated, ML is very essential for creating predictive analytics models. Predictive analytics assists foresee changes based on understanding the model and differences within that dataset.

Supervised Learning

Supervised learning algorithm initiates with a well-known set of data and a definite accepting of how that data is classified. It is employed to discover models in data that can be useful to an analytics process. The data has labeled features that describe the significance of data. In general, regression algorithm is used for supervised learning assists to comprehend the relationship between variables in dataset. The performance of the supervised algorithms is measured with the help of test data. If the model is fit to only signify the patterns that exist in the training subset, then it cause over fitting problem. Judith Hurwitz (2018) discussed that your model is exactly refrained for your training data but may not be applicable for large sets of unknown data. To prevent this issue, testing should need to be done against unknown (new) labeled data. The test data can also help to measure the accuracy of the model in predicting outcomes.

Unsupervised Learning

An unsupervised learning algorithm is suitable for problem necessitates a huge amount of unstructured data (big data) that is unlabeled. It segment data into groups of clusters or groups of features. Understanding the meaning behind this data requires algorithms that can begin to understand the meaning based meaning based on being able to classify the data based on the patterns or clusters it finds.

Reinforcement Learning Algorithms

Reinforcement learning is a behavioral learning model. This algorithm collects response from the data analysis, supporting the user to the best outcome. It varies from other types of supervised learning because the system is not trained with the sample data set. Rather, the system learns through trial and error. Therefore, a sequence of successful decisions will results in the process being reinforced, because it best solves the problem.

Deep Learning Algorithms

Deep leaning algorithm is a subset of ML is especially useful to learn patterns from big data. Deep leaning algorithms are an extension of artificial neural networks. It is composed of several neurons which mimics like human brain. It is mainly used in image recognition and computer vision applications. The convolutional neural network is mainly used to classify medical images with fully connected layer, polling layer and flatten layers. The hyper parameters used in deep learning algorithms are helpful to predict right / correct outcomes as like human brain recognize right ones.

Transfer Learning

If the dataset is huge and unstructured / big data, then deep learning or transfer learning is suitable. Transfer learning fine tunes CNN models pretrained from normal dataset to complex medical image analysis. Judith Hurwitz (2018) stated that the effectiveness of transfer leaning or deep leaning in medical image classification and recognition is huge and magic. It mimics our human brain and predict exactly. The main problem in handling huge dataset is over fitting. In order to prevent over fitting, we can use dropout strategy in the training phase.

Thyroid Disease Dataset Details

Thyroid disease dataset is taken from UCI machine learning repository. The total number of samples is around 7200 with 21 different attributes. The dataset characteristics are multivariate and domain-theory with categorical and real attribute characteristics. This dataset is used to identify the type of thyroid disease and to classify whether it is normal or diseased one. The various phases involved in the classification algorithms. Initially the dataset is preprocessed to identify the outliers and then extract the important features present in the dataset. Feature extraction and feature selection is very essential phase in medical image analysis or medical image classification. If the dataset is images, we can adopt pre-processing, feature extraction, feature selection and classification. Sometime segmentation and image registration is used to clearly identify the diseases portion. Image registration is particularly used to monitor the growth of the thyroid diseases.

LITERATURE SURVEY

Lot of research work has been carried out in Thyroid problem using UCI machine learning repository. This dataset consists of thyroid diseases with three classes of problems- normal, hyperthyroidism, and hypothyroidism. 1n 1997, serpent et al proposed probabilistic potential function in neural network classifier and predicted his diagnosis accuracy was about 78.14%. Ozyilamz et al 2002 diagnosed thyroid diseases using artificial neural networks like Multilayer perception (MLP) with BPN and achieved 88.3%.

Hoshi et al. (2005) proposed multivariate analysis model and two important approaches namely Bayesian regularized networks and Self Organizing Map for thyroid classification problems. Keles et al in 2008 developed expert system for thyroid and diagnose with accuracy 95.33%. Polat et al. (2007) proposed machine learning strategy with AIRS and predict thyroid diseases of about 85%. Temuras (2009) made comparative study on thyroid disease diagnosis using various neural networks and summarized his perception.

Dogantekin et al. (2011) adopted wavelet-based support vector machine and recognized thyroid disease was about 91.86%. He concluded an expert system based on generalized discriminant analysis of thyroid diseases. Chen et al. (2012) designed a three-stage expert system for diagnosing thyroid disease using support vector machines and obtained the accuracy 97.49%.

Ouyang et al. (2012) developed CAD system for thyroid disease using extreme machine learning and achieved the accuracy of about 97.73%. Valanarasi et al. (2014) diagnosed hypo and hyperthyroidism using MLPN framework. In this work, he predicted the sensitivity value as 93.12% for 3 fold cross validation and 89.02% for 10 fold cross validation. Prerana et al. (2015) predicted thyroid diseases using

Table 2. Summary of Literature survey on different machine learning algorithms and its accuracy

Proposed year	Author	Traditional Machine learning algorithm used	Accuracy / Insights
1997	Serpen G., Jiang H., Allred L	Probabilistic potential function in Neural networks	78.14%
2004	Ozyilmaz L., Yildirim T	Multilayer perception (MLP) with BPN	88.3%
2005	Hoshi K, Kawakami J, Kumagai M, Kasahara S, Nishimura N, Nakamura H, Sato K	Multivariate analysis model and Bayesian regularized networks and Self Organizing Map	84.4%
2007	Polat K, Şahan S, Güneş S	AIRS with Fuzzy weighted clustering algorithm	85%
2008	Keleş A, Keleş A. Estdd	Expert system using supervised learning algorithms	95.33%
2008	Kousarrizi, Nazari MR, Seiti F, Teshnehlab	Fuzzy cognitive Map (FCM)	96.01%
2009	Temurtas F	Various neural network algorithms	Comparative study
2011	Dogantekin E., Dogantekin A., Avci D	Wavelet-based support vector machine	91.86%
2012	Chen HL, Yang B, Wang G, Liu J, Chen YD, Liu DY	Three-stage expert system using SVM Principle component Analysis (PCA)	97.49%
2012	Li LN, Ouyang JH, Chen HL, Liu DY	CAD system using extreme ML algorithms	97.73%
2014	Valanarasi Antony Santiagu	Diagnosed hypo and hyperthyroidism using MLPN, RBF, SPSS	93.12%
2015	Prerana PS	Lavenberg-Marquert algorithm with Neural network	94.55%
2016	Hanirex DK, Kaliyamurthie KP.	LDA Linear Discriminant Analysis	95.6%

various data mining and neural network techniques. He used Lavenberg-Marquert algorithm with Neural network and predicted more accurate results compared to radiant descent algorithms.

Judith Hurwitz (2018) discussed several machine learning methods has been applied for ultrasound Thyroid images using artificial intelligence utilized hand crafted features and Support vector machine methods to classify thyroid nodules. A result of this CAD system showed lower specificity (74.6%) and accuracy (81.4%). The table 3 shows the summary of literature survey on Deep learning algorithms and its insights.

Ma et al. (2017) proposed Cascade convolutional neural networks for automatic detection of thyroid nodules using US image. This cascade CNN is a hybrid model consisting of two different CNNs and a new splitting method. It employs a deep CNN to learn the segmentation probability maps from the ground true data. Then all the segmentation probability maps are split into different connected regions by the splitting method. Finally, another deep CNN is used to automatically detect the thyroid nodules from ultrasound thyroid images, experimental results illustrate the cascade CNNs are very effective in detection of thyroid nodules. The results obtained by area under the curve of ROC are 98.51%.

Liu et al. (2017) proposed transfer learning for classification of thyroid nodules using ultrasound images. Author proposed a feature extraction method for ultrasound images based on CNN to extract meaningful semantic features to the classification. He combined deep features with conventional features such as histogram of oriented gradient (HOG) and Local Binary Pattern (LBP) together to form a hybrid feature space. Experimental results on 1037 images show the accuracy of proposed method is 93%.Huang et al. (2017) explained connected convolution networks using DenseNet for thyroid diseases classification. Here author considered three categories of diseases – Graves' disease, Hashimoto disease and Subacute thyroiditis. Modified DenseNet architecture of CNN is employed using trainable weight parameters. Here the training method is improved by optimizing the learning rate with flower pollination algorithm for network training.Ma et al. (2018) proposed CNN to predict thyroid cancer using SPECT images. The sensitivity and accuracy measures are used the performance evaluation. Li et al proposed improved deep learning method for the detection of thyroid cancer using ultrasound thyroid images. The author used faster RCNN algorithm for detection of thyroid papillary carcinoma detection. Besides, he concatenated the shallow and deep layers of the CNN, the detector can detect blurrier or smaller cancer regions. He predicted 93.5% of papillary thyroid carcinoma regions automatically.

Chi et al. (2019) proposed Fine-Tuning Deep Convolutional Neural Network –GoogleNet for classification of thyroid diseases using ultrasound images. Here author used pre-trained GooLeNet model for superior feature extraction. The extracted features of the thyroid ultrasound images are sent to a Cost-sensitive Random forest classifier to classify the images into malignant and benign cases. The experimental results show the proposed fine-tuned googlenet models achieves excellent classification performance attaining 98.29% classification accuracy, 99.10% sensitivity and 93.90% of specificity for the images in an open access database.

Table 3. Summary of Literature survey on Deep learning algorithms and its Insights

Proposed year	Author	Deep learning algorithm used	Accuracy / Insights
2017	Ma J, Wu F, Jiang T, Zhu J, Kong D	Cascade convolutional neural networks	Automatic detection of thyroid nodules using ultrasound images.
2017	Liu T., Xie S., Xu J., Niu L., Sun W.	Transfer learning	Classify thyroid nodules using ultrasound images
2017	Huang G., Liu Z., Maaten L., Weinberger K. Ensely	Connected Convolution networks – DenseNet	Thyroid diseases classification
2018	Ma L., Ma C., Liu Y., Wang X., Xie W	Convolution Neural network	Predict thyroid cancer using SPECT images
2018	Li H, Weng J, Shi Y, Gu W, Mao Y, Wang Y, Liu W, Zhang J	Improved deep learning approach	Detection of thyroid papillary cancer using ultrasound images.
2018	Wang Y., Ke W., Wan P	Deep convolution neural network	Recognize thyroid papillary carcinoma
2018	Han SS, Kim MS, Lim W, Park GH, Park I, Chang SE	Deep Learning Algorithm	Classification of the Clinical Images for Benign and Malignant Cutaneous Tumors
2019	Song W, Li S, Liu J, Qin H, Zhang B, Zhang S, Hao A	Multitask Cascade Convolution Neural Networks	Automatic detection and recognition of thyroid Nodule
2019	Chi J, Walia E, Babyn P, Wang J, Groot G, Eramian M	Fine-Tuning Deep Convolutional Neural Network -GoogleNet	Thyroid Nodule Classification using Ultrasound Images

DISCUSSION AND CONCLUSION

From the above table 2 – literature survey on thyroid dataset by machine learning algorithms for thyroid images on ultrasound image modalities are summarized. It is very clear, that plenty of machine learning algorithms in last 10 years before has been applied on UCI Machine learning repository and shown various classification accuracy results. The metrics used for evaluation of machine learning algorithms are sensitivity and specificity and accuracy rate by cross fold validations.

In the table 3 – literature survey by deep learning algorithms on thyroid images. The thyroid diseases can be diagnosed by ultrasound images. All deep learning algorithms are mainly adopted convolution neural network, transfer learning algorithms with various nets – ReLu Net, Google Net, ResNet and Image Net etc. The main objective of deep learning algorithm is to detect / diagnose the problems automatically and recognize the different stages of thyroid diseases like hypothyroidism, hyperthyroidism, thyroid nodules, thyroid cancer and Hashimoto's thyroiditis. Besides, many authors conducted their research work on the classification of thyroid diseases using various modalities of images. The motivation behind this classification is required by physicians /radiologist and these expert systems can sometimes act as a recommendation system.

The hyper parameters in convolution neural networks like stride, epochs, learning rate, activation functions, and weights plays a major role in classification and recognitions of diseases from medical images. The role of deep learning and AI plays a major role in medical analysis and healthcare datasets. Various research literature studies predict that about 35% of Indian women are examined with prevalent goiter. There are several factors that affect the thyroid functions – T3, T4 and TSH. It is very necessary to take preventive measures at its early stages, otherwise it causes infertility problem among women. The direct relationship / association of thyroid problems in women are the cause of polycystic ovary syndrome (PCOS).

Polycystic ovary syndrome (PCOS) is a widespread reproductive and endocrinology disorder found in 6-10% of the female population. PCOS caused infertility in women if not diagnosed early. The presence of 12 or more follicles in each ovary measuring 2-9 mm in diameter and/or increased ovarian volume (>10ml) is defined as PCOS. The main indication of PCOS is thyroid problem. Ultrasound abdomen scan image is an efficient tool to determine PCOS. The above study / literature review on Thyroid hormonal problems and different thyroid diseases in women using Data science – ML and Analytics – Deep learning algorithms are clearly discussed.

A new algorithm called DBSCAN or Density –Based Spatial Clustering of Applications with Noise, is an unsupervised machine learning algorithm is a new comer in medical image analysis and will bring revolution. Unsupervised machine learning algorithms are used to classify unlabeled data. The main role of DBSCAN algorithm is, it handle medical images with noise. Because most of the medical images are need to be preprocessed by filters. But sometimes very subtle features of noise hold some intricate details of diseases. So definitely DBSCAN is particularly well suited for medical image analysis. Thyroid disorder stands in the second largest disorder in the endocrinology field. The total number of patients with different types of thyroid disorder in India is more than 100 million. So data science and analytics domain should take necessary steps to bring awareness among Indian women to eradicate thyroid disorder completely.

REFERENCES

Antony, V., & Vaz, S. (2014). Diagnosis of hypo and hyperthyroid using MLPN Network. *International Journal of Innovative Research in Science. Engineering and Technology*, *3*(7), 14314–14323.

Banu, G.R. (2016). *Predicting thyroid disease using Linear Discriminant Analysis (LDA) data mining technique.* Doi:10.5120/cae2016651990

Chen, H.L., Yang, B., Wang, G., Liu, J., Chen, Y.D., & Liu, D.Y. (2012). A three-stage expert system based on support vector machines for thyroid disease diagnosis. *J Med Syst.*, *36*(3), 1953-63.

Chen, H.-L., Yang, B., Wang, G., Liu, J., Chen, Y.-D., & Liu, D.-Y. (2012). A three-stage expert system based on support vector machines for thyroid disease diagnosis. *Journal of Medical Systems*, *36*(3), 1953–1963. doi:10.100710916-011-9655-8 PMID:21286792

Park, Han, Seon, Park, Kim, Moon, Yoon, & Kwar. (2019). Diagnosis of Thyroid Nodules: Performance of a Deep Learning Convolutional Neural Network Model vs. Radiologist. *Scientific Reports*.

Dogantekin, E., Dogantekin, A., & Avci, D. (2011). An expert system based on generalized discriminant analysis and wavelet support vector machine for diagnosis of thyroid diseases. *Journal of Expert Systems with Applications*, *38*(1), 146–150. doi:10.1016/j.eswa.2010.06.029

Dogantekin, E., Dogantekin, A., & Avci, D. (2011). An expert system based on generalized discriminant analysis and wavelet support vector machine for diagnosis of thyroid diseases. *Expert Systems with Applications*, *38*(1), 146–150. doi:10.1016/j.eswa.2010.06.029

Han, S. S., Kim, M. S., Lim, W., Park, G. H., Park, I., & Chang, S. E. (2018). Classification of the Clinical Images for Benign and Malignant Cutaneous Tumors Using a Deep Learning Algorithm. *The Journal of Investigative Dermatology*, *138*(7), 1529–1538. doi:10.1016/j.jid.2018.01.028 PMID:29428356

Hanirex, D. K., & Kaliyamurthie, K. P. (2013). *Multi-classification approach for detecting thyroid attacks.* Academic Press.

Hoshi, K., Kawakami, J., Kumagai, M., Kasahara, S., Nishimura, N., Nakamura, H., & Sato, K. (2005). An analysis of thyroid function diagnosis using Bayesian-type and SOM-type neural networks. *Chemical & Pharmaceutical Bulletin*, *53*(12), 1570–1574. doi:10.1248/cpb.53.1570 PMID:16327191

Hurwitz & Kirsch. (2018). *Machine Learning for Dummies*. IBM Limited Edition, Published by John Wiley & Sons.

Keleş, A., & Keleş, A. (2008). Expert system for thyroid diseases diagnosis. *Expert Systems with Applications*, *34*(1), 242–246. doi:10.1016/j.eswa.2006.09.028

Ker, J., Wang, L., Rao, J., & Lim, T. (2018). Deep learning applications in medical image analysis. *IEEE Access: Practical Innovations, Open Solutions*, *6*(1), 9375–9389. doi:10.1109/ACCESS.2017.2788044

Kim, S.-T., Baek, M., & Cho, J.-K. (2015). Analysis on distribution of effective dose rate around patients for treatment of thyroid cancer with I-131. *Indian Journal of Science and Technology*, *8*(S7). doi:10.17485/ijst/2015/v8iS7/70148

Kousarrizi, Seiti, & Teshnehlab. (2012). An experimental comparative study on thyroid disease diagnosis based on feature subset selection and classification. *International Journal of Electrical & Computer Sciences*, *12*(1), 13–20.

LeCun, Y., Bengio, Y., & Hinton, G. (2015). Deep Learning. *Nature, 521*(7553), 436-44.

Li, H., Weng, J., Shi, Y., Gu, W., Mao, Y., Wang, Y., Liu, W., & Zhang, J. (2018). An improved deep learning approach for detection of thyroid papillary cancer in ultrasound images. *Journal of Imaging Science, 8*(1).

Li, L.-N., Ouyang, J.-H., Chen, H.-L., & Liu, D.-U. (2012). A computer aided diagnosis system for thyroid disease using extreme learning machine. *Journal of Medical Systems*, *36*(5), 3327–3337. doi:10.100710916-012-9825-3 PMID:22327384

Li, L.N., Ouyang, J.H., Chen, H.L., & Liu, D.Y. (2012). A computer aided diagnosis system for thyroid disease using extreme learning machine. *J Med Syst.*, *36*(5), 3327-37.

Liu, T., Xie, S., Xu, J., Niu, L., & Sun, W. (2017). Classification of thyroid nodules in ultrasound images using deep model based transfer learning and hybrid features. *Proceedings of IEEE International Conference on Acoustics, Speech and Signal Processing (ICASSP)*, 919–923. 10.1109/ICASSP.2017.7952290

Ma, J., Wu, F., Jiang, T., Zhu, J., & Kong, D. (2017). Cascade convolutional neural networks for automatic detection of thyroid nodules in ultrasound images. *Med Phys.*, *44*(5), 1678-1691.

Ozyilmaz, L., & Yildirim, T. (2002). Diagnosis of thyroid disease using artificial neural network methods. *Proceedings of International Conference on Neural Information Processing*, 2033–2036. 10.1109/ICONIP.2002.1199031

Pandey, S., Miri, R., & Tandan, S.R. (2013). Diagnosis and classification of hypothyroid disease using data mining techniques. *International Journal of Engineering Research and Technology.*

Prerana, P. S., & Taneja, K. (2015). Predictive data mining for diagnosis of thyroid disease using neural network. *International Journal of Research in Management. Science & Technology*, *3*(2), 75–80.

Raghavendra, U., Gudigar, A., Maithri, M., Gertych, A., Meiburger, K.M., Yeong, C.H., Madla, C., Kongmebhol, P., Molinari, F., Ng, K.H., & Acharya, U.R. (2018). Optimized multi-level elongated quinary patterns for the assessment of thyroid nodules in ultrasound images. *Computer Biology Med.*, *95*, 55-62.

Serpen, G., Jiang, H., & Allred, L. (1997). Performance analysis of probabilistic potential function neural network classifier. *Proceedings of Artificial Neural Networks in Engineering Conference*, 471–476.

Shaik Razia, S., & Narasinga Rao, M. R. (2016). Machine Learning Techniques for Thyroid Disease Diagnosis- A Review. *Indian Journal of Science and Technology*, *9*(28).

Song, W., Li, S., Liu, J., Qin, H., Zhang, B., Zhang, S., & Hao, A. (2019). Multitask Cascade Convolution Neural Networks for Automatic Thyroid Nodule Detection and Recognition. *IEEE Journal of Biomedical and Health Informatics*, *23*(3), 1215–1224. doi:10.1109/JBHI.2018.2852718 PMID:29994412

Temurtas, F. (2009). A comparative study on thyroid disease diagnosis using neural networks. *Expert Systems with Applications*, *36*(1), 944–949. doi:10.1016/j.eswa.2007.10.010

Wang, Y., Ke, W., & Wan, P. (2018). A method of ultrasonic image recognition for thyroid papillary carcinoma based on deep convolution neural network. *NeuroQuantology: An Interdisciplinary Journal of Neuroscience and Quantum Physics, 16*(5), 757–768. doi:10.14704/nq.2018.16.5.1306

KEY TERMS AND DEFINITIONS

Analytics: The systematic analysis of data (thyroid dataset).

Data Science: Data Science is an inter-disciplinary field that uses scientific methods, processes, algorithms and systems to extract knowledge and insights.

Deep Learning: Deep leaning is a subset of machine learning to solve complex problems/datasets.

Hyperthyroidism: Hyperthyroidism means over activity of the thyroid gland.

Hypothyroidism: Hypothyroidism (underactive thyroid) is a condition in which thyroid gland doesn't produce enough hormones.

Machine Learning: Machine learning is a subset of artificial intelligence.

Thyroid Hormonal Problems: Thyroid disorders can range from small, harmless goiter to complex cancer.

Ultrasound Image: Ultrasound modality image.

Chapter 22
Influence of Some Sociodemographic Factors on Causes of Death Among South African Youth

Boipelo Vinolia Mogale

https://orcid.org/0000-0003-1147-9283

North-West University, South Africa

Johannes Tshepiso Tsoku

https://orcid.org/0000-0003-0093-6223

North-West University, South Africa

Elias Munapo

North-West University, South Africa

Olusegun Sunday Ewemooje

Federal University of Technology, Akure, Nigeria

ABSTRACT

Youth mortality is a challenge in South Africa, where on a daily basis a number of deaths are reported and are related to youth. This study used the 2014 Statistics South Africa data to examine the influence of sociodemographic factors on causes of death among South African youth aged 15-34 years, using a logistic regression model. The results showed that there is a significant relationship between education and causes of death as well as other sociodemographic factors and that the youth mortality will likely reduce if more youth have higher levels of education. The results of this study could be used to improve national prevention campaigns to reduce death among young South Africans, especially adolescents.

DOI: 10.4018/978-1-7998-3053-5.ch022

INTRODUCTION

South Africa's National Youth Policy (NYP) (2009-2014) defines youth as persons between the age category of 15 and 34 years. According to the mid-year population estimates 2016 produced by Stats SA there is an overall of 42% of young people in South Africa that there has been an improvement in the living conditions of these youth. The youth are now having access to water, housing and sanitation, and are technologically advanced; nevertheless, the high youth unemployment rate, high HIV infection rate as well as the growing number of households that are headed by young people is still some of the significant challenges that they have to grapple with. The education of the youth is also of paramount importance, the National Development Plan (NDP) 2030, is aiming at ensuring that all people have access to education. The World Health Organisation assets that health is one of the key focus areas of the 2030 Agenda. Within the Sustainable Development Goals (SDGs) and with special reference to SDG 3, health and well-being for all peoples of a nation receive special emphasis as a global action item. On the other hand, the African Youth Charter (2006) also emphasises that every young person should have the right to education of good quality and the right to enjoy the best attainable state of health physically, mentally and spiritually. Education level of the nation remains the most vital factor in the absence of cure for some of the diseases. According to Statistics South Africa, Statistical release P0309.3 (2015) there are basically two types of causes of death, namely natural causes or non-natural as certified by medical practitioners. Natural causes are often attributed to an illness or underlying malfunctioning of the body and non-natural causes refers to deaths that are not natural such as accidents, suicide, and so forth. The study focuses on the causes of death of the youth of South Africa and their education level. The study is aimed at determining whether a relationship exists between the two variables.

BACKGROUND

According to Statistics South Africa, Statistical release P0211.4.2 (2015), there was an improvement in the employment levels for the youth as about 44.5% of them are employed. It was noted that one out of every two young people who were unemployed and seeking employment only had education below matriculation. Borode (2011) suggests that the higher education curriculum in Sub-Saharan African countries should be amended so as to deal with the effects of the current education and training curriculum which have led to the observed high levels of unemployment. He asserts that the drive should focus on training in relevant scarce skills to ensure job market readiness. Higher education should be directed at producing graduates that are relevant to the economy, who would apply the acquired knowledge and skills to shape the economy and create jobs, rather than seeking for job opportunities as employees versus being entrepreneurs and employers.

The United Nations (UN, 2016) factsheet on youth and education established that education attainment can be used to reduce poverty and hunger, and also to promote sustainable developments in the world. UN further reports that globally, about 10.6% of the youth are uneducated and lack basic numerical and reading skills. As a result; there is high unemployment rate among the youth, since many do not have sufficient knowledge and skill to apply for decent jobs. The resultant inequality deters development amongst the youth. Over the years in all OECD and partner countries, there has being an increase in the levels of educational attainment. It was reported that 80% of young adults had education up to secondary level in 2000 in about 20 out of 35 OECD members. In 2016 the OECD countries on the average had 84% of the people aged between 25 – 54 years who had at least attained upper secondary education. This number had increased from the 75% reported in 2000. There was also a steady increase in the number of adults (aged 25 – 34) with secondary, post-secondary and tertiary education during the period 1970 to 2016.

There is a probability that young adults who have completed higher levels of education were more likely to attain economic success than those with lower levels of education. The Ministry of education and research (2016), Mailis Reps, further put an emphasis on the point that many young people limit themselves by completing only basic education or failing to acquire professional qualification and therefore, support services and early interventions should be prioritised. Generally, the youth are the most vulnerable group in the population as they are victims of many socio-economic factors such as unemployment, crime, poverty, and many more. Education together with other factors contributes to better health. Income is one of the primary factors that act together with education to have a significant influence on health (Feinstein et al., 2006).

Krueger et al. (2015) also makes reference to a study conducted at three universities, namely, Colorado, New York, and North Carolina at Chapel Hill (2015) which illustrated that certain causes of death are associated with particular levels of education, and that the variations across education level have widened greatly over the study period – 2010. Natural experiments have shown a strong association – which is substantially causal - between education level and mortality. India, on the other hand, which is also a densely populated country and had the largest population of youth globally, estimated 356 million (10 – 24 years) deaths in 2014. Leading causes thereof among the youth in India are self-harm (suicide) which saw 59,366 deaths recorded, followed by road injuries that claimed 37,137 youth and lastly, Tuberculosis claimed 28,676 lives of youth in 2013 to become the third leading causes of death among youth generation (Sawe, 2017). Similar to India, the number of suicides for both boys and girls in Canada has been relatively consistent in the last 10 years and suicide remains the 2nd leading cause of death for young people in Canada. (Centre for suicide prevention, 2015).

According to Mwaniki (2017) HIV/AIDS, malaria and respiratory infections were the main causes of death in Africa. Annually over a million deaths caused by these diseases are reported. In Africa men have the average life expectancy of 58 years while women have 61 years. When compared to other continent it is notable that Africa has the lowest life expectancy. Approximately 1.1 million people were estimated to have died from HIV/AIDS in 2012. Children under the age of five in Africa suffered mostly from lower respiratory tract infections such as pneumonia, influenza and bronchitis. These infectious diseases contributed to at least a million deaths in 2012. Diarrhoea accounted for 6.7% (603.000 people) of total deaths in 2012. Lastly, malaria accounted for an estimated 554.000 deaths in Africa in 2012 (Mwaniki, 2017).

De Wet and Odimegwu (2017) in their study showed that females were more likely to die from natural causes compared to male counterparts. In addition to this, deaths due to natural causes decreased for males during the period 2001 and 2007 as 26 natural causes of deaths to adolescent males (aged 10 – 19) per 10,000 adolescent male population occurred in 2001. This figure decreased to 25 natural causes to males per 10,000 male population in 2007. On the other hand, the cause specific mortality rate showed that 18 adolescent males per 10,000 adolescent males died from unnatural causes in 2001; and in 2007 there was an increase in the number of male deaths, where it was recorded that there were 26 male deaths per 10,000 adolescent males who died.

Analysis of youth death rates as outlined in the Statistics South Africa (2015), show that for all the deaths that occurred in 2013, the youth accounted for 16.4% of the overall mortality rate. In 1997 youth mortality accounted for 18% of the overall deaths in the country, which was deemed high at the time.

In 2004, this figure further increased to 24%, gradually decreasing over the years to the lowest rates observed in 2013 (16.4%). In South Africa the most common cause of death is the natural causes which accounted for 71.9% of the total deaths that occurred in 2013 for the youth, while non-natural causes only contributed approximately 29% of the total death. The report confirms the findings of De Wet and Odimegwu (2017) that showed that young males were at most at the risk of dying from the non-natural causes when compared to females. Females on the other hand were most likely to die from natural causes.

Excellent health was associated with young adults in possession of a bachelor's or higher degree (Aud *et al.,* 2011). The young adults with lower levels of education were linked to poor health. According to Aud *et al.,* (2011) 65% of the young adults did not complete high school, while those who did complete were reported to be at 72% and 82% were reported to have some college education and/or an associate's degree. Hanushek and Wößmann (2007) further argued that the notion that skills and human capital can only be acquired through formal schooling is short sighted as other factors like family, peers and other individuals are more influential to an individual's knowledge level and ability to think rationally.

Hummer and Hernandez (2013) state that "higher educated adults in the United States have lower yearly mortality rate than less-educated people in every age, gender and racial/ethnic subgroup of the population". Education has a potential to create opportunities for better health. The relationship between the education and health of the people in general and the youth in particular has existed for generations, whether tests were conducted or not, in a sense that it was noted that people with no education were most likely to have poor health which ultimately resulted in untimely death. An assumption is that people who are exposed to poverty and high unemployment are unable to get better health cure for many of their ailments. It is therefore believed that eventually there will be an increase in a number of these diseases amongst the least educated. People who have acquired more education tend to have better health, perhaps due to exposure to information that enables them to make informed decisions about their health and life in general and also having the means to look after their health should the need arise (Feinstein et al., 2006).

From theory it behoves one to state that people with lower education levels are the most likely affected by diseases, resulting to their ultimate death; vice versa it seems like the most educated peoples are most likely to die from accidents, murder and the like. In a study conducted by Mwamwenda et al. (2014), results indicated that university students were more knowledgeable on HIV/AIDS as compared to secondary students. According to the SAMRC Burden of disease research unit the causes of death statistics are an essential data source for understanding, monitoring and making policy decisions that are aimed at improving the health of the nation. In relation to education, the study conducted by Garriga et al., (2015) showed that there was proportionately a higher intravenous drug usage amongst a group of patients with lower levels of education, 26%, compared to those with higher levels of education, 1,5%. Additionally, the study further suggests that patients with lower levels of education had a lower CD4 count compared to those with higher levels of education. This further, emphasises that the probability of people with lower levels of education being exposed to some of these diseases were higher.

The Steinhardt School of Culture, Education and Human Development, 2015, found that in the United States, more than 10% of the adults did not have high school degree, more than a quarter, had some college and no bachelor's degree. The study submits that generally, higher education is associated with longevity because of factors such as higher income and social status, healthier behaviours and improved social and psychological well-being of individuals. In support of this finding, Feinstein et al. (2006) suggests that education is directly correlated with income levels which in turn are directly correlated with health status in that better education is likely to lead to improvement in the income levels of individuals which in turn have a positive influence on the health status of that individual.

Generally, life expectancy is increasing for the human population, and people with higher levels of education are realising most of the benefits. Narrowed to a daily basis, being educated implies getting better jobs and access to better health due to the benefits provided by the employer whereas these basics are non-existent for the uneducated who land even more hazardous jobs with no benefits and get exposed to sickness as they are not able to take care of their medical conditions/needs. All need to take care of health equally because poor health can conversely put even hard earned educational attainment at risk. One of the proposed goals by UNESCO in 2014 was to "ensure healthy lives and promote well-being for all at all ages". It further states that educated people are better informed about scientific diseases, so they can take measures to prevent them or act on the early signs. Education plays a major role in ensuring the diseases are contained and not exacerbated.

The Center on Society and Health (2014), reported that in the United States 27% of adults without higher education were unable to consult a medical practitioner as they could not afford the cost of the consultation and medication. The figure for high school graduates was less than 18% while amongst college graduates this figure stood at only 8%. Equally, people need to take care of their health because poor health can put education attainment at risk in more ways than one. Recent studies showed that causes of death differed by educational attainment. Hummer and Hernandez, 2013, argue that mortality rates linked to causes that have less human control have less variability by educational attainment while those that are linked to social and behavioural factors are spread wide amongst the different levels of education. While it has been proven that lower education levels are associated with poor health and therefore higher mortality rates, a report by the New York University, 2015, submits that there are health conditions that are positively correlated with higher education levels. Educated people were more at risk of suffering from cardiovascular diseases.

Although the NDP is aimed at ensuring that all people receive education and access to medical facilities, this does not appear to have any impact on youth mortality in South Africa, since cases of young people dying from stress related illness, TB, HIV, etc. are still reported on a daily basis. South Africa is however making significant progress in its medical efforts to reduce HIV infections, but a lack of education and social changes has left adolescents vulnerable to infections, with teenage girls terribly particularly at risk.

Therefore, this study investigates whether a relationship exists between the causes of death and education level; and some other sociodemographic factors based on data analysis for South African youth in 2014. The two Sustainable Development Goals (SDG) related to this study are; "(1) to ensure healthy lives and promote well-being for all" (United Nations Economic Commission for Africa, 2015:9); and (2) "ensure inclusive and equitable quality education and promote lifelong learning opportunities for all" (United Nations Economic Commission for Africa, 2015:9). The study will contribute by determining if there is a relationship between causes of death and education level of the youth. Perhaps if they had acquired more education they could have lived longer and not died.

RESEARCH METHODOLOGY

Data Source

The study utilises secondary data set sourced from Statistics South Africa (Stats SA). Stats SA sourced this data from the administrative records at the Department of Home Affairs (DHA). The focus of this study is on the youth of South Africa and therefore the data used is for persons between the ages of 15 and 34 who died in 2014.

Statistical Analysis

The data are analysed at two levels, namely; univariate and bivariate. At the univariate level, distribution of the socio-demographic characteristics of the respondents is shown using descriptive statistics such as charts and percentages. At the bivariate level, statistical test such as chi-square test and logistics regression were performed to test whether a relationship exists between the dependent variable (causes of death) and independent variables (education level, age, gender and death province) using p-value < 0.05 as the criterion for significance.

Chi-Square Test of Independence

According to Blalock (1979), when testing the independence of a contingency table, the null hypothesis is such that the two attributes or characteristics of the elements of a given population are not related (i.e. they are independent) against the alternative hypothesis that the two characteristics are related (i.e. they are dependent). The degree of freedom (df) for a test of independence are:

$$df = (R-1)(C-1) \tag{1}$$

where R and C are number of rows and columns (Mann, 2001). Everitt (1977) suggests that the following formula be used for the χ^2 statistic:

$$\chi^2 = \sum \frac{(f_0 - f_e)^2}{f_e} \tag{2}$$

where f_0 is observed frequencies and f_e is expected frequencies. According to Jackson (2005) the assumptions underlying the χ^2 test of independence are the same as for the χ^2 goodness-of-fit test; the sample must be random, the observations must be independent and the data are nominal.

The hypothesis for χ^2:

H_0: there is no relationship between socio-demographic variables and causes of death
H_1: there is a relationship between socio-demographic variables and causes of death

Logistic Regression

Dowdy et al. (2004) explains that one or more independent variables can also be used to predict a dependent variable that is nominal rather than numerical. According to Agresti (2009) the relationships between π (x) and x are usually nonlinear rather than linear. A constant change in the value of x may not necessarily have a high impact on π when it is near 0 or 1 than when π is near the middle of its range. The corresponding logistic regression model formula is:

$$\log \frac{\pi(x)}{1-\pi(x)} = \alpha + \beta_x \tag{3}$$

The random component for the (success, failure) outcomes has a binomial distribution. The link function is the logit function $\log \left[\dfrac{\pi}{1-\pi}\right]$ of π, symbolized by "logit" (π). The parameter β above determines the rate of increase or decrease of the curve.

Freund (2004) state that likelihood ratio tests are based on the generalisation of the Neyman-Pearson Lemma, which provide a means for constructing most powerful critical regions for testing a simple null hypothesis against a simple alternative hypothesis,

$$H_0 : \theta \in \omega$$

$$H_1 : \theta \in \omega'$$

where ω is a subset of Ω and ω' is the complement of ω with respect to Ω. Thus, the parameter space for θ is partitioned into the disjoint sets ω and ω'; according to the null hypothesis, θ is an element of the first set, and according to the alternative hypothesis, it is an element of the second set. In most problems Ω is either the set of all real numbers, the set of all positive real numbers, some interval of real numbers, or a discrete set of real numbers.

Lee and Peters (2016) suggest that instead of predicting specific values of y from the predictors; predict the probability that y will occur given known values of the predictor variables. From the many number of way of arranging the logistic regression equation, the following equation is recommended:

$$P(y) = \frac{1}{1 + e^{-(b_0 + b_1 x_1 + b_2 x_2 + \ldots + b_i x_i)}} \tag{4}$$

The term e refers to the natural logarithm.

Lee and Peters (2016) further states that in essence, logistic regression predicts the probability that some dichotomous outcome will occur for a given case, based on observations of whether or not that outcome did actually occur. So, for any case, the actual value of the outcome y must equal either 0 (did not occur) or 1 (did occur), and the predicted value of y, denoted as either $P(y)$ or $\hat{y}$, will lie somewhere between 0 (no chance of the outcome occurring) and 1 (outcome will certainly occur). As such, it would be a useful indicator of how well the model works if these observed and predicted values were compare. The log-likelihood is the measure used in logistic regression, and the formula for this is shown below:

$$log-likelihood = \sum_{i=1}^{N} \left\{ y_i ln(P(y_i)) + (1-y_i) ln[1-P(y_i)] \right\} \tag{5}$$

Larger log-likelihood values indicate worse-fitting models. The best way to use a log-likelihood is to compare the value for the model with some baseline model.

Lee and Peters (2016) states that the most important thing to look at is the 'Exp (B)' value for each predictor. This value indicates the change in offs (i.e. probability) resulting from a unit change in each predictor variable. It is far more useful than the b coefficient in interpreting a logistic regression. The odds of an event happening are formally defined as the probability of an event happening, divided by the probability of that event is not happening or in equation form:

$$odds = \frac{P(event)}{P(no\ event)} \tag{6}$$

In order to calculate the change in odds, first calculate the odds of the event happening given a unknown set of values for the predictors, using the above equation. Then calculate the odds of the events happening given a single unit change in the value of the predictors, and then use the values obtained to calculate the percentage change in the odds as follows:

$$\Delta odds = \frac{odds\ after\ a\ unit\ change\ in\ the\ predictor}{original\ odds} \tag{7}$$

Rice (2007) further states that if an event B has probability P(B) of occurring, the odds of B occurring are defined as:

$$odds(A) = \frac{P(A)}{1 - P(A)} \tag{8}$$

And can be translated into the following:

$$P(A) = \frac{odds(A)}{1 - odds(A)} \tag{9}$$

RESULTS

Univariate Analysis

Here, data is presented graphical to show the distribution of the causes of death in relation to the sociodemographic characteristics discussed. Figure 1 illustrates the age in completed years of the youth at the time of their death. The table shows a high percentage of 38.99% and 31.16% of the youth aged between 30-34 and 25-29, respectively while the lowest percentage of the death is among youth aged 15-19 years (10.04%). Youth with secondary education recorded the highest number of deaths in 2014 (71.35%) as shown in Figure 2 while the least death was recorded among youth with higher education (4.40%).

Figure 1. Distribution of death among youth by age

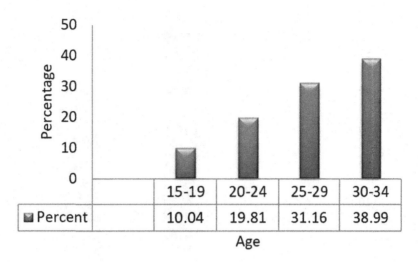

Figure 2. Distribution of death among youth by level of education

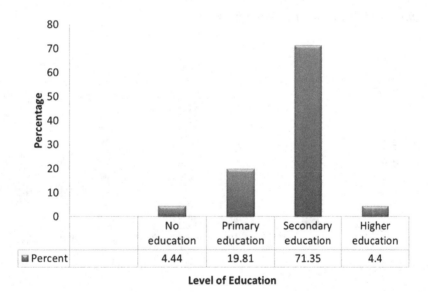

More than half (56.72%) of the registered youth death happened among males while 43.28% of the death occurred among their female counterparts (see Figure 3). In Figure 4, KwaZulu-Natal, Gauteng and Eastern Cape registered the highest deaths among the youth as 23.49%, 17.48% and 15.89%, respectively in 2014. Provinces such as Western Cape and Northern Cape registered the lowest. In Mpumalanga and Limpopo almost the same percentage of deaths were registered. Free State and North West registered 9.12% and 5.87%, respectively. Overall, Figure 5 reveals that about two-third (65.97%) of the youth died from natural causes of death while only one-in-three (34.03%) died from non-natural death.

Figure 3. Distribution of death among youth by gender

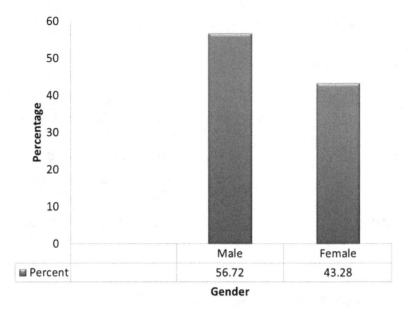

Figure 4. Distribution of death among youth by province

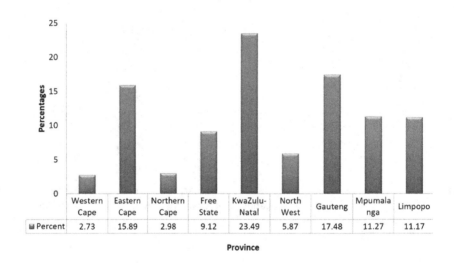

Bivariate Analyses

The chi-square analysis shows that all the sociodemographic variables are significantly related to the causes of death among the youth as shown in table 1. A further covariate analysis shows that there is a very weak positive relationship between education level and causes of death of the youth (Cramer's V coefficient = 0.089). However, a weak positive association is shown by the Cramer's V coefficient (0.212) between the age and causes of death. The Cramer's V coefficient (0.125) also indicates a weak positive relationship between province and cause of death.

Figure 5. Distribution of causes of death among youth

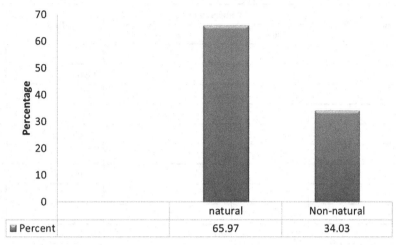

The binary logistic regression is then used in table 2 shows the significance of each level of the sociodemographic variables in relation to causes of death. The odd ratios for age shows that the odds of the youth dying from causes of death increases by 2.96, 3.02 and 1.71 for age groups 15-19, 20-24 and 25-29, respectively as compare to those in their 30s. The odds indicate that dying from the causes of death significantly reduces as the youth increase in age. The odd ratio, 6.48, shows that the odds of dying from the causes of death are more than six times higher for males than for females. It is thus evident that there is a strong significant relationship between males and causes of death than with females.

The odd ratios of causes of death reduce significantly with increase in the level of education among the youth. The results show that the odds of dying from the causes of death are 2.96, 1.85 and 1.40 times higher for the youth with no education, primary education and secondary education than the youth with higher education. It is evident that youth with higher education have better chances of not dying from the causes of death than the others. This indicates that there is evidence that people with no education are most likely to die from these causes of death. Furthermore, the odd ratios show that youth in Western Cape and Gauteng provinces are more than two times (2.08 and 2.03, respectively) likely to die from these causes of death than youth in Limpopo province. Youth in Eastern Cape, Northern Cape, Free State, KwaZulu-Natal and North-West provinces have higher odds of dying than those in Limpopo while youth in Mpumalanga are less likely to die from these causes of death.

DISCUSSION

The study utilised univariate and bivariate techniques to investigate the relationship between some sociodemographic characteristics and causes of death. The results entail graphical presentation of the data and Chi-Square test which was used to determine whether or not there is a relationship between causes of death and these sociodemographic characteristics. Also included in the analysis of the study is the logistic regression which was used to describe and determine the degree of the relationship between the

Table 1. Relationship between sociodemographic characteristics and causes of death

sociodemographic variables	Causes of death		Total	p-value
	Natural	Non-natural		
Age				< 0.001
15 – 19	52.6	47.4	4496	
20 – 24	52.1	47.9	8875	
25 – 29	65.7	34.3	13957	
30 – 34	76.6	23.4	17466	
Gender				< 0.001
Male	50.2	49.8	25407	
Female	86.7	13.3	19387	
Level of education				< 0.001
No education	79.3	20.7	1988	
Primary education	70.5	29.5	8872	
Secondary education	64.5	35.5	31961	
Higher education	56.5	43.5	1973	
Province				< 0.001
Western Cape	54.7	45.3	1224	
Eastern Cape	68.6	31.4	7118	
Northern Cape	59.7	40.3	1334	
Free State	67.9	32.1	4084	
KwaZulu-Natal	66.8	33.2	10522	
North-West	71.1	28.9	2630	
Gauteng	55.3	44.7	7828	
Mpumalanga	71.7	28.3	5050	
Limpopo	71.5	28.5	5004	
Total	66.0	34.0	44794	

dependent variable and independent variables. The data used is based on the deaths that were registered at the DHA in 2014.

The graphical presentation revealed that the deaths among the youth were high for the age category 30-34 compared with other age categories. More male youth died in 2014 compared to their female counterparts' agreement with earlier work of De Wet and Odimegwu (2017). The educational level of the youth that died in 2014 revealed a high percentage of 71.35% for those youth that completed secondary education which was higher than other educational levels. Stats SA (2015) reported that over 80% of deaths in South Africa were due to natural causes for the past 19-year period while in 2010 there was a decline. However, this study revealed that 65.97% of deaths that occurred among the youth in South Africa are due to natural causes, thereby showing increase in non-natural causes of death among the youth. The provinces that recorded most deaths were KwaZulu-Natal, Eastern Cape and Gauteng.

Table 2. Bivariate logistic analysis showing odd ratios predicting causes of death among youth

sociodemographic variables	Causes of death	
	Odd Ratio	**CI**
Age		
15 – 19	2.96**	2.76 - 3.17
20 – 24	3.02***	2.86 - 3.19
25 – 29	1.71**	1.63 - 1.80
30 – 34	1.00	
Gender		
Male	6.48**	6.17 - 6.80
Female	1.00	
Level of education		
No education	2.96***	2.57 - 3.40
Primary education	1.85***	1.67 - 2.04
Secondary education	1.40***	1.28 - 1.53
Higher education	1.00	
Province		
Western Cape	2.08***	1.83 - 2.37
Eastern Cape	1.15**	1.06 - 1.25
Northern Cape	1.70***	1.50 - 1.92
Free State	1.18**	1.08 - 1.30
KwaZulu-Natal	1.25***	1.16 - 1.34
North-West	1.02	0.92 - 1.13
Gauteng	2.03***	1.88 - 2.19
Mpumalanga	0.99	0.91 - 1.08
Limpopo	1.00	

* Significant at 0.05 level, ** Significant at 0.01 level, *** Significant at 0.001 level and 1.00 is reference category

The results also disclosed that there is a statistically significant relationship between causes of death and education in agreement with Albano et al. (2007) study which emphasised that educational attainment is strongly and inversely related to death from all cancers combined, for all black and white men, as well as white women. Previous study by Cutler (2007) reiterate importance of education in reducing death through his work which revealed that educated people have lower death rates from the most common acute and chronic diseases because they are able to afford better health care services.

The results indicate that education does have an impact/effect on the causes of death, as well as the age, gender and province of death of the youth. Hence, logistics regression was adopted to describe the relationship between the socio-demographic variables and causes of death. The results indicated a significant relationship between education and causes of death; same applies for other variables. For education, the odds of dying from causes of death were about three times higher for the youth with no education when compared to those with higher education in agreement earlier studies (Feinstein et al., 2006; Hummer and Hernandez 2013; Mwamwenda et al., 2014). The results for gender indicated that young males had higher odds of dying compared to young females (i.e. males are more than six times likely to die from these causes of death than their female counterparts). The results also showed that younger youth are more likely to die compared to older youth. Western Cape and Gauteng provinces have higher odds of the youth dying compared to other provinces.

CONCLUSION AND RECOMMENDATIONS

The present study has used a nationally representative sample to support many studies that have found that the sociodemographic factors associated with causes of death among South African youth with particular interest in level of education. In conclusion, the study has established the fact that there is a statistically significant relationship between level of education and causes of death among the youth as well as other sociodemographic factors through application of different bivariate techniques. The results of this study could be used to improve national prevention campaigns to reduce death among young South Africans, especially adolescents.

LIMITATION OF THE STUDY

The study examined the relationship between causes of death and education. Other sociodemographic factors such as: age, gender and province of residence were also considered based on available dataset while variables (alcohol usage, drugs abuse, unprotected sex and suicide) are not available in the dataset. The authors also wanted to include the variable for race to study the racial differences but couldn't because Statistics South Africa consider it as a very sensitive variable therefore does not permit researchers to use it for this study. Hence, the influence of these unavailable variables could not be studied, thereby limiting the scope of the study.

This research received no specific grant from any funding agency in the public, commercial, or not-for-profit sectors.

REFERENCES

Agresti, A. (2007). An introduction to categorical data analysis. A John Wiley & Sons, Inc., Publication. doi:10.1002/0470114754

Albano, J. D., Ward, E., Jemal, A., Anderson, R., Cokkinides, V. E., Myrray, T., Henley, J., Liff, J., & Thun, M. J. (2007). Cancer mortality in the United States by education level and race. *Journal of the National Cancer Institute*, *99*(18), 1384–1394. doi:10.1093/jnci/djm127 PMID:17848670

Aud, S., KewalRamani, A., & Frohlich, L. (2011). America's Youth: Transitions to Adulthood (NCES 2012-026). U.S. Department of Education, National Center for Education Statistics. Washington, DC: U.S. Government Printing Office.

Blalock, H. M. Jr. (1979). *Social statistics* (2nd ed.).

Borode, M. (2011). Higher education and poverty reduction among youth in the Sub-Saharan Africa. *European Journal of Educational Studies*, *3*(1), 149–155.

Centre for Suicide Prevention. (2015). *Updated and Expanded: Teen Suicide Resource toolkit.* https://www.suicideinfo.ca/wp-content/uploads/2016/08/Teen-Resource-Toolkit-Web.pdf

Cutler, D. M., & Lleras-Muney, A. (2007). Education and health: evaluating theories and evidence. In J. S. House, R. F. Schoeni, G. A. Kaplan, & H. Pollack (Eds.), *The Health Effects of Social and Economic Policy.* Russell Sage Foundation.

De Wet, N., & Odimegwu, C. (2017). Contextual determinants of adolescent mortality in South Africa. *African Health Sciences*, *17*(1), 62–69. doi:10.4314/ahs.v17i1.9 PMID:29026378

Dowdy, S., Wearden, S., & Chilko, D. (2004). Statistics for research (3rd ed.). New York: John Wiley. doi:10.1002/0471477435

Everitt, B. S. (1977). *The Analysis of Contingency Tables.* Halstead Press. doi:10.1007/978-1-4899-2927-3

Feinstein, L., Sabates, R., Anderson, T. M., Sorhaindo, A., & Hammond, C. (2006). *What are effects of education on health? Measuring the Effects of Education on Health and Civic Engagement: Proceedings of the Copenhagen Symposium.* OECD.

Freund, J. E. (2004). Mathematical statistics with applications (7th ed.). Irwin Miller.

Garriga, C., García de, O. P., Miró, J. M., Ocaña, I., Knobel, H., Barberá, M. J., Humet, V., Domingo, P., Gatell, J. M., Ribera, E., Gurguí, M., Marco, A., & Caylà, J. A. (2015). Mortality, causes of death and associated factors related to a large HIV population-based cohort. *PLoS One*, *10*(12). doi:10.1371/journal.pone.0145701

Hanushek, E. A., & Wößmann, L. (2007). *Education quality and economic growth.* World Bank. doi:10.1596/1813-9450-4122

Hummer, R. A., & Hernandez, E. M. (2013). The effect of educational attainment on adult mortality in the United States. *Population Bulletin*, *68*(1), 1–16. PMID:25995521

Jackson, S. L. (2005). *Statistics plain and simple.* Wadsworth Publishing.

Krueger, P. M., Tran, M. K., Hummer, R. A., & Chang, V. W. (2015). Mortality attributable to low levels of education in the United States. *PLoS One*, *10*(7. doi:10.1371/journal.pone.0131809

Lee, N., & Peters, M. (2016). *Business statistics using Excel and SPSS.* SAGE Publications.

Mann, P. S. (2001). Introductory statistics (4th ed.). New York Wiley.

Mwamwenda, T. S. (2014). Education level and HIV/AIDS knowledge in Kenya. *Journal of AIDS and HIV Research*, *6*(2), 28–32.

Mwaniki, A. (2017). *Leading Causes of Death in Africa.* WorldAtlas. worldatlas.com/articles/the-leading-causes-of-death-in-the-african-continent.html

Organisation for Economic Co-operation and Development (OECD). (2017). *Education at a glance 2017: OECD indicators.* OECD Publishing.

Rice, J. A. (2007). Mathematical statistics and Data analysis (3rd ed.). Thomson Brooks/Cole.

Sawe, B. E. (2017). *Leading causes of death among youth in India.* WorldAtlas. worldatlas.com/articles/leading-causes-of-death-among-the-youth-of-india.html

Statistics South Africa. (2015). *Morbidity and mortality patterns among the youth of South Africa, 2013 / Statistics South Africa.* Pretoria: Statistics South Africa. Report No. 03-09-12.

Statistics South Africa, Statistical release P0211.4.2. (2015). *National and provincial labour market: youth Q1: 2008 – Q1: 2015.* Author.

Statistics South Africa, Statistical release P0309.3. (2015). *Mortality and causes of death in South Africa, 2014: Findings from death notification.* Author.

The Center on Society and Health. (2014). *Why education matters to health: Exploring the causes.* https://societyhealth.vcu.edu/work/the-projects/why-education-matters-to-health-exploring-the-causes.html

United Nation Economic Commission for Africa. (2015). Sustainable development goals for the Southern Africa subregion. Summary report. United Nations Economic Commission for Africa.

United Nations. (2016). *Fact Sheet: Youth and education.* https://social.un.org/youthyear/docs/Youth_Education_Fact_Sheet_FINAL.pdf

KEY TERMS AND DEFINITIONS

Adolescence: A period following the commencement of puberty during which a young person develops from childhood into adulthood.

Death: Permanent cessation of functioning of the organism as a whole or action of being killed i.e. end of the life of a person or organism.

Gender: A range of identities for either of the sexes especially when considered with reference to social and cultural differences rather than biological.

Level of Education: International Standard Classification for Education which represents a board section of education ladder (i.e., progression from elementary to more advanced level of learning).

Logistic Regression Model: A statistical method for analyzing dataset with categorical outcome variable.

Mortality: Number of deaths by place, time, and underlying cause.

Youth: Young persons between age 15 and 34 years.

Chapter 23
Information Technology Act 2000 and the Potential Use of Data Analytics in Reducing Cybercrime in India

Anjali Dixit

Faculty of Juridical Sciences, Rama University, Kanpur, India

ABSTRACT

Cybercrime is increasing rapidly in this digitized world. Be it business, education, shopping, or banking transactions, everything is on cyberspace. Cybercrime covers a wide range of different attacks such as financial cybercrime, spreading computer viruses or malware, internet fraud, pornography cybercrime, intellectual property rights violation, etc. Due to increased cyber-attacks these days, the online users must be aware of these kinds of attacks and need to be cautious with their data online. Each country has their own laws for dealing with cybercrime. The different measures taken by the government of India to combat cybercrime are explained in this chapter. How the potential use of data analytics can help in reducing cybercrime in India is also explained.

INTRODUCTION

The term "Cybercrime" needs no introduction in the present E-world. In this world, where everything is available at a click, infringements are in like manner taking place with just a click. Cybercrime in this way is considered as darker side of innovation and due to this World Wide Web (www) has now turned out to be World Wide Worry due to the digital violations. Web, however offers incredible advantage to society, likewise it also opens doors for cybercrimes utilizing new and exceptionally modern innovative devices.

Digital wrongdoing is rising as a genuine risk. The government, police departments and other cyber units do try to prevent cybercrime. Activities to check across digital dangers are coming to fruition. Indian police has started extraordinary digital cells across the nation to stop cybercrime.

DOI: 10.4018/978-1-7998-3053-5.ch023

The term Cyber "wrongdoing" is a misnomer. This term is not described in any standard/act passed or set up by the Indian Parliament. To battle cybercrime India got equipped with The Information Technology Act 2000. This demonstration got radically revised in year 2008. The Amended Information Technology Act isn't just viable than the previous act, in fact it is even more dominant and stringent than the previous one.

Data analytics can help in reducing cybercrime in India. Data analytics consists of a lot of techniques using which useful information can be extracted from different sets of data. There are different types of data analytics. They are as follows:

1. Descriptive Analytics
2. Diagnostic Analytics
3. Predictive Analytics
4. Prescriptive Analytics

1. Descriptive Analytics: The purpose of descriptive analytics is to show the layers of available information and present it in a digestible/coherent form. It used to understand the big picture of the any institutions process from multiple standpoints.
2. Diagnostic Analytics: It is an investigation aimed at studying the effects and developing the right kind of reaction to the situation.
3. Predictive Analytics: It helps to understand how to make a successful business decisions that bring value to companies.
4. Prescriptive Analytics: It is what to do in the future.

Data analytics can significantly reduce cybercrime in India. To find out how data analytics can reduce cybercrime in India, first what is cybercrime and all its related aspects needs to be understood.

DEFINITION OF CYBERCRIME

"Cybercrime" is not defined in any Indian legislation. Information Technology Act, 2000, is the only legislation which deals with the cybercrimes in India. Information Technology Act, 2000 was amended in the form of Information Technology (Amendment) Act, 2008 like mentioned earlier. However, in these both legislation there is no proper definition for "cybercrime".

Cybercrime is something that includes a lot of malicious activities such as illegally intercepting someone's data, copyright infringements, etc. In various dictionaries, the term cybercrime is defined as a "bad behavior which includes for example, intimidation, burglary, etc. executed utilizing a PC particularly to wrongfully find the opportunity to transmit or control information".

Thus it can be rightly said that the term cybercrime includes various other aspects also like the use of computer and other computing devices, computer network, etc. based on which the cybercrimes can be divided into three categories that are as follows:

1. Crimes in which the computing device is the main target. For example, to gain network access.
2. Crimes in which the computer is used as a weapon. For example, denial of service.

3. Crimes in which the computer is used as an accessory to crime. For example, storing illegally obtained data.

HOW CYBERCRIME WORKS?

There is a growth in digital platforms due to technologies like Artificial Intelligence, data analytics, machine learning, cloud computing and internet of things. All these technologies are helping various digital platforms to sustain and function smoothly. However, the growth of digital platforms has increased the digital data generation.

With a lot of digital data out there, cyber criminals gets various opportunities to attack different cyber networks. Cyber criminals typically create malware by using the internet and computer technology to hack user's personal computers, smart phone data, personal details from social media, business secrets, national secrets etc., Except for creating malware, cyber criminals interfere in cyber world illegally through various more ways.

In cybercrime, cyber criminals use different mechanized awful practices either individually or with the help of the other small or big groups. Offenses like hacking, information burglary, unlawful intruding, etc. could be charged under Section.66 r/w Section.43 of the Information Technology Act. Events of gathering a credit or check card could be charged under Indian Penal Court (IPC).

Information Technology Act was amended in 2008 to secure cyber world and protect data from various cyber offenders. The provisions of the Prevention of Children from Sexual Offences Act, 2012 (POCSO) may also be invoked against the Child pornography crime.

INTENTION BEHIND CYBERCRIME

Cybercrimes are often performed by various intentions like causing someone trouble or achieving wrongful gain, etc. According to authors Aseef, N. et al. (2015), overall hacking comes in different forms and shapes. The intentions of hackers who are performing cybercrime can vary on case to case basis but most of the times the intention behind a cybercrime is either of the one just mentioned above i.e., cybercrime done with the intention of harassing someone or cybercrime done with the intention of achieving personal wrongful gain. For this purpose, cybercriminals many times steal access codes, retina images, etc. to get past security systems and biometric systems.

DIFFERENT KINDS OF CYBERCRIME

Worldwide there are various kinds of cybercrimes. Examples of a few cybercrimes are as follows:

*   Financial cybercrime: Credit card frauds, money laundering, hacking into bank servers, accounting scams etc. all these comes under the financial cybercrimes.
*   Pornography cybercrime: Creating pornographic websites, pornographic online magazines, etc. comes under the pornography cybercrimes.

Besides these two types of cybercrime, there are more various types of cybercrime present for which there is decided punishment in the law. For example, cybercrimes under section 66 (b) of the Information Technology Act 2000, can result up to term of 3 years imprisonment and fine up to rupees two lakhs rupees, or both. Software piracy, copyright infringement, trademarks violations, theft of computer source code etc. comes under the Intellectual Property Crimes. When defamation takes place with the help of computers and/or the internet, it is called cyber defamation which is unlawful.

Repeated acts of harassment and constantly unlawfully monitoring someone or someone's data online and threatening them using internet services comes under the offence of cyber stalking. Apart from this, there is website hacking which is another example of cybercrime.

Sending a large number of emails to the victim resulting in the victim's email account (in case of an individual) or mail servers (in case of a company or an email service provider) crashing comes under the offence of the email bombing.

Cybercrime is also performed by creating computer virus. The computer virus are designed to spread from one computer to another and to interfere with computer operation and harm the computer system. A computer virus might corrupt or delete data on the victim's computer, use the victim' s e-mail program to spread itself to other computers, or even erase everything on the victim's hard disk.

LAWS FOR CYBERCRIME WITHIN THE INFORMATION TECHNOLOGY ACT OF INDIA

Laws for cybercrimes that are mentioned within Information Technology Act are as follows:

1. Tampering with Computer Source Code offence is bailable, cognizable and triable by Court of Judicial Magistrate of First Class (JMFC) and punishable with imprisonment of up to 3 years or fine up to Rs. 2 lakhs.
2. Computer Related Offences are bailable, cognizable offences and punishable with imprisonment up to 3 years or fine up to Rs. 5 lakhs.
3. Sending offensive messages through communication service, etc. offence is bailable, cognizable and triable by Court of JMFC and punishable with imprisonment up to 3 years and fine.
4. Dishonestly receiving stolen computer resource or communication device offence is bailable, cognizable and triable by Court of JMFC and punishable with the imprisonment up to 3 years and/or fine up to Rs. 1 lakh.
5. Identity Theft offence is bailable, cognizable and triable by Court of JMFC and punishable with Imprisonment of either description up to 3 years and/or fine up to Rs. 1 lakh.
6. Cheating by Personation by using computer resource offence is bailable, cognizable and triable by Court of JMFC and punishable with the imprisonment of either description up to 3 years and /or fine up to Rs. 1 lakh.
7. Violation of Privacy offence is bailable, cognizable and triable by Court of JMFC and punishable with the imprisonment up to 3 years and /or fine up to Rs. 2 lakh
8. Cyber Terrorism offence is non-bailable, cognizable and triable by Court of Sessions and punishable with the imprisonment extend to imprisonment for Life.
9. Publishing or transmitting obscene material in electronic form offence is bailable, cognizable and triable by Court of JMFC and punishable on first conviction, imprisonment up to 3 years and/or

fine up to Rs. 5 lakh and on subsequent conviction imprisonment up to 5 years and/or fine up to Rs. 10 lakh.

10. Publishing or transmission of material containing sexually explicit act, etc. in electronic form offence is non-bailable, cognizable and triable by Court of JMFC and punishable on first conviction imprisonment up to 5 years and/or fine up to Rs. 10 lakh and on subsequent conviction imprisonment up to 7 years and/or fine up to Rs. 10 lakh.

11. Publishing or transmitting of material depicting children in sexually explicit act etc., in electronic form offence is non bailable, cognizable and triable by Court of JMFC and punishable with imprisonment of either description up to 5 years and/or fine up to Rs. 10 lakh on first conviction and imprisonment of either description up to 7 years and/or fine up to Rs. 10 lakh on subsequent conviction.

12. Intermediary intentionally or knowingly contravening the directions about preservation and retention of information offence is bailable, cognizable and punishable with imprisonment up to 3 years and fine.

13. Failure to comply with the directions given by Controller offence is bailable, non-cognizable and punishable with the imprisonment up to 2 years and/or fine up to Rs. 1 lakh.

14. Failure of the intermediary to comply with the direction issued for blocking for public access of any information through any computer resource offence is non-bailable, cognizable and punishable with imprisonment up to 7 years and fine.

15. Indian Computer Emergency Response Team (ICERT) is formed to serve as national agency to deal with cybersecurity issues. Any service provider, intermediaries, data centers, etc., who fails to prove the information called for or comply with the direction issued by the ICERT and punishable with Imprisonment up to 1 year and/or fine up to Rs. 1 lakh.

16. Breach of Confidentiality and privacy offence is bailable, non-cognizable and punishable with imprisonment up to 2 years and/or fine up to Rs. 1 lakh.

17. Disclosure of information in breach of lawful contract offence is cognizable, bailable and punishable with imprisonment up to 3 years and/or fine up to Rs. 5 lakh.

18. Publishing false electronic signature certificate in certain particulars offence is bailable, non-cognizable and punishable as imprisonment up to 2 years and/or fine up to Rs. 1 lakh.

19. Publication for fraudulent purpose offence is bailable, non-cognizable and punishable with imprisonment up to 2 years and/or fine up to Rs. 1 lakh.

Apart from all this, Information Technology Act, 2000 has made and added rules for data protection to ensure that all the data including the important and sensitive data remains protected always.

The government of India through this Information Technology Act, 2000 is taking care of reducing cybercrimes in India. Along with it, if data analytics is included in data protection then cybercrime would greatly reduce in India.

Since what is cybercrime and all its related aspects and Information Technology Act 2000 and its laws for cybercrime in India is understood, the proceeding sections will explain how data analytics can help in reducing cybercrime in India.

DATA ANALYTICS

The current era is a computer era. Data analytics plays an important role in this computer era. It helps cyber world harness their data and use it to identify new opportunities.

Data analytics is used for finding out, understanding and communicating different meaningful patterns in data. Data analytics is a science of integrating heterogeneous data from diverse sources and analyzing it and obtaining predictions which can help in decision making.

HOW DATA ANALYTICS CAN HELP IN CYBER SECURITY

Data analytics can help in cyber security in different ways. Consider the following example to understand it.

Analyzing cybercrime pattern: Data analytics generally performs a check on the entire data available. If there are some patterns of cyber threats or some cyber bullying events that took place in the past, then data analytics can detect those patterns and thus help in preventing future cyber threats by exposing them. This is one example of how data analytics can help in preventing cybercrime and thus overall reduce it based on the past events happening.

Similarly there are more such ways in which data analytics can help in cyber security. To protect data and for cyber security there are also various tools, expert analytics techniques and information security teams that help prevent most of data breaches.

This is just one example explaining how data analytics can help in cyber security apart from this data analytics can help in analyzing loopholes and detecting any kind of irregularity in data network, etc.

It can be very difficult to keep data secure as there are always many data attackers as well as copious amounts of data to go through to get insight and in cyber world, the cyber attackers use various techniques to perform a cybercrime so thus altogether it makes it very difficult to maintain data security. For maintaining cyber security, government, non-government and private corporates are given the responsibility but the role of cyber data analyst is the most important in data security.

WHO IS CYBER DATA ANALYST?

Cyber data analyst is a specialized data analyst that performs data analysis in a cyber security context. A cyber data analyst analyzes data from multiple sources in order to produce conclusions that would be useful for improving privacy or security.

Finding loopholes in the data security, making the data security system strong, analyzing the data as well as reporting conclusions about the data, analysis of existing algorithms as well as designing and implementing of new algorithms for dataset, cyber data analyst is responsible for all this work and any other work related to data analysis and data security.

THE ROLE OF CYBER DATA ANALYST IN CYBER SECURITY

The main role of the cyber data analyst is to use data analysis techniques to improve data security and privacy. Cyber Data Analyst is competent in all stages of data collection and processing to secure cyber world. It is the duty of the cyber data analyst to understand what is required and possible in order to keep the data secure.

DATA SECURITY WITH BIG DATA ANALYTICS TOOLS

Data is a valuable asset. Thus privacy and security of data is mandatory. Cyber threats like attacks targeting endpoints can put the cyber security in danger. Data analytics and machine learning tools can help in preventing cyber security threats. These tools provide additional forensic details for quick mitigation of cyber-attacks. Predictive data analysis can be used with machine learning and big data analytics for cyber security. In monitoring and automation data analytics tools monitor and analyze user behavior to detect any unusual activity; while automation enables security teams to respond to threats as they occur.

According to the authors Angin, P., et al. (2019), the combination of data analytics, network traffic, system events, and logs can help organizations to discover anomalies and malicious activities. Big data analytics will be a must-have component of any effective cyber security solution due to the need of fast processing of the high-velocity, high-volume data from various sources to discover anomalies and/or attack patterns as fast as possible to limit the vulnerability of the systems and increase their resilience. Cyber security depends on actionable intelligence. Along with it, cyber security also depends on risk management. With intelligent risk management insights, big data analytics tools can improve cyber security.

CONCLUSION

cybercrime is a case of wrongdoing. The Government of India has instituted Information Technology Act, 2000 which has laws for cybercrime and is quite apt for combating cybercrime. However, the cyber-criminals are constantly advancing their ways of committing cybercrime which is a threat to the human rights as they interfere with one's personal data. In order to reduce cybercrime in India, data analytics can be used along with the Information Technology Act, 2000. Data analytics solutions has the potential to greatly reduce cybercrime in India. Proper monitoring of data and implementation of data analytics using the data analytics tools can provide protection against cybercrimes and can reduce cybercrimes in India. Thus if data analytics is brought into use in cyber world then along with the existing Information Technology Act, 2000, data analytics will truly help in reducing cybercrime in India.

REFERENCES

Angin, P., Bhargava, B., & Ranchal, R. (2019). Big Data Analytics for Cyber Security. *Hindawi Security and Communication Networks*, 1-2.

Aseef, N., Davis, P., Mittal, M., Sedky, K., & Tolba, A. (2005). *Cyber-Criminal Activity and Analysis*. White Paper.

Ministry of Law, Justice and Company Affairs – Legislative Department. (2000). *The Gazette of India Extraordinary Part II*.

Nallaperumal, K. (2018). Cyber Security Analytics to Combat Cyber Crimes. *IEEE ICCIC 2018.*

Rigano, C. (2019). Using Artificial Intelligence to Address Criminal Justice Needs. *National Institute of Justice Journal, 280,* 1–10.

Tatarao, V., & Reddy, B. S. V. (2019). The Cyber Crime under Ground Economy Data Approach. *International Journal of Computer Science Trends and Technology, 7*(6), 70–72.

KEY TERMS AND DEFINITIONS

Cyber Analyst: For digital security of a company, cyber analyst is responsible. Basically, they evaluate, plan, and implement the security systems to protect the organization from cyber threats.

Cyber Security Threat: In general sense a malicious act that seeks to damage data, steal, or disrupt digital life called as cyber security threat.

Data Analysis: The process of collecting, organizing any data in proper order is comes under the data analysis. In analytical and logical reasoning to gain information these data analysis used.

Information Technology: Study, design, implementation, development of whole management of computer-based information systems are called as information technology which includes software applications and computer hardware.

Personal Computer: A multipurpose computer by its size, capabilities including price it feasible for personal use.

Chapter 24

Clustering by K–Means Method and K–Medoids Method:
An Application With Statistical Regions of Turkey

Onur Önay

School of Business, Istanbul University, Turkey

ABSTRACT

Data science and data analytics are becoming increasingly important. It is widely used in scientific and real-life applications. These methods enable us to analyze, understand, and interpret the data in every field. In this study, k-means and k-medoids clustering methods are applied to cluster the Statistical Regions of Turkey in Level 2. Clustering analyses are done for 2017 and 2018 years. The datasets consist of "Distribution of expenditure groups according to Household Budget Survey" 2017 and 2018 values, "Gini coefficient by equivalised household disposable income" 2017 and 2018 values, and some features of "Regional Purchasing Power Parities for the main groups of consumption expenditures" 2017 values. Elbow method and average silhouette method are applied for the determining the number of the clusters at the beginning. Results are given and interpreted at the conclusion.

INTRODUCTION

Data science and data analytics are becoming more and more important with their wide application area. Spending time on the internet, visiting shopping sites, reading the news sites, using search engines, looking social media posts, adding comments to contents etc. each contributes to the formation of datasets. So data is constantly growing from social media, weather stations, government agencies, purchases and so on (Dichev, & Dicheva 2017). Data is very important source of knowledge. In business to design successful strategies and policies data science is widely used (Gibert et al., 2018). Hundreds of scientific studies and real-life applications can be found from the internet in data science and data analytics. A lot of applications can be found according to data which are collected in different areas. Data can be in a

DOI: 10.4018/978-1-7998-3053-5.ch024

variety of formats, such as numeric, text or image and etc. Data science and data analytics can help us understand the data by analyzing various methods. Data science includes mathematical and statistical analysis combined with information technology tools and builds systems and algorithms to discover the information, to detect the patterns, and create useful insights and predictions while doing this it uses techniques, such as classification, clustering, regression and association rule mining (Molina-Solana et al., 2017).

Clustering methods are used as data science methods and that can be used to understand the meaning of the data. The data are grouped into clusters and the resulting clusters are interpreted. There are many types of clustering methods, such as partitioning, hierarchical, grid-based and model-based methods (Kaur et al., 2014). In this study, k-means and k-medoids methods are used which are in partitioning clustering methods. Clusters are arranged with these methods by looking at the distances between the data.

In this study, Statistical Regions of Turkey in Level 2 are clustered with k-means and k-medoids clustering methods. Turkey has three different levels of Statistical Regions. They are "Level 1", "Level 2" and "Level 3". Details of the Statistical Regions of Turkey are given at the section two (background). Turkey has 7 geographical regions and their details are given before the analysis. The dataset 2017 (in Table 3) consists of "Distribution of expenditure groups according to Household Budget Survey (Horizontal %), 2015-2017, 2017", "Gini coefficient by equivalised household disposable income 2017" and some features of "Regional Purchasing Power Parities for the main groups of consumption expenditures" for 2017. The dataset 2018 (in Table 2) consists of "Distribution of expenditure groups according to Household Budget Survey (Horizontal %), 2016-2018, 2018", "Gini coefficient by equivalised household disposable income" for 2018. Statistical Regions of Turkey which are in the same or in a different cluster can be identified and interpreted by the clustering analysis according to datasets. Anyone who knows a region can make inferences about other regions in the same cluster. So data science methods help us understand the clustering of Statistical Regions of the Turkey in Level 2 according to topics of datasets.

There are seven sections in this study. Section one is the introduction. Section two is the background. In this section, there is information about the classification of Statistical Regions system of Turkey and some studies are given as examples from the literature which are related with the study. Section three is the main focus of the chapter part. The information about clustering, k-means, k-medoids, determination of the numbers of the clusters and information of the data are given in section three. Analyses and results are given in section four which is the solutions and recommendations section. Some ideas are given for the future research direction in section five. In the section six conclusions are given. And in final section references are given. The overview of the study can be shown by steps as following;

Step 1: Determine the research problem
Step 2: Do background research
Step 3: Give information of the data and analysis methods
Step 4: Analyze the data
Step 5: Communicate the results
Step 6: Conclusion

BACKGROUND

Statistical Regions of Turkey

Classification of Statistical Regions system has been used since 2002 in Turkey and it has similar logic with the NUTS (Nomenclature of Territorial Units for Statistics) statistical classification system of the European Union. NUTS (Nomenclature of Territorial Units for Statistics) classification system is used for dividing up the European Union's territory on the purpose of produce regional statistics for the Community (Eurostat, 2019) by Eurostat (statistical office of the European Union). Classification of Statistical Region system was published in the Official Gazette of the Republic of Turkey in 2002 and it was started to be used. Gathering and developing the regional statistics, conducting socio-economic analysis of the regions, determining the framework of regional policies were some of the reasons for a new classification of the statistical regions system (The Official Gazette of the Republic of Turkey, 2002). Another reason of the need was establishing a comparable statistical database with the European Union Regional Statistics System (NUTS = Nomenclature of Territorial Units for Statistics) (Özçağlar, 2003; The Official Gazette of the Republic of Turkey, 2002). Because of the listed reasons statistical regions system of Turkey may be called as NUTS of Turkey. There are a lot of studies using NUTS of Turkey, such as Şengül et al. (2013), Bakırcı et al. (2014) and so on.

There are three levels of the Statistical Regions of Turkey (NUTS of Turkey). As it is written in the Official Gazette of the Republic of Turkey (2002); Statistical Regions of Turkey "Level 3" is a degree that consists of all 81 cities in Turkey. Neighbor cities which have similarities in terms of economic, social and geographical aspects are grouped as "Level 2" and "Level 1" Statistical Regions of Turkey by considering regional development plans and population sizes. "Level 2" Statistical Regions of Turkey consists of 26 regions which are produced by grouping Level 3 regions. "Level 1" is produced by grouping "Level 2" regions and it has 12 regions. Hierarchically Statistical Regions of Turkey (nomenclature of territorial units for statistics of Turkey) is obtained as it is shown in Table 1(Official Gazette of the Republic of Turkey, 2002).

Statistical Regions of Turkey (Nomenclature of Territorial Units for Statistics) in Level 2 are grouped by k-means and k-medoids clustering methods in this study. The content of the dataset has two stages according to its year. The year 2017 dataset (in Table 3) consist of "Distribution of expenditure groups according to Household Budget Survey (Horizontal %), 2015-2017, 2017", "Gini coefficient by equivalised household disposable income, 2017" and some features of "Regional Purchasing Power Parities for the main groups of consumption expenditures, 2017". The year 2018 dataset (in Table 2) consist of "Distribution of expenditure groups according to Household Budget Survey (Horizontal %), 2016-2018, 2018", "Gini coefficient by equivalised household disposable income, 2018".

There are several studies in the literature; some of them use Household Budget Survey and are analyzed with various methods, some of them use Gini coefficient and Regional Purchasing Power Parities. Some of the studies are article, some of them are thesis. There are also several studies about different topics of Turkey with clustering methods and other statistical methods. Değirmenci and Özbakır (2018) used clustering techniques and association rule mining technique for their data source which is a household budget survey microdata set in their study; "Differentiating households to analyze consumption patterns: a data mining study on official household budget data". Household income elasticity values of 12 major commodity groups are estimated and they are evaluated as qualifications using by budget survey data of 2014 by Çalmaşur and Kılıç (2018). Living index values of Turkey were analyzed by K-means clustering method and their results were examined by discriminant analysis in the study of Uysal et al. (2017). Bulut (2019) clustered cities of Turkey according to index values of the "Life Satisfaction in Cities" by k-means and EM algorithms. In the study of Giray et al. (2016) European Union countries and Turkey were grouped by fuzzy clustering and robust clustering techniques according to migration rates, Gini coefficient, crime rates and happiness variables. Secgin and Dalkilic (2017) used the Agglomerative hierarchical clustering and the K-medoids clustering methods to cluster 81 cities of Turkey according to 35 topics. Akkuş and Zontul (2019) grouped 214 countries with Self Organizing Map and K-Means clustering algorithms whose the data obtained from the World Bank website in the their study. Topbaş and Unat (2018) investigated the structure of household consumption trend in Turkey for 2005-2016 in terms of expenditure groups by using the data of Household Budget Survey and they use a quantile regression model. Kayalak and Kiper (2006) applied cluster analysis to separate the socio-economic indicators for evaluating regional differences in Turkey. They also used discriminant analysis in their study. Ahi (2015) generated his dataset with Household Budget Survey in 2011 and Survey of Income and Living Conditions in 2012. In his master's thesis, to estimate variables on the basis of Classification of Individual Consumption according to Purpose 12 main expenditure groups for households, Ahi (2015) applied data mining methods related with statistical matching. Erdaş et al. (2017) used regression analysis and ARDL error correction model analysis for determinants of households consumption expenditure in Turkey. Özarı and Eren (2018) used multidimensional scaling method and K-means cluster analysis for life index of provinces in Turkey. Yıldırım (2018) applied hierarchical clustering, k-means and partitioning around medoids (pam) clustering algorithms for the data set of the health indicators for the provinces in Turkey. Dikmen (2018) used clustering analysis investigation of well-being and quality of life of Turkish provinces. Özdemir and Demir (2019) used data mining methods for Survey of Income and Living Conditions data for the year 2015 which is conducted by TurkStat.

MAIN FOCUS OF THE CHAPTER

Clustering Methods

Among of the knowledge discovery techniques from the data, clustering is a technique for exposing the data structures (Khan & Ahmad, 2004). Clustering technics have a lot of usage areas, such as patter recognition, data analyses, image processing and analysis, machine learning, data mining, bioinformatics and so on (Žalik, 2008; Velmurugan & Santhanam, 2011). In partition method, the data set which is a consistence of n data points and m dimensional space, partition into k distinct groups which are called clusters (Han et al., 2011; Khan & Ahmad, 2004). Similarity of the members in each cluster is high, while similarities between members of different clusters are low, namely differences or dissimilarities between data in other clusters are greater (Jain, 2010; Yu et al., 2018; Velmurugan & Santhanam, 2010; Loohach & Garg, 2012).

K-means Clustering Algorithm

K-means is a popular clustering algorithm which is in group of the partitional clustering methods (Zhu et al., 2019) and unsupervised learning technique (Velmurugan & Santhanam, 2010). Let data set and its objects (data points) represent by $X= \{x_i: i=1,2,\ldots,n\}$. K-means algorithm starts by randomly selecting the initial k cluster centers. Clusters have data points which are centers of them and they can be called centroid of cluster. These initial centroids are called seeds (seed-points) (Redmond & Heneghan, 2007; Žalik, 2008). Most similar data are in a cluster that distribute to clusters according to distance between data and cluster centers. In other words data assign cluster according to its nearest cluster center (Liu et al., 2018; Žalik, 2008). Clusters can be represented by C_1, C_2, ..., C_k and centers of K number clusters are represented by C= $\{c_j: j=1,2,...,k\}$. The distance between each data point in the each cluster and its centroid is squared and distances are summed (Han et al., 2011). Each cluster center c_j is updated by the mean of the all x_i members of related cluster C_j (Redmond & Heneghan, 2007). The objective of the k-means is minimizing the sum squared error over all k clusters defined as following (Jain, 2010);

$$O = \sum_{j=1}^{k} \sum_{x_i \in C_j} \left\| x_i - c_j \right\|^2 \tag{1}$$

All data objects are assigned according to new centroids (mean of cluster's member) until the new cluster centers become the same with previous centroids and the clustering is resulted. Otherwise these calculations continue to assignments and specifications of clusters are stabilized (Yu et al., 2018; Han et al., 2011).

K-means algorithm can be summarized as following (Khan & Ahmad, 2004; Kassambara, 2017; Liu et al., 2018):

Step 1: Initial k cluster centers are selected randomly
Step 2: Data is assigned to cluster according to minimum distance from cluster center
Step 3: Update the cluster centers by calculating the new mean of the each cluster.
Step 4: Repeat steps 2 and 3 until cluster assignments and cluster centers do not change

K-means algorithm is sensitive to the locations of the initial centers of cluster so that chosen K values can affect the performance of the clustering (Wu et al., 2008; Pham et al., 2005). Although generally Euclidian metric is used for calculation the distance between members of the clusters and their centroids, there are studies that use different metrics for distance calculations. Mahalanobis distance (Mao & Jain,1996), Itakura-Saito distance (Linde et al., 1980), L_1 distance (Kashima et al., 2008) Bermang distance (Banerjee et al., 2005) are cited by Jain (2010) in his study. In other study, Loohach & Garg (2012) used Manhattan distance.

K-Medoids Clustering Algorithm

K-medoids is the partitioning clustering algorithm like k-means clustering algorithm. Since K-means clustering algorithm has some disadvantages such as sensitivity of outliers although it is useful technique for clustering, k-medoids clustering algorithm can be used to reduce that sensitivity (Park & Jun, 2009; Zadegan et al., 2013; Park et al., 2006). K-medoids algorithm differentiates from k-means by using medoids which are centrally located objects instead of using centroids in the clusters (Sheng & Liu, 2006; Velmurugan, 2012). Data points distribute to the clusters according to their similarities. The dissimilarity can be measured by distance function between data objects. In other words the partitioning method k-medoids minimizes the objective function which is sum of the total dissimilarity between data points and their medoids (Barioni et al., 2008; Lai & Fu, 2011). Distance can be measured by different measures such as; Euclidean distance, Manhattan distance or Minkowski distance (Madhulatha, 2011). Several algorithms were developed for k-medoids clustering. Bhat (2014) mentions that "Partition Around Medoids" (PAM) algorithm is proposed by Kaufman and Rousseeuw in 1987, and cited to their study "Clustering by means of medoids" (as cited in Bhat (2014)). "Clustering Large Applications (CLARA)" is another algorithm that is proposed by Kaufman and Rousseeuw (1990) for large date sets (Ng & Han, 2002) and "Clustering Large Applications based upon Randomized Search (CLARANS)" algorithm is proposed by Ng and Han (Ng & Han, 1994; Ng & Han, 2002).

Partition Around Medoids (PAM) algorithm starts by selecting k representative objects (data samples) which are chosen randomly and called medoids (Khatami et al., 2017). Data in the set (non-selected data (objects)) are grouped with the medoids according to their similarities (Ng & Han, 2002; Ng & Han, 1994). All possible exchanges between medoids and non-medoids are tried and evaluated for every possible combination to improve the quality of the clustering (Paterlini et al., 2011; Han et al., 2011). Each medoid and each data object (non-medoid) swap and total cost is computed. It continues to selecting the pair which minimizes the total cost. When it reaches the smallest value, clusters are determined (the most similar medoid is found for each non-selected object) and then algorithm can stop (Barioni et al., 2008). Readers can find details and algorithmically presentation of PAM algorithm in: Ng & Han (2002) and Ng & Han (1994).

Even though K-medoids method is used for many applications, it may face several disadvantages, such as being trapped in local optima, time consuming because of selecting k medoids randomly and swapping all pairs of medoids and non-medoids, so it can be sensitive to initialization and outliers (Yu et al., 2018).

Determination of the Number of the Clusters

Before starting analysis, both k-means and k-medoids clustering methods need to know the numbers of the clusters at the beginning. Direct methods such as elbow method, average silhouette method and statistical testing methods such as gap statistic method, can be used for determining the number of the clusters. There are also more than thirty methods for solving that problem (Kassambara, 2017).

Elbow Method is one of the methods which determines the optimal number of the clusters. It looks the total with-in cluster sum of square (wss). In other words sum of square errors namely sum of the square of the difference between members of the clusters and their cluster centers (centroids). When the new cluster is added, assessing the improvement performance of wss and numbers of clusters are determined (Kassambara, 2017; Zhang et al., 2016; Deb & Lee, 2018).

Another method for determining the numbers of the clusters, average silhouette method might be used to select the convenient number of the clusters. The optimal number of the clusters is determined by Silhouette method that maximizes the average silhouette width (Kaufman & Rousseeuw, 1990; Rousseeuw, 1987; Jin & Sendhoff, 2004; Jörnsten, 2004; Reynolds et al., 2004).

About Data

In this study, Statistical Regions of Turkey are clustered by using k-means and k-medoids clustering methods.

The study is about to researching and interpreting the nomenclature of territorial units for statistics of Turkey at the Level 2 regions according to "Distribution of expenditure groups according to Household Budget Survey", "Gini coefficient by equivalised household disposable income", some features of "Regional Purchasing Power Parities for the main groups of consumption expenditures" with clustering technics k-means method and k-medoids method. Since the similar regions would be in the same clusters, it might be possible identify statistically by clustering. There are four parts in the study. Data which are used in the study are published by Turkish Statistical Institution (TURKSTAT). It is gotten from the web page of the Turkish Statistical Institution. Names of the features are listed in Table 2 for dataset 2018. Names of the features are listed in Table 3 for dataset 2017.

Part One: Data of the year 2018 consist of "Distribution of expenditure groups according to Household Budget Survey (Horizontal %), 2016-2018 (TurkStat, Household Consumption Expenditures Regional Results), 2018" and "Gini coefficient by equivalised household disposable income, 2018". Data were in two different tables and they were combined for analyzing and the new form of the dataset was comprised. They were analyzed with k-means clustering method.

Part Two: Data of the year 2018 consist of "Distribution of expenditure groups according to Household Budget Survey (Horizontal %), 2016-2018 (TurkStat, Household Consumption Expenditures Regional Results), 2018" and "Gini coefficient by equivalised household disposable income, 2018". Data were in two different tables and they were combined for analyzing and the new form of the dataset was comprised. They were analyzed with k-medoids clustering method.

Part Three: Data of the year 2017 consist of "Distribution of expenditure groups according to Household Budget Survey (Horizontal %), 2015-2017 (TurkStat, Household Consumption Expenditures Regional Results), 2017", "Gini coefficient by equivalised household disposable income, 2017" and some features of "Regional Purchasing Power Parities for the main groups of consumption expenditures, 2017". Data were in three different tables and they were combined for analyzing and the new form of the dataset was comprised. They were analyzed with k-means clustering method.

Part Four: Data of the year 2017 consist of "Distribution of expenditure groups according to Household Budget Survey (Horizontal %), 2015-2017 (TurkStat, Household Consumption Expenditures Regional Results), 2017", "Gini coefficient by equivalised household disposable income, 2017" and some features of "Regional Purchasing Power Parities for the main groups of consumption expenditures, 2017". Data were in three different tables and they were combined for analyzing and the new form of the dataset was comprised. They were analyzed with k-medoids clustering method.

At the metadata (2019(a)) and (2019(b)) of the "Distribution of expenditure groups according to Household Budget Survey"; subject and subtitle of the survey is "Household Budget Survey". It is an annual data. The data for 2017 covers 2015-2017 and the data for 2018 covers 2016-2018. The definition of the "household" is given in the metadata (2019(a); 2019(b)) of the survey; *"Group of people composed of one or more than one members living in the same dwelling either with blood relations or not and meeting their own basic needs together and participating the services and management of the household."* The definition of the "consumption expenditure" is given in the metadata (2019(a); 2019(b)) of the survey; *"It is the monthly average expenditure values of households for the purpose of consume."* And definition continues with adding its components and their definitions such as; "purchase", "consumption from own production", "consumption from income in-kind", "goods and services that are purchased by the

Table 1. Statistical Regions of Turkey (Nomenclature of territorial units for statistics of Turkey) (Official Gazette of the Republic of Turkey, 2002)

Left panel

Level 1		Level 2		Level 3	
TR1	İstanbul	TR10	İstanbul	TR100	İstanbul
TR2	West Marmara	TR21	Tekirdağ	TR211	Tekirdağ
				TR212	Edirne
				TR213	Kırklareli
		TR22	Balıkesir	TR221	Balıkesir
				TR222	Çanakkale
TR3	Aegean	TR31	İzmir	TR310	İzmir
		TR32	Aydın	TR321	Aydın
				TR322	Denizli
				TR323	Muğla
		TR33	Manisa	TR331	Manisa
				TR332	Afyonkarahisar
				TR333	Kütahya
				TR334	Uşak
TR4	East Marmara	TR41	Bursa	TR411	Bursa
				TR412	Eskişehir
				TR413	Bilecik
		TR42	Kocaeli	TR421	Kocaeli
				TR422	Sakarya
				TR423	Düzce
				TR424	Bolu
				TR425	Yalova
TR5	West Anatolia	TR51	Ankara	TR510	Ankara
		TR52	Konya	TR521	Konya
				TR522	Karaman
TR6	Mediterranean	TR61	Antalya	TR611	Antalya
				TR612	Isparta
				TR613	Burdur
		TR62	Adana	TR621	Adana
				TR622	Mersin
		TR63	Hatay	TR631	Hatay
				TR632	Kahramanmaraş
				TR633	Osmaniye
TR7	Central Anatolia	TR71	Kırıkkale	TR711	Kırıkkale
				TR712	Aksaray
				TR713	Niğde
				TR714	Nevşehir
				TR715	Kırşehir
		TR72	Kayseri	TR721	Kayseri
				TR722	Sivas
				TR723	Yozgat

Right panel

Level 1		Level 2		Level 3	
TR8	West Black Sea	TR81	Zonguldak	TR811	Zonguldak
				TR812	Karabük
				TR813	Bartın
		TR82	Kastamonu	TR821	Kastamonu
				TR822	Çankırı
				TR823	Sinop
		TR83	Samsun	TR831	Samsun
				TR832	Tokat
				TR833	Çorum
				TR834	Amasya
TR9	East Black Sea	TR90	Trabzon	TR901	Trabzon
				TR902	Ordu
				TR903	Giresun
				TR904	Rize
				TR905	Artvin
				TR906	Gümüşhane
TRA	North East Anatolia	TRA1	Erzurum	TRA11	Erzurum
				TRA12	Erzincan
				TRA13	Bayburt
		TRA2	Ağrı	TRA21	Ağrı
				TRA22	Kars
				TRA23	Iğdır
				TRA24	Ardahan
TRB	Central East Anatolia	TRB1	Malatya	TRB11	Malatya
				TRB12	Elazığ
				TRB13	Bingöl
				TRB14	Tunceli
		TRB2	Van	TRB21	Van
				TRB22	Muş
				TRB23	Bitlis
				TRB24	Hakkari
TRC	South East Anatolia	TRC1	Gaziantep	TRC11	Gaziantep
				TRC12	Adıyaman
				TRC13	Kilis
		TRC2	Şanlıurfa	TRC21	Şanlıurfa
				TRC22	Diyarbakır
		TRC3	Mardin	TRC31	Mardin
				TRC32	Batman
				TRC33	Şırnak
				TRC34	Siirt
Total	12	26		81	

Source: (Official Gazette of the Republic of Turkey, 2002)

household to be given to the private persons or bodies as gifts or allowances", "consumption expenditures for durable goods", "imputed rent" (Metadata (2019(a)); Metadata (2019(b)).

At the metadata (2018) of the "Regional Purchasing Power Parities for the main groups of consumption expenditures"; subject of the survey is "Prices and Indexes", subtitle of the survey is "Purchasing Power Parity values". A part of the definition of the objective of study is "...*determine the purchasing power of Turkish Liras (TL) in different regions of Turkey. ...*" (Metadata (2018)).

At the metadata (2019(c)) of the "Gini coefficient by equivalised household disposable income"; subject of the survey is "Survey of Income and Living Conditions" and subtitle of the survey is "Number of the poor and poverty rate" and it continues with other definitions of the survey, such as; "objective", "period", "covered period", "data compiling method", "regional scope", "definitions of variables (Equivalised household disposable income, Gini coefficient)" and so on. (Metadata (2019(c))).

Table 2. Features of dataset 2018

Food and non-alcoholic beverages
Alcoholic beverages, cigarette and tobacco
Clothing and footwear
Housing and rent
Furniture, houses appliances and home care services
Health
Transportation
Communication
Entertainment and culture
Education services
Restaurants and hotels
Various good and services
Gini coefficient

Turkey has 7 geographical regions. It may not be possible to see the same feature in all of the areas covered by the geographical regions but they are generally determined by similar natural and socio-economic characteristics. They are listed as; Mediterranean Region, Central Anatolia Region, Eastern Anatolia Region, Southeastern Anatolia Region, Black Sea Region, Aegean Region, Marmara Region (Özçağlar,2003).

In this study, the dataset, which is analyzed, is about Level 2 Statistical Regions of Turkey (Nomenclature of territorial units for statistics of Turkey). The information about geographical locations (regions) of the cities is also given to the readers. Borders of the some cities are in more than one geographic region. In this case, the geographic region of the city is evaluated as region of the city center or from the governorship official web page. For further information about geographic regions and cities, "tourism geography 1" module (2013) and "tourism geography 2" module (2013) can be read which are prepared by accommodation and travel services of the Ministry of National Education of Turkish Republic.

Table 3. Features of dataset 2017

Food and non-alcoholic beverages*	Gini coefficient
Alcoholic beverages, cigarette and tobacco*	Food And Non-Alcoholic Beverages**
Clothing and footwear*	Clothing And Footwear**
Housing and rent*	Housing, Water, Electricity, Gas And Other Fuels**
Furniture, houses appliances and home care services*	Furnishings, Household Equipment, Routine Maintenance Of The House**
Health*	Health**
Transportation*	Transport**
Communication*	Recreation And Culture**
Entertainment and culture*	Education**
Education services*	Hotels, Cafes And Restaurants**
Restaurants and hotels*	Miscellaneous Goods And Services**
Various good and services*	
* from distribution of expenditure groups according to Household Budget Survey	
** from Regional Purchasing Power Parities for the main groups of consumption expenditures	

SOLUTIONS AND RECOMMENDATIONS

Analyses

There are four parts in the study as mentioned above. Elbow method and average silhouette method are used for determining the number of the clusters. Gap Statistics Method is not used for determining the number of the clusters because its results do not provide a usable value for clustering. R-Studio and R packages (The R "Stats" Package (R Core Team, 2019); The R "Base" Package (R Core Team, 2019); "Factoextra" (Kassambara & Mundt, 2017) and "Cluster" (Maechler et al., 2019) packages) are used for analyses.

"Alcoholic Beverages and Tobacco", "Communications" features from "Regional Purchasing Power Parities for the main groups of consumption expenditures" are not included in analyses because their all values are 1. "General" feature from "Regional Purchasing Power Parities for the main groups of consumption expenditures" are not included in analyses.

Part One:

Dataset of Part One consists of combination of the "Distribution of expenditure groups according to Household Budget Survey (Horizontal %), 2016-2018, 2018" and "Gini coefficient by equivalised household disposable income, 2018" which is referred as "dataset 2018". There are 13 features which are shown in Table 2 and Level 2 Statistical Regions of Turkey (26 statistical regions) in the dataset 2018. They are clustered with k-means method. Elbow method and average silhouette method are used for determining number of the clusters. R programming language in the R-Studio is used for analyses. "Factoextra" package (Kassambara & Mundt, 2017) is used for analyses in the R. The R function kmeans() (The R "Stats" Package (R Core Team, 2019)) is used for k-means clustering.

Graphic of the Elbow method is shown in Figure 1 for k-means analysis for dataset 2018. According to Figure 1, there is a bend (or elbow) whose location can be considered as an indicator of the convenient number of clusters at k=4. So dataset 2018 can be grouped to 4 clusters.

Figure 1. Graphic of the Elbow method for k-means analysis for dataset 2018

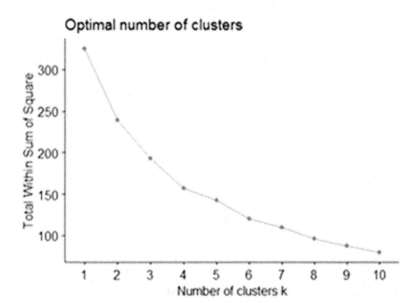

Dataset 2018 is grouped to 4 clusters with k-means method and it is shown in Figure 2.

Four clusters and cluster members (level 2 statistical regions and their cities) are shown in Table 4.

According to clustering with k-means method of the dataset 2018, there are 4 clusters (Figure 1 and Figure 2). The biggest city of Turkey is İstanbul and it is the region TR10, the capital city of Turkey is Ankara and it is the region TR51 and one of the biggest cities of Turkey is İzmir and it is the region TR31. They are clustered in the same cluster, Cluster 3. Geographically, some cities of the Mediterranean Region in the TR63 region; some cities of the Central Anatolia Region in the TR71, TR72, TR82 regions; some cities of the Black Sea Region in the TR82, TR83, TR90, TRA1 regions; some cities of the Eastern Anatolia Region in the TRA1, TRB1 regions and some cities of the Southeastern Anatolia Region in the TRC1 are in the Cluster 1. Some cities of the Eastern Anatolia Region in the TRA2, TRB2 regions and some cities of the Southeastern Anatolia Region in the TRC2, TRC3 regions are in the Cluster 2. Some cities of the Marmara Region in the TR21, TR22, TR41, TR42 regions; some cities of the Aegean Region in the TR32, TR33 regions; some cities of the Mediterranean Region in the TR61, TR62 regions; some cities of the Central Anatolia Region in the TR41, TR52 and some cities of the Black Sea Region in the TR42, TR81 regions are grouped in the Cluster 4.

Graphic of the average silhouette method is shown in Figure 3. High average silhouette width can be considered as an indicator of the convenient number of clusters at k=2. So dataset 2018 can be grouped to 2 clusters.

Dataset 2018 is grouped to 2 clusters with k-means method and it is shown in Figure 4.

Two clusters and cluster members (level 2 statistical regions and their cities) are shown in Table 5.

Figure 2. Dataset 2018 is grouped to 4 clusters with k-means method

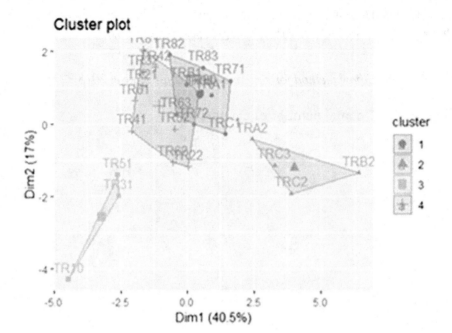

Table 4. K-means clustering of the dataset 2018 with 4 clusters

	TR63	Hatay, Kahramanmaraş, Osmaniye
	TR71	Kırıkkale, Aksaray, Niğde, Nevşehir, Kırşehir
	TR72	Kayseri, Sivas, Yozgat
	TR82	Kastamonu, Çankırı, Sinop
Cluster 1	TR83	Samsun, Tokat, Çorum, Amasya
	TR90	Trabzon, Ordu, Giresun, Rize, Artvin, Gümüşhane
	TRA1	Erzurum, Erzincan, Bayburt
	TRB1	Malatya, Elâzığ, Bingöl, Tunceli
	TRC1	Gaziantep, Adıyaman, Kilis
	TRA2	Ağrı, Kars, Iğdır, Ardahan
Cluster 2	TRB2	Van, Muş, Bitlis, Hakkari
	TRC2	Şanlıurfa, Diyarbakır
	TRC3	Mardin, Batman, Şırnak, Siirt
	TR10	İstanbul
Cluster 3	TR31	İzmir
	TR51	Ankara
	TR21	Tekirdağ, Edirne, Kırklareli
	TR22	Balıkesir, Çanakkale
	TR32	Aydin, Denizli, Muğla
	TR33	Manisa, Afyonkarahisar, Kütahya, Uşak
	TR41	Bursa, Eskişehir, Bilecik
Cluster 4	TR42	Kocaeli, Sakarya, Düzce, Bolu, Yalova
	TR52	Konya, Karaman
	TR61	Antalya, Isparta, Burdur
	TR62	Adana, Mersin
	TR81	Zonguldak, Karabük, Bartın

Figure 3. Graphic of the average silhouette method for k-means analysis for dataset 2018

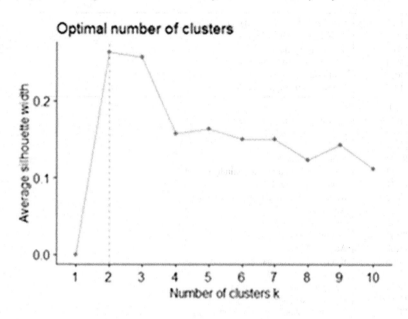

Figure 4. Dataset 2018 is grouped to 2 clusters with k-means method

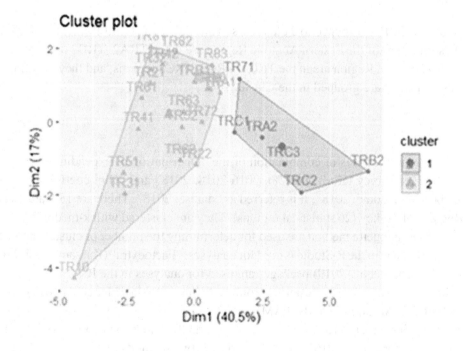

Table 5. K-means clustering of the dataset 2018 with 2 clusters

Cluster 1	TR71	Kırıkkale, Aksaray, Niğde, Nevşehir, Kırşehir
	TRA2	Ağrı, Kars, Iğdır, Ardahan
	TRB2	Van, Muş, Bitlis, Hakkari
	TRC1	Gaziantep, Adıyaman, Kilis
	TRC2	Şanlıurfa, Diyarbakır
	TRC3	Mardin, Batman, Şırnak, Siirt
Cluster 2	TR10	İstanbul
	TR21	Tekirdağ, Edirne, Kırklareli
	TR22	Balıkesir, Çanakkale
	TR31	İzmir
	TR32	Aydin, Denizli, Muğla
	TR33	Manisa, Afyonkarahisar, Kütahya, Uşak
	TR41	Bursa, Eskişehir, Bilecik
	TR42	Kocaeli, Sakarya, Düzce, Bolu, Yalova
	TR51	Ankara
	TR52	Konya, Karaman
	TR61	Antalya, Isparta, Burdur
	TR62	Adana, Mersin
	TR63	Hatay, Kahramanmaraş, Osmaniye
	TR72	Kayseri, Sivas, Yozgat
	TR81	Zonguldak, Karabük, Bartın
	TR82	Kastamonu, Çankırı, Sinop
	TR83	Samsun, Tokat, Çorum, Amasya
	TR90	Trabzon, Ordu, Giresun, Rize, Artvin, Gümüşhane
	TRA1	Erzurum, Erzincan, Bayburt
	TRB1	Malatya, Elâzığ, Bingöl, Tunceli

When the dataset 2018 is grouped to 2 clusters, some cities of the Central Anatolia Region are in the TR71 region; some cities of the Eastern Anatolia Region are in the TRA2, TRB2 regions; some cities of the Southeastern Anatolia Region are in the TRC1, TRC2, TRC3 regions; and they are all in the Cluster 1. Other cities of Turkey are grouped in the Cluster 2.

Part Two:

Dataset of Part Two consists of combination of the "Distribution of expenditure groups according to Household Budget Survey (Horizontal %), 2016-2018, 2018" and "Gini coefficient by equivalised household disposable income, 2018". It is referred as "dataset 2018". There are 13 features and Level 2 Statistical Regions of Turkey (26 statistical regions). They are clustered with k-medoids method. Elbow method and average silhouette method are used for determining the number of clusters at the beginning. R programming language in the R-Studio is used for analyses. "Factoextra" (Kassambara & Mundt, 2017) and "Cluster" (Maechler et al., 2019) packages are used for analyses in the R.

"Pam()" function for k-medoids clustering from the "Cluster" (Maechler et al., 2019) package of the R is used for Partition Around Medoids (PAM).

Graphics of the elbow method and average silhouette method are shown in Figure 5 and Figure 6 for k-medoids clustering for dataset 2018. According to both two methods to determine the number of the clusters at the beginning of the analyses in the Figure 5 and Figure 6, there is a bend (or elbow) whose location can be considered as an indicator of the convenient number of clusters at k=4, and high average silhouette width can be considered as an indicator of the convenient number of clusters at k=4. So dataset 2018 can be grouped to 4 clusters.

Figure 5. Graphic of the elbow method for k-medoids clustering for dataset 2018

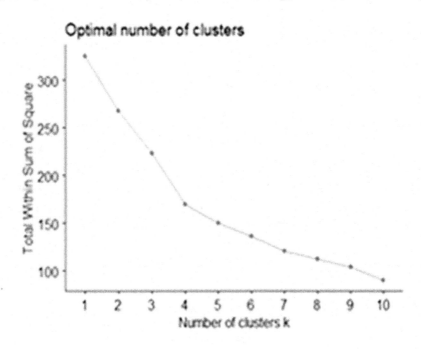

Figure 6. Graphic of the average silhouette method for k-medoids clustering for dataset 2018

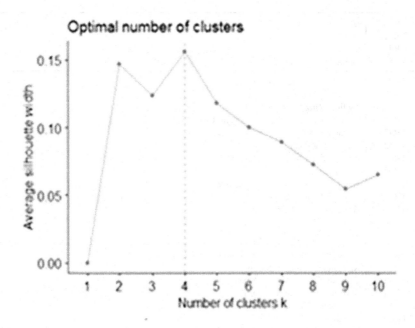

Dataset 2018 is grouped to 4 clusters with k-medoids method and it is shown in Figure 7.
Four clusters and cluster members (level 2 statistical regions and their cities) are shown in Table 6.

Figure 7. Dataset 2018 is grouped to 4 clusters with k-medoids method

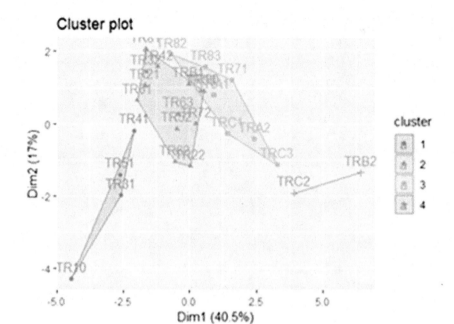

Table 6. K-medoids clustering of the dataset 2018 with 4 clusters

Cluster 1	TR10	İstanbul
	TR31	İzmir
	TR41	Bursa, Eskişehir, Bilecik
	TR51	Ankara
Cluster 2	TR21	Tekirdağ, Edirne, Kırklareli
	TR22	Balıkesir, Çanakkale
	TR32	Aydin, Denizli, Muğla
	TR33	Manisa, Afyonkarahisar, Kütahya, Uşak
	TR42	Kocaeli, Sakarya, Düzce, Bolu, Yalova
	TR52	Konya, Karaman
	TR61	Antalya, Isparta, Burdur
	TR62	Adana, Mersin
	TR63	Hatay, Kahramanmaraş, Osmaniye
	TR72	Kayseri, Sivas, Yozgat
	TR81	Zonguldak, Karabük, Bartın
	TR90	Trabzon, Ordu, Giresun, Rize, Artvin, Gümüşhane
	TRB1	Malatya, Elâzığ, Bingöl, Tunceli
Cluster 3	TR71	Kırıkkale, Aksaray, Niğde, Nevşehir, Kırşehir
	TR82	Kastamonu, Çankırı, Sinop
	TR83	Samsun, Tokat, Çorum, Amasya
	TRA1	Erzurum, Erzincan, Bayburt
	TRA2	Ağrı, Kars, Iğdır, Ardahan
	TRC1	Gaziantep, Adıyaman, Kilis
	TRC3	Mardin, Batman, Şırnak, Siirt
Cluster 4	TRB2	Van, Muş, Bitlis, Hakkari
	TRC2	Şanlıurfa, Diyarbakır

According to clustering with k-medoids method of the dataset 2018, there are 4 clusters (Figure 5, Figure 6 and Figure 7). The biggest city of Turkey is İstanbul and it is the region TR10, the capital city of Turkey is Ankara and it is the region TR51, one of the biggest cities of Turkey is İzmir and it is the region TR31 and the cities of the TR41 (Bursa, Eskişehir, Bilecik) that the Level 2 Statistical Regions of Turkey are clustered in the same cluster, the Cluster 1. Geographically, some cities of the Central Anatolia Region in the TR71, TR82 regions; some cities of the Black Sea Region in the TR82, TR83, TRA1 regions, some cities of the Eastern Anatolia Region in the TRA1, TRA2 regions and some cities of the Southeastern Anatolia Region in the TRC1, TRC3 regions are grouped in the Cluster 3. Two regions of Level 2 TRB2 and TRC2 statistical regions are grouped in the Cluster 4. Other Statistical Regions of Turkey are grouped in the Cluster 2. Some cities of the Marmara Region in the TR21, TR22, TR42 regions; some cities of the Aegean Region in the TR32, TR33 regions; some cities of the Mediterranean Region in the TR61, TR62, TR63 regions; some cities of the Black Sea Region in the TR42, TR81, TR90 regions; some cities of the Central Anatolia Region in the TR52 region and some cities of the Southeastern Anatolia Region and Eastern Anatolia Region in the TRB1 region are grouped in the Cluster 2.

Part Three:

Dataset of Part Three consists of combination of the "Distribution of expenditure groups according to Household Budget Survey (Horizontal %), 2015-2017, 2017", "Gini coefficient by equivalised household disposable income, 2017" and some features of "Regional Purchasing Power Parities for the main groups of consumption expenditures, 2017" which is referred as "dataset 2017". There are 23 features which are shown in Table 3 and Level 2 Statistical Regions of Turkey (26 statistical regions) in the dataset 2017. They are clustered with k-means method. Elbow method and average silhouette method are used for determining the number of the clusters. R programming language in the R-Studio is used for analyses. "Factoextra" package (Kassambara & Mundt, 2017) is used for analyses in the R. The R function kmeans() (The R "Stats" Package (R Core Team, 2019)) is used for k-means clustering.

Graphic of the Elbow method is shown in Figure 8 for k-means analysis for dataset 2017. According to Figure 8, there is a bend (or elbow) whose location can be considered as an indicator of the convenient number of clusters at k=4. So dataset 2017 can be grouped to 4 clusters.

Dataset 2017 is grouped to 4 clusters with k-means method and it is shown in Figure 9.

Four clusters and cluster members (level 2 statistical regions and their cities) are shown in Table 7.

As it is in dataset 2018, there are 4 clusters (Figure 8 and Figure 9), according to clustering with k-means method of the dataset 2017. The biggest city of Turkey which is the region TR10 is İstanbul, the capital city of Turkey is Ankara and it is the region TR51 and one of the biggest cities of Turkey which is the region TR31 is İzmir, and they are clustered in the same cluster, Cluster 3. Geographically, some cities of the Marmara Region in the TR21, TR22, TR41, TR42 regions; Eskişehir is a city of the Central Anatolia Region in the TR41 region; some cities of the Aegean Region in the TR32 region, some cities of the Mediterranean Region in the TR61, TR62 regions and some cities of the Black Sea Region in the TR42, TR81, TR90 regions are grouped in the Cluster 1. Some cities of the Eastern Anatolia Region in the TRA2, TRB2 regions and some cities of the Southeastern Anatolia Region in the TRC2, TRC3 regions are grouped in the Cluster 2. Other cities of the Aegean Region, Mediterranean Region, Black Sea Region, Central Anatolia Region, Eastern Anatolia Region and Southeastern Anatolia Region which are in the TR33, TR52, TR63, TR71, TR72, TR82, TR83, TRA1, TRB1, TRC1 in the Level 2 Statistical Regions are grouped in the Cluster 4.

Figure 8. Graphic of the Elbow method for k-means analysis for dataset 2017

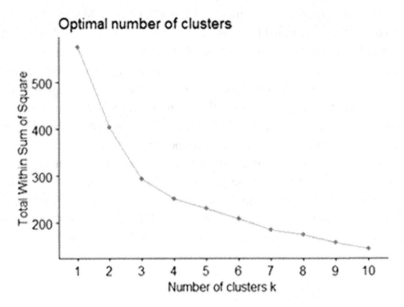

Figure 9. Dataset 2017 is grouped to 4 clusters with k-means method

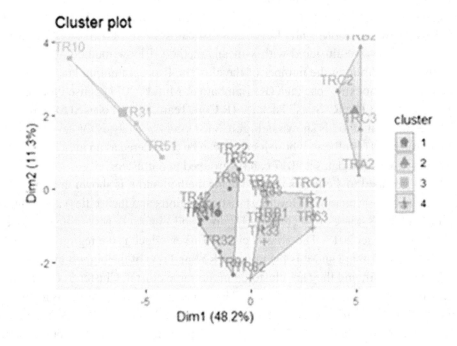

Graphic of the average silhouette method is shown in Figure 10. High average silhouette width can be considered as an indicator of the convenient number of clusters at k=3. So dataset 2017 can be grouped to 3 clusters for k-means method.

Table 7. K-means clustering of the dataset 2017 with 4 clusters

Cluster 1	TR21	Tekirdağ, Edirne, Kırklareli
	TR22	Balıkesir, Çanakkale
	TR32	Aydin, Denizli, Muğla
	TR41	Bursa, Eskişehir, Bilecik
	TR42	Kocaeli, Sakarya, Düzce, Bolu, Yalova
	TR61	Antalya, Isparta, Burdur
	TR62	Adana, Mersin
	TR81	Zonguldak, Karabük, Bartın
	TR90	Trabzon, Ordu, Giresun, Rize, Artvin, Gümüşhane
Cluster 2	TRA2	Ağrı, Kars, Iğdır, Ardahan
	TRB2	Van, Muş, Bitlis, Hakkari
	TRC2	Şanlıurfa, Diyarbakır
	TRC3	Mardin, Batman, Şırnak, Siirt
Cluster 3	TR10	İstanbul
	TR31	İzmir
	TR51	Ankara
Cluster 4	TR33	Manisa, Afyonkarahisar, Kütahya, Uşak
	TR52	Konya, Karaman
	TR63	Hatay, Kahramanmaraş, Osmaniye
	TR71	Kırıkkale, Aksaray, Niğde, Nevşehir, Kırşehir
	TR72	Kayseri, Sivas, Yozgat
	TR82	Kastamonu, Çankırı, Sinop
	TR83	Samsun, Tokat, Çorum, Amasya
	TRA1	Erzurum, Erzincan, Bayburt
	TRB1	Malatya, Elâzığ, Bingöl, Tunceli
	TRC1	Gaziantep, Adıyaman, Kilis

Dataset 2017 is grouped to 3 clusters with k-means method and it is shown in Figure 11.
Three clusters and cluster members (level 2 statistical regions and their cities) are shown in Table 8.

Figure 10. Graphic of the average silhouette method for k-means analysis for dataset 2017

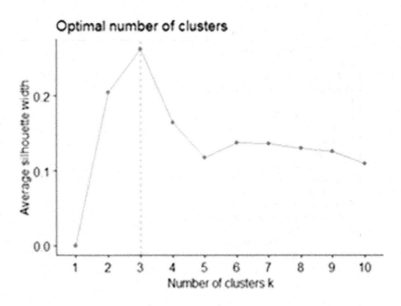

Figure 11. Dataset 2017 is grouped to 3 clusters with k-means method

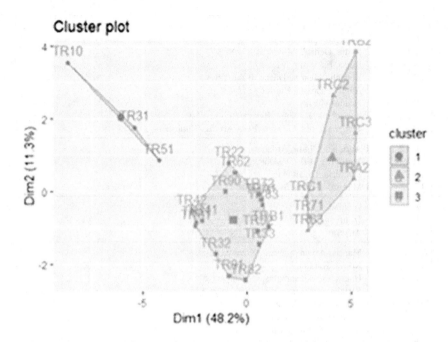

Table 8. K-means clustering of the dataset 2017 with 3 clusters

Cluster 1	TR10	İstanbul
	TR31	İzmir
	TR51	Ankara
Cluster 2	TR63	Hatay, Kahramanmaraş, Osmaniye
	TR71	Kırıkkale, Aksaray, Niğde, Nevşehir, Kırşehir
	TRA2	Ağrı, Kars, Iğdır, Ardahan
	TRB2	Van, Muş, Bitlis, Hakkari
	TRC1	Gaziantep, Adıyaman, Kilis
	TRC2	Şanlıurfa, Diyarbakır
	TRC3	Mardin, Batman, Şirnak, Siirt
Cluster 3	TR21	Tekirdağ, Edirne, Kırklareli
	TR22	Balıkesir, Çanakkale
	TR32	Aydın, Denizli, Muğla
	TR33	Manisa, Afyonkarahisar, Kütahya, Uşak
	TR41	Bursa, Eskişehir, Bilecik
	TR42	Kocaeli, Sakarya, Düzce, Bolu, Yalova
	TR52	Konya, Karaman
	TR61	Antalya, Isparta, Burdur
	TR62	Adana, Mersin
	TR72	Kayseri, Sivas, Yozgat
	TR81	Zonguldak, Karabük, Bartın
	TR82	Kastamonu, Çankırı, Sinop
	TR83	Samsun, Tokat, Çorum, Amasya
	TR90	Trabzon, Ordu, Giresun, Rize, Artvin, Gümüşhane
	TRA1	Erzurum, Erzincan, Bayburt
	TRB1	Malatya, Elâzığ, Bingöl, Tunceli

There are 3 clusters (Figure 10 and Figure 11), when it is clustered by k-means method of the dataset 2017. The Statistical Region TR10 is İstanbul which is the biggest city of Turkey, the Statistical Region TR51 is Ankara which is the capital city of Turkey and the Statistical Region TR31 is İzmir. They are grouped in the Cluster 1. Geographically, some cities of the Mediterranean Region in the TR63 region; some cities of the Central Anatolia Region in the TR71 region; some cities of the Eastern Anatolia Region in the TRA2, TRB2 regions; some cities of the Southeastern Anatolia Region in the TRC1, TRC2, TRC3 regions are grouped in the Cluster 2. Some cities of the Marmara Region in the TR21, TR22, TR41, TR42 regions; some cities of the Aegean Region in the TR32, TR33 regions; some cities of the Mediterranean Region in the TR61, TR62 regions; some cities of the Black Sea Region in the TR42, TR81, TR82, TR83, TR90, TRA1 regions; some cities of the Central Anatolia Region in the TR52, TR72, TR41, TR82 regions and some cities of the Eastern Anatolia Region in the TRA1, TRB1 are grouped in the Cluster 3.

Part Four:

Dataset of Part Four consists of combination of the "Distribution of expenditure groups according to Household Budget Survey (Horizontal %), 2015-2017, 2017", "Gini coefficient by equivalised household disposable income, 2017" and some features of "Regional Purchasing Power Parities for the main groups of consumption expenditures, 2017" which is referred as "dataset 2017". There are 23 features which are shown in the Table 3 and Level 2 Statistical Regions of Turkey (26 statistical regions) in the dataset 2017. They are clustered with k-medoids method. Elbow method and average silhouette method are used for determining the number of the clusters at the beginning. R programming language in the R-Studio is used for analyses. "Factoextra" (Kassambara & Mundt, 2017) and "Cluster" (Maechler et al., 2019) packages are used for analyses in the R.

"Pam()" function for k-medoids clustering from the "Cluster" (Maechler et al., 2019) package of the R is used for Partition Around Medoids (PAM).

Graphics of the Elbow Method is shown in Figure 12 for k-medoids clustering for dataset 2017. According to Figure 12, there is a bend (or elbow) whose location can be considered as an indicator of the convenient number of clusters at k=4. So dataset 2017 can be grouped to 4 clusters.

The dataset 2017 is grouped to 4 clusters with k-medoids method and it is shown in Figure 13 and Figure 14. Distance measures (Euclidean metric and Manhattan metric) cause difference between clustering of the dataset for dataset 2017. It is analyzed with "Pam()" function of the Cluster (Maechler et al., 2019) package in the R.

Four clusters and cluster members (level 2 statistical regions and their cities) are shown in Table 9.

There are different two results according to the distance measures which are used. Dataset is grouped to 4 clusters with k-medoids method for the dataset 2017. The Statistical Region TR10 is İstanbul which is the biggest city of Turkey, the Statistical Region TR51 is Ankara which is the capital city of Turkey and the Statistical Region TR31 is İzmir and they are grouped in the Cluster 1 for both two distance measurements, Euclidean metric and Manhattan metric. Geographically, some cities of the Marmara Region in the TR21, TR22, TR41, TR42 regions; some cities of the Aegean Region in the TR32 region; some cities of the Black Sea Region in the TR42, TR90 regions; Eskişehir is a city in the TR41 and it is in the Central Anatolia Region and they are grouped in the Cluster 2 for Euclidean metric. Some cities of the Aegean Region in the TR33 region; some cities of the Central Anatolia Region in the TR52, TR71, TR72, TR82 regions; some cities of the Mediterranean Region in the TR61, TR62, TR63 regions;

some cities of the Black Sea Region in the TR81, TR82, TR83 regions and Bayburt from the TRA1 region; some cities of the Eastern Anatolia Region in the TRA1, TRB1 regions and some cities of the Southeastern Anatolia Region in the TRC1 region are grouped in the Cluster 3 for Euclidean metric. The difference between clusters with usage of the Euclidean metric and usage of the Manhattan metric is the region TR61, whose cities are in the Mediterranean Region, is added to Cluster 2 for Manhattan metric clustering and it is also in the Cluster 3 for Euclidean metric usage. Some cities of the Eastern Anatolia Region in the TRA2, TRB2 regions; and some cities of the Southeastern Anatolia Region in the TRC2, TRC3 regions are grouped in the Cluster 4. Members of the clusters are the same with usage of the Euclidean metric and Manhattan metric, except the region TR61.

Figure 12. Graphic of the Elbow Method for k-medoids clustering for dataset 2017

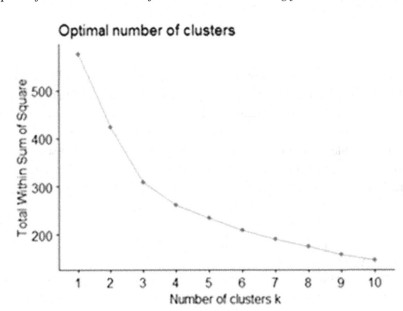

Graphic of the average silhouette method is shown in Figure 15. High average silhouette width can be considered as an indicator of the convenient number of clusters at k=2. So dataset 2017 can be grouped to 2 clusters for k-medoids method.

The dataset 2017 is grouped to 2 clusters with k-medoids method and it is shown in Figure 16.

When the dataset 2017 is grouped to 2 clusters, Cluster 1 is consisted of three regions. İstanbul is the biggest city of Turkey and it is in the Marmara Region. İstanbul constitutes The Statistical Region TR10. Ankara is the capital city of Turkey and it is in the Central Anatolia Region. Ankara constitutes The Statistical Region TR51 and the Statistical Region TR31 is İzmir and it is in the Aegean Region. They are grouped in the Cluster 1. The other Level 2 Statistical Regions, which are consisted of cities from different geographical locations of Turkey, are grouped in the Cluster 2.

Figure 13: Dataset 2017 is grouped to 4 clusters with k-medoids method (Clustering with Euclidean metric)

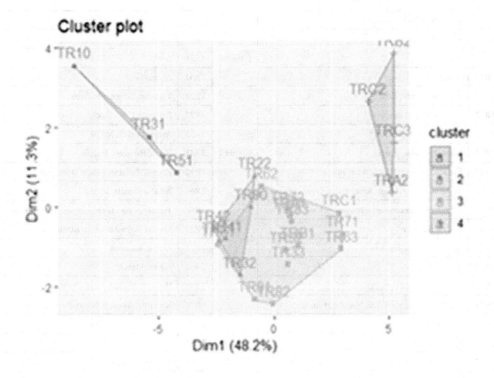

Figure 14: Dataset 2017 is grouped to 4 clusters with k-medoids method (Clustering with Manhattan metric)

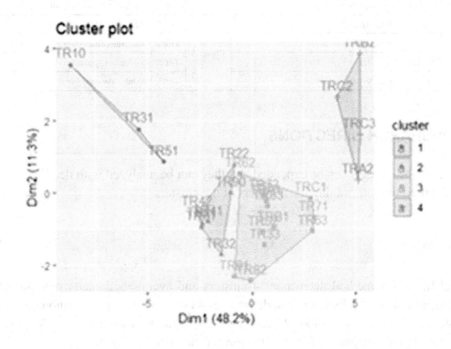

Table 9. K-medoids clustering of the dataset 2017 with 4 clusters

		Euclidean Metric				Manhattan Metric
Cluster 1	TR10	İstanbul		Cluster 1	TR10	İstanbul
	TR31	İzmir			TR31	İzmir
	TR51	Ankara			TR51	Ankara
Cluster 2	TR21	Tekirdağ, Edirne, Kırklareli		Cluster 2	TR21	Tekirdağ, Edirne, Kırklareli
	TR22	Balıkesir, Çanakkale			TR22	Balıkesir, Çanakkale
	TR32	Aydin, Denizli, Muğla			TR32	Aydin, Denizli, Muğla
	TR41	Bursa, Eskişehir, Bilecik			TR41	Bursa, Eskişehir, Bilecik
	TR42	Kocaeli, Sakarya, Düzce, Bolu, Yalova			TR42	Kocaeli, Sakarya, Düzce, Bolu, Yalova
	TR90	Trabzon, Ordu, Giresun, Rize, Artvin, Gümüşhane			TR61	Antalya, Isparta, Burdur
Cluster 3	TR33	Manisa, Afyonkarahisar, Kütahya, Uşak		Cluster 3	TR90	Trabzon, Ordu, Giresun, Rize, Artvin, Gümüşhane
	TR52	Konya, Karaman			TR33	Manisa, Afyonkarahisar, Kütahya, Uşak
	TR61	Antalya, Isparta, Burdur			TR52	Konya, Karaman
	TR62	Adana, Mersin			TR62	Adana, Mersin
	TR63	Hatay, Kahramanmaraş, Osmaniye			TR63	Hatay, Kahramanmaraş, Osmaniye
	TR71	Kırıkkale, Aksaray, Niğde, Nevşehir, Kırşehir			TR71	Kırıkkale, Aksaray, Niğde, Nevşehir, Kırşehir
	TR72	Kayseri, Sivas, Yozgat			TR72	Kayseri, Sivas, Yozgat
	TR81	Zonguldak, Karabük, Bartın			TR81	Zonguldak, Karabük, Bartın
	TR82	Kastamonu, Çankırı, Sinop			TR82	Kastamonu, Çankırı, Sinop
	TR83	Samsun, Tokat, Çorum, Amasya			TR83	Samsun, Tokat, Çorum, Amasya
	TRA1	Erzurum, Erzincan, Bayburt			TRA1	Erzurum, Erzincan, Bayburt
	TRB1	Malatya, Elâzığ, Bingöl, Tunceli			TRB1	Malatya, Elâzığ, Bingöl, Tunceli
	TRC1	Gaziantep, Adıyaman, Kilis			TRC1	Gaziantep, Adıyaman, Kilis
Cluster 4	TRA2	Ağrı, Kars, Iğdır, Ardahan		Cluster 4	TRA2	Ağrı, Kars, Iğdır, Ardahan
	TRB2	Van, Muş, Bitlis, Hakkari			TRB2	Van, Muş, Bitlis, Hakkari
	TRC2	Şanlıurfa, Diyarbakır			TRC2	Şanlıurfa, Diyarbakır
	TRC3	Mardin, Batman, Şırnak, Siirt			TRC3	Mardin, Batman, Şırnak, Siirt

FUTURE RESEARCH DIRECTIONS

In further studies, the datasets can be expanded and they can be analyzed with detailed datasets. Other methods can be used for determining the numbers of the clusters.

CONCLUSION

For dataset 2018; elbow method determines 4 clusters and average silhouette method determines 2 clusters for k-means method. Elbow method determines 4 clusters and average silhouette method determines 4 clusters for k-medoids method. When the results of the k-means and k-medoids for 4 clusters are compared, there are changes of cluster of the cluster members.

Figure 15. Graphic of the average silhouette method for k-medoids clustering for dataset 2017

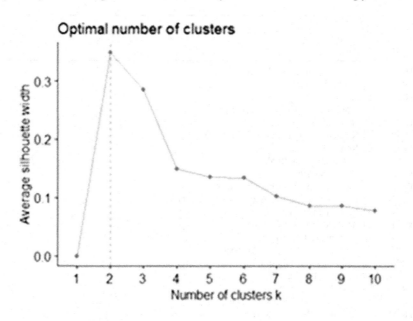

Figure 16. Dataset 2017 is grouped to 2 clusters with k-medoids method

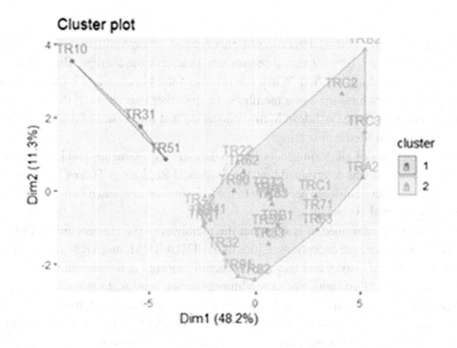

Table 10. K-medoids clustering of the dataset 2017 with 2 clusters

Cluster 1	TR10	İstanbul
	TR31	İzmir
	TR51	Ankara
Cluster 2	TR21	Tekirdağ, Edirne, Kırklareli
	TR22	Balıkesir, Çanakkale
	TR32	Aydin, Denizli, Muğla
	TR33	Manisa, Afyonkarahisar, Kütahya, Uşak
	TR41	Bursa, Eskişehir, Bilecik
	TR42	Kocaeli, Sakarya, Düzce, Bolu, Yalova
	TR52	Konya, Karaman
	TR61	Antalya, Isparta, Burdur
	TR62	Adana, Mersin
	TR63	Hatay, Kahramanmaraş, Osmaniye
	TR71	Kırıkkale, Aksaray, Niğde, Nevşehir, Kırşehir
	TR72	Kayseri, Sivas, Yozgat
	TR81	Zonguldak, Karabük, Bartın
	TR82	Kastamonu, Çankırı, Sinop
	TR83	Samsun, Tokat, Çorum, Amasya
	TR90	Trabzon, Ordu, Giresun, Rize, Artvin, Gümüşhane
	TRA1	Erzurum, Erzincan, Bayburt
	TRA2	Ağrı, Kars, Iğdır, Ardahan
	TRB1	Malatya, Elâzığ, Bingöl, Tunceli
	TRB2	Van, Muş, Bitlis, Hakkari
	TRC1	Gaziantep, Adıyaman, Kilis
	TRC2	Şanlıurfa, Diyarbakır
	TRC3	Mardin, Batman, Şırnak, Siirt

For dataset 2017; elbow method determines 4 clusters and average silhouette method determines 3 clusters for k-means method. Elbow method determines 4 clusters and average silhouette method determines 2 clusters for k-medoids method. When the results of the k-means and k-medoids for 4 clusters are compared two clusters have the same members. In the other two clusters; the cluster of the three cluster members changes in the Euclidean Metric clustering and the cluster of the two cluster members changes in the Manhattan Metric clustering.

In the study, the results of clustering according to datasets with k-means and k-medoids are shown. According to the results, it was determined how the Statistical Regions of Turkey in the Level 2 regions and therefore the cities were clustered according to the information contained in the datasets. Clustering results were compared and evaluated.

When the clusters are examined, it is seen that the members of the clusters are partially geographically close even though there are exceptions. Cities of the TR10, TR51, and TR31 regions are in the high level development cities of Turkey and they were generally located in the same cluster.

Datasets consist of the "Distribution of expenditure groups according to Household Budget Survey", "Gini coefficient by equivalised household disposable income" and some features of "Regional Purchasing Power Parities for the main groups of consumption expenditures" topics, so results of the cluster analyses may assessable in determining economic policies or in determining investment policies.

REFERENCES

Ahi, L. (2015). *Veri Madenciliği Yöntemleri İle Ana Harcama Gruplarının Paylarının Tahmini* [Estimation Of Main Expenditure Groups' Portion With Data Mining Methods] (Unpublished master's thesis). Hacettepe Üniversitesi Fen Bilimleri Enstitüsü.

Akkuş, B., & Zontul, M. (2019). Veri Madenciliği Yöntemleri ile Ülkeleri Gelişmişlik Ölçütlerine Göre Kümeleme Üzerine Bir Uygulama [An Application On Clustering Countries With Data Mining Methods Based On Development Criteria]. *AURUM Mühendislik Sistemleri ve Mimarlık Dergisi, 3*(1), 51–64.

Bakırcı, F., Ekinci, E. D., & Şahinoğlu, T. (2014). Bölgesel kalkınma politikalarının etkinliği: Türkiye alt bölgeler bazında bir uygulama [The Effectiveness of Regional Development Policies: An Application on Sub-Regions of Turkey]. *Atatürk Üniversitesi Sosyal Bilimler Enstitüsü Dergisi, 18*(2), 281–298.

Banerjee, A., Merugu, S., Dhillon, I. S., & Ghosh, J. (2005). Clustering with Bregman divergences. *Journal of Machine Learning Research, 6*, 1705–1749.

Barioni, M. C. N., Razente, H. L., Traina, A. J., & Traina, C. Jr. (2008). Accelerating k-medoid-based algorithms through metric access methods. *Journal of Systems and Software, 81*(3), 343–355. doi:10.1016/j.jss.2007.06.019

Bhat, A. (2014). K-medoids clustering using partitioning around medoids for performing face recognition. *International Journal of Soft Computing. Mathematics and Control, 3*(3), 1–12.

Bulut, H. (2019). Türkiye'deki İllerin Yaşam Endekslerine Göre Kümelenmesi [The Clustering of Cities in Turkey According to Indexes of Life Satisfaction]. *Süleyman Demirel Üniversitesi Fen Bilimleri Enstitüsü Dergisi, 23*(1), 74–82. doi:10.19113dufenbed.444143

Çalmaşur, G., & Kılıç, A. (2018). Türkiye'de Hanehalkı Tüketim Harcamalarının Analizi [Analysis Of Household Consumption Expenditures in Turkey]. *Erzurum Teknik Üniversitesi Sosyal Bilimler Enstitüsü Dergisi, 3*(5), 61–73.

Deb, C., & Lee, S. E. (2018). Determining key variables influencing energy consumption in office buildings through cluster analysis of pre-and post-retrofit building data. *Energy and Building, 159*, 228–245. doi:10.1016/j.enbuild.2017.11.007

Değirmenci, T., & Özbakır, L. (2018). Differentiating households to analyze consumption patterns: A data mining study on official household budget data. *Wiley Interdisciplinary Reviews. Data Mining and Knowledge Discovery, 8*(1), e1227. doi:10.1002/widm.1227

Dichev, C., & Dicheva, D. (2017). Towards data science literacy. *Procedia Computer Science, 108C*, 2151–2160. doi:10.1016/j.procs.2017.05.240

Dikmen, F. C. (2018). Investigation of Well-Being and Quality of Life of The Turkish Provinces by Clustering Analysis [Türkiye'dekı İllerin İyi Oluş Ve Yaşam Kalitesinin Kümeleme Çözümlemesiyle İncelenmesi]. In F. B. Candan & H. Kapucu (Eds.), Current Debates in Business Studies: Current Debates in Social Sciences (Vol. 15, p. 169). Academic Press.

Erdaş, H., Erdoğan, S., & Erdoğan, A. (2017). Türkiye'de Hane Halkı Tüketim Harcamalarının Belirley-icileri [Determinants Of Households Consumption Expenditure In Turkey]. *Trakya Üniversitesi İktisadi ve İdari Bilimler Fakültesi Dergisi, 6*(1), 309–326.

Eurostat. (2019). https://ec.europa.eu/eurostat/web/nuts/history

Gibert, K., Horsburgh, J. S., Athanasiadis, I. N., & Holmes, G. (2018). Environmental data science. *Environmental Modelling & Software, 106*, 4–12. doi:10.1016/j.envsoft.2018.04.005

Giray, S., Yorulmaz, Ö., & Ergüt, Ö. (2016). Classification Of The Countries By Fuzzy And Robust Cluster Methods Based On Gini Coefficient, Migration, Crime And Happiness Factors. *Journal of Awareness, 1*(2), 1–16.

Han, J., Kamber, M., & Pei, J. (2011). *Data mining concepts and techniques* (3rd ed.). Elsevier.

Jain, A. K. (2010). Data clustering: 50 years beyond K-means. *Pattern Recognition Letters, 31*(8), 651–666. doi:10.1016/j.patrec.2009.09.011

Jin, Y., & Sendhoff, B. (2004). Reducing Fitness Evaluations Using Clustering Techniques and Neural Network Ensembles. In K. Deb (Ed.), Lecture Notes in Computer Science: Vol. 3102. *Genetic and Evolutionary Computation – GECCO 2004. GECCO 2004.* Springer. doi:10.1007/978-3-540-24854-5_71

Jörnsten, R. (2004). Clustering and classification based on the L1 data depth. *Journal of Multivariate Analysis, 90*(1), 67–89. doi:10.1016/j.jmva.2004.02.013

Kashima, H., Hu, J., Ray, B., & Singh, M. (2008, December). K-means clustering of proportional data using L1 distance. In *2008 19th International Conference on Pattern Recognition* (pp. 1-4). IEEE. 10.1109/ICPR.2008.4760982

Kassambara, A. (2017). *Practical guide to cluster analysis in R: Unsupervised machine learning* (Vol. 1). STHDA.

Kassambara, A., & Mundt, F. (2017). *factoextra: Extract and Visualize the Results of Multivariate Data Analyses. R package version 1.0.5.* https://CRAN.R-project.org/package=factoextra

Kaufman, L., & Rousseeuw, P. J. (1990). *Finding groups in data: An introduction to cluster analysis.* Wiley. doi:10.1002/9780470316801

Kaur, N. K., Kaur, U., & Singh, D. D. (2014). K-Medoid clustering algorithm-a review. *International Journal of Computer Applications in Technology, 1*(1), 2349–1841.

Kayalak, S., & Kiper, T. (2006, May). İstatistiki Bölge Birimleri Nomenklatörü'ne (NUTS) Göre, Türkiye'de Bölgesel Farklılıklar [Regional Differences in Turkey According to NUTS]. In *Proceedings of IV. Ulusal Coğrafya Sempozyumu*, (pp. 45-54). Ankara Üniversitesi Türkiye Cografyası Arastırma ve Uygulama Merkezi (TÜCAUM).

Khan, S. S., & Ahmad, A. (2004). Cluster center initialization algorithm for K-means clustering. *Pattern Recognition Letters, 25*(11), 1293–1302. doi:10.1016/j.patrec.2004.04.007

Khatami, A., Mirghasemi, S., Khosravi, A., Lim, C. P., & Nahavandi, S. (2017). A new PSO-based approach to fire flame detection using K-Medoids clustering. *Expert Systems with Applications*, *68*, 69–80. doi:10.1016/j.eswa.2016.09.021

Lai, S., & Fu, H. C. (2011). Variance enhanced K-medoid clustering. *Expert Systems with Applications*, *38*(1), 764–775. doi:10.1016/j.eswa.2010.07.030

Linde, Y., Buzo, A., & Gray, R. (1980). An algorithm for vector quantizer design. *IEEE Transactions on Communications*, *28*(1), 84–95. doi:10.1109/TCOM.1980.1094577

Liu, G., Yang, J., Hao, Y., & Zhang, Y. (2018). Big data-informed energy efficiency assessment of China industry sectors based on K-means clustering. *Journal of Cleaner Production*, *183*, 304–314. doi:10.1016/j.jclepro.2018.02.129

Loohach, R., & Garg, K. (2012). Effect of distance functions on k-means clustering algorithm. *International Journal of Computers and Applications*, *49*(6), 7–9. doi:10.5120/7629-0698

Madhulatha, T. S. (2011). Comparison between K-Means and K-Medoids Clustering Algorithms. In D. C. Wyld, M. Wozniak, N. Chaki, N. Meghanathan, & D. Nagamalai (Eds.), *Advances in Computing and Information Technology. ACITY 2011. Communications in Computer and Information Science* (Vol. 198). Springer. doi:10.1007/978-3-642-22555-0_48

Maechler, M., Rousseeuw, P., Struyf, A., Hubert, M., & Hornik, K. (2019). *Cluster Analysis Basics and Extensions*. R package version 2.0.8.

Mao, J., & Jain, A. K. (1996). A self-organizing network for hyperellipsoidal clustering (HEC). *IEEE Transactions on Neural Networks*, *7*(1), 16–29. doi:10.1109/72.478389 PMID:18255555

Metadata. (2018). Regional Purchasing Power Parities for the main groups of consumption expenditures. Retrieved from https://biruni.tuik.gov.tr/bolgeselistatistik/metaVeriEkle.do?durum=metaGetir&menuNo=457

Metadata. (2019a). *Distribution of expenditure groups according to Household Budget Survey (Horizontal %), 2016-2018*. Retrieved from https://biruni.tuik.gov.tr/bolgeselistatistik/metaVeriEkle.do?durum=metaGetir&menuNo=422

Metadata. (2019b). *Distribution of expenditure groups according to Household Budget Survey (Horizontal %), 2015-2017*. Retrieved from https://biruni.tuik.gov.tr/bolgeselistatistik/metaVeriEkle.do?durum=metaGetir&menuNo=530

Metadata. (2019c). *Gini coefficient by equivalised household disposable income*. https://biruni.tuik.gov.tr/bolgeselistatistik/metaVeriEkle.do?durum=metaGetir&menuNo=515

Molina-Solana, M., Ros, M., Ruiz, M. D., Gómez-Romero, J., & Martín-Bautista, M. J. (2017). Data science for building energy management: A review. *Renewable & Sustainable Energy Reviews*, *70*, 598–609. doi:10.1016/j.rser.2016.11.132

Ng, R. T., & Han, J. (1994, September). Efficient and Effective clustering methods for spatial data mining. In *Proceedings of VLDB* (pp. 144-155). Academic Press.

Ng, R. T., & Han, J. (2002). CLARANS: A method for clustering objects for spatial data mining. *IEEE Transactions on Knowledge and Data Engineering, 14*(5), 1003–1016. doi:10.1109/TKDE.2002.1033770

Özarı, Ö. Ü. Ç., & Eren, Ö. Ü. Ö. (2018). İllerin Yaşam Endeksi Göstergelerinin Çok Boyutlu Ölçekleme ve K-ortalamalar Kümeleme Yöntemi ile Analizi [Life Index of Proviences in Turkey Via Multidimensional Scaling and K-Means Clustering]. Afyon Kocatepe Üniversitesi Sosyal Bilimler Dergisi, 20(2), 303-313.

Özçağlar, A. (2003). Türkiye'de Yapılan Bölge Ayrımları Ve Bölge Planlama Üzerindeki Etkileri [The Region Divisions in Turkey and Its Effects on Regional Planning]. *Coğrafi Bilimler Dergisi, 1*(1), 3–18.

Özdemir, O., & Demir, İ. (2019). Data Mining of SILC Data: Turkey Case. *International Journal of Sciences:Basic and Applied Research, 48*(7), 110–138.

Park, H. S., & Jun, C. H. (2009). A simple and fast algorithm for K-medoids clustering. *Expert Systems with Applications, 36*(2), 3336–3341. doi:10.1016/j.eswa.2008.01.039

Park, H. S., Lee, J. S., & Jun, C. H. (2006). A K-means-like Algorithm for K-medoids Clustering and Its Performance. *Proceedings of ICCIE*, 102-117.

Paterlini, A. A., Nascimento, M. A., & Traina, C. Jr. (2011). Using pivots to speed-up k-medoids clustering. *Journal of Information and Data Management, 2*(2), 221–236.

Pham, D. T., Dimov, S. S., & Nguyen, C. D. (2005). Selection of K in K-means clustering. *Proceedings of the Institution of Mechanical Engineers. Part C, Journal of Mechanical Engineering Science, 219*(1), 103–119. doi:10.1243/095440605X8298

R Core Team. (2019). *R: A language and environment for statistical computing*. R Foundation for Statistical Computing. https://www.R-project.org/

Redmond, S. J., & Heneghan, C. (2007). A method for initialising the K-means clustering algorithm using kd-trees. *Pattern Recognition Letters, 28*(8), 965–973. doi:10.1016/j.patrec.2007.01.001

Reynolds, A. P., Richards, G., & Rayward-Smith, V. J. (2004). The Application of K-Medoids and PAM to the Clustering of Rules. In Z. R. Yang, H. Yin, & R. M. Everson (Eds.), Lecture Notes in Computer Science: Vol. 3177. *Intelligent Data Engineering and Automated Learning – IDEAL 2004. IDEAL 2004.* Springer. doi:10.1007/978-3-540-28651-6_25

Rousseeuw, P. J. (1987). Silhouettes: A graphical aid to the interpretation and validation of cluster analysis. *Journal of Computational and Applied Mathematics, 20*, 53–65. doi:10.1016/0377-0427(87)90125-7

Secgin, S., & Dalkilic, G. (2017). A Decision Support System Using Demographic Issues: A Case Study in Turkey. *The International Arab Journal of Information Technology, 14*(3).

Şengül, Ü., Shiraz, S. E., & Eren, M. (2013). Türkiye'de İstatistikî Bölge Birimleri Sınıflamasına Göre Düzey 2 Bölgelerinin Ekonomik Etkinliklerinin VZA Yöntemi ile Belirlenmesi ve Tobit Model Uygulaması [Economic Activities of Regions of Level 2 According to Statistical Regional Units Classification (NUTS) in Turkey Determining by Using DEA and Tobit Model Application]. *Yönetim Bilimleri Dergisi, 11*(21), 75–99.

Sheng, W., & Liu, X. (2006). A genetic k-medoids clustering algorithm. *Journal of Heuristics*, *12*(6), 447–466. doi:10.100710732-006-7284-z

T.C. Millî Eğitim Bakanliği Konaklama ve Seyahat Hizmetleri. (2013). *Turizm Coğrafyasi 1 (tourism geography 1)*. Retrieved from http://megep.meb.gov.tr/mte_program_modul/moduller_pdf/Turizm%20 Co%C4%9Frafyas%C4%B1-%201.pdf

T.C. Millî Eğitim Bakanliği Konaklama ve Seyahat Hizmetleri. (2013). *Turizm Coğrafyasi 2 (tourism geography 2)*. Retrieved from http://megep.meb.gov.tr/mte_program_modul/moduller_pdf/Turizm%20 Co%C4%9Frafyas%C4%B1%20-2.pdf

The Official Gazette of the Republic of Turkey. (2002). Retrieved from https://www.resmigazete.gov.tr/ eskiler/2002/09/20020922.htm#3

Topbaş, F., & Unat, E. (2018). Gelir Ve Tüketim İlişkisinin İstikrarı: Harcama Gruplarına Ve Zamana Göre Kantil Regresyon Modelden Kanıtlar [The Stability Of The Income And Consumption Relationship: Evidence From The Quantile Regression Model According To Expenditure Groups And Time] *Izmir Democracy University Social Sciences Journal*, *1*(2), 103–126.

Uysal, F. N., Ersöz, T., & Ersöz, F. (2017). Türkiye'deki İllerin Yaşam Endeksinin Çok Değişkenli İstatistik Yöntemlerle İncelenmesi [Analysis By Multivariate Statistical Methods Of Life Index Of Provinces In Turkey]. *Ekonomi Bilimleri Dergisi*, *9*(1), 49–65.

Velmurugan, T. (2012). Efficiency of k-means and k-medoids algorithms for clustering arbitrary data points. *Int. J. Computer Technology and Application*, *3*(5), 1758–1764.

Velmurugan, T., & Santhanam, T. (2010). Computational complexity between K-means and K-medoids clustering algorithms for normal and uniform distributions of data points. *Journal of Computational Science*, *6*(3), 363–368. doi:10.3844/jcssp.2010.363.368

Velmurugan, T., & Santhanam, T. (2011). A survey of partition based clustering algorithms in data mining: An experimental approach. *Information Technology Journal*, *10*(3), 478–484. doi:10.3923/ itj.2011.478.484

Wu, X., Kumar, V., Quinlan, J. R., Ghosh, J., Yang, Q., Motoda, H., McLachlan, G. J., Ng, A., Liu, B., Yu, P. S., Zhou, Z. H., Steinbach, M., Hand, D. J., & Steinberg, D. (2008). Top 10 algorithms in data mining. *Knowledge and Information Systems*, *14*(1), 1–37. doi:10.100710115-007-0114-2

Yıldırım, H. (2018). Comparison of Provinces of Turkey In Terms of Accessing Health Care Services by Using Different Clustering Algorithms. *Eskişehir Technical University Journal of Science and Technology A-Applied Sciences and Engineering*, *19*(4), 907–925.

Yu, D., Liu, G., Guo, M., & Liu, X. (2018). An improved K-medoids algorithm based on step increasing and optimizing medoids. *Expert Systems with Applications*, *92*, 464–473. doi:10.1016/j.eswa.2017.09.052

Yu, S. S., Chu, S. W., Wang, C. M., Chan, Y. K., & Chang, T. C. (2018). Two improved k-means algorithms. *Applied Soft Computing*, *68*, 747–755. doi:10.1016/j.asoc.2017.08.032

Zadegan, S. M. R., Mirzaie, M., & Sadoughi, F. (2013). Ranked k-medoids: A fast and accurate rank-based partitioning algorithm for clustering large datasets. *Knowledge-Based Systems*, *39*, 133–143. doi:10.1016/j.knosys.2012.10.012

Žalik, K. R. (2008). An efficient k′-means clustering algorithm. *Pattern Recognition Letters*, *29*(9), 1385–1391. doi:10.1016/j.patrec.2008.02.014

Zhang, Y., Moges, S., & Block, P. (2016). Optimal cluster analysis for objective regionalization of seasonal precipitation in regions of high spatial–temporal variability: Application to Western Ethiopia. *Journal of Climate*, *29*(10), 3697–3717. doi:10.1175/JCLI-D-15-0582.1

Zhu, Q., Pei, J., Liu, X., & Zhou, Z. (2019). Analyzing commercial aircraft fuel consumption during descent: A case study using an improved K-means clustering algorithm. *Journal of Cleaner Production*, *223*, 869–882. doi:10.1016/j.jclepro.2019.02.235

KEY TERMS AND DEFINITIONS

Cluster Analysis (Clustering): It is used to separate the data into groups with using different techniques.

Geographical Regions of Turkey: There are 7 geographical regions of Turkey. They are determined by their features.

K-Means Algorithm: It is an algorithm that is used for cluster analysis.

K-Medoids Algorithm: It is an algorithm that is using medoids for cluster analysis.

Statistical Regions of Turkey in Level 1: Level 1 is one of the types of Statistical Regions of Turkey and it consists of 12 regions. They are produced by grouping Level 2 regions.

Statistical Regions of Turkey in Level 2: Level 2 is one of the types of Statistical Regions of Turkey and it consists of 26 regions. They are produced by grouping Level 3 regions.

Statistical Regions of Turkey in Level 3: Level 3 is one of the types of Statistical Regions of Turkey. It consists of 81 cities of Turkey.

Chapter 25
Descriptive Data Analytics on Dinesafe Data for Food Assessment and Evaluation Using R Programming Language:
A Case Study on Toronto's Dinesafe Inspection and Disclosure System

Ajinkya Kunjir

iD https://orcid.org/0000-0001-7634-4115
Lakehead University, Canada

Jugal Shah
Lakehead University, Canada

Vikas Trikha
Lakehead University, Canada

ABSTRACT

In the digital era of the 21st century, data analytics (DA) can be highlighted as 'finding conclusions based on observations' or unique knowledge discovery from data (KDD) in form of patterns and visualizations for ease of understanding. The city of Toronto consists of thousands of food chains, restaurants, bars based all over the streets of the city. Dinesafe is an agency-based inspection system monitored by the provincial and municipal regulations and ran by the Ministry of Health, Ontario. This chapter proposes an efficient descriptive data analytics on the Dinesafe data provided by the Health Ministry of Toronto, Ontario using an open-source data programming framework like R. The data is publicly available for all the researchers and motivates the practitioners for conveying the results to the ministry for betterment of the people of Toronto. The chapter will also shed light on the methodology, visualization, types and share the results from the work executed on R.

DOI: 10.4018/978-1-7998-3053-5.ch025

INTRODUCTION

Data science can be generally explained as a lifecycle of data gathering, preparation, transformation and pattern generation to achieve milestones. The data collected has many dependencies starting from time, space and complexity. Big Data and Advanced deep learning are the two rapidly growing areas of research and advances. Hence, there is a need to construct or modernize the process that resolves and addresses current challenges in the data development and deployment cycle. Several concepts about data science have been derived by the multinational companies dealing with massive chunks of data in everyday life. Data measurable in TeraBytes (Tb's), Petabytes (Pb's), and Zettabytes are being generated by social media sites such as Facebook, Twitter, and LinkedIn daily. The data collected is unstructured or semi-structured as it comprises images, audio, documents and all other media. The goal is a business outcome rather than improving a measure of accuracy on a specific analytic model. Operational Big Data analytics or systems implementing Operational Big Data Analytics (BDA's) introduce a plethora of difficulties and challenges due to the data distribution, novel approach(s) and partnership with other multiple organizations that are using cloud services (Nancy W. Grady et.al, 2017). Where Big Data is booming in the field of analytics, the decision-making flows along with it. There are four types of analytics to start with: Descriptive Analysis, Diagnostic analytics, Predictive Analytics, and Prescriptive analytics. The more complicated the analytics is, the more value it holds. For instance, to deal with our data in this research, the authors will be going forward with descriptive analytics. Descriptive analytics deal with the question 'What Happened? Descriptive analytics mostly juggles data from multiple sources to deduce insights into the past. The patterns generated simply signal that is something right or wrong, without a proper explanation. With the 'Dinesafe' data, the authors are going to find out 'what happened with what?' for the current and past few years (2017 & 2018). The following questions are to be investigated in this research

- What was the severity of food establishment in 2017, 2018 and 2019?
- How has the progress been from 2017 to 2019?
- How many Food establishments types have a minimum number of inspections = '1/2/3'?
- The ratio of a pass, conditional pass and Closed for all food establishments in 2017, 2018 & 2019?

There may be many more questions arising by looking at the dataset, but we are just going to showcase the ones that have a high impact on the viewers.

Existing System

The current work executed on Dinesafe is reported and embedded in the Toronto Health safe website as an application with inputs. The work is illustrated in the form of a map representation pointing at all the current food establishments according to their result flags such as Pass(In Green), conditional pass (Yellow) and closed (In red). The web application can be queried by the end users and return outputs based on the inputs they feed to the fields. Currently, the app can accept 'Postal code' and 'Food establishment Name' from the end-users and represent the output on the map itself. The existing system is worthy of producing the immediate results to the users but lacks prediction, descriptions and comparative analysis between the years. The lacuna of the current system can be filled in by adding informative layers of technology to the Dinesafe data, elaborated in the next few sections.

Proposed Work

The authors propose efficient data analytics in the form of a pattern generation from the Dinesafe Data picked up from the Open Data library of Toronto City. Dinesafe is the local Toronto Food and inspection agency that has a list of inspecting all the food and drink establishment and rating it as pass, conditional pass and closed (If an establishment has crucial laybacks and court notice). The visualization and analysis displayed on the City's health website are compact and fail to give a wholesome analytical picture. The comparison from the past years is not shown and coded in the system. The system truly displays statistics from the latest inspection data. The authors emphasize analyzing the Dinesafe data ranging from the year 2016-2019 and derive conclusions in the form of patterns for subtle analytics using an R programming language for Data Analytics. The data does not qualify for predictive analytics as it lacks numerical data in any columns but can be transformed into a well available dataset for prediction. For a temporary basis, the data can be loaded in for descriptive analytics and methods such as Clustering and Association rules can be run over the data. More details about Dinesafe, Data and Descriptive Analytics is explained in the later sections.

R: Programming Language

'R' is a statistical computing tool very popularly used by data practitioners to visualize and study data graphs on a wide scale. One can pique their appetite by introducing machine learning techniques on R platform. 'R' is an open-source FOSS (Free and Open-source Software) platform to deal with huge data chunks affiliated with statistical computing. Due to its flexible and convertible nature, R can blend in with all data formats and readily adapt to the tribbles. The Machine learning tutorial for 'R' presented & published in 2018 at the first International Conference on Artificial Intelligence for Industries explained Data Manipulation in 'R' and R-studio (Joseph R. Barr, 2018).

Apart from being flexible, 'R' is a procedural and object-oriented language that consists of a family of appended packages and libraries. The foundation of 'R' is based on native data structures such as arrays, vectors, matrices, lists and others of relevance. Being an Interpreted language, standardized notations with generic functions help coding tasks and code comprehensions. For example, let's consider a simple generic command – Summary (dataset_name): Here 'dataset_name' is a standardized object and is expected to represent a return value/ result for the query fired. Here's the quick list of 'R' commands enlisted in the table given below:

The specific packages used for this research are ggplot2(), tidyverse(), Shiny(), RMySql(), tidyr() and dev tools(). We won't dig deep at explaining the packages as many web sources are giving out a brief description of all the packages mentioned in the above table.

Dinesafe Canada

Dinesafe is the name of an inspection system based on Provincial and Municipal regulations. Based on the Ontario food Premises regulations, Ontario's health board is required to assess and evaluate the conditions of any food establishments. The Ministry of Health gives a direct order to every board of health. Dinesafe Inspection agency has to follow some rules and regulations to identify the risk levels associated with the establishments. Every food and drink establishment in Ontario, Canada or Toronto to be subject-specific has 3 defined risk levels as High, medium, low. All food establishments receive a minimum of 1, 2 or 3 at max agency inspections every year by Dinesafe. Therefore, Dinesafe can be defined as a health food inspection agency that conducts food checks for processing, hygiene, food volume, and quality control.

Table 1. Packages in 'R'

PACKAGE CATEGORY	PACKAGE NAME	COMMAND	PURPOSE
To Load Data	DBI	Install.packages("DBI")	Package that connects R to relational databases
	RMySQL	Install.packages("RMySQL")	If you'd like to read data from MySQL
	XLConnect, foreign	Install. Packages("XLConnect","foreign")	Read and export data from Excel and SAS dataset
To Manipulate Data	Dplyr	Install.packages("dplyr")	Fast data manipulation package for joining, summarizing and rearranging data
	Tidyr	Install.packages("tidyr")	Data layout changing tool. Gather and spread operations at ease
	Stringr	Install.packages("stringr")	Easy learning tool for regular expressions character strings
To Visualize Data	Ggplot2	Install.packages("ggplot2")	Package for building beautiful graphics
	Ggvis	Install.packages("ggvis")	Interactive web based graphics built with grammar
	Rgl	Install.packages("rgl")	3D Visualizations
	Leaflet, DT, dygraphs, threeJS	Install.Packages("Leaflet","threeJS","dygraphs")	Interactive 3D visualization tools
To Model Data	Mgvc	Install.Packages("mgvc")	Generalize Addictive Models
	randomForest	Install.Packages("randomForest")	Random forest methods from machine learning
	Multcomp	Install.Packages("multcomp")	Comparing multiple objects
	survival	Install.Packages("survival")	For survival analysis
To Report Results	Shiny	Install.Packages("Shiny")	Shiny tool makes interactive web tools leading in an innovative way to explore data
	R Markdown	Install.Packages("markdown")	Write R code in the report and when render the report, generate the exact results and export it as pdf, HTMl file, MS word
	Xtable	Install.Packages("xtable")	Package allows you to take an object and return the latex/HTML code.
High Performance Code	Rcpp	Install.Packages("Rcpp")	Write R functions that call C++ code for fast speed
	Parallel	Install.Packages("parallel")	Using parallel processing to speed up code or crunch data
To work with web	XML	Install.Packages("XML")	Read or create XML documents with R
	jsonlite	Install.Packages("jsonlite")	Read or create JSON tables with R
To write your own R packages	Devtools	Install.Packages("devtools")	An essential tools for turning your code into R package
	testthat	Install.Packages("testthat")	Provides an easy way to write unit test for code projects

Table 2. Dinesafe Risk Assessment

Risk Level	Risk Assessment Criteria	Minimum Inspections
High	Criteria for any food establishment are involved in toxic or hazardous food preparation, meeting at least one or many of the following criteria: · Serve a high-risk population · Processes undertaken leading to food illness	3 times a year
Moderate	Criteria for any food establishment: · Prepare hazardous food without meeting the criteria for high risk · Prepare food with extensive handling/ high volume	2 times a year
Low	Criteria for any food establishment: · Serve pre-packaged hazardous food · Food storage facility used for non-hazardous food only	Minimum of One time a year

Adding up to the Risk assessment criteria, there are three types of infractions developed under the DineSafe food Safety Inspection and Disclosure program. These infractions possibly cover all requirements stated under the Ontario Food Premises Regulation.

1. Minor Infraction: The types of infractions that possess minimum risks. Examples include cracked walls, liquid on the floor, equipment repair, hair constraints not worn, and inadequate services.
2. Significant Infraction: The impact of these infractions is much higher than Minor offences but less than the crucial infractions. Appropriate care should be taken and corrected in 12-48 hours after inspection. Examples include Repair of refrigeration, lack of hand wash, garbage

Leak, not enough sanitization, uncleaned washrooms and inadequate supplies in the establishment.

3. Crucial Infraction: Such Infractions present an immediate health hazard and involve food contamination, lack of safe water and other health hazards. Examples include No water running from taps, sewage backup, lack of safe water and adulterated food. Food establishment with crucial infractions can be penalized for a significant amount and can also be dragged to court for not following the OFP regulations.

The web source 'https://www.toronto.ca/health/dinesafe/system.htm' describes more about the Reporting and Disclosure of Dinesafe Canada. The reporting and disclosure system is just about indicating if the food establishment inspected has passed or failed the inspection exam. Besides pass and fail, there is also a conditional pass notice issued when one or more significant infractions are observed during an inspection.

If taken into consideration the current statistics for the Dinesafe Inspection system for the year i.e, 2019 September (Current Month), the real-time application embedded in Toronto's city site displays the diagrammatic visualization for all the food establishments located in Toronto City. Below given is a quick snapshot of the users residing in the city site.

End users living in Toronto or any other city in Canada can view the result status such as pass, conditional pass, closed and multiple establishments by entering a specific Pincode or using the location GPS of the device (Nearby locations). The search can be narrowed down by searching via Establishment Name, Establishment address or both at once.

Figure 1. Quick Map view of the result status for establishments in Toronto

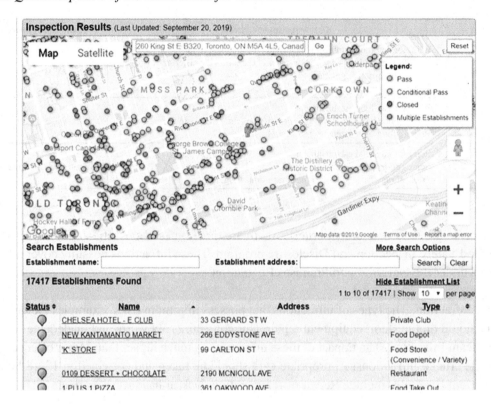

Figure 2: Search Provisions by Establishment Name and Address

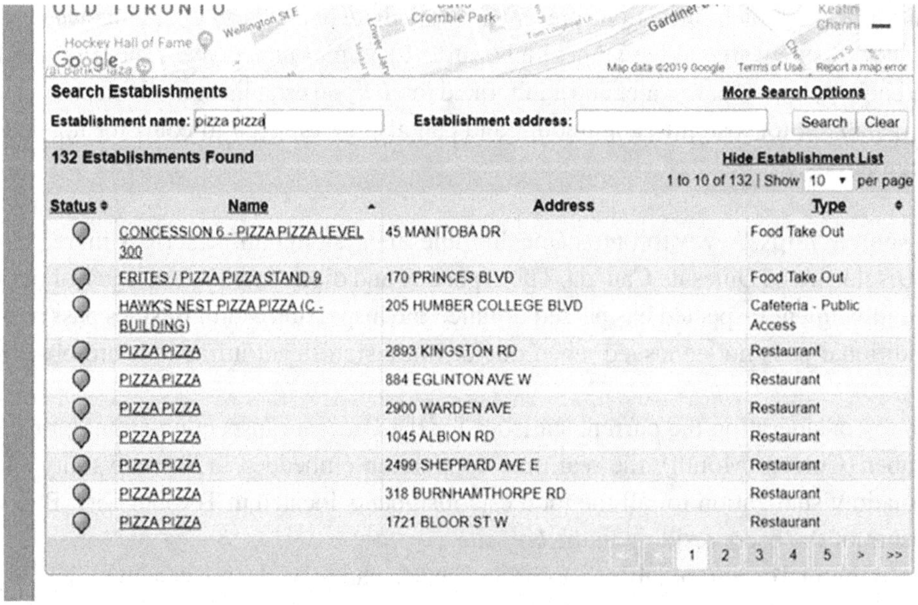

According to the Evaluation report in the year 2002, it was concluded that the Food inspection program hosted by the City was valued by the most food premises operators, public health inspectors and food owners. All the acts and trends were positive and determined improvement in food safety in Toronto. The end-users were feeling better and safe of the food and establishment ambience. All indicators point to a successful implementation of the program, and there is strong support for continuance. The health inspection program's investment had and should continue to yield significant results (Food Evaluation Report, 2002).

The authors in their research 'Dinesafe Toronto: An Evaluation of the Placard System' described their research work on the Dinesafe Data for the year 2004-2016. The data was divided into two time periods, 2004-2006 and the other one 2012-2014. The data were analyzed using a two-sample T-test (Anya Besharah et.al, 2015). The results obtained showed the drop of violations for the second frame (p =0.85). After a successful inspection, the research showed that the second data frame (2012-2014) had higher violations than the first one (2004-2006). The proposed research on Dinesafe data focuses on the data frame for the year 2016-2019 (Current year). Apart from obtaining p-values, means and standard deviations, the authors are going to perform descriptive mining on the data and embed the visualizations in a shiny web application.

Enhancing and Improving the Existing System

The existing system at the City's site is pretty straightforward with a search tree and query results. Visual representation is displayed for the query fired, and results are represented to the end-users. The authors mutually decide to segment the parent dataset (Year range 2016-2019) into 4 equal segments/ datasets as follows for a simplified aggregation process and analytics:

1. A dataset with establishments for the year 2016
2. A dataset with establishments for the year 2017
3. A dataset with establishments for the year 2018
4. A dataset with the establishment for the year 2019

T intends to cover the comparative analytics for all the years to conclude a pattern for establishment status pass, conditional pass and closed. The Dinesafe inspection rate and its increment and decrement ratios can be plotted by finding these analytics. The primary objective of this research would be to clustering the data and follow the descriptive mining principles. Besides having a definite class label, there are severe conditions that resist the motivation for predictive mining. Prediction scenarios for this data might be postponed to future work with other tools and not 'R' and 'Python'. More about Descriptive Mining and Clustering techniques will be elaborated in the lower sections. A shiny web application built using the R programming framework is also proposed for an aesthetic User Interface and running an application without manually compiling it for plots. There is more discussion about this application in the section 'Technical Discussion' as more development for the application lies in future work.

LITERATURE SURVEY

The health industry is extremely notorious for forecasting and concluding results. The demand is highly volatile and has FGC's have short durability cycles (A. Sen, 2008). The FGC sale is influenced by variables such as weather, supply, hygiene and competitors. The authors in their research 'Forecasting Nike's Sales Using Facebook data' displayed the accurate sales forecast for Nike by scanning the Facebook data such as Likes, comments, shares and promotions on Facebook (Linda Bolt et.al, 2016). The dataset acquired for such a forecast consisted of all the Facebook's likes, shares, comments for each day and global sales figures in one column. The authors built simple and multiple regression models on understanding low and high forecast accuracy. Text analysis was performed on the big social data to obtain the company's marketing strategy and enhance decision-making.

Digital Data is growing every other second, with continuous recording of any aspect of life. The data is stored on disks, local systems, cloud or any business lab. Researchers seek robust tools to explore complex relationships in the data and discovering knowledge from the data. The tools should allow us to carve insights from the raw block of data. The authors in their research work described the model-driven analytics with high-quality visual feedbacks to the fresh chunk of data. The data focused on that specific kind of research is 'Big Data', and Visual representations are explored using ethical frameworks and tools (Shenghui Cheng et al., 2016). The geo-spatial data was experimented for visual representations such as pie & bar charts by integrating it into Google Earth and manipulated further. In 2013, a team of climatic researchers made extensive use of this integrated data and later innovated several discoveries (Z. Zhang et al., 2013). Talking about Big Social Data Analytics, the authors in their conference article 'Big Social Data Analytics of Changes in Consumer Behaviour and Opinion of a TV Broadcaster' examined the changes in consumer behaviour and opinions due to the transition from public to commercial broadcaster (Anna Hennig et al., 2016). The researchers prioritized analyzing TV Viewer ratings, Facebook activities and relevant sentiments. Transition observed was from airing NRK to TV2 in Norway affected consumer behaviour and opinions. Visual and text analysis methods were carried out on the social datasets, and patterns were generated. The research questions asked before conducting the experimentation were as follows: (deduced From the article itself)

Table 3. Questions Asked for Research

How did consumer behaviour of the TV2 network change as a result of broadcasting the Olympic Winter Games of 2014?
How was consumer opinion of the TV2 network affected During the Olympic Winter Games of 2014?
How did consumer opinion towards TV2 and NRK differ During the Olympic Winter Games of 2014?

In comparison with the above-mentioned previous work, the authors follow a similar approach to asking research questions in terms of 'What happened' for highlighting descriptive analytics. There will be no transition shift from one channel to channel, but the practitioners impose on comparing the data for the past years with the current year to conclude progress or deprecation. A brief overview of R and its command packages has been mentioned in the earlier sections regardless of the need and advantages. In their research, Ilir Keka and Betim Cico presented in the 8th Mediterranean conference on embedded computing mentioned trend detection in the data of load profiles. This research intended to find the correlation of the variables in the Multiple Linear regression model using R- Programming framework. The trends were later visualized in the form of scatterplots, treemaps, bar graphs, and other important (Ilir Keka and Betim Cico, 2019).

Despite various data analytic techniques, the researcher addresses the efficiency and scalability constraints in big data in their research article "Data-less Big Data Analysis (Towards Intelligent Data Analytics Systems)". Widely used technique AQP (Approximate Query Processing) relies on data sampling and compromises accuracy. To eliminate the existing challenges where data accuracy cannot meet the projections of data-intensive applications, A new paradigm is required. This approach keenly focuses on process-analytics queries which providing access to base data, while providing accurate results. Data-less big data analysis achieves the SEA (Scalability, Efficiency, and Accuracy) analytics and hence provides leverage for analysts. Since queries are injected in the system as before and provides a base "intelligence" model for data which further can be blended with machine learning models to predict accurate results. While advocating the new paradigm, it showed the validity and potential for classes of analytical queries. Hence it can be concluded as a game-changing approach and is highly useful in the case of classified or sensitive data (Peter Triantafillou, 2018). The authors in their transaction on Computational Biology and Bioinformatics revealed the secrets of protein sequences using AP Clustering methods. They discovered the sequence patterns with variations unveiling significant functions of the protein family. AP Clustering, also called Aligned Pattern clustering, was used to find out weak patterns and clusters with superior coverage and entropy (Andrew K.C Wong and En-Shiun Annie Lee, 2014).

The researchers in their article entitled 'Cluster Quality-Based Performance Evaluation of Hierarchical Clustering Method' explained Hierarchical clustering, the working and the breakdown into Agglomerative and Divisive clustering. The authors elaborated three parameters to evaluate the high-quality clusters, such as Cohesion measurement, Silhouette index and Elapsed time. Cluster cohesion is the degree of association between the objects of the group. A high value of similarity corresponds to a high coherence between the objects and vice versa (Nisha and Puneet Jai Kaur, 2015). R. Krishnamoorthy and S. Sreedhar Kumar in their IEEE paper – 'A New Inter-Cluster Validation Method for Unsupervised Clustering Techniques' presented a technique to measure the inter-cluster similarity and dissimilarity over each cluster with other clusters of the unsupervised clustering techniques. The methods are tested over four unsupervised learning clustering techniques such as K-Means, CURE, OAC and LIAC (R. Krishnamoorthy and S. Sreedhar Kumar, 2013).

DINESAFE DATA DESCRIPTION

The Dinesafe data was recorded on June 23rd, 2019 and uploaded on the open data catalogue for public use and research for the Health Ministry of Canada. The dataset loaded in R-Studio (R version x64) for cleaning and transforming the data for noise reduction. Here's a quick glimpse at the Dinesafe tribble imported in R:

As you can see from Fig. 3, the data has been imported without headings for convenient syntax coding. The columns from the dataset using colnames() in R, as shown below:

Matching the heading from Fig. 3 with the colnames from Fig. 4, the following list was concluded:

V1 = ROW_ID, **V2** = ESTABLISHMENT_ID, **V3** = INSPECTION_ID, **V4** = ESTABLIHSMENT_ NAME, **V5** = ESTABLIHSMENTTYPE, **V6** = ESTABLISHMENT_ADDRESS, **V7** = LATITUDE,

V8 = LONGITUDE, **V9** =MINIMUM_INSPECTION_YEAR, **V10** = INFRACTION_DETAILS, **V11** = INSPECTION_DATE, **V12** = SEVERITY, **V13** = ACTION, **V14** = ESTABLISHMENT_STATUS, **V15** = COURT_OUTCOME, **V16** = AMOUNT_FINED

Fig. 5 gives an overall summary of all the columns of the dataset along with their mean, median, standard deviations and categories in the categorical columns of the dataset.

Figure 3. Dinesafe Data Description (2017-2019)

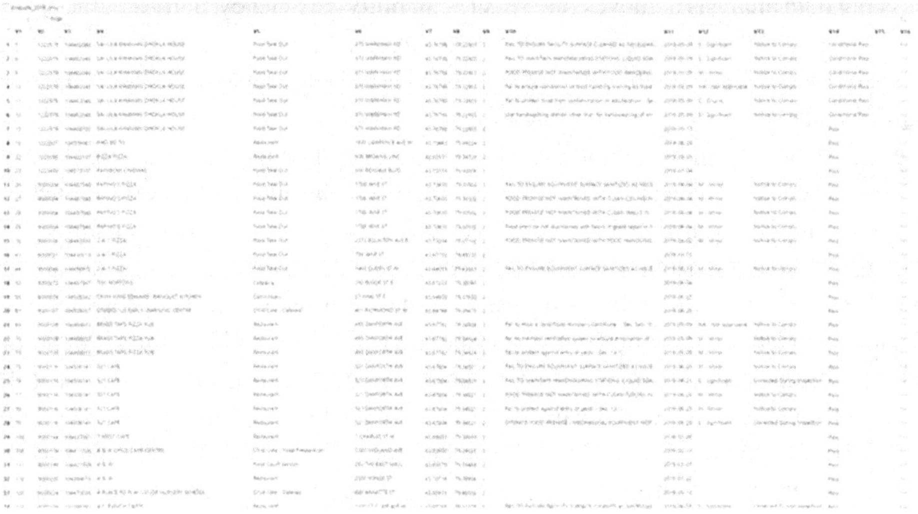

Figure 4. All Column Names from Dinesafe (2017-2019)

```
> cols <- colnames(dinesafe_analytics)
> print(cols)
 [1] "ROW_ID"                    "ESTABLISHMENT_ID"          "INSPECTION_ID"       "ESTABLISHMENT_NAME"
 [5] "ESTABLISHMENTTYPE"         "ESTABLISHMENT_ADDRESS"     "LATITUDE"            "LONGITUDE"
 [9] "MINIMUM_INSPECTIONS_PERYEAR" "INFRACTION_DETAILS"      "INSPECTION_DATE"     "SEVERITY"
[13] "ACTION"                    "ESTABLISHMENT_STATUS"      "COURT_OUTCOME"       "AMOUNT_FINED"
```

DINESAFE DATA OPERATIONS

The aggregated Dinesafe data consists of records from all the three years (2017-2018-2019). Clustering is almost impossible on a dataset with a high number of records, which cause congestion in a categorical column. There are several categorical columns in the chosen dataset and hence make it nearly impossible to execute basic clustering algorithms such as K-means, medians and agglomerative clustering techniques.

The individual results fetched from the isolated datasets can be combined using SQL joint queries. A lump sum dataset can be created by aggregating all the results from queries as an end product for Visualizing statistics in the web application. Analytical visualization such as bar graphs, charts and tree diagrams of every year for the comparative study is given in the below section.

Figure 5. Summary of all Columns of Dinesafe Data

```
> summary(dinesafe_2019_only)
      V1              V2                V3                   V4
Min.   :     7   Min.   :  1222579   Min.   :104100478   TIM HORTONS         :  347
1st Qu.:25267   1st Qu.:10322562   1st Qu.:104413576   SUBWAY              :  222
Median :50106   Median :10508098   Median :104446260   MCDONALD'S          :  116
Mean   :48973   Mean   :10267103   Mean   :104446370   PIZZA PIZZA         :  116
3rd Qu.:74354   3rd Qu.:10608585   3rd Qu.:104479895   SECOND CUP          :  102
Max.   :88989   Max.   :10677965   Max.   :104514068   AROMA ESPRESSO BAR  :   81
                                                        (Other)             :24010
                                       V5                        V6              V7              V8               V9
Restaurant                          :13732   3401 DUFFERIN ST  :  101   Min.   :43.59   Min.   :-79.63   Min.   :1.000
Food Take Out                       : 3755   633 SILVER STAR BLVD:  84   1st Qu.:43.65   1st Qu.:-79.43   1st Qu.:2.000
Food Store (Convenience / Variety)  : 1131   4750 YONGE ST     :   78   Median :43.68   Median :-79.39   Median :2.000
Food Court Vendor                   :  891   1 DUNDAS ST W     :   75   Mean   :43.70   Mean   :-79.39   Mean   :2.359
Supermarket                         :  833   1800 SHEPPARD AVE E:  72   3rd Qu.:43.74   3rd Qu.:-79.35   3rd Qu.:3.000
Bakery                              :  757   900 DUFFERIN ST   :   69   Max.   :48.79   Max.   :-79.13   Max.   :3.000
(Other)                             : 3895   (Other)           :24515
                                                                                                          V10
FOOD PREMISE NOT MAINTAINED WITH FOOD HANDLING ROOM IN SANITARY CONDITION - SEC. 7(1)(E)           : 7939
FAIL TO ENSURE EQUIPMENT SURFACE SANITIZED AS NECESSARY - SEC. 22                                  : 1988
FOOD PREMISE NOT MAINTAINED WITH CLEAN FLOORS IN FOOD-HANDLING ROOM - SEC. 7(1)(G)                 : 1920
FAIL TO MAINTAIN HANDWASHING STATIONS (LIQUID SOAP AND PAPER TOWELS) - SEC. 7(3)(C)                : 1505
Fail to Ensure the Presence of the Holder of a valid Food Handlers Certificate - Sec. 545- 157E(1 7)(a): 764
(Other)                                                                                            : 822
                                                                                                  :10056
      V11                        V12                          V13                        V14
2019-06-20:  345                              :7939                              : 7939   Closed            :   75
2019-06-26:  304   C - Crucial            :  900   Corrected During Inspection : 2924   Conditional Pass: 4841
2019-06-19:  296   M - Minor              : 9814   Not in Compliance           :    8   Pass            :20078
2019-06-27:  289   NA - Not Applicable: 1449   Notice to Comply            :13928
2019-04-16:  287   S - Significant        : 4892   Summons                     :   25
2019-04-04:  281                                   Summons and Health Hazard Order:  15
(Other)   :23192                                   Ticket                      :  155
                                  V15                   V16
                               :24814   Min.   :    0.0
Cancelled                      :    3   1st Qu.:   75.0
Charges Dismissed              :    1   Median :  150.0
Charges Withdrawn              :   10   Mean   :  275.4
Conviction - Fined             :   43   3rd Qu.:  385.0
Conviction - Suspended Sentence:    1   Max.   : 1875.0
Pending                        :  122   NA's   :24942
> |
```

Figure 6. Combined Data Split into 3 segment datasets for 2017, 2018, 2019

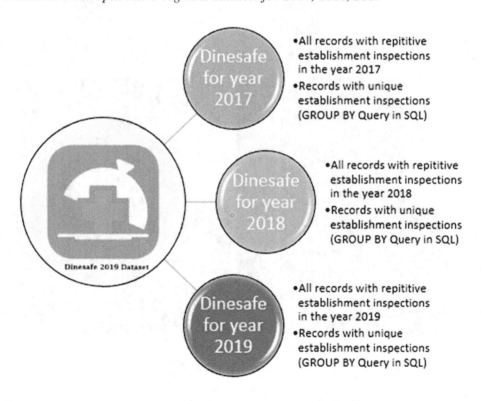

DINESAFE ANALYTICS

• Comparing Inspection Ratio for the year 2017-2018-2019

For acquiring a rough estimate on the graphs, the authors calculated the number of inspections of the first ten restaurants in the dataset segmented for the year 2017. Got 'Number of Inspections' on the Y-axis and Restaurant's name on the X-axis for all the comparisons. For example, for the year 2017, let's consider the restaurant '1000 Variety' for elaborating the comparison as follows:

1. Restaurant '1000 Variety' had 1 Inspection for the year 2017
2. Restaurant '1000 Variety' had 2 Inspections for the year 2018
3. Restaurant '1000 Variety' had 2 Inspections for the year 2019

Figure 7. Restaurants Vs Number of Inspections in the year 2017

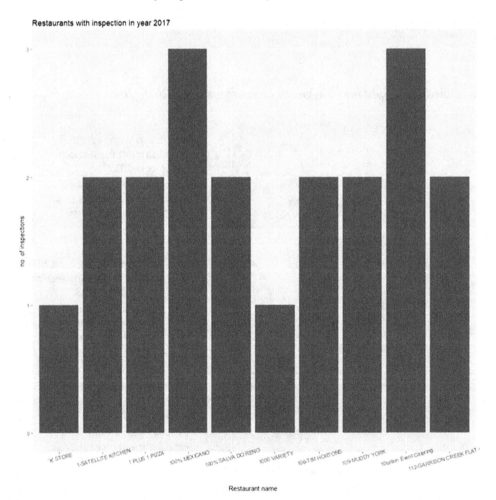

Frequency of 'Severity of Restaurants' for the years 2017-2018-2019

Next, the authors intend to analyze the severity of the restaurants for the years 2017, 2018 and 2019 each, respectively. Below you can see the severity ratio for restaurants with Minimum inspections per year on the Y-axis. Consider 1000 restaurants with Inspection per year = 1. Here there are categories for the restaurants with severity such as Crucial, Significant, Minor and few are 'N/A'.

The severity division for 2017 (Fig. 10) for restaurants with Minimum Inspection per year = 1 would be as follows:

- Not Specified = 779
- Crucial = 2
- Minor = 143
- Not Applicable = 40
- Significant = 120

The statistics for the year 2018 and 2019 with the severity ratios and driven analytics for appropriate comparison has been calculated. The primary objective would be to integrate all the analytics results in the Shiny web application. More about the Shiny web application is explained in section VII.

Figure 8. Restaurants Vs Number of Inspections in the year 2018

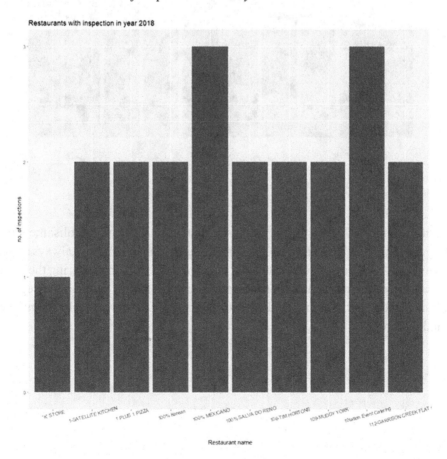

The above-given Tree-map highlights the number of Inspections for the types of food establishments. We can conclude that food establishments such as 'Food Court Vendor' and 'Food Caterer' had the maximum number of inspections in 2018. The output from the latest results after the last check is conducted in December 2019.

Figure 9. Restaurants Vs Number of Inspections in the year 2019

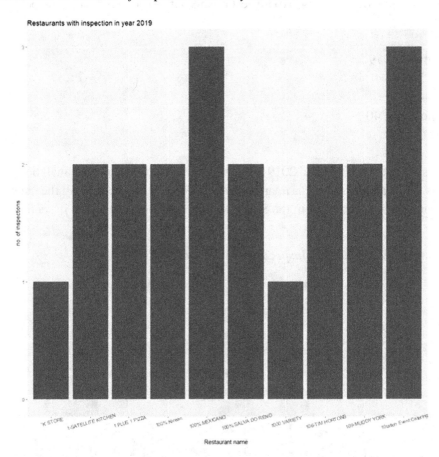

Here's one last example of a logistic bar graph stating the status for all establishment types in 2019. Results for the years 2017 and 2018 can be derived in the same manner. There is always more to Dinesafe when it comes to Data Analytics, but unfortunately, the focus will shift on clustering the segmented data. For further expansion of the research, experimentations can be carried on with the segmented data in the next iteration of the paper, which may deal with predictions for new establishments by comparing the test data and their results.

CLUSTERING METHODS

This section deals with clustering validation and evaluation strategies resulting in measuring the goodness of the grouping. To measure the suitability of our data for clustering, also called as 'Clustering Tendency', the authors are going to scale the data and find out the distances between the records. The classification of observations into groups requires some methods for computing the distance or the dissimilarity between each pair of observations (Alboukadel Kassambara, 2017). The author has described all the unsupervised learning – clustering methods in the book – Practical Guide to Cluster Analysis in R (Edition 1)'. The choice of a distance measuring is a significant step in cluster analysis. Mostly, by default, the option is 'Euclidean Distance'. The other methods for measuring distances are Manhattan Distance, correlation methods such as Pearson correlation, Spearman correlation distance, Eisen Cosine Correlation distance and Kendall correlation distance.

After calculating the Euclidean distance and distance matrix computation, the authors begin with clustering our data by following the 'Partitioning Clustering' method.

Partitioning Clustering

Clustering methods used to classify observations within data into multiple groups based on similarity are called partitioning clustering methods. There are three types of partitioning clustering methods – Kmeans clustering, K-medoids (PAM) clustering and CLARA algorithm.

The R- packages required for computation and visualization in partitioning clustering are:

- 'Stats' package for computing K-means
- 'Cluster' package for computing PAM and CLARA algorithm
- 'Factoextra' for aesthetic visualization

K- Means Clustering

K-means is the most popular unsupervised learning algorithm for partitioning a given dataset into sets of k groups where each 'k' represents the number of groups specified by the practitioner. Each cluster/group represented by its centre corresponds to the mean of points assigned to the cluster. The authors will indicate the number of clusters that will be generated in the final solution. The algorithm starts by selecting random 'K' objects from the dataset to serve as the cluster centres.

The procedure will start with the segmented 2017 dataset, which only contains continuous variables. The k-means algorithm uses variable means from the dataset for computing clusters. K-means doesn't work well with large datasets. Therefore the authors have cut down the 2017 year data segment to 50 records. The dataset is transformed for continuous variables such that the probabilities of establishment Names against the severity types – Significant, crucial, Minor, Not applicable and Blank is represented. The authors scale the data, following the estimation of optimal clusters. The R- function 'fviz_nbclust ()' from the factoextra package provides a convenient solution to estimate optimal clusters. The figure provided below helps us to choose the optimal number of clusters for the k-means algorithm._

From the above Fig. 15, the knee bend on the graph points the optimal number of clusters i.e. '2' in this case for further computation. After computing k-means (data, clusters, nstart) command for the data, the authors get the following results:

Figure 10. Frequency of 'Severity of Restaurants' in the year 2017

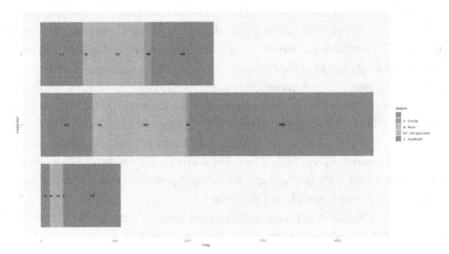

Figure 11. Frequency in 'Severity of Restaurants' in the year 2018

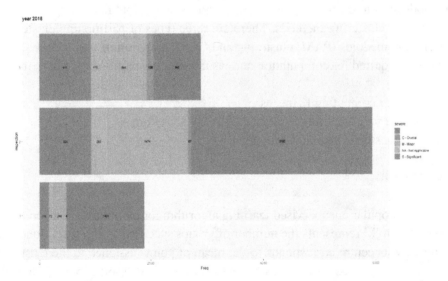

The k-means algorithm in R-Studio calculated 2 clusters for the 50 records with a WSS percentage of 77.6%, which is considered to be satisfactory as per the clustering standards. The more the clusters, the more the WSS (within the square sums), the better the clustering. The clustering can be visualized using the fviz_cluster() command of the 'factoextra' package after PCA is calculated. PCA (Principal Component Analysis) has to be calculated when the dataset has multiple dimensions.

From Fig. 17, it can be seen that the 50 observations have been clustered based on their distances and probabilities of the variable 'Severity'. The establishment names that seem to be isolated or away from the clusters are unknown records, also called 'Outliers'. The outliers have no particular purpose and can be eliminated from the dataset by deleting the files or replacing them with N/A or the mean value of the variable. The clustering plot, which covers all the outliers by edges, is displayed below.

Figure 12. Frequency in 'Severity of Restaurants' in the year 2019

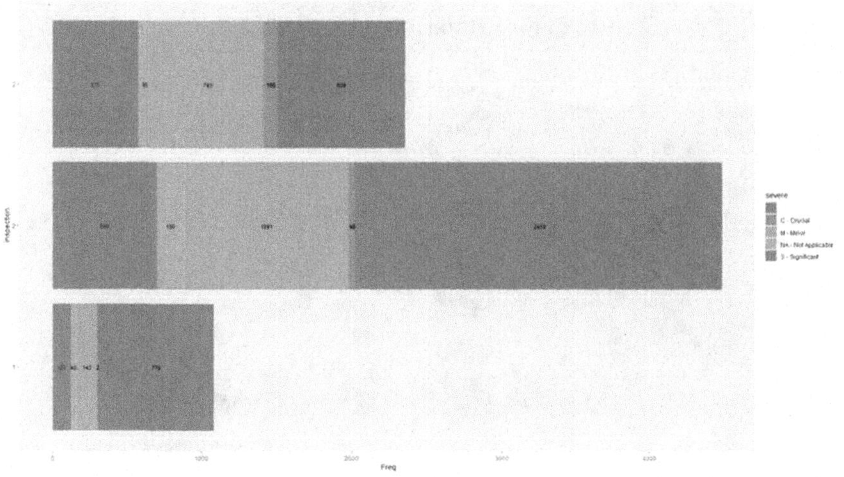

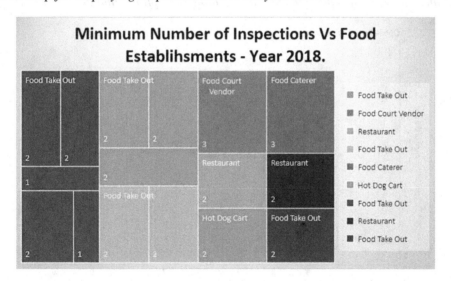

Figure 13. Tree-Map for displaying Inspection rate in the year 2018

Other efficient clustering methods such as K-medoids and CLARA can be performed on the data segments or the aggregated data. The authors will temporarily settle with the k-means algorithm and focus shift the computations and visualizations for the year 2018 & 2019.

Shiny Web Application

The shiny web application is an effort to visualize all the analytical results to the end-users (Web source). The more about the shiny web application is discussed in the future work section. The commands and syntaxes are supposed to be embedded in the client and server 'R' files of the application. This application is expected to display all the visualizations and clustering results (Descriptive Analytics) of all three years, such as 2017, 2018 and 2019.

Figure 14. Bar Graph for establishment status ratio in 2018

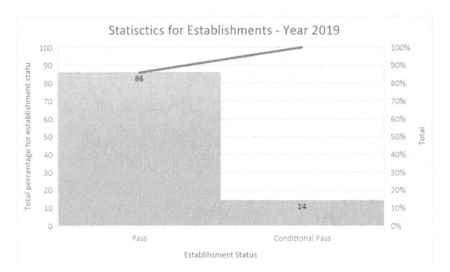

Figure 15. Within the sum of a square method to calculate the optimal number of clusters

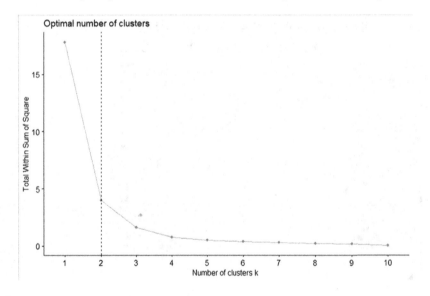

FUTURE WORK

In this chapter, the authors have illustrated all the work on the Dinesafe data frame of the year 2017-2019 and results were obtained and aggregated after the data split operation. Due to the amount of data collected, a number of researches could be conducted. Future researchers can determine the rate of inspections dropping/escalating per year, the progress of 'pass' establishment status, determining the number of establishments with court notice, identifying the closed establishment with the rise in years. This information could also be used by the health units to allocate resources better. The visualization could be enhanced by adding a few facet layers to the plots and charts for better understanding. Other clustering types such as Agglomerative and Hierarchical clustering can be performed on the datasets to improve the clustering results and display them to the users. The work represented to the end-users in the form of a web application can be made efficient, fast and scalable with a massive chunk of data. R-Studio users can customize a better version of the Shiny app than the one described in this chapter. This research can be extended to province level, even at a country level, by concatenating columns from multiple Food health agencies Datasets. For example, at a city level, the food Inspection agency in Toronto is 'Dinesafe', whereas the food inspection agency in Thunder Bay is 'DineWise'. There are different food and health inspection agencies for each City in Canada. The research can be expanded from a city level to a province-level or, moreover, for multiple provinces of Canada. The limit can be set and defined by future research according to the research scope.

Figure 16. K-means Clustering results for Dinesafe segment- 2017 with the first 50 records.

CONCLUSION

The recent advancements and rapid development in the Health Inspection agency have raised the charts for the quality of food served by food and drink establishments in Toronto, Canada. Dinesafe, a health inspection agency that runs and acts under the Ministry of Health orders, is responsible for ensuring and evaluating the health safety parameters in every food establishment of Toronto. Previous researches were conducted on the old data frame (The year 2004-2014) collected by Dinesafe Inspection agency. They uploaded the data on the Open Data Catalogue of Toronto City for public use and experimentation. The research explained in this chapter focuses on the Dinesafe Data frame (the year 2017-2019) conducting analytics for pattern generation. The patterns generated can derive reports on features of Dinesafe, such as Minimum inspections per year, Establishment status (Pass, conditional pass, Closed), Court notice and amount penalized for bad health conduct. The authors suggest segmenting the data into 3 data segments, such as one for each year, from 2017, 2018 and 2019. Clustering and visualization work better with segmented or 'spread' data. To represent the overall work to the end-users, the researchers impose on embedding all the analytics output as an input to the server-side of a Shiny web application built in the R programming framework for data analytics. The web application can be published via R-Studio and integrated into any local or hosted website for displaying the diagrammatic Analytical representations to the public.

Figure 17. K-Means Clustering Visualization (Ellipse Type = Euclid)

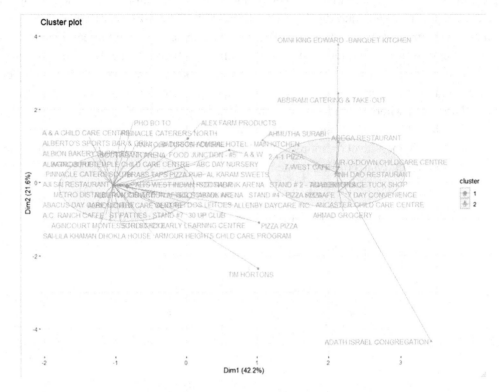

Figure 18.

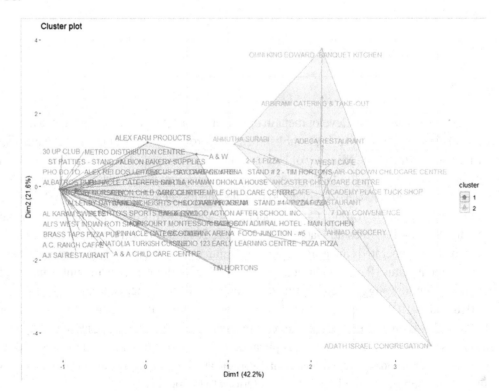

Figure 19. Ideal shiny web application for Dinesafe

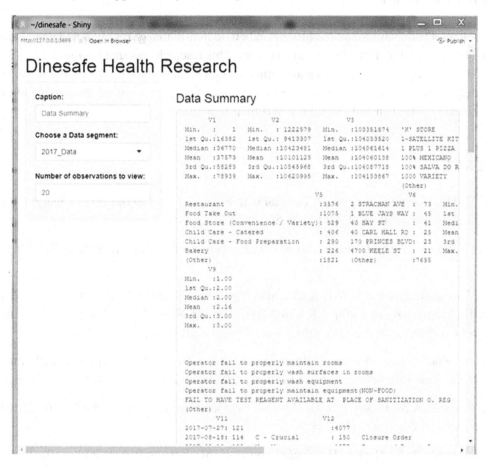

Figure 20. Application displaying data for the selected dataset

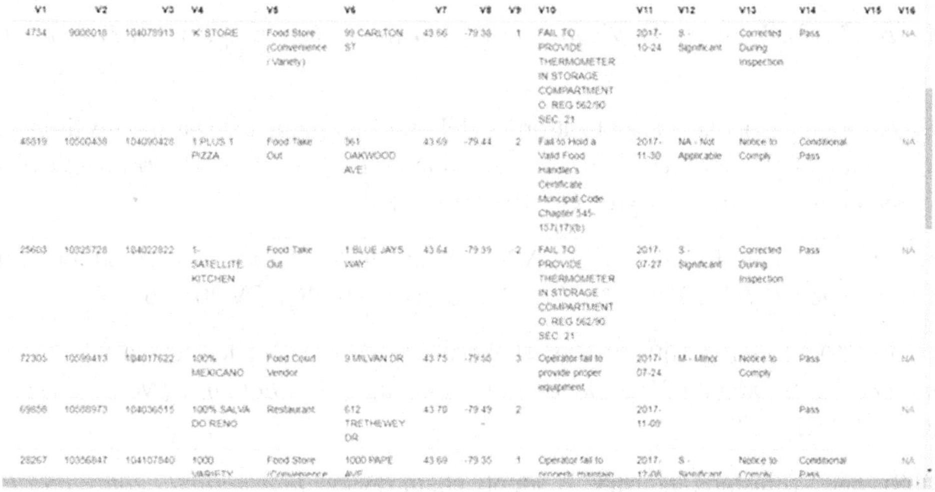

ACKNOWLEDGMENT

We want to thank Dr. Sabah Mohammed for his expertise in this area of research and would also like to appreciate his significant contribution to this chapter. This research was much supported by the manuscript reviewers who provided theories and comments that significantly improved the manuscript. We are immensely grateful to all the previous researchers for their comments on the script, although any errors identified are our own and should not hurt their reputations.

REFERENCES

Barr, J. R. (2018). Machine Learning, A Tutorial with R. *IEEE First International Conference on AI for Industries*, 120-121. doi: 10.1109/AI4I.2018.8665676

Besharah & Heacock. (2015). *Dinesafe Toronto: An Evaluation of the Placard System.* BCIT Institutional Repository.

Bolt, L. C., Vinagayamoorthy, V., Winder, F., Schnittger, M., Ekran, M., Mukkamala, R. R., Lassen, N. B., Flesch, B., Hussain, A., & Vatrapu, R. (2016). Forecasting Nike's Sales Using Facebook data. *IEEE International Conference on Big Data (Big Data).* 10.1109/BigData.2016.7840881

Cheng, Wang, Zhong, Xie, Mahmood, Wang, & Mueller. (2016). Model-driven Visual Analytics for Big Data. *IEEE, New York Scientific Data Summit (NYSDS)*, 1-2. doi:10.1109/NYSDS.2016.7747827

Grady, N., Payne, J. A., & Parker, H. (2017). Agile Big Data Analytics, Analytics Ops for Data Science. *IEEE Conference on Big Data*, 2331-2339.

Hennig, A., Åmodt, A.-S., Hernes, H., Nygårdsmoen, H. M., Larsen, P. A., Mukkamala, R. R., Flesch, B., Hussain, A., & Vatrapu, R. (2016). Big Social Data Analytics of Changes in Consumer Behaviour and Opinion of a TV Broadcaster. *IEEE International Conference on Big Data*, 3839-3848. 10.1109/BigData.2016.7841057

Kassambara, A. (2017). *Practical Guide to Cluster Analysis in R (Unsupervised Machine Learning).* STHDA.

Keka, I., & Cico, B. (2019). Data Visualization as Helping Technique for Data Analysis, Trend Detection and Correlation of Variables Using R Programming Language. *8th Mediterranean Conference on Embedded computing*, 1-4. 10.1109/MECO.2019.8760004

Krishnamoorthy & Sreedhar Kumar. (2013). A New Inter Cluster Validation Method for Unsupervised Clustering Techniques. *1ˢᵗ ICCCV, IEEE, 2013,* 1-5. doi:10.1109/ICCCV.2013.6906741

Nisha, P. J. K. (2015). Cluster Quality Based Performance Evaluation of Hierarchical Clustering Method. *1st International Conference on Next Generation Computing Technologies (NCGT-2015)*, 649-653. 10.1109/NGCT.2015.7375201

Sen, A. (2008). The US fashion industry: A supply chain review. *International Journal of Production Economics*, *114*(2), 571–593. doi:10.1016/j.ijpe.2007.05.022

Shiny. (n.d.). *RStudio*. shiny.rstudio.com/

Toronto Public Health, Healthy Environments Services. (2002). *Food premises Inspection and disclosure system, Evaluation Report*. Author.

Triantafillou, P. (2018). Data-Less Big Data Analytics. *2018 IEEE 34th International Conference on Data Engineering,* 1666-1667. 10.1109/ICDE.2018.00205

Wong, A. K. C., & Lee, E.-S. A. (2014). Aligning and Clustering Patterns to Reveal the Protein Functionality of Sequences. *IEEE/ACM Transactions on Computational Biology and Bioinformatics*, *11*(3), 548–560. doi:10.1109/TCBB.2014.2306840 PMID:26356022

Zhang, Z., Tong, X., McDonell, K., Zelenyuk, A., Imre, D., & Mueller, K. (2013, April). An Interactive Visual Analytics Framework for Multi-Field Data in a Geo-Spatial Context. *Tsinghua Science and Technology on Visualization and Computer Graphics*, *18*(2), 111–124. doi:10.1109/TST.2013.6509095

KEY TERMS AND DEFINITIONS

Clustering: Clustering can simply be referred to as a 'Grouping' based on numerous or similar properties.

Disclosure System: The system that inspects and reveals all the inspected information, insights, and knowledge to public use is called a system that obeys the disclosure policy. The information published may or may not impact or influence business decisions.

FOSS (Free and Open source): The tools and software which are freely available to public use are also highlighted as FOSS tools. Some good examples of FOSS tools include MySQL, MongoDB, R, Python and many more.

OBDA (Operational Big Data Analysis): OBDA can be defined as a concept in which big data technologies can trigger the web application data, which, in turn, can be used to gain valuable insights. OBA is the optimal method for enhancing the speed of KDD (Knowledge Discovery from Data).

OLTP (Online Transaction Processing Tables): The data produced by an organization's daily activities such as accounting, customer files, records, and others in high volume can be stored in a structured table format called OLTP. OBDA strongly supports the concept and architecture of OLTP.

PCA (Principal Component Analysis): PCA is a dimension-reduction tool that can be used to reduce a broad set of variables to a small collection that contains most of the information in the massive game.

Visualization: A Diagrammatic representation of a chunk of information/data leads to a better imagination and eases the viewer's understanding capability.

Compilation of References

Aalipour, G., Kumar, P., Aditham, S., Nguyen, T., & Sood, A. (2018). Applications of Sequence to Sequence Models for Technical Support Automation. IEEE International Conference on Big Data (Big Data), 4861-4869.

Aalst, W. (2018). Spreadsheets for business process management: Using process mining to deal with "events" rather than "numbers"? *Business Process Management Journal, 24*(1), 105–127. doi:10.1108/BPMJ-10-2016-0190

Abbas, A., Abdelsamea, M., & Gaber, M. (2020). Classification of COVID-19 in chest X-ray images using DeTraC deep convolutional neural network. doi:10.1101/ 2020.03.30.20047456

Abbasi, A., Albrecht, C., Vance, A., & Hansen, J. (2012). Metafraud: A meta-learning framework for detecting financial fraud. *Management Information Systems Quarterly, 36*(4), 1293–1327. doi:10.2307/41703508

Abbaszadeh, S., Nguyen, T.-D., & Wu, Y. (2018). Optimal trading under non-negativity constraints using approximate dynamic programming. *The Journal of the Operational Research Society, 69*(9), 1406–1422. doi:10.1080/01605682.2 017.1398201

Abbott, D. (2014). *Applied Predictive Analytics: Principles and Techniques for the Professional Data Analyst.* Wiley.

Accenture. (n.d.). *Financial crime: Data science to the rescue.* Accenture.com.

Acharjya, D. P. (2017). A Survey on Big Data Analytics: Challenges, Open Research Issues and Tools. *International Journal of Advanced Computer Science and Applications, 7*(2), 511–518.

ACL. (2010). *Fraud detection using analytics in the banking industry.* ACL Services Ltd.

Adil, A., Kar, H. A., Jangir, R., & Sofi, S. A. (2015), Analysis of multi-diseases using big data for improvement in health-care. *IEEE UP Section Conference on Electrical Computer and Electronics (UPCON).* 10.1109/UPCON.2015.7456696

Adusei, M. (2016). Modelling the efficiency of universal banks in Ghana. *Quantitative Financial Letters, 4*, 60–70.

Aethon Inc. (2017). *TUG Robots—Healthcare Benefits.* Accessed from https://www.aethon.com/tug/tughealthcare/

Agresti, A. (2007). An introduction to categorical data analysis. A John Wiley & Sons, Inc., Publication. doi:10.1002/0470114754

Ahi, L. (2015). *Veri Madenciliği Yöntemleri İle Ana Harcama Gruplarının Paylarının Tahmini* [Estimation Of Main Expenditure Groups' Portion With Data Mining Methods] (Unpublished master's thesis). Hacettepe Üniversitesi Fen Bilimleri Enstitüsü.

Ahmad, A., Babar, M., Din, S., Khalid, S., Ullah, M. M., Paul, A., Reddy, A. G., & Min-Allah, N. (2019). Socio-cyber network: The potential of cyber-physical system to define human behaviors using big data analytics. *Future Generation Computer Systems, 92*, 868–878. doi:10.1016/j.future.2017.12.027

Ahmad, N. S., Sanusi, M., Wahab, M. H., Mustapha, A., Sayadi, Z. A., & Saringat, M. Z. (2018). Conversational Bot for Pharmacy: A Natural Language Approach. *IEEE Conference on Open Systems (ICOS)*, 76-79.

Ahmed, F., Paul, P. P., & Gavrilova, M. L. (2015). Kinect-based gait recognition using sequences of the most relevant joint relative angles. Journal of WSCG.

AI. (2019). Retrieved from Xpanse AI. https://xpanse.ai/

Ajao, O., Bhowmik, D., & Zargari, S. (2018). Fake news identification on Twitter with hybrid CNN and RNN models. In ACM International Conference Proceeding Series (pp. 226-230) doi:10.1145/3217804.3217917

Akbani, R., Kwek, S., & Japkowicz, N. (2004, September). Applying support vector machines to imbalanced datasets. In *European conference on machine learning* (pp. 39-50). Springer. 10.1007/978-3-540-30115-8_7

Akhavan-Hejazi, H., & Mohsenian-Rad, H. (2018). Power systems big data analytics: An assessment of paradigm shift barriers and prospects. *Energy Reports*, *4*, 91–100.

Akkuş, B., & Zontul, M. (2019). Veri Madenciliği Yöntemleri ile Ülkeleri Gelişmişlik Ölçütlerine Göre Kümeleme Üzerine Bir Uygulama [An Application On Clustering Countries With Data Mining Methods Based On Development Criteria]. *AURUM Mühendislik Sistemleri ve Mimarlık Dergisi*, *3*(1), 51–64.

Akossou, A. Y. J., & Palm, R. (2017). Impact of Data Structure on the Estimators R-Square And Adjusted R-Square in Linear Regression. *International Journal of Mathematics and Computation*, *20*, 84–90.

Alanyali, M., Moat, H. S., & Preis, T. (2013). Quantifying the relationship between financial news and the stock market. *Scientific Reports*, *3*(1), 6. doi:10.1038rep03578 PMID:24356666

Alatabi, H. A., & Abbas, A. R. (2020). Sentiment analysis in social media using machine learning techniques. *Iraqi Journal of Science*, *61*(1), 193–201. doi:10.24996/ijs.2020.61.1.22

Albano, J. D., Ward, E., Jemal, A., Anderson, R., Cokkinides, V. E., Myrray, T., Henley, J., Liff, J., & Thun, M. J. (2007). Cancer mortality in the United States by education level and race. *Journal of the National Cancer Institute*, *99*(18), 1384–1394. doi:10.1093/jnci/djm127 PMID:17848670

Albashrawi, M. (2016). Detecting financial fraud using data mining techniques: A decade review from 2004 to 2015. *Journal of Data Science : JDS*, *14*, 553–570.

Albayati, M. B., & Altamimi, A. M. (2019). An Empirical Study for Detecting Fake Facebook Profiles Using Supervised Mining Techniques. Informatica-Journal of Computing and Informatics, 43(1), 77–86. doi:10.31449/inf.v43i1.2319

Alberti, K. G. M. M., & Zimmet, P. Z. (1998). Definition, diagnosis and classification of diabetes mellitus and its complications. Part 1: Diagnosis and classification of diabetes mellitus. Provisional report of a WHO consultation. *Diabetic Medicine*, *15*(7), 539–553. doi:10.1002/(SICI)1096-9136(199807)15:7<539::AID-DIA668>3.0.CO;2-S PMID:9686693

Alfred, R. (2017). *The rise of machine learning for big data analytics*. Academic Press.

Ali, A., Alrubei, M. A., Hassan, L. F. M., Al-Ja'afari, M. A., & Abdulwahed, S. H. (2020). DIABETES DIAGNOSIS BASED ON KNN. *IIUM Engineering Journal*, *21*(1), 175–181. doi:10.31436/iiumej.v21i1.1206

Aljumah, A. A., Ahamad, M. G., & Siddiqui, M. K. (2013). Application of data mining: Diabetes health care in young and old patients. Journal of King Saud University - Computer and Information Sciences, 25(2), 127–136. doi:10.1016/j.jksuci.2012.10.003

Allam, Z., Tegally, H., & Thondoo, M. (2019). Redefining the use of big data in urban health for increased liveability in smart cities. Smart Cities, 2(2), 259–268. doi:10.3390/smartcities2020017

Alles, M. G. (2015). Drivers of the use and facilitators and obstacles of the evolution of big data by the audit profession. *Accounting Horizons, 29*(2), 439–449. doi:10.2308/acch-51067

Alles, M. G., & Gray, G. L. (2015). *The pros and cons of using big data in auditing: A synthesis of the literature and a research agenda.* Rutgers Business School.

Allevi, E., Basso, A., Bonenti, F., Oggioni, G., & Riccardi, R. (2019). Measuring the environmental performance of green SRI funds: A DEA approach. *Energy Economics, 79*, 32–44. doi:10.1016/j.eneco.2018.07.023

Alteryx, I. (2019). Alteryx: Self-Service Data Analytics Platform. https://www.alteryx.com/platform

Ambekar, S., & Phalnikar, R. (2018). Disease Risk Prediction by Using Convolutional Neural Network. *Fourth International Conference on Computing Communication Control and Automation (ICCUBEA),* 1-5.

Amster, A. (2016). UC Apache spark. Retrieved from https://www.qubole.com/blog/apache-spark use-cases/

Anaconda Inc. (2019). Anaconda. https://www.anaconda.com/

Anaconda. (2018). Numba. Retrieved from http://numba.pydata.org

Anandakrishnan, A., Kumar, S., Statnikov, A., Faruquie, T., & Xu, D. (2017). *Anomaly detection in finance*: Editors' introduction. *Proceedings of Machine Learning Research KDD Workshop on Anomaly Detection in Finance, 71*, 1–7. Retrieved from http://proceedings.mlr.press/v71/anandakrishnan18a/anandakrishnan18a.pdf

Anayiotos, G., Toroyan, H., & Vamvakidis, A. (2010). The efficiency of emerging Europe's banking sector before and after the recent economic crisis. *Financial Theory and Practice, 34*, 247–267.

Angel, J. J., Harris, L. E., & Spatt, C. S. (2015). Equity trading in the 21st century: An update. *The Quarterly Journal of Finance, 5*(1), 1550002. doi:10.1142/S2010139215500020

Angin, P., Bhargava, B., & Ranchal, R. (2019). Big Data Analytics for Cyber Security. *Hindawi Security and Communication Networks*, 1-2.

Anifah, L., Purnama, I. K. E., Hariadi, M., & Purnomo, M. H. (2013). Osteoarthritis Classification Using Self Organizing Map Based on Gabor Kernel and Contrast-Limited Adaptive Histogram Equalization. *The Open Biomedical Engineering Journal, 7*(1), 18–28. doi:10.2174/1874120701307010018 PMID:23525188

Antony, V., & Vaz, S. (2014). Diagnosis of hypo and hyperthyroid using MLPN Network. *International Journal of Innovative Research in Science. Engineering and Technology, 3*(7), 14314–14323.

Antweiler, W., & Frank, M. (2004). Is All That Talk Just Noise? The Information Content of Internet Stock Message Boards. *The Journal of Finance, 59*(3), 1259–1294. doi:10.1111/j.1540-6261.2004.00662.x

Anwaar, M. (2016). Impact of Firms' Performance on Stock Returns (Evidence from Listed Companies of FTSE100 Index London, UK). *Global Journal of Management and Business Research: D Accounting and Auditing, 16*(1), 1-10.

Apache Hadoop Tutorial. (n.d.). Available: https://www.tutorialspoint. com/ hadoop/

Apache Software Foundation. (2019a). Apache Hadoop. https://hadoop.apache.org/

Apache Software Foundation. (2019b). GraphX. https://spark.apache.org/graphx/

Appelbaum, D., Kogan, A., & Vasarhelyi, M. A. (2017a). Big data and analytics in the modern audit engagement: Research needs. *Auditing, 36*(4), 1–27. doi:10.2308/ajpt-51684

Appelbaum, D., Kogan, A., & Vasarhelyi, M. A. (2017b). An introduction to data analytics for auditors and accountants. *The CPA Journal*, 32–37.

Appelbaum, D., Kogan, A., & Vasarhelyi, M. A. (2018). Analytical procedures in external auditing:A comprehensive literature survey and framework for external audit analysis. *Journal of Accounting Literature*, *40*, 83–101. doi:10.1016/j.acclit.2018.01.001

Aras, G., & Yilmaz, M. K. (2008). Price-earnings ratio, Dividend Yield, and Market to Book ratio to predict Return on stock market: Evidence from the Emerging Markets. *Journal of Global Business and Technology*, *4*(1), 2–20.

Artificial Intelligence Techniques, L. (2019). Opennn. https://www.opennn.net/

Aseef, N., Davis, P., Mittal, M., Sedky, K., & Tolba, A. (2005). *Cyber-Criminal Activity and Analysis*. White Paper.

Asness, C. S., Ilmanen, A., Israel, R., & Moskowitz, T. J. (2015). Investing with style. *Journal of Investment Management*, *13*(1), 27–63.

Asri, H., Mousannif, H., Al Moatassime, H., & Noel, T. (2016). Using Machine Learning Algorithms for Breast Cancer Risk Prediction and Diagnosis. Procedia Computer Science, 83(Fams), 1064–1069. doi:10.1016/j.procs.2016.04.224

Association of Certified Chartered Accountants-ACCA. (2019). *Audit and technology*. Report by Chartered Accountants of Australia and New Zealand.

Association of Certified Fraud Examiners. (2018). *2018 global study on occupational fraud and abuse*. Author.

Association of Certified Fraud Examiners. (2019). *Forensic accountant*. Retrieved from https://www.acfe.com/forensic-accountant.aspx

Aud, S., KewalRamani, A., & Frohlich, L. (2011). America's Youth: Transitions to Adulthood (NCES 2012-026). U.S. Department of Education, National Center for Education Statistics. Washington, DC: U.S. Government Printing Office.

Ayuntamiento de Málaga. (2019). Data Set del Ayuntamiento de Malaga. http://datosabiertos.malaga.eu/dataset

Azar, J., Makhoul, A., Barhamgi, M., & Couturier, R. (2019). An energy efficient IoT data compression approach for edge machine learning. *Future Generation Computer Systems*, *96*, 168–175. doi:10.1016/j.future.2019.02.005

Azimi, A., & NoorHosseini, M. (2017). The hybrid approach based on genetic algorithm and neural network to predict financial fraud in banks. *International Journal of Information Security and System Management*, *6*, 657–667.

Bahdanau, D., Cho, K., & Bengio, Y. (2014). *Neural Machine Translation by Jointly Learning to Align and Translate*. CoRR, abs/1409.0473

Baker, A. R., Goodloe, R. J., Larkin, E. K., Baechle, D. J., Song, Y. E., Phillips, L. S., & Gray-McGuire, C. L. (2009). Multivariate association analysis of the components of metabolic syndrome from the Framingham Heart Study. *BMC Proceedings*, *3*(Suppl 7), 1–5. doi:10.1186/1753-6561-3-s7-s42 PMID:20018034

Baker, H. K., & Smith, D. M. (2006). In search of a residual dividend policy. *Review of Financial Economics*, *15*(1), 1–18.

Bakırcı, F., Ekinci, E. D., & Şahinoğlu, T. (2014). Bölgesel kalkınma politikalarının etkinliği: Türkiye alt bölgeler bazında bir uygulama [The Effectiveness of Regional Development Policies: An Application on Sub-Regions of Turkey]. *Atatürk Üniversitesi Sosyal Bilimler Enstitüsü Dergisi*, *18*(2), 281–298.

Ball, R. (1978). Anomalies in relationships between securities' yields and yield-surrogates. *Journal of Financial Economics*, *6*, 103–126.

Bănărescu, A. (2015). Detecting and preventing fraud with data analytics. *Procedia Economics and Finance, 32*(15), 1827–1836. doi:10.1016/S2212-5671(15)01485-9

Banerjee, Bourla, Chen, Kashyap, Purohit, & Battipaglia. (2018). *Comparative analysis of machine learning algorithms through credit card fraud detection.* New Jersey's Governor's School of Engineering and Technology.

Banerjee, A., Merugu, S., Dhillon, I. S., & Ghosh, J. (2005). Clustering with Bregman divergences. *Journal of Machine Learning Research, 6*, 1705–1749.

Bansal, A., & Srivastava, S. (2018). Tools Used in Data Analysis: A Comparative Study. *International Journal of Recent Research Aspects, 5*(1), 15–18.

Banu, G.R. (2016). *Predicting thyroid disease using Linear Discriminant Analysis (LDA) data mining technique.* Doi:10.5120/cae2016651990

Barbee, W. C., Mukherji, S., & Raines, G. A. (1996). Do Sales-Price and Debt-Equity Explain Stock Returns Better Than Book-Market and Firm Size? *Financial Analysts Journal, 52*(2), 56–60.

Barioni, M. C. N., Razente, H. L., Traina, A. J., & Traina, C. Jr. (2008). Accelerating k-medoid-based algorithms through metric access methods. *Journal of Systems and Software, 81*(3), 343–355. doi:10.1016/j.jss.2007.06.019

Barlas, P. (2015). A survey of open source data science tools. *International Journal of Intelligent Computing and Cybernetics, 8*(3), 232–261. doi:10.1108/ijicc-07-2014-0031

Barlas, P., Lanning, I., & Heavey, C. (2015). A survey of open sourcedata science tools. *International Journal of Intelligent Computing and Cybernetics, 8*(3), 232–261. doi:10.1108/IJICC-07-2014-0031

Barr, J. R. (2018). Machine Learning, A Tutorial with R. *IEEE First International Conference on AI for Industries*, 120–121. doi: 10.1109/AI4I.2018.8665676

Barton, D., & Court, D. (2012). Making advanced analytics work for you. *Harvard Business Review, 90*, 79–83. PMID:23074867

Basha & Rajput. (2019). *Classification of Sentiments from Movie Reviews Using KNIME.* Academic Press.

Basu, S. (1977). The Investment Performance of Common Stocks in Relation to their Price to Earnings Ratio: A Test of the Efficient Markets Hypothesis. *The Journal of Finance, 32*, 663–682.

Basu, S. (1983). The relationship between earnings yield, market value, and return for NYSE common stocks: Further evidence. *Journal of Financial Economics, 12*, 129–156.

Bates, D. S. (1991). The Crash of '87: Was It Expected? The Evidence from Options Markets. *The Journal of Finance, 46*(3), 1009–1044. doi:10.1111/j.1540-6261.1991.tb03775.x

Baum, J., Laroque, C., Oeser, B., Skoogh, A., & Subramaniyan, M. (2018). Applications of Big Data analytics and Related Technologies in Maintenance-Literature-Based Research. *Machines, 6*(54), 1–12. doi:10.3390/machines6040054

Bayrakdaroglu, A., Mirgen, C., & Kuyu, E. (2017). Relationship between profitability ratios and stock prices: An empirical analysis on BIST-100. *PressAcademia Procedia, 6*, 1–10.

Beattie, C., Leibo, J. Z., Teplyashin, D., Ward, T., Wainwright, M., Küttler, H., Lefrancq, A., Green, S., Valdés, V., Sadik, A., Schrittwieser, J., Anderson, K., York, S., Cant, M., Cain, A., Bolton, A., Gaffney, S., King, H., Hassabis, D., & Petersen, S. (2016). DeepMind Lab. 1–11. Retrieved from https://arxiv.org/abs/1612.03801

Beaver, W. H. (1989). *Financial accounting: An accounting revolution.* Prentice-Hall, Engle-wood Cliffs.

Becari, W., Ruiz, L., Evaristo, B. G. P., & Ramirez-Fernandez, F. J. (2016). Comparative analysis of classification algorithms on tactile sensors. Proceedings of the International Symposium on Consumer Electronics, ISCE, 1–2. doi:10.1109/ISCE.2016.7797324

Behera, T. K., & Panigrahi, S. (2015). Credit card fraud detection: A hybrid approach using fuzzy clustering & neural network. *Proceedings of the 2015 Second International Conference on Advances in Computing and Communication Engineering (ICACCE)*, 494–499. 10.1109/ICACCE.2015.33

Behera, T. K., & Panigrahi, S. (2017). Credit card fraud detection using a neuro-fuzzy expert system. In *Computational Intelligence in Data Mining*. Springer. doi:10.1007/978-981-10-3874-7_79

Bei, S., Zhen, Z., Xing, Z., Taocheng, L., & Qin, L. (2018). Movement Disorder Detection via Adaptively Fused Gait Analysis Based on Kinect Sensors. *IEEE Sensors Journal, 18*(17), 7305–7314. doi:10.1109/JSEN.2018.2839732

Bell, J. (2014). *Machine learning: hands-on for developers and technical professionals*. John Wiley & Sons publications. doi:10.1002/9781119183464

BerkeleyU. C. (2020). ML Base. http://www.mlbase.org/

Berman, F., Rutenbar, R., Christensen, H., Davidson, S., Estrin, D., Franklin, M., ... Szalay, A. (2016). *Realising the potential of data science*. National Science Foundation Computer and Information Science and Engineering Advisory Committee Data Science Working Group, doi:10.1126cience.1167742

Berman, K., Knight, J., & Case, J. (2013). *Financial Intelligence. A Manager's Guide to Knowing What the Numbers Really Mean*. Business Literacy Institute, Inc.

Besharah & Heacock. (2015). *Dinesafe Toronto: An Evaluation of the Placard System*. BCIT Institutional Repository.

Bhandari, L. C. (1988). Debt/Equity Ratio and Expected Common Stock Returns: Empirical Evidence. *The Journal of Finance, 43*(2), 507–528.

Bhardwaj, R., Nambiar, A. R., & Dutta, D. (2017, July). A study of machine learning in healthcare. In *2017 IEEE 41st Annual Computer Software and Applications Conference (COMPSAC)* (Vol. 2, pp. 236-241). IEEE. 10.1109/COMPSAC.2017.164

Bhargava, M., Dubelaar, C., & Scott, T. (1998). Predicting bankruptcy in the retail sector: An examination of the validity of key measures of performance. *Journal of Retailing and Consumer Services, 5*(2), 105–117.

Bhat, Rao, Shenoy, Venugopal, & Patnaik. (2009). An Efficient Prediction Model for Diabetic Database Using Soft Computing Techniques. In *International Workshop on Rough Sets, Fuzzy Sets, Data Mining, and Granular-Soft Computing*. Springer. 10.1007/978-3-642-10646-0_40

Bhat, A. (2014). K-medoids clustering using partitioning around medoids for performing face recognition. *International Journal of Soft Computing. Mathematics and Control, 3*(3), 1–12.

Bhat, A. Y. (2019). Normal and Abnormal Detection for Knee Osteoarthritis using Machine Learning Techniques. *International Journal of Recent Technology and Engineering, 8*(2), 6026–6033. doi:10.35940/ijrte.B3733.078219

Bhatia, P. (2019). *Data Mining and Data Warehousing: Principles and Practical Techniques*. Cambridge University Press. doi:10.1017/9781108635592

Bhattacharya, S., Xu, D., & Kumar, K. (2011). An ANN-based auditor decision support system using Benford's law. *Decision Support Systems, 50*(3), 576–584. doi:10.1016/j.dss.2010.08.011

Bhosale, H. S., & Gadekar, P. D. P. (2014). A review paper on big data and hadoop. *International Journal of Scientific and Research Publications, 4*(10).

Big, M. L. I. (2020b). BigML Bindings. Retrieved from https://bigml.com/tools/bindings

Big, M. L. I. (2020c). BigML Gas. Retrieved from https://bigml.com/tools/bigml-gas

Big, M. L. I. (2020d). BigML Predict server. Retrieved from https://bigml.com/tools/predictserver

Big, M. L. I. (2020e). BigML Zapier app. Retrieved from https://bigml.com/tools/bigml-zapier-app

Big, M. L. I. (2020f). BigMLer. Retrieved from https://bigml.com/tools/bigmler

Big, M. L. I. (2020g). BigMLx. Retrieved from https://bigml.com/tools/bigmlx

BigM. L. (2019). bigml. https://bigml.com/features

BigM. L. I. (2020a). BigML. Retrieved from https://bigml.com/tools

Black, F., & Scholes, M. (1973). The pricing of options and corporate liabilities. *Journal of Political Economy, 81*(3), 637–654. doi:10.1086/260062

Blalock, H. M. Jr. (1979). *Social statistics* (2nd ed.).

Bland, J. M., & Altman, D. G. (1996). Statistics notes: Measurement error. *BMJ (Clinical Research Ed.), 312*(7047), 1654. doi:10.1136/bmj.312.7047.1654 PMID:8664723

Blazquez, D., & Domenech, J. (2017). Web data mining for monitoring business export orientation. *Technol. Econ. Dev. Econ. Online (Bergheim)*, 1–23. doi:10.3846/ 20294913.2016.1213193

Blazquez, D., & Domenech, J. (2018). Big data sources and methods for social and economic analyses. *Technological Forecasting and Social Change, 139*, 99–113. doi:10.1016/j.techfore.2017.07.027

Blessia, T. F., Kumar, A., Singh, S., & Vennila, J. J. (2011). Application of Knowledge Based System for Diagnosis of Osteoarthritis. *Journal of Artificial Intelligence, 4*(4), 269–278. doi:10.3923/jai.2011.269.278

Bogucki, R., Cygan, M., Khan, C. B., Klimek, M., Milczek, J. K., & Mucha, M. (2019). Applying deep learning to right whale photo identification. *Conservation Biology, 33*(3), 676–684. doi:10.1111/cobi.13226 PubMed

Bollen, N. P. (1998). Valuing options in regime-switching models. *Journal of Derivatives, 6*(1), 38–50. doi:10.3905/jod.1998.408011

Bologa, A.-R., Bologa, R., & Florea, A. (2010). Big data and specific analysis methods for insurance fraud detection. *Database Systems Journal, 1*(1).

Bolt, L. C., Vinagayamoorthy, V., Winder, F., Schnittger, M., Ekran, M., Mukkamala, R. R., Lassen, N. B., Flesch, B., Hussain, A., & Vatrapu, R. (2016). Forecasting Nike's Sales Using Facebook data. *IEEE International Conference on Big Data (Big Data)*. 10.1109/BigData.2016.7840881

Bonthu, S., & Bindu, H. (2018). Review of Leading Data Analytics Tools. *IACSIT International Journal of Engineering and Technology, 7*. Advance online publication. doi:10.14419/ijet.v7i3.31.18190

Borgman, C. L. (2019). The lives and after lives of data. *Harvard Data Science Review*, (1). Retrieved from https://hdsr.mitpress.mit.edu/

Borode, M. (2011). Higher education and poverty reduction among youth in the Sub-Saharan Africa. *European Journal of Educational Studies*, *3*(1), 149–155.

Borthakur, D., Gray, J., Sen Sarma, J., Muthukkaruppan, K., Spiegelberg, N., Kuang, H., Ranganathan, K., Molkov, D., Menon, A., Rash, S., Schmidt, R., & Aiyer, A. (2011). Apache hadoop goes realtime at Facebook. *Proceedings of the ACM SIGMOD International Conference on Management of Data*, 1071–1080. 10.1145/1989323.1989438

Boyle, P. P. (1988). A lattice framework for option pricing with two state variables. *Journal of Financial and Quantitative Analysis*, *23*(1), 1–12. doi:10.2307/2331019

Boyle, P. P., Evnine, J., & Gibbs, S. (1989). Numerical evaluation of multivariate contingent claims. *Review of Financial Studies*, *2*(2), 241–250. doi:10.1093/rfs/2.2.241

Bozzon, A. (2018). Enterprise Crowd Computing for Human Aided Chatbots. *IEEE/ACM 1st International Workshop on Software Engineering for Cognitive Services (SE4COG)*, 29-30.

Brahim, A., Jennane, R., Riad, R., Janvier, T., Khedher, L., Toumi, H., & Lespessailles, E. (2019). A decision support tool for early detection of knee OsteoArthritis using X-ray imaging and machine learning: Data from the OsteoArthritis Initiative. *Computerized Medical Imaging and Graphics*, *73*, 11–18. doi:10.1016/j.compmedimag.2019.01.007 PMID:30784984

Brains, O. A. S. I. S. (2019). OASIS Brains Datasets. http://www.oasis-brains.org/#data

Brejová, B., Vinar, T., & Li, M. (2003), Pattern Discovery. In Introduction to bioinformatics. Humana Press.

Brennan, M. J. (1970). Taxes, Market Valuation, and Corporate Financial Policy. *National Tax Journal*, *23*, 417–427.

Bressler, L. (2010). The role of forensic accountants in fraud investigations: Importance of attorney and judge's perceptions. *Journal of Finance and Accountancy*, *14*(4).

BROAD Institute. (2019). BROAD Institute Cancer Program Datasets. http://portals.broadinstitute.org/cgi-bin/cancer/datasets.cgi

Brogaard, J., Carrion, A., Moyaert, T., Riordan, R., Shkilko, A., & Sokolov, K. (2018). High frequency trading and extreme price movements. *Journal of Financial Economics*, *128*(2), 253–265. doi:10.1016/j.jfineco.2018.02.002

Brown-Liburd, H., Issa, H., & Lombardi, D. (2015). Behavioral implications of big data's impact on audit judgment and decision making and future research directions. *Accounting Horizons*, *29*(2), 451–468. doi:10.2308/acch-51023

Buczak, A. L., & Guven, E. (2016). A Survey of Data Mining and Machine Learning Methods for Cyber Security Intrusion Detection. IEEE Communications Surveys and Tutorials, 18(2), 1153 1176. doi:10.1109/COMST.2015.2494502

Bulut, H. (2019). Türkiye'deki İllerin Yaşam Endekslerine Göre Kümelenmesi [The Clustering of Cities in Turkey According to Indexes of Life Satisfaction]. *Süleyman Demirel Üniversitesi Fen Bilimleri Enstitüsü Dergisi*, *23*(1), 74–82. doi:10.19113dufenbed.444143

Bunney, H. S., & Dale, B. G. (1997). The implementation of quality management tools and techniques: A study. *The TQM Magazine*.

Buttarelli, G. (2015). *Towards a new digital ethics- data, integrity and technology*. Retrieved from https://edps.europa.eu/sites/edp/files/publication/15-09-11_data_ethics_en.pdf

Caldarola, E. G., & Rinaldi, A. (2017). *Big Data Visualization Tools: A Survey - The New Paradigms*. Methodologies and Tools for Large Data Sets Visualization., doi:10.5220/0006484102960305

Callahan, A., & Shah, N. H. (2017). Machine learning in healthcare. In *Key Advances in Clinical Informatics* (pp. 279–291). Academic Press. doi:10.1016/B978-0-12-809523-2.00019-4

Çalmaşur, G., & Kılıç, A. (2018). Türkiye'de Hanehalkı Tüketim Harcamalarının Analizi [Analysis Of Household Consumption Expenditures in Turkey]. *Erzurum Teknik Üniversitesi Sosyal Bilimler Enstitüsü Dergisi, 3*(5), 61–73.

Cambridge University Press. (2019). Dataset. In Cambridge English Dictionary. https://dictionary.cambridge.org/es/diccionario/ingles/dataset

Campbell, J. Y. (1991). A Variance Decomposition for Stock Returns. *Economic Journal (London), 101*, 157–179.

Campbell, J. Y., & Shiller, R. J. (1988a). Stock Prices, Earnings and Expected Dividends. *The Journal of Finance, 43*(3), 661–676.

Campbell, J. Y., & Shiller, R. J. (1988b). The Dividend-Price Ratio and Expectations of Future Dividends and Discount Factors. *Review of Financial Studies, 1*(3), 195–228.

Cao, L. (2017). Data Science: A Comprehensive Overview. *ACM Computing Surveys, 50*(3), 1–42. doi:10.1145/3076253

Capaul, C., Rowley, I., & Sharpe, W. F. (1993). International value and growth stock returns. *Financial Analysts Journal, 49*(1), 27–36.

Cardinaels, E., & van Veen-Dirks, P. M. G. (2010). Financial versus non-financial information: The impact of information organization and presentation in a Balanced Scorecard. *Accounting, Organizations and Society, 35*, 565–578.

Carriero, A., Zavatsky, A., Stebbins, J., Theologis, T., & Shefelbine, S. J. (2009). Determination of gait patterns in children with spastic diplegic cerebral palsy using principal components. *Gait & Posture, 29*(1), 71–75. doi:10.1016/j.gaitpost.2008.06.011 PubMed

Carto. (2019). Data mapping and visualization tools. https://carto.com/builder/

Casadei, R., Fortino, G., Pianini, D., Russo, W., Savaglio, C., & Viroli, M. (2019). A development approach for collective opportunistic Edge-of-Things services. *Information Sciences, 498*, 154–169. doi:10.1016/j.ins.2019.05.058

CaseOLAP. (2019). CaseOLAP. https://caseolap.github.io/

Castro, F. M., Marin-Jimenez, M. J., Guil, N., Lopez-Tapia, S., & Perez De La Blanca, N. (2017). Evaluation of Cnn Architectures for Gait Recognition Based on Optical Flow Maps. In Lecture Notes in Informatics (LNI), Proceedings - Series of the Gesellschaft Fur Informatik (GI) (pp. 1-5). doi:10.23919/BIOSIG.2017.8053503

Cattuto, C., Quaggiotto, M., & Panisson, A. A. A. (2013). Time-varying social networks in a graph database: a Neo4j use case. https://dl.acm.org/doi/abs/10.1145/2484425.2484442

Cengiz, H., & Püskül, A. Ö. (2016). Hisse Senedi Getirileri ve Karlılık Arasındaki İlişki: Borsa İstanbul Endeksinde İşlem Gören İşletmelerin Analizi. *Yalova Sosyal Bilimler Dergisi, 7*(12), 295–306.

Centers for Medicare & Medicaid Services. (2019). Hospital Compare datasets. https://data.medicare.gov/data/hospital-compare

Centre for Suicide Prevention. (2015). *Updated and Expanded: Teen Suicide Resource toolkit.* https://www.suicideinfo.ca/wp-content/uploads/2016/08/Teen-Resource-Toolkit-Web.pdf

Chaboud, A. P., Chiquoine, B., Hjalmarsson, E., & Vega, C. (2014). Rise of the machines: Algorithmic trading in the foreign exchange market. *The Journal of Finance, 69*(5), 2045–2084. doi:10.1111/jofi.12186

Chandrima, R., Siddharth, S. R., & Manjusha, P. (2018). Big Data Optimization Techniques: A Survey. *International Journal of Information Engineering and Electronic Business*, *10*(4), 41–48. doi:10.5815/ijieeb.2018.04.06

Chandrinos, S. K., Sakkas, G., & Lagaros, N. D. (2018). AIRMS: A risk management tool using machine learning. *Expert Systems with Applications*, *105*, 34–48. doi:10.1016/j.eswa.2018.03.044

Chang, H. S., Fu, M. C., & Hu, J. S. M. (2016). Google DeepMind's AlphaGo.https://www.informs.org/ORMS-Today/ Public-Articles/October-Volume-43-Number-5/GoogleDeepMind-s-AlphaGo

Chang, P. C., Lin, J. J., & Dzan, W. Y. (2012). Forecasting of manufacturing cost in mobile phone products by case-based reasoning and artificial neural network models. *Journal of Intelligent Manufacturing*, *23*(3), 517–531. doi:10.100710845-010-0390-7

Chang, R., Lee, A., Ghoniem, M., Kosara, R., Ribarsky, W., Yang, J., Suma, E., Ziemkiewicz, C., Kern, D., & Sudjianto, A. (2008). Scalable and interactive visual analysis of financial wire transactions for fraud detection. *Information Visualization*, *7*(1), 63–76. doi:10.1057/palgrave.ivs.9500172

Chan, J. F., Yuan, S., Kok, K., To, K. K., Chu, H., Yang, J., Xing, F., Liu, J., Yip, C. C., Poon, R. W., Tsoi, H., Lo, S. K., Chan, K., Poon, V. K., Chan, W., Ip, J. D., Cai, J., Cheng, V. C., Chen, H., & Yuen, K. (2020). A familial cluster of pneumonia associated with the 2019 novel coronavirus indicating person-to-person transmission: A study of a family cluster. *Lancet*, *395*(10223), 514–523. doi:10.1016/S0140-6736(20)30154-9 PubMed

Chan, L. K., Hamao, Y., & Lakonishok, J. (1991). Fundamentals and stock returns in Japan. *The Journal of Finance*, *46*(5), 1739–1764.

Chapman, A., Simperl, E., Koesten, L., Konstantinidis, G., Ibáñez, L.-D., Kacprzak, E., & Groth, P. (2019). Dataset search: A survey. *The VLDB Journal*. Advance online publication. doi:10.100700778-019-00564-x

Charles, D., Ramona, F., & Ogilby, S. (2009). *Characteristics and skills of the forensic accountant*. American Institute of Certified Public Accountants.

Chavarnakul, T., & Enke, D. (2008). Intelligent technical analysis based equivolume charting for stock trading using neural networks. *Expert Systems with Applications*, *34*(2), 1004–1017. doi:10.1016/j.eswa.2006.10.028

Chen & Pingjun. (2018). *Knee Osteoarthritis Severity Grading Dataset*. Mendeley Data. doi:10.17632/56rmx5bjcr.1

Chen, H.L., Yang, B., Wang, G., Liu, J., Chen, Y.D., & Liu, D.Y. (2012). A three-stage expert system based on support vector machines for thyroid disease diagnosis. *J Med Syst.*, *36*(3), 1953-63.

Chen, X., Ye, Y., Williams, G., & Xu, X. (2007). A survey of open source data mining systems. Lecture Notes in Computer Science, 4819 LNAI(60603066), 3–14. doi:10.1007/978-3-540-77018-3_2

Cheng, Wang, Zhong, Xie, Mahmood, Wang, & Mueller. (2016). Model-driven Visual Analytics for Big Data. *IEEE, New York Scientific Data Summit (NYSDS)*, 1-2. doi:10.1109/NYSDS.2016.7747827

Chen, H.-H. (2008). Stock selection using data envelopment analysis. *Industrial Management & Data Systems*, *108*(9), 1255–1268.

Chen, H.-L., Yang, B., Wang, G., Liu, J., Chen, Y.-D., & Liu, D.-Y. (2012). A three-stage expert system based on support vector machines for thyroid disease diagnosis. *Journal of Medical Systems*, *36*(3), 1953–1963. doi:10.100710916-011-9655-8 PMID:21286792

Chen, H., Roger, H. C., & Veda, C. S. (2012). Business Intelligence and Analytics: From Big Data to Big Impact. *Management Information Systems Quarterly*, *36*(4), 1165–1188. doi:10.2307/41703503

Chen, J. (2012). The synergistic effects of IT-enabled resources on organizational capabilities and firm performance. *Information & Management*, *49*(34), 140–152. doi:10.1016/j.im.2012.01.005

Chen, J.-S., Hung Tai, T., & Huang, Y.-H. (2009). Service Delivery Innovation: Antecedents and Impact on Firm Performance. *Journal of Service Research*, *12*(1), 36–55.

Chen, K. H., & Shimerda, T. A. (1981). An empirical analysis of useful financial ratios. *Financial Management*, *10*(1), 51–60.

Chen, M., Li, W., Hao, Y., Qian, Y., & Humar, I. (2018). Edge cognitive computing based smart healthcare system. *Future Generation Computer Systems*, *86*, 403–411. doi:10.1016/j.future.2018.03.054

Chen, S. D. (2016). Detection of fraudulent financial statements using the hybrid data mining approach. *SpringerPlus*, *5*(1), 16. doi:10.118640064-016-1707-6 PMID:26848429

Chen, S. W., & Shen, C. H. (2009). Is the Stock Price Higher than that Implied by the Fundamentals? *International Research Journal of Finance and Economics*, *29*, 87–109.

Chew, P. A., & Robinson, D. G. (2012). Automated account reconciliation using probabilistic and statistical techniques. *International Journal of Accounting and Information Management*, *20*(4), 322–334. doi:10.1108/18347641211272722

Chollet, F. (2019). Keras: The Python Deep Learning library. https://keras.io/

Choubey, D. K., & Paul, S. (2016). Classification techniques for diagnosis of diabetes: A review. *International Journal of Biomedical Engineering and Technology*, *21*(1), 15–39. doi:10.1504/IJBET.2016.076730

Chu, C. C. F., & Chan, P. K. (2018). Mining Profitable High Frequency Pairs Trading Forex Signal Using Copula and Deep Neural Network. *2018 19th IEEE/ACIS International Conference on Software Engineering, Artificial Intelligence, Networking and Parallel/Distributed Computing (SNPD)*, 312-316.

Chung, K. H., & Pruitt, W. (1994). A Simple Approximation of Tobin's q. *Financial Management*, *23*(3), 70–74.

Chun, S. H., & Kim, S. H. (2004). Data mining for financial prediction and trading: Application to single and multiple markets. *Expert Systems with Applications*, *26*(2), 131–139. doi:10.1016/S0957-4174(03)00113-1

Chun, S. H., & Park, Y. J. (2006). A new hybrid data mining technique using a regression case-based reasoning: Application to financial forecasting matter. *Expert Systems with Applications*, *31*(2), 329–336. doi:10.1016/j.eswa.2005.09.053

Cielen, A., Peeters, L., & Vanhoof, K. (2004). Bankruptcy prediction using a data envelopment analysis. *European Journal of Operational Research*, *154*, 526–532.

Cielen, D., Meysman, A. D. B., & Ali, M. (2016). *Introducing data science*. Manning Publications Co.

Cleveland, W. S. (2001). Data Science: An Action Plan for Expanding the Technical Areas of the Field of Statistics. *International Statistical Review*, *69*(1), 21–26. doi:10.1111/j.1751-5823.2001.tb00477.x

Cochrane, J. H. (1992). Explaining the Variance of Price-Dividend Ratios. *Review of Financial Studies*, *5*, 243–280.

Codd, E. F. (1990). *The relational model for database management: version 2*. Addison-Wesley Longman Publishing Co., Inc.

Columbus, L. (2019). *AI is predicting the future of online fraud detection*. Retrieved from https://www.forbes.com/sites/louiscolumbus/2019/08/01/ai-is-predicting-the-future-of-online-fraud-detection/

Comai, A. (2018). Beyond patent analytics: Insights from a scientific and technological data mashup based on a case example. *World Patent Information*, *55*, 61–77.

Commission, E. (2019). PALIA suite for process mining https://ec.europa.eu/eip/ageing/commitments-tracker/b3/palia-suite-process-mining_en

Computation and Visualization environment. (2020). Data Melt. Retrieved from https://datamelt. org /

Comstock. (2018). *Skin Vision gets $7.6M to continue expanding skin cancer app Skin Vision*. Retrieved from https://www.mobihealthnews.com/content/skinvision-gets-76m-continue-expanding-skin-cancer-app

Conneau, A., Schwenk, H., Le Cun, Y., & Barrault, L. (2017). Very deep convolutional networks for text classification. 15th Conference of the European Chapter of the Association for Computational Linguistics, EACL 2017 - Proceedings of Conference. doi:10.18653/v1/E17-1104

Connolly, S. (2012). *7 key drivers for the big data market*. Retrieved from https://hortonworks.com

Conrad, J., Wahal, S., & Xiang, J. (2015). High-frequency quoting, trading, and the efficiency of prices. *Journal of Financial Economics, 116*(2), 271–291. doi:10.1016/j.jfineco.2015.02.008

Cooper, W. W., Seiford, L. M., & Tone, K. (2006). *Introduction to data envelopment analysis and its uses: with DEA-solver software and references*. Springer.

Cooper, W., Seiford, L. M., & Zhu, J. (2011). *Handbook on Data Envelopment Analysis*. Springer.

Copeland, T., Koller, T., & Murrin, J. (1996). *Valuation: Measuring and Managing the Value of Companies*. Wiley.

Corrales, D. C., Ledezma, A., & Corrales, J. C. (2015). A Conceptual Framework for Data Quality in Knowledge Discovery Tasks (FDQ-KDT): A Proposal. *Journal of Computers, 10*(6), 396–405. doi:10.17706/jcp.10.6.396-405

Cournapeau, D. (2019). scikit-learn. https://scikit-learn.org/stable/

Cox, J. C., Ross, S. A., & Rubinstein, M. (1979). Option pricing: A simplified approach. *Journal of Financial Economics, 7*(3), 229–263. doi:10.1016/0304-405X(79)90015-1

Craig, J., & Moores, K. (2005). Balanced Scorecards to drive the strategic planning of family firms. *Family Business Review, 18*(2), 105–122.

Crawley, M., & Wahlen, J. (2014). Analytics in empirical/archival financial accounting research. *Business Horizons, 57*(5), 583–593. doi:10.1016/j.bushor.2014.05.002

Creamer, G. (2015). Can a corporate network and news sentiment improve portfolio optimization using the Black–Litterman model? *Quantitative Finance, 15*(8), 1405–1416. doi:10.1080/14697688.2015.1039865

Cukier, K., & Mayer-Schoenberger, V. (2013). The rise of big data: How it's changing the way we think about the world. *Foreign Affairs, 92*. https://www.foreignaffairs.com/articles/2013-04-03/rise-big-data

Curme, C., Preis, T., Stanley, H. E., & Moat, H. S. (2014). Quantifying the semantics of search behavior before stock market moves. *Proceedings of the National Academy of Sciences of the United States of America, 111*(32), 11600–11605. doi:10.1073/pnas.1324054111 PMID:25071193

Cutler, D. M., & Lleras-Muney, A. (2007). Education and health: evaluating theories and evidence. In J. S. House, R. F. Schoeni, G. A. Kaplan, & H. Pollack (Eds.), *The Health Effects of Social and Economic Policy*. Russell Sage Foundation.

Czyz, M. J., Filter, M., & Buschulte, A. (2018). Application of data science in risk assessment and early warning. *EFSA Journal, 16*, e16088. Advance online publication. PubMed doi:10.2903/j.efsa.2018.e16088

Daghistani, T., & Alshammari, R. (2016). Diagnosis of Diabetes by Applying Data Mining Classification Techniques. *International Journal of Advanced Computer Science & Applications, 1*(7), 329–332. doi:10.14569/IJACSA.2016.070747

Dagiliene, L., & Kloviene, L. (2019). Motivation to use big data and big data analytics in external auditing. *Managerial Auditing Journal*, *34*(7), 750–782. Advance online publication. doi:10.1108/MAJ-01-2018-1773

Dai, W., & Ji, W. (2014). A mapreduce implementation of C4. 5 decision tree algorithm. *International Journal of Database Theory and Application*, *7*(1), 49–60. doi:10.14257/ijdta.2014.7.1.05

Dai, W., Zhang, H., Yu, J., Xu, H., Chen, H., Luo, S., Zhang, H., Liang, L., Wu, X., Lei, Y., & Lin, F. (2020). CT imaging and differential diagnosis of COVID-19. *Canadian Association of Radiologists Journal*, *71*(2), 195–200. doi:10.1177/0846537120913033 PubMed

Daniel, B. K. (2019). Big Data and data science: A critical review of issues foreducational research. *British Journal of Educational Technology*, *50*(1), 101–113. doi:10.1111/bjet.12595

Dara & Anuradhab. (2017). *Use of orthogonal arrays and design of experiment via Taguchi L9 method in probability of default.* Growing Science Ltd., doi:10.5267/j.ac.2017.11.001

Dar, A. A., & Anuradha, N. (2017a). One Period Binomial Model: The risk-neutral probability measure assumption and the state price deflator approach. *International Journal of Mathematics and Trends and Technology*, *43*(4), 246–255.

Dar, A. A., & Anuradha, N. (2017b). Value at Risk (VaR) using statistical method. *International Journal of Science. Engineering and Management*, *2*(11), 42–49.

Dar, A. A., & Anuradha, N. (2018). Comparison: Binomial model and Black Scholes model. *Quantitative Finance and Economics*, *2*(1), 230–245. doi:10.3934/QFE.2018.1.230

Das, S. R., & Chen, M. Y. (2007). Yahoo! for Amazon: Sentiment Extraction from Small Talk on the Web. *Management Science*, *53*(9), 1375–1388. doi:10.1287/mnsc.1070.0704

Databricks, I. (2020). MLflow. Retrieved from https://mlflow.org/

Databricks. (2019). Databricks Unified Analytics Platform. https://databricks.com/product/unified-analytics-platform

DataHub. (2018). Climate Change Data. https://datahub.io/collections/climate-change

Dataiku. (2019). dataiku. https://www.dataiku.com/

DataRobot. (2020). Data Robot. Retrieved from https://www.datarobot.com/

Davenport, H. T., & Dyche, J. (2013). *Big Data in Big Companies.* Retrieved from http://www.sas.com/ resources /asset/ BigData-in-Big-Companies.pdf

Davenport, T. H., & Dyché, J. (2013). Big data in big companies. *International Institute for Analytics*, 3. https://coseer. com/blog/what-is-cognitive-computing/

Davenport, H. T., & Jill, D. (2013). *Big data in big companies.* International Institute for Analytics.

Davenport, T. H. (2010). Business intelligence and organizational decisions. *International Journal of Business Intelligence Research*, *1*(1), 1–12. doi:10.4018/jbir.2010071701

Davenport, T. H., & Harris, J. G. (2007). *Competing on analytics: The new science of winning.* Harvard Business Press.

David Kokkelink, L. C. R. (2019). UC Data Wrapper. Retrieved from https://blog.datawrapper .de/create-datavisualization- for-free/

David Maguire. (2016). *Interoperability and the NHS: are they incompatible?* Accessed from https://www.kingsfund. org.uk/blog/2016/08/interoperability-and-nhs

David, A. F. (2009). *Statistical Models: Theory and Practice*. Cambridge University Press.

David, G., Magnus, J., Higinio, M., & Julian, S. (2019). *Review of the Complexity of Managing Big Data of the Internet of Things*. Advance online publication. doi:10.1155/2019/4592902

Day, S. (2017). *Quants turn to machine learning to model market impact*. Retrieved from https://www.risk.net/asset-management/4644191/quants-turnto-machine-learning-to-model-market-impact

DB. (2020). *Big data: how it can become differentiator*. Deutsche Bank Report. Retrieved from https://cib.db.com/

De Clercq, D., Jalota, D., Shang, R., Ni, K., Zhang, Z., Khan, A., Wen, Z., Caicedo, L., & Yuan, K. (2019). Machine learning powered software for accurate prediction of biogas production: A case study on industrial-scale Chinese production data. *Journal of Cleaner Production, 218*, 390–399. doi:10.1016/j.jclepro.2019.01.031

De Gennaro, M., Paffumi, E., & Martini, G. (2016). Big Data for Supporting Low-Carbon Road Transport Policies in Europe: Applications, Challenges and Opportunities. *Big Data Research, 6*, 11–25.

De Laet, T., Papageorgiou, E., Nieuwenhuys, A., & Desloovere, K. (2017). Does expert knowledge improve automatic probabilistic classification of gait joint motion patterns in children with cerebral palsy? *PLoS One, 12*(6), 1–18. doi:10.1371/journal.pone.0178378 PubMed

De Wet, N., & Odimegwu, C. (2017). Contextual determinants of adolescent mortality in South Africa. *African Health Sciences, 17*(1), 62–69. doi:10.4314/ahs.v17i1.9 PMID:29026378

Deaves, R., Miu, P., & White, C. B. (2008). Canadian stock market multiples and their predictive content. *International Review of Economics & Finance, 17*(3), 457–466.

Deb, C., & Lee, S. E. (2018). Determining key variables influencing energy consumption in office buildings through cluster analysis of pre-and post-retrofit building data. *Energy and Building, 159*, 228–245. doi:10.1016/j.enbuild.2017.11.007

DeBerg, C. L., & Murdoch, B. (1994). An Empirical Investigation of the Usefulness of Earnings Per Share Disclosures. *Journal of Accounting, Auditing & Finance, 9*(2), 249–260.

DeBondt, W., & Thaler, R. (1987). Further Evidence on Investor Overreactions and Stock Market Seasonality. *The Journal of Finance, 42*, 557–581.

Deep, K., Jain, M. & Salhi, S. (2019). *Logistics, Supply Chain and Financial Predictive Analytics*. Springer.

Değirmenci, T., & Özbakır, L. (2018). Differentiating households to analyze consumption patterns: A data mining study on official household budget data. *Wiley Interdisciplinary Reviews. Data Mining and Knowledge Discovery, 8*(1), e1227. doi:10.1002/widm.1227

Dejaeger, K., Hamers, B., Poelmans, J., & Baesens, B. (2010). A novel approach to the evaluation and improvement of data quality in the financial sector. *Proceedings of the 15th International Conference on Information Quality*.

Delen, D., Fuller, C., McCann, C., & Ray, D. (2009). Analysis of healthcare coverage: A data mining approach. *Expert Systems with Applications, 36*(2), 995–1003. doi:10.1016/j.eswa.2007.10.041

Deloitte. (2016). Why artificial intelligence is a game changer for risk management. *Deloitte Advisory*. Retrieved from https://www2.deloitte.com/content/dam/Deloitte/ us/Documents /audit/us-ai-risk-powers-performance.pdf

Deloitte. (2018). *The evolution of forensic investigations*. Retrieved July 1, 2019, from https://www2.deloitte.com/us/en/pages/advisory/articles/evolution-forensic-investigations-series.html

Demaagd, Oliver, & Oostendorp. (2012). Practical Computer Vision with SimpleCV: The Simple Way to Make Technology See. Academic Press.

Dempsey, M. (2010). The book-to-market equity ratio as a proxy for risk: Evidence from Australian markets. *Australian Journal of Management, 35*(1), 7–21.

Demšar, J., Curk, T., Erjavec, A., Gorup, Č., Hočevar, T., Milutinovič, M., ... Zupan, B. (2013). Orange: Data mining toolbox in python. *Journal of Machine Learning Research, 14*, 2349–2353.

Deo, R., & Panigrahi, S. (2019, November). Performance Assessment of Machine Learning Based Models for Diabetes Prediction. In *2019 IEEE Healthcare Innovations and Point of Care Technologies (HI-POCT)* (pp. 147-150). IEEE.

Devadiga, N., Kothari, H., Jain, H., & Sankhe, S. (2017). E-banking security using cryptography, steganography and data mining. *International Journal of Computers and Applications, 7*(164), 26–30. doi:10.5120/ijca2017913746

Developers, D. core. (2019). Dask. Retrieved from https://dask.org/

DevelopersS. (2020). SciPy. Retrieved from https://www.scipy.org/

Devlin, J., Chang, M., Lee, K., & Toutanova, K. (2019). *BERT: Pre-training of Deep Bidirectional Transformers for Language Understanding*. NAACL-HLT.

Dhar, V. (2013). Data science and prediction. *Communications of the ACM, 56*(12), 64–73. doi:10.1145/2500499

Diabetes and high blood pressure. (n.d.). Available: http://www. bloodpressureuk. org/Blood Pressure- andyou Yourbody/

Diabetes.co.uk. (n.d.a.). *Pre-diabetes*. Available: https://www.diabetes.co.uk/pre-diabetes.html

Diabetes.co.uk. (n.d.b). *Type1diabetes*. Available: http://www.diabetes.co.uk/ type1 -diabetes.html

Diabetes.co.uk. (n.d.c). *Type2Diabetes*. Available: http://www.diabetes.co.uk /type2-diabetes.html

Dichev, C., & Dicheva, D. (2017). Towards data science literacy. *Procedia Computer Science, 108C*, 2151–2160. doi:10.1016/j.procs.2017.05.240

Dikmen, F. C. (2018). Investigation of Well-Being and Quality of Life of The Turkish Provinces by Clustering Analysis [Türkiye'deki İllerin İyi Oluş Ve Yaşam Kalitesinin Kümeleme Çözümlemesiyle İncelenmesi]. In F. B. Candan & H. Kapucu (Eds.), Current Debates in Business Studies: Current Debates in Social Sciences (Vol. 15, p. 169). Academic Press.

Dilla, W. N., & Raschke, R. L. (2015). Data visualization for fraud detection: Practice implications and a call for future research. *International Journal of Accounting Information Systems, 16*, 1–22. doi:10.1016/j.accinf.2015.01.001

Dogantekin, E., Dogantekin, A., & Avci, D. (2011). An expert system based on generalized discriminant analysis and wavelet support vector machine for diagnosis of thyroid diseases. *Journal of Expert Systems with Applications, 38*(1), 146–150. doi:10.1016/j.eswa.2010.06.029

Dolatabadi, E., Taati, B., & Mihailidis, A. (2017). An automated classification of pathological gait using unobtrusive sensing technology. *IEEE Transactions on Neural Systems and Rehabilitation Engineering, 25*(12), 2336–2346. doi:10.1109/TNSRE.2017.2736939 PubMed

Dolice, Z., Castro, R., & Moarcas, A. (n.d.). Robots in healthcare: a solution or a problem? Workshop proceedings. https://www.europarl.europa.eu/committees/en/ supporting-analyses/sa-highlights

Domenico, B., Caron, J., Davis, E., Kambic, R., & Nativi, S. (2002). Thematic real-time environmental distributed data services (thredds): Incorporating interactive analysis tools into nsdl. *Journal of Digital Information, 2*(4), 114.

Domino Data Lab. (2019). Domino Data Science Platform. https://www.dominodatalab.com/platform/

Donoho, D. (2015). 50 years of data Science. *Tukey Centennial Workshop*, 1–41.

Donoho, D. (2017). 50 Years of Data Science. *Journal of Computational and Graphical Statistics*, 26(4), 745–766. doi:10.1080/10618600.2017.1384734

Dowdy, S., Wearden, S., & Chilko, D. (2004). Statistics for research (3rd ed.). New York: John Wiley. doi:10.1002/0471477435

Dr, B., & Haufiku, M. (2018, May 6). Namibia considers PPP to boost public health care. *Namibia considers PPP to boost public health care*. Retrieved from https://southerntimesafrica.com/site/news/namibia-considers-ppp-to-boost-public-health-care

du Jardin, P., & Séverin, E. (2011). Predicting corporate bankruptcy using a self-organizing map: An empirical study to improve the forecasting horizon of a financial failure model. *Decision Support Systems*, 51(3), 701–711.

Dubey, H., Yang, J., Constant, N., Amiri, A. M., Yang, Q., & Makodiya, K. (2015). Fog Data: Enhancing Telehealth Big Data Through Fog Computing (#4). Proceedings of the ASE BigData & SocialInformatics 2015, 14:1-14:6. 10.1145/2818869.2818889

Edirisinghe, N. C. P., & Zhang, X. (2007). Generalized DEA model of fundamental analysis and its application to portfolio optimization. *Journal of Banking & Finance*, 31, 3311–3335.

Education, L. U. (2018). UC Apache Spark. Retrieved fromhttps://medium.com/@tao_66792/how-are-bigcompanies-using-apache-spark-413743dbbbae

Ekins, S., Nikolsky, Y., Bugrim, A., Kirillov, E., & Nikolskaya, T. (2007). Pathway mapping tools for analysis of high content data. In High Content Screening (pp. 319-350). Humana Press.

Elhadi, M. T. (2000). Bankruptcy support system: Taking advantage of information retrieval and case-based reasoning. *Expert Systems with Applications*, 18(3), 215–219. doi:10.1016/S0957-4174(99)00063-9

Embarak, O. (2019). *Data analytics and visualization using Python-analyze data to create visualization for BI system*. APress California.

Enlyft. (2020). UC Oracle data mining. Retrieved from https://enlyft.com/tech/products/oracle data-mining

EpiData. (2019). EpiData. https://epidata.co/

Erbao, C., Ruotian, G., & Mingyong, L. (2018). Research on the vehicle routing problem with interval demands. *Applied Mathematical Modelling*, 54, 332–346. doi:10.1016/j.apm.2017.09.050

Erdaş, H., Erdoğan, S., & Erdoğan, A. (2017). Türkiye'de Hane Halkı Tüketim Harcamalarının Belirleyicileri [Determinants Of Households Consumption Expenditure In Turkey]. *Trakya Üniversitesi İktisadi ve İdari Bilimler Fakültesi Dergisi*, 6(1), 309–326.

Ernst & Young. (2013). *Demystifying "big data" analytics*. Retrieved from https://www.ey.com

Ernst & Young. (2016). *Shifting into high gear: mitigating risks and demonstrating returns global forensic data analytics survey 2016*. Author.

Ernst & Young. (2018). *Integrity in the spotlight, the future of compliance; 15th global fraud survey*. Retrieved from https://www.ey.com/Publication/vwLUAssets/ey-global-fids-fraud-survey-2018/$FILE/ey-global-fids-fraud-survey-2018.pdf

Esen, M. F., Bilgic, E., & Basdas, U. (2019). How to detect illegal corporate insider trading? A data mining approach for detecting suspicious insider transactions. *Intelligent Systems in Accounting, Finance & Management, 26*(2), 60–70. doi:10.1002/isaf.1446

Eswari, T., Sampath, P., & Lavanya, S. (2015). Predictive methodology for diabetic data analysis in big data. *Procedia Computer Science, 50*, 203–208. doi:10.1016/j.procs.2015.04.069

EUMETNET. (2019). European Climate Assessment & Dataset project. https://www.ecad.eu/

European Union Agency for Network and Information Security (ENISA). (2016). *Big data threat landscape and big data practice guide*. ENISA.

Eurostat. (2019). https://ec.europa.eu/eurostat/web/nuts/history

Evans, C., Pappas, K., & Xhafa, F. (2013). Utilizing artificial neural networks and genetic algorithms to build an algo-trading model for intra-day foreign exchange speculation. *Mathematical and Computer Modelling, 58*(5–6), 1249–1266. doi:10.1016/j.mcm.2013.02.002

Evans, W. (1996). Computer-supported content analysis: Trends, tools, and techniques. *Social Science Computer Review, 14*(3), 269–279. doi:10.1177/089443939601400302

Everitt, B. S. (1977). *The Analysis of Contingency Tables*. Halstead Press. doi:10.1007/978-1-4899-2927-3

Faizura, H., Rosmah, A., Nazri, K., & Sufyan, B. (2017). Descriptive analysis and text analysis in Systematic Literature Review: A review of Master Data Management. *International Conference on Research and Innovation in Information Systems (ICRIIS)*, 1-6.

Falbel, Allaire, & Chollet. (2020). Keras. Retrieved from https://keras .rstudio.com/index.html

Fama, E. F., & French, K. (1992). The cross-section of expected stock returns. *The Journal of Finance, 47*, 427–465.

Fama, E. F., & French, K. (1993). Common risk factors in the returns on stocks and bonds. *Journal of Financial Economics, 33*, 3–56.

Fama, E. F., & French, K. R. (1998). Value versus growth: The international evidence. *The Journal of Finance, LIII*(6), 1975–1999.

Fama, E., & French, K. (1988). Dividend Yields and Expected Stock Returns. *Journal of Financial Economics, 22*, 3–26.

Fang-Ming, L., & Wang-Ching, C. (2010). A precaution diagnosis of financial distress via Grey Situation Decision. *Journal of Grey System, 22*(4), 395–403.

Fangxuan, L., Jinchao, H., Juntian, L., Wengui, X., & Zhiyong, Y. (2019). Multivariate analysis of clinicopathological and prognostic significance of miRNA 106b~25 cluster in gastric cancer. *Cancer Cell International, 19*, 1–10. PMID:30622437

Farrell, K. J., & Carey, C. C. (2018). Power, pitfalls, and potential for integrating computational literacy into undergraduate ecology courses. *Ecology and Evolution, 8*(16), 7744–7751. doi:10.1002/ece3.4363 PubMed

Feinstein, L., Sabates, R., Anderson, T. M., Sorhaindo, A., & Hammond, C. (2006). *What are effects of education on health? Measuring the Effects of Education on Health and Civic Engagement: Proceedings of the Copenhagen Symposium*. OECD.

Feng, Y., Cui, N., Hao, W., Gao, L., & Gong, D. (2019). Estimation of soil temperature from meteorological data using different machine learning models. *Geoderma, 338*, 67–77. doi:10.1016/j.geoderma.2018.11.044

Fernandes, K. J., Raja, V., & Whalley, A. (2006). Lessons from implementing the balanced scorecard in a small and medium size manufacturing organization. *Technovation*, *26*, 623–634.

Figini, S., Bonelli, F., & Giovannini, E. (2017). Solvency prediction for small and medium enterprises in banking. *Decision Support Systems*, *102*, 91–97. doi:10.1016/j.dss.2017.08.001

Figueiredo, J., Santos, C. P., & Moreno, J. C. (2018). Automatic recognition of gait patterns in human motor disorders using machine learning: A review. *Medical Engineering & Physics*, *53*, 1–12. doi:10.1016/j.medengphy.2017.12.006 PubMed

Financial Stability Board. (2017). *Artificial intelligence and machine learning in financial services Market developments and financial stability implications*. Financial Stability Board.

Flach, P. (2012). *Machine learning: the art and science of algorithms that make sense of data*. Cambridge University Press. doi:10.1017/CBO9780511973000

Fleckenstein, M., & Fellows, L. (2018). *Modern data strategy*. Springer. doi:10.1007/978-3-319-68993-7

Floridi, L., & Cowls, J. (2019). A unified framework of five principles for AI in society. *Harvard Data Science Review*, (1), 1–13. Retrieved from https://hdsr.mitpress.mit.edu/

Foley, E., & Guillemette, M. G. (2010). What is business intelligence? *International Journal of Business Intelligence Research*, *1*(4), 1–28. doi:10.4018/jbir.2010100101

Foote. (2016). *A Brief History of Data Science*. Retrieved from https://www.dataversity.net/brief-history-data-science/

Forgo, N., Honald, S., & van den Hoven, J. (2020). *An ethico-legal framework for social data science*. International Journal of Data Science and Analytics., doi:10.100741060-020-00211-7

Foroughi, F., & Luksch, P. (2018). *Data Science Methodology for Cybersecurity Projects*. Academic Press.

Forrester. (2019). Big Data Fabric 2.0 Drives Data Democratization. In *The Insights-Driven Business Playbook*. Forrester Research.

Fortune. (2019). *Big Data Technology Market Size, Share & Industry Analysis*. Fortune Business Insights.

Foundation, T. A. S. (2018a). Apache Spark. Retrieved from https://spark.apache.org/

Foundation, T. A. S. (2019). ZooKeeper. Retrieved from https://zookeeper.apache.org/

Foundation., T. A. S. (2019). Pig. Retrieved from https://pig.apache.org/

FoundationP. S. (2020). Cython. Retrieved from https://pypi.org/project/Cython/

FoundationT. A. S. (2018b). Sqoop. Retrieved from https://sqoop.apache.org/

FoundationT. A. S. (2020a). Hadoop. Retrieved from https://hadoop.apache.org/

FoundationT. A. S. (2020b). Hive. Retrieved from https://hive.apache.org/

Fraser, E., & Page, M. (2000). Value and momentum strategies: Evidence from the Johannesburg Stock Exchange. *The Investment Analysts Journal*, *29*(51), 25–35.

Free Software Foundation. (2018). PSPP. https://www.gnu.org/software/pspp/

Freund, J. E. (2004). Mathematical statistics with applications (7th ed.). Irwin Miller.

Fukuyama, H. (1993). Technical and scale efficiency of Japanese commerical banks: A non-parametric approach. *Applied Economics*, *25*, 1101–1112.

Gale, C. (2019). Time to tackle technology. *Accounting Today*, *33*(6). www.accountingtoday.com

Gallizo, J. L., & Salvador, M. (2003). Understanding the behavior of financial ratios: The adjustment process. *Journal of Economics and Business*, *55*(3), 267–283.

Gandomi, A., & Haider, M. (2015). Big data concepts, methods,and analytics. *International Journal of Information Management*, *35*(2), 137–144. doi:10.1016/j.ijinfomgt.2014.10.007

Garber, A. (2019). Data science: What the educated citizen needs to know. *Harvard Data Science Review*, (1), 1–14. Retrieved from https://hdsr.mitpress.mit.edu/

Gardijan, M., & Kojić, V. (2012). Dea-based investment strategy and its application in the Croatian stock market. *Croatian Operational Research Review*, *3*, 203–212.

Gardijan, M., & Škrinjarić, T. (2015). Equity portfolio optimization: A DEA based methodology applied to the Zagreb Stock Exchange. *Croatian Operational Research Review*, *6*, 405–417.

Garriga, C., García de, O. P., Miró, J. M., Ocaña, I., Knobel, H., Barberá, M. J., Humet, V., Domingo, P., Gatell, J. M., Ribera, E., Gurguí, M., Marco, A., & Caylà, J. A. (2015). Mortality, causes of death and associated factors related to a large HIV population-based cohort. *PLoS One*, *10*(12). doi:10.1371/journal.pone.0145701

Gartner. (2019). *Forecast Snapshot: Prescriptive Analytics Software, Worldwide*. Gartner Research.

Geckoboard. (2019). geckoboard. https://www.geckoboard.com/product/

gephi.org. (2019). The Open Graph Viz Platform. https://gephi.org/

Gepp, A., Kumar, K., & Bhattacharya, S. (2010). Business failure prediction using decision trees. *Journal of Forecasting*, *29*(6), 536–555. doi:10.1002/for.1153

Gepp, A., Linnenluecke, M. K., O'Neill, T. J., & Smith, T. (2018). Big data techniques in auditing research and practice: Current trends and future opportunities. *Journal of Accounting Literature*, *40*, 102–115. doi:10.1016/j.acclit.2017.05.003

Geradts, Z. (2018). Digital, big data and computational forensics. *Forensic Science Review*, *3*(3), 179–182. doi:10.1080/20961790.2018.1500078 PMID:30483667

Gestational Diabetes. (n.d.). Available: https://www.diabetesaustralia.com.au /gestational-diabetes

Ghale, Z. R. (2015). The relation between financial ratio and earnings quality and stock returns. A case study, *GMP Review*, *15*, 6-13.

Ghassemi, M., Naumann, T., Schulam, P., Beam, A. L., & Ranganath, R. (2018). *Opportunities in machine learning for healthcare*. arXiv preprint arXiv:1806.00388

Gianfrancesco, M. A., Tamang, S., Yazdany, J., & Schmajuk, G. (2018). Potential biases in machine learning algorithms using electronic health record data. *JAMA Internal Medicine*, *178*(11), 1544–1547. doi:10.1001/jamainternmed.2018.3763 PMID:30128552

Gibert, K., Horsburgh, J. S., Athanasiadis, I. N., & Holmes, G. (2018). Environmental data science. *Environmental Modelling & Software*, *106*, 4–12. doi:10.1016/j.envsoft.2018.04.005

Gil Press. (2013). *A Very Short History of Data Science*. Retrieved from https://www.forbes.com/sites/gilpress/2013/05/28/a-very-short-history-of-data-science/#37bd1c1655cf

Giray, S., Yorulmaz, Ö., & Ergüt, Ö. (2016). Classification Of The Countries By Fuzzy And Robust Cluster Methods Based On Gini Coefficient, Migration, Crime And Happiness Factors. *Journal of Awareness*, *1*(2), 1–16.

Giudici, P. (2003). *Applied Data Mining: Statistical Methods for Business and Industry*. Wiley.

Glauser, W. (2018). Primary care system outdated and inconvenient for many millennials. *Canadian Medical Association Journal*, *190*(48), E1430–E1431. doi:10.1503/cmaj.109-5688 PMID:30510054

Gmb, H. D. (2020). Data Wrapper. Retrieved from https://www.datawrapper.de/why-datawrapper/

Gobierno de México. (2019). Datos Abiertos de México. https://datos.gob.mx/

Golany, B., & Roll, Y. (1989). An application procedure for DEA. *Omega*, *17*(3), 237–250.

Goloshchapova, I., Poon, S., Pritchard, M., & Reed, P. (2019). Corporate social responsibility reports: Topic analysis and big data approach. *European Journal of Finance*, *25*(17), 1637–1654. doi:10.1080/1351847X.2019.1572637

Google Trends. (2019). *Google trends*. Retrieved August 1, 2019, from www.trends.google.com

Google. (2019a). Cloud AutoML. https://cloud.google.com/automl/

Google. (2019b). Google Dataset Search. https://toolbox.google.com/datasetsearch

Google. (2019c). TensorFlow. https://www.tensorflow.org/

Google. (2020). GoogleAutoML. Retrieved from https://cloud.google.com/automl/

Gopal, M. (2018). *Applied Machine Learning*. McGraw-Hill Education.

Gorgulho, A., Neves, R., & Horta, N. (2011). Applying a GA kernel on optimizing technical analysis rules for stock picking and portfolio composition. *Expert Systems with Applications*, *38*(11), 14072–14085. doi:10.1016/j.eswa.2011.04.216

Government of Spain. (2018). The professionals of Data Science teams https://datos.gob.es/en/noticia/professionals-data-science-teams

Grady, N., Payne, J. A., & Parker, H. (2017). Agile Big Data Analytics, Analytics Ops for Data Science. *IEEE Conference on Big Data*, 2331-2339.

Gray, E., & Fata, C. (2017). Increased use of big data in SEC enforcement. *The Review of Securities & Commodities Regulation*, *50*(12), 145–149.

Greco, L., Ritrovato, P., & Xhafa, F. (2019). An edge-stream computing infrastructure for real-time analysis of wearable sensors data. *Future Generation Computer Systems*, *93*, 515–528. doi:10.1016/j.future.2018.10.058

Gregoriou, A., Healy, J., & Gupta, J. (2015). Determinants of telecommunication stock prices. *Journal of Economic Studies (Glasgow, Scotland)*, *42*(4), 534–548.

Grover, P., & Kar, A. K. (2017). Big data analytics: A review on theoretical contributions and tools used in literature. *Global Journal of Flexible Systems Managment*, *18*(3), 203–229. doi:10.100740171-017-0159-3

Gruda, D., & Hasan, S. (2019). Feeling anxious? Perceiving anxiety in tweets using machine learning. *Computers in Human Behavior*, *98*, 245–255. doi:10.1016/j.chb.2019.04.020

Grus, J. (2019). *Data science from scratch: first principles with python*. O'Reilly Media.

Gubler, B. (2019). UC TensorFlow.js. https://blog.logrocket.com/tensorflow-js-an-intro-and analysis-with-use-cases-8e1f9a973183/

Gul, S., Kaya, M., & Kaya, B. (2016). Predicting links in weighted disease networks. *3rd International Conference on Computer and Information Sciences (ICCOINS)*, 77-81.

Günther, W. A., Mehrizi, M. H., Huysman, M., & Feldberg, F. (2017). Debating big data: A literature review on realizing value from big data. *The Journal of Strategic Information Systems*, *26*(3), 191–209. doi:10.1016/j.jsis.2017.07.003

Gupta, S. C., & Kapoor, V. K. (2013). Fundamentals of mathematical statistics (11th ed.). Sultan Chand & Sons Educational publishers.

Gupta, R., & Gill, N. S. (2012). Financial statement fraud detection using text mining. *International Journal of Advanced Computer Science and Applications*, *3*(12), 189–191. www.ijacsa.thesai.org

Gurovich, Y., Hanani, Y., Bar, O., Nadav, G., Fleischer, N., Gelbman, D., Basel-Salmon, L., Krawitz, P. M., Kamphausen, S. B., Zenker, M., Bird, L. M., & Gripp, K. W. (2019). Identifying facial phenotypes of genetic disorders using deep learning. *Nature Medicine*, *25*(1), 60–64. doi:10.103841591-018-0279-0 PMID:30617323

Gurría. (2017). *OECD Health Ministerial Statement - The next generation of health reforms*. The Next Generation of Health Reforms.

Gutierrez-Garcia, J. O., & Lopez-Neri, E. (2015). Cognitive Computing: A Brief Survey and Open Research Challenges. *3rd International Conference on Applied Computing and Information Technology/2nd International Conference on Computational Science and Intelligence, IEEE*, 328-333.

Gu, W., Foster, K., Shang, J., & Wei, L. (2019). A game-predicting expert system using big data and machine learning. *Expert Systems with Applications*, *130*, 293–305. doi:10.1016/j.eswa.2019.04.025

Gu, X., & Angelov, P. (2018). Self-organizingfuzzy logic classifier. *Information Sciences*, *447*, 36–51. doi:10.1016/j.ins.2018.03.004

Gym. (2020). OpenAIgym. Retrieved from https://gym.openai.com/

H2O. (2019). H2O. https://www.h2o.ai/products/h2o/

H2O.ai. (2020). H2O Driverless AI. Retrieved from https://www.h2o.ai/products/h2o-driverless-ai/

Hadoop Map-Reduce. (n.d.). Available: https://www.tutorialspoint.com/ hadoop/ hadoop_mapreduce.htm

Haenssgen, M. J., & Ariana, P. (2016). The Social Implications of Technology Diffusion: Uncovering the Unintended Consequences of People's Health-Related Mobile Phone Use in Rural India and China. *World Development*. Advance online publication. doi:10.1016/j.worlddev.2017.01.014

Haenssle, H. A., Fink, C., Schneiderbauer, R., Toberer, F., Buhl, T., Blum, A., Kalloo, A., Ben Hadj Hassen, A., Thomas, L., Enk, A., & Uhlmann, L. (2018). Man against machine: Diagnostic performance of a deep learning convolutional neural network for dermoscopic melanoma recognition in comparison to 58 dermatologists. *Annals of Oncology: Official Journal of the European Society for Medical Oncology*, *29*(8), 1836–1842. doi:10.1093/annonc/mdy166 PMID:29846502

Hafeez, K., Zhang, Y. B., & Malak, N. (2002). Determining key capabilities of a firm using analytic hierarchy process. *International Journal of Production Economics*, *76*, 39–51.

Hafner, D., Davidson, J., & Vanhoucke, V. (2017). TensorFlow Agents: Efficient Batched Reinforcement Learning in TensorFlow. 1–8. https://arxiv.org/abs/1709.02878

Hamdan, M. (2018). The role of forensic accounting in discovering financial fraud. *International Journal of Accounting Research*, *6*(2). Advance online publication. doi:10.35248/2472-114X.18.6.176

Hamzacebi, C., & Pekkaya, M. (2011). Determining of stock investments with grey relational analysis. *Expert Systems with Applications*, *38*(8), 9186–9195. doi:10.1016/j.eswa.2011.01.070

Hamzacebi, C., & Pekkaya, M. (2011). Determining of stock investments with grey relational analysis. *Expert Systems with Applications*, *38*, 9186–9195.

Han, J., Rodriguez, J. C., & Beheshti, M. (2008), Diabetes data analysis and prediction model discovery using rapid-miner. In *Future Generation Communication and Networking, 2008. FGCN'08. Second International Conference on* (Vol. 3). IEEE.

Hanchett, W. (2016). *SEC uses big data for regulatory compliance.* Retrieved July 1, 2019, from www.kpm-us.com

Hanirex, D. K., & Kaliyamurthie, K. P. (2013). *Multi-classification approach for detecting thyroid attacks.* Academic Press.

Han, J., Kamber, M., & Pei, J. (2011). *Data mining concepts and techniques* (3rd ed.). Elsevier.

Hanne, T., Dornberger, R. (2017). *Computational Intelligence in Logistics and Supply Chain Management.* Springer.

Han, S. S., Kim, M. S., Lim, W., Park, G. H., Park, I., & Chang, S. E. (2018). Classification of the Clinical Images for Benign and Malignant Cutaneous Tumors Using a Deep Learning Algorithm. *The Journal of Investigative Dermatology*, *138*(7), 1529–1538. doi:10.1016/j.jid.2018.01.028 PMID:29428356

Hanushek, E. A., & Wößmann, L. (2007). *Education quality and economic growth.* World Bank. doi:10.1596/1813-9450-4122

Harc, M. (2015). The relationship between tangible assets and capital structure of small and medium-sized companies in Croatia. *Econviews*, *28*(1), 213–224.

Hasbrouck, J., & Saar, G. (2013). Low-latency trading. *Journal of Financial Markets*, *16*(4), 646–679. doi:10.1016/j.finmar.2013.05.003

Hassan, N., Gillani, S., Ahmed, E., Yaqoob, I., & Imran, M. (2018). The Role of Edge Computing in Internet of Things. *IEEE Communications Magazine*, *56*(11), 110–115. doi:10.1109/MCOM.2018.1700906

Hegadi, R. S., Navale, D. I., Pawar, T. D., & Ruikar, D. D. (2019). Osteoarthritis Detection and Classification from Knee X-Ray Images Based on Artificial Neural Network. *Communications in Computer and Information Science*, *1036*, 97–105. doi:10.1007/978-981-13-9184-2_8

Hendricks, D., & Wilcox, D. (2014). A reinforcement learning extension to the Almgren-Chriss framework for optimal trade execution. In *IEEE Conference on Computational Intelligence for Financial Engineering & Economics (CIFEr)* (pp. 457–464). 10.1109/CIFEr.2014.6924109

Hennig, A., Åmodt, A.-S., Hernes, H., Nygårdsmoen, H. M., Larsen, P. A., Mukkamala, R. R., Flesch, B., Hussain, A., & Vatrapu, R. (2016). Big Social Data Analytics of Changes in Consumer Behaviour and Opinion of a TV Broadcaster. *IEEE International Conference on Big Data*, 3839-3848. 10.1109/BigData.2016.7841057

Hernandez, R. R., Mayernik, M. S., Murphy-Mariscal, M. L., & Allen, M. F. (2012). Advanced Technologies and Data Management Practices in Environmental Science: Lessons from Academia [Article]. *Bioscience*, *62*(12), 1067–1076. doi:10.1525/bio.2012.62.12.8

Herrera, M., Torgo, L., Izquierdo, J., & Pérez-García, R. (2010). Predictive models for forecasting hourly urban water demand. *Journal of Hydrology (Amsterdam)*, *387*(1–2), 141–150. doi:10.1016/j.jhydrol.2010.04.005

Heyns, E., Uniyal, S., Dugundji, E., Tillema, F., & Huijboom, C. (2019). Predicting Traffic Phases from Car Sensor Data using Machine Learning. *Procedia Computer Science*, *151*, 92–99. doi:10.1016/j.procs.2019.04.016

Hibbard, J. H., & Greene, J. (2013). What the Evidence Shows About Patient Activation: Better Health Outcomes and Care Experiences; Fewer Data on Costs. Health Affairs: New Era of Patient Engagement, 32(2).

Hill, C. W. L., Jones, G. R., & Schilling, M. A. (2014). Strategic management theory (11th ed.). Mason: Cengage Learning.

Hindle, G. A., & Vidgen, R. (2018). Developing a business analytics methodology: A case study in the foodbank sector. *European Journal of Operational Research, 268*(3), 836–851. doi:10.1016/j.ejor.2017.06.031

Hirvasniemi, J., Thevenot, J., Immonen, V., Liikavainio, T., Pulkkinen, P., Jämsä, T., & Saarakkala, S. (2014). Quantification of differences in bone texture from plain radiographs in knees with and without osteoarthritis. *Osteoarthritis and Cartilage, 22*(10), 1724–1731. doi:10.1016/j.joca.2014.06.021 PMID:25278081

Holmes, G., Donkin, A., & Witten, I. H. (1994). WEKA: A machine learning workbench. Australian and New Zealand Conference on Intelligent Information Systems - Proceedings, 357-361. 10.1109/anziis.1994.396988

Hoshi, K., Kawakami, J., Kumagai, M., Kasahara, S., Nishimura, N., Nakamura, H., & Sato, K. (2005). An analysis of thyroid function diagnosis using Bayesian-type and SOM-type neural networks. *Chemical & Pharmaceutical Bulletin, 53*(12), 1570–1574. doi:10.1248/cpb.53.1570 PMID:16327191

Hossein Hassani, H., Huang, X., & Silva, E. (2018). Digitalisation and big data mining in banking. *Big Data and Cognitive Computing, 2*(18), 1–13. doi:10.3390/bdcc2030018

Huang, A., Zang, A., & Zheng, R. (2014). Evidence on the Information Content of Text in Analyst Reports. *The Accounting Review, 89*(6), 2151–2180. doi:10.2308/accr-50833

Huang, C., Dai, C., & Guo, M. (2015). A hybrid approach using two-level DEA for financial failure prediction and integrated SE-DEA and GCA for indicators selection. *Applied Mathematics and Computation, 251*, 431–441.

Huang, C.-F. (2012). A hybrid stock selection model using genetic algorithms and support vector regression. *Applied Soft Computing, 12*(2), 807–818. doi:10.1016/j.asoc.2011.10.009

Huang, C., Yang, M., Huang, C., Chen, Y., Wu, M., & Chen, K. (2018). A Chatbot- supported Smart Wireless Interactive Healthcare System for Weight Control and Health Promotion. *IEEE International Conference on Industrial Engineering and Engineering Management (IEEM)*, 1791-1795. 10.1109/IEEM.2018.8607399

Huang, J. T., & Liao, Y. S. (2003). Optimization of machining parameters of wire-EDM based on grey relational and statistical analyses. *International Journal of Production Research, 41*(8), 1707–1720.

Huang, S. Y. (2013). Fraud detection model by using support vector machine techniques. *International Journal of Digital Content Technology and Its Applications, 7*(2), 32–42. doi:10.4156/jdcta.vol7.issue2.5

Hua, Z., Wang, Y., Xu, X., Zhang, B., & Liang, L. (2007). Predicting corporate financial distress based on integration of support vector machine and logistic regression. *Expert Systems with Applications, 33*(2), 434–440. doi:10.1016/j.eswa.2006.05.006

Hui, X.-F., & Sun, J. (2006). An application of support vector machine to companies' financial distress prediction. In *Modeling decisions for artificial intelligence* (pp. 274–282). Springer Verlag. doi:10.1007/11681960_27

Hull, J. C. (2003). *Options futures and other derivatives.* Pearson Education India.

Hummer, R. A., & Hernandez, E. M. (2013). The effect of educational attainment on adult mortality in the United States. *Population Bulletin, 68*(1), 1–16. PMID:25995521

Hunsinger, S., & Waguespaack, L. (2016). A Comparison of Open Source Tools for Data Science. *Journal of Information Systems Applied Research, 9*(2), 33.

Hurwitz & Kirsch. (2018). *Machine Learning for Dummies.* IBM Limited Edition, Published by John Wiley & Sons.

Hussain, S., & Lee, S. (2015), Semantic transformation model for clinical documents in big data to support healthcare analytics. *Tenth International Conference on Digital Information Management (ICDIM).* 10.1109/ICDIM.2015.7381876

IBM. (2013, May 15). *Southern Denmark to use IBM's Shared Care Platform to improve care for patients with chronic illness.* Copenhagen, Denmark: IBM. Retrieved from https://www.news-medical.net/news/20130515/Southern-Denmark-to-use-IBMs-Shared-Care-Platform-to-improve-care-for-patients-with-chronic-illness.aspx

IBM. (2020a). IBM Cognos. Retrieved from https://www.ibm.com/products/cognos-analytics

IBM. (2020b). IBM Watson. Retrieved from https://dataplatform.cloud.ibm.com/docs/con tent/wsj/ gettingstarted/overview-ws.html

ICAEW. (2018a). *Artificial intelligence and the future of accountancy.* ICAEW Thought Leadership.

ICAEW. (2018b). *Big data and analytics – what's new?* ICAEW Thought Leadership.

Implementation of C4. (n.d.). *5 Algorithm using Hadoop Map Reduce Paradigm.* Available: http://btechfreakz.blogspot.in/2013/04/_implementation-of-c45- algorithm-using.html

Inc, A. (2020). Core ML. Retrieved from https://developer.apple.com/machine-learning/core-ml/ intellipaat.com. (2016).

Induja, S. N., & Raji, C. G. (2019, March). Computational Methods for Predicting Chronic Disease in Healthcare Communities. In *2019 International Conference on Data Science and Communication (IconDSC)* (pp. 1-6). IEEE. 10.1109/IconDSC.2019.8817044

INEGI. (2019). Datos. https://www.inegi.org.mx/datos/

Inpatient Telemedicine Study: HIMSS Analytics. (2017). Retrieved from https://www.himssanalytics.org

Insights, H. G. (2020). UC Apache Mahaout. https://discovery.hgdata.com/product/apache-mahout

Intellipaat. (2016). uc hadoop. IntelliPatt. Retrieved from https://intellipaat.com/blog/how-hadoop helps-companies-manage-big-data/

International Data Corporation. (2019). *Worldwide Global DataSphere IoT Device and Data Forecast, 2019–2023.* IDC Corporate.

International Data Corporation. (2020). *Worldwide Big Data and Analytics Spending Guide.* Available at: https://www.idc.com/getdoc.jsp?containerId=IDC_P33195

Investing. (2019). https://www.investing.com

Ip, R. H. L., Ang, L.-M., Seng, K. P., Broster, J. C., & Pratley, J. E. (2018). Big data and machine learning for crop protection. *Computers and Electronics in Agriculture, 151,* 376–383. doi:10.1016/j.compag.2018.06.008

Irons, A., & Lallie, H. (2014). Digital forensics to intelligent forensics. *Future Internet, 6*(3), 584–596. doi:10.3390/fi6030584

Iyer, Jeyalatha, & Sumbaly. (2015). *Diagnosis of diabetes using classification mining techniques.* arXiv preprint arXiv:1502.03774

Izabella, V. L., Barbara, J. D., & Cees, J. M. L. (2019). Internet of Things and Big Data-Driven Data Analysis Services for Third Parties: Business Models, New Ventures, and Potential Horizons. In M. Natarajan (Ed.), *Strategic Innovations and Interdisciplinary Perspectives in Telecommunications and Networking* (pp. 256–289). IGI Global., doi:10.4018/978-1-5225-8188-8.ch014

Jablonsky, S. F., & Barsky, N. P. (2001). *The Manager's Guide to Financial Statement Analysis*. Wiley.

Jackson, S. L. (2005). *Statistics plain and simple*. Wadsworth Publishing.

Jaggi, M., & Templier, T. (2019). *Software Tools for Handling Magnetically Collected Ultra-thin Sections for Microscopy*. Academic Press.

Jagla, B., Wiswedel, B., & Coppée, J. Y. (2011). Extending KNIME for next-generation sequencing data analysis. *Bioinformatics (Oxford, England)*, *27*(20), 2907–2909. doi:10.1093/bioinformatics/btr478

Jain, A. (2015). matminer. http://hackingmaterials.lbl.gov/matminer/

Jain, A. K. (2010). Data clustering: 50 years beyond K-means. *Pattern Recognition Letters*, *31*(8), 651–666. doi:10.1016/j.patrec.2009.09.011

Jalali, F., Hinton, K., Ayre, R., Alpcan, T., & Tucker, R. S. (2016). Fog computing may help to save energy in cloud computing. *IEEE Journal on Selected Areas in Communications*, *34*(5), 1728–1739. doi:10.1109/JSAC.2016.2545559

Jans, M., Alles, M. G., & Vasarhelyi, M. A. (2014). A field study on the use of process mining of event logs as an analytical procedure in auditing. *The Accounting Review*, *89*(5), 1751–1773. doi:10.2308/accr-50807

Japan Science and Technology Agency. (2019). Life Science Database Archive. https://dbarchive.biosciencedbc.jp/index-e.html

Jarvenpaa, S. L., & Machesky, J. J. (1989). Data analysis and learning: An experimental study of data modeling tools. *International Journal of Man-Machine Studies*, *31*(4), 367–391. doi:10.1016/0020-7373(89)90001-1

Jayalakshmi, T., & Santhakumaran, A. (2010, February). A novel classification method for diagnosis of diabetes mellitus using artificial neural networks. In *2010 International Conference on Data Storage and Data Engineering* (pp. 159-163). IEEE. 10.1109/DSDE.2010.58

Jeble, S., Kumari, S., & Patil, Y. (2018). Role of Big Data in Decision Making. *Operations and Supply Chain Management*, *11*, 36–44. doi:10.31387/oscm0300198

Jemrić, I., & Vujčić, B. (2002). Efficiency of banks in Croatia: A DEA approach. *Comparative Economic Studies*, *44*(2-3), 169–193.

Jensen, J. B., Ahire, S. L., & Malhotra, M. K. (2013). Trane/Ingersoll Rand combines lean and operations research tools to redesign feeder manufacturing operations. *Interfaces*, *43*(4), 325–340. doi:10.1287/inte.2013.0680

Jiang, F., Jiang, Y., Zhi, H., Dong, Y., Li, H., Ma, S., Wang, Y., Dong, Q., Shen, H., & Wang, Y. (2017). Artificial intelligence in healthcare: past, present and future. *Stroke and Vascular Neurology, 2*(4), 230-243.

Jiang, M., Fan, X., & Yan, H. (2020). Retina Face Mask: A Face Mask Detector. arXiv: 2005.03950v2

Jiang, H., & He, Y. (2018). Applying Data Envelopment Analysis in Measuring the Efficiency of Chinese Listed Banks in the Context of Macroprudential Framework. *Mathematics*, *6*(184), 1–18.

Jiang, W., & Chai, H. (2016). Research on big data in business model innovation based on GA-BP model. *IEEE International Conference on In Service Operations and Logistics, and Informatics (SOLI)*, 174-177. 10.1109/SOLI.2016.7551682

Jiang, Z. (2019). A Novel Crop Weed Recognition Method Based on Transfer Learning from VGG16 Implemented by Keras. *IOP Conference Series. Materials Science and Engineering*, *677*(3), 032073. Advance online publication. doi:10.1088/1757-899X/677/3/032073

Jie, J., Hu, Z., Qian, G., Weng, M., Li, S., Li, S., Hu, M., Chen, D., Xiao, W., Zheng, J., Wang, L.-W., & Pan, F. (2019). Discovering unusual structures from exception using big data and machine learning techniques. Science Bulletin, 64(9), 612–616. doi:10.1016/j.scib.2019.04.015

Jiménez Gómez, C. E. (2018). Análisis predictivo de datos abiertos sobre el uso turístico del servicio de alquiler compartido de bicicletas de Nueva York Universitat Oberta de Catalunya]. http://openaccess.uoc.edu/webapps/o2/bitstream/10609/81516/9/carlosjgTFM0618memoria.pdf

Jin, X., Wah, B., Cheng, X., & Wang, Y. (2015). Significance and Challenges of Big Data Research. *Big Data Research*, *2*(2), 59–64. doi:10.1016/j.bdr.2015.01.006

Jin, Y., & Sendhoff, B. (2004). Reducing Fitness Evaluations Using Clustering Techniques and Neural Network Ensembles. In K. Deb (Ed.), Lecture Notes in Computer Science: Vol. 3102. *Genetic and Evolutionary Computation – GECCO 2004. GECCO 2004*. Springer. doi:10.1007/978-3-540-24854-5_71

Jofre, M., & Gerlach, R. H. (2018). *Fighting accounting fraud through forensic data analytics*. SSRN Electronic Journal., doi:10.2139srn.3176288

Joglekar, P. & Pise, N., (2016). Solving cyber security challenges using big data. *International Journal of Computer Applications*.

Johnson, M., Hofmann, K., Hutton, T., & Bignell, D. (2016). The malmo platform for artificial intelligence experimentation. *IJCAI International Joint Conference on Artificial Intelligence*, 4246–4247.

Jolly, A., & Tripathi, P. (2019). Role of Big Data Analytics in Healthcare. *International Journal of Engineering and Advanced Technology*, *9*(1), 4174–4177. doi:10.35940/ijeat.A1421.109119

Jones, G., Ding, C., Scott, F., Glisson, M., & Cicuttini, F. (2004). Early radiographic osteoarthritis is associated with substantial changes in cartilage volume and tibial bone surface area in both males and females11Sources of support: National Health and Medical Research Council of Australia, Masonic Centenary Medical Research Foundation. *Osteoarthritis and Cartilage*, *12*(2), 169–174. doi:10.1016/j.joca.2003.08.010 PMID:14723876

Jordan, M. I. (2019). Artificial intelligence - the revolution hasn't happened yet. *Harvard Data Science Review*, (1). Retrieved from https://hdsr.mitpress.mit.edu/

Jordan, C. E., Clark, S. J., & Smith, W. R. (2007). Should Earnings Per Share (EPS) Be Taught as a Means of Comparing Inter Company Performance? *Journal of Education for Business*, *82*(6), 343–348.

Jörnsten, R. (2004). Clustering and classification based on the L1 data depth. *Journal of Multivariate Analysis*, *90*(1), 67–89. doi:10.1016/j.jmva.2004.02.013

Joshi, P. L., & Marthandan, G. (2018). The hype of big data analytics and auditors. *Emerging Market Journal*. Retrieved from http://emaj.pitt.edu

Juliani, A., Berges, V.-P., Vckay, E., Gao, Y., Henry, H., Mattar, M., & Lange, D. (2018). Unity: A General Platform for Intelligent Agents. https://arxiv.org/abs/1809.02627

Jurgovsky, J., Granitzer, M., Ziegler, K., Calabretto, S., Portier, P.-E., He-Guelton, L., & Caelen, O. (2018). Sequence classification for credit-card fraud detection. *Expert Systems with Applications*, *100*, 234–245. doi:10.1016/j.eswa.2018.01.037

Kaggle. (2019a). https://www.kaggle.com/datasets. https://www.kaggle.com/datasets

Kaggle. (2019b). Kaggle: you home the data science. https://www.kaggle.com/

Kalyankar, G. D., Poojara, S. R., & Dharwadkar, N. V. (2017), Predictive Analysis of Diabetic Patient Data Using Machine Learning and Hadoop. *International Conference on IoT in Social, Mobile, Analytics and Cloud*, 619-624. 10.1109/I-SMAC.2017.8058253

Kamath, S. (2014). Closed-loop control strategy for type I diabetic patients. *International Journal of Medical Engineering and Informatics*, 6(4), 345–354. doi:10.1504/IJMEI.2014.065438

Kamrad, B., & Ritchken, P. (1991). Multinomial approximating models for options with k state variables. *Management Science*, 37(12), 1640–1652. doi:10.1287/mnsc.37.12.1640

Kanchan, B. D., & Kishor, M. M. (2016). Study of machine learning algorithms for special disease prediction using principle of component analysis. *International Conference on Global Trends in Signal Processing, Information Computing and Communication (ICGT- SPICC)*, 5-10.

Kashima, H., Hu, J., Ray, B., & Singh, M. (2008, December). K-means clustering of proportional data using L1 distance. In *2008 19th International Conference on Pattern Recognition* (pp. 1-4). IEEE. 10.1109/ICPR.2008.4760982

Kassambara, A., & Mundt, F. (2017). *factoextra: Extract and Visualize the Results of Multivariate Data Analyses. R package version 1.0.5.* https://CRAN.R-project.org/package=factoextra

Kassambara, A. (2017). *Practical Guide to Cluster Analysis in R (Unsupervised Machine Learning)*. STHDA.

Kassambara, A. (2017). *Practical guide to cluster analysis in R: Unsupervised machine learning* (Vol. 1). STHDA.

Kaufman, L., & Rousseeuw, P. J. (1990). *Finding groups in data: An introduction to cluster analysis.* Wiley. doi:10.1002/9780470316801

Kaur, G., & Chhabra, A. (2014). Improved J48 Classification Algorithm for the Prediction of Diabetes. *International Journal of Computers and Applications*, 98(22), 13–17. doi:10.520/17314-7433

Kaur, H., & Kumari, V. (2018). *Predictive modelling and analytics for diabetes using a machine learning approach.* Applied Computing and Informatics. doi:10.1016/j.aci.2018.12.004

Kaur, N. K., Kaur, U., & Singh, D. D. (2014). K-Medoid clustering algorithm-a review. *International Journal of Computer Applications in Technology*, 1(1), 2349–1841.

Kavakiotis, I., Tsave, O., Salifoglou, A., Maglaveras, N., Vlahavas, I., & Chouvarda, I. (2017). Machine learning and data mining methods in diabetes research. *Computational and Structural Biotechnology Journal*, 15, 104–116. doi:10.1016/j.csbj.2016.12.005 PMID:28138367

Kayalak, S., & Kiper, T. (2006, May). İstatistiki Bölge Birimleri Nomenklatörü'ne (NUTS) Göre, Türkiye'de Bölgesel Farklılıklar [Regional Differences in Turkey According to NUTS]. In *Proceedings of IV. Ulusal Coğrafya Sempozyumu*, (pp. 45-54). Ankara Üniversitesi Türkiye Cografyası Arastırma ve Uygulama Merkezi (TÜCAUM).

Kedia, A., Narsaria, M., Goswami, S., & Taparia, J. (2017). Empirical Study to Evaluate the Performance of Classification Algorithms on Healthcare Datasets. *World Journal of Computer Application and Technology*, 5(1), 1–11.

Keim, D. B. (1988). Stock Market Regularities: A Synthesis of the Evidence and Explanations. In E. Dimson (Ed.), *Stock Market Anomalies* (pp. 16–39). Cambridge University Press.

Keka, I., & Cico, B. (2019). Data Visualization as Helping Technique for Data Analysis, Trend Detection and Correlation of Variables Using R Programming Language. *8th Mediterranean Conference on Embedded computing*, 1-4. 10.1109/MECO.2019.8760004

Keleş, A., & Keleş, A. (2008). Expert system for thyroid diseases diagnosis. *Expert Systems with Applications, 34*(1), 242–246. doi:10.1016/j.eswa.2006.09.028

Kellgren, J., & Lawrence, J. (1957). Radiological assessment of osteo-arthrosis. *Annals of the Rheumatic Diseases, 16*(4), 494–502. doi:10.1136/ard.16.4.494 PMID:13498604

Kelly, B. (2019). UC Trifacta. https://www.trifacta.com/blog/how-trifacta-is-helping-companies realize-the-massive-value-in-data/

Ker, J., Wang, L., Rao, J., & Lim, T. (2018). Deep learning applications in medical image analysis. *IEEE Access: Practical Innovations, Open Solutions, 6*(1), 9375–9389. doi:10.1109/ACCESS.2017.2788044

Kesavaraj, G., & Sukumaran, S. (2013). A study on classification techniques in data mining. 2013 4th International Conference on Computing, Communications and Networking Technologies. ICCCNT 2013, 2013(March), 85–97. 10.1109/ICCCNT.2013.6726842

Khan, K. (2013, May). The transformative power of advanced analytics. *Supply Chain Management Review,* 48-49.

Khandani, A. E., Kim, A. J., & Lo, A. W. (2010). Consumer credit-risk models via machine-learning algorithms. *Journal of Banking & Finance, 34*(11), 2767–2787. doi:10.1016/j.jbankfin.2010.06.001

Khan, S. S., & Ahmad, A. (2004). Cluster center initialization algorithm for K-means clustering. *Pattern Recognition Letters, 25*(11), 1293–1302. doi:10.1016/j.patrec.2004.04.007

Khan, W. Z., Ahmed, E., Hakak, S., Yaqoob, I., & Ahmed, A. (2019). Edge computing: A survey. *Future Generation Computer Systems, 97*, 219–235. doi:10.1016/j.future.2019.02.050

Khatami, A., Mirghasemi, S., Khosravi, A., Lim, C. P., & Nahavandi, S. (2017). A new PSO-based approach to fire flame detection using K-Medoids clustering. *Expert Systems with Applications, 68*, 69–80. doi:10.1016/j.eswa.2016.09.021

Khokhlova, M., Migniot, C., Morozov, A., Sushkova, O., & Dipanda, A. (2019). Normal and pathological gait classification LSTM model. *Artificial Intelligence in Medicine, 94*(November), 54–66. doi:10.1016/j.artmed.2018.12.007

Kim, H., & Gardner, E. (2015). The science of winning in financial services — competing on analytics: Opportunities to unlock the power of data. *Journal of Financial Perspectives, 3*(2), 13–24.

Kim, S. Y., & Upneja, A. (2014). Predicting restaurant financial distress using decision tree and AdaBoosted decision tree models. *Economic Modelling, 36*, 354–362. doi:10.1016/j.econmod.2013.10.005

Kim, S.-T., Baek, M., & Cho, J.-K. (2015). Analysis on distribution of effective dose rate around patients for treatment of thyroid cancer with I-131. *Indian Journal of Science and Technology, 8*(S7). doi:10.17485/ijst/2015/v8iS7/70148

Kinds, M. B., Marijnissen, A. C. A., Bijlsma, J. W. J., Boers, M., Lafeber, F. P. J. G., & Welsing, P. M. J. (2013). Quantitative Radiographic Features of Early Knee Osteoarthritis: Development Over 5 Years and Relationship with Symptoms in the CHECK Cohort. *The Journal of Rheumatology, 40*(1), 58–65. doi:10.3899/jrheum.120320 PMID:23118113

Kluzek, S., & Mattei, T. A. (2019). Machine-learning for osteoarthritis research. *Osteoarthritis and Cartilage, 27*(7), 977–978. doi:10.1016/j.joca.2019.04.005 PMID:31002937

KMIME. (2019). KMIME. https://www.knime.com/

KNIME. (2019). KNIME. Retrieved from https://www.knime.com/software-overview

Koh, H. C. (2004). Going concern predictions using data mining techniques. *Managerial Auditing Journal, 19*(3), 462–476. doi:10.1108/02686900410524436

Koksal, B., Orman, C., & Oduncu, A. (2013). *Determinants of capital structure: evidence from a major emerging market economy.* Available at: https://mpra.ub.uni-muenchen.de/48415/

Komal, Ms. (2018). *A Review Paper on Big Data Analytics Tools.* https://www.proschoolonline.com/blog/top-10-data-analytics-tools

Koop, C., Mosher, R., Kun, L., Geiling, J., Grigg, E., Long, S., Macedonia, C., Merrell, R., Satava, R., & Rosen, J. (2008). Future delivery of health care: Cybercare. *IEEE Engineering in Medicine and Biology Magazine, 27*(6), 29–38. doi:10.1109/MEMB.2008.929888 PubMed

Kothari, S. P., & Shanken, J. (1997). Book-to-market, dividend yield, and expected market returns: A time-series analysis. *Journal of Financial Economics, 44*, 169–203.

Kotsiantis, S. B., Zaharakis, I., & Pintelas, P. (2007). Supervised machine learning: A review of classification techniques. *Emerging Artificial Intelligence Applications in Computer Engineering, 160*, 3-24.

Kotsiantis, S. B. (2012). Use of machine learning techniques for educational proposes: A decision support system for forecasting students' grades. *Artificial Intelligence Review, 37*(4), 331–344. doi:10.1007/s10462-011-9234-x

Kotsiantis, S., Koumanakos, E., Tzelepis, E., & Tampakas, V. (2006). Forecasting fraudulent financial statements using data mining. *International Journal of Computational Intelligence, 3*(2).

Koul, S., & Verma, R. (2011). Dynamic vendor selection based on fuzzy AHP. *Journal of Manufacturing Technology Management, 22*(8), 963–971. doi:10.1108/17410381111177421

Kourou, K., Exarchos, T. P., Exarchos, K. P., Karamouzis, M. V., & Fotiadis, D. I. (2015). Machine learning applications in cancer prognosis and prediction. *Computational and Structural Biotechnology Journal, 13*, 8–17. doi:10.1016/j.csbj.2014.11.005 PMID:25750696

Kousarrizi, Seiti, & Teshnehlab. (2012). An experimental comparative study on thyroid disease diagnosis based on feature subset selection and classification. *International Journal of Electrical & Computer Sciences, 12*(1), 13–20.

Koyuncugil, A., & Ozgulbas, N. (2012). Financial early warning system model and data mining application for risk detection. *Expert Systems with Applications, 39*(6), 6238–6253. doi:10.1016/j.eswa.2011.12.021

Kozak, J., & Boryczka, U. (2016). Collectivedata mining in the ant colony decisiontree approach. *Information Sciences, 372*, 126–147. doi:10.1016/j.ins.2016.08.051

KPMG. (2016). *Using data analytics to successfully detect frauds.* Kpmg.com

Krishnamoorthy & Sreedhar Kumar. (2013). A New Inter Cluster Validation Method for Unsupervised Clustering Techniques. *1ˢᵗ ICCCV, IEEE, 2013,* 1-5. doi:10.1109/ICCCV.2013.6906741

Kristoufek, L. (2013). Can Google Trends search queries contribute to risk diversification? *Scientific Reports, 3*(1), 3. doi:10.1038rep02713 PMID:24048448

Krueger, P. M., Tran, M. K., Hummer, R. A., & Chang, V. W. (2015). Mortality attributable to low levels of education in the United States. *PLoS One, 10*(7. doi:10.1371/journal.pone.0131809

Kumar & Garg. (2018). Predictive Analytics: A Review of Trends and Techniques. *International Journal of Computer Applications, 182.*

Kumar Jangir, S., Soni, L., & Goswami, A. (2019). Machine Translation : A Brief Overview. Journal of Analysis and Computation, 1–4.

Kumar Jangir, S., Babel, V., & Kumar Singh, B. (2018). Evaluation methods for machine learning. *Journal of Analysis and Computation, 11*, 1–6.

Kumar, A., Irsoy, O., Ondruska, P., Iyyer, M., Bradbury, J.H., Gulrajani, I., Zhong, V., Paulus, R., Socher, R. (2015). *Ask Me Anything: Dynamic Memory Networks for Natural Language Processing.* ArXiv, abs/1506.07285

Kumar, B. S., & Ravi, V. (2016). A survey of the applications of text mining in financial domain. *Knowledge-Based Systems, 114*, 128–147. doi:10.1016/j.knosys.2016.10.003

Kumari, V. A., & Chitra, R. (2013). Classification of diabetes disease using support vector machine. *International Journal of Engineering Research and Applications, 3*(2), 1797–1801.

Kuosmannen, T. (2009). Data envelopment analysis with missing data. *The Journal of the Operational Research Society, 60*(12), 1767–1774.

Kuo, Y., Yang, T., & Huang, G.-W. (2008). The use of a grey-based Taguchi method for optimizing multi-response simulation problems. *Engineering Optimization, 40*(6), 517–528.

Kurach, K. (2020). Research Lead and Olivier Bachem, Research Scientist, Google Research, Z. Google Research Football. Retrieved from https://ai.googleblog.com/2019/06/introducing google-research-football.html

Kurach, K., Raichuk, A., Stańczyk, P., Zając, M., Bachem, O., Espeholt, L., Riquelme, C., Vincent, D., Michalski, M., Bousquet, O., & Gelly, S. (2019). Google Research Football: A Novel Reinforcement Learning Environment. Retrieved from https://arxiv.org/abs/1907.11180

La Pelle, N. (2004). Simplifying qualitative data analysis using general purpose software tools. *Field Methods, 16*(1), 85–108. doi:10.1177/1525822X03259227

La Porta, R. (1996). Expectations and the Cross-Section of Stock Returns. *The Journal of Finance, 51*(5), 1715–1742.

Lai, S., & Fu, H. C. (2011). Variance enhanced K-medoid clustering. *Expert Systems with Applications, 38*(1), 764–775. doi:10.1016/j.eswa.2010.07.030

Lam, M. (2004). Neural network techniques for financial performance prediction: Integrating fundamental and technical analysis. *Decision Support Systems, 37*(4), 567–581. doi:10.1016/S0167-9236(03)00088-5

Lamon, C., Nielsen, E., & Redondo, E. (2016). *Cryptocurrency Price Prediction Using News and Social Media Sentiment.* Retrieved form http://cs229.stanford.edu/proj2017/final-reports/5237280.pdf

Landers, S., Madigan, E., Leff, B., Rosati, R. J., McCann, B. A., Hornbake, R., MacMillan, R., Jones, K., Bowles, K., Dowding, D., Lee, T., Moorhead, T., Rodriguez, S., & Breese, E. (2016). The Future of Home Health Care: A Strategic Framework for Optimizing Value. *Home Health Care Management & Practice, 28*(4), 262–278. doi:10.1177/1084822316666368 PMID:27746670

Landset, S., Khoshgoftaar, T. M., Richter, A. N., & Hasanin, T. (2015). A survey of open source tools for machine learning with big data in the Hadoop ecosystem. *Journal of Big Data, 2*(1), 24. doi:10.1186/s40537-015-0032-1

Langevin, A., & Riopel, D. (2005). *Logistics Systems: Design and Optimization.* Springer. doi:10.1007/b106452

Larson, D., & Chang, V. (2016). A review and future direction of agile, business intelligence, analytics and data science. *International Journal of Information Management, 36*(5), 700–710. doi:10.1016/j.ijinfomgt.2016.04.013

Lau, C. H., & Sholihin, M. (2005). Financial and non-financial performance measures: How do they affect job satisfaction? *The British Accounting Review, 37*, 389–413.

Lau, S. T., Lee, T. C., & McInish, T. H. (2002). Stock Returns and Beta, Firms Size, E/P, CF/P, Book-to-market, and Sales Growth: Evidence from Singapore and Malaysia. *Journal of Multinational Financial Management, 12*, 207–222.

LaValle, S., Lesser, E., Shockey, R., Hopkins, M. S., & Kruschwitz, N. (2011). Big data, analytics, and the path from insights to value. *MIT Sloan Management Review, 52*(2), 21–31.

Leary, M. T., & Michaely, R. (2011). Determinants of Dividend Smoothing: Empirical Evidence. *Review of Financial Studies, 24*(10), 3197–3249.

LeCun, Y., Bengio, Y., & Hinton, G. (2015). Deep Learning. *Nature, 521*(7553), 436-44.

Lee, S. S., Choi, S. T., & Choi, S. (2019). Classification of gait type based on deep learning using various sensors with smart insole. Sensors (Switzerland), 19(8), 1–15. doi:10.3390/s19081757 PubMed

Lee, C. F., Tzeng, G. H., & Wang, S. Y. (2005). A fuzzy set approach for generalized CRR model: An empirical analysis of S&P 500 index options. *Review of Quantitative Finance and Accounting, 25*(3), 255–275. doi:10.100711156-005-4767-1

Lee, C., & Lee, W. H. (2008). Can financial ratios predict the Malaysian stock return? *Integration & Dissemination, 2*, 7–8.

Leech, N. L., & Onwuegbuzie, A. J. (2007). An array of qualitative data analysis tools: A call for data analysis triangulation. *School Psychology Quarterly, 22*(4), 557–584. doi:10.1037/1045-3830.22.4.557

Lee, D., Oh, K., & Choi, H. (2017). The chatbot feels you - a counseling service using emotional response generation. *IEEE International Conference on Big Data and Smart Computing (BigComp)*, 437-440.

Lee, N., & Peters, M. (2016). *Business statistics using Excel and SPSS*. SAGE Publications.

Lee, S. J., & Siau, K. (2001). A review of data mining techniques. *Industrial Management & Data Systems*.

Lee, S. M., Yoon, S. M., & Cho, H. (2017). Human activity recognition from accelerometer data using Convolutional Neural Network. In *IEEE International Conference on Big Data and Smart Computing, BigComp 2017*, (pp.131-134). 10.1109/BIGCOMP.2017.7881728

Legara, E. F. (2017). *Data science, advanced analytics for modern manufacturing*. Inclusive Innovation Convention.

Legato, M. J., Simon, F., Young, J. E., Nomura, T., & Sánchez-Serrano, I. (2020). Roundtable discussion III: The development and uses of artificial intelligence in medicine: A work in progress. Gender and the Genome, 4, 247028971989870. doi:10.1177/2470289719898701

Lemenkova, P. (2019). Processing Oceanographic Data By Python Libraries Numpy, Scipy and Pandas. Aquatic Research, 2(2), 73–91. doi:10.3153/AR19009

Leonelli, S. (2019). Data governance is key to interpretation : Reconceptualising data in data science. *Harvard Data Science Review*, (1), 1–7.

Leong, P. H., Goh, O. S., & Kumar, Y. J. (2017). MedKiosk: An embodied conversational intelligence via deep learning. *13th International Conference on Natural Computation, Fuzzy Systems and Knowledge Discovery (ICNC-FSKD)*, 394-399.

Lepenioti, K., Bousdekis, A., Apostoloua, D., & Mentzas, G. (2020). Prescriptive analytics: Literature review and research challenges. *International Journal of Information Management, 50*, 57–70. doi:10.1016/j.ijinfomgt.2019.04.003

Lewellen, J. (2004). Predicting Returns with Financial Ratios. *Journal of Financial Economics, 74*, 209–235.

Ley, C., & Bordas, S. P. A. (2018). What makes Data Science different? A discussion involving Statistics 2.0 and Computational Sciences. *International Journal of Data Science and Analytics, 6*(3), 167–175. doi:10.100741060-017-0090-x

Li, H., Leng, W., Zhou, Y., Chen, F., Xiu, Z., & Yang, D. (2014). Evaluation models for soil nutrient based on support vector machine and artificial neural networks. TheScientificWorldJournal, 2014, 1–8. doi:10.1155/2014/478569 PubMed

Li, H., Weng, J., Shi, Y., Gu, W., Mao, Y., Wang, Y., Liu, W., & Zhang, J. (2018). An improved deep learning approach for detection of thyroid papillary cancer in ultrasound images. *Journal of Imaging Science, 8*(1).

Li, L.N., Ouyang, J.H., Chen, H.L., & Liu, D.Y. (2012). A computer aided diagnosis system for thyroid disease using extreme learning machine. *J Med Syst., 36*(5), 3327-37.

Liang, Y., & Kelemen, A. (2016). Big Data Science and Its Applications in Health and Medical Research:Challenges and Opportunities. *Journal of Biometrics & Biostatistics, 7*(3), 1–7. doi:10.4172/2155-6180.1000307

Li, C., Tang, J., Tang, H., & Luo, Y. (2019). Collaborative cache allocation and task scheduling for data-intensive applications in edge computing environment. *Future Generation Computer Systems, 95*, 249–264. doi:10.1016/j.future.2019.01.007

Li, F. (2010). The Information Content of Forward-Looking Statements in Corporate Filings: A Naive Bayesian Machine Learning Approach. *Journal of Accounting Research, 48*(5), 1049–1102. doi:10.1111/j.1475-679X.2010.00382.x

Li, H., Dai, J., Gershberg, T., & Vasarhelyi, M. A. (2018). Understanding usage and value of audit analytics for internal auditors: An organizational approach. *International Journal of Accounting Information Systems, 28*, 59–76. doi:10.1016/j.accinf.2017.12.005

Li, H., & Sun, J. (2008). Ranking-order case-based reasoning for financial distress prediction. *Knowledge-Based Systems, 21*(8), 868–878. doi:10.1016/j.knosys.2008.03.047

Li, H., Sun, J., & Wu, J. (2010). Predicting business failure using classification and regression tree: An empirical comparison with popular classical statistical methods and top classification mining methods. *Expert Systems with Applications, 37*(8), 5895–5904. doi:10.1016/j.eswa.2010.02.016

Li, H.-Y., Zhang, C., & Zhao, D. (2010). Stock Investment Value Analysis Model Based on AHP and Grey Relational Degree. *Management Science and Engineering, 4*, 1–6.

Li, L.-N., Ouyang, J.-H., Chen, H.-L., & Liu, D.-U. (2012). A computer aided diagnosis system for thyroid disease using extreme learning machine. *Journal of Medical Systems, 36*(5), 3327–3337. doi:10.100710916-012-9825-3 PMID:22327384

Li, M. Y. L. (2009). Value or volume strategy? *Finance Research Letters, 6*(4), 210–218.

Lim, J., Kim, J., & Cheon, S. (2019). A Deep Neural Network-Based Method for Early Detection of Osteoarthritis Using Statistical Data. *International Journal of Environmental Research and Public Health, 16*(7), 1281. doi:10.3390/ijerph16071281 PMID:30974803

Lim, S., Oh, K. W., & Zhu, J. (2013). Use of DEA Cross-Efficiency Evaluation in Portfolio Selection: An application to Korean Stock Market. *European Journal of Operational Research, 236*(1), 361–368.

Lin, C. C., Chiu, A. A., Huang, S. Y., & Yen, D. C. (2015). Detecting the financial statement fraud: The analysis of the differences between data mining techniques and experts' judgments. *Knowledge-Based Systems, 89*, 459–470. doi:10.1016/j.knosys.2015.08.011

Linde, Y., Buzo, A., & Gray, R. (1980). An algorithm for vector quantizer design. *IEEE Transactions on Communications, 28*(1), 84–95. doi:10.1109/TCOM.1980.1094577

Lin, K., Pankaj, S., & Wang, D. (2018). Task offloading and resource allocation for edge-of-things computing on smart healthcare systems. *Computers & Electrical Engineering*, *72*, 348–360. doi:10.1016/j.compeleceng.2018.10.003

Lintner, J. (1956). Distribution of Incomes of Corporations among Dividends, Retained Earnings, and Taxes. *The American Economic Review*, *46*, 97–113.

Li, Q., Wang, Y., Sharf, A., Cao, Y., Tu, C., Chen, B., & Yu, S. (2018). Classification of gait anomalies from kinect. *The Visual Computer*, *34*(2), 229–241. doi:10.1007/s00371-016-1330-0

Li, T. R., Chamrajnagar, A. S., Fong, X. R., Rizik, N. R., & Fu, F. (2018). Sentiment-based prediction of alternative cryptocurrency price fluctuations using gradient boosting tree model. *Frontiers in Physics*, *7*, 98. doi:10.3389/fphy.2019.00098

Littley, J. (2012). *Leveraging data analytics and continuous auditing processes for improved audit planning, effectiveness, and efficiency.* Available at http://www.kpmg.com/US/en

Litzenberger, R., & Ramaswamy, K. (1979). The Effects of Personal Taxes and Dividends on Capital Asset Prices: Theory and Empirical Evidence. *Journal of Financial Economics*, *7*(2), 163–195.

Liu, L. (2016). Requirements Engineering for Health Data Analytics Challenges and Possible Directions. doi:10.1109/re.2016.48

Liu, S. (2019). Detectron. Retrieved from https://github.com/facebookresearch/Detectron

Liu, G., Yang, J., Hao, Y., & Zhang, Y. (2018). Big data-informed energy efficiency assessment of China industry sectors based on K-means clustering. *Journal of Cleaner Production*, *183*, 304–314. doi:10.1016/j.jclepro.2018.02.129

Liu, S., & Lin, Y. (2006). *Grey Information Theory and Practical Applications.* Springer.

Liu, S., & Lin, Y. (2010). *Grey systems, Theory and Applications.* Springer.

Liu, T., Xie, S., Xu, J., Niu, L., & Sun, W. (2017). Classification of thyroid nodules in ultrasound images using deep model based transfer learning and hybrid features. *Proceedings of IEEE International Conference on Acoustics, Speech and Signal Processing (ICASSP)*, 919–923. 10.1109/ICASSP.2017.7952290

Li, X., Ma, J., Wang, S. Y., & Zhang, X. (2015). How does Google search affect trader positions and crude oil prices? *Economic Modelling*, *49*, 162–171. doi:10.1016/j.econmod.2015.04.005

Lo, A. W., Siah, K. W., & Wong, C. H. (2019). Machine learning with statistical imputation for predicting drug approvals. *Harvard Data Science Review*, (1). Retrieved from https://hdsr.mitpress.mit.edu/

Lokshin, D. (n.d.). Mobile Telemedicine Treatment-and-Diagnostic Unit (MTTDU) «Baikal» for carrying out of clinical examination, medical inspection, diagnostics and cure of basic nosologies of population in remote and hard-to-access districts project by. Moscow: National Telemedicine Agency Research-and-Production Union.

Loohach, R., & Garg, K. (2012). Effect of distance functions on k-means clustering algorithm. *International Journal of Computers and Applications*, *49*(6), 7–9. doi:10.5120/7629-0698

Lopes, A., Lanzer, E., Lima, M., & da Costa, N. Jr. (2008). DEA investment strategy in the Brazilian stock market. *Economic Bulletin*, *13*(2), 1–10.

Lopez. (2017). *Survey: Hospital supply chain practices are outdated.* Supply Chain Dive. Accessed from https://www.supplychaindive.com/news/hospital-supply-chain-survey-cardinal-inventory/436505/

Loughran, T., & McDonald, B. (2016). Textual Analysis in Accounting and Finance: A Survey. *Journal of Accounting Research*, *54*(4), 1187–1230. doi:10.1111/1475-679X.12123

Lu, C. J., & Shao, Y. J. E. (2012). Forecasting Computer Products Sales by Integrating Ensemble Empirical Mode Decomposition and Extreme Learning Machine [Article]. Mathematical Problems in Engineering. *Article, 831201*. Advance online publication. doi:10.1155/2012/831201

Lugovskaja, L. (2009). Predicting default of Russian SMEs on the basis of financial and non-financial variables. *Journal of Financial Services Marketing, 14*(4), 301–313.

Ma, J., Wu, F., Jiang, T., Zhu, J., & Kong, D. (2017). Cascade convolutional neural networks for automatic detection of thyroid nodules in ultrasound images. *Med Phys., 44*(5), 1678-1691.

Mabu, S., Hirasawa, K., Obayashi, M., & Kuremoto, T. (2013). Enhanced decision-making mechanism of rulebased genetic network programming for creating stock trading signals. *Expert Systems with Applications, 40*(16), 6311–6320. doi:10.1016/j.eswa.2013.05.037

Machine Learning Group. U. of W. (2019). WEKA. Retrieved fromhttps://www.cs.waikato.ac. nz/ml/weka

Machine Learning Repository, U. C. I. (n.d.). *Pima Indians Diabetes Data Set*. Available: https://archive.ics.uci.edu/ml/datasets/pima+indians+diabetes

Machine, S. (2020). SimpleCV. Retrieved from http://simplecv.org/

Madhu, D., Jain, C. J., Sebastain, E., Shaji, S., & Ajayakumar, A. (2017). A novel approach for medical assistance using trained chatbot. *International Conference on Inventive Communication and Computational Technologies (ICICCT)*, 243-246. 10.1109/ICICCT.2017.7975195

Madhulatha, T. S. (2011). Comparison between K-Means and K-Medoids Clustering Algorithms. In D. C. Wyld, M. Wozniak, N. Chaki, N. Meghanathan, & D. Nagamalai (Eds.), *Advances in Computing and Information Technology. ACITY 2011. Communications in Computer and Information Science* (Vol. 198). Springer. doi:10.1007/978-3-642-22555-0_48

Maechler, M., Rousseeuw, P., Struyf, A., Hubert, M., & Hornik, K. (2019). *Cluster Analysis Basics and Extensions*. R package version 2.0.8.

Magenta. (2020). Magenta. Retrieved from https://magenta.tensorflow.org/

Magesh, G., & Swarnalatha, P. (2017). Big Data and Its Applications: A Survey. *Research Journal of Pharmaceutical, Biological and Chemical Sciences, 8*(2), 2346–2358.

Mahmood, T., & Uzma, A. (2013). Security analytics: Big data analytics for cybersecurity: A review of trends, techniques and tools. In *Information assurance (ncia), 2nd national conference on*. IEEE.

Maniraj, S. P., Saini, A., Sarka, S. D., & Ahmed, S. (2019). Credit card fraud detection using machine learning and data science. *International Journal of Engineering Research & Technology (Ahmedabad), 8*(9), 110–115. doi:10.17577/IJERTV8IS090031

Maniruzzaman, M., & Jahanur Rahman, M. (2018). Accurate Diabetes Risk Stratification Using Machine Learning: Role of Missing Value and Outliers. *Journal of Medical Systems, 42*(5), 92. doi:10.100710916-018-0940-7 PMID:29637403

Maniruzzaman, M., Kumar, N., Abedin, M. M., Islam, M. S., Suri, H. S., El-Baz, A. S., & Suri, J. S. (2017). Comparative approaches for classification of diabetes mellitus data: Machine learning paradigm. *Computer Methods and Programs in Biomedicine, 152*, 23–34. doi:10.1016/j.cmpb.2017.09.004 PMID:29054258

Mann, P. S. (2001). Introductory statistics (4th ed.). New York Wiley.

Manning, C. D., Bauer, J., Finkel, J., & Bethard, S. J. (2014). The Stanford CoreNLP Natural Language Processing Toolkit. Aclweb.Org, 55–60. http://macopolo.cn/mkpl/products.asp

Manning, C. D., Raghavan, P., & Schütze, H. (2008). *Introduction to information retrieval*. Cambridge university press. doi:10.1017/CBO9780511809071

Mantri. (2016). Data Science: Literature Review & State of Art. *Technical Report*, 1-3.

Mao, J., & Jain, A. K. (1996). A self-organizing network for hyperellipsoidal clustering (HEC). *IEEE Transactions on Neural Networks*, 7(1), 16–29. doi:10.1109/72.478389 PMID:18255555

maria jesus. (2019). UC BigML. https://blog.bigml.com/2019/03/25/machine-learning-boosts startups-and-industry/

Market Research. (2018). Retrieved from https://www.transparencymarketresearch.com/pressrelease/telehealth-market.htm

Martinez-Millana, A., Lizondo, A., Gatta, R., Vera, S., Salcedo, V. T., & Fernandez-Llatas, C. (2019). Process Mining Dashboard in Operating Rooms: Analysis of Staff Expectations with Analytic Hierarchy Process. *International Journal of Environmental Research and Public Health*, 16(2), 199. Advance online publication. doi:10.3390/ijerph16020199 PubMed

Max Planck Institute for Demographic Research. (2019). The Human Mortality Database. https://www.lifetable.de/cgi-bin/data.php

Max-Planck-Institute of Biochemistry. (2018). MaxQuant. https://maxquant.org/

Max-Planck-Institute of Biochemistry. (2019). Perseus. https://maxquant.net/perseus/

Mazanetz, P., Reisser, C. B. T., Marmon, R. J., & Morao, I. (2013). Drug Discovery Applications for KNIME: An Open Source Data Mining Platform. *Current Topics in Medicinal Chemistry*, 12(18), 1965–1979. doi:10.2174/1568026611212180004 PubMed

McCabe, R. (2008). *U.S. Patent No. 7,386,463*. Washington, DC: U.S. Patent and Trademark Office.

McDonald, J. T. (1999). The Determinants of Firm Profitability in Australian Manufacturing. *The Economic Record*, 75(229), 115–126.

McFee, B., Raffel, C., Liang, D., Ellis, D., McVicar, M., Battenberg, E., & Nieto, O. (2015). librosa: Audio and Music Signal Analysis in Python. Proceedings of the 14th Python in Science Conference, Scipy, 18–24. doi:10.25080/Majora-7b98e3ed-003

McPadden, J., Durant, T. J. S., Bunch, D. R., Coppi, A., Price, N., Rodgerson, K., Torre, C. J., Byron, W., Hsiaol, A. L., Krumholz, H. M., & Schulz, W. L. (2019). Health Care and Precision Medicine Research: Analysis of a Scalable Data Science Platform. *Journal of Medical Internet Research*, 21(4), e13043. Advance online publication. doi:10.2196/13043 PubMed

Meltwater. (2019). Fairhair.ai. https://fairhair.ai/about

Menkveld, A. J. (2013). High frequency trading and the new market makers. *Journal of Financial Markets*, 16(4), 712–740. doi:10.1016/j.finmar.2013.06.006

Merton, R. C. (1973). Theory of rational option pricing. Theory of Valuation, 229-288.

Metadata. (2018). Regional Purchasing Power Parities for the main groups of consumption expenditures. Retrieved from https://biruni.tuik.gov.tr/bolgeselistatistik/metaVeriEkle.do?durum=metaGetir&menuNo=457

Metadata. (2019a). *Distribution of expenditure groups according to Household Budget Survey (Horizontal %), 2016-2018*. Retrieved from https://biruni.tuik.gov.tr/bolgeselistatistik/metaVeriEkle.do?durum=metaGetir&menuNo=422

Metadata. (2019b). *Distribution of expenditure groups according to Household Budget Survey (Horizontal %), 2015-2017*. Retrieved from https://biruni.tuik.gov.tr/bolgeselistatistik/metaVeriEkle.do?durum=metaGetir&menuNo=530

Metadata. (2019c). *Gini coefficient by equivalised household disposable income.* https://biruni.tuik.gov.tr/bolgeselistatis-tik/metaVeriEkle.do?durum=metaGetir&menuNo=515

Mian, M., Teredesai, A., Hazel, D., Pokuri, S., & Uppala, K. (2014). Work in Progress - In-Memory Analysis for Health-care Big Data. *International Congress on Big Data (BigData Congress)*, 778-779. 10.1109/BigData.Congress.2014.119

Michalski, R. S. (1998). *Machine Learning and Data Mining: Methods and Applications.* Wiley.

Microsoft. (2019a). Machine Learning Studio. https://azure.microsoft.com/es-es/services/machine-learning-studio/

Microsoft. (2019b). Microsoft Excel. https://products.office.com/es-mx/excel

Microsoft. (2019c). Power BI Interactive Data Vizualitacion. https://powerbi.microsoft.com/en-us/

Microsoft. (2020a). ProjectMalmo. Retrieved from https://www.microsoft.com/en us/research/project/projectmalmo/

Microsoft. (2020b). SQL Data tools. Retrieved from https://visualstudio.microsoft.com/vs/features/ ssdt/

Mikalef, P., Pappas, I., Krogstie, J., & Giannakos, M. (2018). Big data analytics capabilities: A systematic literature review and research agenda. *Information Systems and e-Business Management*, *16*(3), 547–578. doi:10.100710257-017-0362-y

Mikolov, T., Sutskever, I., Chen, K., Corrado, G. S., & Dean, J. (2013). *Distributed Representations of Words and Phrases and their Compositionality.* NIPS.

Miller, M., & Scholes, M. (1982). Dividend and taxes: Some empirical evidence. *Journal of Political Economy*, *90*, 1118–1141.

Mind, D. (2020). DeepMind. https://deepmind.com/blog

Miniera. (2019). MIRA Analytics. http://www.mira-analytics.com/

Ministry of Law, Justice and Company Affairs – Legislative Department. (2000). *The Gazette of India Extraordinary Part II.*

Min, J. H., & Lee, Y. C. (2005). Bankruptcy prediction using support vector machine with optimal choice of kernel function parameters. *Expert Systems with Applications*, *28*(4), 603–614. doi:10.1016/j.eswa.2004.12.008

Min, S. H., Lee, J., & Han, I. (2006). Hybrid genetic algorithms and support vector machines for bankruptcy prediction. *Expert Systems with Applications*, *31*(3), 652–660. doi:10.1016/j.eswa.2005.09.070 PMID:32288331

Miroslav, K., Fedor, L., & Gabriel, V. (2012). *Multi-Platform Telemedicine System for Patient Health Monitoring.* doi:10.1109/BHI.2012.6211525

Mitsubishi Electric Research Labs. (2019). MERLSense Data. https://sites.google.com/a/drwren.com/wmd/

MLJAR. (2019). ML Jar. Retrieved from https://mljar.com/blog/

Modigliani, F., & Miller, M. (1958). The Cost of Capital, Corporation Finance and the Theory of Investment. *The American Economic Review*, *48*(3), 261–297.

Modigliani, F., & Miller, M. (1963). Corporate income taxes and the cost of capital: A correction. *The American Economic Review*, *53*(3), 433–443.

Modugu, K. P., & Anyaduba, J. O. (2013). Forensic accounting and financial fraud in Nigeria: An empirical approach. *Journal. International of Business and Social Science*, *4*(7), 281–289.

Moffitt, K. C., & Vasarhelyi, M. A. (2013). AIS in an age of big data. *Journal of Information Systems*, *27*(2), 1–19. doi:10.2308/isys-10372

Molina-Solana, M., Ros, M., Ruiz, M. D., Gómez-Romero, J., & Martín-Bautista, M. J. (2017). Data science for building energy management: A review. *Renewable & Sustainable Energy Reviews*, *70*, 598–609. doi:10.1016/j.rser.2016.11.132

Monajemi, H., Murri, R., Jonas, E., Liang, P., Stodden, V., & Donoho, D. (2019). Ambitious data science can be painless. *Harvard Data Science Review*. Retrieved from https://hdsr.mitpress.mit.edu/

Mongo, D. B. I. (2020). MongoDB. Retrieved from https://www.mongodb.com/hadoop-and mongodb

Monreale, A., Rinzivillo, S., Pratesi, F., Giannotti, F., & Pedreschi, D. (2014). Privacy by design in big data abalytics and social mining. *EPJ Data Science*, *3*(1), 10. doi:10.1140/epjds13688-014-0010-4

Morris, R. (2018). *Early Warning Indicators of Corporate Failure: A Critical Review of Previous Research and Further Empirical Evidence*. Rutledge Revivals.

Mortenson, M. J., Doherty, N. F., & Robinson, S. (2015). Operational research from Taylorism to Terabytes: A research agenda for the analytics age. *European Journal of Operational Research*, *241*(3), 583–595. doi:10.1016/j.ejor.2014.08.029

Motl. (2020). *Niblack local thresholding*. Error! Hyperlink reference not valid. 40849-niblack-local-thresholding

Moustakidis, S., Christodoulou, E., Papageorgiou, E., Kokkotis, C., Papandrianos, N., & Tsaopoulos, D. (2019). Application of machine intelligence for osteoarthritis classification: A classical implementation and a quantum perspective. *Quantum Machine Intelligence*, *1*(3–4), 73–86. doi:10.100742484-019-00008-3

Muhammad, N., & Scrimgeour, F. (2014). Stock Returns and Fundamentals in the Australian Market. *Asian Journal of Finance & Accounting*, *6*(1), 271–290.

Mu, J., Liu, X., Luan, S., Heintz, P. H., Mlady, G. W., & Chen, D. Z. (2011). Segmentation of knee joints in x-ray images using decomposition-based sweeping and graph search. *Medical Imaging* 2011. *Image Processing*, *7962*, 159–166.

Mukherji, S., Dhatt, M. S., & Kim, Y. H. (1997). A Fundamental Analysis of Korean Stock Returns. *Financial Analysts Journal*, *53*(3), 75–80.

Muni Kumar, N., & Manjula, R. (2014). Role of Big data analytics in rural health care-A step towards svasth bharath. *International Journal of Computer Science and Information Technologies*, *5*(6), 7172–7178.

Munos, B., Baker, P. C., Bot, B. M., Crouthamel, M., de Vries, G., Ferguson, I., Hixson, J. D., Malek, L. A., Mastrototaro, J. J., Misra, V., Ozcan, A., Sacks, L., & Wang, P. (2016). Mobile health: The power of wearables, sensors, and apps to transform clinical trials. *Annals of the New York Academy of Sciences*, *1375*(1), 3–18. doi:10.1111/nyas.13117 PMID:27384501

Murillo, D. J. H. (2019). UC neo4j. Retrieved from https://neo4j.com/news/graph-database-tech elping-improve-businesses-telcos-airbnb/

Mwamwenda, T. S. (2014). Education level and HIV/AIDS knowledge in Kenya. *Journal of AIDS and HIV Research*, *6*(2), 28–32.

Mwaniki, A. (2017). *Leading Causes of Death in Africa*. WorldAtlas. worldatlas.com/articles/the-leading-causes-of-death-in-the-african-continent.html

Myers, S. C. (1984). The Capital Structure Puzzle. *The Journal of Finance*, *39*(3), 575–592.

Myers, S. C., & Majluf, N. S. (1984). Corporate Financing and Investment Decisions When Firms Have Information That Investors Do Not Have. *Journal of Financial Economics*, *13*(2), 187–221.

Nagorny, K., Lima-Monteiro, P., Barata, J., & Colombo, A. W. (2017). Big Data Analysis in Smart Manufacturing: A Review. International Journal of Communications. Network and System Sciences, 10(3), 31–58. doi:10.4236/ijcns.2017.103003

Nakano, M., Takahashi, A., & Takahashi, S. (2018). Bitcoin technical trading with artificial neural network. *Physica A*, *510*, 587–609. doi:10.1016/j.physa.2018.07.017

Nallaperumal, K. (2018). Cyber Security Analytics to Combat Cyber Crimes. *IEEE ICCIC 2018*.

Nanduri, P. (2017). UC Paxata. Stravium Intelligence LLP. Retrieved from https://www.analytics insight.net/paxata-bridging-link-data-business-value/

Nanni, L., & Lumini, A. (2009). An experimental comparison of ensemble of classifiers for bankruptcy prediction and credit scoring. *Expert Systems with Applications*, *36*(2), 3028–3033. doi:10.1016/j.eswa.2008.01.018

Naqvi, B., Ali, A., Hashmi, M. A., & Atif, M. (2018). Prediction Techniques for Diagnosis of Diabetic Disease: A Comparative Study. *International Journal of Computer Science and Network Security*, *18*(8), 118–124.

National Center for Biotechnology Information & U.S. National Library of Medicine. (2019). GEO DataSets. https://www.ncbi.nlm.nih.gov/gds

National Oceanic and Atmospheric Administration. (2019). NOAA Climate.gov. https://www.climate.gov/maps-data/datasets

National Statistics | Data and Statistics | Arthritis | CDC. (2003). Retrieved from https://www.cdc.gov/arthritis/data_statistics/national-statistics.html

Nawrat, A. (2018). *3D printing in the medical field: four major applications revolutionising the industry*. Retrieved from https://www.medicaldevice-network.com/features/3d-printing-in-the-medical-field-applications

Nelson, A., Sunny, B. M., Joseph, J., Shelly, M., & George, S. (2019). Breast cancer prediction techniques : A review. *National Conference in Emerging Computer Applications (NCECA2019)*, 24–26.

Neo4j, I. (2020). Neo4j. Retrieved from https://neo4j.com/

Neogi, T., Felson, D., Niu, J., Nevitt, M., Lewis, C. E., Aliabadi, P., & Zhang, Y. (2009). Association between radiographic features of knee osteoarthritis and pain: Results from two cohort studies. *BMJ (Clinical Research Ed.)*, *339*(7719), 498–501. doi:10.1136/bmj.b2844 PMID:19700505

NeuroSolutions. (2019). Premier Neural Network Software. http://www.neurosolutions.com/neurosolutions/

New Vantage Partners. (2020). *Big Data and AI Executive Survey 2020*. Retrieved from https://newvantage.com/

Newville, B. J. M., & Ansanelli, J. M. (2017). *SEC continues to use advanced data analytics to investigate insider trading*. Retrieved from https://www.corporatedefensedisputes.com

Ng, R. T., & Han, J. (1994, September). Efficient and Effective clustering methods for spatial data mining. In *Proceedings of VLDB* (pp. 144-155). Academic Press.

Ngiam, K. Y., & Khor, W. (2019). Big data and machine learning algorithms for health-care delivery. *The Lancet Oncology*, *20*(5), e262–e273. doi:10.1016/S1470-2045(19)30149-4 PMID:31044724

Ng, R. T., & Han, J. (2002). CLARANS: A method for clustering objects for spatial data mining. *IEEE Transactions on Knowledge and Data Engineering*, *14*(5), 1003–1016. doi:10.1109/TKDE.2002.1033770

Nguyen, T. N., Huynh, H. H., & Meunier, J. (2016). Skeleton-Based Abnormal Gait Detection. *Sensors (Basel)*, *16*(11), 1–13. doi:10.3390/s16111792 PubMed

Nguyen, T., Zhou, L., Spiegler, V., Ieromonachou, P., & Lin, Y. (2018). Big data analytics in supply chain management: A state-of-theart literature review. *Computers & Operations Research*, *98*, 254–264. doi:10.1016/j.cor.2017.07.004

Nisha, P. J. K. (2015). Cluster Quality Based Performance Evaluation of Hierarchical Clustering Method. *1st International Conference on Next Generation Computing Technologies (NCGT-2015)*, 649-653. 10.1109/NGCT.2015.7375201

NLTK Project. (2019). Natural Language Toolkit. https://www.nltk.org/

Norrie, M.A .(2019).An introduction to machine learning. In *Data analytics: Concept, techniques and application.* CRC Press.

nosql-database.org. (2019). nosql. https://nosql-database.org/

NumFOCUS. (2019). shogun. https://www.shogun.ml/

Nwiabu, N. D., & John, A. O. (2019). Model for Evaluating Hospital Management Performance using Artificial Neural Network. *International Journal of Computer Science and Mathematical Theory*, *5*(1), 30–43.

NYSE. (2020). *Stock market summary*. Retrieved from https://www.nyse.com/market-data/historical

Oh, K., Lee, D., Ko, B., & Choi, H. (2017). A Chatbot for Psychiatric Counseling in Mental Healthcare Service Based on Emotional Dialogue Analysis and Sentence Generation. *18th IEEE International Conference on Mobile Data Management (MDM)*, 371-375. 10.1109/MDM.2017.64

Ohlhorst, F. (2013). *Big data analytics*. Wiley.

Oka, H., Muraki, S., Akune, T., Mabuchi, A., Suzuki, T., Yoshida, H., Yamamoto, S., Nakamura, K., Yoshimura, N., & Kawaguchi, H. (2008). Fully automatic quantification of knee osteoarthritis severity on plain radiographs. *Osteoarthritis and Cartilage*, *16*(11), 1300–1306. doi:10.1016/j.joca.2008.03.011 PMID:18424107

Olaronke, I., Oluwaseun, O., & Rhoda, I. (2017). State of the art: A study of human-robot interaction in healthcare. *International Journal of Information Engineering and Electronic Business*, *9*(3), 43–55. doi:10.5815/ijieeb.2017.03.06

Olavsrud, T. (2019). UC IBM Cognos. Retrieved from https://www.cio.com/article/3391920/5 ways-ibmcognos-analytics-is-transforming-business.html

Olson, D., & Wu, D. D. (2020). *Enterprise Risk Management Models*. Springer. doi:10.1007/978-3-662-60608-7

Open Palladio projects. (2019). Open Palladio. http://hdlab.stanford.edu/palladio/about/

Oracle. (2015). *Big data in financial services and banking*. Retrieved from http://www.oracle.com/us//big-data-in-financial-services-wp-2415760.pdf

Organisation for Economic Co-operation and Development (OECD). (2017). *Education at a glance 2017: OECD indicators*. OECD Publishing.

Oumar, A. W., & Augustin, P. (2019). Credit card fraud detection using ANN. *International Journal of Innovative Technology and Exploring Engineering*, *8*(7), 313–316.

Oyebisi, O., Wisdom, O., Olusogo, O., & Ifeoluwa, O. (2018). Forensic accounting and fraud prevention and detection in Nigerian banking industry. COJ Reviews & Research, 1–8. doi:10.31031/COJRR.2018.01.000504

Özarı, Ö. Ü. Ç., & Eren, Ö. Ü. Ö. (2018). İllerin Yaşam Endeksi Göstergelerinin Çok Boyutlu Ölçekleme ve K-ortalamalar Kümeleme Yöntemi ile Analizi [Life Index of Proviences in Turkey Via Multidimensional Scaling and K-Means Clustering]. Afyon Kocatepe Üniversitesi Sosyal Bilimler Dergisi, 20(2), 303-313.

Özçağlar, A. (2003). Türkiye'de Yapılan Bölge Ayrımları Ve Bölge Planlama Üzerindeki Etkileri [The Region Divisions in Turkey and Its Effects on Regional Planning]. *Coğrafi Bilimler Dergisi, 1*(1), 3–18.

Özdemir, O., & Demir, İ. (2019). Data Mining of SILC Data: Turkey Case. *International Journal of Sciences:Basic and Applied Research, 48*(7), 110–138.

Ozyilmaz, L., & Yildirim, T. (2002). Diagnosis of thyroid disease using artificial neural network methods. *Proceedings of International Conference on Neural Information Processing*, 2033–2036. 10.1109/ICONIP.2002.1199031

Padmanabhan, A. (2019). Trifacta Wrangler. Devopedia. https://devopedia.org/wrangle-language

Palepu, K. G., Healy, P. M., Bernard, V. L., & Wright, S. (2010). Business Analysis & Valuation: Using Financial Statements (4th ed.). Mason: South-Western Cengage Learning.

Pal, L., Ojha, C. S. P., Chandniha, S. K., & Kumar, A. (2019). Regional scale analysis of trends in rainfall using nonparametric methods and wavelet transforms over a semi-arid region in India. *International Journal of Climatology, 39*(5), 2737–2764. doi:10.1002/joc.5985

Panch, T., Szolovits, P., & Atun, R. (2018). Artificial intelligence, machine learning and health systems. *Journal of Global Health, 8*(2), 020303. doi:10.7189/jogh.08.020303 PMID:30405904

Pandey, S., Miri, R., & Tandan, S.R. (2013). Diagnosis and classification of hypothyroid disease using data mining techniques. *International Journal of Engineering Research and Technology.*

Panduranga, V. (2013a). An Empirical Analysis of Black Scholes option pricing model for select banking stocks. *International Journal of Multidisciplinary Research in Social and Management Science, 2*, 23-30.

Panduranga, V. (2013b). Relevance of Black-Scholes option pricing model in Indian derivatives markets–a study of cement stock options. *International Journal of Multidisciplinary Research in Social and Management Sciences, 1*(4), 91–95.

Papageorgiou, E., Nieuwenhuys, A., Vandekerckhove, I., Van Campenhout, A., Ortibus, E., & Desloovere, K. (2019). Systematic review on gait classifications in children with cerebral palsy: An update. *Gait & Posture, 69*, 209–223. doi:10.1016/j.gaitpost.2019.01.038 PubMed

Park, Han, Seon, Park, Kim, Moon, Yoon, & Kwar. (2019). Diagnosis of Thyroid Nodules: Performance of a Deep Learning Convolutional Neural Network Model vs. Radiologist. *Scientific Reports.*

Park, C. S., & Han, I. (2002). A case-based reasoning with the feature weights derived by analytic hierarchy process for bankruptcy prediction. *Expert Systems with Applications, 23*(3), 255–264. doi:10.1016/S0957-4174(02)00045-3

Park, H. S., & Jun, C. H. (2009). A simple and fast algorithm for K-medoids clustering. *Expert Systems with Applications, 36*(2), 3336–3341. doi:10.1016/j.eswa.2008.01.039

Park, H. S., Lee, J. S., & Jun, C. H. (2006). A K-means-like Algorithm for K-medoids Clustering and Its Performance. *Proceedings of ICCIE*, 102-117.

Pätäri, E. J., Leivo, T. H., & Honkapuro, J. V. S. (2010). Enhancement of value portfolio performance using data envelopment analysis. *Studies in Economics and Finance, 27*(3), 223–246.

Patel, J. A., & Sharma, P. (2014), Big data for better health planning. *International Conference on Advances in Engineering and Technology Research (ICAETR).*

Paterlini, A. A., Nascimento, M. A., & Traina, C. Jr. (2011). Using pivots to speed-up k-medoids clustering. *Journal of Information and Data Management, 2*(2), 221–236.

Paul, M., Vishwakarma, S. K., & Verma, A. (2016). Analysis of Soil Behaviour and Prediction of Crop Yield Using Data Mining Approach. *Proceedings - 2015 International Conference on Computational Intelligence and Communication Networks, CICN 2015*, 766–771. 10.1109/CICN.2015.156

Pawletta, M. (2020). UC KNIME. Retrieved from https://www.knime.com/blog?page=1

Paxata. (2020). Paxata. Retrieved from https://www.paxata.com/machine-learning/

Penman, S. H., Richardson, S. A., & Tuna, I. (2007). The book-to-price effect in stock returns: Accounting for leverage. *Journal of Accounting Research*, *45*(2), 427–467.

Pennington, J., Socher, R., & Manning, C. D. (2014). *Glove: Global Vectors for Word Representation*. EMNLP.

Perols, J. (2011). Financial statement fraud detection: An analysis of statistical and machine learning algorithms. *Auditing*, *30*(2), 19–50. doi:10.2308/ajpt-50009

Petroutsatou, K., Georgopoulos, E., Lambropoulos, S., & Pantouvakis, J. P. (2011). Early cost estimating of road tunnel construction using neural networks. *Journal of Construction Engineering and Management*, *138*(6), 679–6. doi:10.1061/(ASCE)CO.1943-7862.0000479

Pham, D. T., Dimov, S. S., & Nguyen, C. D. (2005). Selection of K in K-means clustering. *Proceedings of the Institution of Mechanical Engineers. Part C, Journal of Mechanical Engineering Science*, *219*(1), 103–119. doi:10.1243/095440605X8298

Philip Chen, C. L., & Zhang, C. Y. (2014). Data-intensive applications, challenges, techniques and technologies: A survey on Big Data. *Information Sciences*, *275*, 314–347. doi:10.1016/j.ins.2014.01.015

Philips, P., & Louvieris, P. (2005). Performance measurement systems in tourism, hospitality and leisure small medium-sized enterprises: A balanced scorecard perspective. *Journal of Travel Research*, *44*, 201–211.

Phillips, R. C., & Gorse, D. (2017). Predicting cryptocurrency price bubbles using social media data and epidemic modelling. *2017 IEEE Symposium Series on Computational Intelligence*, 1–7. 10.1109/SSCI.2017.8280809

Picklum, M., & Beetz, M. (2019). MatCALO: Knowledge-enabled machine learning in materials science. *Computational Materials Science*, *163*, 50–62. doi:10.1016/j.commatsci.2019.03.005

Piskorec, M., Antulov-Fantulin, N., Novak, P. K., Mozetic, I., Grcar, M., Vodenska, I., & Smuc, T. (2014). Cohesiveness in financial news and its relation to market volatility. *Scientific Reports*, *4*, 8. PMID:24849598

Poornima, S., & Pushpalatha, M. (2018). A survey of predictive analytics using big data with data mining. *International Journal of Bioinformatics Research and Applications*, *14*(3), 269–282. doi:10.1504/IJBRA.2018.092697

Powers, J., & McMullen, P. (2002). Using data envelopment analysis to select efficient large cap securities. *Journal of Business and Management*, *7*(7), 31–42.

Praharsi, Y., Miaou, S.-G., & Wee, H.-M. (2013). Supervised learning approaches and feature selection–a case study in diabetes. *International Journal of Data Analysis Techniques and Strategies*, *5*(3), 323–337. doi:10.1504/IJDATS.2013.055346

Pramanik, M. I., Lau, R. Y. K., Demirkan, H., & Azad, M. A. K. (2017). Smart health: Big data enabled health paradigm within smart cities. *Expert Systems with Applications*, *87*, 370–383. doi:10.1016/j.eswa.2017.06.027

Preis, T., Moat, H. S., & Stanley, H. E. (2013). Quantifying trading behavior in financial markets using Google Trends. *Scientific Reports*, *3*(1), 3. doi:10.1038rep01684 PMID:23619126

Prerana, P. S., & Taneja, K. (2015). Predictive data mining for diagnosis of thyroid disease using neural network. *International Journal of Research in Management. Science & Technology*, *3*(2), 75–80.

Prieto, I. M., & Revilla, E. (2006). Learning capability and business performance: A non-financial and financial assessment. *The Learning Organization*, *13*(2), 166–185.

Process Mining Group. (2016). ProM. http://www.processmining.org/prom/start

Procházka, A., Vyšata, O., Vališ, M., Ťupa, O., Schätz, M., & Mařík, V. (2015). Use of the image and depth sensors of the Microsoft Kinect for the detection of gait disorders. *Neural Computing & Applications*, *26*(7), 1621–1629. doi:10.1007/s00521-015-1827-x

Project Jupyter. (2019). Project Jupyter. https://jupyter.org/

Provost, F., & Fawcett, T. (2013). Data science and its relationship to big data and data-driven decision-making. *Big Data*, *1*(1), 51–59. doi:10.1089/big.2013.1508 PMID:27447038

Proyag, P., Triparna, M., & Asoke, N. (2015). Challenges in data science: A comprehensive study on application and future trends. *International Journal of Advance Research in Computer Science and Management Studies Research*, *3*(8), 1–8.

Punn, N. S., Sonbhadra, S. K., & Agarwal, S. (2020). Monitoring COVID-19 social distancing withperson detection and tracking via fine-tuned YOLOv3 and Deepsort techniques. arXiv:2005.01385v2 [cs.CV]

PurePredictive. (2020). Pure Predictive. Retrieved from https://www.purepredictive.com/

PwC. (2018). *Global economic crime and fraud survey*. Retrieved from https:// www.pwc.com/fraudsurvey

Pyne, S., Rao, B. L. S., & Rao, S. B. (2016). Big Data Analytics: Views from Statistical and Computational Perspectives. In *Big Data Analytics: Methods and applications*. Springer.

Python Software Foundation. (2019). Python. https://www.python.org/

PyTorch. (2019). pytorch. https://pytorch.org/features

Qlik. (2019). Qlik View https://www.qlik.com/us/products/qlikview

QlikTech. (2020). QLIK. Retrieved from https://www.qlik.com/us

Quah, T. (2008). DJIA stock selection assisted by neural network. *Expert Systems with Applications*, *35*(1–2), 50–58. doi:10.1016/j.eswa.2007.06.039

Quante, R., Meyr, H., & Fleischmann, M. (2009). Revenue management and demand management: Matching applications, models, and software. *OR-Spektrum*, *31*(1), 31–62. doi:10.100700291-008-0125-8

R Core Team. (2019). *R: A language and environment for statistical computing*. R Foundation for Statistical Computing. https://www.R-project.org/

R, S. (2015). Performance Analysis of Different Classification Methods in Data Mining for Diabetes Dataset Using WEKA Tool. International Journal on Recent and Innovation Trends in Computing and Communication, 3(3), 1168–1173. doi:10.17762/ijritcc23218169.150361

Raghavendra, U., Gudigar, A., Maithri, M., Gertych, A., Meiburger, K.M., Yeong, C.H., Madla, C., Kongmebhol, P., Molinari, F., Ng, K.H., & Acharya, U.R. (2018). Optimized multi-level elongated quinary patterns for the assessment of thyroid nodules in ultrasound images. *Computer Biology Med.*, *95*, 55-62.

Raghupathi, W., & Raghupathi, V. (2014). Big data analytics in healthcare: Promise and potential. *Health Information Science and Systems*, *2*(3), 1–10. doi:10.1186/2047-2501-2-3 PMID:25825667

Ragothaman, S., Carpenter, J., & Buttars, T. (1995). Using rule induction for knowledge acquisition: An expert systems approach to evaluating material errors and irregularities. *Expert Systems with Applications*, *9*(4), 483–490. doi:10.1016/0957-4174(95)00018-6

Raguraman, P., Mohan, R., & Vijayan, M. (2019). LibROSA Based Assessment Tool for Music Information Retrieval Systems. Proceedings - 2nd International Conference on Multimedia Information Processing and Retrieval, MIPR 2019, 109–114.doi:10.1109/MIPR.2019.00027. 2019.00027

Rahaman, A. (2018). *Challenging tools on Research Issues in Big Data Analytics.* https://www.softwaretestinghelp.com/big-data-tools/

Rahman, M. M., Haq, N., & Rahman, R. M. (2014). Machine Learning Facilitated Rice Prediction in Bangladesh. Proceedings - 2014 Annual Global Online Conference on Information and Computer Technology, GOCICT 2014, 1–4. doi:10.1109/GOCICT.2014.9

Rahman, G., & Islam, Z. (2011), A decision tree-based missing value imputation technique for data pre-processing. *Proceedings of the Ninth Australasian Data Mining Conference-Volume 121.* Australian Computer Society, Inc.

Rahmani, A. M., Gia, T. N., Negash, B., Anzanpour, A., Azimi, I., Jiang, M., & Liljeberg, P. (2018). Exploiting smart e-Health gateways at the edge of healthcare Internet-of-Things: A fog computing approach. *Future Generation Computer Systems*, *78*, 641–658. doi:10.1016/j.future.2017.02.014

Rai, S., Raut, A., Savaliya, A. A., & Shankarmani, R. (2018). Darwin: Convolutional Neural Network based Intelligent Health Assistant. Second International Conference on Electronics, Communication and Aerospace Technology (ICECA), 1367-1371.

Raj, B. S. (2019). BERT. Retrieved from https://towardsdatascience.com/understanding-bert-is-it a-game-changer-in-nlp-7cca943cf3ad

Rajesh, K., & Sangeetha, V. (2012). Application of data mining methods and techniques for diabetes diagnosis. *International Journal of Engineering and Innovative Technology*, *2*(3).

Rajesh, R., & Mathivanan, B. (2017). Predicting Flight Delay using ANN with Multi-core Map Reduce Framework. In *Communication and power engineering* (p. 280). Walter de Gruyter GmbH & Co KG.

Rallapalli, S., Gondkar, R. R., & Ketavarapu, U. P. K. (2016). Impact of processing and analyzing healthcare big data on cloud computing environment by implementing Hadoop cluster. *Procedia Computer Science*, *85*, 16–22. doi:10.1016/j.procs.2016.05.171

Ramsay, J. O., & Dalzell, C. J. (1991). Some tools for functional data analysis. *Journal of the Royal Statistical Society. Series B. Methodological*, *53*(3), 539–561. doi:10.1111/j.2517-6161.1991.tb01844.x

Ramya, Kumar, & Mugilan. (2018). A Review of Different Classification Techniques in Machine. Academic Press.

Ramya, K., & Sumathi, A. (2019). Big data applications in Aadhar card fraud detection. *International Journal on Computer Science and Engineering*, *7*(3), 865–867.

Ramzan, M. (2017). Comparing and evaluating the performance of WEKA classifiers on critical diseases. India International Conference on Information Processing, IICIP 2016 - Proceedings. 10.1109/IICIP.2016.7975309

Rangra, K., & Bansal, K. L. (2014). Comparative study of data mining tools. *International Journal of Advanced Research in Computer Science and Software Engineering*, *4*(6). https://towardsdatascience.com/comparison-of-data-analysis-tools-excel-r-python-and-bi-tools-6c4685a8ea6f

Rani, S., Ahmed, S. H., & Shah, S. C. (2019). Smart health: A novel paradigm to control the chickungunya virus. IEEE Internet of Things Journal, 6(2), 1306–1311. doi:10.1109/JIOT.2018.2802898

Ranji, R., Thanavanich, C., Sukumaran, S. D., Kittiwachana, S., Zain, S., Sun, L. C., & Lee, V. S. (2019). *Progress in Drug Discovery & Biomedical Science An automated workflow by using KNIME Analytical Platform : a case study for modelling and predicting HIV-1 protease inhibitors.* Academic Press.

Rao, R., Chhabra, A., Das, R., & Ruhil, V. (2015). A framework for analyzing publicly available healthcare data. *17th International Conference on E-health Networking, Application & Services (HealthCom)*, 653-656. 10.1109/HealthCom.2015.7454585

RapidMiner. (2014). Rapid Miner. Retrieved from http://edutechwiki.unige.bch/en/RapidMine r _ Studio

RapidMiner. I. (2019). rapidminer. https://rapidminer.com/

Ravisankar, P., Ravi, V., Rao, G. R., & Bose, I. (2011). Detection of financial statement fraud and feature selection using data mining techniques. *Decision Support Systems*, *50*(2), 491–500. doi:10.1016/j.dss.2010.11.006

Ray, J., Johnny, O., Trovati, M., Sotiriadis, S., & Bessis, N. (2018). The Rise of Big Data Science: A Survey of Techniques, Methods and Approaches in the Field of Natural Language Processing and Network Theory. *Big Data Cogn. Comput*, *2*(22), 1–18. doi:10.3390/bdcc2030022

Ray, P. P., Dash, D., & De, D. (2019). Edge computing for Internet of Things: A survey, e-healthcare case study and future direction. *Journal of Network and Computer Applications*, *140*(December), 1–22. doi:10.1016/j.jnca.2019.05.005

Redmond, S. J., & Heneghan, C. (2007). A method for initialising the K-means clustering algorithm using kd-trees. *Pattern Recognition Letters*, *28*(8), 965–973. doi:10.1016/j.patrec.2007.01.001

Refinitiv. (2020). *Big Data & Machine Learning trends in 2020*. Retrieved from https://www.refinitiv.com/perspectives/big-data/big-data-and-machine-learning-trends-to-watch-in-2020/

Regents, U. C. (2019). What is Data Science? https://datascience.berkeley.edu/about/what-is-data-science/

Restrepo, M. (2019). *Explaining data science, AI, ML and deep learning to management-a presentation and a script-part 1 of 3*. Retrieved website: https://towardsdatascience.com/explaining-data-science-ai-ml-and-deep-learning-to-management-a-presentation-and-a-script-4968491eb1e5

Reynolds, A. P., Richards, G., & Rayward-Smith, V. J. (2004). The Application of K-Medoids and PAM to the Clustering of Rules. In Z. R. Yang, H. Yin, & R. M. Everson (Eds.), Lecture Notes in Computer Science: Vol. 3177. *Intelligent Data Engineering and Automated Learning – IDEAL 2004. IDEAL 2004.* Springer. doi:10.1007/978-3-540-28651-6_25

Rhonda Collins. (2017). *Bringing Nurses Back to the Bedside*. https://www.fortherecordmag.com/archives/0915p10.shtml

Rice, J. A. (2007). Mathematical statistics and Data analysis (3rd ed.). Thomson Brooks/Cole.

Rickman, J. M., Lookman, T., & Kalinin, S. V. (2019). Materials informatics: From the atomic-level to the continuum. *Acta Materialia*, *168*, 473–510. doi:10.1016/j.actamat.2019.01.051

Rigano, C. (2019). Using Artificial Intelligence to Address Criminal Justice Needs. *National Institute of Justice Journal*, *280*, 1–10.

Ritchken, P., & Trevor, R. (1999). Pricing options under generalized GARCH and stochastic volatility processes. *The Journal of Finance*, *54*(1), 377–402. doi:10.1111/0022-1082.00109

Rizkallah, J. (2017). *The big (unstructured) data problem*. Retrieved from Forbes website: https://www.forbes.com/sites/forbestechcouncil/2017/06/05/the-big-unstructured-data-problem/

Rocklin, M. (2015). Dask: Parallel Computation with Blocked algorithms and Task Scheduling. Proceedings of the 14th Python in Science Conference, Scipy, 126–132.doi:10.25080/Majora-7b98e3ed-013

Rosruen, N., & Samanchuen, T. (2018). Chatbot Utilization for Medical Consultant System. *3rd Technology Innovation Management and Engineering Science International Conference (TIMES-iCON), 1-5.*

Rousseeuw, P. J. (1987). Silhouettes: A graphical aid to the interpretation and validation of cluster analysis. *Journal of Computational and Applied Mathematics, 20*, 53–65. doi:10.1016/0377-0427(87)90125-7

Roxanne Nelson. (2016). *Personalized Medicine Delivers Better Outcomes: More Proof.* Retrieved from https://www.medscape.com/viewarticle/863499

RStudio. (2019). Rstudio. https://www.rstudio.com/

Rudini, A. A. (2020). *Implementation of chatbot in the health industry to detect COVID-19 plague.* SSRN Electronic Journal., doi:10.2139srn.3590815

Rueangsirarak, W., Zhang, J., Aslam, N., Ho, E. S. L., & Shum, H. P. H. (2018). Automatic Musculoskeletal and Neurological Disorder Diagnosis with Relative Joint Displacement from Human Gait. *IEEE Transactions on Neural Systems and Rehabilitation Engineering, 26*(12), 2387–2396. doi:10.1109/TNSRE.2018.2880871 PubMed

Russom, P. (2011). Big data analytics. *TDWI best practices report, fourth quarter, 19*(4), 1-34.

Russom, P. (2013). *Managing big data. The Data Warehousing Institute Best Practices Report.* TDWI Research.

Rutledge, R. B., Chekroud, A. M., & Huys, Q. J. M. (2019). Machine learning and big data in psychiatry: Toward clinical applications. *Current Opinion in Neurobiology, 55*, 152–159. doi:10.1016/j.conb.2019.02.006 PubMed

Sabibullah, M., Shanmuga Sundaram, V., & Priya, R. (2013). Diabetes patient's risk through soft computing model. *International Journal of Emerging Trends & Technology in Computer Science, 2*(6), 60–65.

Sadasivam, G. S., Subrahmanyam, M., Himachalam, D., Pinnamaneni, B. P., & Lakshme, S. M. (2016). Corporate governance fraud detection from annual reports using big data analytics. *International Journal of Big Data Intelligence, 3*(1), 51–60. doi:10.1504/IJBDI.2016.073895

Sadhana, S., & Shetty, S. (2014). Analysis of diabetic data set using hive and R. *International Journal of Emerging Technology and Advanced Engineering, 4*(7), 626–629.

Salardini, F. (2013). An AHP-GRA method for asset allocation: A case study of investment firms on Tehran Stock Exchange. *Decision Science Letters, 2*(4), 275–280.

Salleh, K., & Aziz, R. A. (2014). Traits, skills and ethical values of public sector forensic accountants : An empirical investigation. *Procedia: Social and Behavioral Sciences, 145*, 361–370. doi:10.1016/j.sbspro.2014.06.045

Saltz, J., Shamshurin, I., & Crowston, K. (2017). Comparing Data Science Project Management Methodologies via a Controlled Experiment. doi:10.24251/hicss.2017.120

Sandhya, R., Prakash, J., & Vinoth Kumar, B. (2020). Comparative Analysis of Clustering Techniques in Anomaly Detection Wind Turbine Data. *Journal of Xi'an University of Architecture & Technology, 12*(3), 5684–5694.

Sa-ngasoongsong, A., & Chongwatpol, J. (2012). An Analysis of Diabetes Risk Factors Using Data Mining Approach. Paper PH10-2012, Oklahoma State University.

SAP. (2019). SAP Cloud Platform Internet of Things. https://www.sap.com/sea/products/iot-platform-cloud.html

Saru, S., & Subashree, S. (2019). Analysis and Prediction of Diabetes Using Machine Learning. *International Journal of Emerging Technology and Innovative Engineering*, *5*(4).

SAS Institute Inc. (2020). SAS Visual Data Mining. Retrieved from https://www.sas.com/ en_us /software/visualdata-mining-machine-learning.html

Sathyapriya, M., & Thiagarasu, V. (2017). Big data analytics techniques for credit card fraud detection: A review. *International Journal of Science and Research*, *6*(5), 206-211.

Sawe, B. E. (2017). *Leading causes of death among youth in India*. WorldAtlas. worldatlas.com/articles/leading-causes-of-death-among-the-youth-of-india.html

Schmidt-Rohlfing, B., Bergamo, F., Williams, S., Erli, H. J., Rau, G., Niethard, F. U., & Disselhorst-Klug, C. (2006). Interpretation of surface EMGs in children with cerebral palsy: An initial study using a fuzzy expert system. *Journal of Orthopaedic Research*, *24*(3), 438–447. doi:10.1002/jor.20043 PubMed

Scholz, P., Schieder, C., Kurze, C., Gluchowski, P., & Boehringer, M. (2010). Benefits and challenges of business intelligence adoption in small and medium-sized enterprises. *18th European Conference on Information Systems, Proceedings*, 1-12.

Schreyer, M., Sattarov, T., Borth, D., Dengel, A., & Reimer, B. (2017). *Detection of anomalies in large scale accounting data using deep autoencoder networks*. Retrieved from https://arxiv.org/abs/1709.05254

Schultz, T. (2013). Turning Healthcare Challenges intoBig Data Opportunities: A Use-Case Review Across thePharmaceutical Development Lifecycle. *Bulletin of the Association for Information Science and Technology*, *39*(5), 34–40. doi:10.1002/bult.2013.1720390508

Sebastian, M. P. (2017). High-Value Health System for All: Technologies for Promoting Health Education and Awareness. *International Journal of Educational and Pedagogical Sciences*, *11*(8), 2060–2065.

Secgin, S., & Dalkilic, G. (2017). A Decision Support System Using Demographic Issues: A Case Study in Turkey. *The International Arab Journal of Information Technology*, *14*(3).

Secretaria de Modernización. (2019). Datos Argentina-Datasets. https://datos.gob.ar/dataset

Seen Environmental Learning Information. (2012, November 19). Health and the Environment. *Health Services in Namibia*, 4. Retrieved 2017, from http://www.mcanamibia.org/files/files/bd5_Health%20Services%20in%20Namibia%20-%20Seen%20Environmental%20Learning%20Information%20Sheet%20No.%206.pdf

Sen, A. (2008). The US fashion industry: A supply chain review. *International Journal of Production Economics*, *114*(2), 571–593. doi:10.1016/j.ijpe.2007.05.022

Sendak, M., Gao, M., Nichols, M., Lin, A., & Balu, S. (2019). Machine Learning in Health Care: A Critical Appraisal of Challenges and Opportunities. *EGEMS (Washington, DC)*, *7*(1), 1. doi:10.5334/egems.287 PMID:30705919

Şengül, Ü., Shiraz, S. E., & Eren, M. (2013). Türkiye'de İstatistikî Bölge Birimleri Sınıflamasına Göre Düzey 2 Bölgelerinin Ekonomik Etkinliklerinin VZA Yöntemi ile Belirlenmesi ve Tobit Model Uygulaması [Economic Activities of Regions of Level 2 According to Statistical Regional Units Classification (NUTS) in Turkey Determining by Using DEA and Tobit Model Application]. *Yönetim Bilimleri Dergisi*, *11*(21), 75–99.

Serpen, G., Jiang, H., & Allred, L. (1997). Performance analysis of probabilistic potential function neural network classifier. *Proceedings of Artificial Neural Networks in Engineering Conference*, 471–476.

Services, A. W. (2020). Amazon Lex. Retrieved from https://aws.amazon.com/lex/

Services, M. o. (1990, March 21). *Ministry of Health and Social Services*. Government of the Republic of Namibia. Hosted by the Office of the Prime Minister. Retrieved June 20, 2017, from http://www.mhss.gov.na/

Seth, T., & Chaudhary, V. (2015). Big data in finance. In book: Big Data: Algorithms. *Analysis and Applications*, 329–356.

Shahid, N., Rappon, T., & Berta, W. (2019). Applications of artificial neural networks in health care organizational decision-making: A scoping review. *PLoS One, 14*(2). doi:10.1371/journal.pone.0212356 PMID:30779785

Shaik Razia, S., & Narasinga Rao, M. R. (2016). Machine Learning Techniques for Thyroid Disease Diagnosis- *A Review. Indian Journal of Science and Technology, 9*(28).

Shamir, L., Ling, S. M., Scott, W. W., Bos, A., Orlov, N., Macura, T. J., & Goldberg, I. G. (2009). Knee X-Ray Image Analysis Method for Automated Detection of Osteoarthritis. *IEEE Transactions on Biomedical Engineering, 56*(2), 407–415. doi:10.1109/TBME.2008.2006025 PMID:19342330

Shankar, M., Pahadia, M., Srivastava, D., Ashwin, T. S., & Reddy, G. R. (2015). A Novel Method for Disease Recognition and Cure Time Prediction Based on Symptoms. *Second International Conference on Advances in Computing and Communication Engineering*, 679-682.

Shao, H. C., Chiu, Y. S., & Dai, S. Y. (2014). Duplicate drug discovery using Hadoop. In *International Conference on Big Data (Big Data)*, IEEE.

Shapira, Y., Berman, Y., & Ben-Jacob, E. (2014). Modelling the short-term herding behavior of stock markets. *New Journal of Physics, 16*(5), 16. doi:10.1088/1367-2630/16/5/053040

Sharma, A., & Panigrahi, P. (2012). A review of financial accounting fraud detection based on data mining techniques. *International Journal of Computers and Applications, 39*(1), 37–47. doi:10.5120/4787-7016

Sharma, N., Taneja, S., Sagar, V., & Bhatt, A. (2018). Forecasting air pollution load in Delhi using data analysis tools. *Procedia Computer Science, 132*, 1077–1085. doi:10.1016/j.procs.2018.05.023

Sharma, R., Thanvi, A., Menghani, B., Kumar, M., & Kumar Jangir, S. (2019). *An Approach towards Information Retrieval through Machine Learning and its Algorithms: A Review*. Academic Press.

Sheng, W., & Liu, X. (2006). A genetic k-medoids clustering algorithm. *Journal of Heuristics, 12*(6), 447–466. doi:10.100710732-006-7284-z

Shi, F., Wang, J., Shi, J., Wu, Z., Wang, Q., Tang, Z., He, K., Shi, Y., & Shen, D. (2020). Review of artificial intelligence techniques in imaging data acquisition, segmentation and diagnosis for COVID-19. IEEE Reviews in Biomedical Engineering, 1–1. doi:10.1109/RBME.2020.2987975 PubMed

Shi, W., Cao, J., Zhang, Q., Li, Y., & Xu, L. (2016). Edge Computing: Vision and Challenges. IEEE Internet of Things Journal, 3(5), 637–646. doi:10.1109/JIOT.2016.2579198

Shin, K.-S., Lee, T.-S., & Kim, H.-J. (2005). An application of support vector machines in bankruptcy prediction model. *Expert Systems with Applications, 28*(1), 127–135. doi:10.1016/j.eswa.2004.08.009

Shiny. (n.d.). *RStudio*. shiny.rstudio.com/

Shi, X., Chen, G., Heng, P. A., & Yi, Z. (2017). Tracking topology structure adaptively with deep neural networks. *Neural Computing & Applications, 30*(11), 3317–3326. doi:10.100700521-017-2906-y

Shmueli, G., Bruce, P., Gedeck, P., & Patel, N. (2019). *Data Mining for Business Analytics: Concepts, Techniques and Applications in Python*. Wiley.

Shpyrko, V., & Koval, B. (2019). *Models of fraud detection and analysis of payment transactions using machine learning.* Taras Shevchenko National University of Kyiv.

Siegel, C., & Dorner, T. E. (2017). Information technologies for active and assisted living—Influences to the quality of life of an ageing society. *International Journal of Medical Informatics, 100*, 32–45. doi:10.1016/j.ijmedinf.2017.01.012 PMID:28241936

Sigdel, D., Kyi, V., Zhang, A. D., Setty, S. P., Liem, D. A., Shi, Y., Wang, X., Shen, J. M., Wang, W., Han, J. W., & Ping, P. P. (2019). Cloud-Based Phrase Mining and Analysis of User-Defined Phrase-Category Association in Biomedical Publications. Jove-Journal of Visualized Experiments, (144), Article e59108. doi:10.3791/59108

Sikora, R., & Piramuthu, S. (2007). Framework for efficient feature selection in genetic algorithm based data mining. *European Journal of Operational Research, 180*(2), 723–737. doi:10.1016/j.ejor.2006.02.040

Silva, M., & Cunha, C. (2017). A tabu search heuristic for the incapacitated single allocation p-hub maximal covering problem. *European Journal of Operational Research, 262*(3), 954–965. doi:10.1016/j.ejor.2017.03.066

Simone Edelmann. (2019). *6 technologies that will transform healthcare.* Retrieved from https://healthcaretransformers. com/healthcare-business/technologies-transform-healthcare

Singh, A., & Schmidgall, R. S. (2002). Analysis of financial ratios commonly used by US lodging financial executives. *Journal of Retail & Leisure Property, 2*(3), 201–213.

Singh, D., & Reddy, C. K. (2014). A survey on platforms for big data analytics. *Journal of Big Data, 2*(1), 8. doi:10.1186/s40537-014-0008-6 PubMed

Sinitcyn, P., Rudolph, J. D., & Cox, J. (2018). Computational Methods for Understanding Mass Spectrometry–Based Shotgun Proteomics Data. *Annual Review of Biomedical Data Science, 1*(1), 207–234. doi:10.1146/annurev-biodatasci-080917-013516

Sisodia, D., & Sisodia, D. S. (2018). Prediction of diabetes using classification algorithms. *Procedia Computer Science, 132*, 1578–1585. doi:10.1016/j.procs.2018.05.122

SiteWhere LLC. (2019). SiteWhere Open Source Internet of Things Platform. https://sitewhere.io/en/

Sivanandhini, P., & Prakash, J. (2020). Crop Yield Prediction Analysis using Feed Forward and Recurrent Neural Network. *International Journal of Innovative Science and Research Technology, 5*(5), 1092–1096. doi:10.38124/volume5issue5

Sivarajah, U., Kamal, M. M., Irani, Z., & Weerakkody, V. (2016). Critical analysis of big data challenges and analytical methods. *Journal of Business Research, 70*, 263–286. doi:10.1016/j.jbusres.2016.08.001

Škrinjarić, T. (2014). Investment Strategy on the Zagreb Stock Exchange Based on Dynamic DEA. *Croatian Economic Survey, 16*, 129–160.

Škrinjarić, T., & Šego, B. (2019). Using Grey Incidence Analysis Approach in Portfolio Selection. *International Journal of Financial Studies, 7*(1), 1–16.

Skymind. (2019). Deeplearning4j. https://deeplearning4j.org/

Sneha, N., & Gangil, T. (2019). Analysis of diabetes mellitus for early prediction using optimal features selection. *Journal of Big Data, 6*(13), 13. doi:10.118640537-019-0175-6

Sodhro, A. H., Pirbhulal, S., & Sangaiah, A. K. (2018). Convergence of IoT and product lifecycle management in medical health care. *Future Generation Computer Systems, 86*, 380–391. doi:10.1016/j.future.2018.03.052

Software. T. (2020). Tableau. Retrieved from https://www.tableau.com/

Sofya, S. T., Valeriy, N. T., Georgios, A., & Jan, P. (2019). Fast implementation of pattern mining algorithms with time stamp uncertainties and temporal constraints. *Journal of Big Data*, 6, 1–34. doi:10.118640537-019-0200-9

Sohail, M. N., Ren, J., & Uba Muhammad, M. (2019). A Euclidean Group Assessment on Semi-Supervised Clustering for Healthcare Clinical Implications Based on Real-Life Data. *International Journal of Environmental Research and Public Health*, 16(9), 1581. doi:10.3390/ijerph16091581 PMID:31064121

Soltanpoor, R., & Sellis, T. (2016). Prescriptive analytics for big data. *Databases Theory and Applications: 27th Australasian Database Conference, Sydney, NSW, Proceedings*, 245-256. DOI: 10.1007/978-3-319-46922-5_19

Solutions, E. I. (2020). MarketSwitchOptimisation. Retrieved from http://www.experian. com/ decision analytics/ marketswitch-optimization.html

SolutionsS. (2020). VisualAR. Retrieved from https://visualrsoftware.com/index.html

Song, W., Li, S., Liu, J., Qin, H., Zhang, B., Zhang, S., & Hao, A. (2019). Multitask Cascade Convolution Neural Networks for Automatic Thyroid Nodule Detection and Recognition. *IEEE Journal of Biomedical and Health Informatics*, 23(3), 1215–1224. doi:10.1109/JBHI.2018.2852718 PMID:29994412

Sonnati, R. (2017). Improving Healthcare Using Big Data Analytics. *International Journal of Scientific & Technology Research*, 6(3), 142–146.

Son, Y., Byun, H., & Lee, J. (2016). Nonparametric machine learning models for predicting the credit default swaps: An empirical study. *Expert Systems with Applications*, 58, 210–220. doi:10.1016/j.eswa.2016.03.049

Sordoni, A., Bengio, Y., Vahabi, H., Lioma, C., Simonsen, J.G., & Nie, J. (2015). *A Hierarchical Recurrent Encoder-Decoder for Generative Context-Aware Query Suggestion.* ArXiv, abs/1507.02221

Sosna, M., Trevinyo-Rodríguez, R. N., & Velamuri, S. R. (2010). Business model innovation through trial-and-error learning: The Naturhouse case. *Long Range Planning*, 43(2), 383–407. doi:10.1016/j.lrp.2010.02.003

Sperhac, J. M., & Gallo, S. M. (2019). VIDIA: A HUBzero gateway for data analytics education. Future Generation Computer Systems-the International Journal of Escience, 94, 833–840. doi:10.1016/j.future.2018.02.004

SPSS Inc. (2015). SPSS. Retrieved from http://www.spss.com.hk/software/modeler/

Srivastava, N., Baxi, P., Ratho, R. K., & Saxena, S. K. (2020). Global trends in epidemiology of coronavirus disease 2019 (COVID-19). Medical Virology: From Pathogenesis to Disease Control, 9-21. doi:10.1007/978-981-15-4814-72

StackShare. (2020). UC ML Flow. Retrieved from https://stackshare.io/mlflow

Stamate, D., Katrinecz, A., Stahl, D., Verhagen, S. J. W., Delespaul, P. A. E. G., van Os, J., & Guloksuz, S. (2019). Identifying psychosis spectrum disorder from experience sampling data using machine learning approaches. *Schizophrenia Research*.

Stanford. (2019). Stanford NLP. Retrieved from https://stanfordnlp.github.io/CoreNLP/

Stanton, J. (2012). *An introduction to data science in Open Source eBook* (3rd ed.). Retrieved from https://surface.syr. edu/istpub/165/

Statistics South Africa, Statistical release P0211.4.2. (2015). *National and provincial labour market: youth Q1: 2008 – Q1: 2015.* Author.

Statistics South Africa, Statistical release P0309.3. (2015). *Mortality and causes of death in South Africa, 2014: Findings from death notification.* Author.

Statistics South Africa. (2015). *Morbidity and mortality patterns among the youth of South Africa, 2013 / Statistics South Africa.* Pretoria: Statistics South Africa. Report No. 03-09-12.

Stattman D. (1980). Book values and stock returns, *The Chicago MBA: A Journal of Selected Papers, 4,* 25–45.

Staub, R. B., da Silva, S., & Tabak, B. M. (2010). Evolution of bank efficiency in Brazil: A DEA approach. *European Journal of Operational Research, 202,* 204–213.

Subahi, A. F. (2019). Edge-Based IoT Medical Record System: Requirements, Recommendations and Conceptual Design. *IEEE Access : Practical Innovations, Open Solutions, 7,* 94150–94159. doi:10.1109/ACCESS.2019.2927958

Subcretaria del Ministerio de Agricultura. (2019). Biblioteca de Datos climaticos. https://www.climatedatalibrary.cl/?Set-Language=es

Subramonia, M., & Rajini, V. (2013). Local Binary Pattern Approach to the Classification of Osteoarthritis in Knee X-ray Images. *Asian Journal of Scientific Research, 6*(4), 805–811. doi:10.3923/ajsr.2013.805.811

Sui, M., Shen, F., Wei, H., & Chen, J. (2010). Logistics Route Planning with Geographic Data Considering Multiple Factors. *International Conference of Logistics Engineering and Management (ICLEM) 2010,* 2346-2352. 10.1061/41139(387)327

Sule, S., Ibrahim, S., & Sani, A. (2019). The effect of forensic accounting investigation in detecting financial fraud : A study in Nigeria. *International Journal of Academic Research in Business and Social Sciences, 9*(2), 545–553. doi:10.6007/IJARBSS/v9-i2/5590

Sun, E. W., & Meinl, T. (2012). A new wavelet-based denoising algorithm for high frequency financial data mining. *European Journal of Operational Research, 217*(3), 589–599. doi:10.1016/j.ejor.2011.09.049

Sun, J., & Hui, X. F. (2006). Financial distress prediction based on similarity weighted voting CBR. In X. Li, R. Zaiane, & Z. Li (Eds.), *Advanced data mining and applications* (pp. 947–958). Springer Verlag. doi:10.1007/11811305_103

Sun, J., & Li, H. (2008). Data mining method for listed companies' financial distress prediction. *Knowledge-Based Systems, 21*(1), 1–5. doi:10.1016/j.knosys.2006.11.003

Sun, X. Q., Shen, H. W., & Cheng, X. Q. (2014). Trading network predicts stock price. *Scientific Reports, 4,* 6. PMID:24429767

Sun, Z.-L., Choi, T.-M., Au, K.-F., & Yu, Y. (2008). Sales forecasting using extreme learning machine with applications in fashion retailing. *Decision Support Systems, 46*(1), 411–419. doi:10.1016/j.dss.2008.07.009

Sushmitha & Padma. (2016). *Sentiment Analysis on Twitter by using Machine.* Academic Press.

Sutskever, I., Vinyals, O., & Le, Q. V. (2014). *Sequence to Sequence Learning with Neural Networks.* NIPS.

Suvarna, M, & Patil, A., & Mudholkar, R. (2014). Exploring ANFIS Model for Osteoarthritis Disease Classification. *International Journal of Current Engineering and Technology, 4*(3), 2124–2130.

T.C. Millî Eğitim Bakanliği Konaklama ve Seyahat Hizmetleri. (2013). *Turizm Coğrafyasi 1 (tourism geography 1).* Retrieved from http://megep.meb.gov.tr/mte_program_modul/moduller_pdf/Turizm%20Co%C4%9Frafyas%C4%B1-%201.pdf

T.C. Millî Eğitim Bakanliği Konaklama ve Seyahat Hizmetleri. (2013). *Turizm Coğrafyasi 2 (tourism geography 2).* Retrieved from http://megep.meb.gov.tr/mte_program_modul/moduller_pdf/Turizm%20Co%C4%9Frafyas%C4%B1%20-2.pdf

Tableau Software LLC. (2020). UC Tableau. Retrieved from https://www.tableau.com/solutions/high-technology-analytics

Tableau Software. (2019). Data visualization beginner's guide: a definition, examples, and learning resources. https://www.tableau.com/learn/articles/data-visualization

Tableau. (2019). tableau. https://public.tableau.com/en-us/s/

Talend. (2020). Retrieved from Talend. https://www.talend.com/

Talwar, A., & Kumar, Y. (2013). Machine Learning: An artificial intelligence methodology. *International Journal of Engineering and Computer Science, 2*, 3400–3404.

Tang, J. (2018). Intelligent Mobile Projects with TensorFlow. Packt. Retrieved from https://books.google.com/books

Tanizaki, T., Hoshino, T., Shimmura, T., & Takenaka, T. (2019). Demand forecasting in restaurants using machine learning and statistical analysis. Procedia CIRP, 79, 679–683. doi:10.1016/j.procir.2019.02.042

Tan, P. N., Steinbach, M., & Kumar, V. (2016). *Introduction to data mining.* Pearson Education India.

Tatarao, V., & Reddy, B. S. V. (2019). The Cyber Crime under Ground Economy Data Approach. *International Journal of Computer Science Trends and Technology, 7*(6), 70–72.

Taylo. (2017). *By 2020 the Smart Hospital will be a reality.* Accessed from https://www.philips.com/a-w/about/news/archive/future-health-index/articles/20170613-by-2020-the-smart-hospital-will-be-a-reality.html

Tay, M., Low, Y., Zhao, X., Cook, A., & Lee, V. (2015). Comparison of infrared thermal detection systems for mass fever screening in a tropical healthcare setting. *Public Health, 129*(11), 1471–1478. doi:10.1016/j.puhe.2015.07.023 PubMed

Technologies, U. (2020). Unity 3d. Retrieved from https://unity3d.com/machine-learning

Tehrani. (2019). UC Teradata. Retrieved from https://blog.tmcnet.com/blog/rich tehrani/fow/teradata-simplifies advanced-analytics-with-new-solutions-for-future-of-work.html

Tehrani, A. G., & Tehrani, A. (2015). The effect on financial ratios to predict company profits and stock returns. *International Journal of Life Sciences (Kathmandu), 5*(1), 591–599.

Telang, P. R., Kalia, A. K., Vukovic, M., Pandita, R., & Singh, M. P. (2018). A Conceptual Framework for Engineering Chatbots. *IEEE Internet Computing, 22*(6), 54–59. doi:10.1109/MIC.2018.2877827

Temenos. (2019). LogicalGlue. Retrieved from https://www.logicalglue.com/

Temurtas, F. (2009). A comparative study on thyroid disease diagnosis using neural networks. *Expert Systems with Applications, 36*(1), 944–949. doi:10.1016/j.eswa.2007.10.010

TensorFlow. (2020a). TensorFlow. Retrieved from https://www.tensorflow.org/

TensorFlow. (2020b). TensorFlowLite. Retrieved from https://www.tensorflow.org/lite

Teradata. (2020). TeraData. Retrieved from https://www.teradata.com/

Teran, H. E. E., Puris, A., & Novoa-Hernandez, P. (2019). Causes affecting the promotion of students of pre-university courses at the state technical university of quevedo: A study applying data mining. Revista. *Universidad y Sociedad, 11*(2), 61–65.

Terrades, O., Berenguel, A., & Gil, D. (2020). *A flexible outlier detector based on a topology given by graph communities.* Retrieved from https://arxiv.org/pdf/2002.07791

Terroso-Saenz, F., González-Vidal, A., Ramallo-González, A. P., & Skarmeta, A. F. (2019). An open IoT platform for the management and analysis of energy data. *Future Generation Computer Systems*, *92*, 1066–1079. doi:10.1016/j.future.2017.08.046

Tetlock, P. C. (2007). Giving content to investor sentiment: The role of media in the stock market. *The Journal of Finance*, *62*(3), 1139–1168. doi:10.1111/j.1540-6261.2007.01232.x

Thanvi, A., Sharma, R., Menghani, B., Kumar, M., & Kumar Jangir, S. (2019). Bitcoin Exchange Rate Price Prediction Using Machine Learning Techniques. *RE:view*.

The Apache Software Foundation. (2020a). Apache Mahout. Retrieved from http://mah out.apache.org/

The Apache Software Foundation. (2020b). Hbase. Retrieved from https://hbase.apache.org/

The Center on Society and Health. (2014). *Why education matters to health: Exploring the causes.* https://societyhealth.vcu.edu/work/the-projects/why-education-matters-to-health-exploring-the-causes.html

The Official Gazette of the Republic of Turkey. (2002). Retrieved from https://www.resmigazete.gov.tr/eskiler/2002/09/20020922.htm#3

Thomson, J., O'Neill, T., Felson, D., & Cootes, T. (2015). Automated Shape and Texture Analysis for Detection of Osteoarthritis from Radiographs of the Knee. *Lecture Notes in Computer Science*, *9350*, 127–134. doi:10.1007/978-3-319-24571-3_16

Thusoo, A., Sen Sarma, J., Jain, N., Shao, Z., Chakka, P., Zhang, N., Antony, S., Liu, H., & Murthy, R. (2010). Hive - A petabyte scale data warehouse using hadoop. Proceedings - International Conference on Data Engineering, 996–1005. 10.1109/ ICDE.2010.5447738

TIBCO Software Inc. (2019). TIBCO. https://www.tibco.com/products

Titus, M., Hendricks, R., Ndemueda, J., McQuide, P., Ohadi, E., Kolehmainen-Aitken, R.-L., & Katjivena, B. (2015). *Namibia National WISN Report.* Ministry of Health & Social Services.

Tiulpin, A., Thevenot, J., Rahtu, E., Lehenkari, P., & Saarakkala, S. (2018). Automatic Knee Osteoarthritis Diagnosis from Plain Radiographs: A Deep Learning-Based Approach. *Scientific Reports*, *8*(1), 1–15. doi:10.103841598-018-20132-7 PMID:29379060

Tobin, J. (1969). A General Equilibrium Approach To Monetary Theory. *Journal of Money, Credit and Banking*, *1*(1), 15–29.

Togaware Pty Lt. (2019). Rattle. https://rattle.togaware.com/

Togaware. (2019). Rattle. Retrieved from https://rattle.togaware.com/

Topbaş, F., & Unat, E. (2018). Gelir Ve Tüketim İlişkisinin İstikrarı: Harcama Gruplarına Ve Zamana Göre Kantil Regresyon Modelden Kanıtlar [The Stability Of The Income And Consumption Relationship: Evidence From The Quantile Regression Model According To Expenditure Groups And Time] *Izmir Democracy University Social Sciences Journal*, *1*(2), 103–126.

Toronto Public Health, Healthy Environments Services. (2002). *Food premises Inspection and disclosure system, Evaluation Report.* Author.

Totoni, E., Anderson, T. A., & Shpeisman, T. (2017). HPAT: High performance analytics with scripting ease-of-use. Proceedings of the International Conference on Supercomputing, Part F1284. doi:10.1145/3079079.3079099

Toussaint & Mannon. (2014). Hospitals Are Finally Starting to Put Real-Time Data to Use. *Harvard Business Review*. Accessed from https://hbr.org/2014/11/hospitals-are-finally-starting-to-put-real-time-data-to-use

Tracy, J. A. (2004). *How to Read a Financial Report: Wringing Vital Signs Out of the Numbers*. John Wiley and Sons.

Triantafillou, P. (2018). Data-Less Big Data Analytics. *2018 IEEE 34th International Conference on Data Engineering*, 1666-1667. 10.1109/ICDE.2018.00205

Trifacta. (2020). Trifacta Wrangler. https://www.tracifacta.com/data-analysis-tools/

Tsai, C. W., Lai, C. F., Chao, H. C., & Vasilakos, A. V. (2015). Big data analytics: A survey. *Journal of Big Data*, 2(1), 21. doi:10.118640537-015-0030-3 PMID:26191487

Tsui, K. L., Zhao, Y., & Wang, D. (2019). Big Data Opportunities: *System Health Monitoring and Management. IEEE Access: Practical Innovations, Open Solutions*, 7, 68853–68867. doi:10.1109/ACCESS.2019.2917891

U.S. Department of Health & Human Services. (2019). Datasets. https://healthdata.gov/content/about

U.S. General Services Administration. (2019). The home of the U.S. Government's open data. https://www.data.gov/

UC SAS. (2018). uc sas data mining. https://intellipaat.com/blog/what-is-sas-analytics/

Uddin, M. Z. (2019). A wearable sensor-based activity prediction system to facilitate edge computing in smart healthcare system. *Journal of Parallel and Distributed Computing*, 123, 46–53. doi:10.1016/j.jpdc.2018.08.010

Unemyr, M. (2019). UC Data Robot. Retrieved from https://www.unemyr.com/automl datarobot/

United Nation Economic Commission for Africa. (2015). Sustainable development goals for the Southern Africa sub-region. Summary report. United Nations Economic Commission for Africa.

United Nations. (2016). *Fact Sheet: Youth and education.* https://social.un.org/youthyear/docs/Youth_Education_Fact_Sheet_FINAL.pdf

University of California. (2019). UC Irvine Machine Learning Repository. http://mlr.cs.umass.edu/ml/

University of Essex, & University of Manchester and Jisc. (2019). UK data Service-Get Data. https://ukdataservice.ac.uk/get-data.aspx

University of Ljubljana. (2019). Orange. https://orange.biolab.si/

University of Ljubljana. (2020). Orange. https://orange.biolab.si/

Urcuqui, C., Castano, Y., Delgado, J., Navarro, A., Diaz, J., Munoz, B., & Orozco, J. (2018). Exploring Machine Learning to Analyze Parkinson's Disease Patients. In Proceedings - 2018 14th International Conference on Semantics, Knowledge and Grids, SKG 2018, (pp.160–166). doi:10.1109/SKG.2018.00029

Uskov, V. L., Bakken, J. P., Byerly, A., & Shah, A. (2019). Machine Learning-based Predictive Analytics of Student Academic Performance in STEM Education. *IEEE Global Engineering Education Conference (EDUCON)*, 1370-1376. 10.1109/EDUCON.2019.8725237

UW Data Science Team. (2017). *A Modern History of Data Science*. Retrieved from https://datasciencedegree.wisconsin.edu/blog/history-of-data-science/

Uysal, F. N., Ersöz, T., & Ersöz, F. (2017). Türkiye'deki İllerin Yaşam Endeksinin Çok Değişkenli İstatistik Yöntemlerle İncelenmesi [Analysis By Multivariate Statistical Methods Of Life Index Of Provinces In Turkey]. *Ekonomi Bilimleri Dergisi*, 9(1), 49–65.

Vaishnav & Patel. (2015). Analysis of Various Techniques to Handling Missing Value in Dataset. *International Journal of Innovative and Emerging Research in Engineering*, 2(2).

Vaishya, R., Javaid, M., Khan, I. H., & Haleem, A. (2020). Artificial intelligence (AI) applications for COVID-19 pandemic. *Diabetes & Metabolic Syndrome*, 14(4), 337–339. doi:10.1016/j.dsx.2020.04.012 PubMed

Valsamis, E. M., Ricketts, D., Husband, H., & Rogers, B. A. (2019). Segmented linear regression models for assessing change in retrospective studies in healthcare. *Computational and Mathematical Methods in Medicine*. PMID:30805023

Van der Aalst, W. (2016). Process mining: Data science in action. Process Mining: Data Science in Action, April 2014, 1–467. doi:10.1007/978-3-662-49851-4

Van Der Aalst, W. (2016). Data science in action. In *Process mining* (pp. 3–23). Springer. doi:10.1007/978-3-662-49851-4_1

Vanani & hMajidian. (2019). Literature Review on Big Data Analytics Methods. *Social Media and Machine Learning*, 1-22.

VantaraH. (2020). Pentaho. Retrieved from https://www.hitachivantara.com/en-us/products/data managementanalytics/pentaho-platform.html

Vasarhelyi, M.A.,& Tuttle, B.M. (2015). Big data in accounting: An overview. *Accounting Horizons, 29*(2), 381-396.

Vaswani, A., Shazeer, N., Parmar, N., Uszkoreit, J., Jones, L., Gomez, A. N., Kaiser, L., & Polosukhin, I. (2017). *Attention is All you Need*. NIPS.

Vaughan, C. L., & O'Malley, M. J. (2005). A gait nomogram used with fuzzy clustering to monitor functional status of children and young adults with cerebral palsy. *Developmental Medicine and Child Neurology*, 47(6), 377–383. doi:10.1017/S0012162205000745 PubMed

Velmurugan, T. (2012). Efficiency of k-means and k-medoids algorithms for clustering arbitrary data points. *Int. J. Computer Technology and Application*, 3(5), 1758–1764.

Velmurugan, T., & Santhanam, T. (2010). Computational complexity between K-means and K-medoids clustering algorithms for normal and uniform distributions of data points. *Journal of Computational Science*, 6(3), 363–368. doi:10.3844/jcssp.2010.363.368

Velmurugan, T., & Santhanam, T. (2011). A survey of partition based clustering algorithms in data mining: An experimental approach. *Information Technology Journal*, 10(3), 478–484. doi:10.3923/itj.2011.478.484

Verma, P., & Sood, S. K. (2018). Fog assisted-IoT enabled patient health monitoring in smart homes. IEEE Internet of Things Journal, 5(3), 1789–1796. doi:10.1109/JIOT.2018.2803201

Verma, S., & Bhattacharyya, S. S. (2017). Perceived strategic value based adoption of big data analytics in emerging economy: A qualitative approach for Indian firms. *Journal of Enterprise Information Management*, 30(3), 3. doi:10.1108/JEIM-10-2015-0099

Vicente, M. R., López-Menéndez, A. J., & Pérez, R. (2015). Forecasting unemployment with search data: Does it help to improve predictions when job destruction is skyrocketing? *Technological Forecasting and Social Change*, 92, 132–139. doi:10.1016/j.techfore.2014.12.005

Vidgen, R., Shaw, S., & Grant, D. B. (2017). Management challenges in creating value from business analytics. *European Journal of Operational Research*, 261(2), 626–639. doi:10.1016/j.ejor.2017.02.023

Vijayakumari & Holi. (2019) Assessment of Joint Space in Knee Osteoarthritis using Particle Swarm Optimization Technique. *International Journal of Innovative Technology and Exploring Engineering, 9*(1), 502–507.

Vijayarani & Sharmila. (2016). Research in Big Data - An Overview. *Informatics Engineering International Journal, 4*(3), 1-20.

Vimalajeewa, D., Kulatunga, C., & Berry, D. P. (2018). Learning in the compressed data domain: Application to milk quality prediction. *Information Sciences, 459,* 149–167. doi:10.1016/j.ins.2018.05.002

Virtanen, P., Gommers, R., Oliphant, T. E., Haberland, M., Reddy, T., Cournapeau, D., Burovski, E., Peterson, P., Weckesser, W., Bright, J., van der Walt, S. J., Brett, M., Wilson, J., Millman, K. J., Mayorov, N., Nelson, A. R. J., Jones, E., Kern, R., Larson, E., & Vázquez-Baeza, Y. (2020). SciPy 1.0: Fundamental algorithms for scientific computing in Python. *Nature Methods, 17*(March), 261–272. Advance online publication. doi:10.1038/s41592-019-0686-2 PubMed

Visualdata. (2019). Visualdata. https://www.visualdata.io/

Vogels, W. (2017). UC Amazon Lex. Retrieved from https://www.allthingsdistributed.com /2017/06/amazonconnect-with-amazon-lex.html

Vyas, A., & Jangir, S. K. (2019). Advances in approach for Object Detection and classification. Na#onal Conference on Informa#on Technology & Security Applications, 978, 1–3.

Wahyuningrum, R. T., Anifah, L., Eddy Purnama, I. K., & Hery Purnomo, M. (2019). A New Approach to Classify Knee Osteoarthritis Severity from Radiographic Images based on CNN-LSTM Method. *2019 IEEE 10th International Conference on Awareness Science and Technology (ICAST),* 1-6.

Wahyuningrum, R. T., Anifah, L., Purnama, I. K. E., & Purnomo, M. H. (2016). A novel hybrid of S2DPCA and SVM for knee osteoarthritis classification. *2016 IEEE International Conference on Computational Intelligence and Virtual Environments for Measurement Systems and Applications (CIVEMSA),* 1-5. 10.1109/CIVEMSA.2016.7524317

Waller, M. A., & Fawcett, S. E. (2013). Data science, predictive analytics, and big data: A revolution that will transform supply chain design and management. *The Journal of Business.*

Wamba, S., Gunasekaran, A., Akter, S., Ren, S. J., Dubey, R., & Childe, S. J. (2017). Big data analyticsand firm performance: Effects ofdynamic capabilities. *Journal of Business Research, 70,* 356–365. doi:10.1016/j.jbusres.2016.08.009

Wang, B., Yang, X. C., & Wang, G. R. (2015). Detecting Copy Directions among Programs Using Extreme Learning Machines [Article]. Mathematical Problems in Engineering. *Article, 793697.* Advance online publication. doi:10.1155/2015/793697

Wang, Y., Ke, W., & Wan, P. (2018). A method of ultrasonic image recognition for thyroid papillary carcinoma based on deep convolution neural network. *NeuroQuantology: An Interdisciplinary Journal of Neuroscience and Quantum Physics, 16*(5), 757–768. doi:10.14704/nq.2018.16.5.1306

Wang, Z., & Zhao, H. (2016). Empirical Study of Using Big Data for Business Process Improvement at Private Manufacturing Firm in Cloud Computing. *3rd International Conference on In Cyber Security and Cloud Computing (CSCloud),* 129-135. 10.1109/CSCloud.2016.11

Ward, L., Dunn, A., Faghaninia, A., Zimmermann, N. E. R., Bajaj, S., Wang, Q., Montoya, J., Chen, J., Bystrom, K., Dylla, M., Chard, K., Asta, M., Persson, K. A., Snyder, G. J., Foster, I., & Jain, A. (2018). Matminer: An open source toolkit for materials data mining. *Computational Materials Science, 152,* 60–69. doi:10.1016/j.commatsci.2018.05.018

Warren, J. D. Jr, Moffitt, K. C., & Byrnes, P. (2015). How big data will change accounting. *Accounting Horizons, 29*(2), 397–407. doi:10.2308/acch-51069

Washington State University. (2018). CASAS datasets for activities of daily living http://casas.wsu.edu/datasets/

Wei, C. P., Piramuthu, S., & Shaw, M. J. (2003). Knowledge discovery and data mining. In Handbook on Knowledge Management (pp. 157-189). Springer.

Wicklund, E. (2019). *Hospital's Telehealth Program Reduces ER Visits, Treatment Costs*. Retrieved from https://mhealth-intelligence.com/news/hospitals-telehealth-program-reduces-er-visits-treatment-costs.htm

Wier, B., Hunton, J., & Hassab Elnaby, H. R. (2007). Enterprise resource planning systems and non-financial performance incentives: The joint impact on corporate performance. *International Journal of Accounting Information Systems*, *8*, 165–190.

Williams, S. (2018). Amazon Lex. Packt. Retrieved from https://books.google.com

Williams, G. J. (2009). Rattle: A data mining GUI for R. *The R Journal*, *1*(2), 45–55. doi:10.32614/RJ-2009-016

Willmott, C. J., & Matsuura, K. (2005). Advantages of the mean absolute error (MAE) over the root mean square error (RMSE) in assessing average model performance. *Climate Research*, *30*, 79–82. doi:10.3354/cr030079

Wing, J. M. (2019). The data life cycle. *Harvard Data Science Review*, (1). Retrieved from https://hdsr.mitpress.mit.edu/

Wong, A. K. C., & Lee, E.-S. A. (2014). Aligning and Clustering Patterns to Reveal the Protein Functionality of Sequences. *IEEE/ACM Transactions on Computational Biology and Bioinformatics*, *11*(3), 548–560. doi:10.1109/TCBB.2014.2306840 PMID:26356022

Woodall, L. (2017). *Model risk managers eye benefits of machine learning*. Retrieved from https://www.risk.net/risk-management/4646956/model-risk-managers-eye-benefits-of-machine-learning

Woodside-Oriakhi, M., Lucas, C., & Beasley, J. (2011). Heuristic algorithms for the cardinality constrained efficient frontier. *European Journal of Operational Research*, *213*(3), 538–550. doi:10.1016/j.ejor.2011.03.030

World Health Organization. (2016). *Global report on diabetes*. World Health Organization.

Wu, H., Lu, Z., Pan, L., Xu, R., & Jiang, W. (2009, August). An improved apriori-based algorithm for association rules mining. In *2009 sixth international conference on fuzzy systems and knowledge discovery* (Vol. 2, pp. 51-55). IEEE. 10.1109/FSKD.2009.193

Wu, K. Massa, & Lo. (2019). Detectron 2. Retrieved from https://ai.facebook.com/blog/-detectron2-a-pytorch-based-modular-object detection-library-/

Wu, C. H., Tzeng, G. H., Goo, Y. J., & Fang, W. C. (2007). A real-valued genetic algorithm to optimize the parameters of support vector machine for predicting bankruptcy. *Expert Systems with Applications*, *32*(2), 397–408. doi:10.1016/j.eswa.2005.12.008

Wu, D. D., & Olson, D. L. (2015). *Enterprise risk management in finance*. Springer. doi:10.1057/9781137466297

Wu, J.-H., Chen, Y.-C., & Greenes, R. A. (2009). Healthcare technology management competency and its impacts on IT–healthcare partnerships development. *International Journal of Medical Informatics*, *78*(2), 71–82. doi:10.1016/j.ijmedinf.2008.05.007 PMID:18603470

Wu, L. S. (2000). A Survey and An Analysis of Investor's Demands for Listed Companies' Accounting Information. *Economic Research Journal*, *4*, 41–48.

Wu, L., Yue, X., Jin, A., & Yen, D. (2016). Smart supply chain management: A review and implications for future research. *International Journal of Logistics Management*, *27*(2), 395–417. doi:10.1108/IJLM-02-2014-0035

Wu, X., Kumar, V., Quinlan, J. R., Ghosh, J., Yang, Q., Motoda, H., McLachlan, G. J., Ng, A., Liu, B., Yu, P. S., Zhou, Z. H., Steinbach, M., Hand, D. J., & Steinberg, D. (2008). Top 10 algorithms in data mining. *Knowledge and Information Systems, 14*(1), 1–37. doi:10.100710115-007-0114-2

Xia, B. S., & Gong, P. (2015). Review of business intelligence through data analysis. *Benchmarking, 21*(2), 300–311. doi:10.1108/BIJ-08-2012-0050

Yagli, G. M., Yang, D., & Srinivasan, D. (2019). Automatic hourly solar forecasting using machine learning models. *Renewable & Sustainable Energy Reviews, 105*, 487–498. doi:10.1016/j.rser.2019.02.006

Yang, K., & Xu, W. (2019). FraudMemory: Explainable memory-enhanced sequential neural networks for financial fraud detection. *Proceedings of the 52nd Hawaii International Conference on System Sciences 2019*. 10.24251/HICSS.2019.126

Yan, W., & Clack, C. D. (2010). Evolving robust GP solutions for hedge fund stock selection in emerging markets. *Soft Computing, 15*(1), 37–50. doi:10.100700500-009-0511-4

Yaramala, D. (2016). *Health care data analytics using Hadoop* (Diss.). San Diego State University.

Yıldırım, H. (2018). Comparison of Provinces of Turkey In Terms of Accessing Health Care Services by Using Different Clustering Algorithms. *Eskişehir Technical University Journal of Science and Technology A-Applied Sciences and Engineering, 19*(4), 907–925.

Yin, Y., Zeng, Y., Chen, X., & Fan, Y. (2016). The Internet of Things in healthcare: An overview. *Journal of Industrial Information Integration, 1*, 3–13. doi:10.1016/j.jii.2016.03.004

Yip, A. Y. N. (2004). Predicting business failure with a case-based reasoning approach. In *Knowledge-based intelligent information and engineering systems* (pp. 665–671). Springer Verlag. doi:10.1007/978-3-540-30134-9_89

Yoon, K., Hoogduin, L., & Zhang, L. (2015). Big data as complementary audit evidence. *Accounting Horizons, 29*(2), 431–438. doi:10.2308/acch-51076

Yoo, T. K., Kim, D. W., Choi, S. B., Oh, E., & Park, J. S. (2016). Simple Scoring System and Artificial Neural Network for Knee Osteoarthritis Risk Prediction: A Cross-Sectional Study. *PLoS One, 11*(2), e0148724. doi:10.1371/journal.pone.0148724 PMID:26859664

Yousefpour, A., Fung, C., Nguyen, T., Kadiyala, K., Jalali, F., Niakanlahiji, A., Kong, J., & Jue, J. P. (2019). All one needs to know about fog computing and related edge computing paradigms: A complete survey. *Journal of Systems Architecture, 98*(February), 289–330. doi:10.1016/j.sysarc.2019.02.009

Yu, D., Liu, G., Guo, M., & Liu, X. (2018). An improved K-medoids algorithm based on step increasing and optimizing medoids. *Expert Systems with Applications, 92*, 464–473. doi:10.1016/j.eswa.2017.09.052

Yu, S. S., Chu, S. W., Wang, C. M., Chan, Y. K., & Chang, T. C. (2018). Two improved k-means algorithms. *Applied Soft Computing, 68*, 747–755. doi:10.1016/j.asoc.2017.08.032

Yu, W., Liang, F., He, X., Hatcher, W. G., Lu, C., Lin, J., & Yang, X. (2017). A Survey on the Edge Computing for the Internet of Things. *IEEE Access: Practical Innovations, Open Solutions, 3536*(c), 1–1. doi:10.1109/ACCESS.2017.2674687

Zadegan, S. M. R., Mirzaie, M., & Sadoughi, F. (2013). Ranked k-medoids: A fast and accurate rank-based partitioning algorithm for clustering large datasets. *Knowledge-Based Systems, 39*, 133–143. doi:10.1016/j.knosys.2012.10.012

Zagreb Stock Exchange. (2019). https://www.zse.hr

Žalik, K. R. (2008). An efficient k′-means clustering algorithm. *Pattern Recognition Letters, 29*(9), 1385–1391. doi:10.1016/j.patrec.2008.02.014

Zamani, L., Beegam, R., & Borzoian, S. (2014). Portfolio Selection using Data Envelopment Analysis (DEA): A Case of Select Indian Investment Companies. *International Journal of Current Research and Academic Review*, 2(4), 50–55.

Zamora, I., Lopez, N. G., Vilches, V. M., & Cordero, A. H. (2016). Extending the OpenAI Gym for robotics: a toolkit for reinforcement learning using ROS and Gazebo. August. https://arxiv.org/abs/1608.05742

Zhang, B., Mor, N., Kolb, J., Chan, D. S., Lutz, K., Allman, E., Wawrzyne, J., Lee, E., & Kubiatowicz, J. (2015). The Cloud is Not Enough: Saving IoT from the Cloud. 7th USENIX Workshop on Hot Topics in Cloud Computing, HotCloud '15. Retrieved from https://dl.acm.org/citation.cfm?id=2827740%0Ahttps://www.usenix.org/conference/hotcloud15/workshop-program/presentation/zhang

Zhang, Y., Oussena, S., Clark, T., & Kim, H. (2010). Use data mining to improve student retention in higher education: A case study. ICEIS 2010 - Proceedings of the 12th International Conference on Enterprise Information Systems, 1, 190–197. 10.5220/0002894101900197

Zhang, Z. (2016). When doctors meet with AlphaGo: potential application of machine learning to clinical medicine. https://www.ncbi.nlm.nih.gov/pmc/articles/PMC4828734/

Zhang, B., Zhang, Y., & Begg, R. K. (2009). Gait classification in children with cerebral palsy by Bayesian approach. *Pattern Recognition*, 42(4), 581–586. doi:10.1016/j.patcog.2008.09.025

Zhang, Q., Yang, L. T., Chen, Z., & Li, P. (2018). A survey on deeplearning for big data. *Information Fusion*, 42, 146–157. doi:10.1016/j.inffus.2017.10.006

Zhang, Y., Moges, S., & Block, P. (2016). Optimal cluster analysis for objective regionalization of seasonal precipitation in regions of high spatial–temporal variability: Application to Western Ethiopia. *Journal of Climate*, 29(10), 3697–3717. doi:10.1175/JCLI-D-15-0582.1

Zhang, Y., Ren, S., Liu, Y., & Si, S. (2017). A big data analytics architecture for clean manufacturing and maintenance processes of complex products. *Journal of Cleaner Production*, 142(2), 626–641. doi:10.1016/j.jclepro.2016.07.123

Zhang, Z., Tong, X., McDonell, K., Zelenyuk, A., Imre, D., & Mueller, K. (2013, April). An Interactive Visual Analytics Framework for Multi-Field Data in a Geo-Spatial Context. *Tsinghua Science and Technology on Visualization and Computer Graphics*, 18(2), 111–124. doi:10.1109/TST.2013.6509095

Zhao, D., Kuo, S.-H., & Wang, T. C. (2014). The Evaluation of the Business Operation Performance by Applying Grey Relational Analysis. In Intelligent Data analysis and its Applications, Volume I. Advances in Intelligent Systems and Computing, (Vol. 297). Cham: Springer.

Zhao, Z., Xu, F., Wang, M., & Yi Zhang, C. (2019). A sparse enhanced indexation model with norm and its alternating quadratic penalty method. *The Journal of the Operational Research Society*, 70(3), 433–445. doi:10.1080/01605682.2018.1447245

Zheng,L., Liu,G., Luan, W., Li, Z., Zhang, Y., Yan, C., & Jiang, C. (2018). A new credit card fraud detecting method based on behavior certificate. In *Networking, Sensing and Control (ICNSC)*. IEEE.

Zhenhua, W., Yangsen, Y., & Dangchen, J. (2018). Analysis and Prediction of Urban Traffic Congestion Based on Big Data. *International Journal on Data Science and Technology*, 4(3), 100–105. doi:10.11648/j.ijdst.20180403.14

Zhou, L., Pan, S., Wang, J., & Vasilakos, A. V. (2017). Machine learningon big data: Opportunities and challenges. *Neurocomputing Journal*, 237, 350–361. doi:10.1016/j.neucom.2017.01.026

Zhu, C., Idemudia, C. U., & Feng, W. (2019). Improved logistic regression model for diabetes prediction by integrating PCA and K-means techniques. *Informatics in Medicine Unlocked*, 17, 100179. doi:10.1016/j.imu.2019.100179

Zhu, Q., Pei, J., Liu, X., & Zhou, Z. (2019). Analyzing commercial aircraft fuel consumption during descent: A case study using an improved K-means clustering algorithm. *Journal of Cleaner Production, 223*, 869–882. doi:10.1016/j.jclepro.2019.02.235

Zikopoulos, P., & Eaton, C. (2011). *Understanding big data: Analytics for enterprise class Hadoop and streaming data.* McGraw-Hill.

Zou, Q., Qu, K., Luo, Y., Yin, D., Ju, Y., & Tang, H. (2018). Predicting diabetes mellitus with machine learning techniques. *Frontiers in Genetics, 9*, 515. doi:10.3389/fgene.2018.00515 PMID:30459809

Zufferey, D., Hofer, T., Hennebert, J., Schumacher, M., Ingold, R., & Bromuri, S. (2015). Performance comparison of multi-label learning algorithms on clinical data for chronic diseases. *Computers in Biology and Medicine, 65*, 34–43. doi:10.1016/j.compbiomed.2015.07.017 PMID:26275389

About the Contributors

Bhushan Patil is an Independent Researcher. He has published various papers in international journals which also includes the prestigious IEEE Xplore among others. He has also published various book chapters. Currently he is the Editorial Review Board Member and Reviewer of various different international journals. Along with being the Editor of this book titled, "Handbook of Research on Engineering, Business and Healthcare Applications of Data Science and Analytics, he has authored two books which shall be published soon. Also, he is currently working on four books as an Editor which shall be published in 2021.

Manisha Vohra is an Independent Researcher. She has published various papers in international journals which also includes the prestigious IEEE Xplore among others. She has also published various book chapters. Currently she is the Editorial Review Board Member, Associate Editor and Reviewer of various different international journals. Along with being the Editor of this book titled, "Handbook of Research on Engineering, Business and Healthcare Applications of Data Science and Analytics, she has authored two books which shall be published soon. Also, she is currently working on four books as an Editor which shall be published in 2021.

* * *

Minal Abhyankar is currently working with Symbiosis International University.

G. Aghila received her B.E degree in Computer Science and Engineering from Thiagarajar College of Engineering, India, M.E degree in Computer Science and Engineering from College of Engineering, Anna University, Guindy, India and Ph.D. in knowledge representation and reasoning from College of Engineering, Anna University, Guindy, India. She has 30 years of teaching experience for both U.G and P.G. Her research interests includes Artificial Intelligence, Chem-informatics, Image and Audio Steganography, Big data analytics, Edge computing, Block chain in banking and Smart & Secure environment.

Osaheni Thaddeus Akpata is a PhD student in the Department of Accounting in the University of Benin.

S. R. Balasundaram has been working since 1987 at National Institute of Technology (formerly known as Regional Engineering College) Tiruchirappalli. After completing M.C.A. from PSG College of Technology, Coimbatore, he joined REC Trichy during 1987 as Computer Programmer. He completed

M.E. in Computer Science & Engineering in 1992. Currently he is working as Professor in the Department of Computer Applications. He earned his doctorate in "E-Learning and Assessment" from NIT, Trichy. He has published more than 40 papers in reputed Journals and Proceedings of International conferences. His areas of interest are Web & Mobile Technologies, Cognitive Sciences, and e-Learning Technologies.

Ricardo A. Barrera-Cámara is Ph.D. in Computer Systems from the Universidad del Sur, Master in Informatics from the Universidad Autónoma of Carmen. He is a Research professor at the Autonomous University of Carmen in Mexico. He is also National System of Researchers level candidate and Leader of the academic group of scientific and technological computing. Along with it, he is also Leader of the Academy of Administration and information processing. His research areas are Scientific Computing, Data Science, Optimization, Quality and Information Technology.

Ulkem Basdas, after her graduation from Middle East Technical University (METU) Economics Department (with a minor degree in Industrial Engineering on Operational Research), earned M.A. degree in Economics, Bilkent University, and Ph.D. in Finance, METU. She continued her research in finance as Visiting Scholar at the University of Michigan, Ann Arbor, Ross Business School. She started her professional career in Siemens as Project Commercial Manager in 2005, and between 2009 and 2010 she worked as Economic Policy Analyst in the Economic Policy Research Institute of Turkey. Following her experience in Borsa İstanbul over 2010-2016, she joined Philip Morris International, Leaf Planning Department. She has given lectures on financial markets and financial instruments, and her research interests are behavioral decision-making and financial anomalies.

Maria Beatriz Bernábe-Loranca was born in the city of Puebla, Mexico. She received the B.S. degree in Computer Science from Benemérita Universidad Autónoma de Puebla (BUAP), Mexico in 1993 and the M.I. degree in quality engineering from Universidad Iberoamericana (UIA), Mexico in 2003. In January 2010, she received the Doctorate degree in Operations Research from the Universidad Nacional Autónoma de México (UNAM.). Since 1995, she has been a professor at the School of Computer Science of BUAP, where she works in statistics.and operations research. Her research interests are combinatorial optimization, territorial design and multiobjective techniques. She belongs to "Sistema Nacional de Investigadores" Conacyt - México.

Gaurav Kumar Bishnoi is an engineering graduate from Birla Institute of Technology and Science, Pilani, India. He has done projects in data analytics in the logistics industry.

Selvan C. received B.E. degree in Computer Science and Engineering from Manonmaniam Sundaranar University, India, in 2002, M.E. degree in Computer Science and Engineering from Anna University, Chennai, India, in 2007 and Ph.D. degree in Information and Communication Engineering from Anna University, Chennai, India in 2013. During his Ph.D. degree he was a Junior Research Fellow and Senior Research Fellow under University Grants Commission (UGC, New Delhi) in Government College of Technology, Coimbatore. He had been working as a software developer from 2002 to 2005 and has been engaging in various responsibilities in the Engineering colleges, in Tamil Nadu since 2007. He is currently a Post-Doctoral Fellow in National Institute of Technology, Tiruchirappalli, under UGC, New Delhi, India since 2017. His current research interests include Mobile Computing, Data Analytics, and Graph Analytics. He is an IEEE member and a member of the Indian Society for Technical Education.

Ana Canepa-Saenz is a professor at the Universidad Autónoma de Carmen from 1995 to date, currently teaches and conducts research at the Faculty of Information Sciences. She has Ph.D. in computer systems from Universidad del Sur since 2011. It belongs to the academic body in consolidation of scientific and technological computing from 2016 to date, the line of research is scientific and technological computing. She was a representative of the professors before the Technical Council 2014 - 2016. She is a member of the academy of networks and distributed systems, and is part of the editorial committee of the Universidad Autónoma del Carmen.

Saikat Chakraborty obtained his B.Tech from West Bengal University of Technology and M.Tech from Jadavpur University. Currently, he is a Ph.D research scholar in the Computer Science and Engineering Department at NIT Rourkela. He has research experience of 2 years in sentiment analysis and computer vision. In addition, 3 years of research experience in computational biomechanics. He is a reviewer of many international journals in the field of computational biomechanics and human gait analysis. His current research interest includes clinical gait analysis using computational intelligence.

Pavithra D. is a PG Scholar. She is currently affiliated with Avinashilingam Institute for Home Science and Higher Education for Women.

Amir Ahmad Dar is a Research Scholar in Department of Mathematics and Actuarial Science at B S Abdur Rahman Crescent University Chennai. He received his BSc in Actuarial and Financial Mathematics from Islamic University of Science and Technology Kashmir and his MSc in Actuarial Science from B. S. Abdur Rahman Crescent University Chennai. He passed the India Actuarial Common Entrance Test (ACET) in the year 2014. He did Eight weeks Internship at Cluster innovation center the University of Delhi in the year 2014, Six weeks Internship at Jammu and Kashmir Bank in the year 2016 and one month internship at Chennai Mathematical Institute. The area of interest: Financial mathematics, financial economics, statistics and business mathematics.

Abhipsha Das is an undergraduate student in IIIT Bhubaneswar. She is proficient in deep learning and interested in applications of machine learning in various domains.

Frans David is a Namibian citizen and obtained his Master degree in Computer Science. He is currently working as Lecturer and Deputy Director of Computer Center at International University of Namibia (IUM). He specializes in Networking and Cyber Security and has experience and interest in research and education in the areas of Artificial Intelligence, Big Data, Data Center, Cyber Security and Open Source.

Harman Singh Dhami is an engineering graduate from Birla Institute of Technology and Science, Pilani, India. He has done projects in data analytics in the logistics industry.

Nagaraj V. Dharwadkar completed his B.E. in Computer Science and Engineering in 2000, from Karnataka University, Dharwad, M.Tech. in Computer Science and Engineering in 2006 from VTU, Belgum and Ph.D. in Computer Science and Engineering in 2014 from National Institute of Technology, Warangal . He is Professor and Head of the Computer Science and Engineering department at Rajarambapu Institute of Technology, Islampur. He has 18 years of Teaching Experience at Professional Institutes across India and has published 55 papers in various International Journals and Conferences. His area of research interest are Multimedia Security, Image Processing, Big Data Analytics and Machine Learning.

Anjali Dixit is an Assistant Professor of Juridical Sciences at Rama University. She has been teaching law since 2011 and has joined the Faculty of Juridical Sciences, Rama University in November 2018. She did her LL.B. (Gold medal) from Rohilkhand University, LL.M. from the Faculty of Law, Lucknow University, M.B.A. (IB & HR) from A.P.J. Abdul Kalam Technical University, Lucknow. She has also done M.A. (Political Sciences) and is currently pursuing her Ph.D. (Law). As a Law Trainee she served High Court, Lucknow Bench. She has also served EBC Publication Pvt. Ltd. As an Editorial Assistant (Legal Works). Along with it, she has served as Acting Principal at S.B.S. Law College (CSJM University, Kanpur) and Assistant Professor at Invertis University, Bareilly. She has published 25 research papers in reputed International and National journals. In addition to this, she has also presented 30 paper/poster in reputed international/national conferences, seminar, symposiums etc. Also, she has published seven book chapters. Besides, she has also served as a convener and committee member of many committees and has delivered Guest Lecture at Ramswaroop Memorial University. She has been awarded by the Election Commission to help in peacefully conducting 2019 Lok Sabha Election.

M. Fevzi Esen is currently working as an assistant professor on information technologies. His M.A. and PhD degrees are on data mining and stock market applications.

Olusegun Sunday Ewemooje, PhD, is a lecturer at the Department of Statistics, Federal University of Technology, Akure, Nigeria. He is currently a postdoctoral research fellow at the Population and Health Research Entity, Faculty of Humanities, North-West University (Mafikeng Campus), South Africa. His research interest includes Sample Survey Designs and Applications, Population Studies, Demography and Environmental Statistics. He has published many articles both in national and international peer-review journals.

Alejandro Fuentes-Penna is National System of Researchers level candidate. He is Ph.D. on Strategic Planning and Technology Directorate. He has published JCR, indexed articles and books internationally. He has worked in different companies and institutions as researcher, consultant and professor. He is working at Centro Interdisciplinario de Investigación y Docencia en Educación Técnica as researcher. His research line: scientific, intelligent and bioinspired computation.

Niharika Garg received her PhD in Computer Science from Banasthali Vidyapith in 2018. She worked for 12 years as an Assistant professor in Computer Science in several universities. Later, she served as a Quality Engineer in United Health Group, Phoenix Arizona for almost 2 years. She is currently working as a Project Manager from last 2 years in Optum Global Solutions, Gurgaon. During her tenure, in 2015 she submitted and completed successfully the research project sanctioned by Government of India under DST WOS-A scheme.

Kanika Gautam has received her Bachelor's degree from Mody University of Science and Technology, Lakshmangarh in Computer Science and technology (Big Data Specialization). She is currently working in core areas of Machine Learning, Deep Learning, Predictive Analysis and Big Data Analytics.

Kiran Shrikant Gawande is an Assistant Professor in the Computer Department of Sardar Patel Institute of Technology, Mumbai University.

M. Govindarajan is currently an Associate Professor in the Department of Computer Science and Engineering, Annamalai University, Tamil Nadu, India. He received the B.E, M.E and Ph.D Degree in Computer Science and Engineering from Annamalai University, Tamil Nadu, India in 2001, 2005 and 2010 respectively. He did his post-doctoral research in the Department of Computing, Faculty of Engineering and Physical Sciences, University of Surrey, Guildford, Surrey, United Kingdom in 2011 and at CSIR Centre for Mathematical Modelling and Computer Simulation, Bangalore in 2013. He has visited countries like Czech Republic, Austria, Thailand, United Kingdom (twice), Malaysia, U.S.A (twice), and Singapore. He has presented and published more than 100 papers at Conferences and Journals and also received best paper awards. He has delivered invited talks at various national and international conferences. His current research interests include Data Mining and its applications, Web Mining, Text Mining, and Sentiment Mining. He has completed two major projects as principal investigator and has produced four Ph.Ds. He was the recipient of the Achievement Award for the field in the Conference in Bio-Engineering, Computer Science, Knowledge Mining (2006), Prague, Czech Republic. He received Career Award for Young Teachers (2006), All India Council for Technical Education, New Delhi, India and Young Scientist International Travel Award (2012), Department of Science and Technology, Government of India, New Delhi. He is a Young Scientists awardee under Fast Track Scheme (2013), Department of Science and Technology, Government of India, New Delhi and also granted Young Scientist Fellowship (2013), Tamil Nadu State Council for Science and Technology, Government of Tamil Nadu, Chennai. He also received the Senior Scientist International Travel Award (2016), Department of Science and Technology, Government of India. He has published two book chapters and also applied patent in the area of data mining. He is an active Member of various professional bodies and Editorial Board Member of various conferences and journals. He is IQAC Coordinator and Nodal Officer for data collection, Department of Computer Science and Engineering and also Member of Patent Cell, Annamalai University.

Valerianus Hashiyana is a Namibian national and obtained his Doctorate in Computer Science from Russia. Currently employed as Senior Lecturer and Head of Computer Science Department at University of Namibia (Unam). His area of research are Wireless technologies, Computer Networks and Security, IoT, ML to mention few of them.

Sheehama Jacobus is a Namibian national and obtained his Doctorate in Microbiology. He is currently working as Senior lecturer and Deputy Director of academic affairs at Northern Campus of University of Namibia. He specializes in microbiology and has experience and interest in research and education in the areas of Medical Biological Scientist - Medical Microbiology, Biochemistry and infectious diseases.

Rohan Jagtap has done Bachelor of Engineering (Computer Engineering) from Sardar Patel Institute of Technology, Mumbai, India. He has published a paper titled "An In-depth Walkthrough on Evolution of Neural Machine Translation", https://arxiv.org/abs/2004.04902. He is immensely interested in Deep Learning Research and Natural Language Processing. Along with it, his current areas of interest are Transformer based Self-Attention Architectures for Language Modeling.

Sunil Kumar Jangir received his B.E. in Information Technology (with honors) in 2009 and M. Tech degree with the highest distinction in Software Engineering in 2012 and Ph.D. degree in Computer Science & Engineering in 2018.He is currently an Assistant Professor with the Department of Computer Science & Engineering, Mody University of Science and Technology, Sikar, Rajasthan, India. The main areas of his research interest include Design of algorithms, Machine learning, Computer Networks as well as routing protocols for ad- hoc networks.

Judith Justin is currently a Professor and Head of Department of Biomedical Instrumentation Engineering at Avinashilingam Institute for Home Science and Higher Education for Women.

Vandana Kalra is an academician in the Department of Computer Science at SGGSCC, University of Delhi where she has been a faculty member for over 18 years. She is quite enthusiastic about learning and probing into the academic materials with a passion. Her subject's interests are programming languages and core computer science areas artificial Intelligence with machine learning. Her research interests lie in the area of data analytics, ranging from theory to design to implementation. She has collaborated actively with researchers in several other disciplines of computer science particularly Rough Sets and data mining.

M. Kameswari is currently an Associate Professor in the department of Mathematics, Thiagarajar College of Engineering, Madurai, Tamil Nadu, India. She has 21 years of Teaching Experience and 12 years of Research Experience. Her fields of interest include Topology, Operations Research, Fuzzy Mathematics, Discrete Mathematics and Machine Learning. She has published more than 25 research articles in leading academic international journals. She has received best teacher award five times from different organizations and she has received Best Presentation Award in the reputed international conferences. She has organized and executed 12 conferences/workshops/seminars and presented almost 25 special lectures in several establishments in several mental abilities. She is pursuing a project for which grant is received from PMMMNMTT from GRI.

Anil K. Kannur is an Assistant Professor in Department of Computer Science and Engineering, at Rajarambapu Institute of Technology Islampur. He has completed his B.E. in Computer Science and Engineering in 2001, M. Tech.(Computer Science and Engineering) in 2006 and is currently pursuing Ph.D. in Computer Science and Engineering (Registered under Visvesvaraya Technological University, Belagavi, India). He has published 14 research papers in peer reviewed International Journals and Conferences. His research area of interest are Image Processing, Pattern Recognition and Computational Forensics.

Indu Kashyap has more than Thirteen years of experience in teaching. She has done M.Tech and Ph.D. in Computer Science and Engineering. She has guided many M. Tech projects, Dissertations and Ph.D scholars. She has several publications to her credit in various leading International and National Journals in the various areas like, Wireless Networking, Databases, Cloud Computing etc. Currently, she is working as an Professor in the Faculty of Engineering and Technology (FET), MRIIRS and also acting as a Ph.D coordinator for Engineering Programme. She is a member of many technical committees.

Harmeet Kaur is an Associate Professor in the Department of Computer Science, Hansraj College, University of Delhi, Delhi-110007, India. She received Doctoral degree from the Department of Computer Science, University of Delhi, in 2007. She has about 23 years of teaching and research experience and has published more than 42 research papers in National/International Journals/Conferences. Her research interests lie in the field of Trust, Recommender Systems, Grid Computing, Cloud Computing and Crowdsourcing.

B. Vinoth Kumar is working as an Associate Professor with 16 years of experience in the Department of Information Technology at PSG College of Technology. His research interests include Soft Computing, Blockchain and Digital Image Processing. He is author of more than 26 papers in refereed journals and international conferences. He has edited three books with reputed publishers such as Springer and CRC Press. He serves as a Guest Editor/Reviewer of many journals with leading publishers such as Inderscience, De Gruyter and Springer.

Manish Kumar received B.Tech. degree in Applied Electronics and Instrumentation Engineering from Biju Patnaik University, Rourkela, India, in 2010 and M.Tech. Degree in Biomedical Engineering from the Manipal University, Udupi, India, in 2013. He received Ph.D. degree in Electrical and Electronics Engineering from Birla Institute of Technology, Ranchi, India. He is currently an Assistant Professor with the Department of Biomedical Engineering, Mody University of Science and Technology, Sikar, Rajasthan, India. His area of interests are Medical Image Processing and Computational Intelligence.

Ajinkya Kunjir has done Bachelor in Computer Engineering from M.E.S College of Engineering, Pune, India in 2017. He is currently pursuing Masters Degree in Computer science at Lakehead University, Thunder Bay, Ontario, Canada (2018-2020). His research interests include Data Mining, Machine Learning, Big Data, and BCI.

Mrunal Kurhade has done Bachelor of Engineering (Computer Engineering) from Sardar Patel Institute of Technology, Mumbai, India.

Boipelo Mogale received her Master of Commerce in Statistics at the Mafikeng Campus of the North-West University and currently studying for her PhD in the same field at the Mafikeng Campus of the North-West University. She is also a staff of the Statistic South Africa.

Elias Munapo is Professor of Operations Research at the Department of Statistics and Operations Research, North-West University, Mafikeng Campus, South Africa. His areas of specialization include; Applied Statistics & Operations Research.

Anuradha N. is an Associate professor in Department of Management Studies at B. S. Abdur Rahman Crescent Institute of Science and Technology, Chennai, India.

Gaurav Nagpal is an Assistant Professor in Management Department of Birla Institute of Technology and Science Pilani. His area of expertise is Operations and Supply Chain Management, Operations Research, Industrial Engineering, Business Statistics and Data Analytics. He received his Bachelor's degree in Mechanical Engineering from YMCA Institute of Engineering in 2005. Post that, he completed his MBA from Indian Institute of Foreign Trade, New Delhi. He has been a GATE topper with 99.83 percentile (AIR-41) in mechanical engineering. He has also done EPMBD from IIM Calcutta, and is CSCP qualified from APICS. He is currently pursuing his PhD from BITS Pilani in the area of inventory management. He has twelve years of industry experience, of which the former seven years were into Operations and supply chain profiles with NTPC, Daimler India Commercial Vehicles and with Escorts Agri-machinery Group. After that he worked for five years in business strategy, planning and analysis profiles. Before joining BITS as Assistant Professor in 2018, he was working with the leading grocery e-Commerce firm "Grofers" as Associate Director- Business Planning and Analysis.

Anup Nandy is working as an Assistant Professor in Computer Science and Engineering Department at NIT Rourkela. He earned his Ph.D from IIIT Allahabad in 2016. His research interest includes Machine Learning, Image Processing, Human Cognition, Robotics, Human Gait Analysis. He received Early Career Research Award from SERB, Govt. Of India in 2017 for conducting research on "Human Cognitive State Estimation through Multi-modal Gait Analysis". He also received research funding for Indo- Japanese joint research project, funded by DST, Govt. Of India. He recently received NVIDIA GPU GRANT AWARD in 2018 for his research on Human Gait Analysis for Abnormality Detection.

Ziadi Nihel is a Research Scholar at High Business School of Manouba, Tunisia.

V. Nivethitha has done her BTech in Computer Science and Engineering from Sri Manakular Vinayagar Engineering College, Pondicherry University, India and M.Tech in Distributed Systems (CSE) from Pondicherry Engineering College, India. She's currently pursuing her Ph.D. in Edge computing in National Institute of Technology Puducherry, Karaikal. Her research areas are Edge computing and Data Analytics.

James Osabuohien Odia is an Associate Professor in the Department of Accounting in the University of Benin.

Onur Önay is a teaching and research assistant in the School of Business at the Istanbul University. He has PhD degree in quantitative methods. His interest and research areas are operations research, mathematical modeling and their applications in business. He has published several papers in various journals and he has also published several book chapters.

Pankaj Pathak obtained Masters and Ph.D. in 2005 and 2014 respectively. He is working as an Assistant Professor in Symbiosis Institute of Telecom Management. His area of interests are Data Mining, AI, and Smart Technologies. He has Published Several Research papers in the area of Data Mining, IoT security and Speech Recognition Technology.

Kshitij Phulare has done Bachelor of Engineering (Computer Engineering) from Sardar Patel Institute of Technology. He is currently working as a Machine Learning Engineer. His areas of Interest include Artificial Intelligence, Deep learning and Data Analysis.

Samaya Pillai is associated with Symbiosis International University for the past 15 years in the capacity of Assistant Professor. She has completed her BSc, MCM from Pune University. MCA from

Manipal and MPhil from Bharati Vidyapeeth. Her core areas are Databases, NoSQL, IOT and Current trends. Currently perusing PhD from Pune University under the guidance of Dr. Kadam and Dr. Acharya. She is certified in Big Data and Oracle. She has published papers and Books in renowned publications.

Shivananda R. Poojara completed M.Tech in Computer Science and Engineering from University of Visvesvaraya College of Engineering, Bangalore. He has worked as an Assistant Professor in Rajarambapu Institute of Technology, Sakhrale, Maharashtra, India for three years. Furthermore, he has worked as Intern in the Nokia R&D Labs, Bangalore for two years in cloud computing domain. He is currently working as a research scholar at Mobile and Cloud Computing Lab, University of Tartu, Estonia. His research domain is Cloud Computing and Virtualization, Scientific Workflow Scheduling and Big data. He has delivered invited talks on Aneka platform in many reputed organizations including University of Malaya, Malaysia, NIT Silchar, NIT Kurukshetra, WBUT Kolkatta, GJU and many more. He has published more than 12 papers in International and National Conferences and Journals.

J. Prakash received B.E. degree in Computer Science & Engineering and the M.E. degree in Software Engineering from Anna University in 2012 and 2014 respectively. Currently he is pursuing his Ph.D. degree in Computational Intelligence. He completed his internship at Infosys Limited, Mysore in 2014 and joined as an Assistant Professor in the department of Computer Science & Engineering at PSG College of Technology, Coimbatore in 2014. He has published around 6 papers and 1 book chapter in peer reviewed National/International Journals and Conferences. His current area research interests include Machine Learning, Evolutionary Algorithms and Digital Image Processing. His ORCID is https://orcid.org/0000-0002-2228-568X.

Vanithamani R. is currently a Professor in Department of Biomedical Instrumentation Engineering at Avinashilingam Institute for Home Science and Higher Education for Women.

Rajaram was born in Mamsapuram near Rajapalayam in the year 1973. He completed B.E degree in ECE in 1994 from Thiagarajar College of Engineering, Madurai and Master's degree with Distinction in Microwave and Optical Engineering from Alagappa Chettiar College of Engineering and Technology, Karaikudi in 1996. He holds a PhD degree in VLSI Design from Madurai Kamaraj University. He completed his Post-Doctoral Research in 3D wireless system at Georgia Institute of Technology, Atlanta, USA during 2010-2011. Since 1998, he has been with Thiagarajar College of Engineering, Madurai. Currently he holds the post of Associate Professor in the department of Electronics and Communication Engineering, Thiagarajar College of Engineering. He is a former Member of Academic Council of Thiagarajar College of Engineering and Member of Board of Studies for several educational Institutions. His fields of interest are VLSI Design and Wireless Communication. Under his guidance ten research scholars have already obtained PhD degrees.

Miguel Ángel Ruiz-Jaimes is a professor at the Universidad Politécnica del Estado de Morelos. He is from Cuernavaca, Morelos. He has a PhD in Computer Systems from the Universidad del Sur, studied a Masters in Information Technology at the Universidad Interamericana para el Desarrollo, and has professional studies in Computer Science at the Universidad Autónoma del Estado de Morelos. He is the Academic Director of Computer Engineering and Engineering in Electronics and Telecommunications.

Jorge A. Ruiz-Vanoye was born in D.F. Mexico in 1975. He obtained his Ph.D. degree in Computer Science in 2008 from CENIDET, under supervision of Joaquin Pérez and Rodolfo Pazos. He has worked at Electric Research Institute of Mexico government (IIE) and in diverse companies more. He has given classes in diverse Mexican Universities since 1996, He is professor at Universidad Politécnica de Pachuca, México. He is a Senior Member of IEEE, and author of more than 100 publications on Computer Science, metaheuristic optimization and Artificial Intelligence. He was director of 7 Ph.D. Thesis; for publications and more information see www.ruizvanoye.com.

Boško Šego is professor with full tenure at Faculty of Economics and Business, University of Croatia. Currently, he is teaching 7 mathematical courses. His field of study is financial mathematics and modelling. He won prize Mijo Mirković in 1987 and 2014. He is author and co-author of more than 100 publications (books, scientific papers, etc.), among which some he presented on dozens of international conferences. He was mentor for dozens of graduate thesis, master thesis and doctoral thesis.

Jugal Shah has done Bachelor in Computer Engineering. He is currently pursuing Master's in Computer Science from Lakehead University.

Paulus Sheetekela is a CAD/E/M Systems engineer. He has experience and interest in research and education in the areas of Artificial Intelligence, HPC/Supercomputing, Parallel programming to enhance development and innovation in solving problems of scientific visualization, 3D modelling for design and prototyping products and simulation of different phenomena especially in the development of smart industrial solutions with elements of artificial intelligence based on a flexible quasi-model architecture. In addition to this, he also has interest in the development of computer models of complicated industrial complexes, intelligent control systems of technological, energy, transportation, manufacturing processes using embedded systems and various technologies and integration of various systems components in one single technological platform for applying CAD/CAE/CAM systems to solve problems in health, medicine, transport, mining, security and defense and various related fields.

Shatakshi Singh is currently pursuing her graduation in Computer Science and Engineering from Mody University of Science and Technology, Lakshmangarh, Rajasthan. Her area of interest include data science, data analytics and problem-solving.

Prachi Singhal is currently pursuing her bachelor's degree in computer science and engineering from Mody University of Science and Technology, Lakshmangarh, Rajasthan. She is an enthusiast to work in the field of machine learning and data analysis.

Tihana Škrinjarić, PhD, is employed as an assistant professor at the Department of Mathematics at the Faculty of Economics and Business of the University of Zagreb. Her research areas are risk management, econometrics and financial economics, with special focus on regime switching methodology and portfolio management. She has published more than 90 publications in the abovementioned research areas; she has participated at dozens of international conferences on econometrics and operational research. Tihana has been a member of the Croatian Operational Research Society and the Croatian Statistical Association.

R. Suganya currently serves as an Assistant Professor at the Department of Information Technology at Thiagarajar College of Engineering, Madurai. Her areas of interest include Medical imaging, Big data Computing, Software Engineering, Video processing, Wireless Sensor Networks and Automation. She completed her B. E. (Computer Science and Engineering) from R.V.S College of Engineering in 2003. She then completed her M.E. (Computer Science and Engineering) from P.S.N.A College of Engineering. She completed her Ph.D. in Information and Communication Engineering from Anna University, Chennai. She has published papers in 11 International Conference, 12 International Journal and she has also published one Book Chapter. She has publication in eight Scopus indexed journals. She has published a Book on Classification of US liver images using Machine Learning techniques. She is a reviewer for many Journals. She is working with Thiagarajar College of Engineering, Madurai since 2006.

Tomoya Suzuki was an M.Tech student at Tokyo University of Technology & Agriculture during this work. He has 2 years of research experience in computational intelligence.

Vikas Trikha has done Bachelor in Computer Engineering. He is currently pursuing Master's in Computer Science degree from Lakehead University.

Johannes Tshepiso Tsoku holds PhD in Statistics and he is a Senior Lecturer in the Department of Statistics and Operations Research, North West University, Mafikeng, South Africa. His area of specialization are Applied statistics, Multivariate analysis, Econometrics and Time series.

Gentiane Venture has completed an Engineer's degree from the Ecole Centrale of Nantes (France) in 2000 in Robotics and Automation and a MSc from the University of Nantes (France) in Robotics. In 2003, she obtained her PhD from the University of Nantes (France). In 2004 she joined the French Nuclear Agency (Paris, France), to work on the control of a tele-operated micro-manipulator. Later in 2004 she joined Prof. Yoshihiko Nakamura's Lab at the University of Tokyo (Japan) with the support of the JSPS. In 2006, still under Prof. Nakamura, she joined the IRT project as a Project Assistant Professor. In March 2009, she became an Associate Professor and started a new lab at the Tokyo University of Agriculture and Technology (Japan). Since July 2016 she is a distinguished professor with the Tokyo University of Agriculture and Technology. Her main research interests include Non-verbal communication, Human behavior understanding from motion, Human body modelling, Dynamics identification, Control of robot for human/robot interaction and Human affect recognition.

Akshat Vijayvargia is an engineering graduate from Birla Institute of Technology and Science, Pilani, India. He has done projects in data analytics in the logistics industry.

Index

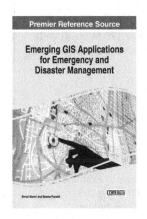
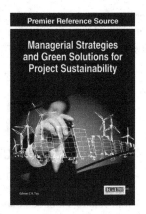

IGI Global Proudly Partners With eContent Pro International

Receive a 25% Discount on all Editorial Services

Editorial Services

IGI Global expects all final manuscripts submitted for publication to be in their final form. This means they must be reviewed, revised, and professionally copy edited prior to their final submission. Not only does this support with accelerating the publication process, but it also ensures that the highest quality scholarly work can be disseminated.

English Language Copy Editing

Let eContent Pro International's expert copy editors perform edits on your manuscript to resolve spelling, punctuaion, grammar, syntax, flow, formatting issues and more.

Scientific and Scholarly Editing

Allow colleagues in your research area to examine the content of your manuscript and provide you with valuable feedback and suggestions before submission.

Figure, Table, Chart & Equation Conversions

Do you have poor quality figures? Do you need visual elements in your manuscript created or converted? A design expert can help!

Translation

Need your documjent translated into English? eContent Pro International's expert translators are fluent in English and more than 40 different languages.

Email: customerservice@econtentpro.com   www.igi-global.com/editorial-service-partners

Printed in the United States
By Bookmasters